THE DAY
THE COUNTRY DIED

First published in Great Britain in 2006 by Cherry Red Books
(a division of Cherry Red Records Ltd.), 3a Long Island House,
Warple Way, London W3 ORG.

ISBN: 1 901447 707

Design: Dave Johnson
Printing: Biddles

THE DAY
THE COUNTRY DIED

IAN GLASPER

PEACE

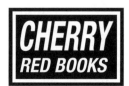

CONTENTS

Leeds squatters 1987, Nick Evans (ex-Slaughter Tradition) in the middle, picture by Andrew Medcalf.

FIRST of all, by even trying to label anarcho punk as 'anarcho punk', you seek to leech away much of its power, by stuffing it into a neat pigeonhole, where, once classified, it can be more easily controlled. Please bear in mind, the term is one used here for ease of reference only.

And please note, for the sake of argument, the bands have been categorized geographically, by their place of origin. For example, Antisect, The Mob and Zounds all ended up in London, but started their musical journey elsewhere, and it was the environment in which they grew up that more often than not shaped them into the people and bands that they became.

Yes, there are several major players in the anarcho punk scene not represented here as fully as I intended. As with 'Burning Britain', I made all efforts to contact every important act of any relevance, but for various reasons known only to themselves, not everyone either wanted to be – or was able to be – involved. This is still the closest you're likely to get to a definitive overview in your lifetime anyway!

I should briefly mention the inclusion of John Cato and AYS, which may surprise many readers, considering the inflammatory nature of his world view. But c'mon, if a book on anarcho punk can't ruffle a few feathers, what's the point? John's story is an interesting and important one, and, as repugnant as I find his politics, the notion of censoring him is even more anathema to me.

Animal liberation badges, as seen on a stall at a Conflict gig, picture by Tony Mottram.

And finally, before we get started, let me state once and for all: I am not an anarchist... I have a wife, two kids, a regular job and, it pains me to say, a hefty mortgage. But I am a lifelong 'fan' (another horrible word, merely used to illustrate a point rather than suggest any sycophantic tendencies) of anarcho punk, with strong anarchistic tendencies, and many of the ideals instilled in me as a direct result of the music I listened to as a youth have remained with me to this day. Respect for myself and those around me, respect for the planet and all its inhabitants, regardless of creed, colour or species. Yes, I've been beaten up whilst hunt sabbing... yes, I've been arrested on demonstrations... but I mention this not for the sake of misplaced vanity, but merely to help reassure you that I do indeed hold strong views and have in the past been prepared to stick my neck out to express them.

But punk music liberated me in so many other ways, and whilst age and responsibility have mellowed me, and to all intents and purposes I'm at the beck and call of the system with my regular life, I certainly know my own mind; I don't swallow all their lies, hook, line and sinker, and I do what I can to have a positive effect on those around me. If personal revolution starts with the honest dissection of one's own hopes and fears, I've been revolting most of my adult life. And believing in yourself is surely the first tentative step towards personal liberation. Maybe I'm more of an 'anarchist', in my own quiet way, than I think...

See you again in 2008 with a book all about UKHC from 1985 – 1989, which will complete my planned trilogy about Eighties punk rock in the UK.

Ian Glasper

I wish to extend my sincerest gratitude to the following wonderful people:

Sean Forbes (for patience, encouragement, proof-reading and invaluable assistance with the discographies), James Sherry, Steve Cotton, Darren 'Rat' Radburn, Dave Marston, Trunt, Sean McGhee, Roy Wallace; Des, Jimmy, Shrew, Al, and all the Cheltenham punks; Pat Poole and Pat Lawlor; Iain Aitch, John Esplen (Overground), Dmitriy Kovlskiy, for all the kind words (good luck with your own book, mate!); John Welsh; Jamie Cartwright (for the postcard!), Mark Brennan, Rebecca Pollard, Lance Hahn, Aston Stephens, Michael Heatley at Northdown, and, of course, all at Cherry Red, especially Iain McNay, Matt Bristow and Doug Shipton.

The following kind folk for many of the incredible pictures: Tony Mottram, Jaz Wiseman and Marc Freeman, Andrew Medcalf, Paul May (dead_brit@yahoo.com), Mick Slaughter, Mick Mercer, Claire McNamee, Mo, Scotty, Dai Joseph, Lee Holford, Per, Chris Low, Mickey Penguin...

Stig of Amebix at the 100 Club, London, September 1985, picture by Paul May.

All the bands involved for their time and patience, especially those that extended me the hospitality of their own homes: Penny Rimbaud, Gee Vaucher, Steve Ignorant, Colin and Paco, Colin Latter, Dick Lucas, Sid and Zillah, Gary Dirt, Rob Amebix, Phil Anti-System, Eddie Icon, Ian Bone, Steve Lake, and Andy System...

Sensei Malcolm McLure and Nigel Lees of OKKO, Sensei Steve Branagan of Ledbury Aikido, and not forgetting Iain Abernethy for being an inspirational karateka, never mind an old punk rocker at heart! All at Terrorizer, especially Jonathon Selzer, Pete Yardley, Damien, Avi Pitchon, James Hoare, and Marion Gardner. Last, and most definitely least, my fellow thrashers in Suicide Watch (especially Richard White) for putting up with my diminishing abilities on the bass guitar!

My wife, Jo, for her unconditional support, my beautiful kids, Amy and Sam, for keeping everything in perspective; mum, dad, Paul, Emma, and everyone else in my immediate family; everyone I work with, for putting up with me... and all the Ledbury punks, past present and future, especially Silv, Dave, Renn, Mobs, Paul, Glynn, Darren, Griff, Kev, Big Barr, Trigg, Mav, Captain and Dorris... the list is endless. My apologies to anyone I've forgotten.

This book is respectfully dedicated to the memory of Andrew 'Stig' Sewell, an overlooked genius if ever there was one, whose articulate sense of right and wrong will be sorely missed.

Also in memory of John Loder, a kind and generous visionary, Iain 'Corrosive Abuse' Shiner, and my late, great mate, Dean Uzzell, whose memory is with me always – RIP.

Ian Glasper, July 2006

Front cover pics (clockwise from top left): *Crass, Liverpool 1984; poll tax riot 1990; Conflict, Leeds Brannigans, 1984; Stop The City, 1984 – all by Andrew Medcalf.*
Central image: *Class War's Bash The Rich march in Hampstead, Sept '85, by Danny Gralton.*
Back cover pics (clockwise from top left): *Rob Miller of Amebix, by Paul May; Subhumans; Corny of The Sears, by Marc Freeman; Icons Of Filth vocalist, Stig, by Paul May; Flux Of Pink Indians banners, by Tony Mottram; Laura And Zillah, of Rubella Ballet.*

THE DAY THE COUNTRY DIED

Steve Ignorant of Crass, picture by Tony Mottram.

In the beginning there was Crass... although as reluctant leaders of an anarcho punk movement that essentially eschewed all leadership, I doubt they'll thank me for saying that. But they were Year Zero, a very literal line in the sand that translated as 'Enough is enough!' No more corporate companies misrepresenting our music; this was the birth of genuinely DIY labels, whose records were sold at virtually cost price, and bearing 'Pay No More Than...' notices to make sure they were. No more big booking agents controlling punk shows, levelling extortionate guarantees; now fans of the music themselves could communicate directly with the bands, and book them into alternative venues at affordable prices, the meagre door takings being ploughed back into worthwhile causes locally. No more glossy magazines dictating how punks should look, sound and behave; anyone who could string two words together and use a stapler was a potential fanzine editor. No more inane lyrics about cider and glue; the kids were taking back control and making a difference.

These things may well have happened without Crass, of course, but every single band in this book cites them as a major inspiration; they were a catalyst, no doubt about it, even if they defiantly refused to be figureheads. Preening rock bands like Guns 'N' Roses may pay lip service to the concept of being 'the most dangerous band in the world', but how many bands of that ilk had their phones tapped by MI5 and were courted by the KGB? Not bad for a bunch of ex-hippies really! And of course it was Johnny Rotten who sneered, 'Never trust a hippy'... but how many ex-members of Crass do you see appearing on celebrity game shows nowadays? None... because they meant it, maan.

Crass ushered in a whole new concept of punk as a movement as opposed to merely an outlandish fashion statement, and that movement – for all its naïve shortcomings – made its mark around the world. Fuelled by the very real evils of Thatcherism, economic depression and the nuclear threat that hung over the UK like a funeral pall during the early Eighties, anarcho punk kick-started the mindset of a generation that would ultimately make serious headway in the struggle for human and animal rights. 1984 came and went, and the world didn't go up in smoke, but the hopes and fears of these bands mean as much today – if not more, in many ways – as they did back then.

Conflict vocalist Colin
Jerwood, picture by
Tony Mottram.

The 'anarchy and chaos' punks, as examined in 'Burning Britain', professed not
to care, but the 'anarchy and peace' punks did care. They wanted their children
to inherit a planet where the sun still shone, where the air could still be
breathed, where you could walk down the street without flashing an ID card,
free of the cold hard stare of CCTV cameras, free of curfews… free of
oppression, free of fear. Just because they've convinced us over the years to
think we're being paranoid doesn't mean that we're not being watched!

The anarcho bands weren't so rigid in their musical approach as the bands
featured in 'Burning Britain' either. Your average 'UK82' punk band had a fairly
generic sound (and what a great sound it was!), but the anarcho bands were
bound together more by their ethics than any unwritten musical doctrine.
Distinctly less ambitious as regards their musical 'careers' than their leather-clad
cousins, they weren't afraid of setting their creative sights significantly higher.
So you had bands as disparate as The Mob, Conflict, Chumbawamba and Poison
Girls sharing stages, all for the common good, influences taken everywhere
from meandering folk via raging hardcore to arty noise and back again. 'No
rules!' was the only real mantra, after all.

And, quite rightly, the natural balance between males and females was far more
representative in the anarcho punk scene… a subculture so yearning for internal
and external peace and freedom was bound to embrace sexual equality after all.
Anarcho punk truly empowered all it touched, encouraging every last one of us
to take control of our own destinies before it was too late.

So, now it's time to see who's who…!

CHAPTER ONE

There's a strong argument for the two most influential punk bands of all time being the Sex Pistols and CRASS; the former encouraged bored teenagers everywhere to get off their arses and start their own bands, the latter encouraged them to think for themselves. Of the two bands, however, the shadow cast by Crass is certainly the one with the most substance; they gave the ephemeral rebellion hinted at by the Pistols specific shape and purpose, and a thousand anarcho-punk bands set sail in their wake. And these bands weren't thrashing against any imaginary opponent conjured by the paranoia of youth... no, they set themselves very real targets and clearly defined – if a little ambitious – objectives. They weren't interested in sensationalist, unworkable notions of anarchy and chaos, they wanted a gradual revolution from within; they wanted anarchy, peace and freedom. The shock tactics of punk had been usurped, given an articulate intellectual make-over, and were now being put to sound social use.

"Well, I don't think that we were leaders of any movement," says drummer Penny Rimbaud (real name Jerry Ratter) modestly, "although we may have helped inspire one. And we ourselves were inspired by some of the earliest punk bands, but what we aspired to do was what they only pretended to do. Commercial punk was a complete sham, part of the whole rock'n'roll circus, operating in the same way as someone like Marc Bolan – which is not to denigrate it as such... after all, music is an industry; it produces product and people enjoy product. But to imagine that the first wave of punk related in any real way to what followed is quite inaccurate, and it was basically finished by late '77.

"And that particular element of rock'n'roll that was called 'punk' would have died a natural death, and the next phase, be it goth or whatever, would have been invented by the music business. It would've required its main characters, of course, but would have just continued along the same line that rock'n'roll has always continued along for many, many years.

"We sort of tail-ended that first wave," he adds, of Crass themselves. "We were playing through '77, playing a lot with bands like the [UK] Subs, for example, and being talked about in the same breath. We didn't see any great disconnection really, but we actually wanted to put into action what had never been the intention of those earliest punk bands. We picked up their pretensions and tried to make them real. We came in with their energy, but also a great deal of political sincerity, and it was the political sincerity that attracted and created a movement. You could never have created a 'movement' out of something as banal as punk rock.

"I mean, they were playing a Clash record on the radio earlier on today, and it struck me that you couldn't really tell the difference between that now and the Rolling Stones. It was just rock'n'roll at the end of the day, just music.

"It was our sincerity, and our authenticity, that made us different. Of course, it's only now that I'm aware of the authenticity part, but I was certainly aware of the sincerity even then; we genuinely meant that anyone could get up and do it. Because we had gotten up ourselves and done it! Most of the bands before us had been pub bands, on some sort of circuit; they'd already tried some form of rock'n'roll, just commercial players looking for a break... but we were saying, 'Have a go!' And we really meant it. And when we set up our own label, at least initially, anyone who said they wanted to get up and play could get up and play. And we ourselves were happy to play with anyone else; we couldn't see that what we were doing was any different to what the Subs were doing, but it soon became clear that we did mean it. And we were quite prepared to put what little money we made –

Penny Rimbaud (AKA Jeremy Ratter), drummer and co-founder of Crass.

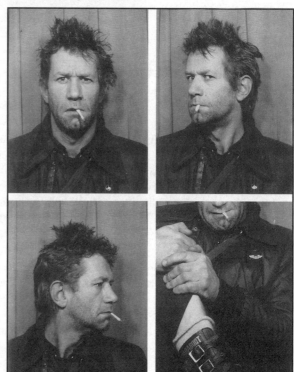

actually it was quite a large amount of money – back into promoting those ideas.

"If what you're saying is that we created the anarcho-punk movement, then we didn't create it as leaders. We were just as hard-working as anyone else, scrubbing floors, knocking out leaflets, carrying our own gear – and everyone else's too! We never separated ourselves; we were a part of it, at one with it. There were those that tried to force that sense of leadership onto us, but I think we were very successful in never, ever accepting that role."

Crass were never your 'typical band' from the off. The truly unique chemistry that set up the claustrophobic tension so inherent in their sound was a result of many factors, including disparate musical tastes, but more importantly differences in age and class. Penny was a 35-year-old ex-art teacher, living a communal life at Dial House, on the edge of Epping Forest, whilst vocalist Steve ('Ignorant') Williams (who's actually anything but) was a fifteen-year-old yobbo from Dagenham.

"It all came about through my older brother, who would turn up at people's places, ask to stay the night and then end up staying three weeks," laughs Steve, by way of explanation of how he and Penny hooked up. "He'd stayed at Dial House for two nights or something, through some hippy types that he knew down in Ongar, and he came over to see me where I lived in Dagenham – this is pre-Crass, by the way, when I was only about thirteen – and he told me about this amazing place where you could go and draw if you wanted to, go and play piano if you wanted to, whatever... and he took me over there. I was totally intrigued by it; I was an ex-skinhead, and I turned up in all this gear, really loud 'Rupert The Bear trousers', checked jacket... and there's all these people walking around bare-foot, with no fucking television! Talking in these accents I couldn't understand, using all these words I couldn't comprehend, and sounding like they had fifteen plums in their mouths!

"But also, for the first time in my life, I was actually being included in the conversation... even though I didn't understand what they were going on about; they treated me like an equal, y'know? If I said something, they would consider it... it was the first time that I thought, 'Well, yeah, I have got something to say.'

"So, I kept playing truant, and going back there to stay, but then I left school and moved to Bristol for about a year, and then punk came along. I went to see The Clash at the Colston Hall, which totally did it for me, and Joe Strummer said, 'If you think you can do better, start your own band...', which became my battle cry. I came back to Dagenham – the week of the Queen's Silver Jubilee, I think it was – with the idea of finding my old drinking buddies and starting a punk rock band of my own. But of course, none of them were having any of it, 'cos they all had wives and jobs and all that bollocks, so I came out to Dial House, to find that Pen was living there on his own, writing 'Christ, Reality Asylum'. Gee [Vaucher, who would become the band's graphic designer] had gone to America, doing illustration work, and so he said, 'What you up to?' And I said, 'I'm gonna start a band...' to which he replied, 'I'll play drums for ya!' And that's how it all started really. His previous band, Exit, had stopped performing properly in '74, but people would still come over at weekends and jam... and what a fucking racket that was!

"Anyway, I turned up wanting to be Johnny Rotten or Paul Simonon... 'cos he was a good looking bloke, always looked a bit tasty... and with my David Bowie background, sort of thing, a part of me always wanted to be famous. And then you had Pen's background, which was much more intellectual, and it just came together. I couldn't even understand what 'Christ, Reality Asylum' was all about, but I knew I liked it because it was having a pop at religion, and it had 'fuck' in it, which was well punk rock, wasn't it? I dunno, we just got on really.

"Dial House was this place where everyone could go; there was this idea that if you were a poet and you turned up, you could earn your night's board by reciting your poetry, for example, and there was going to be all these Dial Houses all around the country. So you had all these people turning up who weren't working class – they tended to be middle class and into photography or film-making – and Pen used to like them turning up and being confronted by me, this spiky-haired, spotty little oik, 'cos punk rockers were still 'frightening' back then. And I used to enjoy seeing that happen as well, my so-called 'elders and betters' being a bit scared of me, so that worked for us as well; it was a little bit of a stage act, a performance. The funny thing was, as soon as Crass started, a lot of the people who used to visit Dial House stopped coming anyway – 'cos the whole place would be full of Italian punks or whatever!

"So yeah, there was a class difference – I remember I always felt really nervous in front of Pen's mum and dad – but it worked for us; it was a good mixture, and I don't really know of any other bands that had that..."

That early poem of Penny's, 'Christ, Reality Asylum', remains a tenet of the Crass canon, an outrageously focused cornerstone from whence the band developed and refined its gleefully confrontational style and approach. With its condemnation of Christ's martyrdom as a 'churlish suicide', exclaiming that Jesus hung 'in crucified delight, nailed to the extent of his vision', it was deliciously, shockingly blasphemous, and was always destined to land the band in trouble with those kind-hearted censors that safeguard our precious morality. When the band's first 12" came out, the song was left off by the outraged pressing plant that manufactured it, forcing the band to name the silence left in its place 'The Sound Of Free Speech'.

"But there were no 'tactics' as such," claims Penny. "I had this friend staying with me, the guy who actually designed the Crass symbol, a bloke called Dave King who now lives in San Francisco [and was later a part of the Sleeping Dogs, who released their 1982 'Beware...' single through Crass]. And we were both from upper-middle-class backgrounds, and we were talking about religion, and I went off on this rant, and I ended up rolling around on the floor, doing all these theatrics. And he said, 'Fuckin' hell, you ought to write that down!'

"I was so in the moment, tearing up all this stupid religious tradition, and I realized that I was 35 years old but still bound up with this superstitious rubbish, and it all started falling away when I started getting into the rant. So I got up off the floor and wrote it down, carried on ranting but onto paper, and that became the 'Reality Asylum' book, and the 'Crass logo' was actually a symbol that Dave designed for the frontispiece of the book. But no, there was no intent there; it was just what I was feeling at the time..."

With Penny on drums and Steve providing vocals, the duo began writing their own material, Steve's searingly blunt approach providing the perfect foil for Penny's more considered, cerebral musings. The contrast between their very differing approaches can best be gauged when comparing 'Reality Asylum' to Steve's first composition, 'So What'.

"Well, actually, the first song I ever wrote was probably something like 'Song For Tony Blackburn', which only ever appeared on a tape or whatever," corrects Steve, "And the first proper song I wrote was 'Do They Owe Us A Living?' The second one was 'So What', I think, and by then I'd sat down and read 'Reality Asylum'. To be honest, it really annoyed me in a way; it was all 'I', 'I', 'I', 'you', 'you', 'you', 'me', 'me', 'me'…

"Then again, when I look at how we laid the lyrics out on [that first 12"] 'The Feeding Of The 5000', with all the obliques and no punctuation, I find that annoying as well, but at the time, I agreed with the others that if we made it difficult for people to read, they'd have to concentrate a lot harder.

"Anyway, little did I know that the first song I ever wrote, 'Owe Us A Living', which I sang under my breath, marching back from the shops going, you know, 'Fuck the politically minded…', would be the main song that I'm remembered for. And all the other songs I've written that I consider far better than that – 'cos I've written some great songs since Crass – no one knows, or cares, what they fucking are! And if I formed another band tomorrow, you know full well that there'd still be people shouting for 'Owe Us A Living' even now…

"To be honest with you, we never thought it would get any further than the music room at Dial anyway; it would just be our little hobby… we never dreamt we'd ever get a gig. We didn't take ourselves that seriously, to start with. Then this guy turned up called Steve Herman – he was a bald, beardy bloke with glasses and sandals… didn't look anything like a punk, but he could play guitar, and we thought, 'Fuck it, it's punk, anything goes!'

"And then Andy Palmer turned up; he couldn't play and he didn't have a guitar, but he nicked one from somewhere and tuned it so he could play a chord by putting his finger straight across. And then [bassist] Pete Wright became involved… but even then, it was like a weekend thing – it was only once we'd done a couple of gigs, that we thought we were maybe onto something. And we were still going on blind drunk at that point, just having a laugh really."

"Yes, it was Steve and myself at first," clarifies Penny, "And Eve [Libertine, real name Bronwen Jones, one of their vocalists] used to live just up the road, a mile or so away. She used to come down, and although she didn't join in with the band for the first year, she was quite instrumental in the nature of how we grew – especially the feminist aspect of it all. It was Eve that disallowed our use of the word 'cunt' in the lyrics.

"And because we've always been this cultural centre [at Dial House], we've always had people coming and going; there's always been an itinerant body of people moving in and out – some of them stuck and some of them didn't. We never ever thought to ourselves, 'Oh, we need to get a bassist', or anything. People just turned up.

"I remember Andy turning up; he was at a local art school, and he'd never played an instrument in his life, but he nicked one from the *International Times* offices, and came round and said he wanted to be in the band, so he was. That's how it worked; we were just mucking about. Me and Steve originally called ourselves 'Stormtrooper'… Eve thoroughly objected to that, and thankfully persuaded us otherwise!

"But really it all just happened, it wasn't by design. Although there did come a point after the first year, when we realised that we were basically fucking ourselves up, drinking quite a lot and using other substances. We couldn't have kept going like that, so we had to say, 'Are we going to take this seriously, or are we just going to carry on pointlessly like this?' So we had this big conference for a whole day, which was very self-conscious, and we made these decisions about what we were going to do, and those things stuck. And by then, all the different people who were going to be in the band were already in the band, and from then on we only incorporated extra people if they could actually add something to it. So we had filmmakers and poets turn up and get involved, and I suppose if a saxophonist had turned up, we might have got them in as well, but they didn't!"

Prior to them sobering up though, the very first Crass gig was during the summer of 1977, somewhere on the Tottenham Court Road… although the band didn't actually get to perform their full set.

Andy of Crass debating with police outside the Zig Zag, picture by Tony Mottram.

"There was a big squat there back then, with a big yard out back," recalls Penny, "and we did three-and-a-half songs, before we got switched off by this retired colonel, who thoroughly objected to what we were saying! It was a very nice squat, very regularized – not at all how one might imagine squats nowadays – and they were basically having a nice afternoon fete, and this bunch of drunken punks came along and spoilt it all! There were a few people there who seemed to half enjoy us, but basically we just fucked up everybody's nice afternoon out, and quite rightly this bloke came along and objected…"

"We got turned off after twelve minutes!" guffaws Steve wickedly. "Some resident from across the road came across and switched us off… and we let him do it! How punk is that, eh? There's some photographs somewhere of us playing, in the background, and two people dressed up as giant teddy bears… it was a fucking weird gig, more like a fete for the people in the squat.

"Then we did our first gig at the Roxy [the legendary Neal Street venue, in London's West End], and that went well, and I met this Deptford punk called Charlie who played in a band called Deceit, doing this sort of percussion-based avant-garde stuff. After that, we somehow got a gig at Covent Garden – some sort of festival when they were about to knock it down – but Pen couldn't make it, so Charlie stood in for us on drums. Someone actually filmed that too, so somewhere out there is this video footage of early Crass, when we all still used to wear different stuff [i.e. before the band adopted a policy of only wearing black onstage], without Pen on drums. Then we did Action Space, in Cheney Street, and the Chelsea Art College… we emptied that place! There was 500 people there when we started; I turned around to talk to Pen after the first song, turned back to say something to the audience and they were all gone. Fuckin' hell! We cleared it out."

About this time, Steve Herman departed for safer climes, and Phil 'Free' (real name Clancey) joined on lead guitar, the band returning to the Roxy for an infamous performance that saw them forbidden to ever return to the club. A moment immortalized in Penny's song, 'Banned From The Roxy', that appeared on the first Crass release, the aforementioned 'Feeding Of The 5000' 12", for Small Wonder Records, where Steve spits vehemently, 'Banned from the Roxy? Okay! I never liked playing there anyway… they said they only wanted well-behaved boys – do they think guitars and microphones are just fucking toys?'

"We were all so out of it," Steve recalls of the gig in question, "I remember throwing up in the street outside. It was partly from excitement as well; I knew all my mates from Deptford would be there and just got pissed too quickly. And then I couldn't hear anything onstage, and kept forgetting the words...

"I remember when we were setting up, every item of the drum kit that came onstage, Pen was looking at it and going, 'What's that?' He was already out of it on three bottles of red wine. The only one who wasn't totally pissed was Pete the bassist; it was a bonkers night... the floor was completely soaked in beer, you couldn't walk on it. And I remember Mick Duffield [the guy in charge of the band's live visuals] being drunk and flinging me across the room for some reason or other... but that's *all* I can remember really!"

"Initially, for the first year perhaps it was just about having fun, although our lyrics were rather serious," ponders Penny, of the self-implication within 'Banned From The Roxy' that Crass were already much more than just a band as early as 1978. "We used to be quite drunk and play rather badly – not following any particular punk ethic really, more just because that's what young-ish lads do, I suppose. But no, I don't think we ever regarded ourselves as a band, and certainly by the time we became known as 'a band', we didn't see ourselves as anything of the sort.

"If anything, and I don't think we were quite so self-conscious about it at the time, we were more a sort of information network. Although all of us had our own interests in music, we also had other interests in art and literature and everything else, so it was a combination of all of those aspects.

"And we didn't really make any effort either; we never tried to sell anything or promote anything. We were picked up by Small Wonder because we did a rehearsal that we recorded, just for a friend of ours to listen to in his van, and he used to do displays at record fairs and stuff, and he took it into [the] Small Wonder [shop]. We didn't make any effort, and we certainly didn't give him the tape with the intention of him doing that.

"We eventually made our own label, of course, but that wasn't because we wanted to make pots of money; it was quite simply because Pete [Stennet] at Small Wonder kept getting hassled by the police because of what we were doing. And it seemed really unfair that there was Pete and his missus in their little shop in Walthamstow having the vice squad going around and harassing them... why should he have to put up with that just 'cos he was nice enough to finance our record?

"I think I can honestly say that we worked very hard, and we were very committed to what we did, but we never ever went out of our way to sell ourselves. And none of the things that we did were about trying to sell ourselves either. We didn't wear all black because it was a natty look! It was initially because it was a very anonymous thing, so although Steve was clearly the front-man/singer, he never became isolated in the same way that generally happens with bands, y'know? That never happened with Crass, and that was partly because we all decided that we would, as much as possible, all look the same. It was a policy decision so that we couldn't be individualised, but eventually it became a practical necessity anyway, because everything around the place was black, and everything came out of the washing machine black. But we really didn't want to be easily definable in the rock'n'roll context."

Recorded completely live on October 29th, 1978, by John Loder at London's Southern Studios, 'The Feeding Of The 5000' (so-called because that was the minimum number of records Small Wonder was allowed to press) was a complete revelation, totally unlike any other record released before or since. Built upon the fierce staccato rhythms of Penny's militaristic drumming and Pete Wright's ruthlessly tight, incisive bass work, the truly unique Crass sound revolved around Andy and Phil's incredibly trebly, distorted guitar tones, weaving jaggedly in and around the thumping rhythm section, and Steve's raw, earthy, 'no frills' vocal delivery. Locked together in their collective rage, Crass were an inexorable musical force – despite claims from their detractors (who couldn't see past those lethal fuzz-boxes all set to '10') that they just revelled in noise for the sake of it. Yes, their latter works did deliberately descend into sonic chaos, but at their leanest, meanest and simplest, they were genuinely untouchable. No wonder then that they quickly inspired a legion of loyal fans in their wake (selling over half a million records in the process), not to mention hundreds of similarly stripped-down bands, encouraged by their defiantly DIY (i.e. 'do it yourself') approach.

"It was terrifying to us that we suddenly seemed to create an army," reckons Penny. "We set off wanting to break through the banality of that first wave of punk, we were just piss-heads having a laugh, but we soon realised that if we were going to have any sort of real effect, we had to straighten ourselves out. People were starting to take an interest in what we were doing, but we would never have survived the way we were going; we were out of our heads all the time! Not in any real sort of hedonistic way, but because we couldn't cope with it. Even now, I only ever drink when I perform, and then only because it's a way of being able to get out of self.

"So, we curbed the drinking, and we started to wear black because it made us anonymous. It was also a statement against that bloody stupid, very expensive clothing that was being flogged down the Kings Road as 'punk gear'... what a load of shit. But we certainly didn't start wearing black so that everyone else in bloody Britain would start doing the same, though all of a sudden, it appeared that was exactly what every young punk was doing. So, we thought, 'Oh shit, now what do we do?' Rather than exploit it, we just ignored it, and hoped it would die its own death, but it never did. And it's since become synonymous with the whole crusty anarcho-punk thing.

"Yet, in the sense that it was considered, it was orchestrated, it was very, very rehearsed; it [the band's live show] was like a Nuremberg rally, and the closer we could get to that sort of undeniable visual and emotional perfection, the better. That's what we were looking for; we wanted to produce a backdrop that was absolutely unbreakable... because we wanted to smash through the banality. We were like a torpedo going straight at all this stupid music business, media crap, and we were strong enough to blow straight through it. And we didn't sit around making conditions on the other side either; we created a breach in their wall, and fuckin' thousands of kids ran through it! And if they wanted to then argue about who was wearing leather shoes or not, that was their fuckin' business. It was nothing to do with us, we just blew the hole in the wall for them, and I don't really think that we can take any responsibility for all those stupid arguments that ensued because we really weren't involved in it all, to be honest."

Prior to the recording of 'Feeding...' however, the band actually played several shows in America, one of the first UK punk bands to play there, albeit on a very low-key level.

"Yeah, we went out to New York, when Gee was living there and knew a lot of the punkers like Richard Hell and Patti Smith. We didn't go out there as any sort of grand tour... we just played half a dozen gigs around New York.

"We didn't do CBGB though; they gave us the ultimatum of either playing there and not the alternative venues, or not playing at all... so we told 'em to stuff it, and played all these great alternative venues, in lofts and places. This was early '78, I think, before 'Feeding...' even came out, but, in the short time we were there, we were getting fucking big audiences. We caused an awful lot of confusion out there; people really didn't know how to take us. And it was there that the fascist thing really got pinned on us...

"Yet we were one of the first bands to organise a mixed race gig there; we set up this gig with a phenomenal reggae band from off the Island... it was in a Polish working men's club, and they wouldn't even allow these 'coloured' guys through the front door! And that was a very, very unusual event, this English punk band playing with a black reggae band; it was a great evening."

Steve reflects candidly on one incident from the New York visit that illustrates the tremendous pressure the band exerted upon itself not to leave any public chinks in its armour: "When Crass went to America, it was heaven for me. The first time I'd ever been abroad... loadsa drugs and what-not, and we were in New York as well, so it was really good quality stuff... even the amyl nitrate was fantastic. Wa-hey!

"Anyway, all these American bands like The Heartbreakers knew we were in town, this English punk band, and there was someone living across the hallway from Gee who knew all these other

Crass live at Cleator Moor Civic Hall 1984 (left to right: Pete, Steve, Andy), picture by Trunt.

bands, so at all times we had to wear black and be punk and... blah blah blah! So Phil Free goes down the stairs in his shorts, and then came running back in, saying, 'Fuck it! I've just been seen by Gladys across the hallway in my shorts!' And I was like, 'Oh no, you wanker! What have you done?' Ha ha!

"And another time, I was at Dial House, and I said to [vocalist] Joy [De Vivre], 'Oh, give us a short hair cut', and she cut it a bit too short, and it looked like a 'suede head' cut... we cancelled a gig because of that – in case we got a skinhead following! They had me in tears over it, I was guilt-ridden...

"But we brought it all on ourselves, 'cos we wrote all those songs, and then we had to stand by them. So, all the time we were scrutinised, and we were scrutinising ourselves as well, examining everything we did under this spotlight, so everything we did was fraught with danger. I went along with that, and even now, if I'm out with my mates, people will be going, 'Are you drunk?' And I'll be absolutely fucking pissed, but I manage to keep straight 'cos of that training in Crass... 'Don't ever make yourself look like an arsehole, 'cos you'll make the whole band look like arseholes!' So we were very self-regulating, it was really difficult. I used to find myself sneaking around, 'cos we had a policy of no drugs at Dial House... quite rightly, because the police had their eye on us and it would've been stupid to have been busted for that... so I used to sneak out and do my thing. I always preferred chemicals in those days – 'blues' and stuff – and I used to hate going back there still stoned or speeding..."

"I always had this imaginary Glaswegian punk in my head," adds Penny, "Because at that time Glasgow was the poorest city in Britain, and I had this mental model of this young punk. I'd think, 'Now would he understand me taking a two-week holiday in Benidorm?' No, so I wouldn't get on a plane and go on holiday. 'Would he understand me going to the local Chinese restaurant for a meal out?' Questionable, better not do it. So, for seven years, I lived as the alter ego of this fourteen-year-old punk in Glasgow. I'm sure I put a foot wrong in places – how could I not do? – but I made a conscious effort to do the right thing whenever I could..."

Keen to take complete control of their recorded output, Crass set up their own eponymous label for all future releases, and although they kept their profit margins to an absolute minimum, enough revenue was quickly generated to allow them to begin releasing records by other like-minded artists. As a general rule of thumb, most bands they worked with were only invited to do one single for the label, and by keeping a tight rein on the production and presentation side of the process, Crass Records quickly developed a distinctive identity all its own, ensuring that each release, beautifully packaged in stark black-and-white poster sleeves, sold respectably well on the strength of the label's reputation for reliably sourcing stimulating new talent. The next four years saw Crass unleash some of the most challenging (and often difficult) music imaginable, from artists as eclectic as The Cravats, Poison Girls, Annie Anxiety and Jayne Gregory. The flip-side of the equation was a whole slew of bands that were basically taking the ideological baton handed them by Crass and running with it in a very similar direction – and with Penny producing their records, they sounded like Crass as well. Ironically though, these more generic releases sold far better than the avant-garde material that Penny more naturally favoured.

"Yes, to some extent, I was guilty of that," admits the drummer. "Because I was largely responsible for choosing what we put out on our label and then producing it, but if we'd only done singles by the likes of Andy T. or Annie Anxiety, we would've busted ourselves quite quickly. Not to say that I chose bands like Dirt or Flux [Of Pink Indians] because they were saleable punk… but nonetheless they were saleable punk. So at least we got our money back and paid for the records! But stuff like Andy and Annie, we lost lots of money on, so there was this funny mixture of bands we worked with: some that were a labour of love, and some giving people a chance that I knew were quite derivative of ourselves. Almost embarrassingly so sometimes, but I only really resented that when I started to find myself at odds with those bands politically. It was like sowing a seed and then the wrong plant comes up! You can't control it – maybe shouldn't try to control it – but you can sometimes regret planting it in the first place…

"But I also think it's very untrue that all the releases we did sounded like Crass. The Mob were certainly an exception to that rule… so were Zounds… most of them were, actually. You had extremes of stuff like Annie, right through to KUKL, for example… who were really just total rock'n'roll, in my opinion. I think we were far more courageous with the material we tried to put out than people give us credit for.

"I remember doing The Snipers single, and people really fucking laid into me for putting that out. But I always thought that punk was about giving people a chance, and I liked what they had to say… yet you wouldn't believe the amount of stick I got for that one. And not just from people like [Sounds journalist] Garry Bushell either, but people in our own camp… people in my own band, in fact. They thought it was a pile of shit, just dour rubbish, but if someone had been there to manage that band they'd have probably ended up on [seminal Manchester label] Factory, who specialised in all that grey raincoat stuff. They were really nice kids too… they did one gig with us, and people just didn't get it. But I said, 'This is what it's meant to be about! Ordinary people who wanna say something, getting up and saying it!'

"But the whole idea was that we were not a label as such… we never signed anybody, never had any agreements other than a spoken promise that bands would get 50% of anything that we made – which was very often next to nothing. The only agreement was, 'You come in, and we'll help put it together…' We wanted the circle design on the front of every record too, our 'corporate image' so we could sell the stuff a bit easier… but they were the only conditions. Most people asked us for help with the artwork as well…

"All we were doing was facilitating, basically showing people how to make records, from the production to the artwork, everything… and that was it: one single, and on your way, once we'd shown you how to do it. We weren't a record label per se; we just wanted to help people create something else. But we then realised that a lot of the bands didn't have the wherewithal or interest to do it themselves, so we then created Corpus Christi as a secondary label. And that had no conditions attached to it whatsoever, and in fact I virtually gave that to John at Southern to run… and he did one or two bands that I would never have touched, but he liked them and that was fair enough because that was his remit.

"I remember we gave the Poison Girls 100% from the first pressing of [their first album] 'Chappaquiddick Bridge', at our own expense, because they weren't selling many records at that point and were so under-funded. We were always looking for ways to help these bands to go and do their own thing, because we certainly didn't want people standing on our back.

"At the other end of the scale, a band like [aforementioned Icelandic pre-Sugarcubes outfit] KUKL [whose name translates as 'witchcraft' in medieval Icelandic] came along, and they didn't really belong in the Crass camp at all, as far as what they were trying to do, as regards making a forceful political statement, but all I tried to do was help them make some bloody good records. It was inevitable really that they should go in the direction that they did, and it was very obvious even when I was working on [their second album] 'Holidays In Europe' that the press and media were only interested in Björk [who subsequently enjoyed massive success

Bjork and Einar of KUKL, picture by Per-Ake Warn.

as a solo artist], grabbing at where the money was and shoving the rest of them back into the bloody Icelandic ocean. So I worked very hard on 'Holidays...' to even that out, to make sure that Björk was no more there than Einar [Örn] was, because the beauty of that band was always the balance of personalities."

As well as the long-awaited, completely uncensored 'Reality Asylum' single (the release of which led to the band living under the threat of prosecution for obscenity from Scotland Yard's vice squad for almost a year), the first Crass record issued on the band's newly-established label was the superb 'Stations Of The Cross' album (its title inspired by the graffiti campaign the band had been waging on London Underground stations), which shot straight to No. 1 in the Independent charts. Regarded by many as the band's defining moment, it spent a staggering two years in the chart, positive proof as if any was needed of the powerful hold Crass had exerted on the imagination of English youth. More subtly produced than 'Feeding...' (despite being recorded virtually live in just one day again, on August 11th, 1979) there were some huge leaps taken in terms of composition and delivery, resulting in two of the band's most chilling moments, 'Mother Earth' (dealing with the general public's guilty obsession with Moors Murderess, Myra Hindley) and 'The Gasman Cometh' (that made unnerving parallels between modern-day state violence and the Holocaust of Forties Germany). Penny maintains however that it was never his intention to discomfit the listener.

"I just wanted to share my feelings about something... and 'Mother Earth' is a good example. It's a pretty horrible subject, but the reason I wrote that song was, I read an article by this bloke who was working for the Daily Express or something like that, who'd been covering the Myra Hindley case. And he was hanging around outside the jail where she was being held, and he began to realise that people weren't there out of criticism for what she had done, but out of some sort of strange affinity – which was a very frightening, unpleasant realisation. So I wanted to create this very creepy sense of something horrible about to happen, to suggest a complicity, which is why it's got this slightly 'heartbeaty' sound. I didn't want to make people uncomfortable, but I wanted them to share my feelings, which is what any novelist or painter would do. Not because I thought my feelings were particularly important, but because the only time I've ever learnt anything in life is through sharing other people's experiences.

"It's a basic artistic approach, and it's the same thing that I do now, except that these days I work with jazz musicians, which is a great freeing up. They're incredibly fast, incredibly sensitive, because that's what their world is – react/respond. So, the net result is an even more unlistenable music than we ever did with Crass, because basically speaking, if you take ten jazz musicians and feed them the kind of questioning lyrics that I'm liable to, then you get some devastatingly heavy responses."

'Stations…' also picked up where 'Feeding…' left off with its harsh criticism of the impotency inherent in the so-called punk movement. 'Feeding…' had 'Punk Is Dead' ('Yes, that's right, punk is dead, it's just another cheap product for the consumer's head; bubblegum rock on plastic transistors, schoolboy sedition backed by big-time promoters…'), which almost certainly prompted The Exploited to proudly call their debut album, 'Punk's Not Dead'. As well as 'White Punks On Hope', 'Stations…' contained 'Hurry Up, Garry' and 'I Ain't Thick, It's Just A Trick' (the former aimed at the aforementioned Sounds scribe, Garry Bushell; the latter at the Oi movement he did much to propagate). Such pointed questioning of punk's real worth, and the subsequent angry retorts from its indignant defenders, created a very definite rift within the scene, between so-called 'peace punks' and their more chaos-oriented counterparts. Colchester's Special Duties took especial exception, even releasing a single entitled 'Bullshit Crass' [Rondelet Records, 1982], that featured the chant 'Fight Crass, not punk!' parodying, of course, the 'Fight war, not wars!' slogan popularized by Crass.

"I really couldn't understand this vicious hatred they had for us," sighs Steve. "I couldn't work that one out at all. When their record came out, it was all over the fucking place, and everyone was like, 'Oh my god, this band doesn't like Crass!' And I was actually surprised that someone didn't do it earlier really, y'know? And what a great way to get your name out there! But we'd done the same thing to The Clash anyway…

"But I thought that it was all a front, and if we ever did meet them, they'd be alright about it and we could have a drink together and that. Then we met 'em in this service station coming back from a gig, and what annoyed me about them was when I questioned [their vocalist] Steve Arrogant and asked him if he really thought we were that bad. He said, 'It's alright for you, being at fucking college and all this…' And I said, 'Well, I never went to fuckin' college! So, you're totally against everything we say then?' And he went, 'Yeah!' I said, 'So you think nuclear wars are a good idea?' And he went, 'Yeah!' 'And what about the police, do you agree with them?' And he went, 'Yeah!' Everything I said, he said the opposite, and it really wound me up… I mean, how fuckin' stupid can you be, just to make a point?

"Anyway, I lost my rag and got him on his own outside and threatened to blow his fuckin' kneecaps off if any of our conversation ended up in the gossip column in Sounds. He said, 'I thought you were a pacifist!' And I said, 'Yeah, I am, but I'm so stupid, I thought it was a 9-to-5 job, and I just finished work and I can do what I like now…!'

"I later met the drummer from Special Duties, who had actually joined Dirt, and I got on alright with him; when asked what it was all about, he just said, 'Oh, it was a publicity stunt, mate.'

"A few years ago, I read an interview with Steve Arrogant in this little fanzine from Colchester, and he was asked about Crass, and he said something like, 'I've got a wife and a kid and a mortgage now, and if me and Steve Ignorant met today, we'd probably get on like a house on fire!' And I thought, 'Yeah, whatever,' and then he said, 'But I'd still like to see the size of his bank account!' Well, I haven't got a bank account; all I've got is a building society account, with about sixteen

Vi Subversa of the Poison Girls, picture by Tony Mottram.

quid left in it… I ain't got no fuckin' money! The whole thing was so strange…"

Sadly Crass and Special Duties never shared a stage together, which might have cleared the air somewhat, as did a low-key, last-minute show they played with one of their other most vocal detractors, The Exploited.

"Yeah, that was a great night, I loved it," smiles Steve, still sounding surprised that it even happened over twenty years later. "That whole Crass/Exploited thing came about when Wattie said that Crass were 'a bunch of wankers'… but that was just because we were in every fucking fanzine going, and even I was getting bored of reading about us, so if someone had said to me at the time, 'What do you think of Crass?' I'd have gone, 'Oh, Crass are a bunch of wankers!' Just to be controversial, y'know? But this whole thing brewed up, aided by the music press, of course.

"Anyway, Annie [Anxiety] was going out with [Exploited vocalist] Wattie… Christ, that would've been a wedding from hell… just imagine those kids! The Exploited were playing the 100 Club, and Wattie asked her to ask us to go and play it unannounced. At first I was dead against it, but then I came round to the idea, and went dressed as a soul boy, wore a short-sleeved shirt, with my hair parted to one side, didn't look punk at all, so no one knew who I was. And there were a few skinheads there looking out for us, and I remember these three in particular: a big one, a little one, and a medium sized one…!

"We went on and played, and then I was stood there watching The Exploited, and they were okay; I didn't rate them that much, to be honest, a lot of stamping about. And suddenly I'm aware of this little bleedin' skinhead stood right behind me, breathing down my neck, and his two mates, the big one and the middle-sized one, were egging him on. So I went to the bar and got a drink, and came back, and his two mates were down the front pogoing, so I stood right behind him and breathed right down his neck. And I fucking kept him there! And in the end, he was rubbing his neck, didn't know what to do, and Pen came and stood next to me and was completely oblivious to this little psychological drama that was going on. And, as we were leaving, I saw this little skinhead outside, and went, 'See you later, mate!' And he was like, 'You fuckin' cunt!'

"But there were no big fist fights, no animosity between the bands; Wattie seemed a nice geezer, y'know? He asked us to play, and good for him; it was a shame that Special Duties couldn't have done something like that as well."

On a related note, as to whether or not Steve Ignorant was an alter-ego character he could 'become' just prior to playing live, Steve adds carefully:

"Yeah, it probably was… 'cos I was always shit-scared about going onstage. But the funny thing about Crass was, 'cos we all lived together, I can't really talk about a personal life and the band; it was all one and the same. It wasn't like we'd do a gig and then say, 'Right, see you Monday then!' With us, it was the band all the time… we'd be talking about it over dinner, getting phone calls all day, people turning up to see us all the time… so eventually, Steve Ignorant wasn't an alter-ego, because that was who I was every minute of the day.

"I don't think there was another band like that, who all lived together… and that was something people used to get pissed off with Crass for, for being 'holier than thou' or whatever. But we lived like that because the band was like that, and the band was like that because we lived like that. Nothing was done for effect… well, alright, the wearing of black and the films were premeditated, but we didn't grow organic vegetables to be trendy or to be punk – that was how we lived! And that's why some of the people who tried to copy Crass couldn't, 'cos if you're living in a squat in Bromley, where the fuck are you going to put your vegetable garden, y'know?

"I was glad that I called myself Steve Ignorant too, purely because I was ignorant of politics. We used to play in Manchester a lot, and every time we played there, this little group of college-goers always used to single me out and surround me in a semi-circle, and be, like, 'Well, what about the trade unions?' All this stuff that I knew fuck all about! It got to the point where people were more worried about whether you had milk in your tea… I used to think, 'Maybe I'm stupid, maybe I ought to read all these intellectual books on anarchy…' but they're all so fuckin' boring, aren't they?

"I always found it very difficult in Crass that it wasn't the done thing to be personal, to write about yourself; everything you wrote had to be about everybody. The stuff I wrote later was much more personal, and I prefer that, because I'm opening myself up for criticism then, and I can defend myself, and defend what I believe, rather than have to defend what Crass believed in as a collective.

"It was weird suddenly getting known, with people coming up to me – not in the street, but in pubs and clubs – and I would feel guilty and stuff. At first I didn't know how to deal with it really, but then I started to enjoy it, and it didn't really matter anymore. It never made sense to me really, 'cos even if I met David Bowie now, I wouldn't ask for his autograph. I'd argue with someone for half an hour about why I didn't wanna sign an autograph, but in the end I found it easier and quicker to just sign the bloody thing! And have they still got it hidden away somewhere…? I doubt it!"

'Stations…' was followed in late 1980 by another bona fide classic (and another Independent No. 1), the 'Bloody Revolutions'/'Persons Unknown' split single with the Poison Girls, a benefit record that raised £20,000 towards the setting up of the London Anarchist Centre. For such a worthwhile cause, both bands offered up some of their finest material, 'Bloody Revolutions' by Crass being their most ambitious, sprawling arrangement to date, and 'Persons Unknown' by Poison Girls a dangerous, stirring exercise in dark, lurching atmospherics. As well as being united on vinyl, the two bands were also inextricably linked by this time on the live front, touring the length and breadth of the country together, taking in en route all manner of alternative venues that most other bands would avoid at all costs.

"The obvious reason that the two bands originally hooked up was that they only lived three or four miles up the road," explains Penny. "Basically speaking, they had a very different sort of agenda to us, a very different story to tell… they were essentially a feminist band – that was always their main preoccupation, even though we actually had more females in our band than they had in theirs – and we felt that given the predominantly male attitudes in rock'n'roll, and especially punk, they brought in this other element, and that was very important. They weren't that liked though, and they had a fucking hard job playing with us… but ultimately they got the respect they deserved. Though when we later toured with the likes of, say, Dirt, as we did straight after we did with the Poisons, the main body of the punk audience were well pleased to be able to just pogo, rather than be confronted with a bit of thought. We were becoming darker and darker ourselves by then – the whole thing was becoming more complex – so it was quite nice not to have that added conflict of a difficult opening band as well. From that point on, we at least started giving people a good time for the first half of the gig… and then we'd come on and wind them up!"

As the turbulent 1981 unfolded like a bad dream, it seemed as if Crass could do no wrong with the record-buying public, who rushed out and bought the 'Nagasaki Nightmare' single (primarily for its frankly brilliant B-side, and the band's best-loved song, 'Big A, Little A'), in sufficient quantities to send it rocketing to the top of the Indies again, and it didn't vanish off the chart's radar for a whole year. Seemingly determined to test the will of their listeners, Crass hurled a well-aimed spanner in the works with the 'Penis Envy' album. Those relishing the thought of another foul-mouthed outburst from Steve Ignorant were disappointed, because he didn't even contribute to the record; those hoping for a long-overdue feminist statement from a band that were rapidly being perceived as fascist 'bovver boys' were gratified by the considered production values and a commanding stint from Eve Libertine as lead vocalist.

"There was a point when we could have become the biggest Oi band going," reckons Penny, "Just after 'Feeding Of The 5000' came out, when even bands like the Cockney Rejects were desperate to come here and see what we were all about. Despite never having met us, they were massive fans, just on the strength of 'Feeding…', but when 'Penis Envy' came out, they were shocked into thinking, 'What a bunch of fucking cunts those blokes turned out to be!'

"We did play it that way – whenever it seemed that our public image was becoming too easily definable, we would do our best to throw people off the scent. Maybe not consciously, but certainly I as an artist have always enjoyed being contradictory, and I've always enjoyed playing with those contradictions."

The release of the 'Rival Tribal Rebel Revel' single, inspired by left wing attacks from the Red Brigade on British Movement skinheads at one of the band's Conway Hall gigs led to yet more confusion as to where the band stood politically, but Crass refused to take sides they didn't feel completely comfortable with.

"Yes, we had quite an argument with the Anti-Nazi League once," recalls Penny, "With whom we had no ideological quarrel, but I objected to the way they divided people in just as prejudiced a way as the people they were condemning. My own experiences with young skinheads who superficially said they supported the British Movement, or whatever it was called in those days, was that they were actually very lonely kids with nothing better to do. And if you gave them something better to think about, they often accepted it gratefully… generally speaking. And left wing prejudice just added fuel to the fire really. We very consciously left the door open to everybody. I've no patience with either the British Movement or the Trotskyite Red Brigade; they all play the same stupid games. I could see what Garry Bushell wanted to achieve with Oi, the unification of all these youths under one banner, but it backfired on him horribly."

Following the rather bizarre 'Merry Crassmas' single (the band's only overtly vegetarian statement), the noisy, over-produced, and rather forgettable 'Christ The Album' emerged during summer 1982, by which time the UK was at war with Argentina in the Falklands. This sad turn of events focused Crass on a specific target once again, our warmongering Prime Minister Margaret Thatcher, who was the subject of their rush-released flexi, 'Sheep Farming In The Falklands', and the next proper single, the poundingly belligerent 'How Does It Feel (To Be The Mother Of A Thousand Dead)?' The uproar these 'traitorous' releases caused amidst the patriotic media led to the band being discussed in Parliament and participating in a live radio debate with Tory MP Tim Eggar. The band ate the hapless fool for breakfast, of course, leading to letters of support from the opposition parties, and Crass found themselves teetering on the edge of a potentially lethal abyss.

Pete Wright of Crass at the Bingo Hall, Islington, March 1984, picture by Paul May.

"I didn't like playing 'Sheep Farming...' live," admits Steve. "I felt really uncomfortable doing it... and I know why now. I know it's their choice to join up [with the army], but I do feel compassion for the squaddie, and I think it was a bit shit to take the piss out of them really. Plus the fact that, it was all well and good to take the piss out of skinheads – the chances of them driving out into the middle of nowhere to do ya were fairly remote – but with Royal Marines, they might actually consider doing just that! I remember once the war had actually really kicked off and people really were being killed, and the '... Falklands' flexi had gone out, talking about soldiers shagging sheep and stuff, I thought to myself, 'Oh gawd, this is where it might get really nasty...'

"The only time I really got a bit scared though was when we started getting letters from the Labour Party, and from the House of Commons, all about 'How Does It Feel?' Up until then, I thought, 'We can really say what we want, we're so well known that no one's going to touch us... we'll just sell more records off the back of it...' But we started reaching those sorts of people... and I suddenly thought, 'This is starting to get a bit serious now...' And there is a point where you can rock the boat too much."

To bolster themselves for the battle looming large on the horizon, members of Crass organized the now-legendary squat gig at London's Zig Zag Club on December 18th, 1982, which was a resounding success on all fronts. Joined by well over a dozen other great bands, they proved that the underground punk scene could handle itself responsibly when it had to, and that music really could be enjoyed free of the restraints imposed upon it by corporate industry.

"I wasn't really involved in the arranging of it," says Steve, "But I remember turning up on the day and being overwhelmed by it all; everyone getting on so well, and no trouble or anything. And such an array of bands as well! You had D&V, and Conflict, and Zounds... and the organisers had done it all perfectly. We could never have done it all ourselves, so they're the unsung heroes of the whole day: the people who got in there and secured it, the people who were cooking food for everyone but didn't want paying for it... someone found some beer barrels in the cellar, so they came up, and that was free, and everyone had a great time.

"The idea was to go in there and squat it as a one-off and then vacate the place, but of course there were a few people who argued they had a right to stay there to live, and then a couple of

Zig Zag gig list, picture by Tony Mottram.

boneheads smashed the bogs up or something. But really I went away thinking, 'Oh, we've done it! All living together in harmony, if only for the day...' And we performed well that night; it was a good sound system, and the place was packed out... it was absolutely fantastic, and, like I said, no fights at all."

Buoyed by their success, Crass entered Southern Studios during March 1983 and recorded 'Yes Sir, I Will'. Possibly their most articulate and lasting statement lyrically (making such powerfully resonating observations as, 'Harrods boasts that it can supply any whim its wealthy clients might express... well, let them supply me an Exocet missile and a starving Third World child, and I'll teach them the politics of choice...'), it was unfortunately their least articulate musically by far. In fact, it was an awful noise that tried the patience of even the most ardent Crass fan... but that was the whole point of the exercise.

"That was our artistic approach," claims Penny. "As a writer now, whenever anyone accepts a piece of my work, I'm glad that's happened, but it gives me a license to push harder. And what I'm writing now is utterly unpublishable! To try and break down more cultural barriers... and my major input into Crass was that whenever we'd gotten anywhere, it was a green light for the next step. We had gained this large following of people who appeared to appreciate our records and wanted to grow with us, so every step we made was more like, 'Great, now let's try this!' And I accept that 'Yes Sir...' is truly one of the most unlistenable records ever made...

"The thing is, after 'Christ, The Album', we decided that we couldn't afford to take another fucking year writing, recording and manufacturing an album; people were very frightened and upset. And I think I wrote 'Yes Sir...' in a week; I just sat in my shed and did it. We didn't edit it or anything; I said, 'Right, here's the script; we're not going to rehearse!' and we went in and fucking did it. It was an immediate heart-felt response to what was going on around us... and that was the general route from the start. As things got worse, so they sounded worse... but it was a very honest process.

"We had realised that if we were to be an effective information service, we couldn't afford to spend an excessive amount of time on production... well, we could afford it financially, but certainly not psychologically... and so, from then on, we did those [subsequent] singles like 'Whodunnit?' and 'You're Already Dead' very quickly. They were like tactical responses, and if we had continued, I think that's how we would have done it. Almost working how a press reporter has to work – they do their thing today, and it's out tomorrow. 'Yes Sir...' was very much like that – we went in and recorded it and got it out, there was no fucking about."

"I didn't like 'Yes Sir, I Will' at all, although I liked what it was saying," adds Steve. "We actually performed that album in its entirety once live, actually holding the scripts up and reciting them, and I swore I'd never do it again, 'cos there was no rhythm, no beat, nothing; I didn't know what to do, and didn't enjoy it at all."

"And it *was* fucking unlistenable," continues a frustrated Penny, "But the majority of the people stuck it out, for no other reason than they were caught up in something other than their own thinking... what we were saying was, 'Back off! Fucking take a look!' We were very angry about the Falklands, and very, very angry that so few people seemed to have anything to fucking say about it. I didn't think that we could go on dancing the night away after the Falklands... so we did a piece of music that wouldn't allow people to have any fun to it. We thought that we would wipe the floor with people – that they would walk out of our gig and have to face what was happening... but they didn't. They jumped up and down, made the most they could out of a bad job, so they didn't have to actually look to themselves as we'd had to when we wrote it. Anything but start thinking... it was just so stupid, it was turning into a joke – which was why we had to stop... why we did stop."

Yes, Crass were rapidly reaching the end of their natural life, and thankfully those involved had the good sense to finish it all on their own terms rather than allow themselves to descend messily into self-parody. They still had one or two tricks up their sleeves though, not least of all sending the 'Thatchergate tape' – a cleverly edited recording of an alleged telephone conversation between then-US president Ronald Reagan and Margaret Thatcher, during which Thatcher admits responsibility for the sinking of the Argentine battleship, General Belgrano – to the world's press. Although blatantly a mischievous hoax, the vehemence with which it was investigated and denied by the authorities, suggested that the band had definitely struck a raw nerve in the corridors of power.

"Yes, it was a hoax," agrees Penny, "But all based on facts at the end of the day. Everything that Thatcher says on it was classified information that we'd gotten from this guy in the Falklands... and what Reagan says on it was all supposition, but all based on what one knew he was up to. It was serious stuff... serious enough for the Pentagon to be totally taken in by it anyway! And that's a very long way from turning up at the White Lion in Putney, half-pissed and having a good laugh...

"Although I can't remember feeling terrified, I can genuinely say that it was terrifying... I remember meeting the bloke from the Falklands who gave us all this information, meeting him at this bar in Victoria Station... it was horrible! Writing down all this information like it was a menu, and getting home and looking at it, and thinking, 'Fucking hell! What are we going to do with this...?'

"That sort of stuff isn't very funny, but that was us actually trying to be responsible, trying to do what we felt was our duty. And I don't think anyone else was getting representatives from Baader-Meinhof [the late Sixties/early Seventies German terrorist faction] turning up in their garden. So, there was this thing called punk rock, and everyone's out there making their records, all arguing amongst themselves about who was still wearing leather shoes, but none of them were getting the IRA claiming to be watching their backs! I mean, some of it was great, but some of it was not so great... we were a rock'n'roll band too... at least we thought we were!

"And that's another reason why we remain unique. All the time we were out on the road, all the time we were making records, all the time we were trying to help other people go out there and make records, all the time we were printing leaflets telling people how to make their own bread or whatever... at the same time, we were also dealing with all this other shit. Like getting letters from the Houses of Parliament... getting embroiled in other people's fucking power games... which we were happy to do in a very unhappy sort of way, because what else can you do when you get given the information? We carried a big, big load... because other people didn't know where to turn. Where else could some skinhead who joined the army and ended up in the Falklands write and say, 'This is what's happening... can you do something about it?' Other people could have fun, but we couldn't; it's hard to have fun when that sort of shit's going on around you."

Rumour has it that Crass had always planned to split up in 1984, and all their records' various catalogue numbers thus counted down to that ominous Orwellian deadline. Questioning their continued relevance, Crass did indeed collapse under the weight of internal and external pressure that very summer, following a rowdy benefit for the striking miners in Aberdare, South Wales, guitarist Andy being the first to jump ship, but it seems it was never written in stone that this was going to happen.

"Yeah, funny that, innit? I definitely didn't know anything about it!" scoffs Steve. "I just assumed that 1984 was a key date, and certainly didn't expect to finish after that Aberdare gig. The funny thing was though, when Andy said he was gonna pack it in, three or four of us – myself included – said, 'Yeah, so are we.' We were just tired of it all, and for me, there was this sense of relief, at not having to think like that all the time, look at all

Joy de Vivre of Crass, Liverpool 1984, picture by Andrew Medcalf.

those horrible images all the time. I was burnt out on it all, but two weeks later, of course, I had itchy feet, missing the adulation, and wanting to go back touring…

"And suddenly we were living with each other as individuals, and not as members of Crass anymore, so personal issues started to come to the fore, and some real antagonisms came to light… some really bitter stuff, and various people left Dial House as a result. While the band was going, we were all there for the common good, but the minute that the band was taken away, it all got directed at each other then… it all deteriorated from there really; once the band split up, so did the household… but I don't wanna go into all that really. It isn't fair, and it'll just set up another myth."

"No, we didn't play Aberdare knowing it would be the last show," confirms Penny, "But it was in the air, and it became fairly obvious travelling home in the van. There was a terrible sadness to that gig… it was a miners' benefit, and we'd put a fair amount of work into helping the miners' families, and we saw all these people broken by the vicious despot we had in power. And we realised that working class honour was being mercilessly trashed during that whole conflict; the dignity of the main force of people in this country was being dragged through the dirt. And we started thinking that it was wrong to be jumping up and down and shouting onstage, when these people didn't even know where their next fucking meal was coming from… everything had been taken from them, and it put a lot of things in perspective for us.

"There was a time when we felt that we could really make a difference to things, and there's no question that we helped shape this movement or whatever, but that gig somehow made us realise the futility of it all as well."

As one last act of clarification, members of Crass issued the 'Acts Of Love' and 'Ten Notes On A Summer's Day' albums, two sensitive collections of poetry that sought to demonstrate that the band's anger was borne of love not hatred. They merely added further to the indefatigable mystique surrounding Crass because they were so completely and unapologetically different to everything they had issued previously.

Steve Ignorant became a permanent member of Conflict – appearing at their now infamous 'Gathering Of The Five Thousand' show in 1987, and recording two studio albums with them in the late Eighties – before immersing himself in Schwartzeneggar, with members of Thatcher On Acid, and, most recently, in Stratford Mercenaries, with Gary from Dirt.

Penny has concentrated on his writing ever since (AK Press publishing his 'The Diamond

Signature' and 'Shibboleth' books), although still performs live on a regular basis and releases the occasional recording as The Crass Agenda, a free-form jazz project that bears little sonic resemblance to his old band but remains as intuitive as ever on a lyrical level. He still lives at Dial House, having fought a long hard battle against property developers to keep it standing, still considers himself an anarchist, and thankfully isn't averse to contemplating his time in Crass.

Meanwhile, Eve set up Red Herring Records with the enigmatic A-Soma, and still performs to this day, often with Penny; Gee remains on the cutting edge of film-making and graphics (her video collages that played a prominent part of the Crass stage show have even been compiled as the 'Semi-Detached' film, whilst all her stunning artwork from their records has been compiled by AK Press as the weighty 'Crass Art And Other Pre Post-Modernist Monsters' tome), and Pete Wright is currently involved with Martin Wilson in the Judas II project.

"I still question the whole concept of democracy," maintains Penny. "You hear that word thrown about so often, but I don't think there's a government in the west that presents a true model of democracy. I think the only true democracy lies somewhere in the anarcho construct. Equally I do acknowledge that many, if not most, people aren't capable – be it through slavery, through bad education, through bad social conditions... whatever – of determining their own lives. I'm not saying that in a condescending way either, but those opportunities don't exist for most people, and we tried so hard to say that they can. We were saying to working class kids that they weren't fucking idiots just 'cos they hadn't been to public school... we can all make our own decisions... they might not be world-shattering, but they can be personally shattering. That's the essence of anarchism: respect for yourself, and respect for others. And I don't mean respect yourself in any narcissistic or egotistical way, but just being able to trust yourself. That was very central to what we were saying, and that's still the path I continue on.

"I would have maybe thought twenty-five years ago that by now, aged sixty, I might have found some sort of solid ground, but it actually goes the other way. Rather than working towards some sort of pyramid point (where you can eventually stand at the top and say, 'Wow, now I understand!'), it's actually the opposite, and I ask bigger, wider questions now than ever before. Fucking hell, back then I was 'just' asking questions about the government and the church, but now I'm deconstructing my own feelings. The process continues, and that is essentially an anarchistic approach. I do not want to be a part of this cult of individuality, or this new age thing... knowing yourself isn't actually good enough. You have to know yourself before you can trust others, but it's the second part of the equation that's most important. Well, it's not most important, because that's like putting the cart before the horse, but if the only reason you're looking into yourself is to improve yourself... that 'Californian dream'... well, you can stuff it up your arse, because I'm not interested in that. I didn't want to destroy the church for my own sense of satisfaction, I wanted to do it because I believed that as human beings we could aspire to something a little bit better than a heaven you'll never see and a god you'll never know. I wasn't sure what it was, else I might have said so, and I'm still not sure what it is, but I do believe that there's something better than that.

"On a political level, I think the whole idea of co-operatives and decentralisation, the whole syndicalism thing, is very sensible ground. But given the fact that we're living in an increasingly globalised world, and the leaders of that globalised world are more than ready to inflict violence upon anyone who opposes it, then it's a bit daft to say, 'Oh, let's base our model on these Catalonian syndicates!' Fuck me, we need to base the model on ourselves, so we are strong enough to resist all of what globalisation is throwing at us right now. I think we should have a long-term political view, but until we're clean enough in ourselves to honestly say we're not just catering to our own little desires, it won't work.

"Fear is the key. We don't need imposed slavery in Great Britain because people willingly put on their manacles every morning because the fear of what will happen if they don't is so deeply instilled in them. We've had four hundred years of 'democratic' conditioning... we don't need to be told we'll be in the shit if we don't get up at 8 o'clock. In less developed nations, people are still asking questions; they think, 'Oh fuck it, I'm going to stay in bed a bit longer,' or 'I'm not going to work today, I'll sit and eat this mango!' They're not yet in the manacles of capitalist economics… although it's trying its best in every corner of the globe.

"The thing is, it is possible to live outside the system, and, with Ringo [Starr]'s 'a little help from my friends', that's how I've lived all my adult life. We live very frugally; we live in a very valuable house, thanks to the generosity of some close friends, on very, very little. I'm not about to feel guilty about it. I've lived by my wits, and one can do that – if one's prepared to do without. Or go out and do something to get whatever you need. I mean, I used to work as a coalman to pay the rent. I wasn't prepared to do that to buy myself a Porsche, but it was worth it to have a place to live where we could all sit around and talk revolution. But that's anarchy, a co-operation, sharing, putting aside one's own little fantasies and desires…

"Yes, what we're doing now is a very natural and logical extension of what we were doing before. No one should be shocked, at least no one who knew us. We're still every bit as radical and confrontational as we were then."

"And I'm not putting myself down as an idiot," ponders Steve honestly, "But all I was was an oik in a band, y'know? Who wanted to be Johnny Rotten! But, not being thick or stupid, I quickly believed in everything we were saying, because I could see that it was fundamentally right, and I still live my life to most of those terms and conditions. But it was a weird thing to have to deal with, because we didn't get people coming up to us saying, 'Oh, great gig!' It was always, 'Oh, about what you said about so-and-so…' And because I was in Crass, I had to deal with that, whether I felt like it or not.

"On the other hand, as well as the people who loved what we did, you also had the people who fucking hated it, and they were even more intense. I remember when all the factions were splitting, and there was a lot of hatred towards Crass, I was thinking, 'This isn't what I set out to do… I thought we were all going to be mates down the pub!'

"It all snowballed out of control really, and went into areas that I didn't understand. Where I got my ideas of anarchism from were the black-and-white Sixties films about angry young men… Allen Ginsberg… Jack Kerouac… films like 'Taste Of Honey', where this woman has sex with a black guy, is having a baby and living with a gay bloke. That was what I thought anarchy was about, being able to speak your mind and break down barriers – not Spanish revolutions and Polish miner strikes. I mean, good luck to 'em if they won, and also if they lost, but it doesn't really have any relevance to my own circumstances.

"I'd be at gigs, hanging about afterwards, and I'd be watching members of the support bands copping off with girls and stuff, and I'd be stuck discussing anarchy and peace with some idiot in an anorak holding a clipboard, thinking, 'Hang on a minute, there's something wrong here…!'

"Once, when I was onstage in Los Angeles with the Stratford Mercenaries, I became aware of this red dot dancing over my chest, and for an instant, I thought, 'Oh shit, here we go, out like John Lennon!' But it was only someone with one of these flashy ballpoint pens with a laser light on it…

"What I'm now finding is, I go to the pub around the corner, where no one knows me as Steve Ignorant from Crass, and it's just normal blokes, people from the [pro-bloodsports] Countryside Alliance and all that, reckoning that we shouldn't have blacks living around here and all that sort of shit, and I'm gradually putting them right on a few things. And the funny thing is, it's like being on the front line all over again, arguing about racism and sexism and all that.

"They all know I was in a band, of course, and they're like, 'Oh, what was the name of your band, Steve?' 'Crass!' 'Oh, right…' And they go off and think no more about it, but then the other night someone came in and said, 'Hey, Steve, I was talking to some girl up in Rochdale who was into punk, and she used to absolutely love your band! So you were famous then?' And I'm like, 'Well yeah, check it out on the internet!'

"Sometimes it really sort of moves me that people are still so interested, all over the world. Alright, so I ain't got a car, and I never ended up rich and famous, and I ain't got my own recording studio, and I don't go to parties with Paul Weller or whatever, but it's comforting that I can go to just about any country in the world, and meet people who know about Crass.

"Also, you can get vegetarian food in every single café now – people are so much more aware of all that – and I was a small part of helping that thought process arrive. I'm not saying it was because of Crass, but we were a part of it, and I can hold my head up... because I did my bit. I did go on the protest marches, even though I sometimes didn't want to; sometimes I hated it, but I'm glad that I went. All those Stop The Cities and that... yeah, I wouldn't have missed it for the world."

By means of a postscript, in November 2002, all the original members of the Crass collective performed at the 'Voices And Music Against War' event, at the Queen Elizabeth Hall on London's South Bank, although they did not appear onstage at the same time. Thankfully, Crass are one band that will never reform, and hence their legacy remains as pure and honest as the day it was created, untainted by the vociferous appetite of profit-driven nostalgia.

SELECT DISCOGRAPHY

7"s:

'Reality Asylum' (Crass, 1980)
'Bloody Revolutions' (Crass/Xntrix, 1980) – split with Poison Girls
'Nagasaki Nightmare' (Crass, 1980)
'Rival Tribal Rebel Revel' (Crass, 1980) – first issued as a limited flexi-disc
'Merry Crassmas' (Crass, 1981)
'How Does It Feel?' (Crass, 1982)
'Sheep Farming In The Falklands' (Crass, 1983) – first issued as a limited flexi
'Whodunnit?' (Crass, 1983)
'You're Already Dead' (Crass, 1984)

12"s:

'The Feeding Of The 5000' (Small Wonder, 1978)
'Ten Notes On A Summer's Day' (Crass, 1984)

LPs:

'Stations Of The Crass' (Crass, 1980) – double LP
'Penis Envy' (Crass, 1981)
'Christ The Album' (Crass, 1982) – double LP
'Yes Sir, I Will' (Crass, 1983)
'Acts Of Love' (Crass, 1984)

At A Glance:

Anyone who has taken the trouble to buy this book and read this far needs to own at least 'The Feeding Of The 5000' and 'Stations Of The Crass', both of which have been reissued on CD by Crass/Southern with full lyrics and artwork, although it has to be said that the CD versions of these releases simply can't do justice to the original stunning gatefold posters that the band wrapped their vinyl releases in. The 'Best Before... 1984' CD collects all the band's timeless singles onto one disc, complete with a thick booklet of lyrics and notes by Penny Rimbaud, and is another essential purchase. Finally, the Pomona book 'Love Songs' compiles all the band's lyrical outpourings (that still work surprisingly well as stand-alone pieces of poetry) in one highly recommended volume, whilst Penny's own book 'Shibboleth' is a must-read experience for anyone intrigued to learn more about Crass.

Hot on the heels of Crass, **FLUX OF PINK INDIANS** also surely rate as one of the most important anarcho-punk bands ever. Hailing from Bishops Stortford, the band produced several classics of the genre – not least of all the rather glorious 'Neu Smell' EP for Crass… a record probably responsible for more punk rockers turning vegetarian than any other – before nose-diving into pretension and eventually self-destructing rather messily. Like their mentors Crass, they ultimately succumbed to the relentless pressures placed upon them by the often-restrictive scene they themselves helped create. Of course, things weren't always so complicated for the band, who began life in 1978 as The Epileptic Fits and actually first picked up their instruments with ambitions no loftier than making a bloody racket for the sheer hell of it.

"It was just totally different really," recalls vocalist Colin Latter of his immediate attraction to punk rock in 1976. "I'd been into all the usual bands before then – Deep Purple, Zeppelin, Yes… all those kind of bands… but punk had such an energy, it was totally new. Plus I remember that, in all the classes in my year at school, there was maybe only the four of us that liked it, so there was the added attraction of liking something that most other people didn't.

"To be honest, I can't imagine that we'd have even had the idea to start a band without punk. We started off as The Epileptic Fits… I think my mum came up with the name! But we thought that was terrible, so we shortened it to The Epileptics. We had a guitarist who could play a

Flux Of Pink Indians vocalist Colin Latter, picture by Tony Mottram.

bit [Clive Griffiths] and a drummer that had never drummed [Richie Coveney]. I couldn't sing either, but that didn't really matter, and we didn't have a bass player, so the early rehearsals were just drumming on cardboard boxes with the guitar going through a little 30 watt practise amp, and me screaming over the top.

"Derek [Birkett] used to hang around with us, and we asked him to play bass, but he thought it was a boring instrument and said he'd never play it. So I bought a bass guitar, and tried to play bass and sing at the same time, but that was impossible from scratch, and in the end Derek picked it up and had a go. We were just school friends, and none of us, apart from the guitarist, had ever touched an instrument before in our lives. We lived in semi-detached houses, in a very average suburban area, and it was great when we went to visit the drummer… 'cos you could hear him drumming about a hundred yards down the road! I always thought that it was unfortunate for drummers, 'cos how the hell do they ever learn when they've got nowhere to really practise? But he used to buy all the punk records of the time and work out how to play them, and he came along really quickly. If you listen to the first single, '1970s' is actually quite a complex drum pattern; fair play to him, he wasn't content to just tap away in the background..."

With the enthusiastic impetuosity of youth on their side, The Epileptics wasted little time taking to the stage to ply their wares in public... even if it was at their local haunt minus their regular bassist.

"It was at the Triad in Bishops Stortford, at an all-day punk gig. Derek had gone on holiday, so we asked Steve [Drewett], the guitarist from the Newtown Neurotics, to play bass for us, but he didn't know any of the songs so he just plodded along. But we were on early in the day anyway, so there weren't many people there to see us.

"The second gig we did was actually with Crass, and that was a bit of a funny one really. 'cos of a cock-up they had a gig arranged at the Basement in Covent Garden, London, the same night that we did, so we decided to combine the two. We'd only done the one gig, and Crass had only been together for about six months then, and no one had done any advertising... so, only two people wandered in during the sound checks, but wandered back out again, and apart from that, not one person came to the gig! So we played to them, and they played to us, but it was a good way of the two bands bonding.

"I'd already seen Crass play at the Triad before then [August 2nd, 1978], and was totally shocked by them really; they were like nothing else I'd ever seen. We weren't expecting anything at all, it was mid-1978, punk was dead apparently, and every band we saw there, week in, week out, was basically crap. A band called The Heat were headlining, I think they were soft punk or whatever, and Crass opened. We were really anti-fascist at the time, and I can remember seeing them with their banners and all their black gear on, and thinking, 'I don't like the look of them!' Then Steve [Ignorant] came over and said, 'You got the time, mate?' And one of my mates thought he was definitely a punk!

"We stood there at the front of the stage, looking at them, and half of them were bald, and we didn't know whether to knock all their water over onstage or what, but after about the third song, one of us turned to the others and said, 'Start pogoing!' and we all went crazy! And then we talked to them afterwards, and told them that we thought they looked like fascists... and Penny wrote me a letter a few days later – I wish I'd kept it – that said all across the bottom, 'And we ain't no fucking fascists!'"

This rudimentary version of The Epileptics, although penning several decent tunes that would later be reworked for use in Flux Of Pink Indians, were still a million miles away lyrically from the serious political statements they would eventually become synonymous with.

"Yes, our songs were dreadful!" laughs Colin. "Some of the lyrics were just foul-mouthed, perverted stuff, mainly written by Clive, like 'I Wanna Give You A 69'! Typical early punk stuff, rather than anything politically correct. Either Crass didn't give a shit, or couldn't hear what we were singing, 'cos they offered us another gig, which was up in Bradford.

"But before that, we played locally again, just after Kevin [Hunter] had joined the band, when Clive left. A local scene was emerging, and Stortbeat Records were arranging all these gigs but they didn't want us to play 'cos they thought we were really bad. Kevin was actually quite a good guitarist and had already played in a local band called The Darlex, so everyone was shocked when he joined us, whom they all thought was the worst local band going."

"Originally we thought we'd call ourselves The Antichrist," reveals Kevin of The Darlex, who settled on their name in March 1977. "After the first line from 'Anarchy In The UK', of course, but we only had that name for a few weeks, then we changed it to Urban SS... obviously nicking the idea from the London SS that we'd read about. By March 1977 we had changed it again to The Darlex. Can't remember why, but it just seemed like a good idea at the time! And we changed the way it was spelt in [popular TV sci-fi show] 'Dr. Who'; I think we imagined we might be big one day and didn't want to get any hassle from Terry Nation, the Daleks creator!

"Our set was made up of songs like 'Sod The Jubilee' [inspired by one of the ad-libs on the fade-out of '1977' by The Clash], 'Routine Day', 'I Hate Work', 'Smash The Councils', 'Born To Rule', and one called 'Boutique Clique', which was taking the piss out of punks who bought their clothes off the peg for stupid amounts of money, rather than taking the DIY route that we did. I used to paint all my own t-shirts; one was a rip of the Seditionaries' 'Destroy' design… it had the word at the top in the same style but a big question mark in white on a red circle (instead of the swastika) with 'negativity' underneath it. I also did one of a wounded policeman being carried by his colleagues, and stencilled 'Riot' at the top. I don't think any of us had any mass-produced punk clothes; we just used to stencil or paint-splash on shirts from chazzers [charity shops] and wear straight trousers and Doc Martens. Paul, our singer used to wear this diarrhoea-coloured boiler suit most of the time which he'd flicked paint all over. I did buy a leather jacket from a motorbike shop once, after seeing Steve Jones and Sid Vicious wearing them in the Pistols video for 'Pretty Vacant' on Top Of The Pops. That was my one concession to the ready-made look.

"After The Darlex disintegrated, I'd noticed some graffiti around the town… the name Epileptics sprayed on walls and stuff, with the legend 'Smash guitar solos', and I was determined to find out who they were. In late 1978, I was at the Triad, and I asked someone if they knew who 'these Epileptics' were. This bloke called Stringy, who later formed The Eratics, pointed to two younger kids, one who looked like a punk with a quiff and one who was a skinhead, and said, 'Well, that's the singer and that's the drummer!' I went over to them and said that I thought their name was brilliant, and even though I hadn't seen or heard what they were like I was intrigued by them. I also said, 'If you're ever looking for a guitarist, let me know', and then Col looked at Richard, smiled and looked back at me, and told me that their guitarist Clive was leaving to go to college. And that was it, I was in, I'd become a member of The Epileptics."

"So, the next gig we did was with this Hell's Angel band, 'cos they were the only people who would give us a gig," continues Colin. "And then we had this CND benefit in Bradford with Crass and the Poison Girls… although we never actually played in the end. The van broke down so we didn't turn up until 11 o'clock… but when we did turn up, just as everything was finishing, at least they realised that we were serious! We got stuck up there that night in the snow and had to sleep in the van…"

Through several more gigs over the next year, Crass helped introduce Epi-x (as they became known briefly, following complaints regarding their name from the British Epilepsy Association) to the London crowds, and even offered them a one-single deal with their fledgling label. But, following an initial demo, recorded March '79 at Romford's Speedway Studios (one song of which, 'Two Years Too Late', was subsequently adopted as their own by Derbyshire band, Anti Pasti), The Epileptics, in yet another pique of youthful naivety, had already signed the next two years of their musical career away to the aforementioned Stortbeat, who released the '1970s' EP in November 1979.

A suitably abrasive debut, '1970s' hinted at the brilliant noises to come, the title track effortlessly stealing the show with its compelling chorus hook built around Colin ranting, 'Plastic crap! Plastic crap! That keeps going wrong!' On the flip-side, despite displaying some strong ideas, neither 'System Rejects' nor 'Hitler's Still A Nazi' manage to rise above the horribly messy production.

"We recorded it at Spaceward up in Cambridge; just went in and did it all in one day [on September 2nd, 1979]. Didn't even know what songs we were going to do until we got there, and we were really influenced by this guy Shane, who was the guitarist in a psychedelic punk band on Stortbeat called The Sods. But you go in the studio and see all these buttons, and get totally carried away, and those three tracks ended up sounding nothing like we really were. It must have been pretty good though, 'cos Peel played it over and over again; he must have played it at least twenty times. But I think it only sold about a thousand copies, 'cos the record label went bust – yet they still held us right until our contract was up!"

Still, with Stortbeat eventually rolling over and releasing them, The Epileptics were at last free to take Crass up on their earlier offer of a single, which resulted in a true genre classic in the shape of the aforementioned 'Neu Smell' EP. But not before they had changed their name to Flux Of Pink Indians and undergone a significant line-up shuffle.

"Kevin and Richard left," explains Colin. "Richard left first; we'd been going for about a year and a half, and getting more and more involved with Crass, who were more politically motivated than musically. That suited me and Derek down to the ground, but not so much Kevin and Richard. The only drummer I knew was Sid [Ation] from Rubella Ballet, and it seemed up in the air whether they were still going or not, so I told Kevin that I was going to try and track him down and get him to play for us, but Kevin didn't like the idea at all."

"Being in The Epileptics had been great although the band did tend to have two factions," reckons Kev. "Colin and Derek on one side, me and Richard on the other. I think it basically boiled down to the fact that Col and Derek were always more political than us, certainly after we'd gotten more involved with Crass, whereas Rich and I were more interested in the musical side of things. It became particularly apparent when we played a couple of gigs outside of our 'comfort zone' (if that doesn't sound too petty) and it almost led to The Epileptics splitting in two.

"On the first occasion we had a gig in Deptford, South London, where we were one of about fifteen bands that were supposed to play sometime between the afternoon and the evening. As was generally the way at these multi-band gigs the whole thing was a shambles – someone had the idea, got all the bands to come along, but there was no organisation whatsoever. A complete free-for-all, and as a result it meant that the bands just hung around for fucking ages, not knowing when or if they would even get chance to play their set. I don't think it bothered Col or Derek at all, but after a couple of hours Rich and I started to get really pissed off, and we decided to go back home. It wasn't as if people had come to see us anyway, so we weren't going to disappoint anyone, but me and Rich buggered off, and Col and Derek weren't happy about the way we'd behaved, and looking back I can't say I wouldn't have felt the same way in their shoes. But we got over it, and were rehearsing again the following week, so not too much harm done!

"Then a month or so later we got the chance to play at Stonehenge, which Crass were also doing. Right from the start Rich had reservations and so did I; we couldn't see why we would want to play to an ostensibly hippy audience, but we went along anyway. Once again, there didn't seem to be any kind of organisation at all, and we arrived at the place mid-afternoon to be told that we'd be playing late afternoon. Nothing happened, and we were then told that we'd be on sometime in the early evening, so we waited and waited, and it was a grim place to be. There was fuck all to do, no decent food to eat… the mobile toilet wagon was set at a jaunty angle and you couldn't get closer than three feet to the urinals or you'd be wading in piss… and these horrible little hippy kids were climbing in the Transit and going through our bags and jackets trying to nick our stuff.

"Well, we still hadn't played by about 7 o'clock that evening so Rich and I said that we'd had enough and got into a big argument with Col, Derek and our so-called 'manager', Dave Direktor – and refused to play even if we were eventually allocated a time. So that was that; we all piled back into the van, not speaking to each other! It all sounds very childish now, but it goes to show how the two factions in the band had quite different attitudes.

"A few days later, we were all okay again, but I think that had definitely caused some damage. Anyway, we made it through to the end of the year, then just before Christmas 1979, Rich decided that he was going to leave the band; at first I thought I'd stick around, but as soon as Col and Derek told me that they were thinking of getting Sid in on drums I realised that the band would end up being a 3-against-1 kind of outfit, with me out in the cold, so I jacked it in too."

Andy Smith and Neil Puncher, both guitarists with local band The U. Samples, were consequently recruited, the latter actually filling in on drums until Sid joined before moving to

The Epileptics live at the Triad, November 1979 (left to right: Derek, Colin, guitarist Kev and drummer Richard.

second guitar. It was this line-up that recorded the 'Neu Smell' single.

"It was Steve from Crass, he was the first person that I knew who was into the American Indian stuff, and I got quite into it through him," adds Colin, as regards the unusual choice of new moniker they settled on in the end. "Originally I suggested calling ourselves Tribe Of Pink Indians, as opposed to Red Indians, of course. We'd been writing loads of new songs, and there was only really me and Derek left from The Epileptics, hence the change of name. The Epileptics was more of a straight punk name really, but Crass actually liked it, and when we turned up to play Stonehenge with them again the following year [a notoriously violent show this time, which ended in a near riot between bikers and punks, with Flux being bottled offstage!] and said, 'We're going to change the name to Flux Of Pink Indians', they just laughed and said, 'We'll pretend we didn't hear that!' They thought it was the worst idea they'd ever heard... but Crass were always lucky to have an 'A' in the middle of their name. The real reason we changed our name from The Epileptics was because there wasn't an 'A' to circle in it!

"It was like starting all over again, but there was no thought given to whether people would know who we were or anything. We never thought about anything like that, but things still just seemed to happen, records and gigs and stuff... but later on, if I fast forward to when I started Hotalacio, you couldn't get anything. No one wanted to know, and I realised what hard work it was when things don't just happen naturally. Flux had stuff offered us all the time, and we just said 'No!' to everything, 'cos it just didn't seem to matter. Then later on, when we actually wanted stuff to happen, we couldn't get sod all."

Recorded – like all releases on Crass – at Southern Studios, by John Loder and Penny Rimbaud, the single was a resounding success upon its release during the summer of '81, spending the better part of a year in the Indies and peaking at No. 2. It was only kept from the coveted 'top spot' by Depeche Mode's 'New Life', a single that actually made No. 11 in the mainstream National Charts – an indication of just how many units Flux actually shifted of their debut.

A cathartic blast of viciously distorted guitars and relentlessly powerful drums, the thrust of the release was the utterly infectious, oft-copied-but-never-equalled-since 'Tube Disaster', which was actually an old Epileptics track that was never even intended for inclusion on the EP.

"Yeah, the night before we recorded it, we went round to the Crass house and played them all our songs, and between us, with Penny, we decided which three songs we were going to record. We'd already decided what we thought we were going to record, but Penny decided on another three, and when we went into the studio the next day, we thought, 'Why have we changed our minds? Let's do it our way!' And Penny basically told us to fuck off; we had to do it his way or not at all. And Derek was like, 'Oh shit, we better do those three songs then!' I suppose we *had* agreed the day before with him to do these three songs, but it was this mate of ours that used to drive us around that said, 'Well, why have you changed your minds?' But in the end we did the three songs that Penny wanted, and it turned out bloody great.

"The song 'Tube Disaster' itself was actually inspired by the Moorgate tragedy [when the 08:37 tube from Drayton Park to Moorgate inexplicably crashed, killing 43 people on February 28th, 1975], but to be honest with you, when I first wrote it, it was just a punk shock lyric, which Derek later on interpreted as something deep and meaningful. But I was working in London at the time, and was always travelling on the Tube, and I wrote it as a shock-horror-type thing. I actually wrote it at the same time as a song about this pompous business man who loses his ticket and is trapped down the underground for ten years, unable to get out 'cos he's too scared to just walk through the barriers, and in the end he thinks, 'Fuck it!' and runs through and no one stops him. And 'Tube Disaster' was intended as a similarly dark, humorous song, but Derek or Penny added the line, 'Vicarious living rids your boredom', and that totally changed the concept of the song. I did used to write a lot of strange songs that made perfect sense to me, but were a bit silly to other people!"

Whatever the ambiguity surrounding 'Tube Disaster', there could be no misinterpretation of the two tracks on the B-side – both 'Background Of Malfunction' and 'Sick Butchers' were specifically critical of man's inhumanity to animals. With lyrics that included the damning couplet, 'You try to stroke me in a field and then go home and eat me as your meal', and a thought-provoking fold-out poster sleeve, complete with horrific images from within the manmade hell known as the abattoir. Strange then that, in the picture on the back sleeve, three of the band are wearing leather jackets… and Colin himself wasn't even a vegetarian when he wrote the lyrics!

"To be honest, Derek was the only person I knew who was vegetarian," admits the singer. "And yes, I wrote the lyrics on 'Neu Smell' under his influence when I wasn't even a vegetarian myself. I can remember playing the 100 Club and going out to get a burger somewhere afterwards… it was only later on that I realised I ought to be taking it all a bit more seriously! Derek wasn't really a songwriter, you see, but I could take his ideas and write about them, even when I wasn't doing them myself.

"And later on, I must admit that I met some people who were so into animal rights they were totally oblivious to human suffering. I remember when Ken Livingstone of the GLC was giving a speech at Crouch End Town Hall, and we all went along as anarchos – anti-Labour and all that… well, we were anti-fucking-everything, to tell the truth… and I shouted out, 'Well, are you vegetarian?' And I'm not sure if I shouted it in response to something he said, or because that was all I could think about. But anyway, he turned around and said 'Yes!' and that shut me up!

"But it's strange really, 'cos the artwork wasn't really us either. When Crass asked us what we wanted for the sleeve, we didn't really know – I wanted [what would become] the 'Spiderleg skull' on the front, with spiky hair and everything, and Derek hated it – he never liked it actually – so Crass went ahead and just did the sleeve without really asking us. I hated it at the time, I thought it was so 'not punk', but now I look at it and think, 'What a great sleeve!'

"And the guy in the cloak on the inside… I think that was 'cos I was into the 'Lord Of The Rings' at the time, all that 'Middle Earth' stuff… then when we bumped into bands from Dorset and the West Country, we realised that a lot of them were quite into all that pagan stuff, and that's when the hippy thing started to come back in, and it was okay to have long hair again."

"I went along to see them in spring 1981 when they played at the Triad," Kev recollects. "And it did feel a bit weird for me, seeing Col and Derek in what was almost a completely different band but playing some of the songs that we'd been doing a couple of years previously. And image-wise they looked quite different too… apart from Derek, who was still into the Mark E. Smith look, just nondescript baggy trousers and jumpers, the others were predominantly decked out in black; they had Crass-style backdrops on stage, and Colin was a lot more focussed, more intense as a vocalist. In the Epileptics he'd been a bit of a nutter, whether kicking a monitor offstage, swinging from a light fitting, or just generally playing the 'punk', but now he was more studied, almost aloof, and it was weird.

"I felt a bit left out actually, as around this time I'd seen Col at a mate's party, and he'd told me about 'Neu Smell' and played a tape of it to me. I thought it sounded a lot more powerful and less commercial than the Epileptics stuff, but I couldn't help feeling a bit jealous that the main track on it was 'Tube Disaster', which me and Col had written together back in late '78, yet I wasn't even on this version of it. It was a real shame!"

Their profile greatly boosted by the leg-up from Crass, and now suitably knowledgeable in the mechanics of record production, the band then set up their own label, Spiderleg – albeit financed and distributed by Southern – with the intention of releasing future Flux material themselves. But not before they'd re-released the Epileptics' '1970s' single, and issued several EPs by the likes of Subhumans, Amebix and The System. And also not before they'd endured yet more predictably pointless line-up disruptions; Andy then Sid both left, the latter to concentrate once again on Rubella Ballet, making way for a brief appearance from Dave 'Bambi' Ellesmere and Simon Middlehurst, drummer and guitarist respectively with Wigan-based punk band, The Insane. An arrangement that was doomed to be temporary given the logistics of writing and rehearsing material with half the band on the other side of the country anyway, and one that broke down rather dramatically in the end as well.

"When 'Neu Smell' did so well, Stortbeat decided that they were going to re-release '1970s', so we went down to Southern one night, and Penny was in there, and we were moaning about them repressing the single. He suggested that we re-record it, and then try to persuade Rough Trade to sell our version rather than Stortbeat's, and we agreed because they'd been so unhelpful with our contract.

"The idea was to get the original Epileptics back together to record it again; Kevin said yes, but Richard didn't wanna do it, so we asked Bambi to do the drums, but didn't ask Simon to play guitar. So they got a bit funny about it, and went and played a gig ['Woodstock Revisited' at the Rainbow] with The Insane that Flux had turned down, the very same day that Bambi was meant to be in the studio with us re-recording '1970s'. We guessed what they'd done, so we went down the venue and had it out with them. Derek went and found them in their dressing room and dragged them both outside to face the music. Simon didn't give a toss, but Bambi seemed quite upset about it all really."

The end result of this confusion was that Penny stood in behind the kit for the new, artist-endorsed '1970s' single, and then Spider from The System helped out when they recorded 'Tapioca Sunrise' for the hugely successful 'Wargasm' compilation for Pax, on which they appeared alongside the Dead Kennedys, Angelic Upstarts and Infa Riot.

Long-time fan and correspondent of the band, Martin Wilson, then joined on drums, but rhythm guitarist Neil also decided to bow out, so Kev became an official member once again, just in time for the band's only Indie No. 1, late '82's 'Strive To Survive Causing The Least Suffering Possible' album. Was there ever a more heroic motto to live one's life by? Possibly not, and the music behind the title was just as forceful and profound. As well as pounding slices of heart-felt protest such as 'Progress' and 'They Lie, We Die' (the two best songs, in the traditional sense of the word, ever penned by the band), the ambitious packaging included detailed information about the government's various nuclear fallout shelters.

Colin: "Derek had this thing that every single line should matter, and that if you were writing a song about a subject, you should include all these different points of view, and make sure that nothing was left out… which is a bit of a flat way to write a song, to be honest. It was like going back to school.

"So, when you get to 'Strive', it was still me writing most of the songs, but Derek would re-write a lot of them. If you hear the demos of that material, the lyrics are one way, but slightly different on the album. But on 'Myxomatosis', Kevin's saying my original lyrics in the background, but the actual lyrics being sung are Derek's rewriting of my song because it hadn't touched on what it could've touched on. We were getting quite serious about it all, which wasn't Kev's cup of tea at all.

"You know? I'm sure Simon [Middlehurst] had something to do with writing some of the guitar bits on both 'Myxomatosis' and 'Blinded By Science'. And Kevin only had one rehearsal tape of it to work out what he'd done, so he ended up reinterpreting it all…"

"We wanted the album to be really punchy, so I got a fat guitar sound," explains Kev. "I was aiming for something like Steve Jones of the Pistols crossed with Tony Iommi of Black Sabbath, and I think Penny was quite accommodating; in fact I laid down three or four layers of chords, recording the same guitar parts one on top of the other to pad out the sound. It was just such a great experience to be able to spend time getting exactly what we wanted down onto tape. We'd carry on recording until late in the night, or into the early hours, then go upstairs (where we had our sleeping bags) and crash out, then get up the next morning, throw some food down our necks and go back in to start all over again.

"It was Penny's idea to have the layers of feedback between each track, to sort of link them all together, so I had to crank up my amp to maximum and just get the strings vibrating... then move the guitar around to vary the feedback, and the volume was set so high that I only had to change my position a few inches to make the squealing sound different. I don't know how long I did this, probably only for ten minutes or so, and it completely knackered my eardrums; then when I'd finished, Penny said, 'That was great... now do it all over again!' I thought he was winding me up, so I said, 'Fuck off!' But then he told me that I needed to record a second layer of feedback so that he could put it on top of the first take, to make it sound really noisy, and I did, but it was really painful...

"I didn't realise it at the time, but I must have killed my amp doing all that, and the following week we played a gig in Milton Keynes, and the bloody thing just wouldn't work at all. Anyway, once we'd finished laying all the tracks down, we had to go back in and listen to a rough mix, and it sounded fucking brilliant. Somehow though, between then and the LP being pressed, Penny remixed the whole thing and compressed the guitar so that it sounded thin and fizzy, more like Crass's own sound. I didn't know it was going to be like that until we were given the white label test-pressings, and when I heard it I was gutted. I can't remember who told me, but apparently Penny doesn't like rock music, and reckoned that the original guitar sound had been 'too macho'! Fucking unbelievable really, but there you go."

Despite such a sterling release in the racks though, behind the scenes it was business as usual for the Flux soap opera, with yet more dissent in the ranks.

"Just before we did 'Strive...', Derek was threatening to leave, because we weren't serious enough, but we managed to convince him to stay and do it," sighs Colin. "At the time it seemed so important to keep him in the band... and I'm not sure why. He was definitely a big influence on what we did, but I suppose he was a bit of a dictator too. Like we were driving to this gig and he told us that Virgin had contacted us, after the success of 'Neu Smell', and offered us a deal, but he'd told them to 'Fuck off!' And Kevin was like, 'How can you make that decision without asking us?' And Derek replied, 'Well, if you wanna do it, I'm leaving...' And that was it, and he would always come out with that; we always had that hanging over our heads. But he would also do some amazing things, like sticking up for you when no one else would, and stuff.

"It would've been strange if he'd left then though, 'cos he was working in the tax office at the time, and we'd have done 'Strive...' with some other bassist, and then we might have signed with Virgin after all, and Derek might never have started [his own label] One Little Indian!"

Recorded over five days at Southern Studios ("The best five days of my life," smiles Colin), with Penny Rimbaud at the helm again, it was hardly surprising that Flux Of Pink Indians were growing ever closer to Crass in both sound and attitude, not least of all in the vocal department.

"We were always one step behind Crass really," admits Colin. "The first single wasn't influenced by them at all, 'cos we didn't even know them then, but by the time we'd done 'Strive...' we'd been gigging a lot with them, and my vocals were just like Steve's. We were just sounding more like them; we were part of that scene and you couldn't sing muck-about songs anymore. We didn't worry about being in their shadow or anything though, and we actually pissed them off quite a bit sometimes.

"I remember that we did gigs with Six Minute War, and they had openly slagged Crass off on one of their EPs, and Crass were shocked that we would endorse that. And we were going to do this record on Spiderleg for a band called This Bitter Lesson – just a girl singer, guitarist and drummer – and it sounded like the song was anti-abortion. Crass heard it, 'cos it was recorded at Southern, and they said that if we ever released it, they would take out a page ad in Sounds disowning us, so

Flux Of Pink Indians, Sunderland Bunker, April 1983, picture by Andrew Medcalf.

it never came out. I still don't know what the song was all about either! So, we did lose a lot of the fun side of being in a band, but we always thought Crass were 'the business' really; they were amazing, even when we didn't see eye to eye on everything."

Many gigs were undertaken to promote the 12" the length and breadth of the UK – but never abroad (Colin: "Derek had this idea that we were an English band and that we were singing about issues that specifically affected people living in England... but basically he had this real fear of flying!"), a period that Kev remembers fondly... for the most part, at least!

"One of the best gigs was at Digbeth Civic Hall [May 3rd, 1982], which we played with Crass and Dirt. It was a massive place, or certainly seemed like it. I'd seen a picture of it on Black Sabbath's 'Volume Four' LP years before, and it shows the band from the back, with the audience out in front of them, and bugger me, there I was looking out at the same hall! It was packed, people everywhere, the place even had balcony seats! And it seemed to me like, 'Wow, we're pretty well known now.' Obviously more people had come to see Crass than Dirt or Flux, but the atmosphere was brilliant, really enthusiastic. I think the response must be something to do with the Midlands, as that part of the country seems very warm, very into whatever music it is. The gigs in the Midlands and the north of England (especially St. Helens, Preston, Burnley, etc.) were almost always better than the ones we played in and around London and the Southeast. Maybe it's always been like that, maybe it still is, but Southern audiences always seemed more jaded, harder to impress... maybe they were spoilt for choice? In the Midlands and the North, people always seemed far more appreciative, more into what we were about. And they were a lot friendlier, more genuine individually, whereas Southerners always struck me as more suspicious and aloof. Somehow it felt as if they wanted to be part of an elite... which is really ironic when you think about it... an elite anarcho scene? But that's how it often felt.

"The only gig that I didn't enjoy at all, and ironically enough it was a Northern one, was at the

Leadmill in Sheffield [4th October, 1982] which we did with Crass, Annie Anxiety, and Dirt. I wasn't really into what Flux wanted to do at the time anyway, and right from the start the place had a bad atmosphere. There were a lot of wankers there that night, lots of glue-sniffers and general idiots around, really aggressive punks, and even when we were playing our set, Col and I were getting wafts of Evo-stik (or whatever shit they were using) vapour coming up from the kids at the front of the stage, and it was sickening, quite literally.

"And fuck knows why, but we'd always been gobbed at during gigs, and that night at the Leadmill it was just atrocious; phlegm rained down on us for the whole set, we were completely covered in it, and it's disgusting. I remember sitting around after we'd played, trying to clean this shit off my shirt, my face, out of my hair, off my guitar, and thinking, 'What the fuck is this all about?'

"Oh yeah, and one other thing about that gig, something else that sticks in my mind… after we'd played and we were packing up, some kid came up to me and started asking me serious questions, and I just wasn't in the mood. Actually, it was always the same…we got these rather earnest and intense young blokes coming up to us and asking us tricky stuff… we never ever got girls asking us for telephone numbers, just pain-in-the-ass blokes being difficult! Anyway, this one asked me something like, 'You talk a lot about anarchy, but what does it actually mean to you?' I wasn't in the mood for one thing, as the gig hadn't been a good one, and secondly he had 'The Exploited' painted in big letters on the back of his leather jacket, so he was hardly into punk for the philosophy, was he? So I just pretended that I hadn't heard his question due to my ears being completely buggered by the sound level that night, but he was persistent, so I said something arsey like, 'Oh, go and ask Derek… he's the thinker in the band!'

"Actually, on occasions, kids would come up and ask us for autographs, sometimes even ask me for my plectrum, and although it might seem a bit like we were playing the 'star trip' by doing that, I didn't have a problem with it, and neither did Col or Martin. I mean, if someone wants your signature, or a memento of the gig for whatever reason, then where's the harm in it? The look on their faces when you scribbled on a slip of paper, or when they could have your plectrum or a drumstick or whatever, just showed that it was a big deal for them, and that's great. But Derek refused point-blank to give autographs or anything like that; he said that it was making a distinction between us as a band and the people in the audience. Hmmm… well, Derek, there was… we were a band and they were the audience…and your point is? Anyway, whenever he refused a request for his signature, the people who asked usually looked disappointed; they probably thought he was actually being more of a 'star' by being so detached! I mean they'd paid to get in, had probably trekked fucking miles to see us, so to follow Derek's line, maybe we shouldn't have played in the first place… after all, by being onstage it would only emphasise the division between us and the audience! Prat!"

Flux were even courted again by a major label during this period. Lured by the enigma of a political hardcore punk band who could top the Indie charts with seeming ease, Island Records were the next corporate whores to be sent packing, but it became ever more apparent that not all of the band shared Derek's (apparently) hard-line views regarding their music and big business. Kevin left the fold in late 1982 after a gig in Nottingham to be replaced yet again by not one but two guitarists, Timothy Luke and Lou, the latter formerly with popular anarcho outfit Dirt. And his departure, although possibly strengthening the resolve of the band as a cohesive political unit essentially marked the end of Flux Of Pink Indians as any sort of enjoyable musical entity.

"I'd felt for some time that I was pulling in a different direction to Colin and Martin, and especially Derek, and they had also been talking about getting a house together, and sharing it. I wasn't into that idea at all – communal living ain't for me – so that didn't sound too good for a start. Then Colin and Derek had suggested that we go for a more noise-orientated sound, less structured, less riffy, and Col mooted this idea of getting Lou from Dirt into the band on second guitar. That was another idea that I didn't agree with, not because I didn't want someone else playing guitar alongside me, but if you have two guitarists in a band I think they've really got to 'spark' off each other, or else work together really tightly, and I wasn't even bothered about Lou as a person, let alone as a guitarist. Don't get me wrong, she was okay, just not my sort of person; completely different in attitude and she used to get really nervy and intense before playing a gig, and I couldn't imagine it working. It was bad enough that we had to go and look for Derek before each gig – he used to get so anxious that he'd get an attack of the shits, and he'd be in the bog for ages before we went on!

"Oh, yeah, and the final straw for me, as far as leaving Flux was concerned, was that the others had all been telling me how great they thought Antisect were. I had never seen them until that gig in Nottingham, and when I did I just thought they were like a poor version of Discharge; I just didn't get it at all. So after they'd played their set, and I heard Col and Martin saying how brilliant they were, and how Flux should sound more like them, I just decided that I wasn't on the same musical path anymore, and I made up my mind that that was my last gig."

The first album for the new line-up was controversially entitled 'The Fucking Cunts Treat Us Like Pricks', and although it actually made No. 2 in the Indies upon its release in March 1984, its success must have been predominantly due to the sensationalism of its title because musically it was as bad as it was utterly pretentious.

"I tend to agree with you!" laughs Colin candidly. "What happened was, Kevin left, and we were playing these gigs with Dirt, and Lou, their guitarist, joined us, along with her boyfriend, Tim. Thing is, whereas Kevin's guitaring was excellent, they couldn't play that well, so our whole sound totally changed.

"Also, Crass had just done 'Yes, Sir, I Will', and we were always one step behind them. They did an album that was just noise all the way through, and we went in and did the same thing. It was originally going to be just a four-track EP, but it ended up a double album! We had the first four songs, but the rest was made up on the spot, so no wonder it's rubbish. A total waste of time.

"Derek's theory was that if you made the music unlistenable, people would have to pay more attention to the vocals and lyrics. The problem was, we didn't sell that many as a result, so no one new read the lyrics anyway. I've talked to so many people influenced by 'Neu Smell' and 'Strive…', but I'm yet to meet one person influenced by anything on 'The Fucking Cunts…'

"Derek had also got into this whole feminist thing that, again, Crass had already touched on, and it was another world really. He even said that it was all a result of one of our band members being raped, and that was rubbish! Lou was the only girl in the band, and she was never raped. An old girlfriend of mine had been, but that was four or five years earlier, when he wasn't even involved.

"But where were we meant to go next anyway? Without Derek, we would've ended up making 'Strive… Part 2'… just ended up repeating ourselves… so we followed Crass's lead a bit really. You weren't meant to have any fun; it was all so serious, rock songs were really frowned upon.

"And there were people like Andy Martin from The Apostles who thought we were really lame anyway, because we were against direct action, and they were full-on, out there smashing windows. So then Derek decided that we had to be 100% as well, out there disrupting stuff, and I always regarded myself as Derek's lieutenant – he would decide what to do, then stand at the back, while I pushed forward and did as he said!"

It wasn't only their peers in the scene with mixed feelings about the band: audiences too were flummoxed by the sharp left-turn in musical direction, and anyone who turned up expecting a 'greatest hits' set that included all their favourite songs from the earlier records would usually leave disappointed. But Flux didn't want to be bound by such expectations and refused to be a part of the rock'n'roll circus… most of the time, at least.

"I remember we played a gig in Stevenage and everyone had turned up to hear 'Strive…' really, and we started playing 'The Fucking Cunts…' before it had even came out, and after the second song so many people were shouting abuse at us that we stopped. Derek started talking to them all, and afterwards he was saying, 'That was so worthwhile... if we'd just played 'Strive...' I would never have got talking to all those people!'

"The interesting thing was though, after all those super-serious gigs for 'The Fucking Cunts...', we did this total piss-take gig in Camden, a real OTT rock'n'roll gig. Chumbawamba were supporting, and they wanted to do their gig as normal, with all their banners and stuff... but we covered the stage in foil, hired in this big light show, got Pete Wright to mingle in Frank Zappa guitar solos, we all came on in shades and shorts... even changed a lot of the songs to make them more ROCK! And it was one of the best nights ever, and we all wondered how we could go back to doing what we'd done before after that. So it was one of our last gigs for a long time."

'The Fucking Cunts Treat Us Like Pricks' also featured a sexually explicit cover illustration; once again the band were keen to provoke a reaction, if only to make a point.

"The original idea was that we were going to have all these full-on pornographic images on the front, and we had all these pictures spread out all over our living room floor, trying to decide which one to use where, and Derek's girlfriend's mum and dad banged on the window, saying 'Coo-ee!' We were like, 'Oh fuck!' and never moved so fast in our lives, shoving them under chairs and cushions and stuff...!

Flux Of Pink Indians, Liverpool 1984, picture by Andrew Medcalf.

"And then Andy [Palmer, of Crass] came up with all these drawings that he'd done years before, so we used them in the end. But really it's a waste of vinyl... there's a couple of good songs on there, but that's it. You're better off playing it at very low volume...

"We couldn't use a 'safe' cover really, because let's face it, it's got to be one of the most offensive record titles ever, and we needed artwork to suit. And, along with the Dead Kennedys, I'm sure that it helped launch that whole 'parental advisory' sticker thing... it was their [H.R. Giger painted] 'Penis Landscape' poster [that had been planned for inclusion with their 'Frankenchrist' record], and our album title, that brought all that in, so whenever I see one on a CD now, I have to smile to myself.

"I never told my mum that we'd even released it," adds Colin with a wry chuckle. "She just thought we hadn't recorded anything for a bit. It was only ages afterwards, when I'd left Flux, that she found out, when she saw a thing in the paper about us being taken to court, and I was like, 'Oh, it was all Derek's idea!'

"But the whole thing was of its time really, and I only hope that there's someone out there doing the same thing now. Well, not the same thing exactly, but the same kind of thing, their own way of stirring things up.

"One of the big regrets that I do have is, the fourth side of 'Fucking Cunts...' is one big, long song, which I wrote. I went into the studio without telling anyone and recorded it all myself, borrowed everyone's instruments and played everything. Annie Anxiety, who we were living with, went and played it to everyone, and they were like, 'Oh, it's alright...' I knew it was a racket though, 'cos I couldn't play at all, but she gave it to Penny, who actually liked it. And he told Annie to ask me if I wanted to do it on Crass, and he'd produce it and play drums on it... but as soon as Derek heard that, he was determined that it was all ours, and it ended up as part of the 'Fucking Cunts...' album."

After March '85's 'Taking A Liberty' single (another Indie success, reaching No. 5), Derek had a disagreement with John at Southern, and the band abandoned Spiderleg to set up their own label, One Little Indian, with new distribution courtesy of Nine Mile Island. The first release was a new Flux album (the band decided to ring the recent changes by officially opting for the shortened monosyllabic name), 'Uncarved Block'. Although infinitely better than 'The Fucking Cunts...', it was still self-indulgent rubbish compared to the likes of 'Neu Smell' and – with the band's following now wise to their game – sold accordingly, barely troubling the Indie Top Twenty upon its release in August 1986.

One Little Indian went on to release comparatively mainstream music by the likes of The Shamen and The Sugarcubes, the latter being the Icelandic rock band previously known as KUKL who had released records on Crass and toured with the likes of Chumbawamba. The Sugarcubes' female vocalist Björk [Gundmundsdottir] went on to find fame with her solo career in the Nineties, and, on the strength of The Sugarcubes, Derek Birkett landed One Little Indian major label distribution – an astonishing about-turn considering his unwavering stance on big business and the music industry whilst in Flux.

Colin, meanwhile, started Hotalacio, in response to Flux's ever-diminishing creative credibility.

"That was about '86, mainly because we were getting asked to do all this stuff with Flux but no one else wanted to do it. I was getting more and more into rap stuff, so me and a friend started making our own backing tapes – bit like Beastie Boys really – and doing this rap band… which Derek absolutely hated! He loathed dance music… he wasn't keen at all, especially as I was doing stuff outside of Flux. I remember when we were recording I used to hear him through the headphones slagging it off up at the mixing desk where he thought I couldn't hear! Calling it 'rap crap' and stuff.

"I also remember being interviewed for Maximum Rock'n'roll by Andy Chapman, as Flux, and he said, 'Oh Colin, do you want to talk about your new project, Hotalacio?' And Derek shot me a filthy look as if to say, 'You see? I knew this would happen!' So I just said, 'Nah, maybe another time…!'"

The band's ambitious musical evolution then ground to a halt; having painted themselves into a corner of such uncompromising extremity, Flux had nowhere left to go that wouldn't appear to be copping out. Any ideas of touring had similarly been shelved, not just due to lack of interest, both internal and external, but also the increasingly insurmountable logistics involved.

"After we just became Flux, we got involved with Adrian Sherwood and the Tackhead stuff, and we reinvented ourselves a bit, totally removed from the Crass thing. But people didn't seem to care by then anyway; they just wanted to hear The Jesus And Mary Chain. We started doing these banners in red and blue, and by shining red and blue lights on them, you could make the images appear and disappear. So you had Reagan and then Thatcher, a swastika then a hammer and sickle… we were still so deadly serious even then!

"We did one gig [at London's ULU] that took six months to rehearse for. We just played all of 'Uncarved Block', and there was about twenty of us onstage, I couldn't hear my own vocals at all. So I couldn't do it anything like the album… and Lou who had such a great voice on the album sang the whole gig out of tune 'cos she couldn't hear herself either. It was a good gig, I suppose, but not really worth the effort.

"A bit later on, just after 'Uncarved Block', we did venture overseas, just the once. We were invited to go and play this New Music festival in Amsterdam. The organisers had heard our album, and thought it was a whole new sound. Of course, Adrian Sherwood had been involved, which tweaked their interest… but he was only on the record and nothing to do with when we were playing live.

"So, when we got there, we were playing with World Domination Enterprises, [DJ] Tim Westwood, Salt 'n' Pepa… a whole host of different bands. And we were really punky, and after our set, these guys who were meant to be interviewing us totally blanked us. It was then that we suddenly realised that they wanted us to be more like the album, not like 'Strive' and 'Neu Smell'.

"Anyway, it was three gigs, two in Holland, one in Belgium, so the next night we played all our set as if it was 'Uncarved Block'. But then, when we turned up in Brussels, we could see from the poster – with the starving boy with a tag on him on it – that they wanted our punky stuff! And that was the only time we ever played abroad, and Derek had to be held down on the ferry because he was convinced that it was going to sink…"

Inevitably Flux came to a halt. There was no spectacular climax to provide a satisfying conclusion to their tale; they just gradually ceased to be a band.

"I left the house where we all lived together in South London and moved back up to North London again, and since then I've only met Derek on three occasions and he's been obnoxious, a real wanker, every time. As if he thinks, 'How dare you leave…?'

"Looking back now, I have to admit that leaving the Flux house was like walking from a compression chamber into a lovely, wide open field. You felt like you couldn't say anything, you'd just sit there and join in a conversation now and again... but no one ever dared start one, in case you said the wrong thing. I always felt like I was the odd one out, and it was only when I left there that I realised that it was the people who I lived with that made me feel like that. I moved into a squat in Hampstead with two friends and we had a bloody great time, I loved it."

Despite the animosity between himself and certain ex-members, Colin, who now designs and fits luxury kitchens, remains quietly proud of the musical legacy of which he was a part. Although he would rather not be remembered as 'the band that turned all those punks vegetarian' or 'that band who did that album about fucking cunts and pricks'...

"I prefer listening to little stories like, 'My girlfriend and I first kissed whilst listening to 'Tube Disaster', and we've been together ever since!' That sort of thing, with no politics involved. Something positive, 'cos we appeared to be so negative – we always seemed to be against everything, and just assumed that that made it clear what we were for.

"In a way I just think that people should live their own lives. I hate it when people say, 'Huh! What've you got your ears pierced for?' 'Why have you got all those tattoos?' I would never say to anyone, 'Why are you doing that?' I don't need their reasons; people have their own reasons for doing things, and people should be allowed to get on with it if they aren't causing anybody else any trouble.

"To be honest, I've never fully understood what anarchy meant anyway!" he ponders, on the subject of the anarcho-punk scene he will forever be affiliated with. "Johnny Rotten's ideas were certainly worlds apart from Penny Rimbaud's. Unless you'd read all the books, it was hard to explain yourself, but Derek was the man who was good at all that anyway. That was one of the reasons that Kevin left, because he was not into it at all. He refused to be vegetarian when he was in the band, but when he left us, he became one!

"We had this idea that we should just go somewhere else, somewhere where we could live our lives how we wanted, rather than trying to change the whole world. Crass had this idea of starting a commune, or buying a couple of houses, a plot of land in France or somewhere... I so wish we had tried it too, but we only ever talked about it.

"I know now that the thing to do is just to get on with your own life. I can remember back then though, I was shit scared that it would all be over any day, and it was a relief living the last twenty years not in fear of a nuclear war. Even all this stuff with Al Qaeda now, it doesn't worry me a tenth of how the bomb worried me in the Eighties! Now I can see how and why my mum and dad viewed me as a bit strange; I used to want to find a cellar to hide in during the Falklands War, in case I was forced to join the army, and that seems a bit silly now, doesn't it?

"Derek wrote quite a good song for 'Taking A Liberty', called 'Pass Me Another Issue', which was all about that really. Sometimes we were just looking for things that were wrong, so we could sing a song about them – but what happens when you run out of issues? Will everything be okay with the world then, or will you always be looking for something else to sing about?"

Kevin has his own take on the importance of the band:

"I think that 'Strive...' still stands up as one of the better anarcho albums of the period, despite my feelings about how the production wasn't what we wanted. There are some great tunes on there, and it's quite an accessible album. I maintain that if you want to get your point across through the lyrics then you have to make the music easy to get into. I could never stand stuff that was just a load of words ranted over noise... even if what is being said is thought-provoking and important, who can honestly say they would want to play it again and again if there are no hooks or riffs to latch onto? To get your message across, you've got to draw people in with a fucking good tune; if they can get into the sound then there's more chance that people might actually take notice of what you're saying.

"So yes, despite having Penny make the guitars sound like Crass, I'm quite proud of what we put on 'Strive...'. It's just a shame that 'Neu Smell' and 'Strive...' are all that there is to show what Flux Of Pink Indians were about, musically speaking. To me, 'The Fucking Cunts...' is just complete bollocks, noise and anger for the sake of it, no redeeming features whatsoever. If it hadn't had such a provocative title, no one would have noticed the album at all, much less have wasted their money on it. And as for 'Uncarved Block'? It's nothing to do with punk in the slightest, a completely neutered record with no balls at all. Trumpets and bongos on a punk album? Arty-farty shite, I'm afraid."

SELECT DISCOGRAPHY

7"s:

'1970s' (Stortbeat, 1979) – as The Licks
'Neu Smell' (Crass, 1981)
'Last Bus To Debden' (Spiderleg, 1981) – live Epileptics recording from 1979
'1970s' (Spiderleg, 1982) – as The Epileptics
'Taking A Liberty' (Spiderleg, 1985)

12"s:

'Neu Smell' (One Little Indian, 1987) – also included the 'Taking A Liberty' EP

LPs:

'Strive To Survive Causing The Least Suffering Possible' (Spiderleg, 1982)
'The Fucking Cunts Treat Us Like Pricks' (Spiderleg, 1984)
'Uncarved Block' (One Little Indian, 1986)

At A Glance:

One Little Indian have issued most of the Flux back catalogue on CD, but Newcastle-upon-Tyne label Overground have compiled the most pleasing posthumous releases. As well as a 28-track Epileptics history, 'System Rejects' (1996), they're also responsible for two Flux discs. 'Not So Brave' (1997) features twenty-five tracks lifted from demos, live tapes and compilations, whilst 'Live Statement' (1999) features a whole gig recorded at Kev's last gig at Nottingham's Sherwood Community Centre in 1982. Californian label Doctor Strange's 'Fits And Starts' (2003) also comes highly recommended and is beautifully packaged, even though most of the tracks are available on the Overground releases already mentioned.

Whilst it's true that London's **LACK OF KNOWLEDGE** didn't look or sound anything like the typical anarcho-punk band (was there really such a beast?), surely one of the most enduring ideals of the whole genre was that of not conforming – something that Lack Of Knowledge did both instinctively and incessantly. They also, of course, released several records through Crass and gigged with many of the more obvious bands to be found in this book, but it's the fierce streak of independence that ran through everything they did that really qualifies them for inclusion here.

"If you listen to a Lack Of Knowledge record, even the ones that were on the Crass label, you'll soon discover that we were not trying to be anything that we weren't," elaborates guitarist Tony Barber. "Most people's idea of anarcho-punk is to do with haircuts, clothing and how fast the music is, or how aggressive the lyrics can be… the thing is, we already existed before anarcho-punk came along, and we only ended up on Crass because we met them before they'd even started their own label, and when we put out our own single, we gave them a copy. But this whole idea of having some sort of template for being anarcho-punk? It's no different really to being a 'teddy boy' or a mod! It's almost the opposite of what it's actually meant to represent. And for us to sit here and say we were an anarcho-punk group – just for us to even label ourselves as such in fact – would

Lack Of Knowledge, November 1984 (left to right: Tony Barber, Danny Drummond, Phillip Barker, and Karen Gower).

be a complete paradox. We never sounded anything like an anarcho-punk group, and that's probably the one reason why we were one – because we never tailored our sound to fit an imaginary mould."

Formed in Edmonton in late 1980, and previously known by such weird and wonderful monikers as Assorted Tools, English Assassin, and, rather unfortunately, Trio Of Testicles, Lack Of Knowledge initially comprised – as well as Tony – Daniel Drummond on vocals (formerly with original London punks, Headache, who released the 'Can't Stand Still' 7" on Lout in 1977), Paul Stevens on bass, and Chiefy (real name Jason Powell) on drums.

"I think I liked the whole DIY aspect of punk, that was what really appealed to me," reckons Dan. "And so, after going to see groups, it seemed almost obvious to form your own; being a part of it was more important than just watching other bands do it. Before that, bands, not that I didn't like a lot of them, seemed totally remote... the idea that you might one day be playing in Alice Cooper's band, for example, was absurd, a complete pipe dream. You couldn't imagine being that... but you could imagine being in Generation X! It seemed like something that I could actually do, something that was for anybody that wanted to be a part of it. Participation was very important... not wearing something that somebody else wore, but wearing something you'd made yourself. And the anarcho-punk thing, of course, was even more focused on there being no divisions between audience and band..."

So, Lack Of Knowledge began booking their own shows wherever and whenever they could, in local youth centres and church halls; hiring out the room, printing and sticking up posters and even manning the door, all themselves, helping create a local punk scene where there was none before.

"I always thought our best gigs were the early ones that we put on ourselves," recalls Tony fondly. "The minute we played in a rock club like the Clarendon or somewhere like that, it completely devalued what we did, and somehow made us feel redundant as a band... I wouldn't have been able to tell you at the time what it was we were meant to be doing, mind you, but it certainly wasn't playing downstairs at the Clarendon on a Tuesday night! We should've carried on doing what we'd already been doing, I suppose, hiring out churches, putting on five local bands and charging 50p to get in. Those were always our best gigs; we played better, it was always a more interesting setting, and you felt a sense of accomplishment at the end of it that you never felt after doing gigs in 'proper' venues, y'know? I look back at that and think, 'Fuckin' hell, we did some amazing things, and there's nothing out there today to compare with it...' Not just because of the nostalgia thing, but if I wanted to go and hire out a community centre now, imagine the amount of bullshit you'd have to go through to get permission to do a punk rock show! There's no turning up and paying four quid to the caretaker any more, is there?

"I think the culture of the country was totally different then, less paranoid, less corporate, and you certainly didn't have the same amount of private money tied up in local government... the culture was so much more sympathetic to you just seeing an empty hall stood doing nothing, banging on the door and booking it for the following Thursday. Everything's 'moved on' now, and I hesitate to use that phrase, obviously, but all the cracks have been plastered over..."

"Playing those early gigs always felt like a bit of a struggle!" adds Dan, laughing. "We were all rather incompetent, and – speaking for myself, anyway – rather nervous people, and the combination of the two things meant that sometimes the gigs would work really well... and sometimes they would spectacularly explode! The gigs we organised ourselves, we kinda controlled the vibe and set the atmosphere, and they were far more enjoyable to play than gigs where we were playing for someone else. I didn't so much mind turning up and supporting other bands, playing before someone else to people who weren't really interested in you, because they weren't there to see you anyway, so you had nothing to lose. It was more when we started playing at venues where we had no control over what was happening and people were turning up to see us, and I didn't really like that so much; I found that quite difficult to handle."

In early 1981, Lack Of Knowledge entered Octave Electronics in Edmonton and recorded their debut single, 'The Uninvited'/'Ritual', which they released on their own LOK Records. An impressively ambitious debut by anyone's standards, the single established the band's rather unique sound, revealing the quirky relationship between guitar and bass that would characterise every release and Dan's richly melodic voice so reminiscent of a young Phil Oakley. It not only got them played on John Peel's radio show but also landed them a prestigious 'deal' with Crass Records.

"We took it over to Dial House and played it to Penny and Gee and whoever else was there at the time," explains Tony. "Rimbaud took it out into the back room and played it, came back in and went, 'Hmmm, it's really interesting! Would you be interested in making a record on our label?' Me and Paul Stevens were sat there going, 'You what?' It was the most instantaneous A&R-ing ever! He literally went and played it, came back and offered us a single! I didn't actually believe he'd even listened to it, 'cos he was only gone for one minute, thirty, and the shortest song is one minute, thirty-two... nah, just kidding, but that's actually what happened. It was very spur of the moment."

It was to be well over a year before the band actually recorded for Crass though, and during the interim period they bade farewell to drummer Chief, replacing him with Philip Barker from Klee. Then, after playing many more shows, including the Zig Zag squat event with Crass, they entered Southern Studios during early August 1983, under the watchful eye of Penny Rimbaud in the producer's chair, to record the grossly overlooked 'Grey' single.

"Oh, it was a whole new experience for us," says Dan of the session. "When we did our own single we did it on eight-track tape, so there wasn't a great deal of producing going on, not in the day we were in there anyway... I really enjoyed working with someone else, doing something different."

"When we did 'The Uninvited', we didn't even get a day in the studio, we recorded it in a fuckin' evening!" guffaws Tony incredulously. "Then we turned up at Southern and they had extra pairs of head phones, spare mikes, all sorts of shit! But we never got carried away... that was the funny thing about us as a band; we just turned up and concentrated on what we were doing. We never went, 'Wow, we're in a big studio!' It was no big deal to me, to be recording for Crass... I didn't exactly consider it to be what we should be doing, but I didn't consider ourselves to have been especially lucky either, and I certainly didn't think to myself, 'Hey, we're on our way now.' It was just happening, so we got on with it, y'know?"

With its dark, lustrous melodies and flirtations with the electronic post-punk pop scene of the time, 'Grey' remains one of the more interesting singles on Crass, but it's hardly surprising that it threw all the hardcore punks waiting on each new release from the label into some much-needed confusion.

Tony: "We used to go down the Centro Iberico, or the old Autonomy Centre, and you literally just wrote your name on the board if you wanted a certain date, and once you'd wrote it on there, that was your night and you just put the gig on. And people would walk past and see that and go, 'Oh fuckin' hell, fuckin' Lack Of Knowledge! What the hell are they doing here again?' We used to hear people saying stuff like that all the time, and it was hilarious; you'd look around and it would be some bloke covered head to toe in patches and badges of every single anarcho-punk group, except us! The kinda bloke who's probably now working in a bank somewhere..."

"But there was never meant to be a hierarchy in the anarcho scene, by definition. So, you put out your own record, and then when you went to see, say, Flux Of Pink Indians, you never thought of them as being 'above' you in any way. In fact, one gig where we played with Conflict and all that, we drew the names out of a hat to decide who would go on last... and that happened with that Zig Zag gig as well – the running order was drawn from a hat. But then we had to ask if we could go on before 4.00pm, because we had another gig that same night, which we were putting on ourselves."

Lack Of Knowledge were then asked by Crass to release an album on their Corpus Christi offshoot, which resulted in 1984's brooding and absorbing 'Sirens Are Back' LP. However by the time of its release, Paul Stevens had left and been replaced on bass by Tony's then-girlfriend Karen Gower – who couldn't actually play when she landed herself the role.

"Uh, yeah, we didn't ever pick the easy option," sighs Dan. "That was because we tended to pick people who we knew. Sometimes it wasn't so much that they were friends, but just because they wanted to play in the band with us, and we thought that was better than having someone who was just turning up and playing with whatever band wanted them to. And seeing as we weren't on any sort of conveyor belt to success, it wasn't a case of not being able to wait for them to learn their instrument. It didn't make any difference to us."

"We weren't on a tight schedule," adds Tony. "And I'd much rather be in a band with someone I'm friends with who isn't very good, than someone who I'm not friends with who I only see on the days we rehearse but happens to be a better player. And all the time we were going, we never ever sent a demo tape to a record company, never ever advertised to get a new bass player or anything... all the things that bands do, we never did. It wasn't planned that way either; it's only now, looking back, that it's apparent. Even when we had a single out on Crass, which was big news at that time, we never sent a copy to anyone! Never said, 'Oh, we're a band, just done a record on Crass, are you impressed? Please sign us!' And I bet there are bands out there that were on Crass who sent copies of their record to the A&R man at EMI and stuff... I bet there is! 'We've got to spread our message further... tour in the south of France and places like that!' Ha!"

It was back to Southern to record their next release with Mel Jefferson in May 1985, the 'Sentinel' 12" for Chainsaw Records (the label ran by members of Living In Texas), a strong, up-tempo offering that was to be their last of the Eighties. Despite the record garnering much critical acclaim – even landing them the lauded 'Single Of The Week' in Sounds – Lack Of Knowledge split after a show in Colchester in August 1986. It was ironically the furthest the band had ever travelled to play a show, during a troubled period when various band members were questioning just how comfortable they felt with how far they had all strayed artistically from their humble beginnings.

"It was just personal problems between the members of the group," claims Dan, of their premature demise. "Although it's absolutely true that we had no ambition whatsoever, we did put a great deal of pressure on ourselves. I'm not sure what all that was about, because playing together now, it's so completely different. But we just made everything really difficult for ourselves and I don't know why, and I just felt uncomfortable, felt that the band wasn't really working. And playing these gigs, expecting people to turn up and be charged money to watch you... and deep down I felt that we weren't providing people with anything that you could really charge money for. Does that make sense? When we were doing it on a totally amateur level, I felt okay with it, but when it moved up a level, I just didn't really feel that we were, uh, good enough? I'm not sure why, but that was just how I came to feel, and I'm not sure how much that had to do with other aspects of the band making me feel that way..."

"If you've got a record on a major label and it sells 400 copies, it's a disaster, a total flop," offers Tony, philosophically. "But if you put it out yourself and sold 400 copies, it would be regarded as an astounding success – but it would still be the same record! And when you do make music with no expectations, and you staple all the sleeves together yourself, you instinctively produce better stuff because you haven't got the pressure of, 'Shit, now we're on a major label, we've got to up the ante and become entertainers...!' It clouds your artistic vision; it taints your purity of purpose. When you first get together as a band, crowded in your little rehearsal room, it's just you, the four or five guys or whatever, there's not even some guy from a punk rock label looking over your shoulder... but somehow we moved up a level from the youth club rehearsals and shopping trolleys [for transporting equipment to their practise room], to still being in the youth clubs and shopping trolleys but also being in the Independent Charts at the same time. And it artificially created this idea that we should move more towards being a conventional band because it seemed like a logical progression, when in reality it was the worse thing we could've done, because as soon as we put one foot in the water, we were drawn by the currents towards that goal. We were a brilliant group putting out records in photocopied sleeves, doing our own gigs in funny little cinemas in Shepherds Bush – we were about as good as you could get – but as soon as we were trying to operate in the mainstream, we were just this rubbish rock band really."

In 2001 however, Californian label Grand Theft Audio contacted 'this rubbish rock band' with a view to issuing a retrospective CD, a communication which stirred Lack Of Knowledge back into tentative action again, regrouping to record properly for the first time some of the songs they had written in the Eighties but had never actually committed to tape. Then, more recently in 2005, another Californian label, Alternative Records from Berkeley, released a newly-recorded self-titled 7", and, no doubt spurred by the sudden interest in the band's back catalogue, Southern re-released the single and LP recorded for Crass as the 'Grey' CD. Against all odds, Lack Of Knowledge are back together, even playing their first shows outside the UK's Southeast – in New York! – during late 2005, but how long they grace us with their presence for this time remains to be seen.

"We won't be writing any new material," explains Tony, who nowadays also plays bass for Buzzcocks. "These 'new' releases are all stuff from 1981 that was never recorded, songs we used to play day in, day out, that we never even did demos of... and the only copies we had of them were old rehearsal tapes or live tapes or whatever. And we consciously made an effort to record them in the most authentic way possible; we didn't change any lyrics, didn't change any song structures... didn't embellish them with anything that we didn't play at the time... I even used the same guitar and amp!

"We don't even profess to have reformed really... it's just that now and again someone rings us up and asks if we're interested in doing another record. But we did say when we first did it, that we would only record the songs we already had written, and we're running out of songs; there's only four or five left that we never recorded, just enough for maybe one more EP. Although we could compile the 7"s onto one CD perhaps, just to tidy up that aspect of it, but then that'll be it. Except for the occasional show, if it's somewhere interesting... when there's some anarchist art festival in Prague or wherever, that realises they can't get Crass, Dirt, or Flux, so they have to ring us up instead!"

SELECTED DISCOGRAPHY

7"s:
'The Uninvited' (LOK, 1981)
'Grey' (Crass, 1983)
'Lack Of Knowledge' (Alternative, 2005)

12"s:
'Sentinel' (Chainsaw, 1985)

LPs:
'Sirens Are Back' (Crass, 1984)

At A Glance:
The Grand Theft Audio CD, 'Americanized', mixes up old and new recordings to great effect, but readers of this book will no doubt be most interested in Southern's 'Grey' CD, that features the Crass-released single of the same name, plus the 'Sirens Are Back' LP originally recorded for Corpus Christi in 1984. Complete with all the original artwork and lyrics, it's a fascinating snapshot of a thoroughly unique band.

Another punk band that were never really 'anarcho' in the traditional sense of the term, **THE ERATICS** were still part of that scene, albeit more by association than design. Their unruly carefree approach, and their blatant irreverence for both authority and peer expectation, endeared them to Crass, who included them on their 'Bullshit Detector' compilation, ensuring their place in anarcho history, but it was only when they evolved into the slightly more sophisticated **LOOK MUMMY CLOWNS**, that they even entered a recording studio, and by then the band had virtually burnt itself out.

"At the beginning, it was me, 'Snout' [real name Martin Seaward] and 'Bondage' [real name Kevin Lester, originally from Mexborough in Yorkshire]," recalls bassist Terence 'Stringy' Castle. "We were all mates from school, living in a place called Waltham Cross, about ten miles north of Stoke Newington; I grew up in Shoreditch, but there was a lot of slum clearance when I was a kid, so I was moved out to the fringes of Hertfordshire.

"We were going to gigs in the West End, getting a train there and back; this would've been late '77 or early '78, when we were only sixteen or seventeen. We also went to gigs at the Triad in Bishops Stortford, when The Epileptics were just starting really, and Crass played there soon after, and all these bands were very inspiring, and we were already thinking, 'Hey, we could be in a fucking band ourselves!'

"When we were going into town and seeing all these second generation punk bands like The Antz, The Lurkers, and 999, we still saw them as being pretty professional – they were punks, but they were proper musicians, in a way that we could never be, just fuckin' about at home. When we went to the Triad, we thought, 'Hang on a minute, these people are pretty much the same as us: they can't fuckin' play either… but they're having a good go, and they're rapidly getting there!'"

Suitably encouraged, the intrepid trio took up instruments, playing their first show at the Triad with The Epileptics, Urban Decay and Rubella Ballet on June 15th, 1979, Stringy attempting to sing as well as play bass, until they recruited Mark 'Roper' Double on vocals.

"Snout was a guitar player, and he'd been playing since about the age of twelve, but I never knew this until punk broke, and we were talking about doing a band, and he said, 'Well, I've got a guitar…' And I was like, 'Fuckin' hell, have ya?' And he's always been the musician amongst us… I'm certainly no musician, never have been and don't wanna be either…

"The thing is, Bondage couldn't play the drums… well, he could, but he had an extremely odd style… I swear that he invented 'hardcore drumming' because he used to do this basic kinda one-two beat, and it was the first time I'd heard anyone do anything like that. I remember after the first gig, everyone talking about 'that drummer'! But I think we made our noise and we were happy that we'd got onstage and done what we wanted to do.

"Roper was a bit younger than us, but he ended up onstage with us a couple of times early on, singing along – he would get a bit enthusiastic at gigs! And so we just asked him if he wanted to do it permanently…"

The Eratics bassist Stringy, live in Southend.

Roper made his official debut with the band at the Focus in Southend, supporting The Sinyx, a band with whom The Eratics would become strong friends.

"We switched from being based around Bishops Stortford and Harlow to London when I got kicked out of home basically," chuckles Stringy. "I had to move into a squat in town. I was sleeping on Roper's mum's couch for a bit, then on Snout's mum's couch, then I moved to London, and the Islington Squatters Group took me in because I had nowhere to go; I was on the fuckin' street, and ended up knocking on their door, and they were all a bit older than me, remnants of the late Sixties/early Seventies hippy thing, and they had this tight-knit, old school squatters' ethic. It was those kind of people, and a few of the new punkier types that were coming in, that set up St. James's, the Pentonville Road squat we all called 'the old church'… we then took it over a bit, if only on certain nights when we arranged our own gigs.

"The politics was there from the beginning," he adds. "Only the second song we ever wrote was called 'Factory Floor'… we were workers, we left school at fifteen and got jobs in factories near Waltham Cross. I went into an electronics factory, and there was plenty to complain about there, but at least it meant we had some money… not a lot, but enough that we could afford to go to some gigs and buy a few records.

"And by the time our band was ready to play, it was 1979, the 'Winter Of Discontent': wage freezes, rubbish left in the streets, the whole thing was kicking off. I was in the union, and we were in and out of fucking work on a regular basis; union activists would come along and say, 'Alright, brothers and sisters, it's now ten degrees below an acceptable temperature and we're fucking out, until they warm the factory up!'

"Mind you, the first song I ever wrote was called 'Tablets', which is on the Urban Decay record that Gordon [Wilkins] put out [on Handy Records], and I'm not credited with writing it. We used to do it originally, and Dean [Tisbury] from that band would sing it with us, and after a bit, they used to do it, and I'd sing it with them! But it was my song… and what happened was: I busted my leg in a car accident when I was fifteen, and spent much of my teenage punk years hobbling around with callipers on my leg. So I wrote 'Tablets' when I was in hospital getting pumped full of painkillers… it wasn't about recreational drugs or anything."

Although garnering a modest following with their entertaining live shows, The Eratics never made an official recording, and their sole vinyl offering was an appearance on the 'Bullshit Detector' compilation in early 1981, with 'National Service', a track recorded in Snout's front room, straight onto a regular tape recorder.

"It didn't seem important at the time to do a proper recording, we were too busy playing gigs, and although I regret that as an artist – that we never documented the songs properly – I don't think it would've really been any different if we had, 'cos we were so un-together. It was all about the gigs for us, the whole social thing; we never really considered ourselves a proper band!"

The Eratics called it a day in late 1981, after a disastrous gig in Walthamstow where the drummer from D&V stood in for Bondage who hadn't turned up… wisely, it would transpire, as the event descended into violent chaos.

"All these guys smashed their way in and wrecked the place," recalls Roper sadly. "We were actually playing when this was going on… I can remember David from Fack coming up to me, armed with a chair leg, and saying, 'We gotta go out front and help sort it out!' There was a proper battle going on."

Stringy: "At one point, I thought, 'Fuck this, I'm off!' and jumped off stage and tried to do a runner with my guitar… but I couldn't get out anywhere…

"The last proper gig we did though, with Bondage on drums, was at the Stevenage Bowes Lyon House, and we went down a like a fucking lead balloon. We were invited up to play, and we were optimistic about it, but we ended up playing this cavernous hall to no one, while everyone stayed in the bar, blanking us. The only people in there were slagging us off, but we were performing pretty fucking badly, if I remember rightly…"

"I think Special Duties were playing or someone like that," explains Roper, "And it was only their people who had bothered to come 'cos it was snowing. And we were trying all this experimental stuff that we'd only previously played in our front room, and Bondage didn't know what to play and just sat there, shaking his head! And that's why he never turned up to the next gig, and we never heard from him again after that night…"

As mentioned earlier, Roper and Stringy, keen to pursue the experimentation began by The Eratics to its logical conclusion, then started up a new outfit, Look Mummy Clowns, with Dan McIntyre of The Apostles drumming; they played their first gig with Lack Of Knowledge in Shepherds Bush.

"That was a weird one, actually," admits Roper, "Because there were some films being shown as well between bands, so there weren't too many people there, but it was a good warm-up. Our first proper gig, where we headlined, was at the Pied Bull, with Hagar The Womb, and it was blinding. We played a good set, and we were really buzzing after that night, because we'd come a long way since everyone who was at the gig had last seen us as The Eratics, and Tony D. was there, and he reviewed it for the NME."

Stringy: "Basically, we'd chucked The Eratics in the bin, and were just writing exactly what we wanted to play, never mind sticking to any anarcho-punk formula. It was quite a jump really, from the one band to the next, and we were really gunning for it at the start."

Although Look Mummy Clowns seemed to hit the ground running, they found it impossible to maintain their early momentum. They recorded a live demo in March 1983, and also had gigs with the likes of Blood And Roses and Urban Decay reviewed favourably by Sounds and Melody Maker, but the writing was on the wall for the band by the time they toured Italy later that year.

"Yeah, we had a connection with this guy out there called 'Jumpy' who was running Attack Records," explains Stringy. "He liked The Eratics, and then he liked the Clowns, and he ended up inviting us over; it was all done through friendship really… we played Bologna, which was a university town and very political, and there'd been all these riots there in the late Seventies. There was a lot of squats there, and a lot of interest in radical music… and we weren't even very political!"

Whilst in Italy, Look Mummy Clowns even recorded a single, the delicate, meandering 'Bardbuster', for Toto Records, a less political offshoot of Jumpy's Attack label.

Roper: "We recorded that in Bologna [at The Krak], and we had to rush off before we'd even finished it properly, because we had to catch the bus to Milan to play the Virus squat! And we got separated on the way to Milan – me and Stringy arrived together, and the other chaps ended up somewhere else…then, when it was time to go home, me and Stringy caught the bus, but they never; they got stranded and had to stay in Italy for another few weeks…"

Stringy: "But they had all our luggage, so I had to come all the way back to England with no fuckin' trousers! I got strip-searched at customs; I was in a right state… I could go on about that trip for ages, 'cos all sorts of shit went down. The bus driver punched one of the passengers… all sorts of shit…"

Unfortunately, Look Mummy Clowns wouldn't be together long enough to see the single be released; after an equally eventful visit to Holland, the band were a tinderbox of tense emotions just waiting for the right spark to set them off – and that spark came at the band's final show, in New Merlin's Cave, Islington, June 11th, 1985.

"The thing is, the Clowns took on a lot," begins Stringy cautiously. "We wanted to be totally fucking original, we decided we'd never support anyone else, we decided we would organise everything ourselves… and we ran out of resources. Me and Roper were falling out over whether we should talk to this one label or not… we had a lot of principles for a 'non-political' band… but we were outstripping our actual capacity to do all these things. The end result was that we'd fall out over who was going to carry the equipment, who was going to sit on the door… and me and Roper got into conflict, and off he went…"

Roper, vocalist with The Eratics, live in Eltham.

"It was all over nothing," sighs Roper, "But I can remember losing it and lobbing this big jar of money I'd taken across the venue! I stormed off to calm down a bit, and when I came back, Stringy just said, 'Do you wanna do the gig or not?' And I said, 'No!' So they played without me…"

Stringy: "We were reluctant to do it, but we had an audience who'd paid to get in, waiting to see a band. And we briefly discussed carrying on afterwards, but didn't."

Roper: "It had gone full circle; we'd played New Merlin's Cave as the second or third gig we played, and there we were back again, worse off than the first time! We'd achieved everything we possibly could, and we were just getting more and more compromised."

Two years after the demise of the Clowns, Stringy attended St. Martin's School Of Art for five years, getting into performance art in the process, but is now back with Roper and Snout in a brand new band, Peckinpah.

"We co-existed with all the other anarcho bands, but we wouldn't wear their badges," concludes Stringy, pondering exactly where they really fit in the big scheme of things. "We were a bit more personal, we were still living under Thatcher, still had no jobs, no fucking money, so what we were saying wasn't that different from what they were saying, but musically we were very far removed. And that variety was important…

"We didn't want to get involved in big arguments about eating meat, even though I was a vegetarian for a long time; it was all getting a bit too black and white, and life is a bit more hypocritical than that…"

"If you choose to do those things, you do them because you think they're right, not because everyone else is doing them," adds Roper. "I think we were in the middle of everything, without really contributing anything to it all. The band's power was always live; it was a very spontaneous thing we did at gigs… too spontaneous sometimes. Some would go well, others wouldn't; we never knew what would happen. We were all over the place… but that was what we did, and we did it the best we could."

SELECT DISCOGRAPHY

7"s:
'Bardbuster' (Toto, 1985)

At A Glance:
Both The Eratics and Look Mummy Clowns have been featured on Overground's anarcho-punk series of CDs, The Eratics on 2005's volume 2, 'Anti-State', and LMC on volume 3, 'Anti-Society' (2006).

"Thank Christ for **RUBELLA BALLET**!" exclaims Crass vocalist Steve Ignorant whilst acknowledging that, "Punk went from being this fun, colourful place to be, to all these miserable bastards wearing black! I knew what I'd see there [at Crass gigs], I knew what I'd hear played there… and bands like Rubella were a breath of fresh air." Indeed they were, being one of the most colourful, mischievous acts of the early Eighties anarcho scene, more concerned with liberating our uptight senses than preaching po-faced politics.

"The thing is, it wasn't a conscious idea to be like that," reckons vocalist Zillah Minx [real name Zillah Elaine Ashworth]. "It was just us; we were punks, making all our own clothes… and back then, you couldn't find a pair of straight trousers for love nor money, and you had to go round all the old teddy boy shops and charity shops looking for jeans that no one else would wear. It was about doing your own thing…

"The funny thing is, my best friend, Sandra, who 'went punk' the same time as me, started to dress all in black, and she was the first person I knew to do that, and people would go mad at her… her mum was like, 'You don't wear black unless you're going to a funeral!' It was that stupid in those days…

"At the beginning of Rubella Ballet, a lot of the clothes I made for the band were cartoon characters: Mr. Men and stuff like that. I think the only direction we had for our band at that point was that we wanted to be child-like…

"But I was an original punk rocker in 1975, hanging out at the Lacy Lady where members of The Damned and other early punks went before the Sex Pistols went on TV. Then the punk scene exploded onto the world – and we all know that story. During this time I was only fifteen, but I saw every band you could possibly name, and went to every known club… and a lot that were unknown! I was part of the evolution of punk and it meant everything to me, as did the bands of the time: the Sex Pistols, X-Ray Spex and The Slits… seeing girls in some of these bands gave me

Rubella Ballet (top row, left to right: lead guitarist Leda Baker, vocalist Zillah Minx, bassist Rachel Minx; bottom row, left to right: bassist Sam, drummer Sid Ation, guitarist Steve Cachman).

an idea. At the time I remember punks saying we were going to change the world, and when Crass came along they described Johnny Rotten's 'Anarchy In The UK' – our punk anthem – as a lifestyle we could actually really adopt.

"Sid [Ation, drummer] saw the Pistols and became a punk immediately, the only one in his little village. Gem [Stone, bassist] and Pete [Fender, guitarist] were the son and daughter of Vi Subversa, the singer of Poison Girls, so were obviously involved in the scene through them and Crass…

"In fact, it was at a Crass gig that I first met Sid, and he ended up living at their house with them and Poison Girls. We then met Gem and Pete [both formerly with the Fatal Microbes, who featured one Donna 'Honey Bane' Boylan on vocals, who later 'went solo' and released the rather good 'You Can Be You' single on Crass], used Poison Girls equipment to jam and write songs, and eventually just got up and played at a Crass/Poison Girls gig. We formed because we had the opportunity to do so; we were young punks having a laugh, being creative and doing what we wanted. Sid had never played drums and I had never sung or written lyrics.

"But punk was about being able to do anything you wanted to; in the Seventies women had only just had a law passed for equal pay [the 1975 Equal Opportunities Act] and just getting onstage as a woman was a political act in itself. We did it because we were breaking stereotypes and doing anything we wanted; it broke rules and changed society's attitudes, but at the time we were just living anarchy, the punk lifestyle. 'Do and be what you want.' Most punks were into peace, so violent activities were not part of our plan, but many 'normal' people in society at that time were violent to us, and as punks we sometimes had to fight back, both physically and mentally."

Adapting the rather unusual moniker of Rubella Ballet from their original choice of name, Rubella Babies ("No one was that bothered what we called ourselves… it didn't seem important at the time!"), the band first got together in 1979, when they were all in their mid-to-late teens, and they quickly began making a name for themselves through countless DIY gigs anywhere and everywhere they could manage to get their gear on a stage.

"Our first couple of gigs were very fragmented," admits Zillah. "At a Crass gig, Sid got up and played drums with lots of other punks, including Gem and Pete, Annie Anxiety, [Andy] Anarchy, and Womble [real name Tommy Harris]. Another time, at a gig in Chelmsford, I sang and Sid played drums after borrowing equipment off the Waxwork Dummies. It was the first time I'd ever sung onstage through a microphone, and I thought, 'Oh, that sounds alright…!' We did about twenty minutes or something, and when we got offstage, everyone was like, 'That was really good…'

"So then, at a gig in Chelmsford Football Club, we asked members of the audience to play all the other equipment. So, for the first couple of gigs, it was Sid, Zillah, Gem and Pete, but at various times it was also lots of other punks. Eventually though, as we were the ones who ended up living together, at the Poison Girls house, we became Rubella Ballet. All of our early gigs went well really, the audience loved us… but maybe that's because so many members of the audience had been in the band?

"It was pretty easy when Sid lived with the Poison Girls though… this was their house in Epping, just down the road from Crass in North Weald… a big, old mansion that had been condemned, because the M25 was scheduled to run right through it, but of course people objected to the scheme, and it was twenty years before they built the motorway, which turned out to be the M11 link road. It was old and decrepit, but it was big, really big, with two staircases… one of them a great big sweeping one; it had five floors… it was a proper mansion, brilliant.

"Anyway, Sid was staying there; he'd just moved down from Birmingham to be a chef at this really posh restaurant called the Capital Hotel, working under Brian Turner, the celebrity chef. Sid's actually a classically-trained chef, but because he was a punk, and got caught washing his pink hair out in the sink where he should've been washing the vegetables, he had a big fight with Brian Turner, and was asked to leave! Thing is, he was a live-in chef, so he lost his job and his house, and stayed for a while in the Notting Hill Cinema with a load of punks, before he moved in with the Poison Girls.

"At the time, Pete Fender and Gem Stone were in Fatal Microbes, and their record ['Violence Grows'] had just come out, but Honey Bane got all the attention and decided to go solo, so Pete and Gemma were looking for a new band. And because Sid was living there, and I was there all the time visiting him, we naturally ended up getting a band together.

"Anyway, they had this gear we could use, rehearsal space, and they were doing lots of gigs where we could also get on the bill. In later years, when we lived in our own flat on the 24th floor of a tower block, it was a lot harder. We had to buy our own equipment, get our own gigs... everything was harder. We drove ourselves to those gigs, set up our own equipment, got the PA and venue, did our own posters and publicity... I remember doing gigs with all the other bands using our equipment and then it'd be broken by the time we did our set. And taking down our equipment and packing the van, only to find that I was the only sober person left to do the seven hour drive back to London..."

The first real gig as Rubella Ballet was at the Theatre Royal in Stratford, opening – of course – for the Poison Girls.

"It turned into a riot," chuckles Zillah ruefully. "It made the front pages of the local press, because it was meant to be a benefit gig to pay for the renovation of the theatre, and all these skinheads turned up and went wild. Mind you, because I came from the East End, I knew most of the skinheads, and quite often, if they were running away from the police after a West Ham football match, they'd come round my house to hide! That was one of the reasons I was always safe at these gigs, 'cos if they threatened me, I'd give 'em hell.

"If on tour, we would usually ask members of the audience if we could sleep at their house, and often the house would be a cold squat. It was hard work and we rarely covered costs – we were all on the dole, and had bills to pay – but we loved it regardless; we were punks who wanted a different lifestyle."

In keeping with this defiantly underground approach, Rubella Ballet's first release was the 'Ballet Bag', a cassette-only offering that came in – surprise! – its very own bag, complete with a booklet and badge, all designed and printed by the band themselves; a labour of love that ultimately went on to sell almost five thousand copies.

"We recorded our own music [at Heart And Soul, on November 12th, 1981], wrote our own lyrics, made our own lyric booklet, even made the stamp that put the ballerina on each tape, and then assembled the whole thing ourselves. It was important because everyone else was always telling us what to do, and we wanted to do it our way."

Sid had by then been briefly poached by Flux Of Pink Indians, playing on their timeless 'Neu Smell' EP for Crass in 1981, which was recorded by Penny Rimbaud and Jon Loder at Southern. A single on Crass for Rubella Ballet was soon on the cards as a result, an opportunity that the band surprisingly chose to gracefully decline.

"Penny moaned that I was playing too many rolls, that I should make it sound more military," recalls Sid, of his time in the studio with Flux. "And I said, 'But I don't wanna fuckin' play like you!' I'd only been playing for about six months then as well, but I was already the nastiest drummer on the fucking planet! And people always say that drummers can't write songs, which is bollocks, because it was the driving tempo of the drums that made 'Tube Disasters' from a really pants tune into such a classic. And I wrote all the music to 'Background Of Malfunction'... but I think the tribal drumming, all the toms I would play, gave that single a different feel to the other stuff on Crass... gave it the Rubella Ballet feel, to be honest..."

"The only reason we didn't do the Crass single though – and we were asked, right after Sid did the record with Flux – was that we just didn't want a black and white sleeve with the round Crass logo on it," says Zillah. "We weren't being difficult; we just wanted it in colour. We were different to Crass, but we were still part of the same thing, still believed in most of what they and the Poison Girls were saying – otherwise we wouldn't have done so many gigs with them both.

"We were a punk band, not a Crass band. Nowadays people go, 'What have The Jam got to do with punk? They're a mod band!' But in those days, all the mods played with us, all the reggae bands played with us… it was one big scene of people who were on the outskirts of society. It was one big mixture at the early punk gigs; there were mods there, skinheads, black people, gay people… now there's an exclusive gay scene, but then there wasn't, and punk was somewhere for people to go if they were different.

Rubella Ballet live at the Marquee, Oct 1984, picture by Paul May.

"One of the first gigs I went to where Crass played was at the Conway Hall, and up until that point I'd been going to see bands like X-Ray Spex, and then I'd started going to a lot of gigs at the Bridge House, which was my local, and everyone used to play there. I met this bloke called Cookie, and he had this badge with the Crass logo on it, and I said, 'What's that then?' And he told me all about them, and I'd just learnt to drive (I was still only seventeen) and had this beaten-up old Morris Minor, but it gave me and my friends freedom, 'cos now we could follow a band like Crass around and have a laugh.

"Anyway, at that first gig where I saw Crass, the audience were punks! And really weird punks at that! They weren't dressed in black, everyone was doing their own thing… and it was only gradually, later on, that their audience became so regimented."

Sid: "The thing is, you had bands wearing all the same clothes, smoking the same tobacco, using the same fucking Rizlas… I mean, Jesus Christ, I've been to Dial House a hundred times, but I'm not going to start idolising Crass. I thought Penny's military drum patterns were really good, but that's as far as it went, and I certainly wasn't going to start playing like him!

"I did do one interview where I slagged off everybody, including Crass, but that was mainly because I can be a self-opinionated twat sometimes… but what I meant was, I wasn't going to toe any party line. Because we were doing something completely different… we, as people, as well as a band, were different… I must have fucked a lot of people off with my stupidity over the years…

"I left home when I was sixteen, 'cos my mum was beating me up, blah blah blah… everyone around me was listening to Status Quo, for God's sake, so I shaved all my hair off, sewed safety pins all over my clothes, walked down the local youth club, told everyone there to fuck off, and moved to London. My mum couldn't find me for about a year-and-a-half, but that was something I had to do: get my life back together again, and not let someone else dictate what I could or couldn't do. Bollocks to the lot of them… and at that point, I thought, 'Oh, I must be a punk!'

"And having Crass tell me what to do would have been no different to having my mum tell me what to do, so we went our own way. We didn't sit around waiting for anyone else to lead us – we just did it ourselves, for a fucking laugh, and if it wasn't a laugh, we stopped doing it! And that's why we're still doing it today: because we're still having a laugh…"

Zillah: "We had our own opinions, our own lives, our own minds… and we were punks; we didn't need someone else to fucking tell us how to think or act."

Consequently, Rubella Ballet decided to go with Xntrix, the label ran by Poison Girls ("We had an extra loyalty to them anyway, because Gem and Pete were in the band…"), for their debut single, 'Ballet Dance'. Recorded during late May 1982 at Xntric Studio, it made the Indie Top Ten upon its release several months later, and whilst a song like (the mildly annoying) 'Krak Trak' demonstrated the quirkiness inherent in the band, it was left to the brooding heaviness of 'Something To Give' to hint at the dark, throbbing power they also had at their disposal.

Rubella Ballet, live at the Leeds Bierkeller 1984, picture by Trunt.

After two well-received radio sessions for John Peel (broadcast on July 6th, 1982, and February 8th, 1983... "The only thing we ever got paid for!"), another solid release came in the guise of spring '84's release by Jungle of the '42 O F' 12". Recorded at Gooseberry 2 Studios during February of that year, it saw a chap name of Sean replacing Pete Fender on guitar, but the three songs chosen, whilst atmospheric, were slightly lacking in the catchy chorus department. Unperturbed, Rubella Ballet embarked upon an ill-fated Italian tour to help promote it.

Zillah: "That was the first time I'd ever been on an aeroplane... and the promoters only sent us single tickets, not returns, so we were a bit dubious! 'Should we or shouldn't we?' Y'know? So, I got someone to lend me some extra money, just in case there was a problem. When we got there, we hadn't eaten for two days, and our first meal was spaghetti with a blob of tomato paste on top of it. We were staying in squats, everyone pretending they couldn't speak English; we were given shit equipment to play on... tying drum kits together with bits of string! We weren't getting paid, weren't even getting drinks for onstage, and it was a hundred degrees, sweat pouring off us... nowhere to wash, couldn't drink the tap water...

"After five days, me and Gemma both had cystitis, which was agony, so we needed the toilet every two seconds, and we were sat on this bucket in this squat, and in the end Sid went fucking mental at 'em all. The next day, they took us to a station and sent us home on the train – another two days without any food or money. Uh, hello...!"

By the time of the superlative 'Money Talks' 12" (Ubiquitous, 1985), Sean and Gem had been replaced by Adam and Rachel Minx (Zillah's younger sister, Rachel Irene Jane Ashworth), and before the band recorded their debut LP, 'At Last, It's Playtime', at London's Alaska Studios, Adam had been superseded by Steve Cachman. Zillah herself admits that such a rapid turnover of personnel obviously had a restrictive effect on the band's creative growth:

"Sometimes I felt that some of the songs on some of the albums were rushed, usually because we hadn't had time or money to rehearse properly. The other thing was, with all these different musicians coming and going, you had to teach them all the songs in your set, before you could get round to writing any new ones, and that kept setting us back all the time. Sometimes I think we should've given up after the original band stopped, or at least changed the name and did something else... but we always kept going as Rubella Ballet, and I'm not sure whether that was a good thing or not, because every new guitarist that joined and left changed the sound. I think me and Sid should've been more demanding of our fellow musicians, and insisted on the sound we wanted them to get for us. We didn't even like all of the stuff we released ourselves – we just did it, and I'm not sure why! But how the band sounded depended upon which guitarist we had at the time..."

Sid: "And to be honest, to this day, I don't think any of the guitarists we had were any good, apart from Pete… and none of them stayed in the band long enough to really become a part of it."

"Or they'd see us as some big band that they could join," scoffs Zillah, "So they'd think they were good, but at gigs they'd get really pissed and wouldn't be able to play! And we'd be like, 'Fucking great! All that effort, teaching them all the songs…!'"

"Like fucking Steve Cachman… who later became a fuckin' copper!" spits Sid. "But I have to admit, I was pissed all the time myself, and doing loads of speed… and I really think that if I hadn't been such a hedonist, we could've been quite a good band!"

The line-up did stabilise considerably around 1986 though, allowing Rubella Ballet to produce their best works, the 'If' LP and the 'Artic Flowers' single, both of them recorded at Slaughterhouse in Hull. Opening with the punishing Killing Joke-like thump of 'Plastic Life', 'If' skips through musical sub-genres with all the mischievous delight of someone dancing in the puddles left by an April shower; from the thoroughly addictive 'Cowboy Heroes' to the heaving dub of closer 'Red Alert', via the rousing feminist anthem, 'Sisters', and the impassioned 'Mescalito', it remains the band's most convincing and well-rounded full length. Whilst the 'Artic Flowers' single was a sublimely graceful slice of post-punk gothic pop that truly revealed once and for all the band's ear for a catchy tune.

"I wrote a lot of personal stuff, about relationships, about my own life experiences," explains Zillah. "I'm actually very political, but there was a big reason for me not being overtly political with my lyrics. My father was an activist; he stood outside South Africa House to protest in 1950, and got thrown down the stairs and beaten up. I came from a family of activists… we lived in this commune, our phone was always being tapped. My mum and dad nearly got put in prison for being so political; they were the people who got rid of Reg Prentice from the Labour Party… it had never happened before, and it'll never happen again, but my mum was all over the front pages of the press… called 'an MI5 agent' on the front of The Sun…I was followed by journalists, my parents were blackballed… and as a result, I would pretend not to be too political in the band, because the implications for my family were pretty dire really. And that always frustrated me, but, I mean, c'mon, I was a girl in the middle of this male-dominated punk scene – which, like I said earlier, was a political statement in itself.

"There were so many hypocrites involved amongst the political bands though, and, I'm sorry, but I don't want to hear it off people, telling everyone else not to eat meat, when they themselves go into McDonalds! Don't do this, don't do that! Do as I say, not as I do!"

1987's 'Cocktail Mix' album was merely a compendium of the earlier 'Ballet Bag' and 'Ballet Dance' releases, whilst 1988's 'Birthday Box' double-LP had been recorded live (at the Savaloy Ballroom, above the Boston Arms pub in Tufnell Park) two years prior to it appearing on vinyl. The next brand new Ballet album, 'At The End Of The Rainbow', released by Brave in 1990, turned out to be their last.

An intoxicating fusion of feisty punk and wispy pop, with a side order of swaggering rock, it even contained several updated versions of older songs, and proved a fitting legacy for a wonderfully innovative act. Rubella Ballet split soon after its release, playing their final show at Camden Palace in 1991.

"At that point, another guitarist and bassist had just left," sighs Zillah, "And we thought, 'What's the bloody point?' And besides, me and Sid had another band together by then, a dance band called Xenophobia... we did 'Kiss Radio' and were No. 1 in the Dance Charts! And we were part of Spiral Tribe... we did that Castlemorton gig [the May 1992 rave near Malvern, Worcestershire, attended by 25,000 people], and our record 'Rush In The House' was playing at every DJ rig all weekend... but a lot of people involved in raves were ex-punks... it was about entertaining yourself for free, organising yourselves, making your own music..."

"But Sid has always been ahead of his time musically. Because he's a drummer and we lived on the 24th floor of this tower block, he couldn't really rehearse at home, so he had this tape-to-tape, and he started sampling in 1980. If you listen to 'Money Talks', that's one of the first times samples were used, on the B-side of that..."

"Although everyone in the band was equal – anyone could write lyrics, anyone could write music – Sid was the musical one; he listened to a lot of diverse music, and he influenced us a lot... to do stuff like 'Krak Trak', with that funky bass line and stuff. But punk was always about being able to do whatever you liked... wasn't it?"

In 2000, Rubella Ballet reformed to play the European Gathering punk festival in Milton Keynes, and have been together on and off ever since, the current line-up consisting of Sid and Zillah, with Pete Fender back on guitar, plus Phil from P.A.I.N. on additional guitar, and his girlfriend Paris Ite on bass.

"Well, we didn't 'reform' as such," corrects Zillah, "It's more a continuation. After the dance stuff... and what I really didn't like about that rave thing was that you had to get onstage and mime – I couldn't stand doing it, it felt really alien! We never really stopped because we wanted to anyway; it was more that people just stopped asking us to play... and when we did, especially in the Nineties, and only five people would turn up or whatever, it just didn't seem worth it.

"Then the Milton Keynes gig we did, that Stu [Pid, from Police Bastard] put on, actually seemed worth the effort. We really enjoyed it too, as musicians, because we were just totally ready for it, we'd rehearsed really hard... in the early days, every gig seemed like one big party, with everyone in it together, but as it went on, and people's expectations grew, and the press were turning up to review us, it stopped being quite so much fun. But we always enjoyed ourselves, except when we started clocking up a big debt... so now we choose our gigs very carefully, making sure there's going to be an audience there, and that we're going to cover our expenses."

Zillah has recently finished work on her long-awaited film, 'She's A Punk Rocker'; a movie as important as anything she's ever worked on musically or lyrically for challenging stereotypes.

"I started it when I went to university, doing 'communications, and audio and visual productions', and in the last year there, we had to make a documentary, and I decided to do one about women in punk. It was only a ten-minute thing, but I got such a good reaction to it from the college and all the students, and because I knew so many other punk women, and no one had ever done anything like it before, I thought, 'I'd better do this properly!' No other punk documentaries touched on any of the underground bands, apart from maybe X-Ray Spex... it was always Blondie...

"At college it started off about the equality of women in punk, about it being a movement for both men and women; for the first time there was a youth movement that included women as equal to men, not just the girlfriends of the blokes in the band. Siouxsie Sioux is as important as any of the men that were there at the time, isn't she? So it began as that, and I wanted to help other people understand what drew us to punk in the first place... I've got Poison Girls in there, X-Ray Spex, Gaye Advert... all the main bands that I thought were important... but it isn't about the famous people at the end of the day, it's just stories from people like Mad Mary, who was Poly Styrene's bodyguard, from when they were hanging out with the Pistols... that's stuff that people want to hear, 'cos it's about Sid Vicious, but they were just friends at the time, they weren't famous people... it'll explain what it was like being a woman in punk. It's all about the attitude... like Gaye Advert hasn't been a punk for a long, long time, but she still has that certain attitude towards life. And if you've got that attitude, you can change the world, and that was what punk was about, and it did change a lot of things... no matter what everyone says.

"I always say I don't need someone else to tell me how to think... however, I do think it's a good idea to put your opinion out there; it's right to try and influence people, as long as you're sincere about what you're saying. And that was where Crass were so successful, influencing so many people to change their lives for the better; punk became so much more interactive: you always had all the lyrics to the songs...

"It was Johnny Rotten that brought up 'anarchy' in the first place though, so it's not like it was exclusively Crass, is it? But Crass did a great job of raising political awareness, because not everyone came from such a political family as I did. They also introduced this idea of punk as a lifestyle, not just a fashion or an attitude... and that's when some people got a bit carried away, expecting everyone to go vegan and stop wearing woolly jumpers... some people did take it to extremes, but it definitely disseminated out into society as real change.

"My idea of anarchy wasn't that I hated society and wanted to go to war with it, but more like, 'Right, I'm a woman, but I'm not going to leave school, get married, have 2.4 children, get a mortgage and all that... I might want to do it later, but I'll do it when and how it suits me. Not to fulfil what society feels is my role as a woman. And as a working class woman, when I took my GCSEs, I was the only girl to do that; no one got them, you weren't even supposed to take them! It's different now... back then just wearing straight trousers and an ear-ring made you a punk..."

SELECT DISCOGRAPHY

Cassettes:
'Ballet Bag' (self-released, 1980)

7"s:
'Ballet Dance' (Xntrix, 1982)
'Artic Flowers' (Ubiquitous, 1986)

12"s:
'42 O F' (Jungle, 1984)
'Money Talks' (Ubiquitous, 1985)
'Artic Flowers' (Ubiquitous, 1986)

LPs:
'At Last, It's Playtime' (Ubiquitous, 1985)
'If...' (Ubiquitous, 1986)
'Cocktail Mix' (Ubiquitous, 1987)
'Birthday Box' (Ubiquitous, 1988) – double live LP
'At The End Of The Rainbow' (Brave, 1990)

At A Glance:
'Greatest Trips' (Brave, 1990) serves as a more than adequate overview of the band's colourful career.

Despite being much-maligned by many as mere 'Crass clones' (quite possibly out of jealousy by others of the close relationship they enjoyed with their Epping mentors), **DIRT** have proven to be one of the most enduring and influential of the anarcho-punk bands, their simplistic rants lent an unique flavour by vocalist Deno's banshee-like shriek. But although she was very much the public figurehead of the band, it was actually guitarist Gary who formed Dirt in 1980.

"Originally it was me and a girl called Mo," he explains. "I used to go round the country watching bands, just to get out of London, and she was a friend of mine who had a car. At the time, I was playing guitar and wanted to get a band together; I'd written all these songs but had no band members! So, I started teaching Mo how to play guitar, and every Saturday morning we'd meet in London and have a jam. And we knew from the outset what we wanted to do, knew that we wanted a girl singer... I was very into female-fronted bands like Poison Girls, Penetration and X-Ray Spex... they held a fascination for me that none of the macho bands ever could..."

"Punk appealed to me, the fact that anybody could do it," he adds. "I already had a guitar, and had been practising in my bedroom playing Beatles songs and stuff, but then I started learning all these punk classics. I had a friend at school, and we used to buy records together, and he had a guitar as well, so we'd sit down and work all these songs out between us. And he had a cellar, so we'd go down there and jam, and from that point on, I knew I wanted to be in a proper band. Every time I went to see a band onstage, I'd be watching them, seeing what they did, checking out what was going on..."

"And I bought so many records! I remember the Adverts' single, 'One Chord Wonders', and it really confused me, 'cos I thought it was one chord all the way through; even though I played guitar, I could hear the chord changing and couldn't understand the concept of it! I'd buy all these records just because they were on coloured vinyl and stuff, I was quite fanatical.

"Then I started seeing Crass logos everywhere. I think I stumbled upon the Poison Girls first of all, completely by accident; I saw them playing at some university or college, and there were no bouncers on the door... it wasn't in the Marquee or the Music Machine. It was a very odd place for a gig, and it was kind of scary – and I liked it! It was different; there were all these people dishing out hand-outs, making their own stencils..."

After meeting Deno on the bus home one night (she was from Dagenham, Gary from Barking), the initial line-up of Dirt was completed by bassist Vomit (real name Vince) and drummer Fox (real name Phil), two brothers from Edmonton, who responded to an ad placed in the Sounds music paper, the latter turning up for the audition with his dad, Leo, who would provide invaluable assistance to the band.

"Yeah, Fox turned up, this guy with a mohican, with 'a friend of his' – who actually turned out to be his dad... although we didn't know that at the time! He was a builder, a demolition guy, covered in tattoos, but just was not punk, and I couldn't see what the connection was between them, this mohican and this builder... they never introduced each other as father or son, just by first names. Fox sat down and I showed him some of my lyrics, which he gave to Leo, who sat there in the corner looking at them... and, of course, my first reaction was, 'Hang on, they're stealing my lyrics!' I was very paranoid at the time...

"Anyway, Fox started playing, and he got into the patterns real quick. I'd never played with a real drummer before, and he upped the tempos, so we got faster... at which point Mo couldn't keep up. At the time we were listening to a lot of Six Minute War, and they were quite slow, and that was the kind of pace she was comfortable with. Mo went home, but I carried on with Fox, and we got faster and faster, and we did about five songs in the end.

"I had a van at that point, so afterwards, I drove Leo and Fox back to their house in Edmonton, and it turned out they lived together... but I just thought they were room mates, I didn't find out for weeks that Leo was his dad. Anyway, we talked about the band and what I wanted to do, and Leo thought it all sounded good; I told him we were called Dirt [contrary to popular belief, the band

Dirt live in Wapping, January 1982, by Davin Storr.

name was inspired by how Gary perceived mainstream society to view the punk subculture, and wasn't an abbreviation of 'Death In Reality Today'; that ominous tagline came as an afterthought much later on] and that we already had a singer, who they'd meet next week. I said that we just needed a bass player... and Fox said, 'I've got a friend who's a bassist!' Friend? It was his bloody brother, but he didn't say 'brother', he said 'friend'! And they brought him along to the next practise, and he was only fourteen. I was about twenty at the time, but Mo was twenty-eight, a lot older than the rest of us, and when Vomit came in, fourteen years old, again with a mohican, she felt very uncomfortable, couldn't talk to them, and she quit that day, and we never saw her again.

"It was only when Deno was chatting to them one night that we found out they were brothers, and that Leo was their dad. It all seemed very strange at the time, but it just worked, and they were a very good rhythm section. And whatever money Leo made during the day on demolition sites, he would spend on equipment for the band... there was no food in their house, but he bought Vomit a bass stack. If they needed it, he'd go out and work to make sure that they had it, he was very supportive of them and the band. He even bought a lighting rig and would do our lights when we played."

The void created by Mo's departure was filled by another woman, Lou, completing the line-up that played the first Dirt show at the Africa Centre in Covent Gardens, June 6th, 1980... although the band actually played an impromptu set at the University Of East London a few days prior to their official live debut, when invited onstage by their friends, The Funeral Directors.

"None of their other support bands turned up," recalls Gary, "And we all happened to be there in the crowd, so they asked us if we wanted to play. We got up and did a set, even though there was nobody there, but it was like a warm-up, which was good, because it helped us get used to setting gear up onstage, moving it all in close to the drum kit so we could hear everything.

"We even had our own banner... the vivisected skull one... although it actually had 'GR' on it, because Fox and Vomit had started their own band Gutter Rats, which never got past two or three rehearsals, so we kept their banner and modified it, Leo adding the beams coming out of the eyes. He was very into Hawkwind and stuff, and it was just his own interpretation of a futuristic holocaust; he had all these visions going on, which to look at him, you'd never have guessed were there. On the outside he was a demolition man, but underneath he was an artist – a poet, a painter... a fantastic character, I still see him every couple of months. He's in his sixties now, but still has a rehearsal studio in his back garden!"

"We turned up there the afternoon of the gig, dragging our equipment, and the old guy that ran the centre didn't like the look of us," laughs Gary, back on the subject of their first proper live appearance. "It was an African culture centre, and all these punks were turning up, but they'd had gigs before and when we got talking to him, we convinced him it would be alright... and then all these skinheads started turning up, by the busload.

"In Edmonton, where Fox and Vomit lived, was a big skinhead contingent, and of course, 'cos they were local, they'd given them all fliers, and they all turned up. The guy on the door at the African Centre locked himself in his office, the girl behind the bar left for the night, and we were told we had to do our own security! We hadn't planned on that.

"Anyway, the PA turned up, but the guy took one look at the crowd, turned straight around and tried to drive off! Luckily someone blocked him in – there was heavy traffic – and we ran down the road and talked him into doing the gig; we had to pay him upfront and swear that we'd cover any damage done to his gear. But there was no trouble there whatsoever; all the skinheads knew Fox and Vomit, so they didn't start anything, and although there was an unnerving atmosphere, it all went really well..."

After several other gigs with the likes of The Sinyx and The Eratics, and even one opening for the Last Resort (that resulted in the band being offered the support slot on Infa Riot's UK tour, a seemingly unlikely alliance that unfortunately never went past the talking stages), Dirt quickly hooked up with Crass, and the rest, as they say, is history.

"Up until that point we were still very much our own band, thinking 'We're gonna do this, we're gonna do that...' But I'd already said to Deno that we ought to play with Crass as soon as we could, 'cos that was the direction I perceived we should go in, and they were already doing it, and I felt we ought to go along that same path.

"Anyway, something went down between Crass and [their then touring partners] Poison Girls, and they fell out, and I had a phone call off [Poison Girls vocalist] Vi, saying that they were going it alone, and they were looking for a band to tour with them. She'd never seen or heard us, but we'd played a few squat gigs, and people had been talking about us. So, I went to see her, and we talked about it, and she said they didn't have anything coming up – one of the band members had just left...

"Then, when I got home, I had a phone call off Steve [Ignorant] saying, 'We've just fell out with the Poison Girls, and we've got a tour coming up in four or five weeks time! We've heard about you guys, have you got something we could listen to?' I told him that we'd done this demo but it was really crap, although I thought it would give him an idea of what we sounded like. He said, 'Alright then, I'll come and pick it up...' I told him that we rehearsed every Wednesday in this church hall, St. Peters, up in Edmonton, and he said he'd bring some of the other Crass guys along to see us, and we could all talk about it.

"And our rehearsals, we always treated them like proper gigs – we'd set the drums up, then the amps around them, and Leo would even set the lights up, 'cos he was still learning how to do that. And Crass walked in on a Wednesday afternoon, and it was like a proper showcase for them! They laughed, until we told them that was what we did every week, that was how we rehearsed, because we wanted to see what was going to go wrong onstage before it actually happened... even down to having a spare guitar handy if a string broke. So, we were very professional for a punk band... we definitely had professional aims at least.

"Anyway, about six or seven of Crass turned up to watch us, and we just got on with it, played for about twenty minutes, and then we stopped and had a fag and a good chat. They liked what we were doing and asked us if we were up for a tour, told us they didn't have all the dates finalised though and would ring us that weekend, and sure enough, Andy phoned us a few days later with ten shows we could play. They had their van, we had ours; they would pay for everything, sort us out with somewhere to stay and stuff. Most of the money they took on the door would be going to various benefits, so all the profit was already allocated elsewhere; the door price was only a pound, but we'd get petrol money every night, just no guarantee how much. But we didn't care about money, so off we went.

"The first show was an experience; it was in Swansea with the Living Legends [at St. Phillips Community Centre, 24th September, 1981], and there was all this football violence. I was used to seeing bands like Crass or whoever policing their own gigs – getting in the crowd, linking arms and pacifying people – so when I saw someone hit someone else right in front of me, I dropped my guitar, jumped off stage and hit him… and he hit me right back again. I thought, 'Oh, fuck this!'

"Anyway, the gig was stopped, and carried on, was stopped again… but I learnt an important lesson – don't just jump off the stage and hit someone, have an aim… or at least be aware of one. It was a big eye-opener, and from that moment on, I was very much more aware of what was going on around me."

Dirt vocalist Deno live at the Zig Zag, picture by Tony Mottram.

The touring that ensued proved a learning curve in many other ways, the band honing their stage craft and garnering quite a reputation as a live band en route, and an EP on Crass Records was the next logical step. The four-track single, 'Object Refuse Reject Abuse', appeared in March 1982 and sold thirteen thousand copies, shooting straight to No. 4 in the Independent Charts. A caustic exercise in distortion, its strength lies in the incredible intensity Deno and Gary manage to inject into their vocal deliveries, a sincere and passionate outrage that helps the rather generic material transcend its minimalist three-chord limitations.

"It kinda came as a package, the tour and the single... 'We're giving you the tour and some exposure, people are going to see you... we'll put a record out for you, and then where you go from there is up to you...' I think it sounds dreadful now though, to be honest. We did it at Southern Studios with Penny producing... and there's one song – 'Unemployment', I think – where every word was recorded separately... although you can't tell that listening to it. But we'd do a take, and Penny would be like, 'Hmmm, there's Steve-isms in that, we can't have that, do it again!' Or, 'Liked the way your voice went on that, we'll keep that bit!' You know? It took all day!

"Luckily the guitars went down pretty quickly, although I remember they wanted me to get some feedback, and I had to stand on the mixing desk, holding my guitar in front of these great big speakers up on the wall, and Penny was going, 'Hmm, turn left a bit!' It was bizarre. It was almost as if he'd mapped it out in his head how he wanted it to sound, and then he just had to coax it out of you...

"We always said that we were better live than in the studio anyway, 'cos we weren't great musicians, we were very basic, and that's where we came across the best. But doing the 'Object Refuse...' EP, we almost set a precedent for how we were going to sound on vinyl... which was rough; it all sounded like it was being played in a tin box with the lid closed on it. Later on, on the [1985] 'Just An Error' album, at least the guitars sound like guitars, and the bass sounds like a bass...

"I remember me and Deno going out to punk gigs, and someone would put 'Object Refuse...' on between bands, and we'd stand there cringing, 'cos it sounded so fucking bad. Especially if it came after a band like Action Pact, or any other band with a girl singer, who had a crystal clear sound..."

After a proposed two-track single with Corpus Christi ground to a halt (when the band found themselves unable to reach a mutually satisfactory compromise on the final arrangement with producer John Loder), Dirt became one of the few bands Crass honoured with a second release on their label. Although the – rather excellent – live album, 'Never Mind Dirt, Here's The Bollocks', didn't come out until January 1983, by which time the band had very publicly split up at the Zig Zag squat gig on December 18th, 1982.

"Crass had done the single, and we'd done a couple more tours with them, and it was more a case that we had to put something new out," admits Gary. "They asked us to do an album, but we didn't have enough material, and then it was suggested that we do this live record, so we hired the Half Moon Theatre in Stepney [April 5th, 1982], and Southern rented in the Stiff mobile recording studio – this big fuck-off semi-artic parked in the back of the venue; it was pretty full-on. We had a few bands playing with us, and we actually did our set twice, just to make sure we got everything. It still turned out that they hadn't miked up Lou's guitar properly, so we went in the studio later... well, I did, 'cos she didn't turn up... and re-recorded her parts. I re-did some of the lead bits, and some of the backing vocals that hadn't come out. Then Lou came in two days later, heard the album, heard me playing all her guitars and knew it wasn't her, and had a tantrum! She'd already made plans to leave Dirt and join Flux at that point anyway – which we all thought was the biggest mistake Flux could possibly make, because they were such a brilliant band and already had a fantastic line-up... 'Strive To Survive...' was one of the best albums of that whole era... and then they took Lou and [her boyfriend] Tim on as guitarists!

"Anyway, what had happened at the Zig Zag was... the show was organised in advance, but no one knew exactly where it was going to be. All the propaganda had said it would be at the Rainbow, but it was at the Zig Zag, so all the bands turned up, and were like, 'Right, who's going to go on first?'

"We were one of the only bands who didn't care where we went on the bill – first, last, in the middle... it didn't matter, as long as we performed. A few weeks earlier, Conflict had a gig at the Clarendon, and they pulled out, couldn't do it, and they asked us to play instead of them, with The Eratics and a few others supporting. We turned up, expecting to play instead of Conflict, who had since decided they were actually going to play. We were still on the bill, but it meant that The Eratics were going to be on earlier, straight after the doors opened, so The Eratics and Fox got into a big argument, and it was all because of Conflict. We said, 'Oh, it doesn't matter, we'll go first, who cares?' But Fox got the hump, and was like, 'No, you said we were going on here, so we're going on here!' He just didn't wanna be fucked about.

"From that day on, we decided we weren't going to get involved in these hassles.

Anyway, on the day of the Zig Zag, you had the main bands like Poison Girls and Conflict, and how were they going to put them all on, without seeming to give one a higher profile than another by creating an order? And someone pointed out that if Crass went on last, it would look like they were 'the main band', so they put all the names into two hats, one for all the early bands, and one for the later bands. And it turned out that Crass would go on before us, and we'd go on last, and that was Crass saying that they were just like us, and they weren't more important or whatever. But Fox said to Andy, 'Everyone will go home after you've played…' and Andy said, 'But that's not the spirit of it…' To which Fox replied, 'I don't care about the fucking spirit of it, we'll end up playing to no one!'

"Then Leo turned up with his lighting rig, to do lights for all the bands for no charge, and he got into an argument with Gee, I think, who told him, 'No flashing lights…' He said that he didn't do flashing lights, but she reckoned that he'd be trying to make Dirt look like popstars or something! And suddenly we're all arguing, and Deno said, 'Let's just go on now and get it over with,' but Fox said, 'I ain't fucking going on now, forget it!' and stormed off and couldn't be found, so we had to go on last anyway.

"The gig went on, and it was a fantastic day, and then it came to us. Everyone had been down the front for Crass, but when we came on, they all went back to where they were before, and it looked like a big void in front of the stage, so Fox threw his sticks down halfway through the set, got up and left. Thankfully Martin from Flux was standing on the side of the stage, sat straight on the drum seat and carried on, and most people didn't even notice. Afterwards, we came off stage, and Fox had quit the band, wasn't talking to anyone. It was a great day, but it ended really badly for us, and Penny came over and was like, 'What're you gonna do now then?'"

What Gary did was start up a new band with 'the enemy', enlisting Stuart Bray from the vehemently anti-Crass Special Duties to play drums in a new project he tried to get off the ground with Honey Bane singing and Daryl from Omega Tribe on bass. Although it never went past more than a few rehearsals, this project paved the way for the resurrection of Dirt, because when Honey Bane – ironically – "fucked off with Fox" and it all fell apart, Deno and Vomit returned, and alongside Gary, Stuart and new rhythm guitarist Paul, toured the UK with Antisect.

"Then Vomit decided it wasn't the same as before," sighs Gary, "Not without his brother on drums, without Leo on the team; it was all new people, and he didn't really know Paul. Also, me and Deno had this relationship where we thrived on being angry, we just argued all the time… and that hasn't changed! But we did this tour with Antisect with him on bass, and he decided he couldn't deal with that. He didn't like the music, didn't like the direction we were going… and he quit.

"I'd actually set up that tour for MDC and Crucifix, and Antisect were going to open. I booked all the dates, and then MDC arrived at the airport with their guitars, but were refused entry. Crucifix were already in the country, Antisect were ready to go, but we needed another band, and I thought, 'Well, I booked the tour, we might as well play!' So we did the tour, and that was when Vomit quit, at the end of those dates.

"He was replaced by this guy Richard, who was one of three guys from Colchester who used to come and stay in our house most weekends. He'd come to Belfast with us on one of the Crass dates, moved into a squat in Brixton, and we'd become good friends. When Vomit left and we needed a bass player, we thought, 'Well, he's always in the van coming to gigs with us…' So he learned to play bass!"

With Richard on bass, Dirt recorded the aforementioned 'Just An Error' album, at Gold Dust Studios in Sidcup, which they self-released on their very own Dirt Records in 1985. Although a fine collection of angry punk tunes that are well worth revisiting, it lacked the fiery desperation of the first single and would prove to be the last Dirt release of the Eighties.

"Yeah, it was fun, but it just didn't have the same momentum as the early days," concedes Gary. "Back then, we had a goal, we had a vision, and we really felt like we were doing something important, but this was more like, 'We've got these songs written, and we want to play them'… but the old anger wasn't there, no one was arguing with anyone. Me and Deno had split, and she was living in the flat upstairs with [Pete] Lippy from Antisect, so we didn't even argue at home anymore, so all the tension had gone. We did a few dates, but it didn't seem as if it was going anywhere. It felt as if we were beating our heads against the wall; we were just a band, nothing more, and we recorded 'Just An Error' but didn't do anything to promote it.

"I think it sounds like a demo that ended up as an album… and later on, we did an album that got put out as a demo ['Feast Or Famine']! But I didn't like it much; it was too… uh… I had a vision of how the band should sound, but Paul wanted his guitar to sound a different way, and Richard thought he knew how he wanted his

Dirt, live in Bolton 1993, picture by Scotty.

bass to sound – but he could only play the one way, so he couldn't really modify anything. And Stuart was a very lazy drummer… whereas Fox was a proper drummer, and if a bridge in a song needed something, he'd sit and work something out, Stuart was basically a metronome sat at the back. Sometimes, instead of doing a roll around the kit with two hands, he'd do it with one hand, and his one hand would wait for the other to come back! And I'd be stood there saying, 'You can't fucking do that!' He was just so lazy!

"We booked into the studio, and it was all on borrowed money, and we were paying sixteen quid an hour to wait for Stuart to come back from having a smoke, or Richard to come back from the off-license… so when they came back, it was always a case of, 'Get it down – now!' And the engineer had his bit of input, with all these ideas of how he wanted it to sound, putting reverb on Deno's voice – and I hate fucking reverb. And we were all pulling in different directions, it just didn't work. When we played live, the tunes were fantastic, but when we recorded them, it was just so middle of the road…"

Deciding that the reincarnated Dirt "wasn't what it was meant to be", Gary folded the band after mini-tours of Holland, Belgium and Ireland, about a year after the recording of 'Just An Error',

and nothing more was heard from him musically until 1992.

"Uh yeah, I stopped going to gigs altogether… basically I gave up on music; nothing was inspiring me. I started my own business and stuff… just plodding along really. Then the girl I was living with at the time started working for the NME, as a photographer, and she was being sent to all these gigs, getting sent passes… before the NME, she worked for Spiral Scratch magazine. Thing is, she'd take all these photos and quite often, the editor would ring her up afterwards and say, 'Great pictures… but the guy who was meant to write the review never turned up at the gig, so we don't need them!'

"Basically she needed someone to write reviews, so I created a character, Mr. Jackson, and started writing for Spiral Scratch, but I didn't like the bands I was going to see, so I was just trying to be funny. Then she started with the NME, but I carried on going to shows with her, just 'cos she had all these passes, and there was this one band, Daisy Chainsaw [One Little Indian recording artists, members of which would later form Queen Adreena], who just blew me away. I hadn't seen anything like it… they were a four-piece with a girl singer who dressed in a wedding dress… looked like something out of a horror film, and she was all over the stage – really full-on. They were a fantastic band, and I called Deno up the next day and said, 'What are you doing?' They got me all fired up again… 'cos I still had all this energy, but just wasn't interested. I thought we had one more go in us, and that would be that, so I rang her and she was up for it… and then we had to find people to play with. There was a bit of messing around, a couple of drummers came and went… Stef became the drummer at the time, he was one of the characters who used to come up and stay with Richard… another friend, Mick, was on bass… this time, when Dirt went out, we had two girls in the band, one white guy and two black guys, so there was this different ethnic look as well, which was good, and it lasted for a while…

"But then mine and Deno's tantrums got the better of everybody. Mick ended up getting argued out of the band; him and Deno had a fight in Belgium and smashed someone's house up – they were throwing things at each other that didn't even belong to them! So that ended badly… so a girl who was on the road with us at the time became the bass player. Stick from Doom joined on drums as well, because Stef had a family and a proper job, driving buses, so he couldn't always get time off to go on tour, so I had two drummers, and we used to alternate them. But it got to a point where I'd book a tour – I always just used to get the dates sorted out and then ring everyone and tell them when they were, and ask could they make it or not? And I'd be ringing people up, and they'd be like, 'Well, who's on bass?' 'Who's on drums?' There was a lot of tension again, and a lot of the people in the band couldn't relate to each other…"

Despite this lack of stability, the early Nineties Dirt was far more prolific than their Eighties predecessors, recording a superb demo ('Feast Or Famine'), two great singles ('Scent Of The Kill' and 'Beast Or Burden', for Skuld and Tribal War respectively… the former featuring the two best Dirt songs ever – 'Lunacy' and 'Plastic Bullets') and another decent live album ('Drunks In Rusty Transits'). Concerted touring was undertaken, both in Europe and the US; they even toured Europe without Deno, who quit scant weeks before the scheduled dates, Stacey from Connecticut band Mankind proving a more than adequate last-minute replacement against all the odds.

"Well, me and Deno always fell out," chuckles Gary knowingly. "She'd always say she wouldn't play a gig, just to wind me up. If I said it was black, she'd say it was white… we never agreed on a thing. I basically paid for the 'Drunks…' album, and I'd got it back from the plant; I had a thousand copies to sell. Final Warning had booked their tickets to fly over here, and I'd booked this tour, but we decided to buy a bus to travel together in, 'cos we couldn't all fit in one van, so me and Neal bought this bus, just to tour Europe with, and then Deno said she wasn't going, and this time I could tell she really wasn't. So what were we going to do? I couldn't cancel the tour, I didn't wanna get the band a bad name, 'cos I knew no one would touch us again if we blew out a whole tour, so I basically decided that I'd have to sing – even though everyone would be expecting to see Deno up there. Then I thought of Stacey from Mankind; we'd played a few gigs together, and she was vocally very similar to Deno anyway. So I phoned her up and said, 'What are you doing for the next six weeks?'

"I told her I'd pay for the flight and everything, and she said she'd think about it… she called me up the next day, telling me she'd booked a flight, and two days later we were on the road in Europe! She arrived, slept on my couch, and the next morning she got in the van and we went… and we pushed our 'new' bus down the road, so we started how we meant to go on – 'cos we pushed it most of the way round Europe as well. It got hit by a train in Poland, so it came back with one side smashed in!

"Actually it was a very good tour; it was certainly different, it was very relaxed, there was no anger… it was good, but it wasn't Dirt. And for the most part, no one cared that Deno wasn't with us, until we got to Poland and the promoter was really worried about it, but hardly anyone at the shows noticed. Stacey really carried it off, she did a great job. I'm glad we did it… I think we had to do it; too many people would've lost too much money if we hadn't.

"And then we got back to London, for the last show, at the George Robey, and Deno got up and sang with Final Warning, which was funny…

"Final Warning had a few gigs in Ireland, and I was going to go with them anyway, and we all ended up going and playing in Ireland, even though we were never booked to… and I think the last ever Dirt show was in Cork [at McCabe's, 10th June, 1995]."

Both Gary and Deno are now parents, so their priorities have changed considerably in recent years, but since the absolute demise of Dirt, Gary started up Stratford Mercenaries with Steve Ignorant from Crass on vocals (they split in 2000 after several well-received albums) and Deno guested on the Toxic Waste album, the Belfast band with whom she also did two European tours.

"Uh, we came, we saw, we left!" deadpans Gary, when asked how he would like Dirt to be remembered. "We got a lot of stick in the early days, as soon as we teamed up with Crass… especially down at the Anarchy Centre in Wapping; every time me and Deno went there, they'd be scowling at us, pointing at us… questioning everything we did… what we ate, what we said. And I really couldn't deal with people like that, slagging us off left, right and centre.

"I remember one night, there was this black guy called Luke, who was always at all the shows, and he fell asleep on the floor. So Fox and Vomit picked him up and moved him over into a corner... looked after him basically... they actually became good friends with him. But Luke went away to France a few days later, and of course there were all these rumours flying about that they'd beaten him up, drew fucking swastikas on his head or whatever... and it was all coming from this one group of people, and they really pissed me off.

"There was always a lot of backstabbing within the anarcho scene, but no one wanted to stand up and do anything about it – in case we drove a wedge in there. Everyone else was already trying to split it up, and we were trying to keep it together.

"Anyway... how to be remembered? Just as a part of it all really. I'm glad I was involved, and I think we opened up a lot of doors for a lot of bands, by taking the likes of Polemic Attack and Anthrax on the road with us; it got them talking to people from other areas, and it had a knock-on effect... it was all about creating a network. It was never about being content with what you had; it was about making something more. I saw what we did as a form of art in many ways, an outlet. And if you feel angry about something, deal with it... but there's no point in pretending to be angry if you're not!"

SELECT DISCOGRAPHY

7"s:
'Object Refuse Reject Abuse' (Crass, 1982)
'Scent Of The Kill' (Skuld, 1992)
'Beast Or Burden' (Tribal War, 1993)

LPs:
'Never Mind Dirt, Here's The Bollocks' (Crass, 1983)
'Just An Error' (Dirt, 1985)
'Drunks In Rusty Transits' (Dirt, 1993)

At A Glance:
Skuld's superb 'Black And White' release compiles everything the band ever released – and even some stuff they didn't – onto two discs, complete with tasteful digipak and an exhaustive booklet of all the lyrics, plus original artwork and entertaining liner notes from Gary.

Of all the anarcho-punk bands from the early Eighties, **OMEGA TRIBE** were one of the most tuneful, their tales of social woes bitter-sweet pills coated in mournful melody. Formed in Barnet in 1981, they were originally a three-piece comprising Hugh Vivian on guitar and vocals, Daryl Hardcastle on bass, and Pete Shepherd on drums, and briefly called themselves Deadly Game ("Although that was a bit crap…!") before becoming the much more evocative Omega Tribe.

"I'd been in a band called Comatose, which was a bit more experimental than Omega Tribe," reveals Daryl. "Hugh was in this hippy band

Hugh and Pete of Omega Tribe, picture by Tony Mottram.

called Whoosh! and Pete was in a band too, but I can't remember what they were called. We were all mates from school basically, just sixteen or seventeen; funnily enough, we got together the day that Charles and Di got married… we had our first rehearsal, down in this basement most of the day, and missed the whole fucking thing – it was great!

"I started off getting into the Pistols and The Clash in the late Seventies, but I'd been into Crass for a few years by the time we got started; I was really into their lyrics, very intelligent, thought-out stuff, rather than just shouting 'Bollocks!' at everybody… and the music was unusual, totally unique compared to all the other bands of the period.

"Hugh was quite a good singer," he adds, on the distinctly tuneful edge they brought to the genre, "And he always preferred to do that rather than just shout and scream… although there was thrash stuff in our sound as well, especially at the beginning – because we weren't that good at playing! But even that was quite melodic, 'cos Hugh's voice was always in key."

Debuting locally at the Monkfrith Boy's Club during the summer of 1981, Omega Tribe somehow managed to blag a support slot at the prestigious 100 Club as their second gig, thus ensuring their tenure around the halls of Barnet would be a mercifully short one.

"Yeah, it was supporting The Meteors," laughs Daryl incredulously, "Just 'cos Pete, our drummer, knew one of 'em! And they said, 'Come and play with us at the 100 Club!' So, that was a bit of a jump up from the first gig! It was a bit of a clash of styles as well, but we just did it for a laugh… and their audience were okay too… pretty subdued really; I think they were just waiting for The Meteors to come onstage, and when they did, they all went fucking ape-shit!

"But then we got more into the Crass thing, and started playing with a lot of those kinda bands. We didn't really do many local gigs at all; we weren't really a 'local band' like that, we got out straight away. We soon realised that we didn't wanna be stuck in Barnet all our lives, y'know?

"The band was all we ever thought about – writing songs, rehearsing, recording demos… we were quite an ambitious bunch really… we definitely wanted to make ourselves heard. Especially Hugh, who was a bit of a poet; he was a good lyricist and he had a lot to say. He still writes poetry now, in fact."

Practising once a week at We Mean It in Barnet, the rehearsal studio ran by Steve Broughton, one-time drummer with radical Seventies prog-rockers, the Edgar Broughton Band, Omega Tribe recorded their first demo in March 1982. One song of which, 'Nature Wonder', found its way onto the huge-selling Crass Records compilation album, 'Bullshit Detector, Volume 2', after which the band found themselves invited by Crass to play their Zig Zag squat gig... the only time the two bands would tread the same stage on the same day.

"I was doing a fanzine at the time, called 'The Realities Of Society', and I went to interview them," recalls Daryl of his initial introduction to Crass. "I met them at one of their gigs, and asked if I could put them in my 'zine, and they said 'Yes!' So I interviewed them, and then met up with Poison Girls as well – they were basically the only two bands in the mag – and that's when I first met Pete Fender [who would become Omega Tribe's fourth member], over at their house. This was about 1980, I think? And when I started hanging about with him at the Poison Girls place, I would bump into Penny and other members of Crass, and get talking to them a bit, and I got to know them all quite quickly. I suppose I was in awe of Penny and Vi [Subversa, the Poison Girls singer] a bit, at least to start with... but I was seeing Pete a lot, and Vi was just 'Pete's mum' to me in the end, y'know? Like anyone else's mum!

"So anyway, when Penny said he was doing a second 'Bullshit Detector' compilation, we quickly recorded some songs in the Poison Girls' basement studio and ran it up to him at Dial House. He liked it and put it on there, and that was what led to the single on Crass..."

Said single being the masterful 'Angry Songs' that crashed into the Independent Top Ten upon its release during spring 1983. Four tracks of acerbic tunefulness, it dared to defy the hardcore thrashings and nihilistic tendencies that were dominating the scene at the time with its optimistic pleas for love and peace. Ably produced by Penny at Southern, it was a typically overblown affair, with 'Another Bloody Day' being an especially ambitious arrangement, with Pete Fender, then a brand new addition to the ranks, handling lead guitars and pianos.

"Well, it took a lot longer for a start," reckons Daryl, on the difference recording with Penny and John Loder made, "Because we'd only ever used a four-track before then, so we were used to bouncing songs down virtually live, but Southern was a twenty-four track studio. It went okay though, even if we were a bit disappointed with the final sound. Penny always went for very harsh tones... that was what he wanted, the sound he tried to create on all the records he did... but if you listen to our album, after the single, it's a lot warmer and fresher, a lot more upbeat.

"But we weren't complaining; it was just a privilege to even be doing a record for Crass. Everything they did sold thousands of copies almost immediately. And I still like the single, but I'd rather listen to [the album] 'No Love Lost'; it's just got a nicer sound, for me at least.

"Pete [Fender] just came in the studio and played some piano and guitar for us. As I said, we already knew him as a friend through the Poison Girls, and he was always at our rehearsals, and he'd help us put bridges in songs and work out harmonies and stuff. He had his own studio in their house, and he did all our demo tapes, but he didn't join officially until about the time we did that first single.

"And yes, it did really well, especially in the Independents. I remember seeing the chart in Sounds, and we were at No. 4 – and The Damned were at No. 5!" laughs Daryl proudly. "And I thought, 'Oh my gawd, this is a bit weird!' I even had my picture on the front page of Sounds – not the whole cover or anything, but just a little picture of me in the 'Featured this week...' box. It was a bit weird walking into my local newsagents and seeing that!"

After undertaking several UK tours with Conflict ("We were really good mates with them; we all got on really well... squeezing into one van and setting off around the country..."), Omega Tribe concentrated on the recording of their one-and-only album, the near-perfect pop-punk gem, 'No Love Lost'... but not before playing what Daryl still remembers as the pinnacle of his time with the band...

"That would have to be when we played Stonehenge in '83!" he beams. "Well, we played in '84 as well, but that was in the afternoon, and everyone was just lying around stoned. But when we played in '83, we were meant to go on at about 9.00 pm, but this band played before us, the Tony McPhee band, and they went on and on and on… every song lasted about half an hour… so we ended up going on at about one o'clock in the morning, and there was about twenty thousand people there. That was the biggest gig we did by far, and it went really, really well… we played well, and the sound was fucking brilliant onstage; that was a real thrill, I can tell you…

"Then, when Penny asked us if we wanted to do an album for Corpus Christi, we said 'Yes!' But we really didn't want to do it at Southern again; we wanted Pete Fender to do it, 'cos he really knew the band and what we wanted to sound like. So they kindly allowed us a recording budget of about £500 – even though it would've cost about five grand or more to do it at Southern! Luckily one of Pete Fender's mates had a twenty-four track studio called Heart And Soul, just round the corner in Leytonstone, and he was just about to move premises to Walthamstow and had two weeks of dead time coming up while he was packing stuff up and moving out. And it was just a lucky break for us, because I think we only actually spent about £300, and it was all because of this dead studio time we utilised.

"And we were two doors down from where Poison Girls lived, so we kept going back there and sitting in their garden when we weren't doing anything. Recording is always so boring, just sat there in a yard out back somewhere, listening whilst everybody else records their bits, so it was great to get away from the studio as much as possible, and that kept the recording fresh, I think."

Whatever the secret ingredient was, it worked, because 'No Love Lost' remains an unsung classic of the melodic punk genre, every song eliciting a powerful gut reaction – be it joy or sorrow, elation or fear – not to mention much tapping of feet and nodding of heads; Daryl's unique and dynamic bass playing proving an irresistible focal point.

"I took influences from everywhere really!" he admits with a chuckle. "A bit of Crass… bits and pieces from lots of other bands… but you put it all together and you sort of get your own style. I'd play some of the stuff with a pick, the faster parts, but found I could get a nicer feel playing with my fingers on the slower parts, so, on something like 'Aftermath', I'd be picking away on the fast bit, and then I'd quickly slip my plectrum into the scratch plate for the slow bit. And I'd bung a few chords in here and there… just to keep it interesting.

"Either me or Hugh would come up with a tune, and play it to the other one, and we'd chop it about, so even if it might have sounded like Crass to start with, by the time we'd finished messing about with it, it sounded like Omega Tribe. Especially once Pete Fender joined fully; that was when we really started to develop our own style…

"We did have some other songs ready for it, but we thought they were a bit crap!" he adds candidly, on the noticeable brevity of the album. "So we went for quality rather than quantity; we didn't want to dilute the good songs with crappy filler tracks."

With 'Freedom, Peace And Unity' being possibly the most intense cut on offer, its ominously brooding opening section ("Well, tell me where's the future in a world that lives in fear?") bursting into frantic life (a welcome ray of sunlight peering nervously from behind the storm clouds during the chorus refrain of "Anything can change if enough people shout, that freedom, peace and unity is what it's all about…"), the most painfully poignant song on offer is 'My Tears', a pacifist anthem if ever there was one.

"Well, I wrote that about the Falklands War, 'cos not a lot of people were saying anything about it," reckons Daryl. "Well, Crass were, but no one else… I mean, a few bands were obviously saying, 'Bollocks to war!' but that was about it, nothing very insightful. It was quite amazing actually, 'cos I went to the pub and got really pissed, came home and wrote the whole song in about fifteen minutes… the music, the lyrics, the whole thing… I'd never done that before, and I've never done it again since! And that was just before we recorded the album, so it only just made it on there."

Elsewhere the tender 'What The Hell' vied with commanding opener 'Duty Calls' for the listener's attention, leaving one in no doubt that this was truly an album that had genuine

Daryl of Omega Tribe (kneeling), picture by Tony Mottram.

potential to cross over to a much wider audience than merely that encompassed by the anarcho-punk scene.

"Yeah, I think that whole movement started to get tedious quite quickly, a bit too stagnant for its own good. We were moving further and further away from the heavy punk thing anyway, and becoming more melodic... Hugh and Pete Fender were proper musicians really, and it's debatable whether they were even 'punk' in the first place. So, when we were recording, Pete would say, 'Hey, let's put some tambourine on... and what about a triangle?' And you just didn't get that sort of thing from other punk bands...

"And it was nice, 'cos when you played it back, it sounded bloody lovely! And we didn't want to stay the same forever; we welcomed change. Some bands do like to always sound the same, but we were happiest when we were moving along, y'know? But yes, of course, some of our stuff did go right over the heads of the punk crowd, especially if we played with Conflict or someone like that. But if we were playing our own gigs, we tended to get more... uh... subtle punks, if you know what I mean? Once they knew what we sounded like, we didn't get the hardcore lot coming along just to see us; they'd only turn up if we were playing with whoever they were into at the time."

January 1984 saw Omega Tribe back in Southern Studios recording a new single, 'It's A Hard Life', which was produced by the keyboardist from Hot Chocolate and made the Indie Top Five when it was released later that year. It was quite a departure for the band that surprised even those who were used to their musical flights of fancy, but lyrically it was still loaded with the band's trademark pathos.

"The producer did the total pop thing with us, which is what Martin Goldschmidt, our manager at the time, wanted him to do. Martin also managed the Poison Girls, and when he said he'd manage us as well, I was happy for him to do it. Up until then I was trying to do all that, and I was getting in from the pub and there'd be twenty-five or thirty phone calls on my answer machine, and I was thinking, 'Fuck this! I've had enough!' I didn't mind writing endless letters, but organising gigs and everything was really getting on my nerves.

"Martin wanted us to go in a much more commercial direction… and you want to move on, don't you? Otherwise you get bored… plus we were so broke; we just wanted to make a bit of money! We were preaching all this stuff about anarchy and that, and then we were going to sign on. So we thought it'd be nice to make a few hundred quid a week just to live off, to be self-sufficient."

An extensive UK tour was undertaken, that also saw the band promoting a live cassette, recorded at the Hammersmith Clarendon just after the release of 'Hard Life', and put out by Rob Challice of Faction and All The Madmen on his 96 Tapes label. However, it was the last concerted trek the band made together, because they quietly and amicably split in 1985.

"We did record another single [entitled 'Hip, Hip, Hooray'], but it never came out," reveals Daryl. "Hugh left – he just didn't wanna do it any more – so I went and started up another band called simply The Tribe, and carried on from there. It was a different sound again, it was more ska, with a brass section and everything… we even played with Bad Manners once, which was quite funny. We did a few demos, and played lots of gigs, but never released anything… and that ended in about '88.

"Hugh went and did a Billy Bragg sort of thing for a bit, just writing his own songs and performing them with an electric guitar, you know? Pete Fender was in Rubella Ballet for a bit… his sister, Gemma, was in them as well, as bass player… and sometimes he was in them, and sometimes he wasn't.

"And Pete Shepherd moved to Spain about fifteen years ago, 'cos Vi from Poison Girls went out there. I see him occasionally… in fact, when Vi comes home to see Pete, I sometimes see her as well… she came to a barbeque I had at my allotment a few years back, and it was nice to see her. She was seventy this year, in fact [2005]!

"A lot of my beliefs are still the same," adds Daryl, who still occasionally performs the odd Omega Tribe number, albeit acoustically, at jam nights in his local pub. "I haven't become a Tory or anything! I still don't vote, and most of the things we said in the band I still adhere to. We called ourselves anarchists then, and I'm still one now… well, I try to be. I work for myself, I'm a gardener, I don't work for a boss… but it's hard, 'cos I pay taxes… but you have to toe some of their lines… you still gotta take your kids to school.

"Actually, Hugh's a teacher now, in a primary school, and he's very good at it; he was always a sensitive bloke. The school's in a rough area, and he handles the kids very well."

And as for that scar across Daryl's face? Surely a reminder of some punk rock showdown with the establishment's boot-boys…!

"I'd like to say it was received during a fight with a load of vicious skinheads!" he laughs good-naturedly. "But really I came off my bike and fell through a window when I was five – I had sixty stitches in my head. Just a schoolboy accident, nothing very exciting… you see, truth isn't always stranger than fiction!"

SELECT DISCOGRAPHY

7"s:
'Angry Songs' (Crass, 1983)
'It's A Hard Life' (Corpus Christi, 1984)

LPs:
'No Love Lost' (Corpus Christi, 1983)

At A Glance:
The only official Omega Tribe retrospective, Rugger Bugger's 'Make Tea Not War' CD, is unfortunately no longer available.

Standing alone in the anarcho scene like diseased lepers, the perverse ramblings of **RUDIMENTARY PENI** remain an enigma to this day; the band still shrouded in mystery, primarily due to their reluctance to perform live, their early thrashier works universally adored by punks around the world, yet much of their later, more experimental output sailing straight over the same spiky heads and careening wildly off into the distant cosmos.

"A punk band? Yes!" ponders bassist Grant Matthews on where they might fit into the grand scheme of things, if one tried hard enough to bludgeon them into a particular pigeonhole. "But anarcho? No, not really, though I had considerable sympathy with Crass's politics. Jon and Nick weren't into the politics at all, and our association with that scene was mainly due to me volunteering to help out at the Autonomy Centre in Wapping, and then the release later on of [the second single] 'Farce' on Crass Records."

Grant of Rudimentary Peni pictured at the front of a Sinyx show, 1981, courtesy of Steve Pegrum.

Formed June 1980 in Abbots Langley, Hertfordshire, as well as Grant, Rudimentary Peni comprised vocalist/guitarist Nick Blinko and drummer Jon Greville, and emerged from the ashes of Nick and Jon's previous band, The Magits.

"Jon devised the name," reveals Nick. "A shortening of the original name, Magit Turds... and a portent of a genuinely uncompromising name to come!"

"Nick and I were at the same secondary school together, Langleybury Comprehensive," elaborates Jon. "And we met through a mutual friend also at the school, Martin 'Drooper' Cooper. This was when The Magits were formed, alongside another school friend, Alex Hawkes. I reckon this would have been in '78 or '79. We used to have the odd rehearsal around my parents' place, and by god we needed it! Musically, it was pretty shambolic and probably naive, but it was just exciting to be a part of the punk thing. I don't have any memories of Magit gigs, but that's not to say there weren't any...

"My interest in drumming started when I was about eight; my uncle was a drummer in the late Fifties/early Sixties, in a jazz band. My parents were always very supportive, and bought me a second-hand kit, and always encouraged me to do my minimum one-hour-a-day practice. Sometimes that pissed me off, but I'm grateful to them now. I started taking lessons at about the age of ten, and after a while, I used to practice at home by putting on a pair of headphones, and playing along to whatever I was into at the time. In the early days this would have been Slade, Gary (the perv) Glitter, Sweet etc. etc. I started getting into punk about the time of the Pistols' 'Never Mind...' album; I asked my snobbish auntie for the album for Christmas, and I reckon that when she went into the shop to buy it, it was the first time she'd ever said the word 'bollocks'!"

Testament to the empowering qualities of punk rock, even a band as obscure as The Magits could immortalise themselves on vinyl; no longer was that a privilege the preserve of larger-than-life rock-stars... no, now anyone could release a record if they merely set their mind to it. Which The Magits duly did in 1979, with the four-track 'Fully Coherent' EP, for Nick's own Outer

Himalayan Records, the rather disconcerting result. Anyone who has heard this perverse, meandering collection of keyboard torture will know that its song titles such as 'Fragmented' and 'Disjointed' are mischievously and knowingly apt.

Jon himself didn't play on the single, it being the creation of just Nick and Drooper. A second single was also recorded the following year, 'A Pawn In The Game', with Alex Hawkes also lending his services, but it never saw the light of day for various reasons that not even Nick himself can – or cares – to remember. And with the premature demise of The Magits, Rudimentary Peni, a much more hardcore punk affair musically, began rehearsing in earnest at Jon's parents' house and made their live debut in early 1981.

"It was in a village hall outside of Watford, with the S-Haters and Soft Drinks; we played quite well… but the small crowd were unimpressed," deadpans Grant.

This dim view of performing live would lead to the band playing but once a month to begin with, and increasingly less frequently as the years went by. Indeed, Nick was quoted in issue No. 1 of IQ32 zine, as saying 'Playing live is a pain in the arse, who needs it?'

With such an attitude, it's hardly surprising then that they never toured (the furthest they ventured south being Brighton, with Leeds being the most northerly of their one-off forays), but their distaste for public appearances merely helped add to the enticing air of mystery that suggestively shrouds them to this day.

"I do remember that the few gigs we did bother to play in the early days were most disappointing," offers Jon. "In the respect that, there would usually be some wanker that thought it was all about spitting at the band and generally being an aggressive, annoying tosser. Wherever did the idea that bands enjoy being gobbed at come from? I'm fucked if I know! And most gigs ran a similar course, i.e. the majority of people clearly disappointed that we didn't have green mohicans and multiple piercings. I think we were all aware that we didn't look as we were 'supposed to', but I don't think any of us gave this too much thought. Basically, if you were the sort of person to be put off by what we looked like, you were never

Nick and Grant of Rudimentary Peni live in Derby, April 1993, picture by Lee Holford.

going to understand or appreciate the songs anyway."

"The worse gig we ever did was in Harpenden in 1981," reckons Grant. "We had so much stuff thrown at us we had to leave the stage! In the early years, it was probably a combination of laziness and a lack of opportunity that prevented us from gigging. Then it was illness that stopped us… and in later years, it was generally half-empty venues and unappreciative crowds."

Rather, Rudimentary Peni concentrated their efforts on recording, steadily racking up an impressive body of work, their innate ability to disturb and provoke the listener on some deep, primal level almost unrivalled in the punk scene.

"We did a short demo first, which I found quite a thrilling experience at the tender age of sixteen," explains Grant. "The results totally sucked though – out of tune and no 'fuzz' on the guitar. Then the first EP was recorded during the summer of 1981 at Street Level Studios in London; the engineer was from a band called Here And Now, and initially he seemed quite appalled by Nick's abrasive vocal style…"

"Yes, that very first demo was quite an experience," laughs Jon. "We did it in a local four- (or maybe eight-) track studio in Watford that was run by a twisted old prune called David Kaye, whom I think made a part-time living entertaining old age pensioners with his organ! I think it was quite an eye-opener for him!

"As far as the recording of the first single went, I didn't have any great expectations going into the studio. I used the house drum kit, and we bashed through the songs at a ridiculous rate; I certainly don't recall there being many second takes. However, as we were mixing, it began to dawn on me that this was sounding rather good, and after [the second album] 'Cacophony', I reckon it's the best thing we've done. Don't you think all punk songs should sound like 'B Ward'?"

Actually, it would be a shame if they did, because then Peni wouldn't stand alone as demented visionaries towering above a sea of all-too-often shallow and generic peers. That first self-titled EP, once again released by Nick on Outer Himalayan, sounds like nothing else released before or since. Although seemingly steeped in the doctrines of punky thrash (everything louder and faster than everything else, etc. etc.), it crawls with an other-worldliness that quite literally has the ability to raise the hackles on the neck of the listener. The demented chorus of 'Hearse', the chillingly laconic, sibilant delivery of 'The Gardener', and, most memorable of all, the completely insane intro of 'Teenage Time Killer', Grant's burbling bass wandering cryptically in and around an eerie guitar refrain before the whole thing explodes into intense chaos. And 'insane' would be a word often mentioned in the same breath as the band's name, with Nick's lyrical meanderings, not to mention his superb – albeit utterly twisted – artwork that adorned each and every release, owing much to his own questionable mental health.

"It took me a while to meet Nick, 'cos he was quite a reclusive character even back then," recalls Mark Farrelly, guitarist with Part One and a close friend of Peni during their formative years. He was especially close to Nick, sharing the same interest in macabre art and literature, and indeed their bands shared the same stage several times in the early Eighties. "I'd seen Grant at the Anarchy Centre, but I never knew who he was; I hadn't spoken to him… but there was this other guy, a really good friend of mine, who used to call himself Scarecrow, and he was in a few Andy Martin [of The Apostles]-related bands… he's still around, he's done a lot of performance art over the last fifteen years or so. Anyway, he would put together these compilation tapes, and he was playing one of these one day and this song came on called 'Teenage Time Killer', and I was just fuckin' blown away by it; it sounded so odd, so fucking peculiar… to say it was eccentric is quite an understatement. Scarecrow was sneering at it, saying that they were 'just a bunch of fucking sixth-formers', but I couldn't believe what I was hearing. And he pointed Grant out to me, and we ended up on the same train home that night, 'cos he was getting off at Watford and I was going back to Bletchley, which are both on the same line. Grant didn't drink, and I was really pissed, but we struck up a conversation, and because they lived relatively close to us, I eventually met Nick, and we really hit it off straight away, because we both had this very morbid outlook.

"And I loved his artwork; it was fantastic, like nothing I'd ever seen before… and he discussed it with me all the time, because no one else was really that interested back then. I'd always been into drawing since I was a kid, but I'd more or less stopped, and then I met him, and he showed me this catalogue he got from the Hayward Gallery in '79 that was a big influence on his artwork, called 'Outsiders', and it was all what we know as Outsider Art now… you know, art from mental institutions, just fairly odd characters who had drawings in their pockets and stuff. And he showed me this thing and I could immediately see his energy, where he was coming from… 'cos he'd actually worked in a mental hospital himself, just outside Watford. He'd gone to Watford School of Art, and left because he couldn't stand it, but he loved the very resonant world of outsider art. I think it had a big influence on his approach to music as well…"

"Yes, when I was seventeen, I was despatched to the London asylum working as a ward orderly," confirms Nick. "Although by the time I worked there, it was called Shenbury Hospital. Soon, such village-like institutions were not deemed too cool, thus care in the community ('community asylum') arose, and Shenbury Hospital, like most of its kind, is now nearly all houses.

"There's nothing wrong with art school though. I attended a few years too early and might well have done better applying at about age nineteen. Oddly enough though, my doctor, who I rarely see now, suggested that I re-apply… and yes, the shrink has seen my artwork!"

The band's first London gig was with Flux Of Pink Indians and the Subhumans at the Red Lion, Leytonstone, on 18th September 1981 (what a bill for £1.50!), and cemented the band's connections with the burgeoning anarcho-punk scene.

Almost inevitably, the next single, 'Farce', was produced by Penny Rimbaud and came out through the Crass label during July 1982. A slicker, but weedier, take on the raw malevolence of its predecessor, it nonetheless showcased Peni's unique sonic signatures for a wider audience, and made No. 7 in the Indie Chart.

Grant: "In the summer of '81, I went down to their [i.e. Crass] place with a fanzine writer [Don of Stage One]. I gave them a copy of our first EP and they offered us the chance to do a record on their label. I think 'Farce' is fine, though Nick's vocal performance was somewhat inhibited by Penny's production. We wanted to make a fast, intense, high-energy punk record, and within the limitations of the budget, I think we achieved that."

"I thought it was a bit of a let-down myself," proffers Mark, "Mainly 'cos Penny lost something in the sound. The work he did on the Crass records is fantastic, but when he came to produce Peni, he definitely lost something that was present on the first single. I mean, just where the hell did that come from anyway?

"But the guitars are very thin and trebly on 'Farce'… the whole sound is very clinical, like a 'white space'-type recording; the first EP was really dirty and mushy. And Nick's voice on 'Farce' is just shit, it sounds stranded."

However, the band's real masterpiece was to arrive in the shape of their debut album, 'Death Church', which was released by the Crass offshoot, Corpus Christi, in September 1983, spending three months in the Indies, peaking at No. 3. Wrapped in an intoxicating, meticulously drawn poster from Blinko (a sprawling depiction of mass graves, suppurating wounds, deformed angels and weeping phalluses), it saw the band applying the brakes considerably and exploring the more subtle shades at work in their sound. Mixing the morbid ('Cosmic Hearse' and 'Vampire State Building') and the surreal ('Martian Church' and 'Alice Crucifies The Paedophiles') with the obligatory earnest politics (the stunningly bleak '1/4 Dead' and 'Dutchmen') and even several songs about animal rights ('Flesh Crucifix' and 'Pig In A Blanket'), it's a dizzying dip into dangerously dark waters. Since its release, many have aligned the introspective psycho-illogical lyrics with Nick, and the political commentary with Grant, a conclusion the latter strongly warns against.

"Never assume that Nick wrote one thing and that I wrote another; people are usually wrong when they try to do this. To sum up though, we have both been responsible for writing both music and lyrics, but in different degrees and at different times. There is no set pattern to it, and there are no set rules about what will or will not be a subject for a song… but certain themes tend to attach themselves to different records. Jon did not write any lyrics though, nor any guitar and bass parts… apart from the last two seconds of 'Cosmetic Plague'! He did, however, write all the drum parts…"

"Nick and Grant would come to me with basically complete songs," elaborates Jon, on the band's writing process, "That they would have worked out with a basic drum machine track, if any drums at all. I would add what I saw fit rhythmically, and it usually worked straight away. Grant and I just seem to click in terms of playing.

"The album was done at breakneck speed, of course, recorded and mixed in two days, but it felt good. It just worked, first time, virtually every time. And again, with the mixing, came the realisation that this was turning out to be a good recording."

The album also includes the poignant 'Cloud Song' and 'Inside', songs delivered at a sombre pace that are steeped in hints of devastating personal revelation… possibly a direct result of Grant contracting lung cancer during the album's gestation period. He happily managed to help cure himself however, with, as well as the more orthodox treatments for cancer, 'the healing powers of meditation and visualisation' (a direct quote from the bassist lifted from one of their few mainstream music paper interviews, in Sounds, 1989).

"Despite many rumours, no member of the band has ever died… yet!" he chuckles wickedly. "I did get seriously ill in late '82/early '83 though, in between the recording of 'Farce' and 'Death Church'. To be honest, I don't think it did much to the momentum of the band, though it was a very grim time for me."

If the relaxed pace of 'Death Church' surprised some of Peni's hardcore fans, the next album threw virtually everyone for six. 1989's 'Cacophony' was even more complex and bizarre than anything the band had attempted before; a deranged concept album loosely based on the life and works of cult horror author H.P. Lovecraft, the hyper-active musical compositions linked by nightmarish spoken word sections, it had Sounds magazine declare the band '… mad alchemists… a million miles from the rest of the thrash field… brewing up a sound and pouring it straight from their subconscious into the world.' Most fans of the band found it too drastic a departure, and opinion was divided even within the ranks of Peni themselves.

"My favourite release is definitely 'Cacophony'," reckons Nick, before admitting, "But Grant is a better judge of that sort of thing really. At the very outset of Peni, I wanted to wear masks and use keyboards as well as guitars… I don't think I'd still be talking about the band today if we'd gone down that avenue of nondescript. Rather than try to keep up with any particular musical fashion or trend, we have a general policy of just doing what we want to do… which, with 'Cacophony' as the exception, has usually taken the form of either '77-style fast punk or Eighties-style slower, heavier tracks, but avoiding the usual trappings of heavy metal.

"Incidentally, I own the grand total of one Lovecraft book, which I bought three months ago. I've been illustrating some of his stories over the years, the 'Cacophony' cover being an example, with the intention of issuing a small number of prints in a folder, but in the late Eighties I sold all of his books. His work fuses the macabre with immaculate, almost poetic prose (he began as a poet, after all). I can't understand why serious critics hate it so, and it's only mentioned in such circles when some current novel is referred to as 'better than Lovecraft'… usually meaning that atmospheres are evoked then marred by personality piffle.

"By the way, on 'Cacophony', the spoken segments between the tracks were intended to be the equivalent of Lovecraft's descriptions of dark matter, or as he put it, 'the mad spaces between the stars'!"

Jon also enthuses about the record: "For me, it was the most interesting thing that we had done musically, in terms of all those weird time signatures, and the lyrics are fascinating… even if I don't understand all of them! I just think that the band as a whole put in a really good performance, and it was the best thing Nick has ever done vocally; I think he was at the absolute pinnacle of his creativity on that album. I don't share his interest with Lovecraft, but I do think his lyrics are amazing, and I think that is one of the main things that distinguished us from other bands of our genre."

"The different style of 'Cacophony' was not intended," adds Grant, more cautiously. "It just came out that way, and in retrospect I regard it as a move in the wrong direction, into self-indulgence. As a result of that, in recent years, I have pushed to build upon and improve the more 'traditional' Peni style."

"I actually introduced him to Lovecraft, and that was part of the reason why we fell out," claims Mark Farrelly. "Because I was getting more and more jealous of the Lovecraftian tomes he was finding… he acquired some lovely books that I didn't have in my own collection, and I didn't like it very much!

"I didn't actually see 'Cacophony' until years later, but when I picked that up, I couldn't believe it; every single song seemed to have some Lovecraftian theme. But, oh, good luck to him, y'know?

"It was all just personal stuff why we went our separate ways; I wanted to get out of Milton Keynes, where I was still

living with my parents… and Nick was with his folks, and wanted to make some kind of break, but didn't know what to do. After all the intensity of Part One and Peni, we were at a bit of a funny crossroads; it had all gone very quiet on the western front. I knew I didn't wanna do music any more, but I didn't really know what I wanted to do instead… so we both just decided to carry on doing gruesome illustrations, writing Lovecraftian horror stories, and then hopefully, by the time we were sixty or seventy, someone would discover this great tome of work we'd created…! That was the plan anyway, and we were both labouring under a similar illusion. Nick had always been more of the recluse when I first met him, but by the end of the Eighties, I was the recluse, and he was the one making connections with the big, scary outside world."

There would be another yawning hiatus before Rudimentary Peni returned to terrorise our world again – an inconsistent work ethic they've maintained to the present day – and, to be honest, when the third album, 'Pope Adrian 37th Psychristiatric', was unveiled in 1995, it was something of a letdown for all concerned. With Nick in the throes of mental illness, and with many of his delusions finding their way into the fabric of the new album, 'Pope Adrian…' was always going to

The enigmatic Rudimentary Peni captured live in Derby, 1993, by Lee Holford.

be a rambling schizoid affair, but it sadly lacks the vital spark of 'Cacophony', with a flat production also adding to the impression of a band just going through the motions.

"The reasons for the gaps between releases are varied," elaborates Grant, "Sometimes illness, sometimes just lack of interest. Now we're at the stage where we just do short EPs every few years, in order to keep the quality as high as possible. 'Pope Adrian...' is my least favourite of all our releases though. A total turkey in my opinion; there are too many long, repetitive tracks which just sound smug and careless to me."

Jon: "I agree; I thought the end result didn't have the intrigue or edge of the earlier stuff, and ended up sounding a bit monotonous."

"The irony of 'Pope Adrian...' is that nobody felt its recording would help," adds Nick. "Most saw it as actually detrimental to my mental health, all excepting one person, my psychiatrist at the time, who put the question, 'Can music make you ill?' And so the racket was condemned to tape, and after great wrangling eventually released, minus a critical effect on the bass guitar. Loathsome but undoubtedly a milestone... and yes, the shrink had heard the Peni!"

The saving grace of the album though: it was adorned by some of Nick's most impressive artwork since 'Death Church', a disturbing gallery of bitter despair brought lurching to reluctant life by his meticulous scratching. The guitarist/vocalist had also by this time turned his pen to writing a novel, the rather compelling 'The Primal Screamer', published by Hackney's Spare Change Books, a semi-fictitious account of the author's illness, not to mention his band and their uneasy battle for acceptance within the punk rock scene, all garishly dressed with Lovecraftian references of ancient evils straining at the parameters of our dimension. If 'The Primal Screamer' is to be believed, Nick was a connoisseur of hallucinogenic mushrooms and a county chess champion before he was three!

"The fun of 'The Primal Screamer' is trying to figure out what's true and what isn't! I did used to collect fungi spore patterns, and I did play chess for the county third team – but when I was fifteen, not two-and-a-half! I still play chess a fair bit, and continue to aspire to mediocrity. Regression therapy – a cornerstone of the book – seems to skew the imagination occasionally, highlighting old paths in new lights; that is to say, it's not a self-help piece..."

Mark Farrelly also figures quite prominently in the book, albeit under the pseudonym of

'Marco Farrelini', a character that Nick wickedly imagines as still suckling at his mother's breast when aged eighteen!

"But he did post me the little model of a coffin," chuckles Mark, "Just like in the book, and I've still got it. It was a little plasticine figure, in this incredible tiny coffin which he made with sticky bandage... this little brown emaciated figure of plasticine, with his own hair on its head. It was about six inches long, an inch wide, and he'd written my name and address on it in his spidery scrawl... the postage stamp was almost too big to go on it! But somehow it got to me safely..."

1997's 'Echoes Of Anguish' EP saw the band returning to their slightly more conventional earlier sound, pitching itself stylistically somewhere between the 'Death Church' album and the two singles that preceded it, albeit far more measured and calm when considered alongside their original outbursts. 2000 then saw the release of 'The Underclass' EP, and 2003 'The Archaic' EP, both comprising, just like 'Echoes...', twelve short, sharp bursts of minimalist gloomy punk rock.

"My favourite release is the 'Archaic' EP," reveals Grant. "It has a good sound and more refined song structures, i.e. with all the irrelevant, waffling, cluttered bits taken out. We're working on another EP right now, though it won't be out for a couple of years yet.

"There's no intention of ever doing another full album though, and there won't be any live performances either. We've really never split up or reformed in the conventional sense; instead we simply get together to record stuff when we feel like it."

"For me, it's been very rewarding," reflects Jon on his time with Peni. "I think we have made a valid contribution, and I am very proud of most of the stuff we've put out. Showing my kids a cutting from Sounds of 'Death Church' at No. 3 in the Indie charts and No. 1 in the punk charts was a very proud moment.

"None of us have ever been that fussed about playing live though; I think that our very early experiences effectively suppressed that desire. Also, it would have been virtually impossible for Nick to recreate most of the vocal stuff off 'Cacophony' live. I would just like the band to be remembered as one that were exceptionally creative, and made people think."

Nick Blinko though, ever the enigma, has a suitably nihilistic parting comment.

"Us? Be remembered? I think not!"

SELECT DISCOGRAPHY

EPs:
'Rudimentary Peni' (Outer Himalayan, 1981)
'Farce' (Crass, 1982)
'Echoes Of Anguish' (Outer Himalayan, 1997)
'The Underclass' (Outer Himalayan, 2000)
'Archaic' (Outer Himalayan, 2003)

LPs:
'Death Church' (Corpus Christi, 1983)
'Cacophony' (Outer Himalayan, 1989)
'Pope Adrian 37th Psychristiatric' (Outer Himalayan, 1995)

At A Glance:
No punk rock collection is truly complete without the 'Death Church' and 'EPs Of RP' CDs, the latter being the band's first two seminal singles compiled on one disc.

Nearby Luton spawned the quite brilliant **KARMA SUTRA**, an anarcho band of exceptional intelligence and tunefulness. They remained sadly elusive during the research for this book, but their 1987 album for Paradoxical, 'The Daydreams Of A Production Line Worker', is an enthralling slab of ambitious, melodic punk rock, and they contributed fine tracks to the Mortarhate compilations, 'Who? What? Why? When? Where?' ('It's Our World Too') and 'We Don't Want Your Fucking War' ('How The Other Half Die').

Karma Sutra, picture by Jaz Wiseman.

Amongst the other Luton bands they so ably assisted whilst in existence were **DOMINANT PATRI**, who played less than a dozen shows and recorded just the one demo, 'Heroes' Glory'. That sole studio session though was enough to ensure their place in the annals of anarcho punk, being of such intense power, it has captured the imagination of all who hear it, and is now finally enjoying a limited vinyl release as part of (Rugger Bugger offshoot) Demo Tape Record's planned series of singles resurrecting obscure treasures from the early Eighties.

"The punk scene in Luton was good fun," smiles vocalist Chris Jones, "And Karma Sutra were definitely at the centre of it all, putting on gigs and arranging transport to various demos and stuff; they were a positive influence on all concerned, and very well organised. In fact, the furthest we ever travelled to play a gig was Liverpool, and that was with Karma Sutra... there were quite a few skinheads in the audience that night, and our bassist Steve [Richards] played most of the gig with his back to them, convinced they were staring at him!"

As well as Chris and Steve, the band, who formed in 1983, comprised Kate Packwood on vocals, Paul 'Bugsy' Hugget on guitar and Gary Pratten on drums, and they recorded the three-track 'Heroes' Glory' demo on June 18th, 1983, at Luton's Midland Road Studio. Unfortunately they split soon after; otherwise the undoubted promise of songs such as the furious, Dirt-like 'Experiment' would surely have catapulted them to popularity in the positive punk scene.

"The studio in Midland Road where we did the demo is no longer there," sighs Chris. "It used to be part of a shop called 'Can U? Music', which literally just fell down one day! Rumour has it that the owner, Paul Gittens, employed some dodgy builders to save a bit of money... there's a moral to the story somewhere, but I'm not sure what it is..."

"As for the split? It was drugs-related, and I'm afraid that I was the culprit; I deeply regret causing the band's demise, but my behaviour became erratic and unpredictable. After Dominant Patri, Steve, Bugsy and Gary formed another band, the name of which eludes me... it was something like Pnumb Pesi, I think! Meanwhile, I did nothing but procrastinate, aided and abetted by copious amounts of exotic herbs and spices!"

At A Glance:

The likelihood of securing yourself one of the limited-to-200-copies 'Heroes' Glory' 7"s is something akin to the UN locating any weapons of mass destruction in Iraq, so the curious reader may have to console themselves with the thumpingly heavy (both musically and emotionally) 'Death Of Thomas', on Overground's 'Anti-Capitalism (Anarcho-punk Compilation Volume 4)' CD.

lthough ex-members of **THE APOSTLES** themselves deny that they were ever an anarcho-punk band, their – primarily overlooked – contribution to said scene was immense, not least of all as a foil that forced the lens of scrutiny uncomfortably back onto one's self. Despite playing just twenty-four gigs, they released an incredible seven singles and seven albums, countless cassettes and pamphlets, and helped set up and run four different Anarchy Centres: the Autonomy Centre (Wapping), the Centro Iberico (Westbourne Park), the LMC (Camden) and the Recession Club (Hackney).

"We also ran an information network," adds vocalist/violinist Andy Martin, "Put homeless people in touch with housing co-ops and squatters groups, put lonely people in touch with other like-minded lonely souls, and organized various social events of a non-musical nature. We also participated in direct action politically… there were other groups that did more than us – but they didn't play music! My main criticism is that we tried to do too much in too many different fields, so that we excelled in none of them. Certainly our music was often ineptly performed and badly produced… our political activities were rather more successful, but only in a small way. The results of our nine years work still exist, but hardly set parliament on fire!

Dave Fanning of The Apostles, recording the second EP, 1983, picture by Chris Low.

"For me, the 1980s are associated with just three things: crap politics, crap fashions and crap music, and anarcho-punk was a musically conservative and rather insignificant side show to the real assault on global capitalism in which I was – and still am – engaged. Dave Morris and Helen Steel, for example, have achieved more for the campaign against McDonald's than every punk band there has ever been. This is not to unduly berate punk bands, but they must be regarded in the correct perspective…"

The very first Apostles line-up was very different to the band that released the aforementioned slew of tape and plastic. Forming in late 1981, they comprised Bill Corbett (vocals), Pete Bynghall (guitar), Julian Portinari (bass) and Dan MacKintyre (drums)… during which time Andy was actually a patient in the Springfield Psychiatric Hospital's secure unit for disturbed children.

"The fact is, punk was already dead by 1981, and really we were all just prolonging its death throes," he claims. "I was not a punk… on the contrary, I regarded punks as out-dated, hopelessly naïve, definitely irrelevant, and very boring to be around. My pals were all into soul, funk and reggae, which didn't interest me particularly, but at least the bands dressed properly.

"I gravitated more toward the industrial and independent pop music scene, where I encountered Twelve Cubic Feet, probably the most unjustly neglected pop group of the past two decades. Their drummer, Andrew Bynghall, informed me that his younger brother, Pete, was also in a pop group, and that they needed a singer as their current incumbent, Bill Corbett, was going off to start university…

"Of course, I never told the lads I had dyspraxia [AKA Clumsy Child Syndrome] and I never told them I was gay; I was ashamed and also a little anxious they might reject me if they knew. After all, I had learned the hard way that most people despise 'spastics' and 'queers'! Being both, I realised I had to be careful if I wanted to maintain the fragile friendship I developed with the band. Trouble is, we were destined never to be a success because I was in the wrong band. They wanted a punk singer in the Crass mode, and I wanted a pop group like Twelve Cubic Feet or an avant-garde ensemble like Five Or Six. It had to end in tears...and it did.

"They'd invite me to gigs with them but I usually declined their offers – a night out having my ears assaulted by 'Flux Of Punk Idiots' did not appeal to me...surrounded by leather clad morons, all beer and safety pins, sharing one damaged brain between them? No thanks. Pete, Julian and Dan were not like that, so I couldn't understand why they moved in such circles; I'd invite them to accompany me to the Africa Centre to see The Lemon Kittens and Eyeless In Gaza, but they'd look at me with just the right amount of pity to ensure I realised how far apart we were culturally."

The first Apostles gig was a chaotic appearance at The Basement youth club in Covent Garden ("We were absolutely wretched... but mercifully brief!"), where Andy met Dave Fanning (then bassist with The Innocent Bystander) and John Soares (then guitarist with Libertarian Youth). A second concert in Southend, organised by The Sinyx, went well, but the band were pulling too violently in opposing directions to last.

"It started when Pete, Julian and Dan arrived one afternoon in my Stoke Newington attic for, I assumed, another rehearsal," reveals Andy. "On the contrary, they came to collect their amplifiers and drum kit: 'Goodbye, Martin, your services are no longer required, and please do not ask us for a reference!' At the time, the story they handed me was that being in a band had become boring, so they had elected to cease operations. I then asked them – calmly and politely (which was considerably out of character for me) – to tell me the real situation. Pete had the decency to reveal, with some reluctance, that they simply couldn't work with me anymore. Dan and Julian hotly denied this and berated Pete for being so cruel. I know they didn't wish to upset me, but I had more respect for Pete because he told me the truth. I had been sacked.

"Were they being unfair? Actually, no. Did I deserve to be sacked? Probably not, but I certainly could not remain in the group. The problem was that none of us was actually 'wrong'. They were in the band to have fun, and could not understand why being in a group was so important to me, nor why it was so imperative we achieve a high degree of technical ability and attain a level of professionalism of which we could be proud. I could not understand how they could be satisfied with anything less... not that I tried very hard to appreciate their point of view."

Hooking up with John Soares and Dave Fanning again, plus Martin Smith, all of them ex-members of Libertarian Youth, Andy set about forming a band of his own, and because he was still smarting from his treatment at the hands of Pete, Dan and Julian, he decided to call it The Apostles as well. This line-up of the band played a few shows and released the cassette-only albums, 'The Apostles' and 'The Second Dark Age' (both through their own Scum Tapes label, in '81 and '82 respectively). The tapes demonstrated the band's far-reaching musical ambitions – an earthy, driving, often hypnotic, punk rock dirge that refused to do what was expected of it, loaded with all manner of rhythmic flourishes and off-the-wall vocal deliveries – but John (now a sought-after sound engineer in the USA) departed soon after, leaving Andy to re-enlist Dan MacKintyre, for the recording of the superb first single, 'Blow It Up, Burn It Down, Kick It 'Til It Breaks'. Chris Low of Scottish anarchists Political Asylum then joined, just in time to play on the band's second EP, 1983's 'Rising From The Ashes'. He still remembers fondly his time with the antagonistic combo.

"Basically I heard a tape of the first [Apostles] demo when I was staying with Miles from Napalm Death, and thought it was amazing. I wrote to Andy, and, as anyone else who did the same would know, got an enormous typed letter, plus half a dozen tapes, back a few days later. We kept in touch and during summer 1983, when I was still only fourteen, I went down to London and stayed with him in the squat he shared with someone who remains to this day one of my best mates: Ian 'Slaughter', who did the notorious 'Pigs For Slaughter' fanzine. Anyway, during my stay, Andy was recording a demo with the Assassins Of Hope, and basically I had a jam with him in the studio. At that time, The Apostles were using 'Razzle' [of Hanoi Rocks] as stand-in drummer, but as I had recently 'parted company' with Political Asylum, he asked if I wanted to fill their drum stool. So, there I was, fourteen years old, drumming for one of my favourite bands, and staying in a squat in Hackney with no running water, where you had to climb up the side of the building to get in, 'cos the door was barricaded up!

"The main thing about The Apostles was that, at that time, there was absolutely no other band who sounded anything like them. For a start, neither Andy or Dave listened to punk music (something that I didn't have a great deal of interest in at the time either, being more into Cabaret Voltaire and Throbbing Gristle), and as for their beliefs… it is hard to understand, but at that time there was this pathetic 'Crass clone' mentality where everyone paid lip service to these vacuous ideals of anarchy, peace and freedom, and were basically like fucking Buddhists in black rags. The Apostles, and Pigs For Slaughter zine, were the only voices in the whole anarcho-punk movement who rejected pacifism and all the bollocks that went with it; they were into armed struggle and class war (long before the paper of the same name ever came out), and in an anti-Nazi group… basically a vigilante squad that, along with other un-affiliated groups, used to patrol around Brick Lane and give any Nazis that were causing trouble a kicking.

"Not only didn't they sound like any of the identikit Crass clone bands, but they didn't look like them either. The first time I saw them at the Anarchy Centre, Andy looked like a mod, and Dave looked like some Berlin hippy in a leather jacket painted with Gong artwork. At the time they were doing a zine called 'Scum', all about the emerging 'power electronics' scene which was, musically, the most exciting thing happening back then.

"Anyway, I used to bunk the overnight train from Scotland down to London; as I was still a kid I'd find a likely-looking couple on the train and hide under the table by where they were sitting. Or spend the night in the toilets, and if a guard came along tell him I was feeling sick and that my parents were elsewhere on the train with my ticket. Once I got down there, we would usually have a day's practice, then we would be in the studio to record another record!"

The winter before Chris joined however, The Apostles appeared at the Zig Zag squat gig organised by Crass, but whereas most bands who performed that day remember it as the highlight of their musical career, Andy has a decidedly different take on the whole event.

"We were never mentioned – not once – anywhere!" he rants. "We were like Leon Trotsky in that famous photograph, airbrushed out of history. For the record, Andy Palmer [from Crass] telephoned Little @ Press and asked to speak to Andy or Dave from The Apostles; he specifically wanted us involved, because (I assume) they trusted us to be sufficiently mature and organised to assist them in the venture without fuss or drama. Well, we did all that was asked of us and more. All three members of The Mob, who also helped with the organisation, arrived at the venue and cleared away mountains of rubbish and made the place habitable and presentable… but at least they received some credit in the press and rightly so. However, Melody Maker, Sounds and NME acted as if we were invisible and silent – we expected them to, but that the whole punk scene treated us in precisely the same manner is an outrage, and I shall forever hate them for it.

"I am fully aware that we were a very minor, obscure little band of whom most people had never even heard. I assume the vast majority of people reading this will never have heard of us – why should they? But even if the band's music was unknown (and, I admit, usually not very good… or certainly not very well played), we do deserve credit for the political and social activities in which we participated, often for causes with which we had only peripheral sympathy.

"Anyway, shortly after we had played our rubbish, we were at the back of the hall picking up the inevitable beer tins, paper cups and cigarette packets, when I was shoved aside by this troll in boots and braces. Five skinheads – just five miserable, thick, stupid, cowardly thugs – barged their way into the gig and pushed people out of the way in order to reach the front of the stage. I wasn't taking that treatment from anyone, so Dave and I followed them, but by the time we caught up with them, this Asian lad – he was probably the only audience member not of white Caucasian origin – was being brutally kicked and punched by all of these fascist thugs... that's right, five onto one. And what were the other members of the 500-strong audience doing while this was happening? They had formed a wide circle around the scene and watched it play out... that's right, these anarchist pacifist rat-bags stood and watched five fascists beat up a fifteen-year-old Asian boy. Punks, is it? I wouldn't even piss on them if they were on fire. They are scum, filth, not fit to lick excrement from the soles of my bowling shoes. From that moment on, I swore I would never ever again give so much as the time of day to any anarchist pacifist punk. I honoured my vow with implacable authority; I despise them to this day.

"In case you're wondering what happened next, yes, we did surge forward to come to the lad's aid, but before we could involve ourselves, both Penny and Andy (yes, from Crass) had jumped between us and grabbed hold of the two biggest skinheads, and shoved them to one side of the hall. Colin Jerwood of Conflict confronted the others with less reasonable force, and threatened to put them all in hospital. Those three fascists virtually wet their knickers at the prospect – it was a joy to see these three 'big tough men' quake in fear before 'The Ungovernable Force'. Colin, if you're reading this, you were a hero that night; I'm proud to have had our records released on your label and I'll not hear a word said against you. I spoke to that Asian lad afterwards (who, fortunately, was not badly hurt), because what had impressed me so much is that he had attempted to fight back, and such courage deserves recognition. He said he would make sure he bought every record that Crass and Conflict released in gratitude for their timely action, but that he would never go to

Andy Martin of The Apostles recording for the third Apostles EP, 1983, picture courtesy of Chris Low.

another punk gig again. He appreciated that myself and Dave had rushed to his aid and, it turns out, the main reason he attended was because he wanted to see The Apostles since John Soares was our guitarist and himself an Indian... sadly, John had left the band a couple of weeks earlier. On the bus home that night, I thought about the contempt for punks held by people such as Martin Wright, Vince Stephenson, Dave Couch and the serious Class War and anarchist circles. I understood their attitude completely and I agreed with it utterly."

The Apostles parted company with Chris Low in 1984, soon after Malcolm 'Scruff' Lewty joined on guitar, and the 'Smash The Spectacle' 7" was released by Mortarhate; he was superseded behind the kit by Chris 'Widni' Wiltshire, establishing what was to prove the most long-standing and stable line-up of the band. 1986 saw the release of not only the 'Punk Obituary' album through Mortarhate, but also 'The Lives And Times Of The Apostles' album on respected Bristol label, Children Of The Revolution – although the band refused to tie themselves in with any one label for long, they were prolific to the point of excess.

"I just wanted The Apostles to be the best independent group in Britain," reckons Andy. "I wanted perfection and I wanted beauty in our work, presumably because I was so far from being either perfect or beautiful myself. In short, I became a tyrant and I must have been utterly abysmal to work under. Oh yes, I am well aware of the fact that people in The Apostles worked under me, not with me. Quite how Dave has managed to remain in a group with me since 1984, I simply do not know... his levels of compassion and tolerance must be of Franciscan proportions!

"And Scruff is liable to speak about me in such a way that he exaggerates my importance when I was in the band... if this occurs then it must be tempered with my own assertion, i.e. that The Apostles was always Dave's band, and I was just fortunate enough to be allowed to participate in it.

"Our big mistake was, we would record dozens of pieces, most of them works in progress, and release them all in the belief that everything we did should be made available. You see, I knew we were extremely obscure, virtually unknown and certainly of no interest to the majority of people who had heard about us, and it was my (probably mistaken) belief that if we released a huge volume of records and cassettes, played dozens of concerts and released magazines by the forest load then maybe a few people might acknowledge our existence and realise we had something to say. It actually meant we released a load of crap which served no purpose other than to deplete natural resources and increase the amount of plastic tossed onto landfill sites...

"Take the ninth audio cassette, for example: that was myself and Dave setting up microphones at strategic points all around the house, and picking up various instruments, radio sets and machine tools at random as we tramped up and down stairs and through different rooms, 'to create a multi-level sonic environment'... as I explained in one of my more amusingly serious press releases. Actually, put like that, it sounds quite interesting, doesn't it? You wait until you hear it... better still, save yourself the bother; it is a sheer racket... a generally very quiet racket, true, but a noisome mess all the same. Believe me, the only good thing about that release was that it was a C60 not a C90. I think we sold about forty copies, and they were either to people so desperate for an escape from punk rock they'd buy any old crap, or those kind-hearted souls who felt sorry for us."

In 1987 – four albums and numerous singles later, during which the band proved themselves second only to Rudimentary Peni when it came to unleashing disturbingly quirky, inaccessible rock music – Widni and Scruff left (the former to attend university, the latter to concentrate on his highly-respected thrash metal band Hellbastard) and The Apostles were joined by two further correspondents, Sean Stokes and Colin Murrell, formerly an avant-garde performance art duo called The Demolition Company. In this guise, the band released several more cassette albums in 1988 and the 'Hymn To Pan' LP, but for their final studio session in January 1989, they were actually rejoined by original Apostle, Pete Bynghall.

"For many people, the end of a band is fraught with emotional stress and sadness; for me, it was a glorious release. My only slight regret is that I didn't leave The Apostles two years earlier. In early '89, shortly after that final session, Pete was due to leave England in March to seek a new life in America, and Sean Stokes had severed all links with Colin Murrell – they refused to see or speak to each other. Basically then, the group was myself, Sean and Dave. I took that as a sign that The Apostles really were way past their 'sell by' date. However, Dave and Sean decided we should at least go out in style and end with one last concert. Now, I hate live concerts at the best of times, but I regard farewell concerts as ridiculous events fit only for sad old bastards like Thin Lizzy and Fleetwood Mac. So, the concept of us performing a farewell concert appealed only to the homicidal part of my nature, but somehow I was persuaded to participate. Even more remarkably, Colin was persuaded to sit in the same city as Sean and play his drums, although he and Sean said not one word to each other during every rehearsal, and studiously ignored each other during the entire performance! Somehow it seemed an appropriate end to the group.

"Ironically, we played almost every number brilliantly. Having Pete there was probably responsible for that. And the gods looked kindly upon me at last: only three people turned up to the gig, and one of those was a dog called Leo. No, I'm not making this up; the other two members of the audience were John Waddingham and Tim Verdon, both friends of Dave... Leo was Tim's dog. We played at Chats Palace, Hackney, adjacent to Homerton Hospital where, five years later, I would work. We were the only group who played, and it was an eerie experience, just us in this large hall, in front of two of Dave's friends and that dog. What I knew (but nobody else did) was that this would be the last time The Apostles played together, at least with me in the group. I had already told Dave I was to quit the band, but it seemed then he might find a replacement singer or carry on as a mainly instrumental group. It was automatically assumed the others would patch up their differences and continue. It never happened."

Andy and Dave went on to form Academy 23, who eventually morphed into UNIT, and remain committed to the furthering of their visionary art to this day; older, wiser, and even more honest than ever.

"Basically, if anyone wants to know what The Apostles should have sounded like – would have sounded like, had we access to a record producer and been top class musicians – I recommend [Academy 23's] 'Kämpfbereit', [UNIT's] 'We Are Your Gods' and parts of both 'Fire And Ice' and 'Dare To Be Different'. I urge readers not to waste time and effort trying to track down the original records by The Apostles – they really aren't very good at all. It's in the past... let it stay there.

"Everyone who reads this who is interested in our work and cares about it must learn and remember this: I will be remembered mainly for my work in UNIT [www.unit-united.co.uk], since The Apostles was nothing more than a testing ground, a sonic laboratory, a temporary frolic of little importance compared to what we're doing now.

"The Apostles prepared the groundwork; that was the drive to 2001, during which we marked time while we waited for the future to present itself. I'm alive, healthy, fit and rearing to go... reflecting on mistakes made in the past was never an option. I'm here to plan new projects and forge ahead; I don't look back, I think ahead. Bugger the past; it's over, forget it. By all means, right those wrongs if it means our work is restored to the map where it had previously been erased by the anarcho-punk censors, but now that's done, let's move on. There's work to do."

SELECT DISCOGRAPHY

7"s:

'Blow It Up, Burn It Down, Kick It 'Til It Breaks' (Scum, 1982)
'Rising From The Ashes' (Scum, 1983)
'The Curse Of The Creature' (Scum, 1984)
'The Giving Of Love Costs Nothing' (Scum, 1984)
'Smash The Spectacle' (Mortarhate, 1985)
'Death To Wacky Pop' (Fight Back, 1986) – split with The Joy Of Living
'No Faith No Fear' (Active Sounds, 1989) – split with Statement

LPs:

'Punk Obituary' (Mortarhate, 1985)
'The Lives And Times Of The Apostles' (COR, 1986)
'The Acts Of the Apostles In The Theatre Of Fear' (Acid Stings, 1986)
'How Much Longer?' (Acid Stings, 1986)
'Equinox Screams' (Andy Brant Inc, 1987)
'The Other Operation' (Active Sounds, 1988) – split with Statement
'Hymn To Pan' (No Master's Voice, 1988)

At A Glance:

With such a vast back catalogue to draw upon, it's surprising that there has been no retrospective overview of The Apostles, although both the 'Smash The Spectacle' (including the track 'Mob Violence' – arguably their finest moment) and 'Death To Wacky Pop' singles are featured on the Mortarhate double-CD, 'A Compilation Of Deleted Dialogue: The Singles'.

Southend's **KRONSTADT UPRISING** weren't exactly an 'anarcho-punk band' in the strictest sense of the words for the whole of their colourful career either, but they are more than worthy of investigation thanks to their startlingly intense 'Unknown Revolution' EP that emerged through Flux's Spiderleg Records in late 1983. A maelstrom of red raw riffs, pounding toms and harsh, croaking vocals, it remains as primal an experience today as when it first burst onto the scene like an ugly boil.

"I think that 1980 was a watershed year for punk rock really," reckons drummer Steve Pegrum, casting his mind back to when and why he first picked up his sticks. "A lot of the original bands, like the Sex Pistols, had either split or, in the case of The Clash, were moving so far away from their original starting point that they didn't seem to have much relevance

An early picture of Kronstadt Uprising drummer Steve Pegrum.

for us any more, so when I heard Crass's 'The Feeding Of The Five Thousand', it had a really revitalizing effect. I'd never heard anything quite like it at all before, and, in much the same way that watching the Pistols do 'Pretty Vacant' on Top Of The Pops in 1977 had profoundly affected me, so too did this record. It was another seismic shift, stripping down the music of all unnecessary baggage, and was really direct and to the point!"

Suitably inspired, Steve started up The Bleeding Pyles, who by late 1981 also featured Spencer Blake on vocals, Paul Lawson on guitar and Mick Grant on bass. After two local shows (at the Thorpedene Community Centre on August 19th and the Cliffs Pavilion Maritime Room on October 2nd) that year, Mick Grant decided to 'find God', and was promptly replaced by Andy Fisher. To ring the changes afoot in the band, The Bleeding Pyles thankfully then became known as Kronstadt Uprising, recording their first demo at Wapping's Elephant Studios and unveiling their new line-up and moniker at Southend's Focus Centre on December 7th, 1981. A venue that lived up to its name, bringing together like-minded individuals to create a thriving scene that also featured the likes of The Sinyx and The Icons.

"We loved the original wave of punk bands to death, but we were also very aware that a change was needed," says Steve of the band's rapid musical evolution. "Spencer and I had seen Discharge the previous year at The Music Machine, which had really inspired us, and we were simultaneously developing a harsher edge to our own sound. And the more we listened to Crass, Flux Of Pink Indians, The Sinyx, and Poison Girls, the more we felt a natural comradeship with these bands who seemed to embody the original punk ethic of doing it for yourself, and who seemed to ramify that you didn't need to be some kind of dinosaur virtuoso before you could step on a stage and play. We found this whole thing tremendously empowering! Plus, there was a real sense of 'camaraderie' about the scene… in that pre-Internet age, a lot of people stayed in touch through the fanzine scene; you'd swap information and addresses in them, and people from all over the country would be getting in touch, saying what life was like for them in their neck of the woods.

"So, by 1981, things on this ultra hardcore scene had, for me, seen a 'rebirth', as it were, of punk's original sensibilities, adapted and updated and streamlined for our generation. There was a sense that this was our time and we were glad to be the right age to be active within it.

"I'd had a jam with Graham Burnett [of Southend band The Stripy Zebras and author of 'New Crimes' fanzine] and a few others that previous summer, and he'd tentatively suggested the name 'Kronstadt Uprising' for the project. Sadly, the band hadn't worked out, but I'd really liked the name and it stayed in my head. I'd read about this uprising at school, and after a visit to the anarchist bookshop, 121 Books, in Railton Road on the Brixton front line, where I'd obtained some more books about it, it really struck me as how it was the perfect name for a punk band – people standing up and saying, 'No, it doesn't have to be like this!'"

Although not overjoyed with the results, a track from that first demo session, 'Receiver Deceiver', ended up on the Crass Records compilation, 'Bullshit Detector 2', which garnered Kronstadt Uprising considerable attention, both nationally and internationally, and – more importantly – brought them to the attention of Flux Of Pink Indians, who were in the process of starting up their own label, Spiderleg. However, on the eve of their 'big break', they parted ways with Spencer, reluctantly slimming down to a three-piece with guitarist Paul Lawson also handling vocals.

Steve: "Basically, a week or so after a gig at the [Leigh-on-Sea] Grand Hotel [in May 1982], Paul, Andy and I had a serious discussion with Spence, and it was decided, that due to his lack of commitment, we'd be better off carrying on as a three-piece. We were taking things very seriously at that point and, for many reasons, didn't feel he was as committed as he should be.

"Paul's vocal style initially was a lot harsher than Spencer's, and can be heard at its best on the EP we did for Spiderleg. I used to write quite complex lyrics at the time (like 'Xenophobia' for instance) and Paul managed to phrase them really well. I don't think some fans quite adapted to his harsh style and probably lost interest in the band at that point, but I have to say the majority seemed to stick with us and liked our new harder edge, and, seeing as we were starting to play out more and more, we probably even increased our following really."

Although it didn't set the world on fire sales-wise, 'The Unknown Revolution' was a fiery enough debut to capture the imagination of many an anarcho-punker hungry for some desperately intense sounds, and for many it remains the band's crowning glory, four exceptionally pissed-off songs perfectly captured in all their frenetic fury by John Loder at Southern Studios.

"We were all aware of Southern's reputation as a great studio, and when we got there we were slightly overawed at first – we were just some punk rockers from Southend for whom things seemed to be working out! – but once Derek and Colin from Flux introduced us to the engineer, John Loder, who was a fantastic chap, that did really help us relax. I remember it taking a while to get the right sound from the gear, but I was immediately impressed that they managed to get a great drum sound that had been immeasurably lacking on the Elephant sessions for the first demo. Paul was similarly pleased that they managed to get his guitar sound down too. Andy's bass playing had come on in leaps and bounds and was now excellently captured as well.

"We didn't start 'till late the first day, and a lot of time was spent getting the right sound levels etc., but once we kicked in, it did seem to go pretty fast. We stayed at Flux's place that night, and I remember Annie Anxiety being around in the studio the next day, providing some much-needed sustenance via some excellent home-made spaghetti of hers! Anyway, we carried on recording and in next to no time it was all done. We felt sad to leave the studio then, because once they'd achieved such a great representation of our sound, we wanted to record all our set like that!

"Anyway, we heard the rough mix and later went back to the studio for the full mix, and once finished I think we thought it would be due out within a month or so. However, this didn't prove to be the case, and basically there were a couple of releases that needed to come out before ours, so by the time the schedule came round it was nearly a year later, in September 1983 – which was a shame as that EP, for most people, is what they associate with Kronstadt Uprising, and I'd say it

Spencer and Paul of Kronstadt Uprising, 1981.

does capture us at our best. But by the time it came out, our sound had changed a bit, so when people came to see us, they expected to see us in that permanently enshrined '82 sound as captured on 'The Unknown Revolution'.

"Nevertheless, with hindsight, I think I am pleased that we got the chance to record it at all; it's a great historical document of the time – it has some great artwork courtesy of Kev from Flux's girlfriend, Celia Biscoe, contains all the lyrics and text I wrote for the sleeve, and I think stands the test of time sonically too. I have great memories of glistening with blood and perspiration as we recorded 'End Of Part One', hitting the tom toms as hard as I could… also of Paul screaming himself hoarse, heart and soul, to 'Blind People'. We definitely captured something there and rather than meditate on its delay in appearing at the time, or the fact that we didn't ever record an album of that quality, I'm just glad we did it at all and hopefully in the process inspired other people to try and do the same."

Possibly disillusioned with Kronstadt's seeming lack of progress, Steve also drummed in The Sinyx for most of 1982, and then in early '83, the Sinyx's guitarist 'Filf' (real name Nick Robinson) joined KU as second guitarist. Making his public debut at Crocs (now known as The Pink Toothbrush) in Rayleigh, he thickened the band's sound considerably as demonstrated by successful gigs around the Southeast with the likes of Fallout [ex-Six Minute War], Allegiance To No One, and Autumn Poison, but his tenure was a brief one, as he departed that summer after a triumphant headline slot at the Focus Centre…

"A key point about our gigs in those days," reflects Steve of their most active period on the live circuit, "especially from 1982 to 1984, is that long before the term was invented, they truly were

DIY; we never had a manager, not ever. And, more significantly, they were 'multimedia' events… sometimes we'd hire a venue, we'd get a couple of other bands in to play with us, maybe print some literature to give out, as well as badges etc., then in between the bands we'd maybe get some poets to do some readings – including, in 1983, Paul Barrett (ex-of The Sinyx) and Ian Fry, calling themselves The Provisional Southend Poetry Group. There'd sometimes be rear projections too, all to increase the atmosphere and make the events unique. They'd usually pass trouble-free, and would mainly feature the local punk contingent from our area, although as the band got better known, people would travel from outside the area to see us as well."

After a self-enforced hiatus during autumn 1983, the band reconvened to pursue a far more rock'n'roll direction, looking to the trashier first wave of punk as a primary musical influence rather than the bleak tones of Crass, although Steve maintains that their sound was all that changed – their attitude and approach remained essentially the same.

"Having been into and playing punk so avidly for such a long time, we just felt we wanted to expand our palette a bit. When it got to the point where you'd go to a gig, and all three bands would come out looking and sounding the same, we felt we needed to evolve ourselves, whilst keeping that punk spirit alive. I mean, we were still using the same instrumentation, I just think we wanted to smash down any barriers people were trying to put in front of us, not accept any boundaries whatsoever in fact. Sometimes it worked and sometimes it didn't… and it certainly confused some of the hardcore diehards who would still come and see us, especially when we played in London. The vast majority really liked what we were doing, as it wasn't that far removed from the original punk sound we'd started with in the first place.

"And in many ways, there was a reappraisal of that '76/'77 style, sound and energy in the Eighties, as exemplified by artists like The Lords Of The New Church, and – combined with the re-emergence of a genuine Kronstadt hero, Johnny Thunders – we felt we'd finally found a niche where we still had relevance and could really fit in. If you listen to the last demo we ever did,

Kronstadt Uprising, live at the Grand, 1982, picture courtesy of Steve Pegrum.

the song 'Stay Free' still deals with the same lyrical concerns that we had at the beginning – personal liberation, freedom and rejecting any form of oppression, perceived or otherwise. I think that recording basically completes the circle of the Kronstadt lifespan, with us starting back where we began."

Before that recording though, Kronstadt Uprising actually split in early 1984, playing a 'final' show in March of that year at the Old Queen's Head in Stockwell with the Lost Cherrees – only for Steve to resurrect the band that same summer (albeit in name alone, as he was joined by an all-new line-up). With the able assistance of vocalist Gary Smith, guitarists Kevin de Groot and Murray Blake (brother of Spencer), and bassist Stuart Emmerton, Steve steered the band through the recording of several demos, a rather good single, 'Part Of The Game' for local label, Dog Rock, and a plethora of well-received gigs. However, when Gary Smith left the band a few months after a show at the Southend College Of Technology on May 16th, 1986, citing the inevitable musical differences as the reason behind his departure, it marked the beginning of the end for Kronstadt who were unable to find a suitable replacement and called it a day for good late the following year.

"I would like Kronstadt Uprising to be remembered for being true to ourselves," says Steve, who went on to do a BA degree in Social Science and then a Masters Degree in Politics, thoughtfully. "Hopefully we provided interesting, enjoyable and thought-provoking material and maybe even inspired a few people along the way. If, on the basis of one person seeing/hearing us, it prompted them to then go out and start their own band, fanzine, club, or whatever, then it was all worth it. The early Eighties was quite a grey, depressing time, and if we helped in any way to bring a change to that, then I'm proud of what we did…

"And I really think my time in Kronstadt gave me a sense of 'Don't let anyone tell you that you can't do something, just do it yourself!' If you've got something you want to say, then say it! Whatever the medium of expression you choose – be it music, the written word, sculpture, whatever – just do it. You don't need to spend hours practicing in your bedroom, and perhaps then end up never playing at all – just get out there and start playing straight away! Who knows what you might achieve if you only try?"

SELECT DISCOGRAPHY

7"s:
'The Unknown Revolution' (Spiderleg, 1983)
'Part Of The Game' (Dog Rock, 1985)

At A Glance:
The 'Insurrection' CD released by Overground in 2000 compiles not only both of the band's singles and their track from the 'Bullshit Detector' album, but also all of their obscure demos, twenty-three tracks in all; complete with original artwork, unseen photos and extensive liner notes from Steve, it's a ruthlessly definitive retrospective.

With a track on the first 'Bullshit Detector' album and a decent single in the shape of 'The Black Death EP' for Reality Attack, the aforementioned **THE SINYX** from Southend-on-Sea were another vaguely influential band from the Southeast that could well have had a greater impact nationally if only they'd held down a solid line-up.

Formed in September 1979, they initially comprised Paul 'Alien' Barrett on vocals, Paul Brunt on guitar, Dave 'Auntie' Godbald on bass, and Vints Hibbitt on drums, and played their first show at Southend's Focus Youth Centre in early 1980 with local punks The Icons in support.

"It can't be stressed enough that those Sinyx/Icons gigs in 1980 were definitely rallying points for the local punk scene at the time," exclaims Kronstadt Uprising drummer, Steve Pegrum. "I knew the original Sinyx guitarist, Paul Brunt, through my friend – and local punk legend – Steve King, and he, Paul and I used to talk about punk all the time, so it was great to see him getting in a band and doing it himself. Sinyx songs like 'Camouflage' and 'Britain Is A Mausoleum' meant as much to the region's local punks as did songs by more well-known bands."

"I got into punk through watching 'So It Goes' [Granada TV's 1976/'77 Tony Wilson-presented music programme] and listening to [John] Peel," recalls John 'Sinyk' Edwards, originally of The Icons himself, who eloped to The Sinyx in 1981, first playing bass and then guitar for the band. "I grew up on Canvey Island so it was pretty much [Doctor] Feelgood/[Eddie And The] Hot Rods territory. A mate I went to school with played in a punk band called The Vicars (I roadied for them), who were shit hot; interestingly enough, Alison Moyet sang for them after she left a band called The Vandals. She later hooked up with that bloke (Vince Clarke, I think) from Depeche Mode and the rest, as they say, is history…

"Anyway, I listened to 'Live At The Roxy', which I still think is one of the best punk albums ever, and thought, 'I can do that'… but found out pretty quickly that I couldn't! I was really into The Vibrators and Slaughter And The Dogs – until it became obvious that there were better things out there. I went to my first Crass gig at the Conway Hall in Holborn, London, with Auntie and Paul, and from then on my whole outlook changed."

Before John even joined however, The Sinyx – named after the Cynics, an ancient Greek rebel movement – entered Wapping's Elephant Studios on March 1st, 1980, and recorded an eight-song demo. A copy was sent to Crass who used the track 'Mark Of The Beast' (an angry little number featuring the classic couplet, 'I don't believe in Jesus, I don't believe in God… I won't go to Heaven, I don't give a sod!') on their 'Bullshit Detector' collection, which helped the band's profile no end and saw them gigging regularly in and around London.

When John joined on bass, bringing with him Nick 'Filf' Robinson, also ex-Icons, as the band's new guitarist, Auntie took over on drums from the departing Vints. After a second (three song) demo was done at the Lower Wapping Conker Company in late 1980, the band, with backing from Rob of Reality Attack fanzine, recorded 'The Black Death' EP at Westcliff's Spectrum Studios, a four-track affair that showcased a slower, darker, more measured direction than that hinted at by 'Mark Of The Beast'. One track in particular, 'The Plague', lurches along brilliantly, with its staccato guitar riff and ominous refrain of 'Bring out the dead!' more than compensating for its rudimentary production values.

John: "I'm not sure how Rob got involved, but I can remember sitting in my bedroom at my mum and dad's on Canvey with him, folding 1000 (it may have been 2000) record sleeves. We couldn't get it printed at first, so we got a contact from Crass; we went to their house in North Weald, Essex, and got some advice, but that's all they got involved in. We duly sent them some copies as a thank you.

"The whole package was poorly produced," he concedes. "But we did it ourselves and sold all the copies in a week, and even got to No. 31 – I think! – in the alternative charts. The record shops asked us to do some more but we couldn't afford it, and didn't want to get Crass involved as we were fiercely independent. We all thought that they were being taken advantage of by certain groups of people (not just bands) anyhow, and didn't want to be viewed like that. We were a live band at the end of the day, so it wasn't really a problem for us."

Then, during Summer 1981, Graham Burnett (he of New Crimes 'zine), who had supported and publicised the band from their inception, included three Sinyx tracks ('Animal', 'Suicide' and 'Fight', all recorded 'live' at 'Dave's Practise Studio', May 10th, 1981) on his popular 'New Criminals, Volume One' cassette, that also featured the likes of Subhumans and Flux Of Pink Indians.

However, instead of pushing home their advantage, The Sinyx underwent yet another extensive line-up shuffle. Auntie moved to guitar, the drum stool being filled by Steve Pegrum from Kronstadt Uprising, whilst John swapped his bass to become second guitarist, his former role being filled by the band's driver/roadie, Andy Whiting.

The new-look Sinyx made their public debut at the Forest Gate Centre in late March 1982, supporting The Mob and Rudimentary Peni. They played with The Mob again that August, at the Centro Iberico; another live highlight.

"I particularly remember the best two gigs I played with The Sinyx," reckons Steve. "My debut performance with them at Forest Gate; it was in a huge hall and rammed to the rafters and the place literally exploded when the band came on and the audience went crazy from the beginning to the end of the set. The Sinyx were first and foremost a live band and the set used to build in intensity throughout the night, usually climaxing in a frenzied performance of 'Fight'.

"I also remember that Centro Iberico gig well; from when we turned up in the van with the PA and Mark from The Mob and everyone else helped unload it, to the actual venue itself which was great, to playing the gig, which for a sweltering August night seemed to encapsulate all the band were about for me…great songs, a high level of intensity in the playing and performance, and a rabid audience going mad…brilliant times!"

"I do think that was our best line-up!" ponders John. "Without a doubt that was the best combination of vocals, guitar noise and drumming that the band ever had, especially from a live perspective. The best shows for me were probably at the Grimaldi Squat, just for the atmosphere really, or the Half Moon in Putney.

"The Grimaldi was an abandoned [London] church which was used for gigs at the time; the famous clown 'Grimaldi' was buried there, hence the name. It was on the Pentonville Road between Kings Cross station and the Angel, opposite McCready's Steel on the north side of the road. I can remember one of our roadies, 'Electric' Dick, having to get the mains electricity hot-wired before one gig there, as it had been cut off that day! Sadly the church was knocked flat about ten years ago, and it's not shown on the London A-Z anymore…

"We played with the Subhumans in Islington once as well; I remember Jello Biafra being in the audience just after he got married or something, and we were shit. Good blokes though, the Subhumans! And we played at a place called the Bowes Lyon House in Stevenage once, with Flux

The Sinyx, 1981 (left to right: bassist John Edwards, vocalist Alien (inset above), guitarist Nick 'Filf' Robinson, drummer Auntie).

[Of Pink Indians], and it was a fucking aircraft hanger-sized place, a sports hall or something... but that was shit, just because it was so massive.

"Our gigs at the Focus in Southend were always great as the lady who ran it liked us 'cos our following always spent lots of dosh behind the bar! Her name was Pam and she really looked after us... although we got the plug pulled on us there once as people in the flats about 200 metres away were complaining about the noise – we'd just got a new PA amp!"

Unfortunately though, Paul Barrett, until then the only constant in an ever-shifting line-up, left the band after a gig with Rudimentary Peni and Riot/Clone, at the Moonlight Club in West Hampstead, London, on September 11th, 1982. Steve Pegrum soon followed suit, opting to concentrate on Kronstadt Uprising who had their debut EP coming out on Spiderleg. Auntie, John and Andy soldiered on, recruiting various local musicians (vocalist Mark Bristow, third guitarist Steve Box, and 'Donald The Drummer'... real name Donald Frame, who ended up with Southend goths, Anorexic Dread) and playing occasionally around Southend. John eventually left to join Allegiance To No One, whilst Auntie and Andy formed Sonic Violence – who made quite a name for themselves on the late Eighties industrial circuit – with bassist Murray Blake (also formerly of Kronstadt Uprising) and drummer Elmer Barrett.

"The band wasn't really the same without Paul," admits John. "Mark was a miles better singer but that wasn't really a requirement at the time; Paul had buckets of stage presence, and for a while we had some good songs and a really intimidating front man. He did go through a stage of wearing make-up though, and looked like a really hard version of Robert Smith! He could be very funny onstage as well, he had some great one-liners. Although the band carried on without Paul when he left, I think we lost half of our creative input, which put more focus on Auntie... it just ran its course really.

"I know I sound old here," he laughs when asked about the state of the current punk scene, "But there's not one modern band that I listen to that I can't compare with an earlier band. I don't really get enthusiastic listening to bands anymore, possibly a consequence of playing in bands of my own for almost fifteen years... sad but true.

"And as for punk being a threat still? No, I don't think so; more of a minor annoyance really. Michael Jackson is more of a threat to the music establishment than any of the current punk bands. I just can't compare the likes of Crass and the Dead Kennedys with anything since, sorry."

SELECT DISCOGRAPHY

7"s:
'The Black Death EP' (Reality Attack, 1981)

At A Glance:
A thorough retrospective Sinyx CD is currently planned by US label, Grand Theft Audio.

CHAPTER TWO

After Crass, when most people think of the anarcho-punk genre they immediately think of **CONFLICT**, a band whose music was as blunt, aggressive and uncompromising as their lyrics. Hailing from Eltham in Southeast London, they were the first anarcho band to militantly make animal rights a major issue, and their dogged refusal to back down from even the most violent confrontation generated much controversy and often placed them at odds with the more liberal, pacifist stance taken by many of their peers in the scene.

Rather surprisingly they were drawn to the punk genre by the shock tactics of the Sex Pistols. Explains drummer Francisco 'Paco' Carreno, who began playing when he was just twelve with an outfit called Strontium Dog:

"I remember seeing the 'Weekend' show, with Janet Street-Porter interviewing them [the Pistols], and seeing how disgusted my dad was – because the Daily Mirror had told him to be disgusted basically. He didn't want me to be into punk rock and he didn't want me to get a skateboard... so I got a skateboard and got into punk rock! I was already into bands like Slade from the early Seventies, who were a lot harder-edged than most, and I was into stuff like ELP, when I was about ten, before I was playing any instruments or anything...

"Then when the Pistols came along, I was like, 'Oh, here we go!' They seemed to be against the whole school thing, which I hated. I was really confused by religion and stuff, because I went to a Roman Catholic primary school, run by nuns and all that, and then went straight to a massive comprehensive – but what I found really strange was that there wasn't much difference between the two! Then I started to look into it all a lot more, which is how I found Crass... by the time I was twelve, I had 'Feeding...' and was waiting for 'Stations...' to come out. I had all the lyrics off pat, y'know? It was like, 'Here's someone else that thinks this way; it's not just me going mad... someone else believes it all enough to put out this record!' It seems weird looking back, thinking I was like that when I was only eleven or twelve, but as far as I was concerned, I was fifty! I knew everything about everything, ha ha! 'What do you mean, 'Only twelve'? I'm all of twelve!'"

Formed in and around the notorious Cold Harbour estate by a group of school friends, Conflict were originally vocalist Colin Jerwood and bassist 'Big' John Clifford, with Graham Ball on guitar (although he was soon replaced by Steve from No Class), with a guy called Ken Barnes actually standing in behind the kit to start with. Their first show was on April 11th, 1981, at Sherwood Church Hall, Eltham, but Paco didn't make his live debut until October 8th, 1981, when the band played the Red Lion in Gravesend with Anthrax.

"It was really, really good actually!" says Colin of that first ever gig. "We already had quite a lot of interest in us by then, because everyone knew that we were doing this single on Crass. We knew Garry Bushell as well, 'cos he'd lived on various estates near us, and he was always putting bits in the press about us. And, although we didn't want him to, he was always having digs at Crass through us as well, saying we were 'the real street punk band' and all this crap... but it all helped. He was there at the first show, and we got a lot of press from it."

Things moved quickly for Conflict in 1981, and on December 11th, the day before Paco's sixteenth birthday, they entered Southern Studios under the watchful eye of Penny Rimbaud to record their 'The House That Man Built' EP for Crass.

"I just used to go and see them all the time with this guy called Paul Friday, who was very involved with Conflict at the start," explains Colin, of their early affiliation with Crass. "Stig [from

Conflict vocalist Colin Jerwood, picture by Tony Mottram.

the Icons Of Filth] was always there too, and Ian [Astbury] from Southern Death Cult... and we'd end up sleeping in doorways and all that after the gigs. I got to know Steve [Ignorant], and he was a really nice guy...

"I mainly got to know 'em, to be totally honest with ya, by kicking off with skinheads at their gigs!" he adds, laughing. "And then getting bollocked for it, y'know? But me and Stig had a different view on how to deal with skinheads at gigs to them really... and in the end I think we were just this little pain in the arse for them, 'cos, although they liked us being there, they kinda knew what was going to happen! And Steve used to pull me to one side and say, 'Not tonight, eh?' I've ended up in a few cells after Crass gigs with members of the band locked up as well, all stood there blaming me!

"I mean, before Crass, we'd already had all that crap with The Clash. I was following them for years, and they used to play with The Specials, and sometimes it was full-on. And then there was the whole Sham 69 thing. And yes, I agreed with Crass that it was a sick joke that everyone was kicking each other's heads in, but I still didn't see the point of standing there and taking it. I was thinking, 'I can't have this...'

"But then I got to know Steve, visited him at their house and we got chatting, and – I suppose like everyone else at that time – said, 'I'm in this band...' He asked the rest of Crass to release a single for us, but I think the real motive for them doing it was mainly because we were getting so much press as this street punk band, and they wanted to take it away from Bushell a little bit. Which in a way suited us 'cos we had two sides to it then; we had Bushell whacking it all over the press and Crass plugging it to their camp, as it were..."

Whatever the reasons behind its success, 'The House That Man Built' certainly struck a chord with the record-buying public, selling 7800 copies in the first three weeks and shooting to No. 3 in the Indies upon its release during June 1982 (it stayed in the chart for well over three months). The house of the title being the corrupt courts of law, the prisons full to bursting with petty criminals, the derelict tower blocks where the poor eke out a frugal existence in squalor, the churches where the insipid masses flock for reassurance and forgiveness, and, of course, the slaughterhouse, a manmade hell on earth, heavy with the stench of innocent blood.

Colin: "Gee [Vaucher, of Crass] actually made a model of that house, 'the house that man built'... a purpose-built model, and they put a camera in every room of it, and then – after spending a month working on it, making it out of papier mache – she set it alight for the back cover. I was gutted really, 'cos I wanted to keep it! But they really took it seriously, and put 100% into everything they did."

Although thinly produced, the single still throbs with ferocious intent to this day, the brooding

Early Conflict line-up shot by Tony Mottram (left to right: Colin, Paco, John, Steve).

'War Games' in stark contrast to the bouncy feminist anthem, 'I've Had Enough' (vocals courtesy of Pauline Beck), and the high-speed thrash of 'Blind Attack', the latter song being inspired by Colin almost losing the sight in his right eye in a street brawl.

"The real story of it all, the actual truth of the matter," chuckles Colin, in acknowledgment of the many tall tales circulating about the incident, "is that we were drinking in this pub in Leigh, and there was this group of rockers and Hell's Angels in there, and we'd all had a drink, shouted insults backwards and forwards, and a couple of 'em came after me and Jon outside. One of 'em hit me over the head with this cider bottle and then whacked the broken bottle in my eye.

"It perforated the eyeball, so I've got no lens in there, which means I can't ever focus; I've basically got 10% vision, like looking under water. The bottle actually cut the top of my eye off, it made quite a mess. It doesn't really affect me now, I've gotten used to it; I had a couple of major operations on it, but to start with, they thought I was going to lose the entire eye."

Following up the success of their debut single with a live EP for the Poison Girls' label, Xntrix, 'Live At The Centro Iberico' [the Iberico being the squatted ruins of a Harrow Road Victorian girl's school turned 'Spanish anarchist centre'], Conflict then began work in earnest on their celebrated first album, 'It's Time To See Who's Who', which, in keeping with the Crass policy of only doing one-off singles, came out through Corpus Christi; however, it broke with all other anarcho-punk traditions by coming in a full-colour, lavishly illustrated gatefold sleeve.

Actually spending three weeks at the top of the Independent Charts upon its release during April 1983, it was an awesome assault on the senses that married relentless street punk sounds to the peace punk sensibilities of tracks such as 'Meat Means Murder', a song responsible for converting many a spiky-top to the enlightened ways of vegetarianism.

"We painted a slaughter house as part of a school project," explains Colin, of why he initially rejected a carnivorous diet, "And saw what went on inside there, but up until then I couldn't give a monkey's what I ate, didn't even think about it. That was what sent me overboard, seeing what went on in those places, realising what was involved… I didn't ever really think that bands were into that kind of thing, but then reading some of the Crass lyrics, they flirted with it as such… and I thought someone really needed to whack it home.

"Someone asked us on our website if I thought that bands were singing about animal rights issues to get more popular, but to be honest, I think it makes you less popular now! I know of bands who sang animal rights songs then, who eat meat now – they may have even eaten meat then – but it sold records… it was a popular thing, but now, especially in America, a lot of kids write Conflict off because of the animal rights thing.

"We never had a problem with Paco eating meat though; there was never any way I was gonna try and create a vegetarian band. It has to be down to individual choice, in my opinion… I mean, I know what I'd like everyone to do, but it has to be their own decision, it has to be."

Despite such tolerance within Conflict however, Colin has always advocated a hard-line approach outside of it, and, contrary to many a popular rumour about the band, his beliefs appear to have wavered little over the years.

"No, that's right. I mean, I've had to stop certain bits of it, for obvious reasons, tone down others, 'cos it all got a little bit too heavy. I was wondering, 'Well, are we next?' Having seen, like, [prominent members of the Animal Liberation Front] Ronnie [Lee] and Vivian [Smith] getting eighteen year sentences for ridiculous stuff, we knew we were getting very, very close to going the same way. And the laws are changing every two minutes about what you can and can't print, and we were physically being told that we would be nicked if we kept on producing the kinda stuff we'd been producing. At the end of the day though, we didn't stop doing it, we just got more careful. We've probably done more this time around than we've ever done, especially against people like the Countryside Alliance. Before it was very blasé, and 'Let's get some attention for this,' but now it's a lot quieter. I, especially, was like, 'Get out and do this!', but I saw so many people – especially youngsters – getting put away, put away, put away… eventually you have to think to yourself, 'Well, where does it end?'

"I've got hundreds of letters from inside prisons – not having a go at us, but actually proud to be there. And although they're right, it still feels like you're sending your foot soldiers to the front line. I've never had any complaints, mainly lots of letters thanking us for 'helping them see the light'.

"Before, you used to be able to go on demos, and break whatever the fuck you liked, and you'd get a £300 fine or something… but now you're getting three years! If you're lucky… if you go and mindlessly wreck a telephone box, you're gonna get a fine, but if you stick something through a window because you disagree with it, you're gonna get banged up!

"I'm no good on demos at all, no good standing outside somewhere peacefully protesting… if I know something's going on in there, I'm the kind of person who'd rather throw a bomb over the wall than wait for legislation to be passed. I can't take that – things are getting cut up in there right now, you know what I mean?

"People often ask me why I don't go on demos any more, and a) I got fed up of being filmed, and b) I just don't see the point. I mean, at Huntingdon, they've done fantastic, but if I'd have gone on some of those recent demos, I just wouldn't be here. It's good to show opinion if you can take it, but I just can't take it, and I can't handle being pushed around by policemen, I'm too easy to bait. I've had just one too many closed-door beatings off the Old Bill."

After the album, guitarist Steve was replaced by Kevin Webb, who made his recording debut with the 'To A Nation Of Animal Lovers' EP, which as the title suggests was an even more focused statement about man's inhumanity towards animals, the expletive-laden choruses balanced out (at least in the case of 'Whichever Way You Want It', a furious rant against the modern witchcraft that is vivisection) by some genuine pathos reluctantly wrung from the lead guitars. It was also the first Conflict recording to feature guest vocals from Steve Ignorant of Crass, who would eventually join the band on a more permanent basis during the late Eighties. Kevin's more metallic guitar style thickened and tightened up the Conflict sound considerably, a song like 'Berkshire Cunt' especially utilising the formidable intensity of the crossover scene to hammer home its impassioned (anti-fox hunting) message. Issued by Corpus Christi in August 1983, it was another runaway Indie success for the band.

Finding themselves in a strong position as regards profile, Conflict's next move was to set up their own label. Mortarhate, which not only issued all their own records from then on, but also a slew of strong releases from their peers in the anarcho-punk scene – although it was never plain sailing for the label, despite the band's unwavering popularity.

"Uh, the intention originally was to stay on Crass," offers Colin. "But we had offers from Secret and several other record labels, although nothing major, not back then. We'd done these two tapes, the Icons [Of Filth] one ['Not On Her Majesty's Service'] and our own 'Crazy Governments' one, which was basically just our first demo with our first drummer – some songs that never even made the first album, they were that bad! From then on in, it became known as Mortarhate, and Mort 1 through 6 went through IDS... [second album] 'Increase The Pressure' sold fucking truck loads, and we were waiting for the money when IDS went bankrupt! And I had to buy all the parts for our records back off the receiver! Which was quite a knock-back, so then we took it to Jungle, 'cos I knew Steve Brown there, but he was such a good mate of mine and so easy-going, he let me over-spend ridiculously, on anything that we did on Mortarhate, and it ended up that I owed him £30,000! Thankfully [third studio album] 'The Ungovernable Force' cleared that debt, but it's been one tussle after another really..."

"The whole scene around that 'Hagar [The Womb] period' was really nice though," he adds, as regards the criteria involved in getting 'signed' to Mortarhate. "I was going to loads of gigs then... and it was just bands I saw, that I liked as people, that we worked with. For example, I can't say that I ever actually liked Liberty, their sound or anything like that – they didn't really do anything for me – but I really liked them as people, and liked some of their lyrics."

Of course, as with all things concerning Conflict, speculation and rumours were rife that they weren't paying the bands on Mortarhate the royalties they were due.

"The way we do it now is we give bands copies, but I wish we'd done it back then 'n' all. 'Cos we never used to get sales figures ourselves off Jungle until way after the event, but if all those bands were to see those statements now, they'd realise that 99% of it lost money, especially the singles. And we can prove it to them. But now, with every new release we press, we're giving the band 200 copies in every thousand to sell for what they want.

"Yeah, we heard all the rumours too, but no one has ever actually confronted us and asked for figures – 'cos if they wanna see 'em, they can have 'em... I think some people prefer to just moan about how they got shafted by Conflict rather than actually sit down and work it all out. But I'd like to state categorically that we've never, ever withheld anyone's money... although sometimes, if a release had broken even it may have got caught up in the bigger picture with the distributor going under or something... but if we've been accounted to, money has never not been passed on, never. Although, to be honest, it's only really the last album and some of the reissues that have been making money; the rest of it was in such a deficit, it just wasn't selling, not after the early days had passed anyway... I'm sure a lot of these bands are convinced that they sold a lot more than they did. A lot of them thought they were selling similar to Conflict, but they weren't, there was a world of difference."

The first release for Mortarhate was 'The Serenade Is Dead' 7" EP. Recorded at Greenhouse Studios, London, in September 1983, and appearing in January 1984, it was quite a departure for the band at that point, a mournful bass-line ushering in a rather profound and deeply personal contemplation of the system and its restrictive ways. Backed by the powerful one-two of 'The Positive Junk' (a scathing attack on the hypocrisy of self-seeking, mainstream punk rockers) and 'The System Maintains', 'The Serenade Is Dead' even saw Conflict breaching the lower echelons of the National Charts for the first time.

The band then peaked with what this writer considers their finest work, 1984's 'Increase The Pressure' album, which took all the musical and lyrical fury of the preceding releases and distilled it into seven of the finest anarcho-punk songs ever committed to vinyl. Only the album's glorious A-side featured new studio recordings however; the B-side being a (comparatively) substandard live set from a Brixton Ace show the previous October.

Colin: "We just didn't have enough songs for a whole new album. We didn't have the time or money to write and record a whole record, but we needed something new out just to survive. 'Cos we were putting out all these singles on Mortarhate, but we weren't making anything from them 'cos they were so cheap…"

Still, such is the strength of the studio songs, 'Increase The Pressure' stands as not only Conflict's crowning glory, but also as a watershed in political punk, the band not only unleashing some of their most passionate compositions to date but also daring to print the home addresses of various individuals involved in the barbaric seal cull on the Orkney Isles, a provocative step that raised the ire of even their close friends in Crass.

"I had some real debates with them over that," remembers Colin. "They got quite upset with me, because they felt that those guys were only doing what they had to do to make a living. And I said, 'Well, they should fuckin' do summat else!' And Crass were like, 'But there's nothing else to do up there…' And I was like, 'So they should fucking move somewhere else then!' I wasn't prepared to hear any excuses for what they were doing, but Crass were a lot more liberal than us, too liberal for their own good sometimes…"

A heavy touring schedule was undertaken to promote the album; in fact, Conflict were veritable road-dogs throughout the Eighties, gigging across the entire country several times a year… and, of course, in true Conflict style, the shows were often not without incident.

"We have had some run-ins, I must admit," concedes Colin. "But we've not backed down from it, y'know? We've had to get out of a venue only once, and that was the White Lion in Putney; we didn't even get to play that night, it was wall-to-wall with skinheads. We was set up, 'cos there was thousands of British Movement skinheads there when we arrived, and it was bad, we coulda been killed… and to be honest with ya, that was when we went up a gear outside of Conflict. I thought, 'I'm not having it!' And we knew where certain people were, and we targeted a few of their top guys and put 'em straight… 'It's different rules now, it's not just about gigs, it's us and you… and we know where some of you are and we'll come and get ya!' And there was this kind of acceptance after that, an uneasy truce… it sounds like a thick notion, but it was almost like, 'They're alright, they don't mind a fight!' Well, it was either that or they knew we weren't kidding when we said that one of 'em would be coming out of bed one night…"

Paco: "That was when we realised that the most important part of the band's equipment was the tool kit! We carried several weapons of mass destruction! But we had to do it really, 'cos it was them or us…"

Colin: "And when people saw us really go off, it started to change things. I remember we were in Exeter, and a load of skinheads and marines kicked off, and we went for 'em… and the whole hall went with us, it was amazing. It was as if everyone decided at the same time that they weren't gonna take it anymore."

Paco: "If we'd have backed down and just ignored it, then the audience would've done the same, and those thirty or forty guys would've probably killed someone."

It was at this point that Conflict picked up rather a bad name on the live circuit as an often unreliable act that seemingly cancelled as many shows as they played – but once again, the truth of the matter is quite different to that perceived by an outsider.

"Do you know why that really was? I'll tell you why!" spits Paco with feeling. "It's 'cos people would think, 'Oh, they're nice blokes, they'll turn up', and they'd organise gigs without telling us in advance. This is the truth now; we never once bumped a gig because we couldn't be bothered to do it."

"Or pulled out for fear of what was meant to happen there or whatever," interjects Colin.

"I remember sitting around Colin's house once, and answering the phone, 'cos I was nearest. 'Hello?' 'Where are you?' 'Well, in Eltham! Where are you?' 'Fucking Skegness, waiting for you to play, you bastards…!' And we didn't even know about this gig! But it happened all the time, people would organise gigs just assuming we'd do it, or they'd mention this gig they were planning in six months time to us, and we'd never hear from them again until we saw the fliers somewhere! Or they'd speak to someone else, like the Icons, who'd assumed that they'd also get in touch with us directly or whatever."

"Don't get us wrong, there are gigs we've had to pull out of," admits Colin. "And some of them have been a bit late in the day, but people have always been informed, and it's never been too late to warn people not to travel. No way! But of course, people would say, 'Oh, you're 'big' now, you can't be bothered…' Or shit like that."

Paco: "This is a classic joke from 1985, which someone told me on the way to the Ambulance Station in the Old Kent Road. 'Why don't Conflict ever get girls pregnant? 'Cos they always pull out at the last minute!' But yeah, I'd say that maybe 40% of the gigs we were meant to play, we didn't even know about."

During August 1984, Conflict played their first shows in the USA, most noticeably headlining the Olympic Auditorium, LA, as part of the Nagasaki Nightmare festival, commemorating the fortieth anniversary of the atomic bomb being dropped on Japan. A recording of the show was later released as the 'Only Stupid Bastards Help EMI' album, the title an attack on New Model Army who had just betrayed their independent roots by signing to the aforementioned major label, the record itself a benefit for the Anarchist Bust Fund, an organisation who helped pay the fines of incarcerated anarchist activists.

"We went out there and did four gigs," recalls Paco candidly. "Three of them were great; we did this huge self-sufficient squat in San Francisco, and that was good. It depends what you call 'good' really… is it good to play to thousands of people in LA, but have police on horseback rioting outside? Or is it better to play two nights later in a little venue with no security to a few hundred people? You know, it was crazy. We played Fenders at Long Beach, and there were thousands of people there who'd been waiting to see us for years, but the security were working with the Old Bill, and they were all lined up in the streets with baseball bats! It was already a done deal, no one stood a chance, every body was gonna get slapped.

"And the skinheads were doing there what they were doing here in '82, so everyone was getting intimidated but we were like, 'We're not having this!' So we waded in, and they were all like, 'Who are these crazy limey guys?' Ha!

"But we were pleasantly surprised at how much they lived and breathed what we were about over there. You gotta remember that, at the time, there was no internet, no mobile phones, everything was done by regular mail and word-of-mouth… yet these kids were really deeply into what we were doing."

Another benefit record followed, this time a single, 'This Is Not Enough' – cheekily backed by 'Neither Is This'! Recorded again at Greenhouse, it was released in March '85 to help fund the Stop The City campaigns that bravely attempted to bring the capitalist machinery at the heart of

London to an all-too-brief halt in an effort to raise awareness of corporate globalisation, although more money would have been raised if the band hadn't decided to price the record at a paltry 49p, in an optimistic act of defiance that backfired somewhat.

"Yeah, we actually lost 2p a time on that – and it sold fucking thousands!" chuckles Colin wryly. "We thought we could break dead even with it, and to be honest we just wanted to take the piss a bit. You can do it in the DIY scene okay, but we got it in all the stores, and they hated stocking it, but they had to 'cos there was so many copies wanted. But then, when we worked it all out a year later, 40,000 copies sold, and all these 'minus two pences' on the statements, it really added up!"

Conflict live at the 100 Club, December 1984, picture by Paul May.

Adds Paco: "We knew we couldn't do it as cheap as [the debut Crass single] 'Reality Asylum', which was 45p, so it was gonna be 50p, then we said, 'Fuck it, make it 49p!' But then we found out we were just mugging ourselves…"

"I even got a fucking load of stick when I put it back out at 99p," says Colin incredulously. "Off people saying, 'It used to be 49p, you're ripping us off…!' Yeah, alright, mate, whatever… it'd be three-and-a-half quid now!"

Musically, 'This Is Not Enough' picked up the baton where the studio side of 'Increase The Pressure' left off, revealing a confident band at the height of their powers, as did the band's next single, 'The Battle Continues'. Recorded during August 1985, for an October release, it actually went on to become Conflict's best-selling single. And not without reason, because it features not only some of Colin's most inspirational lyrics ("If it's a fight they want, they've got it, but we had better be prepared!") but also some of the band's most dynamic arrangements, the acoustic mid-section of 'Mighty And Superior' especially capable of sending shivers down the spine.

Not so great though the next recording, 'It's Time To See Who's Who Now', which was basically a re-worked version of the first album, with a few of the best tracks from the '… Animal Lovers' single thrown in for good measure. With Kevin handling both guitar and bass duties (John was busy tending to some personal issues at the time), it's a decent enough, hard-nosed punk record, but fairly redundant considering how good the original recordings sounded in the first place, and then it wasn't actually released until May 1994 anyway.

"That was just taking the piss out of Southern basically," explains Colin of the sessions. "Because we wanted our first album out on our own label, and they wouldn't release the rights to it. They had paid for the recordings, so officially they owned it… it had sold fantastic amounts when it came out, it really went… I think it sold about 26 or 27 thousand copies straight away – and then it stopped, because it got deleted! I dunno why, but you couldn't get it for years, it was just one of those catalogue titles that they pulled…"

Ex-Crass vocalist Steve Ignorant whilst singing with Conflict, Woolwich Poly 1987, picture by Jaz Wiseman.

"It was more a drunken moment of anger than anything else, to be honest with ya," confesses Paco. "We went out for a drink with Derek [Birkett, bassist with Flux Of Pink Indians], and he'd had problems with Southern as well, and he had his own studio, and we were, like, 'We'd love to record that fucking album again!' And he said, 'Come back and record it then!' And we were, like, 'Fuck it, we will!'"

Colin: "It gave Kevin a chance as well, 'cos he played guitar and bass on that, and we just whacked it out…"

Paco: "Which is exactly what it sounds like! But if it sounds fucking angry, it's 'cos it was!"

Thankfully the band's next studio album proper was about as raging as anything they ever put their name to, 'The Ungovernable Force' being released autumn 1986 and climbing straight to No. 2 in the Independent Charts. Opening with the atmospheric 'You Cannot Win', it remains an impressively diverse work, still maintaining the high levels of aggression that helped define previous releases yet also taking in the almost poppy melodies of 'Custom Rock' and

'Statement', effective spoken word pieces such as 'The Arrest' and '1986, The Battle Continues', a montage dedicated to the strong foundations laid by Crass ('C.R.A.S.S.') and even some moments of high comedy, in particular the damning satire of the Metropolitan police, 'Force Or Service?'. Not bad for a record that was written entirely in Rockfield Studios (Monmouth), the band not having a single note written for it prior to recording, not even rehearsing for a month leading up to the session!

It was also the first release to feature new bassist Paul 'Oddy' Hoddy, who had previously played with D-fekt and Broken Bones.

"He used to come and see us when we played Manchester," recalls Paco. "And he basically used to come up to us and say, 'I'm going to be in your band!' and he was really into it, almost like a dog hanging on your leg! He was well up for it…"

"And I went to see him at the 100 Club, playing there with Broken Bones," adds Colin. "I watched from the side of the stage… and, as much as we love John – we've known him for years – he'll be the first one to admit that he's not a great bass player! And so I stood there watching Oddy, thinking, 'Fucking hell, you might be a pest [laughs], but I really wanna play with you!' Bones were pretty big then too, packing out the 100 Club, so it was kind of a compliment that he even wanted to play with us in the first place. And he's been really good ever since, really, uh… 'loyal' is the wrong word… but he always puts his back in, y'know?"

Possibly as a rite of passage with Conflict, Oddy even had to endure the band leaving 'deliberate mistakes' in his bass-playing on the intro to the title track of the album.

"At the beginning of 'The Ungovernable Force', it was all meant to fall to bits before the band kicks in together really powerful and all that," explains Paco. "It was meant to be a big mess until the snare brought everything crashing back in. Thing is, me and Kev did it really tight, so it wasn't a mess at all, and it sounded like Oddy fucked up on his own!"

Colin: "He was the only one who did what he was told, the rest of 'em said, 'Bollocks, we like it the way it is! Don't go all Crass on us!' Oddy still hates us for that even now…"

And whilst on the subject of 'going all Crass', Conflict organised and headlined the extremely ambitious 'Gathering Of The 5000' show at the Brixton Academy on Saturday April 18th, 1987, that saw Steve Ignorant joining the band onstage for a spirited run-through of many a Crass classic, as well as the regular Conflict set. What could have been a triumph for the underground punk movement was scuppered by the overwhelming logistics involved in booking such a huge venue for such a huge event, with costs spiralling out of control and co-operation between the band and the Academy breaking down at a crucial point in proceedings. Guest lists were ignored, the vegetarian catering refused access to the venue, farcically resulting in beef burgers being offered as sustenance amongst the multitude of animal rights stalls!

Outside the venue after the show, police intimidation of punks leaving the building resulted in scuffles breaking out which quickly escalated into a full-scale riot that saw fifty-two Conflict fans arrested and ten police officers injured. The show left Conflict hopelessly in debt, and banned from most major London venues.

"I was in New York in 1980," says Steve, by way of explanation. "And was walking along the boardwalk on Coney Island, and I heard these amazing sounds coming from this ghetto blaster, so I went over and asked these black guys what it was, and they were like, 'Haven't you ever heard of scratching?' And they were intrigued by this punk guy asking them all these questions. So, even during Crass I was getting into the rap thing, and writing more in that style, but after Crass had finished, I rang Colin from Conflict up, and said that I'd written this rap song, and would he want to do it as a single… it never came out in the end, but he asked me if I wanted to do this Gathering Of The Five Thousand gig. Of course, it ended in a fuckin' riot, in true Conflict tradition, but what do you expect?

"Anyway, it was meant to be a one-off, but I enjoyed hanging out with them all so much, having a right old laugh, that I did another one with 'em, and in the end I joined them properly for a while."

The Gathering was recorded (and filmed, although the video tapes have been in contractual limbo ever since) and later released as the – rather good – double live LP, 'Turning Rebellion Into Money', which actually made No. 1 in the Indies upon its release during summer of '87.

Unfortunately it would be the last Conflict record to feature Kev's not-inconsiderable guitar skills, with him leaving the fold soon after the Gathering, and tragically taking his own life in more recent years.

"I'm not sure what happened, I haven't heard the full story, but I believe he got back into drugs again," says Colin sadly. "He was into heroin before he even joined Conflict, and we suspect during his time with us a little bit as well…"

"I'd heard he was on Prozac too," adds Paco. "But at the end of the day though, the only person who really knows why he did what he did is Kevin…"

Colin: "It was a real shame 'cos he was good at what he did, and he was very into the beliefs too. He'd been out on ALF stuff with me, and he was right bang into it – to the point of fearlessness really. But he never wanted to listen to anybody… me and him clashed many, many times… over really stupid stuff! We'd openly row in front of people at the front of the stage over the set we were playing and stuff like that… you just don't need it, do you? But he was a great guitarist, probably the best guitarist we ever had. He brought a whole new style to the band, that sort of Motörhead/crossover style, which was nice… he was great when he was knuckling down and working at it, but he couldn't handle the pressure, I don't think. What used to get to him was that he lived up in North London, and a whole little lot of 'em up there started to go all anti-Conflict, and he had to listen to it all the time, and it was doing his head in."

Paco: "Of course, we all lived in Eltham, near each other, and he was up there on his own, and with what all his mates were saying to him all the time, he probably felt alienated. We tried to make him feel a part of the band – we bought him a guitar and good quality equipment – but it got quite awkward towards the end of his time with us. The official reason he gave was that he wanted to spend more time with his missus, Gillian, and their kid… but straight after that, he went back on tour, as roadie for [US hardcore act] Scream, so Gillian and the kid fucked off, which set the whole depression ball rolling really…"

Colin: "And it made the reason he gave us for leaving the band seem like an excuse to get away from Conflict really, 'cos he fucked off on tour again straight away!

"I do know that he kicked in a load of windows of a record shop in Islington a few years ago, 'cos he wanted to destroy the Conflict CDs in there that he'd played on! And I know that to be true 'cos I knew the shop owner who didn't prosecute him… but it's strange, ain't it? It must have really got to him, and he ended up hating the thing he helped create."

Kevin's replacement was Chris Parrish, another troubled individual if the rest of the band are to be believed, whose tenure with Conflict was a short one, although he did end up on two albums, 1988's 'The Final Conflict' and '89's 'Against All Odds', which were recorded 'back to back' during the same sessions at the Lodge Studios, Clare, Suffolk.

"Again, a very good guitarist," concedes Colin. "But you just couldn't get any humour or personality out of Chris at all. I remember we went up there and recorded, and I made a meal the one night, just a big stew, and we all sat down round the table to eat it, but he went and sat in the corner with a piece of dry bread! I'm sorry, I started laughing, 'cos I thought it was fucking hilarious, which didn't help at all, and he was going, 'I won't eat anything that anyone else has touched.' And I went, 'Well, I've just cooked it!' And he went, 'I don't care, I'm eating this in the corner…' which to me was just a little bit strange.

"The next day, or a few days later, me and Ignorant were in there, and we picked his guitar up, when Chris was asleep upstairs, only to learn how to play something, just mucking about really, but he heard it and came down and went mad. He kicked a cup straight across the studio, which smashed against the wall…"

Paco: "Picked up his guitar and fucked off! Left the studio, left the session, left the band…!

Luckily he'd finished doing all his guitar parts though!"

Possibly as a result of 1988 being an atrocious year for the band as they struggled to regroup following the Gathering fiasco, 'The Final Conflict' was more defiant than ever, opening track 'Let The Battle Commence' declaring vehemently, 'So what if we don't change a thing? We'll have a fucking good try! Mobilise, fight, against all odds!' And one of the most obviously heart-felt tracks on the album is 'I Heard A Rumour', a knee-jerk reaction to the constant backstabbing and verbal sniping between the various cliques of the punk movement. It's sad but true: Conflict have wasted far too much time and energy over the years feeling it necessary to justify themselves and their actions to all and sundry.

"Yeah, we have, and it's a shame really," sighs Colin. "I was actually talking to Jay from IT [Inner Terrestrials] about this the other day, because he's now having shit written about him on the net and stuff, and I just told him that eventually it'll all go over your head. It actually forced me out of the scene, in '91 or '92, I couldn't take it any more, but I said to Jay, 'Don't waste your time worrying about it... me and you have spent the last hour talking about this, when we could've been talking about something much more worthwhile.' 'Cos I've wasted months defending myself, and in the end it does get to you, especially when someone gets personal.

"Eventually, you just say, 'Fuck it, I ain't taking this!' What gets me though is, I'm supposed to have to put up with violent threats, and people saying stuff to me in the streets, but if you were walking down the road and someone from outside the punk scene said the same thing to ya, you'd whack 'em! Do you know what I mean? And I think that's wrong, you shouldn't be allowed to speak to people like that.

"Yeah, we've been mouthy about a lot of bands and a lot of things – fair enough, I'm happy with that – but it's when people who are meant to be onside turn on ya. They're just waiting for you to slip up, the slightest thing and they're there, gloating... it's mad. That's why I like the forum on our site now, 'cos it's so open. If people are asking something, they're getting a straight answer... and it wasn't that they didn't get a straight answer before, but now I don't care... 'cos what's there to lose? They can either take it or leave it, can't they?"

"And when we did 'The Final Conflict' album, we had three days left of studio time," adds Paco on how they produced two albums for the price of one. "So we said, 'Let's knock out a single... no, fuck it, let's try and do another album!' And we wrote, recorded and mixed 'Against All Odds' right there in the studio in three days.

"I'd always wanted to do a piece of music which had a bit of everything in it," he elaborates on the genesis of the album's ambitious fourteen-minute title track. "Slow rock, fast rock, fast punk, slow punk, and finishing with a little dub section at the end just for the sake of it. But that then set the mood for about fourteen different sets of lyrics...!"

Colin: "Me and Steve [Ignorant] wrote well together, we just sat and took it in turns with the lines. Back then, I had books and books full of one- and two-liners, where I'd just jotted down bits and pieces, so we'd just start with something and see where it went. I liked writing with Steve; he had a quality that I didn't, especially at the time... although I'm getting there a bit now. I was always 'Black, white, fuck, cunt...', but he could write a story around 'Black, white, fuck, cunt...'

"There's not that many Conflict albums that I do still listen to, but now and again I dig out 'Against All Odds', and I do like that song itself. It's got some good changes in it, and I like some of the vocal patterns."

It would be four more years before Conflict issued another album, and when 'Conclusion' was issued in 1993, it had an air of finality about it that wasn't just attributable to the title. With Ferenc Collins and Marshall Penn now heading up a twin-pronged guitar attack, Jackie Hanna providing female vocals, and Mark Pickstone [of Schwartzeneggar] manning keyboards, the album was a mature, considered and well-produced collection with more than its fair share of great tunes (not least of all the lurching 'Someday Soon' and the heavily rhythmic 'Climbing The Stairs', which also appeared as the B-side of the simultaneous single, 'These Colours Don't Run'), but all was definitely not well in the Conflict camp. Apart from a few one-off shows in 1994, an ill-fated tour of Australia in '97, and a string of obligatory retrospective compilations, the band ground to a halt, its members concentrating on other projects.

"Yeah, we just kinda stopped, to come up for air," reckons Colin. "We never said, 'That's it!' And it just kinda drifted, even though we were getting loads of mail and that... and I don't know if it was just a total physical and mental shutdown on my part or what, but I didn't wanna open any more. I'm not sure how the other guys felt, 'cos they all kept on with their other bands and stuff, but personally I just didn't wanna do it any longer...

"It wasn't that I wasn't into it, but we were getting one knock back after another, and to get all the crap we were getting with it, I just couldn't see a way forward any more, there was nothing fresh about any of it. It was always time to do another gig, or time to do another fucking record, and none of it was really inspiring me..."

"And it's like when there's someone who you mean to get in touch with, but the longer you leave it, the harder it is to do," offers Paco. "But when we left it, there's no denying that it was turning into a chore... gigs were like glorified rehearsals, playing to the same thirty people... the live music scene was dead on its arse; no clubs wanted to put bands on, 'cos they could get some DJ wanker down there with his decks for a tenth of the cost and twice as many people.

"Also, when you've been doing something for that long, it's good to get out of the bowl and check out what's going on outside in the real world! I did a band called Experiment for a couple of years, and then I did Fear Of Fear with John... I even took my HGV lorry test and did a bit of that as well! 'Cos I was fifteen when I joined Conflict, so I'd never done any of that 'career' stuff – I'd come straight from being a rebel at school to being a rebel in a band! Before I knew it, I was thirty... so, I did a bit of lorry driving, and it didn't take me long to realise that I definitely fucking hated that game, so that quickly got knocked on the head. Then I did the Inner Terrestrials... but everywhere I was going, people were asking me where Conflict were."

Colin meanwhile had turned to the burgeoning rave scene for inspiration, and even ended up running several dance clubs.

"Well, I got into that afterwards," corrects the vocalist. "First of all, I got into open air field parties – I loved it! It was totally fresh, the first thing since punk that wasn't a shit revival, this was brand new. Taking over a field, totally illegal... until the drugs thing kicked in, it was a great atmosphere. It wasn't political or anything, but it was keeping one step ahead of the police as well...

"Then I got asked to help out at a club and ended up running a night there, and I enjoyed that for a while, but again, drugs moved in, and certain people moved in, and it got a bit too violent, just got too much and that was that."

Approached by Paco to do a one-off reunion for the Across The Decades show that was staged in Milton Keynes in 2000, Colin thankfully agreed, and found it such a positive experience it kick-started Conflict back into full operations once again.

"I wasn't really interested to start with. He rang me up and asked me if I wanted to do it for nostalgia's sake, and I didn't really, to be honest, 'cos I'd got so far out of the scene. But it was so good in the end, I realised how much I'd missed it all.

"It's not that I don't wanna play to people," he tries to explain his trepidation at being mentioned in the same breath as the countless bands that have reformed in recent years to play Darren Russell's Holidays In The Sun/Wasted festivals. "But it is a hard fucking set that we do and I like to do it the right way, and you think to yourself, 'Do we wanna become like that? After what went before?' You know what I mean? And I hate seeing old, wanked-out, overweight punk bands that are not cutting it, and I never want to become that, so the minute I don't think we're vital, that'll be that.

"That's one of the reasons we're putting so much effort into it now; we've gone up a gear, to make sure we don't end up like that. We're certainly not doing it for money – I can go and earn

Conflict live at Salisbury City Hall, November 1985, picture by Marc Freeman.

more money in one day than I do with Conflict in six months! And Paco will tell ya, I don't rehearse if I can help it – I hate it, I just can't do it. I do it when I have to, but it's hard, stood there shouting at a wall…"

But no one bangs their head against that hateful brick wall harder than Conflict, now joined by (John's partner) Sarah Taylor on additional vocals, as proven by their recent studio offerings, 2001's incendiary 'Now You've Put Your Foot In It' EP (released in response to the outrageous cattle culls that were a result of the Foot And Mouth disease which ravaged the British countryside in 2000) and the quite brilliant 2003 album, 'There's No Power Without Control'.

The passing of the years has done little to quash Conflict's ability to stir up fierce controversy, and their most recent sparring partners have been the Countryside Alliance whose primarily bloated, conservative membership and staunch stance in favour of fox-hunting placed them directly in the band's firing line.

Spits Colin with feeling: "I'd have more respect if one of those bastards stopped making silly excuses about controlling foxes and just went on TV and said, 'I enjoy it, I enjoy killing foxes… it's what I like doing, I like killing!' Just be honest, and stop the fucking lies, 'cos I've got some crazy undercover footage of that lot, that shows exactly what they like to do, given half a chance.

All that nonsense about protecting the countryside…? Just admit you like killing.

"They have a good knack of winding me up, and we've had a few run-ins between us. They got us through our PO box, and then through Ferenc's website, and they actually arranged a meeting to have it out with us properly behind Kings Cross station during their big [2002] march, to have a good sort-out… which, to be honest, we were up for. I had a lot of proper people there to support me, and all they sent was a load of police! They bottled it, and we were set up. They're brave in numbers, of course… but there's only one way you can really deal with people like that, only one language they understand…

"It's like that whole A-Team thing we set up, to help the saboteurs when they started getting beaten up by hunt security… there was Daz from Exeter, from The Waste, and we basically co-ordinated a little team so that if sabs were getting bashed, we'd go down there in the van, march over with bats and do the security right back! Which at the end of the day is a bit silly, but what do you do? It's an ongoing battle, and it ain't gonna get any easier.

"What I do find funny though is a lot of the so-called anarchists quoting the law on our website, 'cos for me, I don't need there to be a law, I know that hunting's wrong and I want it stopped right now. But it's a fine line, like I said earlier, between waiting for legislation and chucking a bomb over the wall…"

So, the ungovernable force hasn't mellowed with the passing of time, sticking to its guns where so many others were tempted by the lure of major labels and mainstream airplay.

"We actually got a big offer from EMI a few years ago, which we turned down," reveals Colin. "We thought about it for ages, thought about all the money we could get out of it that could benefit a lot of people like the ALF, but when we spoke to them about it, they just said, 'We'd rather do it the long way, wait and do it independently…'

"The main thing that stopped me though was when this bloke called Mike Smith, their publishing man who wanted to own all the songs outright, said to me as a joke, 'We can all have our pictures taken together and you can wear a 'I'm A Stupid Bastard' T-shirt!' He thought it was humorous, but I just thought 'You wanker!', and walked out of there.

"But a part of me really wants to sort something bigger out for America, 'cos we'd only shipped 1200 copies of '… Power…' just before we last toured there, which is fucking shit for America, but we still did well at the gigs. Having it out there would be so good, but it's knowing how to do it and still live with ourselves. Some people say that it would be a demoralising slap in the mouth for us to go with a major, others say that this shouldn't be a private fan club… that we really should be getting heard and we're not."

Despite Paco having just had to retire from the band because of serious health issues that are now affecting his playing, stamina and ability to travel (he suffers from chronic cellulitis, and has been replaced by Nathan from Lab Rat), Colin sees no reason for Conflict to bow out of the game just yet, and indeed the band have just celebrated their twenty-fifth anniversary with several high-profile shows.

"For me, it's probably the black-and-white-ness of it all," he says, pondering just what set Conflict apart from their peers. "There was no beating about the bush, no pissing about skirting issues, we'd just get straight in there and say it as we saw it, and that was that really. Rather than all the little gimmicks that go with it… we just came out and said it, and what happened, happened. There was never any compromise with the band, and perhaps that's the hard thing now, realising that that's what we're gonna have to do, especially with some of the music channels. I know what kind of video I'd like to give them, but it'd get kicked off after one screening and it would be a waste of time and money. There has to be some kind of compromise somewhere along the line, and as much as I don't wanna do that, I also think it would be a big waste if we don't try something out of the ordinary. I mean, there's a hundred and one publicity stunts we could pull, but they don't last five minutes, and they're never gonna sell us a hundred thousand more records or get us over to a lot of new people, which we're gonna have to use the media to do.

"The trouble is, no one wants us on the same bill as them. It's true! They go, like, 'Fuck that lot! They're all mad, there'll be too much violence!', or whatever. I suppose it all depends on what the next album and single are like, 'cos we're not easy on the ear, you can't sing along to Conflict, can you? Even the people who like us tell us, 'You're the hardest band in the world to show that we're enjoying it!' It's just too manic.

"A lot of my original ideas for the next record were kind of, still up-tempo and powerful, but more like a 'Safe European Home'-type style… but how it's coming together at the moment, it's definitely not progressing that way! We never learn, do we?"

SELECTED DISCOGRAPHY

7"s:
'The House That Man Built' (Crass, 1982)
'Live At The Centro Iberico' (Xntrix, 1982)
'To A Nation Of Animal Lovers' (Corpus Christi, 1983)
'The Serenade Is Dead' (Mortarhate, 1984)
'This Is Not Enough' (Mortarhate, 1985)
'The Battle Continues' (Mortarhate, 1985)
'These Colours Don't Run' (Mortarhate, 1993)
'Now You've Put Your Foot In It…' (Mortarhate, 2001)

12"s:
'From Protest To Resistance' (Konnexion, 1987)
'The Final Conflict' (Mortarhate, 1988)

LPs:
'It's Time To See Who's Who' (Corpus Christi, 1983)
'Increase The Pressure' (Mortarhate, 1984)
'Only Stupid Bastards Help EMI' (Modern Army, 1986)
'The Ungovernable Force' (Mortarhate, 1986)
'Turning Rebellion Into Money' (Mortarhate, 1987)
'The Final Conflict' (Mortarhate, 1988)
'Against All Odds' (Mortarhate, 1989)
'Conclusion' (Mortarhate, 1993)
'It's Time To See Who's Who Now' (Mortarhate, 1994)
'There's No Power Without Control' (Mortarhate, 2003)

At A Glance:
There have been many Conflict compilations over the years, two of the most notable being Cleopatra's 'Employing All Means Necessary' and 'Deploying All Means Necessary, Issue Two', which were re-released in 2001 by Anagram in an attractive digipak, complete with enhanced live and interview footage. But for a comprehensive overview of the band's singles output, Mortarhate's twenty-track 'There Must Be Another Way' collection is a must, whilst their career-spanning 2005 'Rebellion Sucks' compilation even comes with a bonus DVD of a whole live set from the London Underworld, making it the definitive Conflict anthology. Mortarhate have just struck a distribution deal with Cherry Red, and the first three albums are now available again, re-mastered with numerous bonus tracks.

ADMIT YOU'RE SHIT are probably the most controversial of all the bands included in this book, at least for people involved in the punk movement. Closely tied to an anarcho-punk scene they basically despised by two brilliant releases on Mortarhate, they refused to conform to peer expectations at the time, either musically or lyrically, but have since become even more notorious, as a result of their ex-vocalist John 'Weeny' Cato's widely publicised racist beliefs.

"We formed in London, mid-1984, primarily just to play music…" reckons John, "The same as it's always been for anyone who has ever played music, despite every pretentious and arrogant claim you've heard of wanting 'to spread the message'. That bullshit annoys me as much now as it did twenty years ago… and we certainly had no problem expressing our distaste and revulsion for it either.

"The name is actually the chorus words to a Buzzcocks B-side ['Oh Shit'], and just sounded so fucking brilliant, so fucking right, for what we wanted to empathize, were we ever to dare presume that we had a purpose with the band.

"Actually though, and significantly, we never played under the full name, not once ever. Every gig was always 'AYS', even when using acronyms… even when we introduced ourselves, obviously joking as well, as 'Neon Christ'!

"It was only when Mortarhate released the [['Expect No Mercy…']] 7" that we agreed, reluctantly, to the full name being used on the cover. Granted, we were sometimes billed as 'Admit You're Shit' on the Conflict press adverts for gigs, but I think that was always because Colin liked the name far more than we did, and certainly far more than our influence to only use the three letters would permit us to get our own way."

AYS were a completely different take on the fast-developing thrash/punk scene; playing at velocities in excess of even Conflict or Discharge, they also had a manic edge-of-the-seat intensity about them, not to mention a certain innate arrogance, that took considerable influence from the American hardcore scene of the time.

"Oh yeah, without question, I'd even say that [USHC] was our sole inspiration, musically and ethically. To us, it was just better, more thought out, more important. It was even more than what it felt like when you first got into punk – when records had to be sought out and their discovery meant something, not just commodity. It was like having that little scene all over again, where basically every record felt different and new, fresh and exciting; the buzz was indescribable.

"And the lyrics, mostly, talked of things you'd never considered or been exposed to; it was just more honest, so different from every UK band saying exactly the same thing… all these bands who didn't dare to really think for themselves or lay bare any tiny bit of emotion they may have had. Here was passion, something which to me punk was nothing without.

"And the music… wow! Every record just seemed to explode with intensity immediately. No long, slow, sometimes acoustic, intros… no intros that were just bass or guitar or drums – just fuckin' everything all at once. How could you not be moved?"

Joining John were guitarist Johnny Lee (real name 'Tom Horror', formerly with Smegma), bassist Sean Kenney (formerly of Sub Squad, who had one track, 'Capital City', on the Mortarhate compilation 'Who? What? Why? When? Where?') and drummer Simon Rimini, the band making their live debut at the Metropolitan in Farringdon, during October 1984, with the Lost Cherrees.

"We were basically fucking awful!" laughs John. "I remember feeling a mixture of nervousness, excitement, embarrassment and desperation at those early gigs. Nervousness because no-one then was playing the music we were, and, irrespective of not being bothered generally what anyone thought, you'd still like to be given half a chance. Excitement because at least we were doing something, over here, that no-one had seen or heard before, and that, just maybe, even one person might have been excited enough to check out all these amazing, relatively new bands that had inspired us, seek them out for themselves and feel the same rush of excitement that we did.

"And that is why there was embarrassment as well; that we had to accept that we too were

Admit You're Shit, picture by Mick Slaughter.

arrogant enough to believe that we could affect people as well by being different, and good enough that we could expose others to that music and its ideas we had felt so moved by.

"But fucking hell, yeah, more than anything else, the greatest desperation I (wrongly) believed it was ever possible to feel as well. Here was this lazy, self-congratulatory, back-slapping, absolutely and unbelievably conformist 'youth movement', which gave so much credence to 'free speech' and 'freedom of thought', now scared shitless 'cos someone came along and really did that, and – to hell with the short-term consequences – showed it all up for the joke it really was.

"We rarely used to rehearse," he adds, "Certainly not as any sort of Sunday morning ritual anyway; a couple of times prior to a gig, at best, or when arranging new songs before recording, and that was it. I know it showed sometimes as well, but we didn't care. For some reason, we didn't seem to have to try too hard, it just clicked. I didn't like having a good practise just before a gig anyway – it invariably meant that we would play badly… and a bad practise usually meant a good gig; never quite worked that one out, but it always seemed true.

"I remember Hazel O'Connor knocking on the door of our rehearsal room at Bow once and asking to come in and listen for a while. That was quite nice, and very flattering, to hear how this consummate professional was in shock and intrigued enough to interrupt another band's practise, to ask to come in and listen, because she couldn't see how it was possible to sing and play that fast. We were smugly chuffed that it genuinely seemed to confuse her, these young kids who looked 'normal'… well, not 'punk' anyway, even though that was sort of what we were playing… although it was 'nearly metal' as well – how many times were we to hear that? When she left, she was totally shell-shocked, while we were laughing our heads off…"

Playing regularly around London, AYS quickly built up a strong rapport with Conflict, with whom they shared many a stage during the mid-Eighties, a collaboration that naturally resulted in AYS joining the Mortarhate roster despite the confused scratching of heads this unlikely union caused amongst punk purists. As well as an early track ('You're Just A Joke') on the 'We Don't Want Your Fucking War!' compilation, AYS even had ex-Conflict member Pauline Beck singing with them at some of their first gigs (she would perform 'her' song, from the first Conflict EP, 'I've Had Enough', albeit at a much more frantic tempo than with Conflict), and Colin Jerwood himself was rumoured to have played bass for them once.

"The relationship with Conflict, as a whole, was like that between nagging father and errant son!" reckons John. "Don't get me wrong, we were always fully aware that Conflict had been there and done it, and that we were mere pups. So we would've been foolish not to have listened to them when it mattered, even though it would not have meant us altering our core values and compromising.

"As a band to band thing, I think they appreciated the music, and, being mates and close to us, they trusted us and cared enough for us to always be on hand, to rein us back in if they felt we had pushed it too far. Still, by the very nature of the two bands, it could never always be sweetness and light, and there were certainly enough fall-outs and times of enmity… but it was mostly good, all the same.

"I was certainly closer to Colin, man to man, though, than AYS was, and could be, to Conflict, band to band. In fact, I have probably been closer to Colin, friend-wise, than I have been to anyone else, whether it was twenty years ago or not. And even further still, when Colin used to tell everyone that we were brothers, I don't recall a single person not believing it was any different, and we had some fucking great times.

And yeah, it's true: Colin did play bass for us, but only once. And it was a great day out, and such a laugh at the gig…

"It was our first gig outside of London, in Ipswich, with The Stupids and Skumdribblerz. The Stupids had also just started, and Dig (Earache) put me and Tommy, their drummer, in contact. You know how it goes – the quick correspondence, the tape trading, the phone calls… and soon, too soon really, Tommy asked us to play Ipswich with them. This was on a Thursday, and the gig was on the Saturday. Me being eager, and chuffed that not only did someone else like the same music as we did – unheard of at the time! – but had also formed a similar band, I immediately agreed. Fucking great, I thought, brilliant… the only problem was that Sean, our bassist, had a prior engagement that he couldn't get out of. And why should he anyway?

"Me and Colin went out that night as usual, and I told him all this. Remember, we'd only played a handful of gigs at this stage, so Colin, he admitted later, couldn't believe that we had gotten a gig off our own backs, far removed from the tutelage of Conflict as well, let alone outside

London... and he thought I was using the Sean thing as an excuse just to give it the big 'un, and that really there wasn't any gig!

"He should've known better really, but we used to wind each other up something chronic, so he decided to call my bluff and said he'd play bass for us. I knew he could play bass, but what about that fast, bearing in mind that we would have no chance to rehearse? Still, things always seemed to work out right one way or another, so I thought, 'Fuck it, let's do it!' Besides, and Colin will laugh at this, even if we didn't get to play, I would have had just as much pleasure from Colin bottling out at the last minute!

"Typical fuckin' Colin though, he didn't. So, we drove up there Saturday lunchtime, stopping really briefly so that he could get a basic grasp of the songs, and fair play to the geezer, he got them pretty damn quick, and the rest behind closed doors at the venue. Bearing in mind that our song structures were not exactly the simplest, and certainly faster than anything he'd played before, as the boys ran through them while I watched from the back of the room, I may still have been – justifiably – nervous, but I was also now well excited that this was actually going to work, and not be a shambles!

"Even there, and I still don't know how or why, word had spread about 'this band, AYS', who might be ringers and were 'really a USHC band, not from London at all'. So, Tommy made us headline... nice one, mate, the nerves came flooding back.

"No one knew that Col was playing bass for us, so even beyond the other rumours, there was massive intrigue as to what he was doing there, and the level of attention we received was immense. I think Colin just stuck to what he always did: he was there 'to look after me, his little brother.'

"By the time we went on, I was nervous as hell. We played about nine songs in the fastest time ever – even by our standards – and I tell you what, I don't actually remember Colin missing a note or even forgetting the somewhat awkward song structures either. I don't remember who was most amazed though, when halfway through covering 'Punk Innit?' (still don't know why we did it, but it was only the once, and we learnt it that night during the sound-check)... whether it was me, singing this song by someone else, and that someone else was thrashing fuck out of it on bass for us? Or whether it was the audience tormenting themselves with the realisation that, 'But isn't that Colin up there? Yeah, but Colin...!' Or Colin himself at the surrealism of it all... and how he managed to get us back in one piece after the gig? But that's another story...!"

"I hated the blatant obviousness of the jealousy in others of my friendship with Colin, as if that was why he supported AYS so much. Fuck 'em all, I couldn't care less if it meant sleepless nights for them, sweating about how we were 'getting on', this band diametrically opposed to the accepted 'politics' of the norm... but it did bother me that it showed an utter lack of respect for Colin, as a man. This man they viewed as their 'leader', in a world where they apparently wanted no leaders? And it was only because their needs were so selfish that men as human beings didn't matter. And I didn't mean just 'fuck 'em all', I meant 'kill 'em all!' The selfish, vile, hypocritical, lying cunts – and no apologies for that word, either – that they were."

AYS entered Alaska Studios in Waterloo with engineer Iain O'Higgins and recorded six songs for a proposed 'split-cassette' release with The Stupids, that was being mooted as the first release for a Mortarhate offshoot. However, when Colin heard the session he decided it was way too good for merely a tape release, and it became 1985's 'Expect No Mercy...' single.

"The 7" was okay, but I think the overriding thing about it that confused us was that it didn't sound like the bands we listened to and loved, who had inspired us so much. Well, how could it? We liked its rawness and obvious sense of urgency, and we liked the guitar sound and the Bad Brains snap of the snare, and also that it was like nothing else from the UK at the time... and certainly like nothing else on Mortarhate.

"We recorded it mostly in one take, and it was over in an hour. Fucking great! Poison Idea did it with 'Pick Your King', so that was good enough for us, and, more importantly, professionalism as such meant nothing. We loved leaving the mistakes on it, just as much as we loved the good parts!

"I also liked the fact that Colin would let us have a plain white ink on black card cover – like the first Dr. Know LP on Mystic, of course – and that we could have an insert like our favourite US bands, and I'd even admit to liking the unanimously great reviews it had; all the opinions it generated and the comments it received... it was all very flattering and surprising.

"By its nature, the kind comments justified its release, but, concomitant with that, it led, and still does, to what we hated about it all. The discomfort, that feeling of self-betrayal, that the record condemned us to. While we laughed at and despised all those other bands who denied forming bands for any other reason other than ego, here we were doing exactly the same."

John Cato of AYS, live at the Old Arts Centre, London, November 1985, picture by Paul May.

An energetic, rampant slab of emotionally charged hardcore, held together by the skin of its teeth with some instinctive yet impressive musicianship, the single boasted amongst its tracks an effectively brutal rendition of 'In My Eyes', a tee-total anthem originally by Washington straight edge legends, Minor Threat.

"I wrote to [Minor Threat vocalist] Ian [MacKaye], yeah of course, but he generally used to telephone back. A busy man, Ian; we met a few times whenever he was in London, and Minor Threat were undoubtedly one of those very few bands that have influenced everyone at some time or another, to varying degrees, whose whole essence is capable of moving the listener on a very profound level. Well, they did it to me, and we were just fortunate enough that all of us in the band felt that, and at the same time...

"I think that was because, like The Antz and Crass, they marked a time in the development and movement of our lives. And let's face it, any band could be cited as an example of that for one reason or another, but we're not that cheap, not so easily bought, and the world of difference between those bands and any contemporaries they may have had, is the unflinching moral compunction to be so completely and openly honest, following what they felt was right at whatever cost, because it had to be done.

"But I've got to make clear that AYS were never a straight edge band 'in extremis', certainly not by today's standards, and we definitely didn't feel that because Minor Threat were, we had to be too. Their influence wasn't that domineering. Our objection was to overindulgence, where oblivion was the goal above all else. And it was because this was especially prevalent among those that had the audacity to pretend they had greater goals to achieve – that were lying again – that we hated it so much.

"We never, even in the slightest, had a problem with anyone having a few beers, for example, but we did with the excessiveness of ten, and the problems it would invariably cause, the time it would waste… but mostly just with the hypocrisy and pretence of it all.

"Let's face it: everyone has something they use as a crutch, that's all we were pointing out, be it drugs, sex, alcohol, records, coffee, shopping, food… whatever. We didn't even have a problem with that, just that there is a world of difference between indulgence and obsession. Reliance is a weakness; it's very easy, it's lazy, it's a cop-out, and it's only a very small step from use to abuse. And that's why we would have had just as much of a problem back then with the straight edge kids of today, when common sense fails and extremity becomes the norm."

The band then entered the studio to record their blinding 'Someplace Special' 12", which would prove to be their epitaph, it being released posthumously in 1987 after they'd split late the previous year. Opening with a thumping instrumental that recalled COC or the Bad Brains with its impromptu time changes, it was another high-octane excursion into the realms of USHC that built upon the strong foundations laid with the preceding single. And with uncomfortably honest lyrics such as 'Bad Blood', it seemed that AYS were still intent on antagonising as many people as they possibly could before they inevitably self-destructed.

"I wouldn't agree that we were antagonistic to the exclusion of all else, but neither were we not gonna call people on their bullshit as we saw it, if we thought it warranted that. We were just going to be honest, and if that meant upset and condemnation, so what? Fuck 'em, we felt it necessary, and at least we could look ourselves in the mirror each morning.

"And so, it wasn't antagonism that refused to allow us to play certain gigs if we didn't support the cause or group the benefit was for; it was just a refusal to be hypocritical. And it was not antagonism that questioned the crazy ideas and myths propagated by certain bands who wilfully conducted their own lives completely contrarily to the words that came out of their mouths.

"And it was not antagonism that overrode the disgust and revulsion we had for that falseness and cheapness which motivated our desire to expose it. It was not antagonism and its intent which prevented us from really caring about what was happening in Ethiopia at the time – as expressed by the 12" song 'Bad Blood' – or remaining completely unaffected and unmoved by it, tragedy though it undoubtedly was… just the grim realisation that I didn't care, couldn't trick myself into wanting to either. I just wonder how many others might, truly, deep down, have felt the same?"

If AYS fitted in anywhere with the ideals capitulated by the anarcho-punk scene, it would have been with the nihilist strand of the movement, proclaiming belief in nothing but themselves.

"I don't even know if we were nihilists… or anything really. I don't actually think we were wholly at odds with every part of the anarcho-punk movement either – just some of it… those parts which were so disgusting, their vileness could only reflect on the whole of that scene and overwhelm the good there was in it, a lot of which we even admired. We even got on well with most of the bands, some obviously more than others, and always only those that we respected. Others we appreciated and liked as decent, truly caring people, as friends. Others were just a joke, a truly sick fucking joke.

"Though they and we may have seemed to ostensibly be diametrically opposed politically, if you wish; essentially the goal was the same… just completely different ways of expressing it. Those who meant it, truly meant it, and of course, we respected and admired them; we were just sick and tired of the contradictions, the clichés, the lies, and basically just hearing the same thing over and over again. If the cause was so right, then the people involved were so wrong!"

Despite the 12" coming with no proper track-listing or lyric insert – all the packaging in fact looking like something of an afterthought – John still rates it as his favourite AYS release.

"The vinyl output is merely what it always was: nineteen-odd songs by four kids from twenty years ago. I'm proud of a lot of things we did, and cringe at others; I still wouldn't change a thing though, not even the bits that half-a-lifetime on still make me squirm. It was good in its time; we had fun, made a point, got people to think, even when they disliked the manner it was conveyed in... but mostly we had fun.

"I much preferred the 12" though, not only because we were much more musically competent by then, but also because we really had done our best, and most of all, it could not have been bettered lyrically as a definitive articulation and expression of the band. Even now, if we had to do it all over again, I would put the same words to those songs as we did then.

"Occasionally I still regret, although nowhere near as much as I used to, that the songs on the 12" were cut in the wrong order, which was, we felt, extremely important at the time, and it came out with no lyric sheet or our design in the middle of the record where the Mortarhate 'N's were. But I've got to be honest, that was solely down to me and nothing to do with Mortarhate. It didn't come out for over a year after we recorded it, and about nine months after we'd split. At the time my partner was heavily pregnant with our daughter and had about two weeks to go, when I was informed of the date of the cutting and asked to send the insert artwork and label design...

"Well, to be frank, if I didn't care before, I certainly cared a whole lot less by then, and with the imminent arrival of our first child, let's just say it wasn't exactly high on my agenda. Yeah, I regret it because I think the record deserved it, and I regret Mortarhate being blamed for letting it ride when it was really down to me."

AYS played their last ever show, with Conflict of course, at the Camden Electric Ballroom in September 1986, and in true AYS fashion it was a frustrating anti-climax.

"It was the worst gig we ever played. It was two weeks before my 21st birthday, and we had no further gigs planned; we had enjoyed ourselves, but it just wasn't fun anymore. Subconsciously, even if the others didn't, I knew that I wanted to call it quits; I'd had enough.

"We didn't even play well, although whether that was because our interest had waned that much or not, I don't know... maybe. And if we were that jaded already, being denied a sound-check made it worse. The sound was god-awful, and I think it amplified our general lack of enthusiasm.

"If I had any regret I was being forced to admit to, it would be not trying – all of us – to play well, and not finishing in the manner we had started. The one redeeming thing, the only consolation, is that we didn't do that whole grandiose bullshit thing of announcing it was our last gig ever, to declare that it was over. And yeah, it was over, even before our last twenty minutes onstage.

"But personally I couldn't give a fuck how AYS are remembered – I didn't care then, and care even less now. We did what we thought was right, we did it properly; we had no regrets or remorse because, for good or ill, it was honest and we knew it.

"I admit it would grate when people tried to convince themselves that we did it purely out of mischief because the truth was unpalatable... that we had no greater purpose, or, at least, they could not grasp what it was. And so, if I did care twenty years on, I'd hate to think it was the same now. But I really don't care at all... they're not worth it, nor were we, and it is twenty years ago, after all. Nostalgia is nothing more than record collecting, and how did Peni put it? 'The past is past is farce, is farce...'."

And as for the apparent about-turn in his ideals – from the libertarian ambitions he seemed to nurture whilst fronting AYS, to the deplorable white separatist stance taken in later years – John, now a father of "the three most beautiful children in the whole world", remains defiantly unapologetic... although he is careful to point out that the views he expresses on this subject are purely his own, and shouldn't reflect on the other band members.

"Ideals? Nothing has changed over those twenty years!" he spits with feeling, and it's worth pointing out here that John was a member of the British Movement long before he ever fronted a hardcore punk band. "Those who knew us – okay, especially me – will say, 'He's always been like that, he always will be; John is John... whatever he has done, or is supposed to have done, it's no surprise... he was always like that!' And it's true: nothing is different, for good or ill.

"I guess if there was any reason that people would want to read about AYS twenty years on, it would be this somewhat morbid curiosity about 'dodgy politics' – as if AYS weren't bad enough already. And sometimes there is truth in the world of bullshit punk rumours, and usually no smoke without some sort of fire, but I have nothing to hide, and certainly nothing to be ashamed of.

"I've already explained what motivated AYS, that we weren't purely intent on antagonism, that we weren't cynical to the expense of all else – there really was a higher and greater goal. And personally, I haven't changed my whole world-view one iota in those twenty years. That libertarianism that you rightly believe prompted 'Flex Your Heart' back then is the same libertarianism I still feel today...

"It's just that it might not seem acceptable in the parameters set by your own ideas of freedom, and it's articulated in terms you could not fail to feel uncomfortable with. But there's still no difference now from then, whatsoever.

"I may 'hate' – it's a healthy and vital emotion – but I am not a 'hater', and there's a world of difference. And that is why I hate the right wing as much as I hate the left, both of whom are guilty of being incapable of love and mostly lead by hatred.

"Look, I'm no angel, but I'm no demon either. In fact, you know what? Ask me if I'm racist now, and was I back then? And I'll tell you, fucking right I am! And damn right I was back then too. Like I said, I haven't changed in twenty years; nothing ever does.

"But my racism is rooted in love – of my own kind – not in hatred of anyone else."

The burning question that needs to be answered for many reading this book though is: has John Cato ever deliberately hurt anyone simply because of their race?

"No, I can truthfully answer that I have never, ever hurt anyone because of their race. And as for those who have, I can think of nothing more vile. What sort of creature would do such a thing anyway, whether provoked or not?

"Of course, if it was unavoidable, then yes, I would defend myself to whatever extent necessary – as would anyone – but that has nothing whatsoever to do with race. To be honest, it is not something I have even had to deal with; I tend not to put myself in situations where it may happen. Others do, seek it out in fact, as though it is almost desirable. Well, it's not; not only does it serve no purpose... it damages the long-term goal, which they are probably unable to understand anyway. It is people like this that I despise as much as the collaborators and agents of our real enemies. Real racism, real National Socialism, is borne of positive and profound ideals – not the psychotic hatred of non-whites! It's a shame more people don't understand this."

The controversy continues unabated...

SELECT DISCOGRAPHY

7"s:
'Expect No Mercy...' (Mortarhate, 1985)

12"s:
'Someplace Special' (Mortarhate, 1987)

At A Glance:
In 2005, Mortarhate released 'Someplace Special' on CD complete with the 'Expect No Mercy...' single as bonus tracks, and whatever your feelings on John's twisted political leanings, there's no denying the potency of the musical legacy AYS left behind.

Despite an all-too-brief existence, during which they never really managed to extricate themselves from the shadow of their mentors Conflict, **LIBERTY** from North Kent still quickly established themselves as one of the more musically ambitious and politically militant of the second wave of UK anarcho bands.

Although formed in 1980 by three school friends – vocalist Mark Wallis, bassist Graham Clench and drummer Derek Banks – they didn't play their first show until 1982, at the Dartford YMCA, and didn't really get up and running properly as a band until Mick Harrington (who had played briefly with Admit You're Shit) joined on guitar in May 1984.

"Kalibir Bains was our first guitarist, then a guy called Alan, and then Terry," explains Mark. "And we even had a female singer, Lisa Dillon, for a short time, but she left due to musical and personal differences. We used to gather at the Red Lion pub in Gravesend, where bands such as Conflict, Flux, Dirt, and Anthrax would play for 50p… great days! That was where it began for us: fanzines and protest bands, a weekly event. None of us had been in bands before either, until we met Mick at the Red Lion.

"The Red Lion was the root of the scene in Gravesend, where the beat of the drums and the rumble of the bass guitar and the hard-hitting vocals rocked the foundations of the system we all loved to hate. That was the reason we formed the band anyway, to get our message across on the many issues in life; we were dissatisfied with the system, we wanted to create an alternative, a voice for the little man on the street."

"We used to practice at a church hall near to Derek's house in Dartford," recalls Mick. "I lived in Gravesend, a train ride away. We used to practice every Tuesday night, but none of us could drive so getting equipment to practices was a nightmare. I'd have to lug my guitar and amp, with the help of a willing (or unlucky!) mate on the train and then we'd have to walk about two-and-a-half miles to the practice. Even later, when we had Steve, Ray and Oggy in the band, we still practised in Dartford. That meant Steve had to travel from North London, Ray from East London and Oggy from Sevenoaks.

"When I joined Liberty we had quite a good scene in Dartford, with a few local bands we would play in church halls, youth clubs, etc. We never had much aggro at the early gigs, the odd divvy skinhead but not a lot else, which is surprising. Crass wouldn't play Dartford or Gravesend because of the local (Bexleyheath, Crayford and Welling) skins… and, sure enough, when they did eventually make it to Crayford for a gig, there was trouble with Nazis."

Like so many of the bands in this book, Liberty were quick to pick up on the raw, righteous anger being peddled by Crass as an alternative to what the media perceived as punk rock, and it was a logical step from there to the heavier-handed approach of Conflict.

"I remember my first hearing of Crass; it blew my mind," says Mark fondly. "They gave me answers to my confusion, and later I visited them at the Epping commune which still stands today… the house that Crass built!

"Punk was the vehicle to vent our frustrations, but anarcho-punk had the lyrics that educated us. It was also a movement for everyday people to build an alternative music network, independent of the big bosses of capitalism and popular music. Anarchist squat gigs were our examples; anti-system videos, books, collectives and, of course, the message of Crass, all in black to mourn the system. Steve Ignorant made Johnny Rotten sound like Gary Glitter!"

"I'd grown up listening to the [Angelic] Upstarts, [Cockney] Rejects, Menace, and The Lurkers," adds Mick. "So I'd always been drawn to the more 'street' punk scene than the hippy sounds of Crass, but the first time I saw Conflict all that changed. They were a band that talked sense but played street punk. I remember seeing them at the Red Lion when John Jacobs [of The 4-Skins] was their roadie; I think he might even have been playing drums that night…? Anarcho-punk just made sense to us; the idea of being in control of your own destiny and not having MPs, etc., telling you what you can and cannot do is everyone's dream, surely?"

In September 1984, Liberty entered DTS Studios in Chatham to record their first demo, which they began selling at shows. With actual 'product' to hawk, and growing friendly with bands such as State Hate and Stigma, they began gigging with increasing frequency around South London, including several shows at the Woolwich Polytechnic. A song recorded at one of these shows, 'As Fools Rush In', was even included on the 1985 compilation, 'Communicate! Live At The Thames Poly', on TPSU Records, that saw Liberty rubbing shoulders with an eclectic mix of artists that included Sonic Youth, The Mission and The Membranes.

"We also joined the Greenwich Musicians Co-operative, which was a really diverse collective," says Mick. "It was 'home' to all sorts of people and bands. The collective was based in and around Greenwich and we used to meet at the old dockyard at Woolwich. The co-op would organise gigs and we all took turns in arranging gigs for the bands in it. We played some lovely places in and around the area – old houses converted into community centres etc. – and it was here that we met a poet called Pete Dog and also the Bulbous Skunk Cabbages, who both became part of the Liberty collective.

"We liked playing to different crowds and in new venues as a lot of the scene had become stagnant; the same bands, the same people… and most of the anarcho bands were singing about the same stuff we were. But we'd play with anyone willing to play with us. We wanted and needed to open up new avenues of interest, so we asked the Cabbage guys to play flute and saxophone on a couple of our songs, just to see what it sounded like; we liked it, and so did they, which was cool."

It was about this time that a strong, lasting friendship began to form between Liberty and Conflict, which resulted in Colin Jerwood inviting the band to appear on the 'We Don't Want Your Fucking War' compilation, with the track 'Diluted Rebellion', alongside many of their partners in musical crime such as AYS, State Hate and Stigma. It was issued through Mortarhate in early '85 and went Top Five in the Indies, boosting the band's profile overnight.

"We walked alongside Conflict from their first days of gigging in Eltham, Mottingham, and Gravesend," reminisces Mark. "We grew close to them as mates, performed live together, played in the studio together and shared an anarchist vision inspired by Crass. In the early days, Colin was an anarchist living on an estate in Eltham with John and Paco, surrounded by NF skinheads. Colin stood by his beliefs and fought his way there; every time Conflict faced an obstacle they would kick it down – hence the name! We joined in their fight for the anarchist movement, both mentally and physically. They stood on their own and did it alone, great days… good lads, always; that will never change. Colin, with his spiky hair, one side black, the other white, fronted a band that's really stood the test of time. Conflict gave Liberty their first real chance to record; they brought the message of challenge from the commune to the street, and we took up that challenge with them."

The actual song 'Diluted Rebellion', with its vehement closing couplet, 'So, punk is dead and anarchy's a farce, because people still use it to wipe their arse', was a damning indictment of a glue bag-infested punk scene that so often seemed to wallow apathetically in its own self-pity. Like many other anarcho bands, Liberty dreamt of a punk scene that could mean so much more than just music and escapism.

"Punk music without protest words is just another sell-out fashion vehicle," spits Mark with feeling. "Worshipping punk bands as pop stars? Obsessed by individuality, yet we couldn't stand together… but anarchy should have been the common goal. Something new had to take place, a wake up call; the system remained well while we were all sleeping. Actions always speak louder than words; I wanted to know then, as I do now, what we will all be doing in ten or twenty years time… part of capitalism or an alternative to it? Sold out or still resisting? So many bands had gone before that preached the message, we had no excuse. People were using the punk movement for their own private gains, modern day perverts like McLaren of old. The anarchist movement had the ideas and the numbers, the ability to be a proper force; the danger was not to become another cardboard cut-out clown in the rock'n'roll circus, peddling yet more state-controlled pop music.

"Liberty wanted to spread the message of anti-state to a wider audience by whatever means possible, to change minds was the objective. Playing to an anarchist/punk audience was becoming like preaching to the converted, where's the challenge? You can only see the light in the darkness. We wanted to change the anarchist punk movement, to link with all alternative music, united in the message of protest as the left wing was alongside the anarchist movement in direct action. Strength in numbers, for punk was an attitude not a style of music."

Following the positive feedback from 'We Don't Want Your Fucking War', Colin offered Liberty the chance to do their own single on Mortarhate, and the band entered Alaska Studios in April 1985 to record the 'Our Voice Is Tomorrow's Hope' EP. By this time Steve Flack (then-partner of occasional Conflict vocalist, Mandy Spokes) had joined the band as second vocalist, adding yet more intensity to Mark's already passionate vocal delivery. Four fine tunes quite literally crackling with anger, the EP made No. 12 in

Liberty live at Salisbury Arts Centre, November 1985, picture by Marc Freeman.

the Indies, with the band undertaking concerted gigging in support of the release... and more discreet activities in support of the ideals espoused therein.

"I still listen to the EP," reckons Mick. "The production is a bit weak; we were very naive and did all the tracks live, but the sentiments covered in the songs all still stand today – just think the Iraq war, fox hunting, etc. And all of us were involved in some form of direct action or other; wrecking butcher shops, hunt sabbing and the passive things, like marches. We also went to Greenham Common and Molesworth airbases, and played a lot of benefit gigs for the ALF [Animal Liberation Front], SEAL [South East Animal Liberation] and the striking miners. The dream of anarchy was wearing a bit thin though; unfortunately you realise that there are just too many idiots around for

it to work. People were wearing leather jackets with 'Meat Means Murder' painted on the back of them, for fuck's sake!"

Soon after the single though, Graham Clench left, and was replaced by Rob 'Gonk' Lovelock, formerly bassist with The Unorthodox, who only lasted a few gigs himself, and then Paul Forster of The Spice Of Life joined… only to be replaced himself by Ray Searle. Hope you're following all this?

"We met Ray at the Plough And Harrow pub in Leytonstone, East London. He and his mate, Graham Adkins, were putting together a fanzine called 'Activated' and they asked us for an interview. We were playing with the Arch Criminals – who were sort of label mates as they had recorded for the Mortarhate offshoot, Fight Back Records – and we hit it off right away as we all shared the same passions in life: punk, politics and football."

But before Liberty could relax into the stability of a steady line-up, yet another founding member, Derek Banks, left for pastures new ("He had left college and got a job in a bakers, but the combination of late nights and early mornings had started to catch up with him…"), with Oggy from State Hate stepping in to fill the vacant drum stool just in time for an eventful national tour with Conflict in early 1986.

"That tour with Conflict was the best! Wales, Leeds, Birmingham, Sunderland, Brighton, Deptford, Woolwich, Islington… up and down the country… always skint, of course! Empty pockets, touring in a van, crushed together; sitting on amps, guitars and drums… card games and counselling sessions would take place, in the belief that one day we would all be able to rule ourselves. We had good times and good vibes; the crowds were great and the memories even better, meeting other bands and seeing the scenes in other areas.

"One night we were dropped back in the early hours and missed our trains home, so we slept in Eltham Park, freezing until the next day… then it was off again to another gig somewhere. On a number of occasions police arrived when we clashed with Nazis, and on one night there was virtually a mini-riot against NF skins and casuals… beer bottles, broken pool cues and the whole she-bang, but victory was ours in the end. During the tour at Brighton, a whole coach load of us hit the beaches and funfair, taking over the giant slide; we had a right laugh on the road."

"The bond between the bands was very strong," confirms Mick. "The threat of violence was never too far away, a lot of gigs used to end up in mini riots, but Lancaster was a particular exception. We'd travelled all the way up there from Kent in a box van with Conflict and a few mates, and we never got to play a fucking note. The venue was quite small – held about 200 punters – and we were told by the owners and the police not to exceed this. Anyway, when everything was set up and sound-checked, Conflict nipped out to get something to eat, leaving us on the door. The venue soon filled to bursting point and, as we began to turn people away, 30 or 40 local punks turned up. We couldn't let them in but they decided they were coming in anyway. A mass brawl started in the entrance hall and we got kicked up the fucking staircase. Someone ran out to get Conflict and, when they turned up, it was a 'them and us' situation, a sort of Mexican standoff; us at the front of the stage, a few locals from Sellafield with us, and all these arseholes facing us.

"Conflict had a bag of 'surprises' for just such an occasion, and we all armed ourselves with coshes, baseball bats and starting handles, etc. Just as we were about to steam the bastards, the Old Bill turned up in force. The owner had phoned and told them that we were only defending our equipment, but it must have been a bizarre sight – a tooled up crew asking the police to leave us alone for ten minutes, so we could dish out some much-deserved justice. But the Old Bill wouldn't – couldn't – do it. All good, clean fun, I suppose. I don't want to forget any of that tour, it was excellent. Unfortunately, the last date was Newcastle and only those who were there know what really happened that night…!"

After the tour, Liberty returned to Alaska Studios to record their album, 'The People Who Care Are Angry', once again for Mortarhate. A wonderfully diverse set of protest songs, delivered with a vigilante fervour, that saw the band incorporating a whole range of eclectic influences into their sound, the album hinted at great things to come from a band seemingly unconcerned about musical and social barriers. Sadly it was to be their last release, as a disillusioned Steve left before it was even finished, and the band fragmented soon after, but even without the final flourishes that were planned as the icing on the cake, the LP stands as a sterling reminder of Liberty's potent vision.

"We were becoming frustrated playing to the converted in punk ghettos," offers Mark. "We wanted to press on with taking the message to a wider audience by playing with more diverse bands. The tracks for the LP were songs we had played live for many years, but we wanted to cross boundaries too, so we had an acoustic song sung by a local Dartford socialist folk singer, Tony Chater (R.I.P), and a classical piano track by a trained musician, 'Shemy'. The horns were courtesy of chart musos, Pig Bag, who were friends of Colin, and the poetry by our mate, Pete the Dog. We wanted to make a difference by raising awareness in all circles. It doesn't matter if you listen to Crass, Conflict, Bob Marley, Nas, Sizzla, Capleton, Grandmaster Flash, Bounty Killer or Billy Bragg… as long as it's protest songs for revolutionary minds, a poor people's movement from the ghetto."

Mick: "The album was recorded at the same time as Conflict were recording 'The Ungovernable Force', so it was an unforgettable time; the Liberty/Exit-stance 'choir' feature on a couple of tracks. The studio was like an open house for us at the time; we would wander in at any time and someone would be recording: Conflict, AYS or Exit-stance.

"The Conflict/Liberty/Mortarhate thing was like one big family. We used to meet up in Eltham

Park on Sundays and play footie, with jumpers for goal posts. Colin and Paco used to do a disco down the Poly and we'd go week in, week out; sometimes we'd do the door. Colin also put on gigs at the Crypt in Deptford, under St Paul's Church, and we would do the door or the record/T-shirt stall. We would also do stage security at their bigger gigs. So the recordings and the tour were just an extension of all that."

Despite having tours of Ireland (with Stalag 17) and America (with Conflict) in the offing, Liberty split before the album was even in the racks.

"We had experienced many changes, we were tired and skint," says Mark regretfully. "We all decided to go our separate ways; losing Steve was the final blow and personal pressure took over. There was a need to move away for some of the band, to channel energy from music into action, to do what we had been singing about."

True to his words, Mark, still a committed vegetarian (and now a father of two and a social worker in London), travelled Africa and the Middle East doing aid work, and spent several years living in the Bobo Shanti Rasta community.

"After Liberty split, I pissed around in a few bands for a while and then settled down," Mick's story is a very different one, but no less genuine or valid. "We all lost touch, but recently I've met up with Mark, Paul and Derek again. I still go to see bands and I still love punk. I'm nearly 40 and it's still fun going to gigs and seeing kids enjoying music. It's funny to see the British punk bands trying to sound like American emo stuff and the Yanks trying to look like the old British style of punk. I think it was the Icons of Filth who said, 'If the label fits, fuck off!' A lot of individuality has gone and bands tend to try to pigeon hole themselves in categories, i.e. emocore, skacore, hardcore, etc., but, let's face it, from Agnostic Front to Zounds, it's all punk, innit? And I still love it.

"We may have started out as an anarcho-punk band; we had the same hopes and ideals as a lot of the bands/people in the movement, but I think we soon realised that in order to better one's self you have to progress. Anarchy is a state of mind; it's something very personal, and every person will have a different view on what they want out of life. But that's freedom, the right to choose your own path..."

"That Liberty left our mark as a protest band is enough for me," quips Mark. "Lyrics first, music after... trying to unite the left wing activists with the anarchist movement, a common struggle to complement music with action. We did not put ourselves in boxes... challenge brought the truth and caused offence, but if only one word, one song, one lyric, opened up one person's mind to challenge the system, it would have all been worth it."

Liberty have recently reformed, with a new single recorded for an as yet undecided label, and several gigs scheduled to promote it.

SELECT DISCOGRAPHY

7"s:
'Our Voice Is Tomorrow's Hope' (Mortarhate, 1985)

LPs:
'The People Who Care Are Angry' (Mortarhate, 1986)

At A Glance:
Mortarhate's 2004 CD release of 'The People Who Care Are Angry' also includes the 'Our Voice...' EP as a welcome bonus, neatly compiling all the band's major Eighties releases on one disc, complete with artwork and lyrics.

Not to be confused with the fun-loving New York metal act of the same name, Gravesend's ANTHRAX were a convincing anarcho-punk band, that dwelt musically somewhere between Crass's unforgiving rants and Conflict's violent bluster, but with a pleasing edge to their sound that was all their own.

"We started when we were at school," recalls vocalist Gary 'Osker' Budd, "Although [second guitarist] Shaun [Connolly] joined later on; he was a friend of Gareth [Davies], our bass player. We all went to Longfield School together in the beginning, which is where we started the band up, then a lot of 'em left – Dee [David Cubitt] went to Gravesend Grammar, and Shaun was at Meopham School with Gareth...

David and Osker of Anthrax, early 1982.

"We were still in contact with each other though, and we used to rehearse every dinner time in the church hall. Rob Challice was on bass, Paul ['Fod'] Forder was the singer. It was Fod that got me into punk, if I remember rightly; he used to bring all these records round, and we started listening to John Peel and stuff. I was on drums to start with, and we had this geezer called Willie on guitar.

"Eventually I moved to vocals, Gareth came in on guitar, 'cos Rob was still on bass, and we got Peter [Stratton] in on drums – we kept badgering him 'cos his father had bought him a drum kit and he'd had some drum lessons... and then we got Dee in on guitar as well; he used to live at the end of my road and I knew him 'cos his brother used to go banger racing with my brother, but he was a bit of a recluse... he never came out of his house! I used to call for him on a Friday night and he would give me money to go and buy him punk records from the Gravesend market on Saturday morning, and I'd take them back to his house, and he'd vanish back inside! But then his mum bought him a guitar from the Kay's catalogue and he went from there..."

Initially called Vivisection, although they never played a gig under that name, Anthrax also had a female vocalist, Sue Huntley, in their ranks for a short while, although she and Rob left after the first gig and moved to Hackney, where they formed Faction.

"When we were all at Longfields School, I used to do a fanzine with Rob and Fod called Enigma, which was quite big at the time... it was pretty well established on the anarcho-punk scene anyway; it even came with a free patch! We printed them ourselves on this old roll press in the church hall where we practised. It used to all get mailed to my dad's house, and the parcels kept getting opened, and my dad used to really worry about his mail being tampered with!

"And we had the fanzine before the band, which really helped when it came to contacts for gigs and stuff... there was another fanzine in London we were in touch with called Fack, ran by this couple, Dave and Julie, and we knocked about with them for a while, and they were a lot older than us, and introduced us to a lot of people like Conflict... we actually went to their first gig in Eltham.

"We got quite friendly with Conflict early on, although we got beaten up when we went to see them a second time in Eltham! By the Eltham skinheads, too... who were all Conflict's friends, but for some unknown reason didn't like other people coming into their area. We knew 'em all, but they still beat us up after the gig, which was quite bizarre.

"Most of our early gigs were with Conflict [although their first gig – the only one with Rob and Sue in the band – was actually at an Irish pub in Gravesend, the Hit 'N' Miss, in late 1980], and a bit later on, we played a lot with X-Cretas and Naked... we had quite a little community going in the Kent area really, with Carnage and The Committed and so on. We could always fill a coach for gigs further afield, which was good, 'cos we'd turn up mob-handed and have fifty Anthrax fans there straight away, even if most of them were in other bands that we knew! We'd play every week... we played once a week for years in fact..."

And many of those gigs were at the Red Lion, a much-loved Gravesend venue, where Anthrax

had a weekly residency and were able to invite many of their anarcho-punk peers to play alongside them, in exchange for gigs with those same bands in their own areas.

"The Red Lion was really good," remembers Osker fondly. "It was a Hell's Angels pub originally, but we played there every Tuesday night, and had all these different bands travel down here. The landlord used to let us do what we wanted there, and the gigs used to do really well; it was only a small place, with a small stage... we could barely all fit on it... but we used to ram it to the rafters.

"The best thing about it was: we never got any trouble there, none at all. It was only when we went outside Gravesend, when we started playing London and stuff, that we had trouble at our gigs. We played the Blue Coat Boy in Islington, sometime in '82 [Saturday March 26th, with The X-Cretas and Lost Cherrees], and we were the only band that night to get out of there alive! We were pretty lucky if I remember, 'cos someone ran through the bar with an axe. We seemed to have this tendency to get out of places at just the right time...

"That was the only thing I really dreaded about it at the end, the constant violence. I remember we did this anti-glue-sniffing gig once, in Bishops Stortford, and it was full of glue-sniffers! And it really kicked off, but luckily enough, the guys who did the PA sorted them out... but it was all trouble, every gig was trouble. Except the ones in Gravesend... well, it did kick off in Gravesend once, but that wasn't at the Red Lion; that was at the Town Hall, when all the Gravesend soul boys started..."

"That was a Naked gig," adds Shaun, "And all I can remember was Tony, their singer, flying off the stage with the microphone stand and giving it some... our drummer was outside launching dustbin lids at 'em all... it was a bit mad."

In 1981, Anthrax saved up the £90 required for a day in Oakwood Studios, Herne Bay, and recorded seven tracks, one of which – 'All The Wars' – made it onto the 'Bullshit Detector 2' compilation released by Crass the following year. Although an obviously inexperienced recording done on a shoestring budget, there's a compelling simplicity about the buzzing guitars and thundering toms that ensures repeated listening.

"That was what made the Anthrax sound," observes Shaun, of their distinctive guitar tone. "Because Dee played so fast, and had his overdrive set to maximum, it was like one, long constant noise, like a buzzing chainsaw basically – you could hear the notes changing as he played, but not his actual picking. His right hand was so fast, none of us could keep up with him!"

The track on 'Bullshit...' also brought the band to the attention of Pete Stennet's Small Wonder Records, who released their striking debut EP, 'They've Got It All Wrong'; it subsequently spent six weeks in the Independent Charts upon its release in early March 1983, peaking at a very respectable No. 9. The provocative artwork, depicting a gang of punks jerking mindlessly at the end of puppeteer strings, being controlled by the bands that apparently sought to liberate them, was provided by 'The Tasty M.', a graphic designer friend of Dee's, who also provided the cover for the band's second single.

"It was a group called The Snails who took a copy of our demo they'd bought off us into Pete's shop, and he just rang us up," reveals Osker. "It was weird really, 'cos we used to travel all the way across London to the Small Wonder shop to buy records – and all of a sudden he rang us up and asked us to do a single! We had to sign a contract and stuff, because he'd just been shafted by The Cure – he'd recorded 'Killing An Arab' with them, with no contract binding them to him, and they'd gone off with Polydor on the back of it. Anyway, he gave us these contracts but we didn't read any of it, we just signed 'em...

"We recorded it at Southern Studios, but unfortunately it was with an engineer who didn't like Pete! So that wasn't very successful sound-wise... it was a bit of a push anyway, 'cos we recorded it in the evenings, every night after work. But Pete used to live next door to John Peel, and they were good friends, so at least we got plenty of airplay..."

Gareth was replaced by Lawrence from The X-Cretas on bass (who would later join the mighty Antisect), and Shaun was recruited as an additional guitarist, just in time for Anthrax to make the first of two trips to Holland during spring 1983.

"Because of the fanzine, I was in contact with The Ex over there," reckons Osker, "And I wrote to them and said we wanted to play on the continent, and they set up this mini-tour for us, saying they would set up so many gigs in this certain period of time. Then they said, 'How many of ya are coming?' To which I gingerly replied, 'Thirteen!' And they just said, 'No problem...' They paid us, fed us, put us up, and gave us two crates of beer per gig..."

Osker of Anthrax, pictured relaxing at the Moonlight Club.

Anthrax live at
the Red Lion,
Gravesend, 1982.

"It was amazing," smiles Shaun. "We'd be ushered into each venue to have a meal, while someone else unloaded our gear! We'd never been treated so well...

"But we even had trouble over there with skinheads, though thankfully one of the geezers we took with us sorted all that out... the Dutch lot we were with were really nervous about it all, but we had this rather large guy with us, who wasn't an aggressive bloke, but really went for it when the occasion demanded!"

A single on Crass followed just a few months later, 'Capitalism Is Cannibalism', the record that many consider the band's defining moment, and although there's no doubting its lyrical potency ('You might have a title in front of your name, but everyone's shit still smells the same!') and understated musical power, Osker isn't overly keen on it as a representation of Anthrax's real sound.

"After the 'Bullshit Detector 2' album, Eve Libertine [from Crass] rang us up and asked if we wanted to do a single. It was weird, 'cos we recorded for three days with Penny and John Loder [at Southern Studios], and when they mixed it, they took our bassist Gareth off the recording! And added all these little bits... and it ended up sounding nothing like the original songs. Basically we ended up sounding like Crass! Personally I prefer the first demo we did, but we were young, and it was good; we enjoyed it, no real regrets or anything."

Licking their wounds somewhat – morale not helped any when an interview with Winston Smith for Sounds never actually made it to print ("Garry Bushell pulled the plug on it, deciding he didn't want any more of 'that kind of punk' in there!") – the band returned to Oakwood, where they had tracked their very first demo, to cut a track, 'It'll Be Alright On The Night', for Mortarhate's [early 1984] compilation, 'Who? What? Why? When? Where?' It was to be the last thing Anthrax would record together (although the 1982 demo version of 'Violence Is Violence' was included posthumously on the 'We Don't Want Your Fucking War' compilation in 1985), with the band splitting before the record was even out, right after a disastrous second tour of Holland.

"We never meant it to turn out so different to the singles," says Osker carefully, of the surprisingly melodic 'It'll Be Alright On The Night', "But the engineer bought a Mini Moog into the studio, and Dee started tweaking about on that, and suddenly the Mini Moog is on the recording! You know what I mean? Dee was like, 'Oh, what else you got?' It was that kind of session...

"I just got pissed off with it all in the end though," he adds, on his reasons for quitting the band. "I'd been doing it for so long, and I was just wondering how many more gigs we were going to do that were going to get trashed... it was such a caper, trying not to get beaten up all the time. And we were really lucky not to get seriously hurt a few times, we really were...

"I remember we were meant to be playing this gig with Conflict, at the Moonlight Club, and when we turned up, the promoter said we weren't even on the bill. So we got back on the train to come home, and we had a gang of skinheads trying to nick our guitars off us; we had to run for our lives... it was just everywhere you went!

"Then we played the Half Moon [in Putney], and it kicked off big time, loads of claret [i.e. blood] flying everywhere... Crass got done with scaffold poles! We were lay under my car, hiding, and people were just hitting the pavement all around us. That was also the gig where our drummer did a drum roll and fell off his stool at the end of it 'cos he was so drunk..."

"He fell off his stool backwards another time, at Portsmouth Polytechnic," adds Shaun, who played with the blues/rock outfit X-It in the wake of Anthrax. "We looked around and he'd vanished off the back of the stage, leaving us standing around, wondering what to do next..."

In recent years, the members of Anthrax have actually reunited to jam out their old material, with a view to possibly recording something new, but nothing came of it other than a few enjoyable rehearsals.

"Everyone had moved on a lot musically, and all of us in different directions," explains Shaun, "But it was nice to have us all back in one room again, even though it was obvious that the band had run its course."

"I wouldn't change any of it for the world though," says Osker. "Nor the fanzine... although I was only actually involved in the first two issues, before I pulled out 'cos they wanted to charge a pound for it. It had been free up 'til that point... and I felt really strongly about that. Everything we did was free, wasn't it?"

Shaun: "Yeah, the only gig we charged for in Gravesend was a twelve-band benefit gig, to raise money for a leukaemia and cancer equipment fund, and that was only 50p to get in. All the bands played for free, and did four songs each, and the place was packed."

Osker: "I think the most we ever got paid for a gig was £30, and it cost us more than that to get a van and put the petrol in it. But that was what it was all about, wasn't it? The money was never as important as just being involved."

SELECT DISCOGRAPHY

7"s:
'They've Got It All Wrong' (Small Wonder, 1983)
'Capitalism Is Cannibalism' (Crass, 1983)

At A Glance:
Both the Mortarhate compilations that Anthrax appeared on have seen a reissue on CD in recent years, and thankfully Overground have a comprehensive Anthrax discography CD, compiling all the studio recordings, planned for 2007.

It's surely the dream of every band to release at least one great record they can be remembered by, and although the aforementioned **NAKED** literally did just the one single for Bluurg, they can at least rest happy knowing they left behind a genuinely fantastic testament to their time together as a band.

Formed in and around Sheerness in 1979 by vocalist Tony 'Bandy' White and guitarist Chris Counsell, alongside bassist Kevin Nash, second guitarist Alan Dann (not an original member admittedly, and only in the band six months) and drummer Kevin Morgan, Naked actually made their live debut in Holland, at Vlissingen's Hoppit Club, and were joined by bassist Chris 'Midge' Midgley and drummer Kev Arnold in August 1980, by which time the band had already garnered a considerable local following.

"Yeah, they were already playing before we came along," explains Midge. "In fact, we saw them at the [Gravesend] Red Lion several times prior to us joining… Naked did loads of gigs there, so did Anthrax and Conflict… in fact, most of the bands in your book probably played there at some time or other; it was a good venue, and Gravesend had a good little scene going on.

"Me and Kev Arnold were in another band together before Naked, but we never did a gig or anything… it was a punk band, but if we had a name, I honestly can't remember what it was. I was thirteen or fourteen when I started playing bass, and it was 'cos of The Stranglers really – I loved Jean-Jacques Burnel's bass sound… that was the whole reason I ever wanted to join a band in the first place. The Stranglers actually played in [nearby] Rochester last year, up at the castle, and they were really good as well…"

Midge and Kev made their live debut with the band, headlining the Red Lion, in August 1980, supported by Vocal Attack, which served as a much-needed warm-up for a rather prestigious show the following week, opening for the UK Subs at Gravesend's Woodville Hall.

"I think Midge and Kev joining changed our direction quite a bit," ponders Chris. "They were both punks, and the music went more that way for a while. I remember Midge was very raw and didn't really know what notes were which on the bass, so we had a bit of a learning process to go through, but after that… well, you've probably heard the results.

"I don't think we ever set out to be 'a punk band', in the sense that we wanted to play the music we liked, rather than copying everyone else. We all had our own musical influences which I think tended to show through at times; if we had all been the same age, and always listening to the same stuff, we probably would have ended up sounding like every other band we were playing with.

"I was – and still am, of course! – the oldest of the band by about three years, and had grown up listening to Pink Floyd, the Stones, Led Zeppelin, Bowie (who I still listen to), and so on. So punk music was a bit hard to grasp at first: all thrash, no tunes, screaming vocals, 'no talent' etc. etc. But then I did catch on, and found myself thinking how wonderful it was that even these people who didn't know one end of a guitar from another were at least trying – and a lot of it was great to listen to. I expect I sound very pompous, but it was just that it was initially so different… and I don't think I am pompous either! Anyway, then it all got more serious, and the more we were involved, the more it all made sense. I did personally have a struggle with some aspects of it at times, as I had a job in the civil service (in the dole office, of all places!) and responsibilities at home, as my dad had died a couple of years before we formed the band. So, I sometimes felt like a part-time punk, but then, for me, the music was always the No. 1 priority."

Rehearsing in Sheerness Rugby Club ("Which was handy 'cos they had a bar, and we used to help ourselves!" guffaws Midge), Naked began penning new songs for their first studio recording with the new line-up, which they undertook at Rochester's DTS studio; material that was much harder, faster and angrier than how the band had first sounded. And despite its barely-polished rough edges, that earliest recording especially showcased Tony's great voice, a natural talent that lent even the band's thrashier numbers a distinctly tuneful edge.

"Yes, he could really sing!" agrees Midge. "A lot of people said that. In fact, when I first saw them at the Red Lion, I thought to myself, 'This band are good, and that bloke can fucking sing!' But before me and Kev joined, they were much more poppy… definitely a long way from how they sounded after we joined anyway… and I think that when Tony had these two new members, he really exerted his influence on the band, to make it sound a lot more how he wanted it to be; he steered it more in the direction he wanted it to go. It was the ideal opportunity for him to do that."

The demo not only landed them many more mini-tours in Holland ("We practised right by the ferry port anyway…"), it also brought them to the attention of Crass, who included their track, 'Mid 1930s (Pre-War Germany)' on the 1982 'Bullshit Detector 2' compilation. With their crisp guitar sound, tight burbling bass and competent production – not to mention Tony's urgent melodic vocals – Naked were a genuine

Naked (left to right: Midge, Chris, Carl and Tony).

revelation, and they quickly found themselves welcomed with open arms by the anarcho-punk scene, consequently being invited to play shows alongside the likes of Dirt, Flux Of Pink Indians and near-neighbours Anthrax.

Midge: "Tony, the singer, who wrote all the lyrics, was the one most into the anarcho scene, and it was through his contacts that we got as far as we did, to be honest. I didn't really see ourselves as an 'anarcho-punk band'… not even as a 'punk band' really… we were just a band, if you know what I mean? I listened to all sorts of music; I used to really love Killing Joke, although I haven't seen them play live since Youth left; they were a big influence on me, but whether they influenced the rest of the band…? I don't know! But Tony was really into Crass and all the stuff they put out, and after the 'Bullshit…' compilation, we started playing a lot more gigs with all those kinda bands and, before we knew it, that was the scene we were associated with.

"Not that that was a bad thing or anything, don't get me wrong! And what I liked about it all was how everyone tried to help each other out; it was very co-operative. I wasn't too sure about some of the politics of it all, but I liked the general vibe, you know what I mean? It certainly opened a lot of people's eyes to things; I mean, I went vegetarian after hearing 'Sick Butchers' by Flux, and I'm still a vegetarian to this day… although I must admit I wasn't a great lover of meat prior to hearing that anyway. None of the others were veggies though."

After an ill-fated UK tour with Anthrax ("It wasn't particularly well advertised," sighs Midge, "And we ended up doing a few gigs to no one! I remember turning up in Leicester, and no one

knew about it; there were literally no posters for the gig anywhere!") Kev Arnold left and was replaced by Carl Carrick from Westgate, the drummer that actually played on the superb 'One Step Forward Towards Reality' EP for Bluurg.

"He just got pissed off, I think; he didn't drive, and he lived all the way down in Ramsgate. But he was working in Chatham dockyard with me, just across the river here, and he had digs up here as well; I basically used to ferry him around. When the dockyards shut in '83 or whatever, after the Falklands War, he was stuck back down in Ramsgate... but he did re-join eventually; he was a better drummer than Carl anyway. Carl kept trying to put in too many drum rolls, and Kev was a lot steadier, much more solid."

Recorded at DTS in late July 1983, with Dick and Bruce from the Subhumans travelling down to lend the band their production expertise (and backing vocal skills on the enjoyably rampant 'Evil Faces'), the single was a perfectly-formed, vibrant pop punk gem that bothered the lower echelons of the Indie Top Thirty for about a month upon its release in late '83, all five uplifting tracks as memorable as each other.

"I was so chuffed when it came out," says Chris proudly, "just on a personal level even, because I only ever had two ambitions until that stage in my life, and making a record was one of them. I was also really pleased that we, as a band, had achieved it and hoped it would lead to more; we had built a fair following and I was confident we could go a long way.

"Of course I thought it was a great record at the time, the best thing since sliced bread... but then I would! Now, with the benefit of hindsight, I'm still proud of it, and now that I have a copy on CD, I have something to play my son one day. But I also feel that it could have been a lot better and tighter, and without so many out-of-tune or out-of-time bits. It also makes me sad to think we never did get any further with it all, I'm not really sure why; I recall Bruce saying they would want us to do a follow-up, but for whatever reason it never materialised, and we didn't have the means to do it ourselves."

"But it did pretty well," adds Midge, "especially around here, in all the local papers and stuff... whatever that means! It did well in Holland too; I think it made the Top Five of their Independent Charts. We loved playing there, which was why we went over so often; it was so much better organised than over here. I always remember we'd get a roll of drink vouchers to do what we wanted with... which was nice!

"The most memorable gig was probably one we did in Breda, and unknown to us it was an anti-Dutch monarchy gig, arranged to coincide with the Dutch Queen doing a walk-round visit to the town. The whole place got busted by the police; we all got arrested… we had about thirty English people with us, and we were all carted off at gunpoint! It was a great gig though, and we managed to play most of our set before the police burst in on us…

"The worse thing we did there was this live Rhythm 'n' Booze festival in Flushing, and it went out live on the radio. It wasn't just punk bands; there were folk and rock bands playing as well… we were on just before the [American] headliners, Queen Ida and her Bon Temps Zydeco Band. Anyway, my bass amp blew up halfway through our set, so it sounded bleedin' horrible, and everything else went wrong that could go wrong… and it was all broadcast live on Dutch radio."

Surprisingly enough, after such a well-received single, and great shows with the Subhumans at the 100 Club, Tony White left the band ("He lost interest and just wasn't that bothered any more;

Naked - taking a break from rehearsals…

it all seemed a bit of a chore, getting him motivated to practise and stuff..."), leaving Naked to struggle on as a three-piece for a while, with Chris and Midge attempting to fill his rather big vocal shoes between them.

"It didn't work that well though," admits Midge, "so then we had this girl singer, Paula, join; we did a four-track demo with her, sometime in '85, in Gillingham. I think it was one of the best things we ever did, personally, although it was obviously a lot different to what we did with Tony, and we had all these people moaning about the new style.

"The thing is, she sounded alright on tape, but when we played live, she didn't have a very powerful voice, and couldn't really project herself to be heard over the rest of the band."

In fact, Naked only played the one show with Paula fronting the band, in Sevenoaks in 1986, before they quietly disintegrated once and for all.

"I'm not so sure that she had that much of an effect on our sound," reckons Chris, who now works with people that have learning disabilities. "Maybe other people will think otherwise, but as I said previously, for me, making good music was always the most important thing. I'm pretty sure Midge felt the same to be honest too, so I think the main effect Paula had was just that the vocals were different. I think lyrically things had been changing for a while before she joined, and perhaps becoming less political. I can't really tell you how the die-hard fans reacted as I didn't speak to that many of them at the time, but those I did speak to were actually keen and said they liked what we were doing towards the end.

"Anyway, I went on holiday to America, and we were due to rehearse only a day or two after I got back. I was really jet-lagged and rang round to say I wanted to leave it until the next week... but 'next week' never came! How strange and sad is that? We just never got back together. Midge even left his gear, or some of it, at the rehearsal place and never retrieved it. I regret that so much, and have done for many years; I always thought we could get somewhere with our music and still think the same. That's not meant to sound clever or anything either, although I suspect maybe it does; I just honestly thought – and still think – that we had something a bit special, and it was a shame we never got the chance to take it any further."

"I've even been talking about playing again recently," says Midge, now a self-employed builder. "One of the blokes I work with is a really good singer, and we've been talking about doing something, just to keep our hands in really, for something to do... I still pick my bass up and have a little tinkle now and again, but not enough really. The thing is, I broke my wrist five years ago, and lost a lot of movement in it, which is a hindrance. I loved my time in Naked though, wouldn't change a thing... wish I was back there now, to be honest; everything seemed a lot simpler back then."

SELECT DISCOGRAPHY

7"s:
'One Step Forward Towards Reality' (Bluurg, 1983)

At A Glance:
Overground have recently stepped up to the plate and announced a 2007 release for the sort of thorough retrospective CD a band of Naked's calibre undoubtedly deserves.

The quietly influential **RIOT/CLONE** actually formed in Ashford from the remains of Hounslow act, The Replacements, a short-lived band that featured Riot/Clone vocalist, Dave Floyd, on bass and a female singer, Kathy. The other two members, Kenny and Howard actually left the week before the band's first gig, in Ashford, supporting Mod band The Vespas, leaving Dave and Kathy to draft in last-minute replacements.

"And even Kathy was having throat problems, so I reluctantly took over vocal duties as well," recalls Dave. "I don't remember much about the show itself. That morning, however, I had bought the only copy of 'The Feeding Of The 5000' by Crass from our local record shop, and, kinda blown away by there being another band out there with seemingly similar ideas, plus not having that long a set rehearsed, had got together with the guitarist and learnt 'Do They Owe Us a Living?', which we played as our final song. Some twenty years later, I actually met

Riot/Clone (left to right: Pete Spence, Mells, Dave Floyd).

up with someone who had been at the gig who was adamant that I had written the song but Crass had stolen it! No end of arguing would convince him, and he probably still firmly believes it to this day, based on the 'evidence' that the local record shop didn't get any more copies in for a few weeks so he wasn't aware of its release until then..."

With Kathy's throat problems making her continued role as vocalist impossible, Dave decided to sing – until a more permanent vocalist could be found – and recruited next-door neighbour Hammy as guitarist, bassist Pooch (real name Mick Carroll) and drummer Steve Speight. Becoming ever more interested in the Crass way of doing things, Dave changed the name of the band to 'Riot', but two other members wanted to be called 'Clone', and the hybrid compromise of 'Riot/Clone' that was used on the posters for the first gig soon became a permanent arrangement. But not before The Replacements (or at least, a version thereof) enjoyed fifteen minutes of fame supporting The Ruts at The Nashville in West Kensington.

"Yeah, as time went on, I became more and more interested in the political and DIY aspects of punk; the first wave of punk had disintegrated and it became clear that most of the bands had really just been pop star wannabes. I felt cheated and let down, but rather than do what most people in my area seemed to be doing, and leaping onto the mod bandwagon, I decided to concentrate on my own band, working on the theory that the only band I could always trust would ultimately be the one that I was actually involved in myself.

"Anyway, I had been lucky enough to come across The Ruts before they had any real exposure and were still playing to a small crowd of friends at most gigs, so had got to know them pretty well... to the point of being beckoned up onstage to sing backing vocals for them at some gigs. I had obviously told them that I was starting a band, and [their vocalist] Malcolm [Owen] came over to me at the bar at the Nashville show, asking if we were all there, because the support act, Vermillion And the Aces hadn't turned up. 'Yes!' I said, and he went off to arrange for us to play instead... it was then pointed out to me by Pooch that Hammy wasn't in fact with us, having gone to The Marquee instead to see the Angelic Upstarts.

"Malcolm came back and said it was all arranged, and I told him we had no guitarist. 'No problem,' he said, 'I can find you one!' And he disappeared again. Now was the point where Pooch and myself had a serious debate over who should sing; neither of us were overly confident and both knew the bass lines, though admittedly Pooch was a far better bassist than I was. It was eventually decided, by Pooch and Steve ganging up on me, that I should sing; firstly because I'd got us into this, and secondly, because I was the oldest. That settled, Malcolm returned and told us to come backstage so we could teach the guitarist our songs. We were gobsmacked to find that it was none other than Rat Scabies, [drummer] of The Damned. Pooch managed to teach him three songs before it was time to go on, and we decided to do those three, plus any covers that came to mind.

"So on we went: me, Pooch, Steve, Rat Scabies, some guy called Pat, who had overheard the original conversation with Malcolm and blagged himself into the deal, and Vermillion, who had showed up having not found her band. To say I was nervous, walking out in front of over 400 people, would be an understatement. Word had gone around that we were a last minute stand-in though, and with me knowing all The Ruts crew, and Pat knowing a fair percentage of the remaining audience, we were greeted by a resounding roar. My nervousness disappeared immediately, and Pooch was later to say he always regretted forcing me to sing that night, as he could see that the moment I walked out onstage, any thoughts of playing bass had completely vanished from my mind. We went down really well too – even our own songs, which was very pleasing – and, three weeks later, Riot/Clone would play our first proper gig."

Said well-received gig being on October 8th, 1979, at the Grove Tavern in Kingston-upon-Thames, after which, flushed with their early success, the band recorded their first demo (in Steve's bedroom!), which, when coupled with a live recording on the B-side, became the band's aptly-titled 'Musical Destruction' cassette.

However, it would be two years before Riot/Clone found themselves with a stable enough line-up to release anything else; 1981's 'Crime Pays' cassette was another collection of DIY demos and live material, and by the time it emerged, Dave had been joined by guitarist 'Roo', bassist Pete Spence, and drummer 'Mells'. It was this line-up that entered Pet Sounds Studio in South London and recorded the first Riot/Clone EP, 'There's No Government Like No Government', which, inspired by bands such as Six Minute War who were releasing all their own material, they issued on their own Riot/Clone label in early 1982.

"I just got a copy of Melody Maker and phoned all the pressing plants advertised in there, asking questions about the process and their prices," explains Dave, of how he started up the label. "Once I'd done that, I also rang the mastering plant that was most used at the time, and concluded that the whole adventure would cost us £450 plus the covers. So, armed with this knowledge, all we needed now was the £450! We played a gig that paid us £30 and decided to all chip in the rest, in instalments, until we had it all saved. Luckily, we only had to make one £30 injection each, after which someone Mells knew through work offered to lend us the balance, so we could do it there and then, without having to wait. It may have taken some time otherwise, what with two of us being unemployed. A mate of ours who worked in a print shop then offered to do the covers for us at the weekends, when he was on overtime and the boss wasn't around, so that saved us having to dig any deeper, and also dictated the style of the covers as the largest he could print was A3…

"So off we trotted to South London, having rehearsed five songs repeatedly for the recording session. First off, we had to get the sound right and there seemed to be a problem with it, as the engineer pointed out. This is something that will make kids nowadays just starting out in bands crease up with laughter, and shows how inexperienced we were at the time. The engineer asked Roo and Pete if they were in tune, after fiddling with various knobs, trying to rectify the sound. 'Yes!' they both replied. So, they tried again, but again the engineer asked the same question – and got the same reply. He finally hit on the problem though. 'Are you in tune…together?' Blank stares were all he got. Yep, Roo and Pete both had their guitars in tune, but they had both tuned separately, without a thought for the other. Once that was sorted out, we got stuck into the recording, though Mells and myself made sure we took the piss out of our wannabe axe heroes all the way home for that!"

One of the four tracks from the single, the ultra-fast and raw 'Death To Humanity', a tirade against mankind's widespread and despicable abuse of animals, was then included on Anagram's extremely popular 'Punk And Disorderly' compilation, which gained the band many new fans from outside of the peace punk camp. Very aware that their appearance seemed like some sort of 'cop out', having gone to such great lengths to release their own record, Riot/Clone requested that any royalties due them for their contribution should be donated to the Animal Liberation Front.

"That ['Death To Humanity'] is actually my least favourite song of ours. I like the lyrics, but the song itself seems to start, drone on for what seems like hours, then stop – without doing anything remotely interesting in between. Of course, with that being the track that appeared on 'Punk And Disorderly', everyone always wants to hear it, so it has to be included in the live set every time we play, making it something of an albatross I have hanging around my neck forever! The best feeling that came from splitting the band up last year was that I'd never have to sing that damned song again!"

Another four-track EP, 'Destroy The Myth Of Musical Destruction', followed in late '82. Better produced than the first single, it featured four more simple-yet-memorable tunes, the best being 'H-Block', all about the infamous Maze Prison (at Long Kesh, County Antrim, Northern Ireland) where republican hero (over 75,000 people attended his funeral) Bobby Sands was amongst ten men who starved themselves to death on hunger strike, protesting against the institution's appalling conditions and refusal to segregate political prisoners, in 1981.

"I think the second EP captures the best balance between sound quality and energy," offers Dave. "I only finished the lyrics to 'Sick Games' [that include the immortal line, 'If this system's the answer, then it must have been a stupid question…'] in the car on the way to the studio, and it replaced 'Running', which once again proved to be a stumbling block when it came to recording it without making any mistakes [it was left off the first single for the same reason]. This was why we always rehearsed five songs, so we had a back-up in case one didn't work for any reason.

"I do have a soft spot for the first EP though," he adds fondly. "I can remember how great it felt to record it and finally get copies in our sweaty paws, but despite the spirit managing to somehow overcome the dreadful production, the quality of the recording does detract from what could have been a great single had we had a little more money to spend on the recording. Also, lyrically, I'm very pleased that most of the songs remain relevant, whereas quite a lot of output from the early Eighties was of its time, and sounds pretty naïve or dated now."

A third EP, 'Blood On Your Hands?', actually appeared in December 1984, and managed to dent the Indie Top Thirty, despite the band that recorded it (at Fair Deal in Hayes, where The Ruts recorded their first single, 'In A Rut') having split up long before its eventual release.

"We actually split in January 1983, before the third EP had been recorded [hence Dave and Roo re-recruiting original bassist Pooch and enlisting the services of 'a friend of a friend called Kevin' on drums]. The reason was that good old rock'n'roll cliché, the girlfriend! Pete had been seeing Janice since they had hooked up at our Liverpool gig, and as time went on she had become more and more intrusive in the workings of the band. It had reached the point where I pretty much had to get permission from her before booking any gigs… although Pete was blissfully unaware of this, 'cos she always answered their phone.

"One night we were due to play in Cheddington with the Lost Cherrees [whose first single Dave released on Riot/Clone Records soon after], but neither Pete nor Mells, who had just got a job, turned up to meet the van. Steve of the Lost Cherrees already knew the bass lines and was cool with filling in for Pete (the Cherrees actually used to play the Riot/Clone set at rehearsals as a warm up before doing their own stuff), although their drummer Nuts was rather more nervous about having to fill in for Mells. Roo and myself weren't happy; only a couple of months earlier we had all agreed to put more energies into the band, yet with Mells doing overtime at every opportunity and Pete being vetoed by Janice every time she didn't want him to do something, the opposite seemed to be happening. We decided to ask Pete to leave, and ascertain from Mells where

Riot/Clone live at the Genesis Youth Club, Stanwell, June 1982, picture by Mick Mercer.

his main interest lay. Mells turned up ten minutes before we were due to go onstage that night, and wasn't happy to hear that we wanted to ask Pete to leave, saying he would have to consider his own position in the band. Pete agreed to leave, and a couple of days later Mells left too."

Unfortunate really, because at the time of the band's premature demise, they were well on their way to completing the writing of their debut album, which was to have been entitled 'From The Cradle To The Grave' – until the Subhumans released their sophomore album of the same name, and the working title was then shortened to just 'Life'.

Pete and Janice formed Evil I, before Pete went on to do stints with Rubella Ballet and Daisy Chainsaw, as well as some time with Dave in Mad Dog. In 1989, he and Dave reunited with Roo for a brief Riot/Clone reformation, to celebrate what would have been the band's tenth anniversary (minus Mells, who couldn't be located, so the drums were handled by an old friend, Andy Willis), resulting in the early Nineties' ambitious 'Dead… But Not Forgotten' set – all three of the band's singles reissued, and bound together by a 72-page booklet.

However, what was intended to put a satisfactory 'full stop' on the Riot/Clone story actually had the opposite effect and led to them reactivating on a more permanent basis. In early 1995, Dave, Pete and Pooch entered The Studio, Brixton, with Conflict drummer Paco behind the kit, and recorded the forty-track 'Still No Government Like No Government' CD (which was issued on vinyl two years later by Step Forward). Featuring brand new versions of most of the band's old material (much of it previously unreleased), plus some impressive new numbers (some of which were penned under the Mad Dog moniker), it came with an astoundingly thick 142-page booklet of lyrics and in-depth articles about the many varied topics they touched upon. Although a bit much to digest in one sitting, it was the first time the band was blessed with a sound that did them justice, breathing new life into much of their back catalogue, and the accompanying literature certainly lent a credible depth and meaning to the band's message.

In 1997, Bomb Factory released the 'To Find A Little Bluebird' album, which, although wrapped in a serene cover, was the band's most musically uncompromising offering to date, a genuinely hardcore collection of hard-hitting thrash. It was followed in 2000, after various line-up changes and much touring of Europe and North America, by the full-on animal rights album, 'Do You Want Fries With That?' and then, in 2004, by a brand new EP, 'Mad Sheep Disease', for Californian label, Alternative. Both releases demonstrated beyond any doubt that Riot/Clone had lost none of their outspoken invective, and yet another new album was being written when Dave decided to relocate to America for a while in 2005, and the band he left behind recruited a new vocalist and became Refuse/All, who issued the 'Have A Happy Holiday In Guantanamo Bay' LP on D-Restricted Records during 2006.

"There was also another Riot/Clone EP recorded in 2000," explains Dave, "During the same session as 'Do You Want Fries With That?', titled 'Acts Of Floccinaucinihilipilification'. It was due to be released through Catchphraze Records from Arizona, but due to various problems the release never happened. It contained three tracks [including 'Collapse (Is On Its Way)' – a reworking of 'H-Block' with new lyrics], that will appear on the CD version of the new album, that will be out shortly on [Californian label] Dr. Strange Records. As yet, I've no title to give you, but it is by far the best Riot/Clone album ever recorded, and will be a fitting end to the band... though I don't discount the possibility of a final US tour when it is released.

"We dared to be different, unlike those who slavishly followed the Crass model," he adds on what helped Riot/Clone stand apart from their peers. "We never tried to emulate their sound, instead just wrote songs as best we could that we liked. We also never copied the look; in fact I went from always wearing black to purposely making sure I rarely did, once it became a 'scene rule' that all-black was the way to go. We seem to have managed to get a fair crossover audience over the years due to this, but by the same token are destined to remain relatively obscure, straddling the fringes of the normal punk and anarcho scenes. Many people into more standard punk still discount Riot/Clone without ever hearing us, because they assume we are 'just another Crass band', something I've constantly heard from those who stumble across us by accident.

"We also went it alone, despite the obstacles put in our path along the way, such as Fresh Records going bust whilst owing us £600. Damn, we're the only band I know of who turned down a possible record deal with Rough Trade, because we had our own label and wanted to remain as independent as possible. And let's face it: you didn't get much more independent than Rough Trade back then!"

SELECT DISCOGRAPHY

7"s:
'There's No Government Like No Government' (Riot/Clone, 1982)
'Destroy The Myth Of Musical Destruction' (Riot/Clone, 1982)
'Blood On Your Hands?' (Riot/Clone, 1984)
'Dead... But Not Forgotten' (Riot/Clone, 1993) – re-release of the first three singles
'Mad Sheep Disease' (Alternative, 2004)

LPs:
'Still No Government Like No Government' (Step Forward, 1997) – double LP
'To Find A Little Bluebird' (Bomb Factory, 1997)
'Do You Want Fries With That?' (Tribal War, 2000)

At A Glance:
The excellent 1995 'Still No Government Like No Government' CD, although little more than a re-recorded 'Best Of...' collection, remains the perfect way to check out the band's Eighties output because of its superior production values and incredible packaging.

One of the more tuneful anarcho bands were **LOST CHERREES**, although don't be fooled by that past tense because the band are back together, recording and gigging with great success even as we speak. Their 1984 'All Part Of Growing Up' LP was an accomplished slice of melodic punk rock, heavily tinged with both reggae and pop, and remains the defining moment of their Eighties output, although the band were considerably more raw when they first picked up their instruments in late 1981.

Formed in Sutton, Surrey, by bassist Steve Battershill, that first incarnation of the Cherrees also consisted of vocalist Sian Jeffries and guitarist Dave Greaves. In the absence of anyone else willing or able to do it, Steve actually played the drums to start with... until they recruited Warren 'Nuts' Samuels, author of an acclaimed local fanzine 'Hit Ranking', to man the kit.

Lost Cherrees live in Bristol, November 1983 (Sian on the left, Bev on the right), picture by Paul Mahoney.

The first gig was undertaken during July 1982 at The Swan, in Mill Street, Kingston-upon-Thames, with Riot/Clone ("It was fast, noisy, chaotic and brilliant!" recalls Steve), and it wasn't long before the band were blazing a trail on the punk underground. Both with their live shows and also their debut single, the 'No Fighting, No War, No Trouble, No More' EP, for Riot/Clone Records, by which time Dave Greaves had been replaced by Andy Rolfe.

And it was from the outset of their existence that they found themselves aligned with the anarcho-punk movement, by virtue of not only the company they were keeping on the gig circuit but also their thoughtful lyrics and the obvious anti-sexism stance of their moniker.

"We became aware of anarcho-punk the day Crass released 'Feeding Of The 5000'," reckons Steve. "And although we never really applied the term to ourselves, we were more than happy to be mentioned in the same context as most of those bands at the time. If you had to put us in a box, I guess that would be the right one! Although labels and pigeonholes are things we are all born into and have to exist within, and freedom from them begins and ends inside your own head. We were always the same, never changed and never will. Our style of music developed as we improved as musicians, but our lyrics have always been about the things around us that directly affect us.

"The feminist stance was struck very early on and has never wavered; equality in all walks of life is essential to us. The issue had already been raised by Crass and Poison Girls, so, although it wasn't that widespread, people were starting to seriously address such problems."

That debut EP was a spirited affair, undeniably generic with its rather tuneless high-speed approach yet charming in its boisterous naiveté.

"It was recorded at Hart Studios, Kingston," explains Andy. "Between the hours of 10.00pm and 6.00am, because it was cheaper to record at night... seven tracks in eight hours, it really was '1,2,3,4... go!' We mixed all the songs in that time as well. A pro-plus frenzy of chaos and toilets! And sound-wise it was exactly what you'd expect a bunch of sixteen- and seventeen-year-olds who can't play very well to sound like, but it was our first single, and we still look back at it fondly."

Despite its obvious shortcomings, 'No Fighting, No War...' made the Indie Top Thirty for a few short weeks during July 1983, and saw them gigging up and down the country with the likes of Flux Of Pink Indians, Omega Tribe and Conflict. Indeed it was the latter's Mortarhate Records that ended up releasing the second Lost Cherrees single early the following year, although originally the release was slated for Dick from the Subhumans' Bluurg label.

"Yeah, Dick was actually at the session," confirmed Steve. "But when Colin [Jerwood] heard it, he offered to put it out and we went with Mortarhate in the end, because we'd already done a lot of work with Conflict by then. We did release some compilation tapes with Bluurg though [the 'Nothing New' demo and the 'Live At Brannigan's, Leeds' cassette].

Lost Cherrees, live in Bournemouth 1985 (left to right: Debbie, Bev, Gail), picture by Jaz Wiseman.

"Twenty years on and nothing much has changed between us and Mortarhate; they're still really good to deal with. Of course there's always a few horror stories about them, but they usually come from people who don't really know anything about them, or bands that want paying for every fucking note they ever play."

'A Man's Duty, A Woman's Place', as the sophomore EP was known, was an infinitely stronger release than its predecessor and crashed into the Indie Top Ten and spent three months in the chart during spring 1984. Opening with the brooding, evocative 'Blasphemy', 'No Trouble' had a heavy dub reggae influence, but the best track was probably the upbeat 'Living In A Coffin', a damning indictment of the sterility of modern life in the fast lane. And of course, 'Sexism's Sick' remains as relevant now as then in its condemnation of the bigotry inherent in so many traditional institutions.

"My favourite Cherrees release!" enthuses Andy. "It was recorded and engineered by Jon Hiseman, who was the drummer for this jazz/rock band, Colosseum. The experience of recording properly in a top studio was great... you must remember we were still in our teens and so inexperienced. The sessions were really good, though, and the end product still sounds fantastic today."

"Personally my fave track is 'Blasphemy'," elaborates Steve. "Because it came out exactly how I imagined it would, with all the sound effects, the child voice-over [perfectly realised by Hiseman's daughter, Anna], the music, the whole nine yards really. I dreamt that song... and wrote it in five minutes, but it only came together bit by bit; there's a great vocal by Sian too."

Just before they recorded 'A Man's Duty', the Lost Cherrees expanded to a five-piece line-up with the addition on keyboards of Gail Thibert, former lead vocalist with Adventures In Colour, who had previously supported the Cherrees at Feltham Football Club.

"Before I left Adventures In Colour, I did a demo in the studio with what was basically the Lost Cherrees minus Sian," reveals Gail. "In other words, me singing, with Nuts, Andy and Steve. We recorded two tracks, 'Ooh La La La' and 'Lavender'; Steve then invited me to join the Lost Cherrees.

"We came home with the demo, which was called 'Lost In Colour', as it was part Lost Cherrees and part Adventures In Colour, and Steve announced that I was joining the band, but, as Sian was already the singer, it was agreed that I would play keyboards. I laughed and pointed out that I couldn't actually play keyboards, but Steve said that that was okay as they couldn't play either! He then set about teaching me, placing coloured stickers on the keys with numbers on, and nodding his head when it was time to hit one. So there you have it; my secrets are revealed... and I still can't play keyboards!"

The single was followed by the inclusion of 'The Wait' on Mortarhate's popular 'Who? What? Why? When? Where?' compilation album, that saw the band's line-up further expanded by additional vocalists Bev Cook-Abbott and Debbie McKenna just before the aforementioned 'All Part Of Growing Up' LP. Says Bev of her recruitment:

"I was a friend of the band from when they played gigs with other local bands Warning [who appeared on the third volume of Crass Record's 'Bullshit Detector' series] and Panik in Steve's mum and dad's single car garage that had egg boxes stuck to the walls for sound-proofing. We'd all bring our two-litre bottles of cider and the bands would watch each other... I think me and my friend Cindy were the only ones there not in any of the bands!

"Anyway, just as the second single was coming out, Sian was planning to leave to go to university and she rang me out of the blue to see if I fancied replacing her as singer. I've no idea why though, as I'd never sung in my life; I guess no one else wanted to! I'd only heard the first single and that was a while ago so she brought the second single round. I loved it and did an audition tape of me singing along to it, 'cos I was too embarrassed to sing in front of them. Shockingly, it turns out Steve still has that tape...

"The idea was for me to replace Sian but she didn't go to uni in the end and, by the time she was thinking of moving on again, we liked the way it worked with two vocalists, so Gail brought her friend Debbie McKenna in. Then we would still have two vocalists when Sian finally left. Hence the 'All Part Of Growing Up' album had all three of us on it, but Sian eventually left to join Blythe Power just after it came out."

With its heavy musical bias, the album, recorded at Brixton's Ariwa Studios, still shines like a lighthouse towering above a sea of so-often bleak, insular thrash, and it was no surprise when it went Top Ten in the Indies upon its release in November 1984. With the three girls harmonising over some delightfully delicate guitar melodies, and the pace generally carefully measured throughout, it's one of the more listenable, upbeat records of the period. A fact reinforced by the peaceful cover shot – of a Cornish coastline – and a most enjoyable version of 'Pleasant Valley Sunday' that pays suitable homage to the pop overtones surrounding it ("We were the only anarcho-punk band to cover The Monkees!" chuckles Bev).

With such a prominent female force at work in the ranks, it was inevitable the record would continue to confront the thorny topic of sexism, and 'You're You, I'm Me' provides an articulate and balanced take on the theme. Elsewhere the Cherrees ponder the mundanity of everyday life for the average Joe/Jo ('F-Plan, G-Plan' and 'Young And Free'), and there are several songs that deal with animal abuse, in particular hunting and vivisection. No mention is made of eating meat though – possibly because the band would've felt hypocritical addressing such an issue when not all of them were vegetarian.

"I only actually went veggie about eight years ago!" confesses Bev. "I wasn't back in the Eighties… although I would've liked to have been but hated vegetables! Still do, but now you can have Quorn and other meat substitutes, I'm sorted. Give me a plate of ratatouille and I'll give it back to you… give me a nice Quorn roast with all the trimmings, and I'll be your friend forever. I couldn't care less if it looks or tastes like meat – it isn't and that's all that matters. And I have got more into animal rights with each passing year; I won't go to certain countries that have terrible animal rights records, I will only use cosmetics and household stuff that are cruelty-free etc. And I certainly won't wear leather, which I also did back then."

After contributing 'War, Parts I and II' to the 'We Don't Want Your Fucking War' collection, and with Sian now departed, Lost Cherrees entered Alaska Studios to record their last EP of the Eighties, the 'Unwanted Children' 12". Released in September 1985, it only bothered the lower echelons of the Indie Top Thirty for but a few weeks, possibly because the average punk who followed the band was a little disconcerted by the slick rock production and the catchy use of horns on the bouncy title track.

"That's the ironic thing about the musical progression between our releases," sighs Steve. "The better we became, the less people liked us! But I'll be fucked if that mattered. The 'Unwanted Children' EP was a bloody good listen, but people would still stand at gigs and yell out for our old Discharge rip-offs!"

Disillusioned with dwindling sales and indeed with the ignorance that was still rife in the punk scene, despite all efforts made to the contrary, the Cherrees called it a day after a particularly miserable gig at The Mermaid in Birmingham in early 1986.

"It was probably the worse gig we ever did," spits Steve. "In fact, it was so bad we split up after it, because we decided we really could do no more. There we were playing 'Sexism's Sick', and there they were shouting, 'Get your tits out!' A right bunch of wankers, to be honest, and we just felt like we'd been head-butting a wall for the previous four years. What was the point?"

"Apparently I announced halfway through our set that it was our last gig," adds Bev. "And that was that. Listening back to tapes of our last few shows though, we really sounded like a band who couldn't be arsed; we were terrible, and if you can't get yourselves up to play for people who have paid good money to see you then you really shouldn't be there, so we stopped."

For a while at least. Bev formed a band intriguingly called Bubble-Eyed Dog Boys, Andy started up Apex Beat with Andy Kemp from Warning, whilst Nuts put together Instant Reactor with yet more ex-members of that band. None of these acts amounted to anything more than a few demos, and then Andy and Nuts reunited in 1988 for Good Question, a light-hearted covers band that eventually metamorphosed into Pipe. In 2003, Steve decided to resurrect Lost Cherrees…

"I felt bored and boring, and I missed it a lot over the years. And seeing other bands still doing it made me wanna try and see if we could maybe give it another crack, so first I announced on a few punk websites that we were reforming, recording a new single and album, and touring the States, UK and Europe! Then I set out trying to contact the band, and by the time I first heard back from Bev and Nuts, I was already getting loads of emails from America saying how great it was that we were back! Fuck, sometimes you gotta roll the dice a little… but if you build it, they will come…"

"We tried to contact the other three via email, the internet, word of mouth, and a message on our website for them to get in touch," elaborates Bev. "But we got no joy until Gail and Debbie turned up at our very first gig back together, in Hackney in July 2003. It was great to see them; Debbie came up and sang 'Unwanted Children' with me and we had a great catch up. The thing was though, by that time the four of us had worked really hard on gelling the new setup with me and Andy on vocals and we really didn't want to start again, so we actually chose to keep to just the four of us. I think they were a little disappointed, but hopefully they understood."

Since then, the band have been busy spreading the word of their return on the live circuit, even playing as far afield as Italy and America ("Yes, we've finally gone international," laughs Bev). A cracking new studio album ('Free To Speak… But Not To Question') and retrospective DVD ('There Are No Fucking Rules') are the latest additions to the band's canon, and recently they've expanded their live sound by recruiting a second guitarist, Jeremy 'Buzz' Buzzing, and vocalist Joey Hill.

"I don't think we actually differ that much now to then though," reckons Nuts. "After nearly twenty years, I was gonna say that we now sound much better, but, after revisiting all the old tracks, I'd have to say that we sounded pretty good even back then, on a good day at least. Speaking for myself, I would say my ideologies are more or less the same as they were then too; it's sad to say that not much has changed in the world. And even when politicians claim they are gonna change it, and you begin to think that this is the start of something new, they always let you down.

"I think we're just taking it as it comes really. When we got back together it was just to play a few gigs and see how it went down, from that came the Mortarhate anthology CD, and then the new singles, and now the album and DVD. As long as we're all enjoying it, then we'll keep doing it. I've been playing drums for over twenty years now and I can't see a day when I don't want to anymore… and while the Cherrees still want a drummer, I'll be there for them."

SELECT DISCOGRAPHY

7"s:
'No Fighting, No War, No Trouble No More' (Riot Clone, 1983)
'A Man's Duty, A Woman's Place' (Mortarhate, 1984)
'Another Bite Of The Cherrees' (Alternative, 2003)

CD/EPs:
'Fathers 4 Justice' (Fathers-4-Justice, 2004)

12"s:
'Unwanted Children' (Mortarhate, 1985)

LPs:
'All Part Of Growing Up' (Mortarhate, 1984)
'Free To Speak… But Not To Question' (Mortarhate, 2006)

At A Glance:
The excellent 2003 Mortarhate CD, 'In The Beginning…', compiles almost all of the bands early Eighties vinyl releases, and comes complete with a 12-page booklet of lyrics, artwork and rare band photos. It was re-released, with extra tracks, in early 2006 as a double-disc set in a deluxe digipak.

In much the same way as chapter one's Rubella Ballet, **HAGAR THE WOMB** threw a brightly-coloured spanner in the works of pedantic claims that the anarcho-punk scene was a drab and dreary place, where bands only dressed in black and never dreamt of having fun for the sheer hell of it, and they were a very necessary breath of fresh air in an often claustrophobic pressure cooker of mangled power chords and heated political debate. Formed in London in 1980, it was apparent from the outset that Hagar would not conform to any party line, not even that of the non-conformists!

"At the time, we girls were really pissed off with the guys who had 'elected' themselves the movers and the shakers of the Wapping Anarchy Centre," explains vocalist Ruth 'Radish' Elias of the band's inception. "Obviously, being an Anarchy Centre, I don't really mean we had elections, but these guys were mostly in, or connected with, bands that had started to play there, and were busy fixing up gigs and other things to keep the Centre going. They had an attitude and an almost unshakeable sense of authority and we, the few girls there, were finding it hard to get ourselves heard or involved in any sense. Anarchy in Wapping or no, the battle of the sexes continues… so there we were, naffed off because we had just been laughed at for making some suggestion or other, huddled together in the loo – the natural habitat of the female species at venues – and we thought we should form a band, because then they would have to take notice of us. I make no apologies that the Hags were not formed for worldlier reasons, but that's actually why we came about.

"And I am ashamed to say I made the name up in the one whole week we had between forming and doing our first gig. As you can see, it was a rush job and immense advertising pressure was laid to bear to have a name to put on the poster. It doesn't actually mean anything and I never liked it!"

A 'rush job' indeed, especially seeing as none of the original line-up (comprising Ruth, Karen Amden and Nicola Corcoran on vocals, Janet Nassim on guitar and Steph Cohen on bass) could even play an instrument, but punk rock has always been blissfully indifferent of such minor inconveniences as musicians who aren't the least bit musical, hasn't it? And after all, the show must go on – and what a first show! Opening for scene luminaries, Zounds and The Mob…

"The Anarchy Centre was a collective, and thankfully some of the regulars helped us out. In the

Hagar The Womb and friends, Darlington 1986, picture by Andrew Medcalf.

week between our 'band of defiance' being created and our first gig, Andy Martin from The Apostles lent us his habitat to rehearse in, and sorted out a drummer for us, Scarecrow. None of us wanted to drum, or indeed learn to play an instrument; that was all getting a bit too serious really. That's why we started off with three 'singers', and why drums, guitar and bass – despite the brave stabbings of Janet and Steph – became, through musical necessity, the more male preserves within the Womb. That's not to say that other females couldn't play them, just that there was a more plentiful supply of males who played within our circles.

"It was one of the biggest gigs, pre Crass-invasion, to be held at the Centre, and the only reason we got offered it by the guys organising the gig (who I mentioned earlier) was because they didn't think we'd actually get it together to perform live within a week. Everything that followed was because of them... thanks, guys! Bold, if not entirely fearless, proof that anyone really could get up and do it!

"After killing Andy Martin and co. with our noises for a few days, we arrived on gig Sunday armed with a few songs, a drummer, a borrowed guitar, bass and amps, and plentiful supplies of peanut butter sandwiches and alcohol for bribery purposes. These we used to great effect... the 'Hagar Cocktail' (anything went in!) being particularly effective in getting a lairy vocal crowd to the front of the stage to drown out our efforts in encouraging drunken cheers...! These poor souls were then ear-marked for our badges – crudely superimposed over other bands' badges as we didn't have any proper ones. They read 'Number 1 fan', 'Number 2 fan' and so on... we even reached double figures at one show I seem to remember. Those badges must be worth a fortune now... ha ha!

"Our first songs included 'Puff The Magic Dragon' ('... lives by the sea, he doesn't have a lot to do but believes in Anarchyyyyyyyyyyy!'), 'Dressed to Kill' and 'Babies'. Anyway, we were all chuffed with the gig, or rather all the support we got, despite being so knowingly dreadful, and decided to continue..."

JFB (AKA 'Jon from Bromley') was soon drafted in on second guitar, to boost the band's live sound, whilst Scarecrow was replaced behind the kit by Chris 'Elephant Face' Knowles, previously with Cold War. When Nicola left ("She was very little and couldn't reach the mikes!"), the band continued with just two vocalists, Ruth and Karen... for a while, at least.

Through some concerted gigging with like-minded bands, the Hagars began to quietly build a respectable following around London and a name for themselves on the anarcho-punk scene... although whether they were actually 'anarcho punk' remains open for debate.

"I suppose we were always considered a bit different because a) we were not overtly anti-war, or anti-anything actually (apart from anti-labelling which didn't count); b) we were mostly female which was rare, and c) we didn't wear black a lot... apart from that, you couldn't tell us apart from any other 'Crass band'!

"I remember a friend at school lent me Crass's 'Feeding Of The 5000'; I was blown away by it and scared at the same time because it was just soooo angry, it made the Sex Pistols' seething seem like mild disdain. But for me, Crass weren't there at the outset so were not an initial influence on our sound. They did have a massive, positive impact on the anarcho-punk movement though – they shaped it really – and there was no doubting their overriding influence on that scene.

"I lived in West Hampstead at the time; I had been kicked out of home for dying my hair red and ended up at 'Puppy Mansions', the local residence of Tony D. and his seminal 'Kill Your Pet Puppy' fanzine. It was a great place to live, creatively if not hygienically... I admit that I was one of the worst offenders; I remember Tony explaining that I not only had to clean inside a pot, but around it as well – I was amazed!

"The giraffe on the cover of 'Word Of The Womb' originated in my bedroom there – I wonder how many times it's been painted over now? We had the Moonlight pub/club just around the corner, which put on a lot of punk gigs at the time. We, and a lot of bands we hung out with, played there; it was definitely a fave rave of mine. We weren't far from the 100 Club or Marquee either, the Fulham Greyhound and several other great venues, so we were lucky in that respect."

This line-up recorded the band's first demo, a track of which, 'For The Ferryman', eventually appeared on Mortarhate's 'Who? What? Why? When? Where?' compilation. Compared to the heavy-duty thrashings elsewhere on the album, Hagar's contribution bounces along rather inoffensively, a subtle examination of self-knowledge and the adverse effects of peer pressure on individual thought. By the time the compilation was released however, Steph had quietly said 'no more', the bassist slot being subsequently filled by Mitch Flacko, formerly with The Crux, The Snork Maidens and Flack. He quickly immersed himself in the band's light-hearted approach.

"Maybe it's true that booze and other drugs fuck your memory, but I can't remember a single rehearsal!" he laughs. "Getting gigs was easy though; you played the Anarchy Centre in Wapping, or the Centro Iberico in Westbourne Park by asking for a gig, then other bands who liked you put you on the bill when they got gigs and vice versa. People were always trying to put on gigs in their local pub, youth centre, park or whatever, and whoever was the local band, or the popular band with a record contract that could buy their own gear, shared all their backline. Here was a bunch of teenagers doing their own thing... venues, recording studios, record companies, fanzines, theatre companies, cafes, the squat scene. Fuck Thatcher? We did better; we ignored our elders and betters.

"But were we really anarcho punk? I'm a communist and was at the time. The majority of the scene didn't know the difference between anarchy and chaos! The chaos – music, drugs and sex – were what people really liked. The Anarchy Centre had Stalinists, Trotskyites, apoliticals and even Tories coming along... although I think most people were Libertarians of one sort or another. The predominance of anarchists as singers/songwriters probably made it seem as though there were more anarchists around than was actually so. Go and listen to the words of bands like The Mob, Rubella Ballet and Hagar again; there's a lot of personal politics, but very little anarchist rhetoric.

"And I think that the major difference between Hagar and our peers is that we didn't push anarchy, peace, vegetarianism or teenage angst as much as the others. We were more into fun for fun's sake; we were sometimes called 'The Silly Girls' behind our backs. But as I mentioned before, political theory was not the strong point of most, and they'd certainly never heard of personal politics."

"It was the DIY aspect that was most inspirational," ponders Ruth. "That anyone and everyone could do it; I think that's the one thing that has hung on in our lives since. Chris 'Elephant Face' is now one of three seminal acid-techno DJs called The Liberators, and of the three I reckon he is the best known and most sought after – because he made tapes of all his stuff and sent them to whoever requested them, getting himself valuable grass roots exposure. It's how we worked and it still works for him now. Some of the values are still there... I've always worked in not-for-profit organisations since, being much more comfortable in those settings. And a healthy disregard of authority in any shape or form seems inbuilt...

"The only real friction in the punk scene was between the anarcho-punk and Oi! factions around at the same time, two very different camps under the 'punk' umbrella that looked similar but were worlds apart. It makes me laugh now, when I see young punk pretenders in Camden Market with Crass and Exploited badges on the same lapel... that would never have happened back then! The anarcho-punk bands were positive and purposeful – with ideals, social consciences, a sense of responsibility and the ability to use their bands and the scene to strive for positive change. They never advocated blind anger, mindless destruction or hatred – many of the negative connotations associated with Oi!

"However, despite these worldlier aspirations, in our scene there was always bickering about which bands should get higher billing at gigs, or who was more 'anarcho' or who had been veggie longer. Those ideals considered as being in tune with being 'anarcho', such as vegetarianism, took a strong hold very quickly, but led to elements of righteousness amongst those who adopted them, and hypocrisy amongst those who didn't but didn't want others to know. I remember finding it funny at the time that, shortly after the release of Flux's 'Neu Smell', so many people around me went veggie overnight, and fundamentalist veggie at that. The same people who would rant at you if you still ate meat were those who had been doing so themselves up until a week ago. Their bands would push out their anti-slaughter lyrics while some of their own members would make great efforts to hide the fact that they were still eating meat. Still, if efforts like Flux's made veggies of a few thousand of us – for any length of time – that's progress…"

Following their well-received contribution to the compilation, Mortarhate duly offered the band a chance to release a full-blown 12" EP, 1984's 'The Word Of The Womb', the recording of which took place at Heart And Soul Studios, Walthamstow.

"We played with Conflict a lot, they gave us our first gigs outside of London," explains Mitch. "When Conflict decided to start their own label they asked us if we would like to be on it. And when Colin [Jerwood] says 'Come on then!' you don't say no!

"I'd been in studios before to see other bands record, and was pleased at the way Colin and Pete Fender [guitarist with Rubella Ballet, who engineered and produced that first EP] just made us belt it out. Of course, now I know to listen to the final mix before it goes to the pressing plant. What I had put down as guide vocals, on 'True (Love And Faith) Part 1', actually turned up on the record – I can't sing well, but I'm not that bad! I've just listened to the records for the first time in years though, and I still like them."

"We were around bands like Conflict a lot as they played at all the venues we hung out at," elaborates Ruth. "Colin came up to us after we'd played a few gigs and had got Chris, Mitch and Paul [Harding] in the band, who made us more musically-digestible. He noted that we were more mature in the tune department and offered us the EP. I remember the conversation well, as we came up with a condition which he, unsurprisingly, promptly met. 'Can we have badges?' 'Yes.' That was it!

"We recorded it shortly after, an all-night affair in some tiny studio; we kept coming out for bouts of cool, dark London air. We were rough, the recording was rough… and that's about it! I would've been happier with some technology slapped on, even some basics like echo to beef up the vocals, or to patch over some mistakes as most were one-take efforts, but our limited budget wouldn't allow it. Now that EP has a fond place in my heart – like an imperfect teddy-bear!"

Released early 1984, 'The Word Of The Womb' was a great success, spending over five months in the Indies and peaking at No. 6. 'Dressed To Kill', probably the best track on offer, is a ludicrously catchy pop punk ditty, drenched in youthful charm, with an insistent hook that once lodged in the listener's head refuses to let go.

"Janet and I wrote that on a 253 bus after school one day," sniggers Ruth. "With a little help from Boney M!"

Ruth of Hagar The Womb, picture by Mick Slaughter.

Karen and Ruth of Hagar The Womb.

Many gigs were undertaken to promote the release, including one noteworthy all-dayer at the Brixton Ace, supporting Conflict, where, in the resulting live review in Sounds magazine, the band were accused of being Nazis!

"The reviewer thought that the movements our singers did during 'Dressed To Kill' were fascist salutes!" scoffs Mitch incredulously. "She also claimed that, at some point, we said 'Sieg Heil'! At a later date, when we confronted her about her comments, pointing out that there were some people of African and Asian descent in the band, she admitted to being blind drunk at the bar all evening!"

"The article showed a picture of one of us waving in the air," explains Ruth. "There was actually a stage invasion during our set, and the picture was taken as we were flapping around trying to get people off it. We were well miffed and insisted on an apology for 'misconstruing hand movements'… which happened in a subsequent edition."

Such sensationalist coverage aside, Hagar The Womb went from strength to strength, even landing themselves a coveted [Dale Griffin produced] John Peel radio session off the back of the EP, by which time Elaine Reubens had joined Ruth and Karen on vocals.

"He played a song from 'Word Of The Womb' on his show," says Mitch. "Then announced afterwards that if anybody knew how to contact us, he wanted them to get us to phone him… I didn't believe the first two people who rang up to tell me! A big thanks to Conflict here as well, for lending us their backline to do the session, 'cos we still didn't have any at that point…"

"We were just so shocked when it happened," adds Ruth, who has mixed feelings about the session itself. "We had been listening to his show for ages and never thought we would be session material; to be honest we weren't savvy in marketing ourselves at the best of times as we were never ambitious in the sense of selling stuff and 'making it big.' The session itself was a bit of a [night] 'mare because it all had to be done in one day, and the drum-kit promised to us never materialised so we had to scour London for a replacement when we should've been recording. Then there was a problem with the use of the word 'fuck' in 'A Song of Deep Hate.' We were told to replace 'fuckin' hate' with 'hate, hate, hate' which just didn't flow as well and caused no end of trauma and delay.

"In the end, we got what we could down in the time we had, and I still cringe listening to it because it was so much rougher than we were at the time. I don't really know what the exposure did for us, if anything; John championed so many small bands and some got bigger as a result while others faded – I don't think it really opened any doors, but then again we never really tried to capitalise on it."

After falling out with Mortarhate (Ruth cites 'bad feeling and a lack of trust'), Hagar The Womb signed with Abstract Records, then home to the likes of New Model Army and The 3 Johns, the latter being good friends of Mitch's. The resulting 'Funnery In A Nunnery' 12" again made the Indie Top Ten upon its release in February 1985 and marked a significant musical progression for the band. More confident vocals and mature, relaxed arrangements resulted in a captivating EP that took its influences right across the board, from gothic rock to pop punk. Only 'Armchair Observer', with its rather remedial chord progression, tied the band to their primitive roots, whilst the likes of 'Once Proud, Now Dead' and 'Come Into My Soul' were so atmospheric and subtle they almost sounded like a brand new band.

"I think the major difference between the two EPs was the recording technique," reckons Mitch. "For the second one, we actually compiled 'Come Into My Soul' whilst in the studio. We had a much more proactive producer, Dave Woolfson [at Alaska Studios in Waterloo], who suggested changes to our arrangements and stuff. We also had a lot more time, and a better idea of what we could and wanted to do, so there were a lot more overdubs happening."

"That song, 'Come Into My Soul', was my statement of how you lose yourself in a relationship," adds Ruth. "But it was forever changed when Mitch got hold of my lyrics which ended, 'For the price of security rises but never erupts,' and added, 'For the pride of monogamy, what must we give up?' Obviously a strong sentiment of his, but one that changed the emphasis of the song completely. That spoilt it a bit for me really, but that's songwriter's prerogative.

"I also liked the pointed upbeat feel of 'One Bright Spark' – 'We're so happy in the midst of all this sadness' was a comment on how so many bands around us felt they needed to dwell solely on war and death etc… it all got very gloomy! 'Song Of Deep Hate', which Chris penned, got my greatest respect though, because it showed our musical maturity; I would never have believed that song could come from the likes of us!"

'Funnery…', however, would prove to be the band's final release. Mitch left mere hours before a scheduled gig with The 3 Johns at Dingwalls in Camden ("The rest of the band thought the gig was too expensive, but I thought we should play it as we were meant to be onstage in an hour and people had already paid to get in…"), only to be replaced by Paul 'Veg' Venables, who was plunged into the rigours of touring Holland the following week.

"I first saw Hagar some time in 1980 or 1981," recalls Veg. "It was with Krondstadt Uprising and The Snork Maidens at some community centre in Covent Garden; this was when Mitch was in The Snorks and Steph was playing bass for Hagar. My first thought was, 'This band have got some great songs… but they can't play them!' I fucking loved them instantly! At the time, I think me and my mate Calvin were the only two punks in London who had 'Hagar The Womb' on our jackets, which caused Ruth constant confusion… 'Hi Veg,' she would say… 'Uh, no, I'm Calvin! Put your glasses on!'"

"I was so impressed, I went out with Calvin for many years," laughs Ruth, "Or was that Veg?"

"My first proper gig with them was at Woolwich Poly with The 3 Johns," continues Veg. "It was a benefit gig for Mitch who had just been sent down for mistaken identity at some Stop The City demo in Brixton. I remember it being great, but I was so nervous I totally fucked up the first song… I'm sure it was fine after that though. In the dressing room afterwards, Karen was trying to give me £5 and I didn't understand what for. She was going 'But this is what you get paid!' And I'm thinking, 'This is such great fun – and you get paid!' Mind you, I never got paid again after that…"

There was no dramatic split to speak of, but over the next year or so, Hagar The Womb simply fizzled out, and by 1987, Chris, his girlfriend Julie Sorrell (who had been drafted in briefly as a singer after Karen left with Mitch), Paul, and Veg were permanently ensconced in We Are Going To Eat You, who went on to record for All The Madmen (1987's 'I Wish I Knew' 12"), Cat And Mouse ('Heart In Hand' EP, 1988), Big Cat and TVT before changing their name to Melt and splitting in 1991. Mitch meanwhile went on to roadie for The Mekons and play with the likes of [country-flavoured punkers] Some Dogs and Big Bottom, an art-concept band comprising five bassists, but he still remembers his time with 'the Hags' fondly.

"We'd all like to be remembered, wouldn't we? But for me, if someone, somewhere, thinks 'Oh, that Hagar The Womb gig was fun', that's good enough for me."

Ruth: "Twenty-five years on, and I am constantly surprised when I still get e-mails about the band, or see our stuff going for what seems like mega-bucks on e-bay. It's an inexplicable world, but I do like to think we chimed with others out there, if only for a short while."

SELECT DISCOGRAPHY

12"s:
'The Word Of The Womb' (Mortarhate, 1984)
'Funnery In A Nunnery' (Abstract, 1985)

At A Glance:
There are no official Hagar The Womb retrospective releases available, but the 'Who? What? Why? When? Where?' compilation, featuring 'For The Ferryman', has recently (2004) been reissued on CD by Mortarhate.

Thanks to the uniquely powerful vocal chords of singer Kay Byatt, London's **YOUTH IN ASIA** were another of the more distinctive of the early Eighties anarcho bands, yet they only wrote a dozen songs during their brief tenure, resulting in but one cassette release and an acclaimed appearance on 'Bullshit Detector 2', with the defiantly simple yet eminently memorable 'Power And The Glory'.

"I'd met these brilliant girls at a little village festival, who were all dressed so outrageously," recalls Kay, of her initiation into the intoxicating world of punk rock. "They told me to get down to the Greyhound in Croydon on a Sunday night, because that was the nearest venue to me putting on punk gigs. None of my friends wanted to go – being the boring, old hippies that they were, bless 'em – so one Sunday evening I plucked up courage and went on my own... for what proved to be a life-enhancing experience. It was totally amazing, like being transported to another world, full of misfits and outcasts who thought and felt just like me.

"The venue was buzzing, and I immediately got talking to various colourful characters. Tom Robinson, The Damned and The Cowards played, and it was so loud and raw, and there was a huge mass of people pogoing and throwing themselves about, so naturally I joined in. It was an exhilarating experience and I was immediately hooked. Thereafter I became a regular at the Greyhound [AKA 'Foxes Club'], and saw some of the finest punk bands around; everyone who was anyone played there.

"I made some amazing friends, and began to let loose with my clothes, makeup and hair; the emphasis being on second-hand, DIY, anti-fashion – the more outrageous, the better! My mother still laughs about the time I crept home with a huge vibrator around my neck..."

After making an appearance onstage as guest vocalist for The Cowards when they played an impromptu set at Croydon's Pied Bull, Kay formed the, briefly-lived but brilliantly-monikered, Kaysa Lazerbeam And The Gammatrons, with Cowards singer/guitarist Mark Lemming, which only actually lasted for one rehearsal, with Dave and Fred Berk from The Johnny Moped Band on drums and bass ("It was a totally liberating experience, and very punk rock at the time!"). Kay began dating Johnny Moped soon after, travelling all over the capital with his band and soaking up the energy of the emerging punk scene first-hand, but it was an eye-opening encounter with an infinitely more serious troupe that really prompted her to form her own 'proper' band.

"Yes, in 1979 I went to see Crass play for the first time. After two years of constant gig-going, I could see the punk scene changing... a lot of the early bands had sold out or disbanded, and the scene was becoming more commercial, which most original punks resented. The whole essence of punk was being lost.

"I'd read about Crass in the music papers, and when I heard they were playing Red Lion Square in Central London, with Poison Girls, The Eratics and The Straps, duly went along to check them out, and it was unlike any other concert I'd ever been to. There were screens showing films on either side of the stage, and all these banners with anarchist slogans on them, and a lot of the punks – and the band – were dressed all in black; it was very dark and intense, and a totally different vibe to previous gigs I'd attended.

"Nevertheless, the bands were superb, Crass especially, and I was given loads of hand-outs and fanzines, all about anarchy, all anti-state and anti-religion, far more menacing and to-the-point than anything I'd read before. I bought 'Reality Asylum' and played both sides over and over again, and decided that I really had to form my own band as I had plenty to say and protest about myself, and I needed an outlet badly.

"I saw an ad in a music paper from a bloke wanting to form a band along the lines of Crass, who lived in Clitheroe, Lancashire, and was desperate to get a band together, and although we lived 200 miles apart, we managed to meet up, and ultimately became a couple, with Mark moving down to London. He was an avid Crass fan, and had been communicating with them regularly, and he took me to their commune, where I was amazed at how friendly and down-to-earth they all were.

"Then me and Mark went travelling all round Europe for six months, and ended up living in a squatted commune in Freiburg, Germany, but we were always discussing the band we intended to form when we returned home. We moved back to London, into this squat near where Wayne Preston, one of Mark's old friends from Clitheroe who said he wanted to play bass, now lived.

"Mark and I had already come up with the name Youth In Asia, a play on the word 'euthanasia', during our travels, and I began writing lots of lyrics, fuelled with angst and inspired by Crass and Poison Girls. We followed them around on a nationwide tour during this time, and kept bumping into this bloke called Punky Pete and his girlfriend, Olga. It turned out that Pete also wanted to form a band, and was willing to play drums... like Mark on guitar and Wayne on bass, he had no previous experience, but was willing to give it a go!"

Eager to ensure that Youth In Asia wasn't a male-dominated affair, Kay asked Olga to join as second vocalist/keyboardist ("Mark had just bought one of those early Casio keyboards – about 12" long..."), and the fledgling band made their live debut in December 1981 – in Brussels, of all places!

"Well, Wayne knew this Belgian girl, Marlene, who used to hang about with Crass, and she was trying to get an English band to play over there. We did it all on the cheap, of course, because it was self-funded, although we did have accommodation laid on at the other end. I think the venue was a squat, and it was packed with Belgian punks and hippies... we were abysmal, but they loved it – probably because we were from London!

"Afterwards everyone wanted to talk to us, and we were all taken into the toilets and given lots of free drugs, then taken to some club. I remember some young lad saying that he knew I was English because of my animated face... must have been the drugs! We stayed on the floor of some girl's flat, but were kept awake all night by this dog roaring around the room like a greyhound. The next day we wandered around Brussels in the snow, freezing cold and totally skint, and then spent the night in Marlene's posh flat, and all got bitten to death by fleas! Fond memories..."

After a few more gigs back home, Punky Pete (who totally vanished off the scene and sadly died in prison during the mid-Eighties) was replaced by another of Mark's friends from Clitheroe who had freshly relocated to London, the much more dependable Eddie, and Lou from The Witches also joined on rhythm guitar, making Youth In Asia a six-piece band with a 50/50 gender split.

"To be honest, we had it pretty easy when it came to getting gigs," admits Kay. "By the time we got going as a band, the anarcho-punk scene was alive and kicking. We were very much a part of it all anyway, what with our friendship with Crass and knowing lots of other people in bands, and as soon as we were ready to play we had loads of gig offers coming in. Olga is Zillah from Rubella Ballet's sister, so Zillah made sure we always played with them, which was a great start for us... plus they always let us use their equipment, which was really decent of them. We had none of our own stuff, apart from guitars and the Casio, and we had no transport either... although most of our gigs were held in London, so it was merely a case of bunking the underground. All the bands we played with shared their equipment actually; there was a lot of trust and sincerity around in those days, and everyone mucked in to help one another.

"We became regulars at both London Anarchy Centres, and it became a bit of an arrangement that if they were short of a band, YIA would always oblige. No one ever got paid, of course, because most of the gigs we did were benefits... although we might have gotten a free beer on occasion!

"Another reason we later began playing more prestigious gigs was that Wayne worked for an independent badge company called Better Badges. Badges were big back then, and Wayne craftily began doing deals with some of the bigger bands; he'd let them have so many badges free in return for a gig, and that's how we managed to play places like the 100 Club etc.! In fact, we very nearly ended up doing a tour with Sex Gang Children because of Wayne's dodgy badge dealings, and we never had to pay for any YIA badges either."

Their friends Crass gave the band's national profile a healthy boost by including the aforementioned 'Power And The Glory' on 'Bullshit Detector 2', and soon after the compilation's release, they also invited Youth In Asia to play their Zig Zag squat show in December '82.

"That was fucking amazing; out of all the gigs I've played over the years, that is still one of my all-time favourites. Crass proved that you could squat an old venue, fill it with bands and equipment and a non-paying audience – all via word of mouth – and there didn't have to be any trouble. The vibe was something else, and there was a genuine respect amongst everyone there, a real feeling of unity – a very rare thing. Anyone who was there will always remember it; it was like one big party. We managed to get on the bill quite late, and played between Omega Tribe and Poison Girls, and went down a storm for once. I don't think you could get away with anything like that now though, not with all the rules and regulations this government imposes upon us, which is a shame."

In 1983, Youth In Asia recorded their 'Sex Object' cassette in the basement of the Poison Girls house, with Pete Fender helming the mixing desk, a ten-track release that ably captured their hypnotically quirky, unconventional sound. It sold well too, landing the band many more shows in and around London, and even some further a-field.

"Yeah, most of our gigs were in London, but we did a few up in Clitheroe, where Wayne, Mark and Eddie were from, and they were always good, with everyone in the town coming out to see the local lads play. One was especially memorable because of the band we played with, Potential Threat. They turned up late and the place was already heaving, but they had this ridiculous prima donna attitude, saying the venue was too small for them, and they wanted their petrol money back

Kay Byatt and Wayne Preston of Youth In Asia.

home, refusing point-blank to play. Naturally we were appalled, and I started laying into them, saying I'd seen Crass play a tiny air raid shelter with a leaky roof in the pissing rain, where the electricity kept cutting out on them... and this load of arseholes were refusing to play a well-organised gig in a nice church hall! We played the gig with the local band anyway, and it was a blinder, and when we got back to London I told everyone what had happened, and they didn't get invited down to play very much after that.

"Another memorable show was when we headlined downstairs at the Clarendon, which was quite a prestigious place at the time. The trouble started when the bully-boy bouncers started pushing the audience around, stopping them from dancing. It was so good to have people up to you, I didn't want to lose them, so I made an announcement through the mike telling everyone to ignore the bouncers and carry on regardless... which they did. Then, at the end of the gig, I got set upon by these bouncers, threatening to do me for causing trouble! We never did any more gigs after that where bouncers were involved... you live and learn, don't you?"

In late '83, Eddie was forced to move back to Clitheroe, to cure himself of a heroin addiction, and Lou also had to leave due to ill health (she recovered, going on to marry Faction's Rob Challice and form Hysteria Ward, who were briefly slated to release something on All The Madmen); the pair were replaced by guitarist Mick Clarke and drummer Bernie, both formerly of Windsor's Disease. Although it made for a tighter band, it was the beginning of the end for Youth In Asia.

"They were both great musicians and slotted in well, giving us a much more stable sound," explains Kay. "The problem was: we'd written no more than twelve songs in our three years together, so it was time to write some new stuff. We'd just been asked to do a 7" for Crass, and had recorded a demo at Dan [AKA the aforementioned Pete Fender]'s studio of two new songs ['When The Wind Blows' and 'Four Minute Warning'] prior to Mick and Bernie's joining. I did my bit and left Mark and Dan to mix it, and afterwards Mark confessed that Dan had redone the bass himself because Wayne couldn't keep in time. When Bernie joined he also began complaining about Wayne's rigidity, and I guess that was the heart of the problem – we wanted to progress musically, but we were unable, which ultimately led to frustration. Mick and Bernie had played together in Disease for a while, so they were a tight unit, and whilst Mark had no problem keeping up with them, poor old Wayne couldn't manage it.

"Also we'd begun to move in separate directions outside of the band as well; Wayne had a business to run, Olga was expecting her second child, so they both had important personal matters to attend to, whilst the rest of us were concentrating on writing new songs and making some musical headway.

"Hagar The Womb had just split, or were on the verge of doing so, and their bassist Steph was looking for a band to join, and Mark was keen to work with her. The next part got a bit messy, and I've always felt bad about it, so this is my feeble attempt to clear the air with Wayne and Olga...

"I was personally fed up with the increasing tensions; I was pleased that we had a single lined up on Crass, but thought it would be a waste of their time, to be honest, seeing as we might not even be together by the time it came out. But I wanted to stick with Mick, Bernie and Mark, but none of us wanted to kick anyone out (we were all friends with Wayne and Olga, for heaven's sake!), so between us, we decided to end YIA and start a brand new band, Decadent Few, away from the anarcho scene, with a different sound and a different bassist.

"The thing is: I dropped the bombshell in a very shoddy manner; before discussing it with Wayne and Olga, I told a mutual acquaintance, who immediately went and told them, and they were understandably pissed off. It was very immature, although I don't regret the decision; just the way I handled it, which was very underhand."

Steph didn't continue for long with Decadent Few and was replaced on bass by Gary Smith; Mark then bowed out, to concentrate on a career as an electrician, leaving the band as a four-piece. Wayne and Olga even did a few gigs as Decadent Two, and had a track on the Mortarhate compilation, 'We Won't Be Your Fucking Poor', billed as Duet; they eventually married and had several children together.

As well as Decadent Few, Kay also went on to sing with Radical Dance Faction (RDF) for a while – whilst married to Phil, their guitarist – and then The Astronauts. She now lives on the south coast, bringing up her son, but is working on some new songs with Mick, who still runs Inflammable Material distribution, that they hope to record in the near future.

"Once a punk, always a punk!" chuckles Kay. "But seriously, inside I've not changed that much. I've still got that burning inner rage that made punk seem so appealing in the first place. I always was, and always will be, a square peg that won't fit into any nice, convenient pigeonhole, and that's what punk was about – a freak show for the freaks so they could freak everyone else out! Wonderful times…

"Youth In Asia were odd in our own strange way, but now, when I listen back to 'Sex Object', I can appreciate our oddness for what it was, and although we were musically limited, we did dabble with some mad ideas. Our hearts were certainly in the right place too, we were never about preaching anarchist slogans for the sake of them, and it might be hard to believe, but we had a great laugh as well. They were bloody excellent times looking back.

"But I did tire of punk's formality after a while; I thought the scene was about breaking rules, not making them. It became a very 'right on' movement, and maybe a little too puritanical for its own good, with Crass looked upon as virtual gods towards the end!

"Of course, I still feel very strongly about most of the issues I wrote about in YIA, and that inner anger keeps me going. I'll always be a non-conformist in my own way, and will undoubtedly end up one of those silly old biddies in a twilight home with bright purple hair and a nose stud and stuff, singing along to the classic old punk songs on a dodgy cassette, annoying all the other residents! I'd like to think that the other ex-members feel the same… I know Mick does."

At A Glance:
There's no official CD release of Youth In Asia, although 'When The Wind Blows', from their last ever recording session before they split, is included on Overground's 'Anti-War, Anarcho-Punk Compilation, Volume One'.

If anarcho-punk was just about raging against the system at 1000 mph, then London's FLOWERS IN THE DUSTBIN wouldn't be in this book. But thankfully the scene had far more substance than that, despite what its detractors would have us believe, and defiantly eclectic bands such as Flowers... helped add a convincing depth and diversity to the anarcho canon. Rising from the gory remains of the Anabollic [sic] Steroids, they were instantly discernible from many of their peers, and considerably more ambitious sonically than their first outfit suggested they might be.

"When I look back on the Steroids, it was kind of like performance art," reckons vocalist Gerard Evans. "We were that unconcerned about being musical, we didn't even tune up... we didn't know how to tune up, in fact. Our bassist only had one string. We were taking the Sex Pistols' adage that anyone could do it to a real extreme, even more so than The Slits. What was influencing us wasn't so much 'Never Mind The Bollocks', although we loved that, it was more 'The Great Rock'n'roll Swindle'; we knew that McLaren wasn't being serious when he said, 'Find yourself four kids and form a band', but we thought it was funny and tried to take that kind of angle. We were doing it for a laugh.

"I was doing a fanzine at the time as well, called 'Ability Stinks'. There used to be these classified ads in the back of Sounds, and people used to put little statements on their ads, and there was this band called The Bollocks, and they just put 'Ability Stinks' at the bottom of their ad, which I thought was great. And the Anabollic Steroids even had a song called that as well; we really built this ethos that all the local punk rockers got into, that you really didn't have to be able to play, and we did all these chaotic gigs."

Indeed the Steroids actually played several shows at the Wapping Anarchy Centre at the bequest of Andy Martin of The Apostles and his Scum Collective, but split before they could be immortalised on vinyl.

"Yeah, I stopped the Steroids because I didn't like all these appalling punk bands that were about, I just wanted to do something more musical. I was very into Adam And The Ants, and when 'Kings Of The Wild Frontier' came out, I thought it was fantastic... as did most punks, I think, until Adam started appearing on kids' television and stuff. But when it originally came out, they were still a punk band, and they did this incredible album that I was completely inspired by.

"I loved 'Dirk...' ['... Wears White Sox', the 1979 debut by the Ants] as well, but I could never aspire to play music like that because I knew I'd just end up sounding like a tenth-rate version... just like you had a lot of tenth-rate versions of Joy Division and all that. But 'Kings...' had this huge tribal thing going on, the whole Red Indian vibe, with the Western guitars... 'Western' as in Spaghetti Western, of course. More than anything, it made me realise that I could do a lot more than I was with the Steroids; I wanted to do something more colourful, in every possible sense of the word."

The original, short-lived incarnation of Flowers saw Gerard and bassist Chas [real name Charlie Loft] playing alongside Joanne Mead and Samantha 'Noname' – on drums and guitars/vocals respectively – and the band's 1983 public debut was predictably eventful.

"Well, Chas had been temporarily kicked out of the band, for reasons far too long and boring to go into, and we played our first gig at the Lee Centre in South London. Where I cut myself up onstage quite badly with a razor blade... a half-Iggy Pop, half-Ian Curtis moment... I've still got the scar, see? I had started [to self-harm] in my personal life, so as an artist I figured I had the right to take it onstage with me, I suppose...

"Consequently, two of the four band members – two of the women – left immediately, because I hadn't told anyone that I was going to do it! They were upset... people in the audience were quite upset too, because I cut myself really badly... we only did two songs, one of them about fifteen minutes long. A few of the girls were going out with some of the guys from King Kurt, who were really 'Ha ha, let's have a laugh!'-kinda blokes, and they weren't impressed either... well, it was hardly a King Kurt moment, was it?

"So, that was the first gig, but I don't really count it as a Flower... show, to be honest, even though we were called Flowers... at that point. The first 'real' gig was in Wolverhampton, with a [Telford] band called Curse Of Eve, at the Archers Club. It was normally a night club, with all the mirrors and disco lights and so on. We were good friends with a load of the Telford punks, which is how that came about really, and we had an affinity with Curse Of Eve... they were a bit like The Slits, but with a feminist angle... the 'empowering women' angle though, rather than the man-hating one."

The 'Always Another Door' demo was duly recorded, and what it lacked in musical finesse compared to later Flowers... recordings, it compensated for with intelligent, positive energy – qualities that were too often sadly lacking in early Eighties UK punk rock.

"Yeah, me and Chas did that, just the two of us," reveals Gerard. "We went to this really shit studio in Catford, and he did guitar and bass and I did drums and vocals... though obviously not at the same time! It was called 'Always Another Door', because

one of my main inspirations for the band apart from Adam And The Ants was this novel called 'Always Another Door', a '50s novel, a true story about a woman called Pamela Russell. She fell off her horse or got knocked over by a car or something, and was made disabled, confined to a wheelchair, and it's all about how it didn't stop her in life. I was full of teenage angst at the time, and saw some sort of analogy there with my own life, so called our demo 'Always Another Door'."

As they clocked up shows in and around London on the back of the tape, including dates with the likes of Omega Tribe, Lost Cherrees and Flux Of Pink Indians, the band began to build a modest following amongst the anarcho squatter and anarcho goth scenes (two pedantically named sub-genres that were all just part of the burgeoning punk scene at the time), aligning themselves in particular with the Kill Your Pet Puppy collective and the Black Sheep Housing co-op, that also numbered amongst its ranks members of The Mob and Sex Gang Children.

"It was a bit of both really," ponders Gerard, on whether the band found themselves hailed as anarcho punks by accident or design. "It's not a word I'm comfortable with, but we were all anarchists... more or less... politically active a lot of the time. We were involved with organising the first Stop The City... we were the only band involved with Stop The City, in fact... and that put us firmly in that scene to an extent. But we never used to go onstage and shout, 'Fuck the system!'

"Yes, originally there was a very broad umbrella of anarcho bands, before it all split off into goth

Flowers In The Dustbin, live in Telford, 1984.

or positive punk or hardcore or whatever... and there was indeed a strand somewhere in there that we were a part of. I'd say that we belonged to the same scene as The Mob, Poison Girls and Rubella Ballet. We certainly related to all those bands, but where we differed from a lot of them was that we were never contained within that scene, we'd go off and play with other kinds of bands, as long as it wasn't at rip-off prices. We did refuse gigs if the entrance fee was too much... we refused a gig supporting Mercenary Skank at the Marquee once, although we did gigs elsewhere with them, and our place on the bill that night was taken by a young goth band called Stone Roses...!"

Elaborating on just why he felt restricted by the 'anarcho' pigeonhole, Gerard adds:

"We were doing a gig once with some offshoot of UK Decay... essentially some goth-type band anyway... at the Hammersmith Clarendon, and I was outside the venue when I heard someone say, 'Oh, Flowers In The Dustbin... they're that squatter's band, aren't they?' And I thought, 'Jesus, is that how people see us?' Y'know?

"I mean, yeah, admittedly we were a squatter's band... well, we were a band who squatted, but we weren't a squatter's band... do you know what I mean? And I was worried that we would just get tied in with all those tired clichés. We didn't live on buses, we didn't go to Stonehenge... in fact, we always refused to play festivals because we knew how badly organised they were. We didn't want to wait around for eight hours to go onstage, we couldn't handle that.

"So I suppose we were a maverick anarcho band. Politically we were very active, to the point where both Chas and I had the police try to frame us in court and stuff, but we just never felt the need to talk about all that, I guess.

"I think it's important to remember that alongside the generic scene that anarcho-punk will almost certainly be remembered for, there was a completely parallel scene that was nothing like that – people who had been into the New York Dolls, who wore make-up, bands like Blood 'N' Roses and Brigandage... those people were just as much anarcho punks as the people with all the patches and the ripped jeans... in fact, more so, in many respects. And we would have been comfortable if that had been the way the scene had been portrayed... you know, these Adam And The Ants offshoots but with sincerity. Which is what I thought Southern Death Cult were going to be, but they weren't in the end. There was a lot of excitement about them when they came out, because they were everything you could want from an anarcho band really, except Ian

Flowers In The Dustbin (Cold Harbour promotional shot, left to right: Bill Mahoney, John Howells, Gerard Evans, Antje Klaehn, Chas Loft).

wasn't an anarchist anymore. He was a big Poison Girls fan, did you know? I don't blame him for anything though… I mean, he's ended up singing for The Doors, hasn't he? I would've settled for that!"

1984 saw the band finally cementing their nebulous line-up long enough (with guitarist Simon Barry and drummer Bill Mahoney, formerly of London's Fear) to record and release the nefariously diverse 'Freaks Run Wild At The Disco' 12" for All The Madmen Records, the label initially set up by members of The Mob.

"It was more the Puppy collective than The Mob themselves," corrects Gerard. "Mark from The Mob lived with Tony D. and Alistair [Livingston] and Mick Lugworm from the Puppy collective, and I never really got to know any of the other people from The Mob. Tony did the first ever review of us, he was writing for the NME at the time and reviewed us when we played the Burn It Down Ballroom, this squatted venue on the Finchley Road… and he gave us a good review, of course. There was a sense then of almost being a Fifth Column; there were certain writers who were biased towards that scene because it was a culture. There wasn't a culture around any other bands… there was no culture around a band like Nirvana, I don't think. They had long hair and they were pissed off, which is fair enough, and they might have been the greatest band ever or whatever, but it wasn't a culture, was it? And anarcho-punk was a culture, certainly in London, and whenever it entered the mainstream there was this Fifth Columnist mentality, so it was almost a given that Tony would give us a good review.

"And then Mick Lugworm, who was a bit of a mover and shaker – he was at every gig in London – came up to us and asked us if we wanted to do a record for ATM. And we were gob-smacked, 'cos doing a record hadn't even occurred to us… it was the culmination of all my ambitions, because I thought, 'If I can get a record out, it means I'm not completely untalented, not completely deluding myself!' I probably formed a band to shag girls like everyone else does, but I was also looking for some sort of self-validation as well, grasping for a sense that I had some sort of worth."

Indeed, the artistic worth of 'Freaks…' is beyond question, the 12" being a volatile cocktail of impassioned vocals, delicate guitar harmonies, and dramatic atmospherics. Only the thumping 'Last Tango In Vietnam' is instantly classifiable as punk rock; elsewhere the mournful, piano-led 'True Courage' throbs with a quiet intensity, whilst 'Pocketful Of Gold' is a craftily-composed, yet tragic, tale of innocent dreams being swept aside by the trials and tribulations of adulthood.

'All The Best People Are Perverts' was the next release, a lo-fi cassette-only affair on Rob Challice's 96 Tapes, a label named as such because it was run out of No. 96, Brougham Rd., Hackney.

"There was no real effort made there," reckons Gerard. "It was just a collection of demos and live stuff. They'd recently done this tape of Blood 'N' Roses, and to be honest, if they hadn't, we probably wouldn't have bothered, 'cos cassette was definitely a sort of second-class release as far as I was concerned."

Much more convincing was the 'Nails Of The Heart' 7" that the band issued in 1985 through Conflict's Mortarhate label, a surprising alliance considering that Flowers… were not only at considerable odds with Conflict's own musical style, but also out on a limb as regards all the other bands on the roster.

"That's right, yeah. I was living in Bromley, and Conflict were in Eltham, which is just a bus ride away… but Mortarhate had their office in Bromley. In actual fact, Colin was living in Bromley too, he had a flat there, but we didn't bump into each other in the street or anything, so I'm sure that wasn't the reason. For all the so-called differences though, we had a lot more in common with Conflict than, say… oh, I don't know… Skrewdriver or someone! I still went to see Crass play, and I'd see the Conflict guys there… we were doing different things when we were onstage, but we were doing very similar things offstage. All The Madmen didn't have any more money to put anything else out by us, and Mortarhate asked us, and we just said, 'Yeah!' We didn't know where our next record would be coming from, but we knew that we wanted one out.

"And the Conflict single was a lot more professionally accomplished than 'Freaks Run Wild'… we'd recorded that in Gold Dust Studios in Sidcup, Kent. I literally got it out of the Yellow Pages, y'know? I wanted a 24-track studio at the right price, and we had two days in there to record the five songs, but I got this horrible throat infection, and I had to go home. So we had to do a third day, which probably didn't do ATM's finances any good at all!

"The second single we did at Alaska though, a bloody good studio, and Conflict just let us get on with it. Rob Hendry, who ran our rehearsal studio and had become our soundman and our driver, produced it. He used to be a big session musician; he was in Twiggy's band, he was in Nashville Teens, Renaissance… he'd already recorded our demos, the ones that came out on the 96 tape, but with 24 tracks to play with, he could make a bit more of a go of it. But they put the record out, and then we lost contact with them. I think it sold out just because it was on Mortarhate, so it was hard to gauge how well it was received, because 'X amount' of people bought all those records anyway, if only to put them in their collections.

"We gave a copy to John Peel; we hung around and handed it him as he was going into work… he did play it, but about three months after we gave it him, and said, 'That's really good, I wish I'd played it before!' Mmm, so do I! But that was another culmination of some of my dreams, to get John Peel to play us."

Following the moderate success of the Mortarhate single, Flowers In The Dustbin signed with Cold Harbour, a new label started up by two ex-EMI employees keen to branch out on their own, Steve Fernie and Mark Walmesley (who was also then manager of The Cardiacs, and would later go on to manage Napalm Death).

Originally signed for two singles and an album, which the band recorded onto an eight-track Portastudio provided by Cold Harbour, only one single ever materialised, dissent setting in between the core members of the band at a crucial point in their potential career.

"We were all on the dole throughout this period, which was okay because we were 'artists' and we just looked at it like an art grant, but we were starting to wonder what it would be like to be full-time musicians. Because the job centre were on our backs, and the last thing any of us wanted was an actual job; we'd always made a point of being absolutely committed to what we were doing with our music, so having a job was just not on the cards at all…

"Which is where the schism with Si came along; he'd been off to do a part-time college course… and just as we were planning to do this album, he sat us down and asked us to put the writing on hold while he did his exams. Of course, he wasn't just saying that, he was asking us to put our lives on hold while he did his exams. I wasn't happy – I thought it was completely insulting – so I sorta said 'It's me or him!' to the other guys, and at the end of the day it was my band, so it wasn't really much competition."

Simon was replaced by German-born Antje Klaehn, with John Howells also being drafted in on keyboards ("to beef it up a bit, because Antje had a much more delicate style of playing than Si…"), a line-up change that brought the best out in the band's inherently quirky sound, the keys adding a hint of Sixties psychedelia to proceedings.

The subsequent single, 1986's 'Lick My Crazy Colours', was a heady concoction of introspective, rolling bass lines, pseudo-folk guitar harmonies, and Gerard's endearingly vulnerable vocals conveying beautifully a desperate sense of yearning.

To promote the release, Flowers… undertook an extensive UK tour in support of all-female Birmingham post-'punks' Fuzzbox, which although an enjoyable experience was the final nail in the band's coffin.

"We were smoking a lot of dope by this time, and drinking a lot of beer," sighs Gerard. "And we'd always had this strict rule about going onstage straight, but me and Bill had just about kicked that into touch by then, and we were really getting into hedonism, the whole rock'n'roll lifestyle really. We crossed the line basically… nothing bad happened though, and the tour was probably the best time of my life. I defy anybody to travel to a different place every night, be the centre of attention when you get there, show off onstage, and get paid for it, but not enjoy it! It's such a buzz, and when it isn't a buzz, you can always take lots of drugs! But ultimately all the art had gone… all the heart had gone as well…

"This was December '86, and the whole scene had finished in a lot of ways. Chas was still really involved with Hackney Community Defence, but it was all going through a real lull. It was pre-Poll Tax but post-anarcho, and there was a bit of a cultural dirge in that respect. Critically though, the Miners Strike had just been lost, and essentially the class war with it, and there was an empty, 'Shit, what do we do now?' feeling. The war was over and the good guys lost… everyone was bailing out in their own personal way."

Despite morale being through the floor, Flowers persevered and half-heartedly played a few more shows, one of which almost resulted in tragedy.

"That was at Surrey University, Guildford, with The Primitives, who were having their big hit at the time. Chas and Bill had a really bad fight in front of the venue… we weren't subtle enough to have it backstage… and we weren't rock'n'roll enough to have it onstage! Anyway, I got between them and had my leg broken really badly. To a point where I was almost crippled for life… it was a hairline fracture, and I walked around on it for ages, and I developed a calcified haematoma… where basically another bone grew in between my two thigh muscles, and when I finally went to hospital because I couldn't even bend my leg anymore, they said that they'd never seen one that big before. I was an outpatient for six months, and, to start with, they didn't think I'd walk properly again.

"That was essentially where it ended, but ironically, despite all that, we soldiered on for three or four gigs, but I can't remember where they were. By then we were all falling apart as human beings, taking drugs and drinking an awful lot, falling into that whole thing we'd always been careful to avoid. We all felt a bit lost, we didn't know what to do or where to go."

Gerard has continued to write music to this day, most recently starting up a successful web design company and even writing a well-received book on folk music heroes, The Levellers. His most recent book, published in September, 2006, is – aptly enough – all about Crass.

"I've got no regrets musically," he reflects. "All my regrets are from our lack of internal organisation really. Maybe if someone had shaken us by the scruff of the neck, we'd have been a more effective unit. That's what I most admired about Crass; they were such an effective unit, they really were living the dream... the music was what I admired least. That was one of the themes with Flowers... the gap between talking about it and living it. Certainly me and Chas – probably all of us, to be honest – really believed in actually doing it; we weren't pissing about, it wasn't some showbiz façade, we really meant it. And we thought that a lot of other people didn't mean it, a lot of bands were hiding behind a political façade.

"A lot of the anarcho-punk scene was very black-and-white... 'This is right, that is wrong!' But we weren't afraid to reveal our emotions... I was coming from a very Patti Smith angle on that front. When I heard 'Horses' by Patti, that blew all my parameters wide open about what you can do with music. I realised that bands like The Clash and the Pistols were stuck in just one dimension, but Patti Smith was trying to achieve something more, she was writing real poetry, expressing real pain and loss. A lot of other bands were screaming against external things, but we were screaming against the effects that those things were having on us inside.

"On an even greater level, I think we were dealing with similar areas to William Blake, the loss of our own innocence... trying somehow to keep hold of the innocence of our childhoods. A lot of it was about post-puberty angst, about hating the thought of joining the adult world. On songs like 'Pocketful Of Gold', where I sang, 'I just wanna stay pure, don't wanna grow old', that was very heartfelt; I didn't want to end up all broken and forgotten."

SELECT DISCOGRAPHY

7"s:
'Nails Of The Heart' (Mortarhate, 1985)
'Lick My Crazy Colours' (Cold Harbour, 1986)

12"s:
''Freaks Run Wild In The Disco' (All The Madmen, 1984)

At A Glance:
At the time of writing, Honey Bear Records, ran by Lance Hahn of US punk band J. Church, has in the works a 22-track Flowers In The Dustbin compilation CD, 'It's Okay To Be Ugly'.

Blood And Roses signing to Kamera Records in St Paul's Cathedral (left to right: Bob Short, Jez, Saul Galpern from Kamera, and Richard).

BLOOD AND ROSES have been described as 'one of the best goth punk bands of all time', and they almost certainly were just that, despite their own resistance of the gothic tag, and all the 'doom and gloom' trappings that accompanied it. So, why are they here, nestled in a book on the UK anarcho-punk scene? Well, as suggested by Gerard from Flowers In The Dustbin earlier, for a brief period back then, it didn't matter whether you wore eyeliner or bondage trousers – or both! Anyone who felt ostracised by regular society could be a punk. And whilst Blood And Roses most certainly bore little resemblance to the likes of Crass or Conflict musically, their take on the concepts of right and wrong were virtually the same, and their lifestyle – ensconced deep in the trenches of the London squatting scene – certainly warrants examination here.

"I hadn't even heard of such a thing as a goth (outside of the history books) until long after Blood And Roses had bitten the dust," reckons guitarist Bob Short, who actually grew up in Wollongong, just outside Sydney, Australia, and moved to London in 1979 when he simply got bored of his band, the Urban Guerrillas, and the life he was living 'down under'. "I'm told that makes us 'proto-goth'… and I still don't know what that means. I saw the Banshees and the Sex Pistols and PiL, and a thousand lesser bands on Top Of The Pops and I just figured they were bands, and we were a band. In the same way, that I just thought of Crass as a band… I've always either liked something or not liked it.

"I never really referred to us as any particular kind of a band; I don't really think we fitted into any convenient package. When we played at the Anarchy Centre, we didn't sound out of place… and they were without doubt the best gigs we played. That was where we felt at home, they were the people we liked playing to. My very favourite gig we ever did was at the Centro Iberico, when we got up at the end of the night to play a short set, just because we were all there. We played three songs and the whole place just exploded. In the gaps between songs, the roar that came back at us seemed louder than the band; it was like some giant animal roaring… that was cool."

Whilst back in Sydney, Bob took note of Radio Birdman who were dominating the Sydney scene at the time: a band who forged success on their own terms, despite encountering nothing but apathy for their cause to start with.

"Yes, I particularly liked the way they thought," explains Bob. "They picked an unpopular road and beat their heads against it until people started listening… 'No one will book us, so we'll start our own club… no record company will touch us, so we'll do it ourselves!' Whilst that became a fairly standard avenue to follow over the next couple of years, these were amazing ideas at the time: the notion that you didn't need to wait for permission.

"In Brisbane, The Saints had pretty much done the same thing; their self-pressed '(I'm) Stranded' single hit the shelves the day after the Ramones LP. The UK bands at the time were all hanging out for major labels. The only place the Saints could play was in the front room of their house, nobody would have them. Yet live, they were amazing. I remember sitting outside a hall listening to their sound-check, and just the sound of the bass drum sent shivers down my spine. Finally, they hit the stage and just ploughed through their set; they stood there looking like men braced against a storm, screaming feedback against the wind.

"One of the biggest influences on my life has been this notion that you do what you do, no matter how many times you're told to fuck off and die. You don't do it for fame or recognition or money; you do it because you don't have any other choice but to do it."

Before the Urban Guerrillas, Bob cut his teeth in Filth, alongside vocalist Peter Tillman, who would later front the Lipstick Killers, a messy, anarchic punk band who only played a handful of shows, but left their mark on anyone who witnessed the impromptu chaos of their performances.

"The 'anarchy' was more youthful nihilism than anything else," admits Bob, "Although there was a definite political consciousness developing in my song-writing. To me, the songwriting was the most important thing; learning to play guitar was a way to let off steam, but writing songs was something else. Something (and I use this word advisably) magical. I figured that if something could just appear in your head like that, you had a duty to share it with others. Lisa [of Blood And Roses] later identified my greatest need as to communicate and be understood.

"The Urban Guerrillas could definitely have been described as an anarcho-punk band though. The political themes hardened up… we were anti-war, anti-government, anti-religion. We called ourselves punks, and we looked like punks; we were unified in that kind of identity. There was safety in numbers and it doesn't take a genius to work out why I would find that an appealing concept. Everyone looked at us as if we'd come from another planet; the villagers would light their torches and start sharpening their pitchforks whenever we walked by. Along the way, I copped more than a few beatings…"

Upon arriving in London, and having nowhere else to go, Bob quickly found himself a part of the burgeoning squat scene, and although this initially seemed a far more tolerant crucible than the Australian outback, prejudice is sadly a worldwide trait, the narrow minds it relies on for succour a truly international phenomenon.

"Squatting was fun and terrifying, sad and boring. It was like living in an X-rated version of [popular UK soap operas] 'Coronation Street' or 'East Enders'; there was sex and drugs and rock and roll… there was also squalor, disease and death. I felt feelings of belonging and community I will probably never feel again, but there were also times marked by emotional pain and loneliness.

We had nothing but each other's company, but sometimes we hated each other's guts.

"Different squats had different vibes. It's difficult to, say, compare the Fire Station at Old Street with the Campbell buildings in Waterloo, or Derby Lodge in King's Cross. Different people, different music and different drugs... two months was a long time in London. One day everyone was doing speed and listening to the Ants, and then suddenly we're all dropping valium and someone upstairs is playing Public Image's 'Theme' over and over and over again. There you are, too 'off your tree' to go upstairs and change the disc, and someone has crashed out with the bar on the record player up, so it is on eternal repeat. Twenty-four-hours-a-day exposure to John Lydon wishing he could die can have devastating effects on the human psyche...!

"'We have nothing to fear from chaos, we have always lived in holes in the wall...' It's almost definitely misquoted, and I

Lisa of Blood And Roses, live at Clissold Park.

forget who said it, but the point is obvious. Poverty is a great politicising force. Whilst the working class were growing enough enfranchisement to vote Tory at the general election, an underclass was growing... and in many ways, the system encouraged it. If you were on the dole, private rental was not an option in London and council housing was primarily targeted at families. If you were young, broke and pursuing any kind of alternative lifestyle, the system had no need or place for you.

"I think it's fairly important to discuss the violence of the period as well," he adds regretfully. "It was pretty much like a small war going on, far away from the prying eyes of the world. Initially, skinhead violence was purely territorial – they would claim a band for their own (Sham 69 or one of their ilk) and aggressively drive punks away from the gigs – but towards the beginning of '79, the violence shifted to direct assaults on squats.

"The first time a Crass gig was targeted was at a community centre in Waterloo. A group of thirty skinheads burst through the entrance and moved three-quarters of the way up the hall before turning and herding people out. This left the hardcore of fans (although I hate to use that word because it is so patronising) at the front of the hall. After clearing the back of the venue, the skinheads moved forward to beat up everyone at the front. It all happened very quickly, and there had obviously been a fair degree of forward planning.

"Everyone remembers the Conway Hall gig Crass played, when the Socialist Workers came in to do battle with the skinheads. I remember being extremely pleased they had come because I, for one, was getting a little pissed off with having the shit kicked out of me by bald-headed freaks. I think the fact that Crass decided to criticise the SWP said a lot for their ideology, but lost them one or two friends on the scene. They were living happily in their Essex commune, while we were living in fear of having various objects shoved up our arseholes – literally!"

It was at the Old Street squat that Bob met bassist Ruth 'Ruthless' Tyndall, although a proper band didn't really begin to take shape until they were holed up in the Campbell building and met vocalist Lisa Kirby and drummer Richard Morgan. They made the deliberate, not to mention, novel decision to not have a name, just a symbol.

"Yeah, it was like a hammer and sickle barred by a swastika and formed into a question mark, and provided the opportunity to bombard a variety of sites with some mind-fucking graffiti, but we were low-life scum – quite literally street people – and no one was going to let us anywhere near a venue.

"We scraped some money together and tried to record a demo tape at Alaska studios. The results were dreadful – bad enough to make you want to throw your instrument in the dustbin. Some guy from Essex actually stole the one copy we had... and we are eternally in his debt!

"Finally, at the start of 1981, we got a gig at a pub in Bethnal Green. We were so dreadful that someone should have taken us out the back and put us out of our misery. We plodded through about eight of our ten songs, unable to hear each other. After trying to get it together for a year and a half, we just fucked it up. Ruth made the sensible choice and left the band and abandoned the self-destructive lifestyle..."

After a brief stint with "one of Richard's drug buddies" on bass – the aptly-named 'Clapham' (he was, after all, from Clapham) – and a gig in Stoke Newington's Clissold Park under the Cramps-inspired moniker 'ABCDEFG', Jez James was recruited as bassist and the band finally played their first gig as Blood And Roses at the Anarchy Centre during early January 1982.

"Ten days or so earlier, on Christmas Eve, a gang of skinheads had broken into the squat on a 'smash and injure' mission. Some things seemed to never change! For the next couple of months, it was the only place we played. Then, when it closed down, we started to play the Centro Iberico a lot, although we got the odd gig at the Moonlight and a few pubs here and there, but the 'mainstream' circuit remained closed to us. Later, I was told that this was because we had been one of the Anarchy Centre bands which had pulled the crowds away from the Lyceum and led to its closure... which is a ridiculous story; the Anarchy Centres rarely pulled more than two or three hundred people, no matter what anyone says. You wouldn't have been able to fit many more people into Wapping if you tried. Of course, these days, if some of the tales I hear are true, the Anarchy Centre must have been double the size of Wembley, the amount of people who were allegedly there."

In late '82, this line-up of Blood And Roses recorded both a well-received session for John Peel and the 'Love Under Will' EP, which was released in February the following year (the band insisted on signing to new label Kamera in St. Paul's cathedral!). 1983 also saw the 'Life After Death' cassette (a collection of live and demo recordings) emerge through 96 Tapes, and the inclusion of 'ShM YHShVH' on 'The Whip', a Kamera compilation that has since acquired something of a cult following.

Although thinly-produced and held in low regard by Bob, that debut EP has some great moments, not least of all the ponderous, brooding 'Necromantra', a powerful anti-war dirge draped seductively in the velvet frippery of gothdom. It led to them appearing on the ITV programme 'South Of Watford', a documentary about the positive aspects of punk rock hosted by the writer Michael Moorcock.

"Fed up with all the attention" they were getting, the band actually split for a short while, before regrouping, with Ralph Jezzard on bass, and striking a deal in 1985 with Norwich-based Backs Records to put out future releases on their own Audiodrome label. The 'Enough Is Never Enough' album and '(Some) Like It Hot' EP were the impressive results, both mixing imposing soundtrack sensibilities with some wonderfully dark, atmospheric rock, Lisa's commanding, ethereal vocals soaring over the rumbling toms and Bob's expansive guitar scratchings, all demonstrating a tremendous growth in the band's confidence and abilities.

By the end of the following year however, Blood And Roses were no more, having split once again, at the seeming height of their musical powers, and this time for good, depriving the world of an artistic band of great substance.

"After the album came out, Lisa became pregnant and that meant we had to back off from playing live," explains Bob. "We started recording another album with a drummer called Kate, but we were recording in the 'dead time' of a studio that was dying faster than we could lay down our tracks! There was talk of going on tour to America with the Only Ones but there was no funding, and the drugs were coming down like rain on a blocked drain. We called it a day in the end, and by then we went out with more of a whimper than a bang."

After playing in various bands ("Junkyard Blues were a personal favourite of mine, whose one gig supporting the Subhumans at a Uni in Strathfield was a minor miracle of major property damage, rioting and drunken abandon!"), Bob returned home to Australia, where he now makes low-budget films and is the musical director for the Horizon theatre company.

"My belief in the potential for an anarchist-based society probably took a hammering when I went out for a train ride to a girlfriend's parents' house. I think I'd spent the bulk of the previous five years in the tight confines of the squat scene, and my world had become very small. Even when touring I was huddled in the back of the transit [van] and I didn't stop to watch the world go by. On the train trip, I was suddenly struck by just how vast suburbia actually was, and how the bulk of Western civilization lives like that, aspires to that and wants nothing else but that. I thought the chances of them giving it all up were remarkably slim…

"That said, I continue to believe you should try to act as a moral beacon. You should live in a way that is true to your beliefs. Do I succeed in that? I try. When I write, make a film, or make music, I continue down a path I've been walking since a dumb song entered my head in 1977. Do I think music can change the world? I know music can change the world because music changed me… it changed others like me… and it brings me together with other people. When we give voice to our ideas, we give them to the world in direct contrast to the voices that would oppress us.

"I believe the world is shaped by media. If the airways are filled with pretty young things singing about love and cars, they are changing the world too… for the worse. Anyone who does anything to the contrary is changing things for the better."

SELECT DISCOGRAPHY

7"s:
'(Some) Like It Hot' (Audiodrome, 1985)

12"s:
'Love Under Will' (Kamera, 1983)
'(Some) Like It Hot' (Audiodrome, 1985)

LPs:
'Enough Is Never Enough' LP (Audiodrome, 1985)

At A Glance:
There are no definitive Blood And Roses collections available, although the interested reader can contact Bob at: kxv666@hotmail.com.

Sadly, ANATHEMA, a tuneful punk band from New Malden, Surrey, never ever made it onto vinyl, despite a planned split single with The Apostles and one of their tracks being billed for inclusion on the Mortarhate compilation, 'We Won't Be Your Fucking Poor' – their name actually appeared on the cover of the album, but their music was omitted in error! Such near-misses would seem enough to make anyone bitter, but not vocalist Lawrence 'Lol' Cooper, who merely shrugs philosophically:

"I do still feel a little frustrated about it, but I think at the time we were just doing our thing. And besides, on a more positive note, there was such a big underground network of tape labels and fanzines around then, a lot of people still got to hear us anyway… just not on vinyl.

"You have to remember that we were very young at the time, compared to a lot of the other people out there doing stuff; we were all still at school when Anathema started in 1983, and I think that if we had been just that little bit older, we would have done more, vinyl-wise. But at the time we were just enjoying being a part of it all."

And Lol really was right in the thick of it, doing his own tape label and fanzine ('Persons Unknown'), as well as fronting the band and helping build the thriving scene around the Kingston-Upon-Thames area.

"Yeah, I ran Love Of Life [i.e. LOL] tapes, releasing stuff by us and many other bands from all over the world; there was a big underground network in those days, of like-minded people exchanging different, creative stuff from around the globe. It was good because we could put out what we wanted, how we wanted, and people would get the chance to hear it… no big bucks or business plans, just being really into something and sharing it with others. I don't think you have that now, which is a shame. That's how you knew about all these different bands and stuff, not the mainstream music press; it was all done for the people, by the people. Those days are sadly long gone now; it's gone completely the other way, in fact."

Joined by guitarist James Jenkins (whose searing lead work helped lend the band a uniquely slick edge), bassist Edwin Glass (both of whom were also with London metallers Maniac) and drummer Joe Daldorph, Anathema began gigging at such local venues as the William Morris Club, The Dolphin and The Swan, with bands such as The Throbs, Menace Dancers and Fungus, but it was Lol's politically-charged lyrics that got them so heavily associated with anarcho punk.

"We were just happy to be in a band, and never gave a thought to which scene we fitted into," claims the singer. "But timing plays a big part in things, and I was singing about events happening in the world around us – Thatcher, riots in the streets, the miners striking, IRA bombings etc. etc.

"But no, we weren't all on completely the same wave length… which I think is healthy, and that was never the most important thing to us, as long as we could all get along. Besides, any pigeon-holing is restrictive, and in the end we had had enough of it; everyone mouthing the same empty statements. It just got boring and sounded the same; there was no conviction or honesty. You had a few good bands and people, and a load of parrots and puppets. Everything isn't always so black and white, and it was so shit that people thought they had to act and say certain things to fit in. That's not what it's about at all; my idea of anarchy is living by your own rules. If you want to change the world, change yourself first, simple as that."

With drummer Joe being replaced by Lee Duffle, and bassist Ed leaving to focus on Maniac, Anathema made their first 'official' recording in early 1985 at Toad Hall Studios in Leatherhead, and although James ended up playing bass as well as guitar, it was a spirited session that captured more than adequately the band's uplifting positivity, not to mention some extremely adept musicianship. It was promptly sold at gigs in its own right, but was then later released as a split cassette album, entitled 'Smash The Illusion', with the excellent Systematic Annex.

"Funny, I can't remember a 'best gig', but I can definitely remember some bad ones," laughs Lol. "Once we played at an all-day punk festival in Birmingham, which should have been great [it was at the Digbeth Civic Hall supporting the likes of Antisect, Lost Cherrees, Instigators, A-Heads, The Sears and Karma Sutra]; we travelled down with our guitars and bass, on a train full of football hooligans, and it just got worse from there. When we got up to play and I opened my mouth, they hated us straight away because we were from London. Cue shouts of, 'You Cockney wankers! Fuck off, you fucking anarchists!' Beer and glasses were being thrown at us – and this was the second I opened my mouth, before we'd even played a note! And it just got worse... in the end, we just walked off... so that wasn't a good night.

"Also, we played with Exit-stance in a pub in Islington which was a skinhead stronghold, rough as fuck. A girl was being shagged on the stage while we played, and people were thrown through the drum kit, which meant we had to keep stopping to put it back together again. What was even funnier though was that our bass player at the time, Rob [Murphy] was a bit of a goth and had brought all these

fishnets and make-up down to change into before we played... he never did get changed for some reason...!"

Rob was but one of a string of bassists ("It was always just friends coming and going...") that also included Steve Hayward and Seamus D'Arcy, the latter of whom joined Anathema from another local band, N.M.B.D. (which originally stood for New Malden Bowie Division, but became No More Bloody Destruction, with the onset of Crass!), and ended up playing with the reformed Riot/Clone.

Another – superior – demo led the band to a friendship with The Apostles, with whom a split single was slated to appear on Mortarhate, but the record never made it into production, despite reaching the test pressing stage, with promotional posters even being printed in readiness for its release.

"Colin from Conflict had said he was interested in releasing it on Mortarhate, but then things ground to a halt... I think Colin was releasing anything and everything at the time, and ours just didn't happen in the end. Funnily enough, James paid £70 for one of the test pressings years later...

"Unfortunately, we had a similar mix-up with the Mortarhate compilation we were meant to be on, when our artwork made it onto the sleeve but the track didn't! And that was the end of our studio career as Anathema – short and sweet..."

Not surprisingly, faced with such persistent setbacks, the band fizzled out in 1986 ("It wasn't planned or anything, it just happened, so there was never a 'last gig' as such..."), with Lol and James starting afresh as Compassion, enlisting Mark Cooper on bass and Pablo Videla on drums. They continued in much the same vein as Anathema, self-releasing cassette-only albums, but did

Anathema (left to right: Joe Daldorph (back of head), Lol Coopog, Seamus D'Arcy and James Jenkins).

make it to vinyl on the 1992 Sisters Of Percy compilation, 'Liberty? We Want The Real Thing!?'

James continued with Maniac, who released one single, the 'Killing For Pleasure' EP on Rentaracket in 1985, before becoming March Of Anger, who released a vinyl album, entitled 'A Beautiful World', for The Record Label in 1991; he also played guitar for Surf Weasel, with Pablo on drums, who existed from 1990 until '93, and released an EP, 'A Mind Of Your Own', for Sisters Of Percy.

Then, when Compassion split in the early Nineties, Lol and Ed formed Compassion Family, "a punkadelic dance outfit specialising in techno terrorism," who released several minor trance classics on Inter 1, Boom and Full Moon Records, before once again setting up their own label, Greedy Dig Productions.

"Just so we could release our own stuff exactly how we wanted it: full artistic control, DIY... old habits die hard, eh? LOL tapes all over again, just different. I still produce music under the name Liquid Chaos, a more avant-garde experimental ambient project, and there are even some plans to do some updated dance versions of Anathema/Compassion stuff some time in the future..."

Both Lol, who has travelled the world extensively during the last decade, and James became parents in 2005 (Lol fathering a little girl, Missy Asia, and James a son, Oscar), and Lol maintains that his involvement in the anarcho-punk scene played a crucial role in his own personal development.

"Everything shapes you as a person, doesn't it? All experiences, all places, all the people you meet. I think I still have pretty much the same beliefs as I always did; maybe more refined and a little wiser, but the core beliefs are the same. I still hate politicians and politics; they're never gonna save us, are they? It's all about money and power; they'll suck us dry. Bush can get helicopters to Iraq for war, but not to New Orleans to help the dying... that's the politics of choice.

"But of course music can change the world!" he adds, as an optimistic postscript. "By changing the way someone thinks about something, you are changing the world... it's 'the butterfly effect'... by just challenging the way people think about things, encouraging questioning. The Sixties changed the world, and so did the anarcho-punk thing for a lot of people... myself included."

At A Glance:
All the old Anathema and Compassion recordings are now available direct from Lol c/o Greedy Dig Productions: www.greedy-dig.com

CHAPTER THREE

O f all the anarcho-punk bands featured in this book, the **SUBHUMANS** are by far the most consistent, having never released a bad record and rarely played a bad gig. Even their reformation in 1998 revealed a band that was still as vital and exciting as in their youthful heyday, and they continue to delight audiences both young and old every time they set foot on stage. As to whether or not they actually are an anarcho-punk band remains open to debate, with even the band themselves nursing reservations as to whether they should be labelled thus.

"To be honest, I was always fairly uncomfortable being lumped in with the whole anarcho thing at all," admits vocalist Dick Lucas. "I was still living at home back then, and when I got a car I was obviously buying petrol that was polluting the earth… I was still eating meat until 1983. I didn't think I was 'anarcho' because I wasn't '100% anarcho'… whatever that is! I was a bit scared by the whole nature of the politics really, I didn't think I was cut out to be that serious… I just wasn't that angry, and I'd got into punk 'cos it was fun. It was about getting drunk with your mates and making noise… obviously that's a generalisation and there was more to it than that, otherwise we would've been little better than a load of football hooligans, but essentially it was fun… fun to say something meaningful.

"At the time, I liked all the Crass bands, I thought their lyrics were great, and it made me realise that I wasn't wrong to think the whole world was fucked up, that I wasn't alone not liking discos. The anarcho thing said that it was okay to be fucked up, and it was okay to say so, and in the process of saying so, you became less fucked up. But sometimes you could become a bit too overconfident, and you could start saying stuff like, 'Don't do this, don't do that!' And the whole point of punk rock was, 'Don't tell me what to do!' There was a fine line between suggesting an alternative lifestyle and being dictatorial, so, anyone who didn't like anarcho-punk could always accuse the anarcho bands of being the latter. It's a quick lesson to know that to suggest something is way more influential than demanding or accusing… you can't go round splitting people up even more than they already are.

"I read about Crass before I heard the music, but I was well into 'Feeding Of The 5000'," adds Dick. "I really had the lyrics to 'Banned From The Roxy' down; I could sing that song one-and-a-half times on the way to work! Yes, they did influence us, but I can't tell you exactly how or why, 'cos I only read all the stuff they wrote with their records once… fully intending to come back and read it again, but never getting around to it! I liked the way they didn't wanna talk to the media, I liked the way they talked about 'The System' like it was something real and tangible… this mixture of religion, authority, the police, the government, the media… no one had really said, 'Fuck the system' before, had they? They had these ideas that no one had had before, and it was more real than just singing about 'Anarchy In The UK', or whatever. And they were really pissed off, they were really angry; they shocked you into thinking about things. It wasn't the shock of breaking windows or wearing orange sunglasses, it was the shock of saying something so angrily; you just had to take it seriously. And they were also saying, 'We can do this together, it's us against them.'

"It was very, very straight down the line, so much so that Garry Bushell got really pissed off… 'cos he couldn't join in, I suppose… and he slagged them off for being elitist, and separatist, and living in their country house and being ex-public school types and stuff. But for a while, Crass were like any other punk band, and they hadn't been labelled 'anarcho punk' or anything, and neither had any of the other bands that sounded like them. That almost happened because of Garry

Subhumans (left to right: Trotsky, Bruce, Dick, and Grant), picture by Tony Mottram.

Bushell and his invention of Oi, 'the sound of the streets'… as opposed to anarcho's sounds of wishful thinking. This reincarnation of what the hippies had been saying, just a lot more angry."

Confirming his dilemma on the subject, the philosophical vocalist even wrote a song entitled 'Are You Anarchist?' which was never used by the band but suggested that, 'Putting 'anarchy' labels on things is naïve… if you believe in yourself, you'll know when you're free…'

"I really don't know whether I'm an anarchist or not, but I have ideas linked to the whole massive canopy of anarchist ideas… but as soon as you start trying to define which are the right anarchist ideas, and telling people which ones they should be following, it's like, 'Fuck off! Don't tell me what to do!' It depends how serious you wanna take it, from the literary angle, or the hippy angle, where we're all meant to love each other… or is it, go break a window, smash things up… the 'live fast, die young' angle. All the other angles are intensely personal, but I've never met anyone that says, 'Hi, I'm an anarchist!' It doesn't really happen! People are anarchistic 'cos they do things their own way, they ignore all the limitations that most other people seem to live by, and they can be very inspiring people.

"We were doing things that we thought would exclude us from being anarchists. We thought it involved a very strict sense of values, a morality that we couldn't maintain, 'cos we got the impression – wrongly – that there was no fun in anarchy, it was all very, very, very serious. And it was, but we tried… well, we didn't plan anything, and there were no conscious decisions about whether we were anarcho punks or not. Even that song 'Are You Anarchist?' was probably too heavy a statement on the subject for us to ever want to put it to music… I just wrote it all down in case anyone ever asked me about it!"

Such wordy analysis is fairly typical of the Subhumans who, as well as enjoying challenging themselves musically, like to challenge the preconceptions of their listeners with cerebral, witty lyrics, often far removed from the standard nihilism offered by many acts of the early Eighties. But such intellectual aspirations developed organically over time; Dick's first band, The Mental, were far less subtle, as are most initial forays into the world of music.

Dick Lucas of the Subhumans, picture by Craig Thompson.

"My brother Steve was the bassist, and we had Si 'Kick' on guitar, Tony on drums, and Toby on second guitar. We were all at boarding school together, and at weekends we'd go to Si Kick's house, which was near Basingstoke, and practise in his mum's garage. We'd make a right racket, but we wrote some quite basic, solid tracks. We got better as we went on, but gigs were a complete shambles, it was very chaotic; things wouldn't work, tunes were forgotten, but we'd struggle through it…

"Oh crikey!" he then laughs endearingly, when asked about his initial induction into the world of punk rock. "I heard 'Bored Teenagers' by The Adverts on the Alan Freeman show on a Saturday afternoon on Radio One… and it totally encompassed all the bits I'd previously liked from the bands I was listening to beforehand. It was like all the loud bits from, say, a Yes album… I'd realised quite quickly that I'd liked the Yes albums for the faster, more intense bits… and here were The Adverts doing it non-stop. And then it was finished, it was only like two minutes long… and I was, 'Wow, fantastic!'

"So I was straight down to Woolworth's to buy the Adverts single, then The Buzzcocks album… and almost any other punk rock I could find and afford. This was late '77, or '78… then my brother [Steve] got 'Never Mind The Bollocks' the same time as I got [Buzzcocks' debut] 'Another Music In A Different Kitchen'…

"And then the holidays finished and we were back to our boarding school… which is something you keep quiet about in the punk rock scene 'cos you're not meant to go to boarding school unless you're stinking rich, which was not the case at all with us!

"Anyway, I could pick up Radio Luxembourg at school, and they were playing a lot of punk rock, mainly on a Sunday night, and I was taping that and making these C90 cassettes full of punk, and I was religiously buying Sounds and NME, and sometimes Melody Maker, once a week, and cutting out all the pictures and sticking 'em on my wall, and I was just totally interested in all these bands.

"I was a complete wimp, a very insecure character, before punk rock came along. Then I carried on being insecure, but I felt stronger about it, because punk rock allowed you to say anything you wanted to say. You could get rid of all your inner demons, and blame the rest of society at the same time. So being fucked up a) wasn't your fault, and b) was now public knowledge, so fuck you… that sort of thing.

"I suppose that being at boarding school had an effect on us too. We would get six holidays a year, including the half terms, but the rest of the time, from eleven until eighteen, we were living there. It taught me all about the nature of authority, how groups of people work, how hierarchies are set up by physical and mental intimidation, how friendships can shatter under peer pressure… a lot of stuff. But deep down I thought it was a lot of immature kids, and the real world would be so much more together and welcoming and respectful of what you were like… but then I started work and found out that it was exactly the same as school had been!

"Anyway, back to The Mental; I read a fanzine from Southampton recently, which is entirely based on old punk rock memories. And the guy who writes that can remember seeing us at a gig in Salisbury, and the rumours he heard before that show were that we were called The Mental because some or all of us came from an asylum like Rampton or whatever, and we smelt of glue…! Apparently we had this quite huge reputation of being rather weird preceding us, which I didn't know about at the time and was all entirely untrue!"

Several of those chaotic shows were with Warminster band, Stupid Humans, who would basically merge thereafter with The Mental to become the Subhumans.

"Because I was at boarding school, and you couldn't just go out and watch a gig, the only gigs that I got to see were the rare ones that happened in darkest Wiltshire. One of them was the Angelic Upstarts, who played in Trowbridge; I had a phone call off a mate there saying, 'The Angelic Upstarts are playing the Civic Hall!', and I was, like, 'Yeah, right!' But it was true, so we went along, and that was where I met Bruce [Treasure] and Julian [Newby] out of the Stupid Humans. Something about them suggested that they were in a band, so I said, 'Are you in a band? So am I! Yaay!' It was almost like everyone was in a band, or knew someone who was in a band, or said they did. But we were all happy to meet new punk rock people in a world that was mostly not punk rock people, and it all felt very new and exciting. I started going over and watching them practice, and then we did a couple of gigs together, and when The Mental split up, and the Stupid Humans became the Subhumans in 1980 and needed a singer, I did that."

Before they disintegrated though, The Mental actually released a single. The 'Extended Play' EP, on their own Kamikaze Pig Records was limited to 600 copies when the pressing plant damaged 400 units of the 1000 press run, and featured such enjoyably generic shock tactics as 'Kill The Bill'. They even recorded a second EP, that never came out but saw them making significant musical headway.

"We did that with this guy called Adrian who was a friend of Bruce's. It was the best thing we ever did, but we split up before it could come out. It was going to be called 'Shoot The Hostages'... it was a bit topical 'cos there was a bunch of hostage-taking going on somewhere in the Middle East, so we were just trying to wind people up a bit. It's a shame that never materialised, 'cos it would've been really good, but we'd all left school, and it became a bit stupid, travelling 60 miles to go to practise at Si Kick's house, and things started breaking down and not really working out."

By mid-1980, as well as Bruce on guitar and Julian on vocals, the Stupid Humans comprised 'Herb' on bass and Andy Gale on drums. Things fizzled out after two decent

Bruce, guitarist of the Subhumans, pictured drumming for The A-Heads, 1983.

demos (that featured slower embryonic versions of several songs that would later become staples in the Subhumans set) and Ju went on to front Organised Chaos with bassist Herb joining Wild Youth.

Bruce (now handling vocals as well as guitar) and Andy teamed up with Grant, formerly of Warminster combo Audio Torture, as Subhuman (i.e., the Stupid Humans minus one!) despite Bruce's mother's persistent suggestions that they name themselves 'Superhuman'. When Dick joined, they naturally became the Subhumans, and they soon set about playing frequently, at first locally but then anywhere they could get a foot in the door.

"Yeah, 'Superhumans' just sounded way too positive; the whole thing of calling yourself a negative name was settling in by then. I still haven't worked out why the punk rock way of thinking became so naturally negative; the amount of times I say the words 'die', 'dead' or 'dying' on, say, the first LP is... well, heaps. I think it was a subconscious reaction against all the love and happiness of the previous generation of lyrical writers... 'cos apart from a few protest writers in the Sixties, everything up until the Sex Pistols had been 'Baby, baby, baby...' We were saying that the real world is full of death, misery and struggle.

"Our very first gig was in Bradford-on-Avon, and it was brilliant," he recalls fondly. "It was at the St. Margaret's Hall, 19th September, 1980, supporting a local pop band The Waiters who headed straight for obscurity. I don't think they actually got to play in fact; the police turned up, there was a bit of a fight... it was quite messy, the whole of Bradford-on-Avon was freaking out with these punk rockers everywhere, and the gig got stopped. Luckily we'd already played by then, but it was an eventful first gig!"

Other notable shows took place with the likes of The Mob and even Discharge (in Stevenage), but then Andy, frustrated at the complete absence of any studio work, left the band, ironically mere months before Subhumans would record their first single, and was replaced by 'Trotsky'.

"Surnames don't really matter, do they?" laughs Dick. "I still don't know when exactly people started knowing me as Dick Lucas as opposed to Dick Mental or Dick Subhuman or Dick Fish or whatever. In a truly anarcho spirit, surnames are merely a result of a patriarchal society, you see, so they don't count. Plus I wanna be Dick Mental, 'cos it sounds better than Lucas, ha ha!

And there's always the fear that one day we might make loadsa money and the taxman will come after us!

"Anyway, Trotsky was the brother of Martin, who went to school with Bruce. We turned up for practise and there he was, this guy with long hair and an Afghan coat with a Led Zeppelin patch on the back of it – and he had a drum kit! He was only fifteen, but it was rare for anyone to have a drum kit back then, and he really got into it. He was a bloody good drummer, too; even used to write down all this musical notation for his drum patterns, he really wanted to know all about drums. And it turned out brilliantly for us…"

Indeed it did, with Trotsky gelling quickly and fluently with the rest of the band, the chemistry between the four youths immediately apparent, and the Subhumans coming to the attention of Flux Of Pink Indians, who not only took them out on the road but also released their earliest recordings on Spiderleg Records.

"Yeah, Flux were totally into us, and they liked the way we sounded, what we said… and we liked their whole approach and attitude, the way they did the 'Pay no more than' thing on all their sleeves; I really did love that idea. If you're going to be backed by EMI and it costs £10, or more like £5 back then, to hear your band, what's the price of your value system? Music should be as cheap as possible to make it accessible to as many people as possible, and I still totally believe that. The love of money is the root of all evil; it's really insidious, and it wrecks people's lives, and it promises nothing that ever comes true."

The first fruit of this union was the impressive six-track 'Demolition War' EP. Recorded at Pickwick Studios in Corsham by Steve Collinson on August 8th, 1981, and released December that year, it crashed into the Indies at No.13, remaining in the chart for ten weeks. The gatefold cover introduced the record-buying public to the band's 'skull with microphone' logo that has adorned thousands of leather jackets worldwide ever since ("It was my idea, but Grant drew the first one and then I redesigned it a bit," reckons Dick), not to mention their ambitious musical diversity. As early as their debut release they juxtaposed all-out thrash ('Who's Gonna Fight In The Third World War?', 'Drugs Of Youth' and the bass-driven 'Society') with moodier mid-tempo numbers ('Animal' and 'Parasites', whose scratchy guitar intro ushers the EP in with great style) and even a reggae-heavy dirge (the poignant 'Human Error'). The buzz surrounding the release saw them being interviewed for Sounds magazine by Winston Smith, which had their profile rocketing quickly beyond their expectations.

Maintaining their momentum, no sooner was the first single cooling in the racks than the band was in London's Southern Studios recording the next one with John Loder, the furious 'Reasons For Existence' that spent three months in the Indies during Spring 1982.

"Yes, we were prolific, we were banging 'em out! We wrote four songs in one practice once, which is insane – 'Love Is', 'Cancer', and two others… I forget which ones. But we always wrote at least one song every week for ages; there was big motivation, and so many ideas flying about, you couldn't fail to get a new track out of it all.

"For me, the nature of singing was just a backlash against people having a go at me and telling me what to do," adds Dick, on his own personal inspiration. "I was pretty passive and never really fought back, I was always receiving all this shit and not reciprocating… and then suddenly I could! Just by using words. I like words, and language and rhyming; I really hated violence, physical strength over intelligence, so it was nice to be able to fight back without resorting to fists."

The four-track 'Reasons…' EP has an almost minimalist vibe about it, both in terms of production and composition. Simple riffs and simple sounds, but everything exactly where it should be, resulting in an instantly memorable collection of speedy tunes. 'Big City' and 'Peroxide' ("Why would people put such a dangerous chemical on their heads?" laughs Dick incredulously) rattle around enjoyably enough, but it's the heart-felt anti-conformity rant of the title track that commands most attention here, with the ponderous, and rather morbid, 'Cancer' acting as its perfect foil.

"I wrote 'Big City' after I went to see The Cramps with a mate of mine from Scotland. We stayed at his mate's place in London, and he had this skinhead mate who was really twitchy and horrible, and we went to the gig in Hammersmith, and this skinhead robbed me basically. I was scared shitless; he mugged me at the gig and made off with my last tenner! So that's where that line 'spend your money on a skin's flick knife' came from. But I didn't really like the big cities at all, especially not London – it was just too big, scary, horrible, noisy, dirty, polluted… frightening really, I didn't like it. Still don't."

The next single finally made the Indie Top Ten upon its release during July 1982 and, for many a listener, remains to this day the band's defining moment. Recorded back at Pickwick with Steve Collinson again, 'Religious Wars' was/is a driving, sublimely anthemic punk classic. It was also the first cover to feature the painstakingly detailed artwork of one Nick Lant, whose imagery became synonymous with the band, even though he only actually did four (five, if you count the inlay of 'Worlds Apart') pieces for them.

"He just wrote me a letter asking for a list of tapes or whatever, and he drew this punk rocker's head at the top of the letter, about 2" high, in such brilliant micro-detail. We were stuck for a cover for 'Religious Wars' – covers were always a complete pain in the arse – so I sent him the lyrics to 'Religious Wars' and asked him to do a drawing for this single we had coming out. We didn't hear anything back from him for like three weeks, and then suddenly it turned up in the post, this picture in this 7" card mailer. And we thought, 'Holy moly, this is amazing!'

"Then he did 'The Day The Country Died' [the band's debut LP], which took him weeks obviously. I phoned him up to see how he was doing, and he told me he had this punk with a mohican getting shot through the head… and I said, 'Whoah! A mohican? Can you make it spikes, not a mohican?' You know, mohicans just weren't us, and spikes were more general. Some of my best friends had mohicans, but there were more spikes about. And when it came through, we were staring at it for ages, it was amazing – I swear the cover was 50% of the reason that record sold so well…"

"Anyway, he did 'Evolution' and 'Rats' [the 4th and 5th singles] as well, and then he vanished off the face of the planet. There's a rumour that he fell in love and went to Paris! But he never wanted paying for any of the art; he wanted a pint of beer, so we bought him one when we met him at a gig in Nottingham. We were dead lucky to find him to do stuff with us."

Whether it was the cover that helped propel it to No. 3 in the Indies upon its release in January 1983 is open to speculation, but the musical content of 'The Day The Country Died' certainly wasn't lacking in either power or tuneage, and it remains one of the stronger debut albums of the genre. The chillingly intense opener, 'All Gone Dead', was actually a souped-up version of an old Stupid Humans number, as were 'Killing', 'New Age' and 'Ashtray Dirt'. The latter track raising eyebrows with its anti-smoking lyrics being sung by a singer who liked more than the occasional fag!

"Okay, let's clear this one up, shall we? Julian out of the Stupid Humans, who also smoked, wrote 'Ashtray Dirt', so you'll have to ask him what he was thinking at the time! Yes, it's a bit of a bad habit – it goes with coffee – but it's a good song to sing. And the fact that I smoke like a chimney is ridiculously hypocritical, but I sang it when I joined because it was an existing song. But in the end we dropped it, mainly because it was just ridiculous to sing an anti-smoking song when we all smoked!

"'Cancer' on the other hand is not about smoking per se," adds Dick on the similarly themed song from the 'Reasons For Existence' EP. "It's not so much about the habit or what it does to you as about raising cigarettes up to be some sort of tonic for being depressed. I had this image of this guy at work, all depressed, and all his mates say, 'C'mon, cheer up, have a cigarette!' And he says, 'No, I don't want a cigarette, 'cos I've got cancer!' And that's why he's depressed! And that's all it is really, a little story, a bit ironic… the basic subtext being, cigarettes ain't gonna cheer you up – especially if you've got cancer! It's pretty dark humour is all, but there's more to it than it just being about not smoking.

Subhumans vocalist Dick Lucas live in Kansas, 1984, picture by Brent Stafford.

"There's not a lot of real-life stuff in the songs really… personal experience didn't come into that many of our songs… personal thoughts do, of course…"

'Til The Pigs Come Round' must have been from a real story though, surely?

"No, not really real, it was just a summation of things, of what parties felt like, with everyone making loadsa noise, and just extrapolating that into having it in your own mum and dad's house or whatever. But I don't remember being at many parties where the police actually came around and smashed them up… to be honest, it was probably most influenced by watching that episode of 'The Young Ones'!"

The week after the album stormed the Independent charts, the Subhumans appeared on the front of Sounds with what was actually the magazine's first ever full-colour cover.

"We were well chuffed," recalls Dick happily, before rebuking the suggestion that they perhaps copped a load of flak from holier-than-thou scensters for their troubles. "No, no, no, the only stick anyone ever gets for stuff like that is from themselves! There were a few people out there who used to pick at bands for doing this, that and the other, and we ourselves used to snipe at bands who signed to EMI or whatever… or whatever labels they were on, all these various degrees of hipness. But a lot of that, if I could remember every comment we ever made, I'd probably regret having said a lot of it. It was elitist and nit-picking…

"But as far as the Sounds thing went, it was, like, 'Yes!' We thought there was absolutely nothing wrong with going on the front cover of Sounds… Crass didn't wanna do it, but fair enough. I can understand the theory of rejecting all the media and stuff like that, but we were tempted by Satan, and we went for it!

"We weren't as serious and never had as much attitude as Crass, anyway, which is why we shied away from the anarcho tag, like I said. Because people would then say, 'Oh, well, you don't do this… you shouldn't be doing that… you should be doing this…' and laying down all these rules. We were more like, 'We're just a fuckin' punk band! We've got summat to say, and we think it should be heard when we say it… but we also have a lot of fun doing it! We don't mind being on the front cover of Sounds, we don't mind getting drunk and having fun whilst we're doing it! And being at the top of the charts is a wonderful feeling; no one's getting hurt by any of it…'

"The main thing we were concerned about was that people shouldn't get ripped off coming to

Subhumans live in Camden, June 1982, picture by Paul May.

see us or buying our records… the more people that turned up at our gigs, the better. But we didn't wanna sign contracts with third party people who wouldn't understand where we were coming from."

Which would go a long way towards explaining why Dick began his own label, Bluurg, although he maintains, quite simply, "I just wanted to put out our own records really." After starting out as a basic, DIY tape label, Bluurg graduated to releasing vinyl in February 1982 with the 'Wessex '82' compilation EP. Featuring one track each from the Subhumans, the Pagans, Organized Chaos and the A-Heads, the single was a neat snapshot of the enthusiastic underground scene that was flourishing in the 'Melksham-Trowbridge-Warminster punk rock triangle.' Perhaps because the Subhumans opened the record with a previously unreleased track ('No Thanks'), or perhaps because it's a damn fine listen regardless of who's playing what, 'Wessex '82' sold well, made the Indie Top Five, and ensured that Bluurg Records was here to stay. Indeed the very next Subhumans single, 'Evolution', was issued by Bluurg, in June '83.

"It was a logical step to start putting out the Subhumans too, because Spiderleg were folding and severing connections with Southern Studios," reveals Dick, whilst reminiscing of his earlier days as a tape label: "I was inundated! I'd cycle the seven miles home from work, have something to eat and lock myself away in the attic with the ten to twenty-five letters that arrived every day… and 60 or 70% of those wanted tapes off me! I had rows of tapes to record, and three cassette decks linked to each other, little realising that the sound on some of the copies was fucking awful. It was all very idealistic and great fun to do. Suddenly people were writing letters… I mean, the novelty of people writing letters has worn off now, but it was amazing back then, complete strangers were getting in touch with me, saying they liked the music. Computers have killed all that, to an extent."

As well as Subhumans material, Bluurg went on to release some excellent challenging anarcho-punk by the likes of Naked, Faction and The Sears, offering the bands a no-bullshit 'handshake deal' based on trust and mutual respect.

"Yeah, I started out just releasing bands from around here, but I eventually spread my wings to the [Dewsbury-based] Instigators, who just blew me away when I first saw them. So I thought, 'Fuck this 'local' thing, I'll put out any bands that I like!' It just started as a really cheap, easy way to get these bands out there. I was getting people to send me a blank tape and 20p towards the postage – I guess the postage was fuck all back then to post a tape – so the idea was to give people virtually free music. And I remember I had this crisis of conscience about raising the price from 20p to, like, 25p!"

'Evolution' meanwhile – well, the title track, at least – was a 100mph riff on the traditional 12-bars boogie, with vehemently anti-vivisection lyrics that were reinforced by Nick Lant's graphic cover illustration of animal torture. Elsewhere, 'So Much Money' was classic Subhumans (energetic, catchy, intelligent…), 'Germ' was memorably quirky, and the furious 'Not Me' proved that the band could still thrash it up with the best of 'em.

The 'Time Flies But Aeroplanes Crash' 12" followed in October, and again opened with, not one but two, revamped Stupid Humans tracks, 'Get Out Of My Way' and 'First Aid'. But the half studio/half live 12" was most notable for unveiling two of the more unusual songs the band have ever recorded, the piano-led 'Susan' and the cheeky, vocals–only (for the first half anyway), sailor-shanty-feel of 'Work, Rest, Play, Die'.

"It was originally meant to be a whole live album [recorded at Feltham Football Club, June 4th, 1983], but it sounded awful apart from a couple of tracks that we somehow salvaged from the mix, so we went back into Pickwick and did the rest there," reveals Dick. "And I didn't actually write 'Susan', that was by Steve Hamilton, an old punk rock mate from Bradford-on-Avon; never in a band or anything, but he liked his music, and he just gave me these lyrics. The Psychedelic Furs had a song called 'Susan's Strange', I think, so we didn't call it 'Susan Strange' as originally planned, just 'Susan'… and I played the piano on it, Bruce's grandmother's piano to be exact.

"I even had piano lessons when I was a kid, but gave up when I hit puberty 'cos it wasn't on, it was too effeminate to learn proper music…! Plus I found it very boring 'cos the teacher was totally uninspiring… that's one of my regrets really, having not carried on music lessons, 'cos maybe now I'd be able to do something with my left hand on the piano as well as the right. And did you know that if you take the melody to 'Susan' and speed it up, it's the same as the bass line to 'Ashtray Dirt'…?"

With the 12" another Indie Top Ten hit, and the band proving a strong draw on the live circuit thanks to their charismatic stage presence and concerted touring, it seemed everything was going right for the Subhumans. Which, of course, is when fate stepped in with a predictable and well-aimed spanner in the works: original bassist Grant announcing his departure.

"Yeah, Grant had a hand in writing most of [the celebrated second album] 'From The Cradle To The Grave', but he left about a month before we recorded it. He actually left right at the end of this tour in 1983, and it was all a bit bizarre. During that tour I had my legs completely burned by an exploding radiator in the van on the way to Gateshead, and I had to go to the hospital every day to get my bandages changed, and this cream rubbed in. It was absolutely agony walking around, doing anything in fact, and I thought about sitting down onstage… tried it for about half a note and thought, 'Val Doonican!' So I suffered for my art, but I had no fuckin' choice really!

"Anyway, possibly because I was so fucked up with my legs, Grant never mentioned that he was thinking of leaving to me. I think he said something to Bruce and Trotsky perhaps, but at the end of the last gig, at the Fulham Greyhound, he came up to me and shook my hand and said, 'Well done, Dick!' And I thought it was a bit weird… until a week later, Bruce rang me up and said, 'Oh yeah, Grant's going to leave.' It turns out that he didn't think he was in the same head space as the rest of us, not on the same frequency…"

He was quickly replaced by local musician – and, more importantly, good mate – Phil from The Pagans.

"After The Mental split up, my brother went on to form Wild Youth with a couple of mates," explains Dick. "And they eventually became The Pagans, who included Phil on bass. They split up and became The Flying Fish Band, with Phil on guitar, I think… and Bruce from the Subhumans on drums! It was all very incestuous; there were a lot of bands, most of them based around Warminster, and partly Trowbridge. There was lots going on, it was a brilliant time."

And from such a fertile breeding ground emerged 'From The Cradle To The Grave', the band's hotly-anticipated sophomore album which was recorded by John Loder at Southern during October 1983 and released May 1984. It was only kept from the coveted No. 1 spot in the Indies by The Smiths' eponymous debut, and remains a most remarkable album, not least of all because the title track was a seventeen-minute epic that took up one whole side of the vinyl!

That mini-epic made its first public appearance on April 4th, 1984 at the Leeds Bierkeller, when the Subhumans blagged onto a bill that featured Hagar The Womb, the A-Heads and Naked.

"We said we'd only play the one song!" laughs Dick. "And we still play that live… it's quite easy really. I just said to Bruce one day that I had this three-and-a-half page song in my lyric book, and that we should do something with it. I'd been banging out these lines in 4-beat all about birth, and childhood, and kept going with it to see where it ended up. And Bruce had all these ideas that we hadn't used, and over a few weeks of practices we glued it all together…

"Trouble is with playing that song live though, I've got nothing to do for literally minutes at a time, during the instrumental bits, and I have to hop about a bit, go with the flow like… ha!"

As well as the ambitious, meandering title track, the A-side of 'Cradle…' features such daring compositions as the lurching, ominous 'Rain' and the haunting 'Wake Up Screaming'. Rubbing shoulders with the break-neck 'Reality Is Waiting For A Bus'… and even 'Us Fish Must Swim Together', a catchy little oddity based around the tune of 'God Rest Ye Merry Gentlemen'!

"We made very few conscious decisions to write specific songs about this or that, it just didn't happen really. I rang Dan from The Apostles once, and we were talking about whatever, about reality and stuff… and he said, 'Well, reality is waiting for a bus…' and I thought, 'Wow!' And went

Subhumans drummer Trotsky, at the Ad Lib Club, Shepherds Bush, London, September 1984, picture by Paul May.

upstairs after putting the phone down and wrote a song around that line. Because reality *is* waiting for a bus, isn't it? There you are waiting, and your faith in that bus is huge, and when it doesn't turn up, you're so disappointed... not only in the bus, but in yourself for having so much faith in the bus and the system in the first place...!

"And 'Wake Up Screaming' is a bit of a rare song for us, 'cos it's written as if it's very personal – it's all written from my point of view – but none of it actually happened to me. And I only had the tiniest inkling of what drugs did to your head, 'cos I'd only been stoned twice at that point... but there were all these rumours of people overdosing, and people's friends dying. But you didn't know what these drugs were like, and you had to figure out what 'OD' meant... and I just put myself inside someone's mind who had become addicted to something based on what their friend had told them, and then their friend dies..."

'Us Fish...' meanwhile seemed to decry all those technological advances that just fill our lives with essentially unnecessary clutter and blind us to the bigger, far more important picture of what's actually happening right outside our window!

"Most definitely. [Quoting the song] 'Food and sex and water is all you really need'... 'cos it is, really, isn't it? Technology offers freedom of communication but in the case of, say, computers, you end up staying indoors, learning stuff you don't really remember anyway. It's another screen, like a television, but because you're controlling it so much, you fool yourself that it's not controlling you. I'm sure that the invention of remote controls for televisions was partly to give people that feeling of control. But the more channels that come in, all these digital boxes and stuff, the lower the lowest denominator becomes – until it's all crap. You waste twenty minutes flicking through the channels just to discover there's nothing on anyway.

"Things used to happen slower before computers admittedly, but the same amount of things still happened, albeit by having to write letters and wait for the return answer to come back a week later. But we used to get all our gigs like that, by people just asking us, ringing us up or writing to us, and offering us a date. Or we'd ring up bands we'd played with before and sort stuff out. But the circuit is a lot smaller nowadays, there used to be a load of venues... and now there's just night clubs."

January 1985 saw the release of the 'Rats' EP, the title track inspired by the Stop The City demonstrations of the period that sought to highlight the corruption and cruelty that greases the wheels of the Stock Exchange. But the standout cut was 'Joe Public', a scathing attack on the mundane ideals aspired to by Mr. and Mrs. Average, whose mid-section saw Bruce indulging his Hendrix fetish to great effect. However, despite its success – yet another Indie hit that spent over four months in the chart, peaking at No. 2 – it was sadly to be the last Subhumans single. With their blossoming popularity came the inevitable internal disputes over not only musical direction but also, perhaps more importantly, the increasing difficulty with which to maintain control over the band's finances – or lack thereof. Also, with Dick having been the band's sole spokesman as regards lyrics, interviews and newsletters, for five long years, his idealistic concept of the Subhumans had slowly but surely grown further and further away from the reality of the Subhumans as a collective of four individuals.

"It's largely wishful thinking to assume that all members of every anarcho-punk band think exactly the same way as the singer… I mean, granted, the singer probably has the most to say – that's why he wanted to be the singer! I'm not saying that the rest of the Subhumans are out there chopping up cows and doing cocaine whilst shagging thirteen-year-old goats. They're not as overly concerned or analytical about life in general as I am… and they're probably the better for it too!

"We didn't really grow apart as such, but in terms of thinking about what to do next, there was a lot of dissatisfaction. I thought we were on a steady, if slow, progress upwards, and we were doing good and it was gradually getting better all the time… but no one else really agreed with that. They thought we'd done all we could, thought it was getting very repetitive, and wondered where we were going next…"

So, amidst much protest from dedicated followers worldwide, the Subhumans disbanded, but, nice chaps to the last, they left us with not only their greatest album, '85's perfectly-realised 'Worlds Apart', but even a posthumous afterthought in the shape of the '29:29 Split Vision' 12". After the 'final' Subhumans show at the Warminster Athenaeum on November 10th, 1985, supported by Organised Chaos and Steve L., the rest of the band sat back to gather their thoughts, but Dick, a road-dog through and through, was soon to be seen fronting the increasingly popular Culture Shock.

"Yes, we did our last gigs, then invented side two of 'Split Vision', then recorded it after we'd broken up… it wasn't really a messy break-up as such, but it was drawn out. As you can tell by the music that ended up being on that last 12", Bruce's musical ideas really were expanding way beyond what was punk rock.

"The opportunity to sing for Culture Shock came along in the middle of all this – Nige just came over the pub and asked me to sing for this band he was getting together with Paul and Bill – and I thought, 'Yeah, why not?' And it turned out a treat."

Dick was later reunited with Phil and Trotsky in the thoroughly enjoyable politico-ska-punk combo Citizen Fish and, after much deliberation, several low-key Subhuman reunion shows were undertaken in 1990. And then in 1998, the band reunited on a more permanent basis.

"Bruce had been running a music shop in Warminster, and he got married, had two kids, bought a house, was teaching music at a local school, and he played in a band called Switch, this mixture of pop and King Crimson, which eventually fell apart. So, he kept well busy, in all directions; he knows an awful lot about music, does Bruce.

"Anyway, Phil and Trotsky had this idea to get back together and see if it worked, and I was really dubious, but thought it was worth a try. Bruce agreed to try it too, and as soon as we played a few old tracks, we all thought, 'Wow!' It felt really good, and most of it came back with no revision, and it was a nice change from playing stuff that wasn't as angry or hardcore, or whatever… it just felt great. So we did a gig, and it was packed out, and went brilliant, so we planned to do a UK tour, a European tour, a US tour, and thought that would be it, but since then, we've carried on doing things when we can. We've never really discussed how long it's going to go on for or anything."

Since '98, the band have proved their continued worth and relevance with worldwide touring, a MCD of newly-recorded old songs, 'Unfinished Business', and even a superlative live album ('Live

In A Dive') and DVD ('All Gone Live'). Yes, they've reformed, just like a million other Eighties punk bands, but by doing it for all the right reasons, out of a genuine love for the music they've created and a respect for the fans of that music, rather than any desire to make a quick buck, they still loom over the international punk scene as a force of tremendous creative and artistic integrity. Whether we'll ever see a new studio album still remains to be seen though... in the tradition of true temperamental geniuses, they'll no doubt finish it when they finish it.

"Yeah, 'reformation' means dragging all these old punk rockers out of the pubs they've been running ever since, to reform and play slower, and not move about the stage with the energy they used to have, and be a laughable, sorry representation of how good punk rock used to be and how bad it can get. So, we didn't wanna be anything like that, and also it's looking backwards and not forwards, which I still feel about the whole thing really..."

"It's a complicated issue. People like it so much, and to be honest, we reformed so long after we originally split up, we're playing to some people now who were only five years old when we it first happened, and who never saw us live, which contradicts the negativity of repeating ourselves. People had been buying the records ever since we split up anyway, so it was for them as well as for us really."

So, we leave the Subhumans story just as we joined it, immersed in debate, nothing as simple as it first appears. And if to question everything is the essence of anarcho punk, where the Subhumans succeed is by wrapping that simple act of personal liberation in a good, honest, memorable tune.

SELECT DISCOGRAPHY

7"s:
'Demolition War' (Spiderleg, 1981)
'Reasons For Existence' (Spiderleg, 1982)
'Religious Wars' (Spiderleg, 1982)
'Evolution' (Bluurg, 1983)
'Rats' (Bluurg, 1984)

12"s:
'Time Flies But Aeroplanes Crash' (Bluurg, 1983)
'29:29 Split Vision' (Bluurg, 1986)

MCDs:
'Unfinished Business' (Bluurg, 1998)

LPs:
'The Day The Country Died' (Spiderleg, 1982)
'From The Cradle To The Grave' (Bluurg, 1984)
'Worlds Apart' (Bluurg, 1985)
'Live In A Dive' (Fat Wreck Chords, 2003)

At A Glance:
All the band's back catalogue has aged well and stands up to repeated listening, but the 'EPLP' CD on Bluurg compiles the first four singles onto one disc and comes especially recommended. The three albums are all superb in their own way, but 'Worlds Apart' is the most accomplished, satisfying full length. The much more recent 'Live In A Dive', with its excellent production values and fan-friendly track-listing, acts as a veritable – and essential – 'Best Of' collection.

Also part of the thriving Warminster scene, The A-HEADS are probably destined to primarily be remembered in the shadow of their mentors Subhumans, yet they produced some fine, potent punk rock of their own – Mel Bell was a distinctive and powerful vocalist – and were an important thread in the fabric of the underground, public profile be damned!

"Just listening to the music of the Pistols and The Clash really; the teenage years needed something energetic and music was my personal buzz," reckons guitarist Jock

Mel of The A-Heads at Cleator Moor Civic Hall, picture by Trunt.

McCurdy, who formed The A-Heads in 1980 with bassist Nigel Johnston, on the reasons he ended up starting his very own punk band. "I could play a few basic chords on a Woolworth's guitar, so, along with a few friends, we started playing in our bedrooms. My family were in the army though, so, in 1978, we moved to Germany for two years and I missed out on the 'birth' of all the local Warminster bands. Stalag 44, who included Nigel, were the originals, and, from there, The Addics, OPM etc. etc. were formed.

"90% of the English kids at school in Germany appeared to be totally oblivious of the UK punk scene, which made those who knew what was going on more focused in believing their own beliefs and questioning everything that was thrown at them. The music scene there consisted of Boney M. cover bands and ZZ Top look-alikes. Herford and Hannover were the places to see any touring acts; the big cities were a good place to be, the scene there was similar to what I saw when I returned to England. The only difference was that Special Brew was not on the German bar menu!"

Upon his return to the UK, Jock wasted no time locating suitable musicians to help realise his own musical vision, and along with Nigel, he recruited the aforementioned Mel Bell on vocals, and one Andy Gale (the original Subhumans drummer), behind the kit.

"The band name actually came from a toilet wall in Germany. Little did I know the arty matchstick man with the traditional anarchy symbol as a head was sprayed in honour of a Lemgo-based German punk band of the same name. This only came to my attention when a friend who designed the revamped 'Dying Man' single cover, sent me their demo tape along with the art work!

"Anyway, Nigel had played in various bands like OPM and Audio Torture, as had Andy. He became a close friend through a mutual love of music and the pub. We jammed for a few weeks and realised that we had a few good tunes, so we set about finding a drummer and singer. Andy liked what we were doing and had just left the 'Humans, and with Mel being Bruce [also from the Subhumans]'s girlfriend, she knew all of us, so it seemed natural for her to sing. She had good lyrics and a good voice, and, like Andy, liked the tunes.

"Warminster Youth Centre was the place to be on a Saturday afternoon back then. All the local punks would turn up there after a few pints in the Ship And Punchbowl pub. Everyone had their own gear from previous involvement with bands, although the 'Humans lent us the odd microphone – and drummer! There were three bands taking turns in sharing two rooms: ourselves, Organised Chaos and the 'Humans. As word spread, we had people cycling fifteen miles just so they could listen to the bands, chat and drink. None of us had a problem with people watching us trying to write or rehearse; it created a great atmosphere and a feeling of a community.

"As soon as we'd got a set together, the 'Humans asked us to support them along with Organised Chaos; we normally took it in turns as regards support slots. I don't know if people wanted all of us as a kind of package, but when we all did gigs together it felt really good, crammed in a van with a dozen or so really great people, meeting new faces in new places…

"We were all mates and really enjoyed what we were doing; there was no competition, friendship was the important factor. The inter-connecting family tree of all the bands through the years speaks volumes, I think."

The band's public debut came on 11th July, 1981, when they supported another local band, Silent Guests, at the Warminster Regal Cinema. The headliners were with Melksham-based TW Records, who were so impressed with The A-Heads, they offered to sign them as well, and subsequently released their first single, 'Dying Man', in May 1982.

"I think their aim was for the mainstream market simply because their guitarist Dave Coles wrote with a commercial flair," says Jock of the Guests. "Dave helped produce 'Dying Man', and was well respected for his playing. He had been involved with a band called Moskow who had recently split after a decent first single ['Man From UNCLE' b/w 'White Black', TW Records, 1982]. The bassist Wally [real name Dave Stevens] was also in Moskow and later became involved with us when we had problems finding a drummer. An old friend, Paul [Collyer], who I jammed with whilst still at school was the drummer; he had played in a few local bands and had recently left Animals And Men, an early Adam And The Ants-inspired outfit from Frome. Paul set the gig up at the Regal and asked us to support them. The owner thought it would be a good idea to try and help local bands by promoting gigs… but an offer of selling the land to build an old folks home proved slightly more interesting!"

'Dying Man', all about the short-sighted, self-destructive stupidity of glue-sniffing, is an enjoyable, up-tempo rocker, with an infectious chorus, backed by 'Changing Places' (as insistent as it is speedy) and 'Hell Cell'; the latter being probably the most intense track of the EP, powered by dramatic chord changes over a thick, burbling bass line. Like all their releases, it was recorded at Pickwick Studios, Corsham, with Steve 'Splice' Collinson helming the desk.

The first 1000 copies were released in an utterly tasteless sleeve (a pink 'A' on a starry blue background!) that ably demonstrated how devoid of any feel for real punk aesthetics TW Records really were. Thankfully the initial pressing sold quickly and garnered a great response, so the band were able to have it reissued with an approved – not to mention less embarrassing – cover.

"The glue sniffing thing bugged the life out of me," spits Jock with feeling, of the single's subject matter. "There's no inspiration in watching lives being wasted through shit chemical highs fuelled by cheap crap beer. How constructive can you be fucked up on that crap 24/7? I saw a lot of that… pure nega-fucking-tivity.

"There were a lot of positives about the scene though. The squats were great. And the people who were committed to their beliefs had to be admired. The only negative aspects I found were the people who wouldn't give you the time of day. This was an era when there was no tolerance from the local councils etc., a time when, come winter, there was a bizarre law where the pubs would shut at 10.30 pm and any copper could stop and search you day or night!

"Nigel was a great Ruts fan, as was I," he adds, on where the band looked for their major influences. "Both of us spent time structuring our songs simply, because we both loved music and enjoyed what we were doing. Nigel's Crass tattoo spoke volumes for his appreciation of that band, and whilst I admired what they were doing and what they said, the person who really took my attention was [Subhumans' singer] Dick… still does, in fact, and always will. His commitment, knowledge, energy and whole persona made a lasting impression on me, and I think anyone who has spent time with him will agree."

In August 1982, Andy left the band to settle down with his family, and Bruce from the

Subhumans, stood in on drums. A track, 'No Rules', that featured a rather unorthodox (for the punk scene, at least) acoustic intro and falsetto vocal turn from Mel, was recorded on September 12th, 1982 and contributed to Bluurg's successful 'Wessex 82' compilation EP.

Unfortunately, Mel and Bruce, who were living together at the time, split up soon after its release, which, as mentioned previously, led to Wally from Silent Guest stepping in on drums. This line-up recorded the excellent 'Forgotten Hero' single during July 1983, which was issued through Bluurg. Three tracks of subtle brilliance, the pathos of the lyrics superbly communicated through some understated, anguished melody and a considered, spacious production.

"That was always my favourite song of ours," reckons Jock. "At the time there were loads of anti-war songs played at breakneck

speed; we slowed things down a bit to make a point of what the song was about. I don't think Mel enjoyed that period much though, because of splitting with Bruce and stuff. Hence 'Love Or Pain' [one of the songs on the B-side of the 7"]... but the lyrics and feelings at that time went through all of us; hardly anarcho-punk really... but something much more personal."

Indeed, one of The A-Heads' great strengths was that they set their lyrical sights on more than just Thatcher, the police, and, uh, more Thatcher. The third song on 'Forgotten Hero' was 'Isolated', a brave attempt to address the ostracising of gays by mainstream society.

"We just voiced our opinions and did what we believed in. Many bands opened people's minds, like the Chumbas and Crass etc., and if people thought about what was happening around them, and did something constructive to change things, then that's good. We were part of the anarcho scene because we were fucked off with what was being presented to us as the society we were meant to live in, but were we an anarcho-punk band? It's open to debate.

"I was educated with an expectancy to be something... but whose expectancy? I was preached to by teachers who said that the education system they were involved in was the best for my generation. Guided by a career officer who wanted me to sign away my youth to the British army... I asked questions and nobody would listen. The reality was that the teachers' kids were all tucked away safely at boarding school somewhere, and the recruitment of cannon fodder for the army was an easy solution for kids that had moved around all their lives from country to country, without having any grip on reality.

"All of us in the band believed in asking such questions and fought for living our lives as we wanted. We still do and always will. That's why I have respect for Nigel's decision to commit suicide [in 1993] because he believed in what he was doing. Before this event he spoke about the death of another friend and his opinion reminded me that self-belief is all-important. If fighting for your beliefs falls under the anarcho label, then fine, I'm happy with us being regarded as anarcho punks. As regards arming myself with a Kalashnikov and running through the streets? That's another matter altogether. Every generation will question authority and the structure of their society; maybe mine just questioned a little bit louder than others? The likes of [gay and human rights campaigner] Peter Tatchell should be admired – hopefully a generation will take notice and

The A-Heads, Warminster 1980 (left to right: Nigel, Andy Gale, Jock, and Mel).

follow his and other such outspoken people's pursuits – but is he called an anarcho activist? I think not."

Sadly, for such an articulate and sincere band, 'Forgotten Hero' was to be their last vinyl release. 1984 saw a game of musical chairs within the A-Head ranks – Nigel was asked to leave ("A big fucking mistake," sighs Jock. "Put it down to the naivety of youth…"), so Wally replaced him on bass with Bruce re-joining on drums. However, when Lester Carpenter ("Another friend from the pub!") joined on bass, Wally moved back behind the kit, the band even demoing new material for a planned album, but alas, no one seemed interested in putting it out (they issued the recordings themselves though, as the 'Vox Populi' cassette).

Everything ground to a disillusioned halt when Lester left in 1985, with The A-Heads playing their final show on March 13th, at the King Arthur, Warminster, with Blyth Power – just 50 yards from the Regal Cinema where they first appeared in public almost four years earlier.

Mel went on to front The Tiny Giants, who released the 'Death By Chocolate' demo tape on Bluurg in 1992, and even numbered Jock amongst their ranks for a short while, until Nigel's suicide led the guitarist to reassess his whole reason for playing in bands.

"I drifted away from the scene we were involved in due to a renewed passion for football; the tribal effect sucked me in!" admits Jock. "Over the past fifteen years or so, the only bands that took my interest have been the Manic Street Preachers (pre-'Everything Must Go') and The Libertines. There's no urge to play anymore, just to listen. Life these days is spent playing with PCs instead, without any sort of master plan.

"Yet I find the ideals of anarcho-punk more important now than ever. The innocence of youth is well gone, but the 'I'll do it my fucking way' attitude is very much still there. But there's no real desire for the band to be remembered at all; we didn't do anything especially important after all… we just did what a lot of people did at the time and got active."

SELECT DISCOGRAPHY

7"s:
'Dying Man' (TW, 1982)
'Forgotten Hero' (Bluurg, 1983)

At A Glance:
There is an 'official bootleg' CDR, 'EPs '82 – '88', available from Bluurg, that features all of the 'Forgotten Hero' single alongside various other 7"s from the likes of Faction and Instigators. The track 'Forgotten Hero' also featured on Overground's 'Anti-War: Anarcho-punk Compilation, Volume One' (2005).

he band themselves openly admit that they feel uncomfortable being tagged as anarcho punks, but despite their imbibing vast quantities of drugs, AMEBIX had a fiercely revolutionary streak running through their pitch black core, and they certainly lived by their own rules outside the constraints of conventional society for several years. Musically they owed as much to heavy metal and hard rock as they did to punk and hardcore, their heaving noises striking the same primal chord in the listener as the ominous rumblings of an approaching storm. Indeed, even today, putting on their debut album, 'Arise', is like standing before the open door of a blast furnace and melting into the white-hot miasma of pagan savagery.

Predictably enough though, such ambitiously epic soundscapes can be traced back to humble origins, when the band first formed near Tavistock in 1978 as The Band With No Name.

"I'd never really thought about starting a band," admits bassist/vocalist Rob Miller. "Basically my [older] brother Stig [real name Chris Miller] came back from Jersey and he had a guitar and a little practise amp, and he just said, 'Oh shit, let's get a band together!' There was myself and Billy Jugg [real name Andy Hoare] and Clive [Barnes] in school together, we were in the 5th year at the

Amebix at the Boat Club
Nottingham, April 1983,
picture by Paul May.

time, and he presented us with this idea and we thought, 'Great!' 'Cos I'd just been kicked out of the ATC, where I was a sergeant at the time; I'd disgraced myself terribly by getting pissed up in Holland on this big march over there with six-and-a-half thousand allied troops, so the RAF wasn't an option for me after that. But as one door closed, so another one opened…

"We got a bass guitar and just started fucking about, practising at home. We lived out in the country at the time, and we'd hitch to and from Tavistock, which was the nearest big town, about seven or eight miles away… so we used to be pretty fit. We'd walk in on a Friday night, try and get served in as many pubs as possible, then stagger home pissed at 2 o'clock in the morning. Great fun, brilliant days… and when you look back at those times, it seems like it was always summer, real nice balmy evenings with the smell of flowers and hedge rows, y'know? Never any days of discomfort or difficulty!

"Then we got in with this guy called Ali, and he was from this correctional facility up at Kilworthy House, a school for bad kids from London, and a lot of these kids were punkies! And we started hanging out with them when they were allowed to come into town, and they were all allowed to smoke in front of the teachers and stuff. Ali mentioned this band he was into called Crass, and gave us a copy of 'Feeding Of The 5000' – he had all the regalia too – and we were fascinated by it all. I'd been collecting Discharge at the time… I used to watch the charts in Sounds and stuff… well, it was more the NME then, really… and I kept seeing their name cropping up, so we'd go into Plymouth and get the latest singles, and I thought they were pretty good. But oddly enough, I didn't really respond to them that much… looking back I still think they were a great band, but we weren't really into the hardcore stuff at all, the thrash side of punk… absolutely not. Stig had grown up in a different generation, and he was into Bowie and stuff like that, and the Pistols were just the latest elaboration on the whole idea of ostentatious rock'n'roll."

With Rob (who was then known as 'Aphid') just handling vocals to start with, the band played locally around the village halls ("And got canned off stage as everyone did during that period!"), before replacing Clive with Rick Gatsby from the Tam Beat Music Co-Op band, Bop Apocalypse. After a name change to Amebix, a six-track 'demo' was recorded, which Rob, who was writing for a local music paper at the time, proudly presented to Crass when he went along to review one of their shows in Plymouth.

"Yeah, they came down to play Plymouth's Abbey Hall, this old converted church, and I went along to write the gig up. And we'd just done this absolutely crap recording that me and Stig had banged out to sell to friends – and I gave them a copy, never expecting to hear back from them. But they were compiling the 'Bullshit Detector' album, and they asked us to go on it, this album full of all sorts of bollocks from all over the place…! But good on them, because they gave a lot of people a little bit of a boost, and that kick up the arse was all we needed. They sent us twelve copies and that was it, but we were chuffed as punch to be on it; we thought, 'Well, shit, we're actually doing something now.' The choices we had were suddenly opened up… we were basically a lazy bunch of fuckers who couldn't be bothered to work – like everybody else back then – waving a political flag to cover up that fact… 'I prefer the dole to going to work… do they owe us a living? Of course they fuckin' do!' Fucking lazy cunts!"

The track 'University Challenged' was chosen by Crass for inclusion on the album, a frankly awful song that hinted little at what Amebix would be capable of when they found their true direction, yet the national exposure was just the kind of encouragement the band needed.

"Yes, it was the first recognition we ever got for the crap we were producing, but it was just a puerile punk song by a bunch of naïve sixteen-year-olds, an attack on the trendies. We'd just left school and were bumming around, and they'd gone to university. We'd go and gatecrash their parties and stuff, and they'd be looking down their noses at us… it wasn't any great social statement, it was just us saying, 'Wankers! You went to university, fuck you!' It didn't mean anything much at all really, looking back. We had another song at the time called 'Disco Slag', which was approximately twelve minutes of pseudo-Public Image ramblings."

A major step towards that 'true direction' was taken via a chance meeting with Martin Baker ("A huge Sid Vicious look-alike," recalls Rob, "We met him outside the Co-op in Tavistock!"), who became the band's new drummer and invited Rob and Stig to go and stay with him at his parents' house on Dartmoor.

"Martin was 6'6", a massive bloke… a paranoid schizophrenic, but a very interesting character. He came from very well-bred stock, but, ahem, like the old gentry, they're all completely fucking batty 'cos they've been shagging each other for far too long, and they produce these very weird sons and daughters, and he was a perfect example of that. But he really is a lovely, gentle soul trapped inside the body of a paranoid, schizophrenic giant! So, as a consequence, they need to sedate him very heavily indeed, because if he gets angry it's going to take a lot to put him down. His mother was St. Anne, his father was Satan, and they held black masses together underneath the local church in Peter Tavy, sucking the dick of a priest, and all this kind of stuff… and that was the way things would go with him!

"Basically, his parents had this very old manor house called Glebe House on the hill at Peter Tavy, right on the edge of Dartmoor – it was very 'Scooby Doo'… large, wide staircases… oil paintings of all their predecessors going up the stairs… built on a Saxon burial ground, little cubby holes and hidden places everywhere… absolutely reeking with history. And he was left in charge of it in the winter while his parents buggered off to live at their flat in London in modest comfort… and he made the great error of inviting us all round to stay with him. We all lived in the kitchen, huddled around this big Aga, and we'd sit down there and eat and listen to music, get stoned, and then practise upstairs all night long, make little tapes and go back downstairs in front of the fire, get a bit more stoned and listen to what we'd done! A really great, inspirational time, but also very isolated, very secluded… it really brought us an appreciation of making very strange, intense sounds."

At this point Amebix were developing an unhealthy obsession with the mesmeric sounds of Killing Joke, a band whose tribal poundings changed Rob and Stig's perceptions about what constitutes genuine musical power.

"Yeah, we were developing all these influences from people like Bauhaus and Joy Division, but especially Killing Joke, who were just absolutely fucking incredible… we saw them at the Trafalgar Square CND rally in 1980, and they came onstage and just fucking blew everybody else away. It was a bit pretentious, I suppose, but Jaz Coleman came on and said, 'We're the only honest thing that's happened here all fucking day!' And all the CND people were looking at each other, shocked!

"And we were obsessed with this idea of building as big a musical architecture as possible – but we didn't have any musical ability. We still had no idea how to tune our guitars… seriously. Right up until the end of the band, we were still saying to each other, 'This is on the fat string… this on the second fattest!' We didn't know the name of these fucking notes – I used to look at Stig and copy what he was doing, and I'd use my spare time to work out all the fiddly bits, all the bass chords. What we were trying to do was use the very basic tools that we had at our disposal and get as much power and energy out of it as we could. We were all about bringing up something that was really primeval… the phrase that we locked into at the time was atavism. And we got this idea from Austin Osman Spare, an occultist who drew the Amebix face… he was loosely involved with the Neo-Rosicrucian groups, Alistair Crowley and all that. Atavism is all to do with this direct reflection upon the ancestors, like a door that you open that goes right the way down through. And that appeared to be what we were doing, tapping into a very primeval root… probably because we had so little musical ability. Like tribal groups in Africa or whatever, we were getting to the core even without technical ability, it was completely instinctive. It was just about feel, y'know?"

When Martin's parents returned home and found their house in disarray as a direct consequence of him inviting his new friends around to stay, they had him sectioned and he was bundled off to London under heavy medication, a woeful story that later inspired one of the finest Amebix songs, 'Largactyl'. With nowhere to live, Stig and Rob recruited Norman Butler as synth player, moving in with him for a while in Gunnislake, Cornwall.

There was still a volatile ingredient missing from the Amebix tale though, about to be added by a girl called Kay, who Rob still refers to knowingly as 'an angel of death', an ingredient that no good rock'n'roll story is complete without.

"She turned up one day and wheedled her way into our group," he sighs. "And she was the one who gave a twist to the whole thing, she brought the drugs basically. She took us to London – me, Norman and Stig, not as a band, as friends – and put us up in a West Kensington flat, and she would go down to Harley Street and pick up amps of Phiseptome, which was pretty much pure smack, and Ritalin... they used to prescribe the two together in those days, because they would keep you conscious, stop you couching out all the time. Then we'd all get in a taxi, and go round Piccadilly, picking up the junkies and selling the gear to them... it was a pretty cruel initiation into what was going on. These old, fucked-up hippies with gaping, maggot-infested wounds in their arms; it was pretty disgusting, and she brought all that into our world.

"She came from the edge of the moors, up near Yelveton, which is between Tavistock and Plymouth, from a very well-to-do family, and was well into smack long before we ever met her, so I think she was involved with the tail end of the Seventies, all that post-Hippy dream stuff. Because she had rich parents though, they could afford to give her a Harley Street clinician, who always gave her good gear, and basically if you've got clean drugs, it's not going to do you that much harm. And it's a 'good' thing to introduce your friends to, and she introduced Norman and Stig, and that was a very important turning point in all our lives when they made that decision and decided to go down that road. And they've walked it to this day."

Feeling ostracised by their surroundings and with little happening on the band front, the Amebix relocated to Bristol, then a veritable hotbed of musical debauchery, moving from squat to squat, befriending in the process the likes of Disorder and Chaos UK. They eked out a frugal existence there for several years, in abject poverty really, before moving to Radstock, Bath, where they finished out their career.

"The Bristol scene was fucking hardcore; we were all living the lifestyle, and most other people really weren't. We were under the impression at the time that everybody was like that, but then it dawned on us that they weren't, and that we were really fucking out there! And it was hard; it took its toll on a lot of people. I still don't know how we managed to be quite so prolific living in such conditions really, because we did produce a fair body of work in the short time we were around. We didn't do an album a year or anything like that, but it was pretty good going for a band that were living in places where there were no roofs, no toilet facilities, junkies hanging out the windows... it was a funny time in Bristol, and it was four years that I really should have got done in a year. But we never know how it's going to end, do we? Not at any time in our lives... and the end only came when we were presented with the possibility of getting out, and I never knew that that was going to be there until it was. My last poignant memory of Bristol is of being up in Redland in this squat, bouncing from one place to another, and there weren't really any people left in any of these places by then, and returning to this one place where Disorder used to live, and staying in this room upstairs where the roof had actually collapsed... the weight of all the pigeon shit had brought the attic down. I was looking up at the night and there was fucking snow drifting in, settling on my pillow... all I had was this pillow, this sleeping bag, a piss-stained mattress and some pain killers. I'd take a few when I got up, until I could walk around a bit, then I'd go and bum some money, try and get some food, try and get some drugs, and then take a few more when it was time to sleep again. And I was thinking, 'What the fuck is going on here?' That was the last straw... and we were just lucky to even get out really."

Whilst in Bristol, the Amebix procured the services of Disorder drummer, Virus, and released two singles and a 12" EP, all for Spiderleg Records. Strangely enough, it was actually Kay, who had unleashed so much negative chemical energy within the band, that helped land them such a coveted deal.

"She was into different bands to us altogether, nothing to do with the punk scene, and we were telling her about the bands we were into like Crass. So when she was up in London dealing drugs, she went along and saw them, and it turned out that she recognised the woman called Joy de Vivre up onstage. She actually used to go to school with her; they both went to the same nice girls' school, so she was like [effects posh accent], 'Fucking hell, Joy, what are you doing here?' 'Oh, I play for Crass who are frightfully lovely people!' And she got an invitation for me and her to go up to their place and stay, which we did, and that opened things up a bit more for the band. I think they suggested that we try Spiderleg, and they put us onto Flux... but it was essentially a Crass subsidiary in many ways, all based around John Loder at Southern Studios."

Despite the affiliation Spiderleg had with Southern, Amebix recorded their debut EP, 'Who's The Enemy?', locally, at Bristol's eight-track SAM Studios, with Mark 'Sooty' Byrne (who would later join punk heavyweights Vice Squad) helming the desk. A heavily distorted, rather rambling offering, it nonetheless made No. 33 in the Indie charts upon its release during August 1982, and featured the track 'No Gods, No Masters', a phrase that would become something of a motto for the band.

"That was all about the concept of gods really, because I would never have described us as a non-religious band. We live amongst conceptual gods, if you will, all the time... the gods of science, of religion, of sex, politics, all the rest of it; these are almost like Roman household gods. For me we were talking about a god that was beyond religion – but it's a horrible thing to have to use that word because you immediately get confused with religion anyway.

"The Gnostics had this belief that's reflected directly in the film 'The Matrix'; they believed that

Rob 'The Baron' Miller of Amebix, live at the 100 Club London, Sept 1985, picture by Paul May.

the created world was the creation of the demi-urge, which is like a reflection of the true god, but that god himself is actually evil... that concept of god is to do with the created universe. So, they were still hung up with materialism and guilt, but they maintained that it wasn't the whole picture. Their initiates were given certain sequences of words and images that they were made to remember, so when they died and left this mortal sphere, they would be able to travel as souls throughout the universe, meeting certain guardians at certain gates, and they had to give these passwords to get through. So, the heresy of the Gnostics, was that one can understand God through knowledge – which was exactly contrary to the Catholic belief that one understands god through subservience to the priesthood and blind faith... but for a lot of people, blind faith isn't enough.

"And it's a reflection of the punk thing too – if you like, punk was a form of Gnosticism, because it was saying that through true knowledge of yourself and your surroundings, you can attain a better perception of the world itself. I'm sorry, I tend to talk in these heavy terms because it's something I spent a lot of time with my head involved in..."

The 'Winter' single followed (b/w 'Beginning Of The End') in early '83, a poorly produced offering with insistent tom patterns drowned beneath waves of fuzzed-out guitars and Rob's repetitive wailing of the title, that actually spent almost two months in the Indies, peaking at No. 18.

"A lot of the stuff we were writing back then was just garbage," scoffs Rob. "But a lot of it was fundamental as well, building blocks for what we were trying to create. Unfortunately we wasted a lot of time in this melange of stuff that was trying to be Killing Joke... trying to imitate their sound because they were the most realistic interpretation I'd heard of what we were trying to get to ourselves... that whole primitive rhythmic thing that didn't really break into verse/chorus, verse/chorus, middle-eight... it was just about creating this big, big presence."

One thing that was certainly beginning to assert itself within the band though was Rob's bleak, evocative artwork, vaguely disturbing images of people struggling against the chains that held them, that perfectly complemented the minimalist vibe of their early works.

"That bound figure was a recurring motif, pulling against his shackles, trying to rise; it was a personal thing that I was trying to express. It was all about anchor points... in psychological terms, it was all about the Axis Mundi, the centre of the earth, an important theme in all primitive mythologies. It's the place where the central mountain is, the central spike that's driven into the earth, the point from which all creation has evolved. It's a graphic representation of that, of someone trying to break away, albeit just a primitive representation, 'cos I was never a great artist, I couldn't even draw faces. I do like the fact that I invented this particular style of writing that a lot of people are using these days though!"

Norman was replaced on synth by John 'Jenghis' Borthwick, 'The Mad Scotsman', just in time to record the 'No Sanctuary' 12" at Southern Studios, the first Amebix release to even come close to capturing the band's visceral edginess on vinyl. It actually made the Indie Top Ten upon its release in November 1983, and brought the band to the attention of Jello Biafra, lead singer with US politico-punks Dead Kennedys who also ran the highly-respected Alternative Tentacles label. He was in London to play a show with the Bad Brains at the Brixton Ace, and called into Southern where he heard the band recording, liked what he heard and promised to put out their next record

Amebix kicking back in Italy (left to right: Stig, Virus and Rob).

for them. Amebix would be the first of only two UK bands to ever ink a deal with the cult American label (the other being Iowaska). Meanwhile the band embarked upon the first of several forays into Europe, even undertaking an eventful tour of Italy.

"We got arrested in Bologna," chuckles Rob, "Had Uzi sub-machineguns shoved into our backs and everything, for scrawling 'Death to false metal, all men play on ten' on this squat wall! They took it as some sort of political commentary, and threw us straight into the cells. We had to have this Italian girl come in and explain it was a joke! Italy was always pretty wild...

"Stig had his first epileptic fit onstage there, this place called Cazenozia, down towards Sicily. We'd been travelling all day on this sweaty train, and there were two distinct parties there, the fascist party and the communist party, and we were playing for the communists, who were basically the students union. They gave us this budget for food, so we invited everyone we saw to this big last supper-type gathering in this restaurant. And then we played in this cobbled courtyard, and the audience were old women in black robes carrying babies, and men in shirts and ties. And there we were, giving it some shit, and in between songs, they were clapping politely. And there were these sinister Mafiosa dudes hanging about backstage, offering us heroin, and Stig was gagging because he hadn't had a hit since we'd left the UK.

"Anyway, we were about five songs in, and the guitar solo was going on even longer and more discordant than usual, and I looked over and there was Stig lying on his back, his legs twitching, his body convulsing... he'd swallowed his tongue, shit himself, the works, and we had to drag him offstage. They had a big headline in the local paper next day, 'English band... drug addicts... blah blah blah!' He wasn't epileptic up until that point when he'd tried to get off smack, but he was epileptic from then on. So we had to get some liquid valium – we all had valium and vodka cocktails – and flew back to Heathrow."

Such antics didn't prevent the band from penning a genuine masterpiece in the shape of 'Arise', which made No. 3 in the Indies during late 1985; their only release for Alternative Tentacles and an album that towers over most other attempts at fusing punk and heavy metal undertaken since. In fact, the album still casts impenetrably influential shadows over the extreme music scene of today, such is its majestic power and poise. And the new weapon in the band's arsenal that allowed them to land such a devastatingly effective sucker punch? None other than new drummer Spider (real name Robert Richards), formerly with SCUM, who replaced a departing Virus, and had a much more forceful playing style; his intense driving rhythms ignited the band's simplistic riffing and breathed new life into Amebix, lending 'Arise' a throbbing, ferociously heavy, almost physical, presence. Keyboards were provided for the album by George 'The Dragon', then guitarist with the Smart Pils, a psychedelic punk troupe from Bath who released an album 'No Good, No Evil' on Bluurg, and whose drummer Richard Chadwick would later join Hawkwind.

Unbelievably it wasn't a record that Alternative Tentacles relished putting out.

"Well, this is the funny thing. Jello met us when we were recording at Southern Studios and obviously recognised something a bit weird in what we were doing… bear in mind this was the 'No Sanctuary' period, and he loved tracks like 'Moscow Madness'. But when we gave them 'Arise', there was this uncomfortable silence… Jello didn't know what to do really, it was almost embarrassing. He wasn't very happy, he'd been expecting something else, but I'll give him his credit, he still fucking put it out. And these days he'll probably regard that as the right thing to have done, and fair play to him for that, but back then it was unacceptable, it wasn't right for the label at all.

"I've since watched some live video footage of us, and it's weird. We go on looking like rocked-out bikers, giving it some shit with our instruments, and everybody just stands there thinking, 'What the fuck is going on here? Is this cool enough to dance to? Is this a punk band?' And the first three or four songs were always like that, nothing happening at the front of the stage, just us going, 'Arrrgghh!' And then people realised we were serious and the next fast song we'd play, something like the break in the middle of 'Axeman', and all hell would break loose and the gig would get better and better and better. But it only ever peaked during the second half of the gig.

"And 'Arise' was the same, the reviews were very, very unsure, just like Alternative Tentacles, but our saving grace was we didn't go [blatantly heavy metal] like Onslaught or Discharge, because there wasn't any point; what we were doing was quite enough, we'd already found the power we'd always been looking for, as well as a way to deliver it with a punch… and that punch came from the drums.

"But it was never about trying to actually understand what we were playing," ponders Rob on just what makes 'Arise' such a profound listening experience. "We just knew that certain sound we were striving for. We had no fucking idea how to make it though, whereas a lot of bands these days understand intellectually how to create the music they want to make.

"Talking about stuff like this, it makes me realise that I do feel very passionately about what we did as a band. A lot of people do heap a lot of praise upon us, but I read an American review of 'Arise' the other day and the guy was pretty much spot-on. He didn't go, 'Amebix are progenitors of this and that,' and all the rest of it… he actually said, 'These guys wear their influences on their sleeves. You can hear Joy Division, you can hear Killing Joke, you can hear Black Sabbath and Motörhead…' But he was quite disparaging at the end, adding, 'It's just a shame that they didn't leave us anything half as good as these other bands!' Which is fine, y'know? It's his opinion, and good on him, because we did wear our influences on our sleeves in many ways.

"Venom weren't an influence though, that's one thing I strongly need to state to everybody. We were before Venom, and I got their first single and I wrote to them when they brought out 'In League With Satan'… I wrote this letter to Abaddon saying, 'That's the funniest thing I've ever heard in my fucking life!' 'Cos I thought they were taking the piss! And the twat wrote back, 'Do not mock the way of Venom…' and all this sort of thing!

"We didn't take too much from Sabbath either, contrary to popular opinion… what we did get from them was, uh, the vibe of 'War Pigs'. And what was really unsettling was that first album cover, those woods with the old house in the background. It was really quite deep to me, very suggestive – very simple, this horrible old photograph, but it took me right back to the sixteenth century witch trials."

The band's harsh punk/metal sounds, on-the-edge lifestyle and gung ho approach to live performances ultimately helped win them over fans in the biker community, who until then had traditionally been at odds with the whole punk subculture.

"Myself, Jamie [Rob's younger brother, who drove the band for a while and later played in Sidewinder with Scruff from The Apostles] and Stig had always grown up around bikes; dad always had big bikes, and when we were sixteen he would buy us our first mopeds and stuff. And it was something I returned to after Bristol, when we got the place in Radstock… I hooked up with this woman over there, Jen, who was the absolute bane of my life, and she was 'biker, biker, biker…' She was a biker bitch, in fact! Right into all the clubs, the whole attitude… and we fit right into that scene at that time, because we were playing music that was easily accessible to these people. It was like she had half the cards, and we had the other. And on my twenty-first birthday, we brought the two halves together, when she invited down this guy from The Outcasts in Wolverhampton, and some other biker dudes from Weston-Super-Mare, and places like that. And all the punky crew turned up from Bristol, and there was this uneasy truce to start with, then someone put on Amebix downstairs, and all these bikers upstairs were tapping their feet and getting into it. And that broke the ice, and this twenty-one-skin spliff was made, and the whole party erupted; it broke down a lot of barriers and things started to blur. We had people roadie for us who were involved with the biker scene and stuff… although, to be fair, the barriers had been coming down since Motörhead really."

A strange turnabout seeing as bikers had trashed the Stonehenge festival when Flux played just a few years earlier…

"Yeah, I was there when they caused a load of trouble in '82 as well… they can traditionally be arseholes and cause a lot of trouble, but this was more like inter-club rivalry, and people got caught up in it really. It's a load of egotistical shit, to be honest, and I got involved in that later on as well, when I was with a bike club up in Wiltshire, a patch club and all that, and things got pretty rough and all the rest of it. But it was just bollocks, just children really… children with beards! Who haven't sorted out any security in their own lives yet, y'know? It goes back to this infantile desire to create security within your own sect…"

Such a unique aesthetic certainly helped set the band apart from their peers in the punk scene at the time, with only Antisect coming close in terms of sheer belligerent sonic power.

"Yes, but Antisect were friends of ours; we loved what they were doing, and they liked what we were doing – and we were all into Sabbath… we made a point of playing 'Mob Rules' at gigs, just to piss everybody off – but they were still really tied in with the traditional anarcho scene. At that time there were a lot of people trying to do the right thing… it was all tied into the agenda, and the agenda was often being dictated by Crass. Everybody seemed to think that, because they had seniority, they should be the ones to tell everybody how they should be thinking…

"One classic moment was when we were recording 'No Sanctuary', and we were staying at Flux's place… they didn't like that very much, having these smelly bastards who didn't really care about anything sleeping on the floor of their nice house. The Falklands War had just started and they were waiting to hear what Crass had to say about the war before they made their own statement. They were like, 'Okay, we have a copy of the single coming in today…' and they all sat down and played 'Sheep Farming In The Falklands', and then they knew what they were expected to produce, they knew the party line. And there was something cruelly ironic about that, that really changed my mind about the whole scene, because no one was really thinking for themselves. Not to be unkind to either Crass or Flux, but that's the way it was… there was something all-enveloping and warm about being a part of 'the family'. And that's often the way with these pseudo-revolutionary movements, the 'dictators' of the trend themselves often haven't got their own lives sorted out all that well in the first place, y'know?"

Paradoxically, when Amebix settled in the more stable climes of Bath, their musical output faltered quite drastically, suggesting that here was a band whose creative muse genuinely thrived on adversity, and it would be several years before 'Monolith', their hotly-anticipated sophomore offering, was completed. In the meantime, Rob had a son with the aforementioned Jen, and the band kept themselves busy by adding new keyboardist Andy 'A. Droid' Wiggins and undertaking plenty of roadwork, building themselves a formidable reputation as a scarily-intense live act, their onstage presence a veritable force of nature that had to be witnessed to be believed.

"That was how it felt to us as well," reckons Rob. "I remember reading an interview the Bauhaus did in Sounds once, where they claimed – quite pretentiously really – that there was another member of the band, a spirit, that joined them onstage, and there was something about when we were playing that really did echo that sort of thing. There were moments when we were playing live when I felt something coming up, rising up through me... like channelling really. And there was one moment I found quite disturbing, because it was like having someone else looking through my eyes... the whole spatial thing had expanded and something else was looking through me. I really did feel like that, and it was quite overwhelming, to tell you the truth. I wasn't on anything at the time either, it was just the music. To be honest, and at risk of sounding like a hippy, I think it was a total willingness to open up and let something through, and I became a doorway... and some people saw that doorway at the time and were quite taken aback. They thought, 'What the fuck are these guys about?' And I almost felt like, 'Shit, maybe I should have kept that door shut!' It was like a dungeon and god knows what was going to come out.

"I don't like to get ego-bound about the whole thing really, because we were just four guys playing music, but we did create quite an intense experience, and we really put all of ourselves into it as well. It was like mesmerism, getting so focused on an idea that you draw everyone else into it. And it just shows how easily we can get sucked in, we're all looking for this belonging... we long to belong. We don't know where we come from, and at the end of the day we don't know where we're going either... and when people raise flags, proud to be English or Scottish it means nothing. We don't know how to express any of these things properly other than by clinging to our mummy's breast, this whole notion of security, and it's good to unhook from that now and again, and just let things roll."

Unfortunately Amebix were unable to even approach their live power with 'Monolith', which appeared through Wolverhampton's Heavy Metal Records (a division of FM Revolver) in 1987. Despite some savage riffing, oodles of atmosphere and more than a few tracks the equal of anything on 'Arise', the album was seriously hampered by one of the most subdued productions to ever come out of SAM and sank without trace, taking the band with it.

"Basically we just soured," admits Rob. "We'd released 'Monolith', and then when we went to write more songs, it was as if we couldn't draw from the well anymore. We really had done all that we could do, and everything we wrote seemed to be too much in the mould of what we'd done before... there was nothing pushing ahead, nothing that struck us as particularly interesting or new. We were spent.

"I don't regret 'Monolith' at all though, I think it's a very good album... it's cruelly underrated... it could've done with better production values, and we could've done with sitting down and thinking about things a bit more before we rushed it out, but we desperately wanted to put something out that we felt was deeper and heavier than 'Arise'. 'Arise' was punk meets heavy metal, but 'Monolith' was much deeper, much more grungy, a lot heavier in the way that the songs were put together... but we just couldn't seem to move any further into that territory without sounding like a parody of ourselves.

"You may have heard that [final] 'Right To Ride' demo we did? Whereas I liked vocally where I was trying to go at that point, it was beginning to get a bit cheesy, and I'm glad that we ended it where we did, just said, 'That's it!' There was definitely an awareness there that we were going to blow the whole thing if we carried on."

The band played their last show of note in Sarajevo, and quit while they were ahead, ensuring in the process their rightful place in the enigma department of rock history.

Stig and Spider went on to play with the much less convincing Zygote alongside George from the Smart Pils (Spider, who now suffers with tinnitus, later drummed for Muckspreader as well), whilst Rob eventually moved to the Isle of Skye where he still crafts collectible swords by hand today.

"I purposely didn't listen to the band for twelve or fifteen years, because I found it disturbing to do so. Because I wasn't sure that we had any positive impact… it was only during the last ten years, as the internet has really come into its own, that I started to hear from people, and have found out that yes, some people did get something positive from what we were doing. Some people even said that if it wasn't a life-changing thing, it at least helped them get through difficult times. One guy even said that it helped him and his brother relate when they didn't have a relationship at all! One liked punk, one liked heavy metal… and then along came Amebix! Really nice things like that, because I went though a part of my life when I was very naked and vulnerable, psychologically, like someone had peeled off my skin and I could feel every cold wind that blew…

"That was as a long-term consequence of a lot of things that had gone before – in particular, a relationship that had gone bad, but also the band, the time in Bristol… and those things drew me to a place… we talk about 'the dark night of the soul', that everyone faces at some time or other in their life… and how we deal with that is very critical. Personally? I had to deal with it very, very, very carefully, because I was right on the edge and in danger of spinning off. Any adverse stuff at that point could've thrown me one way or the other, so I just had to find my space, sit down, be quiet and just observe… and I spent a lot of years observing… and that was long-term fall-out from a lot of different things. And thank god that's well behind me now, y'know?

"But remember, we never made anything out of what we did… and one of the things I do feel resentment about is that a lot of other people did. And still do! And none of them have bothered to tip the cap to us at all, and I condemn them absolutely. It's not about money, it's about the ethics of the situation – it was all about being good, and right, to one another, and how we deal with one another reflects upon the way we deal with our world. And that's what makes change… if you can't deal with your mates and be fucking honest with them, what hope is there for you?"

SELECT DISCOGRAPHY

7"s:
'Who's The Enemy?' (Spiderleg, 1982)
'Winter' (Spiderleg, 1983)

12"s:
'No Sanctuary' (Spiderleg, 1983)

LPs:
'Arise' (Alternative Tentacles, 1985)
'Monolith' (Heavy Metal, 1987)

At A Glance:
Alternative Tentacles' 'Arise (+ 2)' CD is an expanded version of the band's definitive debut album that includes their two-track final demo as an interesting little bonus, whilst the widely-available bootleg CD, 'Beginning Of The End', compiles all of the Spiderleg releases onto one disc, but is obviously totally unofficial. There are also plans afoot to issue a comprehensive live DVD as well as a long overdue re-mastered version of 'Monolith'.

Where bands like Amebix armed themselves with the most pulverising sounds possible, **THE MOB** succeeded by expressing their vulnerability… laying bare their deepest fears… through raw, honest emotion. Especially with their one and only album, a profound demonstration that was as powerful as any show of brute force.

Formed in the late Seventies by three school friends – guitarist/vocalist Mark Wilson, bassist Curtis Youe and drummer Graham Fallows – in Stoke-sub-Hamdon, a sleepy Somerset village just outside Yeovil, The Mob actually started gigging as 'Magnum Force'.

"Me and Curtis were the first punks for miles," reckons Mark. "And Graham was such a madman, the best drummer ever. Those two gigs as Magnum Force were just at our school… we weren't much good but we'd trash the place every chance we got!

"It was very hard to be different in such a small town – and we were very different! We would be attacked by everyone… bikers, teds… everyone. Anyone who has never

Mark Wilson of The Mob, juggling, picture by Mick Mercer.

lived in small town, redneck land can't begin to imagine how much shit we used to get. You simply can't describe the loneliness unless you've lived it. We were so envious of punks in places like London and Manchester… because we could only read about it…

"When I left school in '77, I had a choice of two jobs – one involved an apprenticeship in Weymouth, making helicopters, and the other was in Plymouth, plumbing. Plymouth was on the itinerary of every punk tour at the time so I obviously became a plumber! I saw bands almost every night after that… The Clash, Generation X, Siouxsie, The Slits, Buzzcocks, and many more…

"I'm not sure why or when we became The Mob exactly, but it suited how we lived. I've never really liked the name much, but as time passed, that was very much what we became, a mob, and there are lots of people who were as much a part of it as the three of us in the band…"

"Personally I think we are all products of our environment to some degree," chips in Curtis. "We were definitely shaped by boredom, frustration and a very strong desire to make something new happen. The arrival of the punk scene in '76 was a very natural progression for us."

"I read an article on punk in the NME in 1976," adds Mark. "And by the time I got to the bottom of the page I knew I was a punk! And I remember praying that I'd like the music as much as I liked the message.

"Before that, I was really into 'Quadrophenia' by The Who – not the film version, but the original opera – and Bob Dylan's 'Hurricane'. I love a song that tells a story; I've listened to both recently and realize now how much they affected my life and beliefs."

As with most punk bands from rural backwaters, and in the absence of any real alternative scene, The Mob had to work hard to create one of their own. Forced to book themselves into village halls until they could blag their way into 'proper' venues, they did everything themselves, printing fliers, manning the door… even producing their own fanzine, 'All The Madmen', to sell to those that turned up.

"Nobody would ever want us near their place!" confirms Mark. "We would rehearse in skittle alleys mostly, and even that would always draw a crowd... although 'the crowd' often included several bikers wanting to kill us! But we also always had lots of people coming to rehearsals just for the 'event' as well.

"We basically begged, borrowed and stole our equipment... at one gig in Bridgewater, we had to persuade one of our entourage to take the house PA out of the van and give it back to the venue. We were still lifted on the way home though anyway, by the local constabulary.

"Actually my first involvement in guitar was stealing a book on guitar chords from a shop in Yeovil. Having nicked the book, I then got a job at £2 a week in a skittle alley and paid for a guitar over the next year. This was a couple of years earlier, when I was still at school, but I had that guitar throughout the whole Mob period... until I threw it into the crowd one night in East London and never saw it again. And the truth is, I never felt the same about music after that; though not because of losing the guitar really... it just happened at the same time."

As well as organizing their own gigs in and around Yeovil and Weymouth, The Mob managed to beg onto several of the larger punk shows they regularly attended, most incongruously as support to Sham 69 in Plymouth. Even in their earliest incarnation though, it was quite apparent they had little in common with the boot boy strand of punk rock, and with their enthusiastic penchant for drink and drugs, they soon found themselves gravitating towards the hippy culture, playing squats and free festivals rather than the professional venues on the rigid rock circuit, and eventually they found their niche as part of the burgeoning anarcho scene.

"Speaking personally, definitely!" comes Mark's instant reply, when asked whether he felt comfortable with the anarcho tag. "The term could have been made for my beliefs! Of course, we are all full of

Josef and Curtis of The Mob (and friends!).

contradictions, but fundamentally I was an anarchist and still am. Someone said to me at work the other day, 'Oh, you're a bit left wing, aren't you?' To which I replied, 'I'm so far to the left, I make Ryan Giggs look like he plays on the right!' Ha!"

"We went through many natural progressions as The Mob," offers Curtis. "And playing the free festivals in the late Seventies was a strong influence. The many friends we made at that time nurtured the peace and love philosophy, yet happily embraced the angry frustrated youth aspect as well. Independence... rebelliousness... it's all anarchy to me!"

Mark again: "Very early on in our career, we blagged a spot with a band of freaks and anarchists called Here And Now, who were doing free tours of the UK and shaking a tin at the end to pay for it. It was called 'The Floating Anarchy Tour'. We were always fond of getting out of it ourselves, and this introduced us to a whole load of possibilities for fun and chaos. We toured and played gigs many times with Here And Now, both in England and Holland [in June, 1979, performing in Amsterdam and Arnheim]; it introduced us to communes and squatting and festivals and many other wonderful things. And, of course, being punks we were welcomed with open arms by alternative society which had grown bored of guitar-solo, hippy bands.

"Through Here And Now we met Zounds, the Androids Of Mu [whose 1980 album, 'Blood Robots', on their own Fuck Off label made No. 15 in the Indie charts] and The Astronauts, and we set up our own free tour, Weird Tales. We performed free all over the UK and shook the tin to pay for it each night… we had some great times, and got arrested and pissed up on Moss Side with a band called The Hamsters who were the best ever. One night we didn't have a gig so we went to a working men's club in Manchester that was having a talent night and pretended to be a punk Wurzels… we won the competition as well!"

Deciding it was high time to immortalize their growing repertoire of material on vinyl, The Mob unveiled their debut single, 'Crying Again', in late 1979, through their own label named after the band's self-produced fanzine; as with all their subsequent releases, with the notable exception of the 'No Doves' single, it was recorded at the popular Spaceward Studios, Cambridge.

"Basically no one was ever going to sign us," admits Mark candidly. "We sent a few tapes out to labels but we never got any offers, so the obvious thing to do was do it ourselves. We were very used to doing everything off our own backs anyway. So All The Madmen became a label as well as a fanzine and everything else. It was all done from Geoff's mum's house really, where we lived most of the time as she tolerated our outrageous behaviour better than anyone else. I see those early records on e-bay now, and I find it amazing to think of us all sat in Geoff's room folding the sleeves and sticking those stickers on, oh so very long ago."

Whilst undeniably crude compared to later offerings, 'Crying Again' laid out the band's stall well enough, a bubbly tempo and insistent simple riff providing a neat contrast to the poignancy of Mark's vocal delivery. Dressed in a bleak picture sleeve depicting a lost teenage soul forlornly hanging around in the rain outside Yeovil bus station, it also spoke volumes about how the band's frustratingly mundane childhoods had coloured their melancholic approach to songwriting. And the dirge-like B-side cut, 'Youth', just emphasized the point.

But if 'Crying Again' was a decent enough opening gambit, it was their second single, 'Witch Hunt', that landed later the same year, that really brought The Mob to the attention of the record-buying public and established themselves as a band of genuinely formidable power. Unfurling from a chilling shriek of anguish, and based around a deceptively simple, repetitive riff, the song subtly builds in atmosphere, whispered backing vocals adding to the quiet intensity of its condemnation of the mainstream's intolerance towards the things it doesn't understand.

In 1981, sick of being ostracised in the Southwest, The Mob relocated to London. Graham chose to stay in Somerset however ("I believe he's still there," offers Mark. "He was a fantastic drummer and went on to play in various club bands – probably still does…") and was eventually replaced by Joseph Porter from the aforementioned Zounds.

"Their drummer quit and they phoned me up and asked me to stand in," recalls Joseph. "I actually stayed as a 'stand-in' for most of the time I was drumming for them. I was in Zounds at the time, and I can't remember if, and when, I ever 'officially' joined The Mob. I know I was replaced a couple of times by other drummers who didn't last…"

Mark: "Those other drummers being a fella called Adie from Yeovil, who was a regular at all our early gigs, and a friend of ours called Tim, who played with us for a while as well. We bought a bus with the intention of travelling around, playing, and the first place we drove to was Brougham Road in Hackney where Joseph lived. A fella came out of No. 74 and asked would we give him £40 for the keys and the plumbing he'd just bought for it, so in we went.

"Brougham Road is still there today… we formed a housing co-op [the Black Sheep Housing Co-Op, with – amongst others – members of Blood And Roses and Crass] and the council eventually leased us the houses we had squatted for so long. Every house in the street was squatted and we moved some friends from the emerging peace convoy into the empty bus station behind the road. London at that time was a place you could live the dream; there were thousands of likeminded people and, every day, new visitors from abroad who were drawn to the anarcho scene there."

The much-maligned (by the band), but highly sought-after, 'Ching' demo was recorded during this period at Brougham Road, a cassette-only release which the band issued themselves.

"It was played live onto a ghetto blaster in the practice room upstairs in my squat at No. 62," reveals Joseph. "The sound was very rough as you can imagine. I can't remember the track listing, but it did have a song on it called 'White Niggers', which vanished shortly thereafter without trace. I know 'Youth' was on it as well, and probably 'Gates of Hell', 'Slayed', 'Never Understood', 'Witch Hunt', 'Shuffling Souls' and others, but I haven't even seen one for over twenty years so I can't be sure."

Brougham Road, picture by Mick Penguin.

Impressed by The Mob's enthusiastic sincerity, Crass offered to release their next single for them, and the resulting 'No Doves Fly Here' was – for many – the band's crowning glory. Released in late April 1982, it spent almost four months in the Indie charts, peaking at No. 8, and remains to this day one of the most profound anti-war statements ever committed to vinyl. Drastically different to the two singles that preceded it, an epic scope lends the band's customary understated simplicity and lilting bass lines an impressive air of grandiosity more than suited to the gravity of the desperately sad truths imparted by the lyrics.

"The Crass release was really brought about by lack of funds on our part," claims Curtis. "And I would say was the only recording we did that was produced beyond what the song was; every other recording we made had a natural feel. We wrote a song and recorded it. But Penny Rimbaud was unhappy with our original finish of 'No Doves…', which had a much more live feel, and went on to create more of a typical Crass production."

"I have a copy of that original recording that didn't have the synthesizers on it," reveals Mark. "There were only two pressed and I somehow kept one. The song was always much more powerful live, I think; it would often move me near to tears. I recently heard a version of it by [US melodic hardcore band] J. Church and liked it better for having a decent guitar and vocal track…!"

"I still think 'No Doves…' is one of the most beautiful singles of the whole punk era," claims Penny, who produced the single at London's Southern Studios. "I really loved the words, so I put huge effort into recreating the atmosphere they suggested to me. I mean, it was still their tune, but on its own, it was… well, a bit bland really, and I helped them transform it into this huge, wonderful soundscape…"

Mark himself is also under no illusions as to the influence Crass had on The Mob: "It was while doing that Weird Tales tour that we first met Crass; our van broke down just up the road from their house. Over the years, we shared houses with various members of the Crass entourage and obviously spent a fair bit of time with them. I always loved their whole ideology, the symbols and what they stood for, although I actually thought the Poison Girls, who shared the stage with them at nearly every early gig, were a far better band. I always felt that Crass liked to have bands playing with them that were no real threat to them musically… yet the Poison Girls were far superior I think.

"They also liked to work with bands that toed 'the party line' better than we could. We always had a fondness for drink and drugs that was at odds with their puritanical approach. Though I for one loved Crass for their politics and commitment, we were perhaps too colourful and out of it for them."

Soon after the release of their third single, The Mob found themselves the surprise cover stars of 'Punk Lives' magazine (issue five), a glossy magazine dedicated primarily to the more obvious acts of the genre that had also begun to take great notice of the thriving anarcho scene. Nevertheless, appearing on the front cover of a mainstream magazine was tantamount to treason for many of the more elitist anarcho punkers, but The Mob took it all in their stride and treated such judgmental snobbery with the contempt it deserved.

"I honestly don't know why I did it," laughs Mark. "And I don't think I gave a shit what anyone thought either. It was something to do with Tony D. who lived in our house in Islington [and was responsible for the popular Kill Your Pet Puppy fanzine]… but real Mob fans would have known that it was just a laugh anyway."

"Besides, Mark was the only member actually interviewed that day," interjects Curtis. "None of us were even photographed either; the pictures were just of friends who lived with Mark at the time. Bit of a joke really…"

With their profile bolstered by such publicity, not to mention the single on Crass, The Mob's 'Let The Tribe Increase' album stormed the Indie charts upon its release in Spring 1983, crashing in at the dizzying heights of No. 3. A wonderful collection of scintillating, uplifting tunes, albeit imbued with an almost tangible aura of profound sadness, the band's album stands as testament to the depth and maturity of their compositions, every single track as memorable as the next. With the disturbingly surreal 'Roger' hinting at the band's more mischievous side, a fine counterpoint to the impassioned pleas for peace and love that make up the bulk of the record.

"The album artwork – all of our artwork, in fact – was done by this genius from Yeovil, Wilf, although me and Joseph contributed bits and pieces as well. I did the back of 'Tribe…' and Joseph did the insert. Wilf sadly died a couple of years back, but he did absolutely masses of paintings during the early punk years that chronicled our lives in Yeovil… and the world. Some of the work he did for 'Tribe…' was just brilliant, but at the time we couldn't use it 'cos printing more than two colours was outside our financial abilities."

Such glories were short-lived however, as The Mob split in late 1983, their final gig being at the Doncaster Co-op Hall on November 19th, a mere month after the release of what Mark considers his favourite single, 'The Mirror Breaks'.

"I'd had that song in my head since I was fifteen or sixteen, and we had played it in several forms all along. I loved the imagery of it and I thought it summed up life at the time. We were all terrified of war and nuclear power and especially Thatcher. It's really hard for people today to understand what it was like to be different under the extremes of Thatcherism.

"As for the split, well… we had some gigs organised in the North of England, and then some more came in for Southern Italy. And there was a clash of interest, 'cos Joseph wanted to go north as there's a great railway hub at Crewe he wanted to see. I thought this was nothing short of madness!

"In addition, I had completely run out of new songs and we had been trotting the same ones out for years. I didn't want to continue to just do it for the sake of it, and I wasn't interested in Joseph's style of songs, which he went on to use with Blyth Power [where he was joined initially by Curtis, who is now working as a chef in South Wales]. I had begun to hang around with the peace convoy and the new age travellers as well, and had very little interest in playing music anymore.

"I've spent most of the intervening years living in caravans and enjoying a traveller/gypsy lifestyle near Bristol. I have been living in a house again for the past eight years… but would consider myself still well off the wall. I run a business recycling vans, which comes from the early days of travelling with The Mob and always having to mend our own!"

Joseph remembers the band's demise slightly differently however.

"Actually I only started [train] spotting again after the band split and Mark went off to become a traveller… I think he simply got bored with it all. I remember we had four days booked for rehearsing at Allan Gordon's studios in Leytonstone. The idea was to get songs worked out for a second album, but we got fed up after a day and a half. I think all we worked out was one new song, which never got played, and a cover of Lou Reed's 'Pale Blue Eyes'. We spent a couple of hours jamming old ATV songs, then knocked it on the head – and that was the last time we ever played together. I never heard anything about an Italian tour… but if I had, I'm sure both Curtis and I would have been happy to go.

"As far as I recall, the band just fizzled out. After the rehearsals Mark told us he wanted to take a break for a few months, then we simply never got back together. Technically, I suppose, The Mob hasn't even split up yet… of course it may well have simply been a plan to ditch me and Curtis. Who knows?"

The years following their premature end saw several posthumous Mob releases, including the 'Crying Again' 12" for All The Madmen (basically a re-release of the first single, bolstered by three live tracks recorded at Meanwhile Gardens, Westbourne Park, London, on June 25th, 1983), and a split live LP with The Apostles on Cause For Concern ('Live At The LMC, 22/1/83', it began life as a cassette release in 1983, but was issued on vinyl, as a completely unofficial bootleg, in 1986). Also, a split live cassette (shared with Faction and D&V), 'No, No, No, Don't Drop Yer Bombs On Us, They Hurt!', recorded during May '83, was released the following year by 96 Tapes, the cassette label ran by Rob Challice, who actually inherited the running of All The Madmen in the wake of The Mob's passing.

Despite having essentially hung up his guitar in late 1983, Mark is philosophical about the band's legacy and the long-term effect his involvement had on shaping the course of his life.

"Our best gigs were nearly always in London. We could fill most places there, which is a great feeling for a band. We did a gig for Raymond's birthday at the Fulham Greyhound, and my sister came along but couldn't get in, so she sat on the pavement outside with a few dozen others. She said she'd never been so proud!"

"Raymond needs a book all to himself," offers Joseph, by way of explanation. "'Father Raymond' we used to call him. He was a Transylvanian ex-Benedictine monk! He'd been studying for a priesthood in the Romanian-speaking part of Hungary, but had fled to escape the Russians, crossed Europe 'on the lam', joined the Foreign Legion to get a pair of boots, then deserted and finally wound up in England where he became a weaver at Downside Abbey in Somerset. Eventually, and probably well into his sixties, he met a bunch of punks in London who took him to see Penetration… and he never looked back. He used to turn up at gigs all over the country with a car full of hitch-hikers and a picnic in his boot for everyone! Blyth Power did an annual birthday gig for him every year until he died… probably the only benefits we ever played that ever did anyone any good."

"And we did a gig at the Brixton Ace and there was a row with a band called 1919, who thought they were something big at the time," scoffs Mark. "They insisted on going on last… there were about 1500 people at the gig and we played second from last. We finished our set and the whole place emptied, leaving 1919 to play with themselves!

Mark of The Mob, by Mick Mercer.

"Our gigs in Europe were always good, especially in Belgium. There was a large group of people who came to every gig we did there and they were all speed freaks; they never paid to get in and were genuine street kids. We loved each other and, later on, several of them came and joined up with us in London…"

"I wasn't aware of any profundity about what we did then, and am even less so now," says Joseph with disarming honesty. "There were some spectacularly badly organised events as well, benefits and the like. I remember one time we went all the way to Rochdale, and all seven of the support bands played too long, and we wound up doing just three songs. Stuff like that was always happening... I believe it's called 'anarchy'!

"For me the whole thing was personal. Looking back I remember people and places, but have never seen them as part of a bigger picture. I recall we were narrow-minded, arrogant, cliquey, vainglorious, and concerned with little beyond our giro cheques and what drugs we were going to spend them on. If others want to construct a memorial to the whole thing then I'd prefer to leave them to it. As for what we brought to the alternative music scene that was uniquely ours? The only answer to that is Mark... although he brought himself really. Curtis and I were just along for the ride."

"I was talking with someone last week who was on about another Zig Zag show," continues Mark. "And I said that I'd be up for doing the breaking-in and that, but I wouldn't want to play. I probably can't play now, anyway... I wasn't much good then, and I used to practise every day! But I like to think that we brought some colour and a sense of hope to people. I sang for the lonely and tortured, and I know of several who have told me since that our music helped them.

"Whether The Mob shaped me or not, I'm not sure, but I do believe strongly in the power of people to change things and that anything is possible. I'm not easily put off and I still believe more fervently than ever in the politics of my youth. It sickens me to see the 'bling' and money culture of today's kids. I believe we were very lucky to have shared the comradeship and family of our movement in its infancy, and, to some extent, up to the present day."

Joseph: "That pretty much sums it up for me as well. I loved that comradeship at the time, and I love the memory of it still... but it happened over twenty years ago, and is no part of my life now. People think I'm pretty cynical about it, but I look back and I see [fellow Black Sheep Co-opers] Tony, Mark, Mick 'Lugworm', Nicky and Val, and the rest of the tribe. I don't see black flags and slogans. It's all intensely personal, and the idea of nailing it all down into a book just doesn't work for me. At the end of the day we weren't revolutionaries; we were just a bunch of confused children huddling together to keep warm."

SELECT DISCOGRAPHY

7"s:
'Crying Again' (All The Madmen, 1979)
'Witch Hunt' (All The Madmen, 1980)
'No Doves Fly Here' (Crass, 1982)
'The Mirror Breaks' (All The Madmen, 1983)

12"s:
'Crying Again' (All The Madmen, 1986)

LPs:
'Let The Tribe Increase' (All The Madmen, 1983)

At A Glance:
Rugger Bugger's excellent CD version of 'Let The Tribe Increase' was far and away the definitive retrospective Mob release, featuring all the band's singles as bonus tracks, in an attractive digipak, complete with comprehensive 24-page booklet. Essential, in every sense of the word, it's thankfully still available through US label, Broken Rekids.

Named after a lyric in the song 'Motorcade' by Howard Devoto's Magazine, Yeovil's **NULL AND VOID** may never have reached the dizzy heights of popularity enjoyed by their mentors, The Mob, but they penned many a great tune, released a fine slice of vinyl in the shape of the 'Still' single, and even recorded with the late Joe Strummer… not bad for a bunch of (self-confessed) 'angry hippies'!

"The hippies were influenced by LSD and hash, and were all laid back and 'far out'," ponders vocalist/guitarist, Andrew Barker, "Whilst the punks were influenced by speed and were usually hyper. There were quite a few hippy types and leftovers from that scene hanging around in the West Country at that time, and they mixed with the punks, with inevitable consequences, not adversarial. We were in between the two camps, sort of mutant hippy punks. The Mob, who were a few years above us at school [Stanchester comprehensive in Stoke-sub-Hamdon, Somerset], had toured with the hippy band Here And Now, so I guess this must have been an influence too. This was before I had left school, so being young, and them all being older and doing music, meant they were kind of role models…"

Andrew began his musical career as 'Andy Stratton', basically a one-off one-man-band, where he sang, and played both guitar and bass, and was assisted on the drums by Graham Fallows, the original Mob drummer. In 1980, whilst still at school, he released the 'I Don't Know' single on The Mob's label, All The Madmen (which was later re-released in 1999 by US label, Hyped-To-Death, as part of their series of CDRs of long-lost English DIY records).

"The Mob had just released 'Witch Hunt'," explains Andrew. "I wasn't sure what I was doing when it came to releasing a record, so I sort of followed their lead. My single never had the street cred of 'Witch Hunt' though, because I wasn't doing any gigs and therefore had no following. However, listening back to the record now, I think it sounds all right actually. I recorded at Spaceward studios in Cambridge, as did The Mob, cut it at Porky Prime Cuts, and pressed it somewhere in High Wycombe. That's really how Graham got involved: he was playing in The Mob, and I was hanging around them a lot and asked him to help out. I felt that he was a very good drummer and versatile enough to play several different styles.

Null And Void (left to right: Mark Hedge, Adie Tompkins, and Andrew Barker).

"All The Madmen was just a banner under which you could release records then; it wasn't a record company as such, it had no money or management. It was just a bunch of punks in Geoff's bedroom at his mum and dad's house in Yeovil, with records all over the floor, out of their sleeves, smoking cigarettes and going to the pub, or hanging out at the Yeovil precinct. To get a record out, you just had to beg, steal or borrow enough money and

*Andrew Barker
of Null And Void.*

then go for it. I begged the money for my record from my wonderful aunty! And the undoubted highlight of Andy Stratton was John Peel playing the record on his show."

With bassist Mark Hedge, a friend from school, and drummer Adie Tompkins, a punk they met whilst hanging around Yeovil bus station (who himself also did a stint playing for The Mob), Andrew then started up Null And Void in 1980, a proper band, able to tour. Who all promptly moved to Seend, Wiltshire, into a communal house with The Mob ("A bunch of punks living communally in a country house with hardly any neighbours? It just seemed to fit with the philosophy…"). It wasn't long before the two bands converted an old coach into a tour bus, and embarked upon a series of dates around the country, finishing up in London with a gig at the Grimaldi Church Hall in Pentonville Road. Said bus, however, as detailed previously, broke down that night in Brougham Road, Hackney, where the bands were partying after the gig, and there it stayed… and so did the bands.

"Brougham Road was really far-out," recalls Andrew, "hippy meets punk meets artist meets anarchist… a world unto itself, and a unique moment in history; there were lots of different people with different ideas to meet and talk to. And Hackney was like a forgotten part of London, the area around Broadway Market and London Fields appearing unchanged since the days of the Blitz. There were many broken- and run-down houses, and so many squats… lots of far-out people.

"I particularly remember the winter being really cold that year; the snow was coming in the back door, and my bedroom had a hole in the floor, so the cold was coming straight up through. The electricity wasn't connected at the time either, and, to be honest, it wasn't much better than sleeping in a doorway outside somewhere."

But it was amidst these salubrious surroundings that Andrew and Mark met Joseph Porter, then drummer with Zounds (who agreed to take up the sticks for Null And Void when Adie went home to Wiltshire, he ended up drumming for The Mob, of course, before forming Blyth Power in the mid-Eighties). A self-titled cassette album was recorded live in their rehearsal room (in No. 62, Brougham Road) and sold at gigs in and around the capital.

"It was an upstairs room padded out floor-to-ceiling with old mattresses found in skips. We just put a cassette recorder in the room and played live. There you go, that's how you do it!

Unfortunately, I don't even have a copy myself, and can't remember what the songs were… but I'm sure there were some greats on it. Oh well!"

As the band became more established around London, they managed to raise sufficient funds for a more substantial recording, and on February 11th and 12th, 1982, they entered the cellar of the Poison Girls' house in Leytonstone, where Pete 'Dan' Fender had set up his own eight-track studio, to record the cassette album, 'Four Minute Warning'. The resultant nine tracks definitely tipped their hat to The Mob, but were jaunty enough to stand on their own two feet, Joseph's strident rhythms tastefully overwritten with some imaginative interplay between guitar and bass.

"I think we recorded all the songs one day, and then went back the next to mix them. We were used to gigging a lot, so we just got in there and recorded the bass and drums together, then the guitar and vocals together. It was pretty much live, mistakes and all, but that was just the way we preferred to present our art. Polishing and overdubbing everything didn't seem authentic; we wanted it raw, naked… warts and all. This approach was reflected in our stage performances as well – we didn't run around the stage, jumping off the PA system; we just gave all our energy whilst standing in one spot, crying into the mike. It wasn't about 'showmanship' to me; it was about messages, and the delivery of artistic ideas. These were the self-imposed parameters within which you could do what you like…"

Gigging took the band further and further afield, first around the North of England, and then on short skirmishes to the continent, most memorably an eventful show in Paris.

"What a day that was!" laughs Andrew. "We stayed in this squat, in some part of Paris; I don't even know where. You needed a key to get out as well as in. It was a four- or five-storey house, in what seemed to be a run-down area. As the evening approached, we went to the venue, which was a big factory and not really like a venue at all. There were many bands playing, and, by the time we went on stage, the place was heaving, with easily more than a thousand people packed in there. During our performance there was the occasional bottle or can being thrown at the stage; one of them hit Adie, the drummer [who was standing in for Joseph, who was unable to do the tour], on the head, so he was none too chuffed. I think if he could have worked out who'd thrown it, he would have started a fight with them.

"Anyway, we battled on. The crowd were so volatile, nothing like the UK at all; I don't think they liked us much… they wanted real thrashy punk music, which we weren't at all. They probably thought we were too soft, and we were quite relieved to finish and get offstage. Afterwards, we did an interview on a French pirate station, Radio Libertaire, upstairs in the venue in this little control room, full of all these crazy French Punks. We were paid with two crates of beer and a bag of French francs. "When we went back to our digs, we drank the beers and I dozed off. However, later that night, or so I was told, some crazy French punk turned up with a gun, looking to kill someone who had upset him at the gig. Some dope let him in and he fired the gun in the house… I must have been quite drunk, because I didn't wake up! Within a short period of time, armed police turned up and were outside the house, pointing their guns at the squat and asking, through a megaphone, for this guy to come out. Somehow he'd got away though, and after a little while the police left too. My goodness!

"Next morning, this French woman woke me up, and told me she needed to get across the border out of France; apparently it was really important, and she wanted to hide under the seat of our van as we drove through customs. I thought she was a nutter, but she wouldn't take no for an answer, so when we left, we didn't tell her we were going and went without her. On the way out of France, we stopped in a motorway service station and spent what little French money we had left on junk food…"

It was on a short tour of Belgium that Brussels-based label, Not So Brave, approached Null And Void about releasing a single, and upon their return to London, they once more visited Pete Fender's basement studio and recorded the mournfully melodic 'Still' 7" (b/w 'Crap'), another fine exercise in Mob worship, but with a distinctive flavour all its own.

By early 1983, the band had parted ways with Joseph, and found a new drummer in the shape of Ralph Parker, with whom they recorded a two-track ('Slow Down'/'Harder To Remember') cassette single in Walthamstow, that was ably produced by Andy 'Nana' Palmer of Crass.

A copy of the 'cassingle' found its way into the hands of The Clash's Joe Strummer, who offered to co-produce their next studio effort, in early '84.

"Working with Joe Strummer was just great," enthuses Andrew. "He was the most down-to-earth, genuine person you could hope to meet. We recorded four tracks in his Lucky 8 studio in Camden Lock during the course of one long day. He had an office above the studio where he did his paper work, and he would come down and help out with the production from time to time. He didn't sit in on the whole session, but when we finished recording, we all went to the pub over the road; I think it was called 'The Railway', but I can't be sure. He got the landlord to put the tape on, so we could listen to it while we were having a pint. I remember him saying that putting the tape on in the pub would be a good way to see if anyone subconsciously liked the music, because they would be tapping their feet without thinking. I remember we looked around and saw a few feet on the go, which was nice! Also, I remember he thought we should change the name of the band, because he felt it was too negative; he said that he liked names such as The Men They Couldn't Hang, because they conjured up images in your mind... and he thought we should choose a name like that."

Such considerations unfortunately turned out to be academic though, as in 1985, Ralph died of a heroin overdose, and Null And Void folded in the wake of the tragedy.

"The band was actually on the way out before then, in fact; life was changing, it was becoming harder and harder to keep things going. We were earning no money, literally existing on a shoe-string, and were getting sick of being so poor all the time. It became more and more difficult to get anything together, so I started working at a furniture shop, to bring a bit of money in. We were all starting to do other things, because if you're not making money, it's difficult to maintain your interests. When Ralph died though, it came as quite a shock, because he had by then settled down with someone and had two kids, was quite a family man. I remember him saying what an impact it had had on him, when his children were born. It was very sad that he died; it really hammered home how fine the line is between life and death when you take heroin. And after he died, we never did any more music as Null And Void."

However, Andrew Barker continues to sporadically make music to this day, and although it's a radical departure from his time fronting Null And Void, it's undertaken in much the same spirit... and, at the end of the day, it's the spirit that counts, right?

"My last major effort was in 1996, when I wrote some songs for an album called 'Why Me?' by themush.com. Themush.com was all about writing for my own benefit without the slightest regard for the listener; it wasn't a band, it was just a creative outlet. In 2000, I recorded it all properly in a 24-track studio, then copied it onto recordable CDs and sold them to anyone I met using my questionable sales technique... 'Complete satisfaction or your money back!' I would then make myself scarce fairly rapidly, ha ha! I am intending to record another album one day, but as you get older, it becomes more and more difficult to find the time. For now, I'm just happy that Null And Void be remembered in the pages of this book."

SELECT DISCOGRAPHY

7"s:
'Still' (Not So Brave, 1982)

At A Glance:
Andrew Barker now has a website where re-releases of the original Null And Void recordings can be obtained: www.null-and-void.com

Ben Corrigan of Thatcher On Acid, picture by Jaz Wiseman.

Another band influenced immensely by the quietly seminal Mob were **THATCHER ON ACID**, who formed in Somerset during 1983 and released many enjoyably cerebral records during the Eighties, before several of them teamed up with ex-Crass vocalist Steve Ignorant for the rather excellent Schwartzeneggar.

"We formed chiefly as a name really," laughs vocalist/guitarist Ben Corrigan, of Thatcher's humble beginnings. "It was just me and Martin [Hosken – drums], and we had this idea of gate-crashing gigs and playing for as long as possible before being kicked off stage. This only ever really happened once though, as I'm sure that you can imagine, in practice, it was way too much like hard work. That one time was at Wincanton racecourse, where we played one 'song' and were joined on bass by Spike [real name Simon Hughes], a guy I had previously been in a band with [Accumulative Poison] at school.

"Initially, I guess, we were influenced by a sort of 'sixth form' idea of utopia, freedom and co-operation. This was when the threat of nuclear war was entirely feasible and even seemed quite likely, what with Britain having just been at war in the Falklands; we definitely felt frightened of the world 'out there' and 'them' anyway. Much of the early Thatch lyrics I wrote at that time were literally under the influence of LSD. I took a lot, and listened to plenty of Jimi Hendrix, Pink Floyd and Gong, as well as Crass and the usual staple diet of '76 – '79 punk rock. The only local bands of any real influence on us were without doubt The Mob and Zounds… I say 'Zounds' because Gary Hatcher (AKA Josef Porta) was their drummer, and he went to our school! We were terrifically impressed when they started releasing records…"

During September 1983, Thatcher On Acid played at The Centre, Shepton Mallet, with the Blind Dogs, after which Spike left, to read English at Reading University, and was replaced by Matt Cornish, resulting in the band's first 'proper' line-up.

After much gigging around the West Country and the recording of a basic demo onto four-track at Matt's parent's house during April 1984 (one song of which, 'And I Thought You Said', owes a huge sonic debt to The Mob masterpiece, 'No Doves Fly Here'), Thatcher On Acid entered Brixton's Cold Storage studio for two days to record 'The Moondance' 12" for All The Madmen Records.

"Actually, we already had the record recorded, and were looking for distribution through Rough Trade and the Cartel," corrects Ben, "But we bumped into Rob Challice [who had by then taken over the reins of All The Madmen from The Mob] at Rough Trade in Kings Cross, and he offered to release it, and that was that. No contract or anything… the first time we saw any money that we could actually spend was when we played at a gig in Wood Green with Stump; we got £40… and bought some beer and cigarettes, probably. This was a year later. Rob did sort us out with a lot of gigs, most with Blyth Power, who were also on ATM, but we never made a bean.

"Anyway, it's got a good cover, but it's a crap record! I don't like it much at all; it sounds as flat as a pancake. And, to this day, I'm not sure if Matt ever got his money back for the recording…"

1987 saw the band back in Cold Storage, which by then had been upgraded to a 24-track facility, recording their debut album, 'Curdled', again for All The Madmen. Boasting a much more impressive production than the 12", it rocked considerably harder as a result, although it wasn't without its fair share of throwaway filler material either. It also marked the departure of Martin, who was replaced behind the kit by Andi Tuck.

Just prior to its release, Thatcher On Acid secured their place in the anarcho-punk history books by opening up Conflict's notorious 'Gathering Of The 5000' show at the Brixton Academy on Saturday April 18th, 1987.

"Again, Rob Challice had some connection with Colin Jerwood; in fact, it seemed more like Colin owing Rob a favour than anything else, although I think he liked the test pressing of our first album or something. And so we played first, along with Benjamin Zephaniah; he was fucking great, and really riled the audience massively... the tension in the place just before Conflict actually came on was so strong, it was almost physical.

Thatcher On Acid's Matt Cornish, picture by Jaz Wiseman.

"We had the thankless task during our set of asking the audience to stop dancing onstage, after the stage manager guy said he was going to pull the plug if they didn't. That went down a storm, as you can imagine; we were greeted with lobbed glasses and chants of 'Fucking popstars!' from the front few rows.

"Then, as time dragged on, we were later refused backstage, despite our 'AAA' [Access All Areas] passes; the bouncers had Rottweilers at the side of the stage, and there were fights breaking out left, right and centre. I picked up my guitar, went out the back doors and walked home. I could hear yelling and smashing glass at the end of Stockwell Road, behind me; not wanting to turn into a pillar of salt, I kept walking! Couldn't bear to watch Barnardo's getting trashed...

"As for that whole anarcho-punk scene? I was only fourteen when Crass started releasing records around 1979, but we quickly got into the idea of mucking in and trying to behave responsibly. We were always blathering on about trying to decipher Crass and their ilk, without ever really feeling as if we were a part of the same thing as them. The 'anarcho' tag just came with the territory of being anti-war, anti-racism, anti-sexism, anti-whateveryoufuckinggot... and also the record label we happened to have a deal with. We never really had a problem with that until much later on, when I for one became very disillusioned, but hey! That always happens..."

Promoting 1988's 'Garlic' live album for the newly-formed Rugger Bugger Discs saw Thatcher On Acid undertake the first of many European tours, which of course was a total 'eye-opener' for the band.

"We missed the Harwich to Hoek ferry for starters," groans Ben, "Which meant we had ten hours to kill in fucking Harwich; that got us off on the wrong foot 'cos we drank too much and were knackered for the first gig. Andi was terribly homesick the following night too, and that set the precedent for the tour really. I loved Holland though, and was inspired by the squatting scene there; they seemed to have it so totally together... I initially felt very backward in the presence of these really organised people!

"Germany was terrible; we played (or rather nearly did) in this peculiar little hut by a railway line near the town of Peine. The place was packed, but the power was fed from outside by a tiny generator that kept conking out. The promoter had a hardcore band that were playing before us, but their bass player was so pissed off with waiting around to play, that he went home! But when the power eventually came on, the promoter guy still insisted on playing, even without the bassist. They were really, really terrible, and they played for what seemed like hours. Seconds after they finished, the generator went again. We waited and waited, and even had our instruments on ready to play, and fffzzzzzzzzzzz – the power went yet again.

"The outside toilet had the generator in it; we went out to investigate the problem only to see a drunk punk guy with a mohican hitting the generator with a piece of wood, over and over, yelling 'Scheisse! Scheisse!' at the top of his voice. We packed up and left."

The next album, this time for (Dan and Sofahead bassist) Ian Armstrong's Meantime Records, 'The Illusion Of Being Together', not only saw the band briefly replacing bassist Matt with (old drummer) Martin Hosken, but also saw them exorcising some of their aforementioned frustration at the often stifling and hypocritical nature of the underground punk scene, much of it inspired by the thought processes of guest vocalist, Dave Kirkby of Slave Dance. Recorded over three intense days at the Yeovil Icehouse, with producer 'Head' (who would later enjoy much success producing PJ Harvey), the album remains the band's most energetic and challenging work.

"Dave was a frighteningly sharp and intelligent guy, that me and Andi spent a lot of time with during the late Eighties," explains Ben. "And the subject matter was mostly his idea; we'd had many discussions about just what the hell was going on in music around us… it was pretty much a critique of the way we saw the scene.

"Admittedly, a lot of the lyrics were lifted from J. Krishnamurti and Vaneigem, but so what? We felt that, even though there were an awful lot of bands and people involved within it, the scene itself was fragmented, permeated with a kind of inverted snobbery and was actually largely fake. And so we didn't really feel a part of it and wanted to comment as such… talk about 'us' rather than 'them' for a change. And draw a few parallels, think about daily life and the things that immediately affect us rather than bemoaning far-reaching targets that, to be honest, we really had no chance of properly addressing. The whole idea that we are guilty ourselves of preventing our own dreams coming true through fear, constantly being distracted from doing anything worthwhile by consumables… stuff like that. Sounds really boring now, I know, but that's the gist of it, and at the time it was quite relevant.

"The music itself was one long song in three parts, and pretty much improvised; although we did have three basic riffs to follow, we had no real idea how it was going to turn out. I liked the results though, despite its lack of humour, which was funny in itself really, because we were always going on about the lack of humour in music at that time! A lot of people didn't like Dave's voice on it either, but I like the real warts 'n' all feel it has… there are some heinous sounding keyboards on there, mind you!"

Matt rejoined in time for 1991's 'Frank' album on Chumbawamba's Agit Prop label, a record that sported guest appearances from both Boff and Mave of the Chumbas ("Another patchy effort," admits Ben, "Nowhere near enough time spent on it…"), and more international touring, including a stint across the USA.

"For many reasons, my favourite Thatch gig was in Santa Barbara in 1991. There was some straightedge kid [actually Kent McLard of Ebullition Records] who had put on the original gig, but then pulled out of promoting it, on account of us having the word 'acid' in our name. We ended up playing in someone's backyard in broad daylight to about fifty people… but it had everything: sun, warmth, absurdity, laughs, and spontaneity. Can't really ask for much more than that from a gig, can you?

"As for gigs I'd prefer to forget? I don't actually know if I regard any gigs as ones I would want to forget completely… it's just that some were more enjoyable than others. We had more 'stinkers' than 'winners', but I think that suited us as we tended to be a bit lukewarm live… and on record! We had flashes of good stuff, but not often enough…

"We rarely stuck to a formula and took a lot of musical risks, most of which didn't work at all, but what the hell? That's why we didn't sell any records. Lyrically we were saying much the same thing as everyone else – anti-this, -that and -the other – but not seemingly for anything. When we realised this, we became better musically, certainly… still not sure about the lyrics though! But at least we were heading in the right direction, or trying to."

'Squib', a split album with the hilarious Wat Tyler, came out in 1992, through John Yates's Allied Recordings, but turned out to be the final TOA recording, because Matt decided to leave to become a full-time doctor. The band's final tour was across Scandinavia and Germany in September 1992 with Alice Donut; an old friend from Yeovil, Bob Butler, stood in on bass.

As mentioned earlier, Ben, Bob and Andi then became three-fifths of Schwartzeneggar, the band fronted by Steve Ignorant of Crass, whom they had met the previous year when he travelled to Yeovil to sing on the superb 'Our Gods Are Falling Down' track for the 'Squib' record. Meanwhile, a posthumous TOA single, 'Yo-Yo Man', was released by K-Records in 1993, and 1998 actually saw them briefly reform for two benefit shows, raising money for the McLibel campaign, at Chat's Palace in Hackney and the University Of London.

Nowadays, Ben works as a tour manager for bands such as The Kills, the Black Keys and the 5678s; Matt still doctors in Somerset, Andi installs electrical systems, whilst Martin teaches ceramics at Brixton College. Spike is somewhere in Spain.

"Schwartzeneggar had a much more aggressive approach than Thatch, who were definitely more about pop sensibilities," concludes Ben. "We were great live – after a while, at least – but generally pretty bad in the studio. As for Thatcher On Acid? People can remember us any way they like, really; I couldn't care less either way."

SELECT DISCOGRAPHY

7"s:
'Flannel 905' (Rugger Bugger, 1990)
'No Fuckin' War' (Clawfist, 1992) – split with 7 Year Bitch
'Frank Jnr.' (Subcorridor, 1992)
'Yo-Yo Man' (K, 1993)

12"s:
'The Moondance' (All The Madmen, 1986)

LPs:
'Curdled' (All The Madmen, 1986)
'Garlic' (Rugger Bugger, 1988)
'The Illusion Of Being Together' (Meantime, 1990)
'Frank' (Agit-Prop, 1991)
'Squib' (Allied, 1992) – split with Wat Tyler

At A Glance:
In 1997, US label Broken Rekids released 'The Moondance' and 'Curdled' together on one CD, a neat snapshot of the band's early period, whilst 'Pressing: 84-92', the 1995 retrospective on Desperate Attempt takes in some more obscure demo and live recordings, providing a fascinating overview of this intelligent, eclectic outfit.

Dorset's **VIRUS** are a fairly typical example of so many anarcho-punk bands of the early Eighties, in that they formed with the best of intentions but disbanded out of frustration to achieve them, played many enjoyable gigs but never really broke out of their local scene, recorded several demos but never managed to capture their live sound on tape, and eventually found their way onto one of the many compilation albums released at the time but narrowly missed out on an exclusive release in their own right. A classic case then of 'So near, yet so far', but talking to the band it quickly becomes apparent that they still cherish their

Virus bassist/vocalist Jaz Wiseman (Dave Oliver in background), live Warminster 1985, picture by Patricia Crew.

memories of that time and are just grateful that they were able to play some small part in it all.

Formed in Gillingham during 1983, when all the band were still in their mid-to-late teens, the first line-up consisted of Des Hoskins – vocals, Jaz Wiseman – bass and vocals, Marcus 'Bowzer' Bowering – guitar, and Rich Brocklehurst – drums, and made its inauspicious public debut at Sherborne's Digby Hall.

"That was in January 1984, supporting Nymphomania, and was a pretty scary event," recalls Jaz. "Both bands were bottled by an audience that consisted of skinheads, soul-boys, trendies, and very few punks; we ended up having to leave the building in fear of being beaten up. Digby Hall is quite large and Sherborne is a very conservative town, with public schools and a real 'He's not a local' mentality, but I don't think it helped that both bands were playing support to the local Saturday night DJ, who was very against the idea of having punk bands play at his disco.

"To top it all off, Des couldn't make the gig due to ill health, so I had to sing as well as play bass… a pretty disastrous start to say the least! I do recall thinking we needed to try and make contact with 'our kind' of bands, so we could at least play to a more sympathetic audience. We did have the last laugh in the end though… it was our performance at the Pulsebeat Club in Sherborne, a venue for horrible trendy Indie bands, that got such a high number of complaints, the club was forced to close. I don't think bands like The Chesterfields [who ran the club] ever forgave us for that…"

Des left in March '84, following a disappointing first foray into Milborne Port's Monitor Studios; he was quickly replaced by seventeen-year-old Dave Oliver, who played his first show with the band that August in a Bournemouth squat, supporting Dirt, Polemic and Eat Shit. A second demo was recorded at Monitor during late '84, 'You Can't Ignore It Forever', which captured the band's measured discordant mix of early Amebix and Subhumans more than amply; adorned with their striking logo (that left no doubt as to the fact the band considered themselves anarchists), it sold well at gigs around the Southwest with the likes of Disorder, Blyth Power and Subhumans, but Jaz remains unconvinced of its musical potency.

"Both the demos sound very rushed, and we really didn't know how to capture our live sound, which was much harder. I think this was basically down to us having never been in a studio before and not using our own equipment.

"As for the logo, I designed it in the summer of 1984, and it became a visually important part of the band, appearing not just as cover art on the second demo, but on backdrops when we played live, on leaflets, etc. etc. I was pissed off to see that, over ten years later, a group called Afro Celt Sound System had copied it exactly and were using it on the cover of their albums.

"Virus were definitely anarchists, and as time progressed we got heavily into green issues. We were a band of committed vegetarians (23 years later and all five original members are still veggies), hunt sabs, and environmentally conscious people… I think this was because we were from the wilds of Dorset and not the inner city. Of course, we had anti-war, Thatcher/Reagan, animal rights songs too, but our surroundings certainly had an impact on the band, and made us more aware of green issues."

Des rejoined as a second vocalist during the summer of 1985, having seen a drastic improvement in the band's song-writing at several of their gigs he'd attended, and played his first show back with them in Swansea supporting Shrapnel. Further gigs were undertaken, including an all-day anti-apartheid benefit in Portsmouth with The Varukers, and dates in Salisbury and London with Conflict, the London show being a Mortarhate night at the Deptford Crypt with Liberty and Hex, to coincide with the release of the 'We Won't Be Your Fucking Poor' compilation, an album that included a Virus track (the rather throwaway 'Turkey Song', complete with a 'chorus' refrain of 'It's about fucking time that a turkey had its say!') lifted from the second demo.

"We sent Mortarhate a copy of that demo in the summer of '85, and, within a few days, Colin [Jerwood] had written back to me, inviting us to submit a song, lyrics and artwork for the '… Fucking Poor' LP. It stated that we had to get the song to them as soon as possible, so we got the eight-track master tape from the studio and sent them that. I asked them to simply reproduce the logo from the front of the cassette, and to use either '3rd World Wonders' [the band's strongest, most atmospheric track, opening with the sibilant intonation, 'Eat the flesh of starving people, eat the flesh, eat the flesssh…'] or 'No Bloody Use', but I sent the lyrics to all of our songs. We then played with Conflict in Salisbury towards the end of the year, before the LP was released, and they were decent blokes… they even ended up stopping a gang of skinheads beating up all the punks while we were playing!

"So, we were somewhat surprised and disappointed when the album was released that they had decided to include 'The Turkey Song' (which was actually entitled 'Oven Overture') as it was something of a 'Merry Crassmas'-style song, and not really reflective of our overall sound. In hindsight, we had plenty of time to record a brand new song, but we were under the impression that the record release was imminent, so it ended up that we didn't really feel it was us on the album. It was a shame, but all just a case of crossed wires between us and Colin."

Disillusioned with their showing on the album, and arguing internally over both musical direction and how they could raise funds to record an EP of their own, Virus split rather acrimoniously in late May 1986, playing their last two shows with Culture Shock and the Hippy Slags at the Crown in Trowbridge and the Cornwall Hotel, Dorchester.

A one-off reunion gig in 1996, that saw Jaz, Bowzer and Dave recruiting drummer Charlie Barber from local thrash act Spudgun, unfortunately failed to reignite interest in the band, and, for better or worse, that was the end of Virus, although Jaz intimates that he still has plans to one day finally record all the old songs that were never taken inside a proper studio.

"An old friend called Jon Jon, who used to follow Virus around and by then had his own punk band [Fat, Drunk And Stupid] asked if we'd do a gig with them, as it was ten years since we'd split," explains Jaz of the ill-fated '96 reformation. "He'd even spoken to Dave who was keen to bury the hatchet with me, so I agreed. But the gig was awful! Even though we'd rehearsed quite a bit, Charlie forgot all the songs on the night (he was on a mix of cider, speed and joints!), and the audience had certainly changed. They didn't want to hear our political noises; they just wanted to have a good time. This took us by surprise really, so we decided not to continue. However, we have done various sticker and graffiti campaigns since, so, as I've said before, true to our name, we're more mutated and dormant than outright deceased!"

At A Glance:
There is a My Space website for Virus, where Jaz can be contacted and possibly persuaded to copy you highlights from the Virus demos and various live recordings still in his possession:
http://www.myspace.com/virus8386

Metro Youth outside their rehearsal room, 1981 (clockwise from top left: Nigel, Rich, Andy, Heff and Tim).

METRO YOUTH also never really secured the same profile as many other bands within anarcho punk, but this sometimes overlooked Exeter six-piece did make a memorable appearance on 'Bullshit Detector 2' before morphing into the even less well-known, but often rather good, **SANCTION**. But more importantly they had a wonderfully unconventional style, sounding not dissimilar to a manic cross between The Ruts and Poison Girls, with a hint of X-Ray Spex for good measure... and who in their right mind would argue with such a hybrid?

Formed during the spring of 1979, when all the members were still at Exeter's Hele's School together, albeit in their last year, Metro Youth (named when they were dabbling with the idea of having a band logo based on the symbols of the London Underground train network) were Andy Southard – drums, Tim Lyddon – guitar, Nigel Stopard – vocals, and Rich Cross – bass, Nigel and Rich having previously been in the "no-hope garage band", XLR8.

"And Metro Youth started out life as a genuine 'garage band' too," adds Rich. "But bitter complaints from the neighbours drove us into a makeshift soundproofed front room. My parents were both Quakers, and we got permission to rehearse downstairs at the Exeter Friends' Meeting House on Friday nights, when the place was empty. From the very beginning, we took the DIY ethic very seriously; we believed in the idea, but in any case, from a practical point of view, there really wasn't an alternative – most times if we didn't organise it ourselves, it just wasn't going to happen."

For all four founder members, Rich is clear that, "The political and social elements of what we were about were present from the very beginning – some of the earliest songs were concerned with anti-nuclear and anti-militarist issues, racism, the power of the media..." For Tim, these themes were, "Very important – it was who we were." Not all of Metro Youth's first songs were overtly 'political' though, but, as Nigel suggests, as the band evolved, "This became an integral part of what we were doing."

The band's memorable first gig was, Rich remembers, "At The Methodist Church Hall in St Thomas, Exeter [August, 1979], in front of a crowd of our mates and some bemused members of the youth club. The main set was pretty chaotic, but in the encore we pulled it together and things started to click. The most striking thing was the chance to play songs that we'd written and arranged ourselves in front of other people for the first time."

But not all self-booked gigs left such a sweet aftertaste, with one at the village hall in nearby Whitstone an especially low-point for Rich.

"We arranged everything," he sighs, "including transport from the city centre for next-to-no money – 20p 'all in' or something like that – and a section of the audience who came trashed the hall, smashed up the toilets and then attacked one of us! That really marked the end of our naïve belief that 'all the punks' might actually be in it together and interested in the same things."

The very talented Heather 'Heff' Dean joined Metro Youth as saxophonist and additional vocalist, after seeing them support The Bodysnatchers at Exeter's St. George's Hall in October 1980 [the same venue where Rich later booked Crass to play, once in 1982 and again in 1984], bringing an exciting eclectic edge, not to mention a fiery female voice, to the band's previously more traditional punk sound.

"She opened our eyes a little further to feminist issues and was able to broaden our song-writing to include a woman's perspective on life," reckons Andy. "She was also a very good musician and I think the rest of us felt that we should 'raise our game' and push for more complex musical arrangements. It must have been difficult for Heff, joining an all-male band, especially three lads who had been friends for years, but she was soon an integral part of it all."

In early 1981, Metro Youth demoed several songs, recording them onto a basic four-track reel-to-reel recorder in their rehearsal space at Catharsis Studios ("We had an excellent relationship with Len Gammon, who ran the place and was closely involved in all aspects of the local music scene," says Rich), one of which – 'Brutalised' – was included on the Crass compilation, taking the band's profile up several rungs… on a national scale, if not locally. According to Tim, "It would have been good to secure an independent single release as well, but hey, I'm not complaining."

"Exeter was not even close to the middle of nowhere," scoffs Rich. "In fact, you couldn't even see the middle of nowhere from there. Culturally, socially and politically, things were spare and conservative…"

"I always thought that the local 'scene', if there was one, was a bit exclusive and not really into what we were about," agrees Nigel. "We did have some small following, but much more support from elsewhere really. The feel of Exeter was very parochial; there were a few punk bands locally, but none as explicitly political as us. We felt more a part of the national punk movement as a whole, I think."

Soon after the recording, the band recruited a second guitarist, Brian Abbott from Airport Delay, giving them even more scope for musical experimentation, but sadly Metro Youth split late in 1981, after two memorable gigs supporting Tenpole Tudor, one in Portsmouth, the other at St. George's Hall, long before they could ever realise their true potential.

"It had a real community feel to it, and a great ideology, and I loved the mix of instrumentation," explains Brian of the chemistry and atmosphere of the band he joined so late in their short existence. "I adored the sax and she was such a good player. Yeah, it was anarcho-punk, but it had a real creative energy about it. We did thrash, but also had some awesome moments where the music took on a life of its own. I think it entered areas that were not strictly 'punk' at all; I think we definitely were creating our own sound."

Change was forced on the band when Tim decided to leave Exeter to attend art college. It was a decision that left him, "Gutted really. I obviously would have liked to have stayed and focused more on improving my contribution to the band both technically and creatively."

Soon after, Brian decided that the time was right for him to quit as well, and the head of creative steam that Metro Youth were accumulating dissipated almost as quickly as it had built, leaving behind just curiosity at what might have been. The band tried to continue with Nigel moving to guitar, but it became apparent that it was time to move on to something new.

The four remaining members became Sanction during the winter of 1982, and were soon ensconced in Queen Street rehearsal studios, penning a new set of musically challenging, and explicitly political, material.

"Definitely!" agrees Rich. "We could still 'thrash it up' with the best of 'em, but we were also interested in trying out different musical and writing styles alongside that, mixing up how we used vocals, experimenting with different song structures, and rethinking how we could use tempo and volume. Metro Youth had been both a fun and a political project, but right from the very beginning, Sanction was entirely concerned with expression and communication; we were keen not to be restricted by ideas of what was acceptable and orthodox, and we wanted to find a sound and a style that was genuinely our own."

Sanction's Heff appearing at Glastonbury 1985 whilst in Toxic Shock, picture by Marc Freeman.

"We had always been open to varying influences," adds Andy, "And we always encouraged each other to contribute to song-writing. We had also progressed with our individual playing by this time, so we tried to push ourselves to the limits of our ability. Probably our best work came from this period, when we were a four-piece with Nigel playing guitar, Heff the sax, Rich the bass, and myself the drums, with all four of us vocalising... please note, I didn't say singing!"

The summer of 1983 saw Sanction making their only official recording, the 'Eight Songs' demo, which, despite the unimaginative title, is an ambitious collection of angry progressive punk; Heff's incredibly raw vocals and quirky sax flourishes elevating songs such as 'Butchery' and 'Unknown Soldier' to such a level that it's a minor tragedy the material never enjoyed a nationwide release.

Unfortunately she left soon after the recording, before Sanction had even performed live, moving to Birmingham and forming Toxic

Shock, leaving the three remaining male members to move into a shared house, where they wrote new music and Rich produced the 'Catalyst' fanzine, performing just one gig, with Wounded Knee at Exeter's Caprice Club during May 1984, before calling it a day for good a few months later.

At that solitary gig, Andy recalls the muted reception of a "rather bemused audience" which left the band feeling as if, "They were in the wrong place at the wrong time."

Nigel agrees, "I don't think Exeter was ever ready for us, but that was their loss!"

"And the live recording that we got through the PA was so badly misbalanced," adds Rich, similarly disappointed. "The guitar was almost entirely absent, and the vocals were way too prominent. It was the right mix for the room, because the back-line was so loud and didn't need much routing through the PA, but it meant that our one and only live recording was a very poor reflection of our real sound."

"I think it was a great idea," muses Andy, on Sanction setting up house together. "It felt like a natural extension of what we were doing, emphasising how central our work with the band had become for all of us, but it didn't turn out to be everything we had hoped. I think we worked harder at keeping warm than anything else. The walls and roof were paper-thin and we literally froze when it got cold!"

After Sanction's demise, Brian went on to forge a varied solo career (his latest album, 'Tara', all about a Tibetan deity, is also a comment on the political situation there… "It won't be a big-seller in China!" he laughs), and two of the other ex-members are still actively involved in music, remembering their formative years with Metro Youth and Sanction more than fondly.

"I think our ideas were of the time," admits Andy, who now plays bass for The Fab Beatles tribute band. "Of course, we honestly believed that there were wrongs that needed righting and we wanted our voices to be heard, to make a difference. We may have been naïve to think that we actually could, but we had to have a voice and ours was conveyed through our music. The world has changed since then, but for me personally, the basic egalitarian ideal is still relevant."

Reaffirming such a view, Tim also insists that he "will always resist lies and deceit in all their forms"; Nigel retains, "A fundamental belief in social justice, seeing that very much in personal terms"; while Brian is clear that he, "Believed in, and still believes in, all the things the band stood for."

"The occasional over-earnest lyric is basically the only thing that makes me really wince looking back," adds Rich, who now plays with Nottingham punk band, Pointy Boss. "But in a sense, that simplicity, that sense of clear conviction – 'let's put an end to war, exploitation, injustice and inequality, and let's use punk rock as the tool to mobilize people to achieve it' – is part of what made the movements we were involved in so attractive.

"For all the naivety in evidence, the social and political aspirations that motivated me then are still the same ones that animate me now, although my view of what's required of a movement wanting to remake the world anew is very different…"

At A Glance:
Metro Youth's 'Brutalised' was included on Hometown Atrocities Exeter punk retrospective CD, 'Year Zero' (2000), and both Metro Youth and Sanction appeared on Overground's first anarcho-punk compilation, 2005's 'Anti-War'.

Hardly the most prolific of punk bands either, what Exeter's **THE WASTE** lacked in releases (they did just the one single for Mortarhate) they more than compensated for in steadfast devotion to the causes they expounded upon. Formed in the summer of 1983 as Toxic Waste, the original band featured Darren Brown on vocals, Rob Stevens on guitar, Sarah Chapple on bass and Andy Horseman on drums.

"We formed primarily out of sheer boredom," confesses Darren. "Three of us had just left school and, with no real prospects to look forward to, something had to be done to fill the days. As far as I can remember, none of us had been in bands before and none of us had any real technical ability. The only thing we did have going for us at the time was this overwhelming desire to play music…

"Initially, as I remember it, we got the name 'Toxic Waste' from the poster that came with the Dead Kennedys album, 'Fresh Fruit For Rotting Vegetables' – the 'dealing with toxic waste' bit on it. We were all pro-C.N.D… well, the ideals of it anyway… and anti- nuclear, so it just sounded right really."

After one local gig as Toxic Waste ("It was on a Sunday night, and it was shit… it gave us the courage to carry on, but it did make us realise that we needed a lot more practice before we could take on the world!"), the band became simply The Waste in late 1984, after they became aware of the Belfast band that had already laid claim to their original choice of moniker.

"They were just about to release their 12" with Stalag 17, and once they had a record out, we really had to change our name. It was strange though, because a couple of years later, one of their singers moved to Exeter and we were trying to get her to join the band!"

After the first gig, Andy was replaced on drums by Jim Litchfield, with Pete Moggeridge and Jez Baker taking over from Rob and Sarah not long after, this overhaul of the line-up another good reason behind the name change.

"The early days tended to consist of bragging to each other about how great we were gonna be, and how we would change the world for the better!" laughs Darren. "We didn't have anywhere regular to rehearse, and no money to hire anywhere, so at first it was in Andy's bed-sit that we tried to knock some songs together, then it was at Rob's house… then, for quite a while – until we found somewhere more permanent and out of earshot – it was in my mum's garage.

"Slowly we borrowed – and 'acquired' – enough equipment to start rehearsing regularly and properly, but at the time it seemed to take forever, with all our best laid plans constantly falling through. Eventually it all came together, but it's not easy trying to find somewhere that's soundproof, has electricity and is cheap! There was a point later on that we were rehearsing for a while in a church hall on Sundays, and that was definitely a strange one, though the congregation wisely tended to make sure that they had departed the area before we arrived!"

After taking their initial influences from the Sex Pistols and Clash, not to mention the myriad punk bands already operating in and around Exeter such as DV8, Field Of Crosses, Rat Patrol and Another Voice, The Waste became firmly entrenched in the anarcho-punk scene via their close friendship with Conflict.

"I first met up with Conflict at a gig in Plymouth in the early Eighties," Darren recalls. "I went to see them as a fan at first, but then we developed a friendship, and it all went from there. I was doing a fanzine at the time and asked if we could do an interview with them, but when they agreed, we couldn't actually think of any serious questions to ask! After that, we went to their gigs when we could and generally kept in touch. As a band we got a few gigs supporting them, and, as a friend, after The Waste finished, I went with them on most of their tours as a roadie… and we joined up on more than one occasion to put some of their lyrics into action!

"So yeah, we did regard ourselves as anarchists, and we regarded ourselves as an anarchist band. At first it was about personal politics, challenging authority – asking questions like, 'If not, why not?' – and challenging attitudes – 'Why can't I?'! Just trying to make our world a better, more humane, place to exist in, I guess.

"Then, as we grew more confident in ourselves, our targets were raised: smash the hunts, smash vivisection, smash the fur trade, smash Cruise, smash the BNP/NF scum, smash the bastards that have given us nothing to aspire to... I mean, when I was growing up, there was a very real threat of nuclear war and three million people were unemployed – did they really expect me to believe that their system was a just and right one?

"We were all active hunt saboteurs, and we did leave our mark in several other places... actions always speak louder than words! Hopefully we also inspired and encouraged other people to get involved in the various causes and struggles that were worthy at the time. There were other things close to our heart too, especially the squatting of the old DHSS [Department Of Health And Social Security] building in Exeter. In the space of six months, before the bailiffs finally got the building back, it was turned into a vegetarian/vegan café, with places for people to stay or live, and regular gigs on a Saturday night, plus a practice space for local bands. In fact, there was space to do anything that was considered constructive! 'The Pig And Bailiff' – as it was affectionately known – really pulled everyone together; it was ours, we all worked for it, and we all put the effort in to get it going, and keep it going."

The Waste, pictured live at The Printers Pie, Exeter.

Once Jim Litchfield had been replaced on drums by Paul Austin, The Waste recorded their first (six-track) demo at Monitor Studios in Sherborne, Dorset, in February 1985, and visited the same studio twice more over the course of the following year to further refine both their song-writing skills and recording technique. 'Dig Up The Duke' from the third of these sessions appeared on the Mortarhate compilation, 'We Won't Be Your Fucking Poor'.

By the time they came to record the 'Not Just Something To Be Sung' single for Mortarhate in February 1986, Spike [real name Anthony Hooper] had replaced Jez on bass and they were a tight, focused unit, with the palpable anger in songs such as the aforementioned – and re-recorded – 'Dig Up The Duke' ('Animal liberation ain't just something to be sung, the bastards that go hunting are scum that should be hung...') and 'Drunken Sailor' ('Watch out, we're rising up, we'll burn your palace down!') very apparent, despite the slightly weak production. Unfortunately though, following Darren's four month incarceration for hunt sabbing activities and direct action against a meat haulage company (a period during which Jez resumed bass duties from Spike, despite such a move being an obvious musical regression), The Waste succumbed to internal disagreements over direction almost before the single even hit the shops, and promptly split up.

"The single was recorded at Alaska Studios underneath Waterloo station in February 1986," explains Darren, before conceding, "and yes, it was a bit weak. Not so much in the content, but more in the sound. Again, it was all done in a day, the recording and the mixing, and by the end of it, we were all knackered, and realised that we should have had a break in the middle to clear our heads and ears a bit.

"Twenty years on and I'm still happy with the sleeve and the songs themselves, but I know we could have done a better job on the overall sound of it. By the time it came out, we had gone our separate ways anyway, so although we had quite a lot of other songs on tapes, none of us thought it would be right to push them.

"The split happened in September 1986; we were meant to play at the Electric Ballroom, in Camden, with Conflict, A.Y.S, Liberty and a few other bands. The rest of the band didn't turn up and that was it for me. Looking back, I think we were starting to drift apart anyway; I wanted to immerse myself in it all full-on, but the others just didn't seem as committed. I felt totally let down by them, and from that point on, there was no way back. I didn't want the band to split up, but at the time thought that we'd run our course. Hindsight is a wonderful thing, I know, but you have to do what you think is right at the time, and that was the decision I made; regardless of what I think now, that's the way it was and is."

Despite the brave words though, Darren still nurses a few regrets regarding the band's impromptu disintegration, especially as Paul Austin committed suicide during the mid-Nineties. "Personally, if the band are going to be remembered by anyone, I would like it to be for the fact that we cared and gave it a go. Simple as that really, just proving that if you want to, you can, as long as you just believe in yourself. I do regret the way that we split, that we all fell out for a while, and if I could've done more for Paul, I would have. After the split, he was in and out of rehab, and every time I saw him afterwards, he would talk about getting the band back together again, or starting something new. Looking back now, Paul lived for the band, and we all took that away from him. I saw him for the first time in a few years in 1994, and we were starting to get back to how things were between us originally, but the next thing I knew was that he had hung himself. I wish I could have done more."

And does Darren still hold true to the same ideals he did back then? "Most of them I think, yeah; I mean, you don't just stop believing in things because your band has split up, do you? I just think that I was lucky to be the right age at the right time… firstly to hear the music, and then to be a part of it. I wouldn't be the person that I am today without having been involved; I met so many good people with fantastic attitudes through being in a band that I couldn't help but be inspired and influenced by it all. Obviously, with time, some of the attitudes mellow, but some of them strengthen, and I still have the belief that we can change things, if we want to…

"As I said earlier, after The Waste split up, I went on several tours with Conflict and carried on hunt sabbing. Since then I have been involved in several major demonstrations; I was in Genoa a few years ago when Carlo Guilliani was shot dead by the police – a couple of days of absolute mayhem, but the people made their voices heard, and now it's up to all of us to make sure that the people who need to hear are forced to listen…"

SELECT DISCOGRAPHY

7"s:
'Not Just Something To Be Sung' (Mortarhate, 1986)

At A Glance:
The 'Not Just Something To Be Sung' EP appears in its entirety on the Mortarhate double-disc retrospective, 'A Compilation Of Deleted Dialogue'.

SELF ABUSE were a Bournemouth-based band that formed in January 1982. Having only done one single in their Eighties heyday, and having never actually played a major London show during their short existence, they remain to this day another of the more obscure bands from the period, which is a shame as they obviously had a lot to offer the scene. Said single has aged quite well, and is reminiscent of prime period Chron Gen with its energetic tempos and melodic overtones.

The band met and formed in a local studio, Studio 95, where several members were having music lessons. Comprising Dave Brown on guitar, Andy Nazer on bass and vocals, Roger Smale on guitar, and Steve Ridgeway on drums, they not only coalesced at Studio 95, but also bought most of their gear from there, rehearsed there, and recorded their first demo there.

"We formed the band because we had to… I think!" ponders Andy. "I can't imagine not having done it… playing punk rock just

Self Abuse live in Bournemouth, July 1984 (left to right: Dave Brown, Steve Ridgeway, Andy Nazer, and Roger Smale).

seemed so important, exciting and vital – and a great way out of the normal humdrum rigmarole routine. Not only that, but there was certainly a need to be singing about what it was like living under Thatcher's Tory regime of the time… not that we were the most politicised band of that era or anything!"

The first Self Abuse demo, 'State Of Mind', was an eight-track affair, and featured their first version of '(I Didn't Wanna Be A) Soldier', a song which would later become the title track of their 7" the following year. Although a little uncertain and rough around the edges, the demo is a surprisingly good first effort and definitely hinted at the potential inherent in the band, and, encouraged by the response they received, Self Abuse played their first show on October 14th, 1982 at the Sloop Hotel, a biker's pub in Poole.

"Steve booked it saying we were a rock band!" remembers the bassist. "But when we showed up we were shocked to find four punks had already turned up! We were well chuffed! The gig went well, even if we were somewhat ropy. Barbed Wire played as well and were really good, and a decent crowd showed up. Although we weren't booked again, there was no trouble, apart from the odd scuffle, and I think the bar takings were up! Can't remember if we got paid though; I doubt it…"

The band's second demo, 'Teenage', saw them gigging around the Southwest with the likes of Cult Maniax and the Subhumans, and got them signed to Radical Change Records, the label ran by Norwich anarchos The Disrupters, who released the '(I Didn't Wanna Be A) Soldier' single in

May 1984. Recorded the previous September at Arny's Shack in Poole, it was a cracking release, tuneful, energetic and very catchy. Backed by 'Bombscare' and the excellent, driving 'State Of Mind', it actually made No. 2 in Melody Maker's alternative chart.

As part of the drive to promote the single, Self Abuse played a well-received set at the Trowbridge Punk Festival, on July 13th, 1984, with the Subhumans, A-Heads and Organised Chaos.

Unfortunately, apart from two tracks off their third demo – 'Another Nightmare' and 'Strange Life' – being included on the 1985 Xcentric Noise compilation album, 'Party Pooping Punk Provocations', that was all they ever released officially in the Eighties.

"There wasn't a second single because Radical Change decided not to pick up our option," admits Andy. "And we weren't entirely happy with them either. Eventually after a phone call or two, we got the contracts back – in pieces! Which was good, 'cos we shouldn't have signed to them in the first place; in effect we were signed for life, both as individuals and as a band. We were even told not to sign with them by our mate Rich's dad who was a lawyer or something, but being young and daft we still did anyway! We just wanted to get a record out, and we didn't know if we'd get another chance."

Wanting to expand their horizons, they added one Andy Rogers on keyboards, a brave move for a punk band in the early Eighties, but he only lasted a few months anyway, before the band ran out of steam without ever fully realising their true worth.

"We just wanted to try something new, I think. Andy was a really nice guy… and he had a van! I think he only actually gigged with us once. I don't remember any particularly negative feedback, although Andy Anderson, our manager guy, hated it and told us we were turning into Hawkwind and smoking too much pot or something! Or maybe it was just a case of too many Andys spoiling the broth…!"

Self Abuse split in late '84, playing their last show on December 29th at the Pembroke Arms in Bournemouth.

"We split because… you know what? I'm not really sure! We just decided a few hours previous to that last gig. We were all pulling in our own directions, I guess. There were no arguments or falling-outs, though we really should have stayed together and written some more kicking punk songs – but hindsight is an exact science!"

Dave, Steve and Andy went on to form Pale Shade Of Black, a more goth-tinged affair, who became The Dragonflys after Andy left. He then played with several other bands over the years, including Inside Out, the Zimmer Frames, and Bad Penny (with Dave again), but now plays guitar in Sludgefeast and sings/drums for The Stand Ins. And, following interest from US label Grand Theft Audio to release a discography CD of the band, Andy and Dave have even persuaded the original line-up of Self Abuse to start playing together again.

"Dave gave me a call in autumn 2004 with the idea of doing a punk gig at Christmas, just playing a load of covers, which we've done from time to time over the years with a few friends calling ourselves Gash. He suggested doing a couple of Self Abuse songs and getting Roger, the S.A. guitarist, along as well. As it panned out, some of the guys from Gash couldn't do it, and after a few calls, we discovered that not only was Roger into the idea, but so was Steve, the old drummer, who now lives up in Derby…"

Adding yet further to the authenticity of the reunion, the resurrected Self Abuse entered Active Studios (formerly known as Arny's Shack, where they recorded their 'Soldier' single) in October 2004, to track four new songs. These materialized as the enjoyably boisterous 'No Change' EP on the band's own label, which in turn landed them a slot at the 2005 Wasted Festival.

"As long as we enjoy it, that's good enough reason for getting up there. And there's quite a few younger punks round here enjoying it 'cos they never saw us back in the day. I think a lot of our lyrics, although sometimes naïve, are still relevant… and there's nothing like having a few beers, plugging in and having a good thrash!

"As for our original punk principles? I think it's safe to say that I've mellowed quite a bit over the years… bloody hell! Makes me sound like a right fuckin' hippy! But I've been a veggie for twenty years now (and Dave is these days too), a direct result of listening to bands like the Subhumans and Conflict. And I still get mad at all the crap that's going on… let's face it, the world's hardly a better place now than then, is it? Different governments (or should that be corporations?)… same old shit!"

SELECT DISCOGRAPHY

7"s:
'(I Didn't Wanna Be A) Soldier' (Radical Change, 1984)
'No Change' EP (Abused, 2005)

At A Glance:
Grand Theft Audio are planning a Self Abuse retrospective CD, that will feature the '…Soldier' EP in its entirety and the best tracks from the various demos, plus liner notes from the band and a wealth of photos from their own collections.

From nearby Dorchester came **ATROX**, a promising punk band with definite anarcho tendencies, who played with the likes of the Subhumans and A-Heads, as well as near-neighbours Self Abuse and Butcher, and recorded two decent demos before metamorphosing into Hate That Smile and then Shot Away (who themselves became the popular melodic UKHC act, Wordbug). Atrox themselves lurched into life as the much more primitive **SHOCK TO THE SYSTEM** in July 1982, and comprised drummer/vocalist Alex Vann (formerly of Chaotic Disorder), guitarist/vocalist Dave Redfern and bassist Alex Russell. The latter was soon replaced by Andy Gouldson, and in late '82, Bryan Brown from Weymouth band, Manic, was recruited to front the band, with Paul Simmons from Dorchester's Screaming Disorder joining on second guitar, and the band making their public debut at the Hardye's Boys School that they all attended.

Atrox in the studio, late 1984 (left to right: Charlie Mason, Alex Vann, Paul Chambers, Paul Simmons and Dave Redfern).

"The sense of rebellion was central to my sense of excitement about it all," reminisces Alex of his induction into punk rock. "I felt I had little in common with a lot of kids my own age, and the music seemed to represent that and make it okay to feel like that. My own political awakening was happening at the same time as the anarcho scene was blossoming, so it was inevitable that I would gravitate towards bands dealing in issues such as animal rights, anti-war, anti-religion…

"About a third of the Hardye's pupils were in the CCF – the combined cadet force, a school version of the armed forces! And even took time out of lessons to parade about the playground! This was a world I felt no affinity with whatsoever, and definitely increased my sense of alienation and fuelled my interest in rebellious music."

Shock To The System recorded their one-and-only demo, 'Last Breathe [sic] For Humanity', July 14th, 1983, on the school's four-track recorder, with Trevor Lee of the RE Department handling the engineering and mixing duties! The four studio tracks – 'Total Blackout',

'Obnoxious Governing', 'Army Song' (an old Chaotic Disorder number, not an Abrasive Wheels cover…) and 'Last Flight Of The Phoenix' – were bolstered with numerous live and rehearsal recordings, and the resulting cassette album sold at gigs, the best being at Wareham Parish Hall with Anthrax, Naked and Mad Are Sane, although the band even did an unofficial beach party supporting Omega Tribe!

"The beach gig was great," reckons Alex. "No promoters or dingy club; just bands, a generator and some amps. Although I think only us and Omega Tribe got to play before the police stopped it all…"

Soon after the demo, Bryan and Andy left and were replaced by yet more Hardye's boys, Mark Hodder and Charlie Mason, on dual vocals, with Paul Chambers from nearby Wareham joining on bass. The new line-up prompted the change in band name to Atrox, and a corresponding, albeit slight, shift in musical direction, with Shock To The System playing their last gig billed as such on Friday 21st October, 1983, at Bournemouth's Christchurch Regent Centre, with Self Abuse, Idiom Tribe and Admass.

"By that stage we all just felt that Shock To The System sounded like a joke punk band name," admits Alex.

"We found Atrox in a Latin dictionary… we were in the sixth form, after all!" laughs Charlie. "We thought it sounded pretty cool, and, by coincidence, it meant 'shocking to society'… so, similar in meaning to the previous name but not as dumb-sounding! Musically, we carried on as usual, but were all listening to increasingly varied stuff – punk, hardcore, psychedelia, Hawkwind, prog rock, folk rock etc. We all became a bit obsessed with Hüsker Dü by 1984 as well, and used to do a couple of their tracks live. 'Recollections' on the second Atrox demo is our 'Dreams Reoccurring'! If anything, Alex's song-writing skills really kicked up a gear in '84/'85 too; you can hear the seeds of Wordbug in some of those last songs he wrote…"

Atrox recorded their 'Hit The Oxide!' demo (self-released on their own Xorta Tapes) during early March 1984 at Monitor Studios, Milborne Port, Dorset, and despite several disposable 'filler' songs (not least of all, the instantly forgettable 'Mark's Car' and the well-meant, but appallingly delivered, poem, 'The Carcass Lies Red'), a considerable musical growth was in great evidence. In particular, 'In For The Kill' delivered a vehement anti-hunting message without sacrificing a great tune to convey the band's anger at the odious subject matter.

Mark Hodder then left, to go to college, but not before playing the band's most prestigious gig, supporting the Subhumans and Self Abuse at Bournemouth's Winton Continental Cinema, July 1984.

"I suppose it was prestigious for us," admits Charlie. "Even though the venue was a seedy local cinema that showed soft porn… given the politics of the crowd, the front seats got ripped out fairly quickly, and no bands ever played there again!

"But we were all major fans of the Subhumans, so it was nerve-racking on that front – a gig with your heroes! Self Abuse were great live too, and for me were the best live band in our immediate vicinity… although the Cult Maniax played around Dorset quite a bit too, and were always good live. No mention of them would ever be complete without the 'support act' they used to bring with them – Vern The Carrot, this guy that used to recite poems while pissing in a beer glass… he'd then drink it as a finale! He allegedly had another routine called 'The Disappearing And Reappearing Mars Bar'. Thankfully I never saw that one!"

A second demo, 'Screaming At Deaf Ears', again on Xorta, was recorded at the same studio in late November 1984, and was another sonic evolution, with opener 'Protest With Action' an especially rousing, jaunty condemnation of punk rock's seemingly inherent complacency. Elsewhere though, Atrox again overreached themselves in terms of musical experimentation; the 'DB: Interlude' was a clever drums and bass instrumental almost worthy of their beloved Subhumans themselves, but both 'Belfast Hornpipe' and 'Recollections', although brave forays into other genres, failed to hit any of the right buttons.

In early 1985, Shaun Hemsley, a friend of Paul Chambers, joined the band as second vocalist ("A much-needed shot of 'singing in tune'!" laughs Charlie), and later that year, two tracks from the 'Screaming...' demo ('Protest With Action' and 'Is This Tomorrow Or The End Of Time?') were included on the aforementioned 'Party Pooping Punk Provocations' compilation, alongside the likes of Stupids, Death Zone, The Samples and Annihilated.

"I was a fan of the label," explains Charlie, who also provided the cover art for the LP, "And had some of his [Andy Thompson from Hull, who ran Xcentric] compilation cassettes, 'Raw War' and 'Grievous Musical Harm'; I greatly admired his attempts to promote international punk and hardcore to a UK audience, at a time when foreign punk bands, apart from a few American exceptions, were seemingly ignored in the UK. I sent him our second demo in hope, and he offered to put two tracks on the next compilation. Same goes for the LP cover; I sent him a photocopy of a big drawing I'd taken a fortnight to draw, saying, 'Use this if you want,' and amazingly he did! I remember the package of freebie copies arriving one morning and taking them into technical college... opening it and seeing our tracks on vinyl was unbelievable!

"I'd traded tapes with Tommy of The Stupids for a year or so by then, so it was good to end up on the same LP; we were all impressed with them and had wanted one of our songs, actually called 'Short Songs', to come out sounding similar... but it didn't quite work [it actually sounds more like Disorder!]..."

After more gigs along the south coast, Charlie departed the band in September '85 to further his education, playing his last show at Southampton's West Indian Club, supporting Pale Shade Of Black. Still rapidly evolving, the remaining members of Atrox, minus Dave Redfern, became Hate That Smile, who later mutated into Shot Away and then the rather brilliant Wordbug, although Paul Simmons moved to Manchester and formed Stretch.

"I haven't given that time together as a band much thought over the years," confesses Alex, "But looking back now, I see it as being quite significant. It feels like it was one of the last youth cults with a very strong identity. Also, the politics of the scene are still very much alive today in the hearts of the people that were involved. I know that I still carry through life the opinions and attitudes I formed during that crucial period..."

At A Glance:

There is talk of a Shock To The System/Atrox discography CD, and Grand Theft Audio is apparently putting a track by each band on a volume of their upcoming 'High Road To Obscurity' compilation CDs of rare Eighties punk, but until then, the curious reader could contact Charlie direct for a copy of the demos:
charlie.m@unisonfree.net

POLEMIC ATTACK formed in Fareham in 1980 as a means for the various members to voice their discontent with society's multifarious ills. They never released anything in their own right, but recorded several decent demos, the first of which provided one of the stronger tracks ('Manipulated Youth') for the second of the 'Bullshit Detector' compilations. The reality of the situation is though, that the band, like so many others never blessed with a vinyl release in their own right, deserves to be recognised and remembered as an integral part of the anarcho-punk scene they helped nurture and propagate with their well-meant lyrics and the very real commitment they held for the ideals expressed therein.

Drummer Terena Plowright, guitarist Heather 'Toxi' Todd and vocalist Gareth Richards first made music together as the Living Dead, but never performed publicly under that moniker. For

Polemic's Heather Todd with Living Dead bassist Mick Roberts, picture by Paul Postle.

Polemic Attack, they were joined by Rob Lynch on bass, and his brother Mike on guitar, and played their first show at the Fareham Technical College. When they recorded their 1981 demos at Hayling Island's Toucan Studios, the band had slimmed down to a trio, with Heather taking up a bass keyboard to replace the departing Rob, Gareth then handling guitar as well as vocals. They also shortened their name to just Polemic.

"I can remember we would practice day after day, as none of us were actually trained in our instruments," says Terena, of the band's uncertain genesis, "And so we were learning as we went along, and often the 'music' was made up as we went along as well. It was great fun though, as the enthusiasm and conviction we had in what we were doing was something I felt completely, and I don't think anything has quite captured my whole being in the same way since. It was just so simple and right, a whole ethos for life... and death. I lived in a pretty big house, with an understanding family, so we rehearsed there..."

"And for gigs, we all used to pile into Gareth's little Mini or Terena's Ford, with our equipment on our laps," adds Heather. "On one occasion, I sat on Terena's lap while she drove and I changed gear! Sometimes there was equipment and six people in the car; we used to drive to London and do gigs for a tenner... two quid each and a couple of quid for petrol. I bought my keyboard on HP [i.e. hire purchase] and paid £7 a month for it..."

Terena: "We used to put on our own gigs and would charge 50p entry: local bands such as 11th Commandment, the Mysterons, and Tears Of Destruction, plus the likes of Flux Of Pink Indians, Subhumans, and Dirt."

Polemic were fairly unique from the off. For starters, hardly any punk bands had female drummers, and the use of the bass keyboard as opposed to a bass guitar also lent their material – especially that of the third, and best-recorded, demo – a distinctive edge; some songs could even out-rant the likes of Dirt, while others were more reminiscent of the brilliant Chron Gen, except they also used female backing vocals to good effect, and the lyrics were far more serious.

"Yeah, we did take it all very seriously," agrees Heather. "Terena and I both had anarchy tattoos; she did mine herself, by drawing around a penny, using Indian ink and a pin – ouch! I considered myself an anarcho-feminist... but into peace. Which may seem like an oxymoron, but I believed that people had the right to live their own lives the way they chose, not be told what to do or think, and that society – the world – should stop fighting everything and everyone. Naïve and simplistic perhaps, but I still believe that it could be that way... if only we weren't so restricted by greed, want, destruction and fear.

"I produced a fanzine called 'Lost Faith', which focused on feminist, anarchist and veggie issues. I felt that the punk scene was more enlightened than regular society obviously, but that was partly to do with the attitude of the feisty, independent, opinionated female punks... we would sometimes have male punks tell Terena that she was a good drummer – 'for a girl!'"

The band themselves produced their own fanzine as well, 'Black Sunday', that was, of course, fiercely anti-war and included all their home addresses, should people care to debate their beliefs further with them. But Heather and Gareth's respective fathers, who both held senior positions in the Navy, were less than impressed, and the fanzine was printed with their particular addresses blacked out and the legend 'Freedom of speech? There is no fucking freedom!' included in the makeshift editorial.

"It was, and is, about complete freedom though," laughs Terena. "Anarchy is about respect for everyone and every being that feels and breathes, and promotes the right of others to treat you in return with freedom and respect. To do as you please basically, so long as it does not harm another.

"I got into animal rights first, and then, at about seventeen years old, was captured by the amazingly simple, perfect concept of 'anarchy and peace'. I heard a Crass album that someone lent me, and I could not stop playing it, as it all made total sense. I was soon going to as many Crass gigs as I could, and discussing different thoughts with them. I got hit at the Stonehenge festival, when it all kicked off the one year, and Crass picked me up and took me to safety, and then gave me and Gareth a lift the next day. I guess that was a turning point really... I then spent time learning from them at their house, and discovering how advanced their thoughts and dedication to peace was. I ended up sharing a house in London with Annie [Anxiety], Lou and Deno from Dirt, and a good friend called Sally."

In fact, Crass discussed with Terena the possibility of issuing a Polemic single – about the same time that Dick Lucas from the Subhumans asked them to do a release for his Bluurg label ("It was all very exciting," says Terena, before admitting, "But we were hanging out for the Crass one really...") In the end, neither 'deal' came to fruition and a frustrated Heather and Gareth left soon after, feeling that the band had achieved all they were going to by that point. But not before they participated in what was surely their live highlight, a slot at the legendary Zig Zag squat gig that Crass organised in December 1982, where they went on between The Mob and the Poison Girls, and played to a thousand enthusiastic punks. Terena continued for a short while, recruiting Caroline, Rich, and again Rob and Mike Lynch, but the band soon found themselves pulling in different directions and decided to quit whilst they were ahead.

"We were outspoken both on- and off-stage," says Heather, who is now an arts programmer. "We were always very active. I won't name names, but one of the band went to prison for raiding an animal lab, and another still has an outstanding libel case for handing out flyers about the same company. We were all hunt saboteurs, and glued up the locks of butcher shops; we raided an abattoir, set light to a fur coat outside a fur shop before staging a sit-in there, marched to [the military research facility at] Porton Down, where I got trampled on, trying to pull a fence down. We protested at [the RAF airbase] Greenham Common [where NATO deployed cruise missiles in 1983], stuck labels saying 'pornography degrades women' over the centrefolds in newsagents... one member of the band was even bitten on the face by a fox that was tucked in their jacket, having just rescued it from a fur farm... to name but a few incidents!

"It was my beliefs that got me into Polemic in the first place, and I'm still vegetarian after 25 years, still anti-fur, anti-violence/war, against animal testing, still a feminist, still don't like being told what to do, still support Greenpeace, Amnesty etc., and I honestly can't see any of that changing. Being in Polemic was important to me, as I felt I was part of a movement that was going to change the world for the better – and I actually think that some of things we protested for then have definitely come to fruition. The world is a better, fairer place, but there is still a lot of work to do... and we should never give up."

"I went and opened a shop called 'Live And Let Live'," adds Terena, "Selling veggie food and books. The police raided it several times though, in case there was a bomb in the lentils... I went on to be in several other bands, but I never found that same conviction from other artists, or the same connection, that we had in Polemic. I now manage the Sustainability Centre in East Meon, Hampshire; my love is still of peace, and that may be why I appreciate the company of sheep and sheepdogs so much!"

At A Glance:
The excellent 'Deceptive Ideals' from the band's third demo appears on 'Anti-State', the second volume of Overground's anarcho-punk series of compilation CDs.

ormed in the wake of Polemic Attack's untimely demise, **TEARS OF DESTRUCTION** aren't exactly a household name in the world of anarcho punk, but they left behind a damn fine seven-track demo, 'Death Of A Nation', which enjoyed distribution via Bluurg, and were an important part of the fabric of the alternative music scene on the South coast, the underground shows they tirelessly booked and promoted allowing more established bands to exert their influence over the needy youth of the area.

Ian from Tears Of Destruction (right) and Nick from The Sears.

As well as Polemic Attack, members of another Fareham band, Infamy, helped spawn Tears Of Destruction, who quickly settled on a stable line-up of Rob and Mike Lynch (bass and guitar respectively), drummer Chris Blackman, guitarist David Hodge, vocalists Rebecca Treloar and Ian Davidson, and, for a brief period at least, 'Bubbles', "A girl we met at a party, who joined for a few rehearsals… until it was decided she was surplus to requirements!

"We had a deep-seated wish to express ourselves and our opinions of the world," recalls Ian, of their earliest motivations. "Not to mention a passion for the anarcho-punk scene. Playing with Tears Of Destruction made us feel that we were doing something creative, and – for myself and at least a few others in the band – the political side of things was as important a part of our lives as the music."

Playing their first gig at Fareham Technical College, supporting Dirt, Tears Of Destruction quickly established themselves as a competent and enthusiastic live band.

"The show with Dirt was amazing; so many people turned up!" smiles Ian. "It was the first show we had put on, and we only went by word of mouth… I think we put up just three posters, in record shops in Fareham, Portsmouth and Southampton! The DIY network was really strong on the South coast; we played a lot and worked with several local bands: Polemic, of course, Ad Nauseam from Portsmouth, and 11th Commandment from Winchester. The gigs were very easy to run and the bands all turned up on trust… very different to promoting these days!

"And there was never any of the problems that some areas had with skinheads in our region; in fact, trouble at gigs was nearly non-existent. The only trouble we ever had was when we played Skunx in Islington; the venue was a small but happening affair, and we did one of our best ever gigs there, supporting The System, but the evening was marred somewhat by violence.

"On the subject of skinheads though, I remember we went to see Poison Girls in Oxford once. The skinheads there were fairly intense and they tried to get onstage, but Vi grabbed one of them by the nuts and squeezed... that put most of them off for a start!"

The band's sole recording – the aforementioned 'Death Of A Nation' demo – showcased their drivingly powerful, yet mournfully melodic, take on the male/female vocal attack style so popularised by the likes of Dirt and Toxic Waste, and even included the kind of subtly pleasing arrangements that eluded many of the 'bigger' bands. It was an impressive offering, and although self-released to begin with, it was no great surprise when it was picked up by Dick from the Subhumans and given a 'proper' release through Bluurg.

Tears Of Destruction, writing in the garage (left to right: Dave, Beki, Chris and vocalist Ian... on bass!).

"Recording the demo [at Toucan Studios, Hayling Island] was one of the best experiences of my life, even though the engineer got us stoned, and our guitarist Dave went white and puked all over the studio! It was only an eight-track desk, and we were completely unaware of what we were doing, but we didn't hang about, putting down seven tracks in a six-hour day... I really liked the simplicity of that live recording approach too, and took it with me to subsequent bands. I appreciate some of the effort that goes into the separation of different instruments in the recording process but for me, although the result of live recording can seem a little harsh at times, the energy that it retains is unbeatable...

"Anyway, we hooked up with Bluurg when we played a gig with the Subhumans in Southampton; they liked us and offered to help us out. And being associated with them did help a lot... it seemed to give us an instant credibility. Although we were nothing like them, and it didn't improve our music or anything, it was almost like a seal of approval."

Backing up their words with actions, members of Tears Of Destruction did view themselves as actual anarchists, and were regulars on many marches and demonstrations, some of their protests occasionally straying beyond the limits set as 'acceptable' by the state and her myriad bully boys.

"Without going into too much detail for obvious reasons, two members of the band found themselves looking at the possibility of long prison stretches for their troubles," sighs Ian. "But those were the days, eh? What is it with the youth of Thatcher's generation though? They don't seem to want to get their hands dirty now. I wonder if it would be possible to mobilise as many people as we did back then on a regular basis? Stop The City, CND, animal rights etc. etc. The demonstrations against Iraq were amazing in recent times, but the fight seems to have gone out of our culture now. There doesn't seem to be as much of a network keeping people in touch and informed... although the breakdown of trade union power and the criminalization of gatherings [the Criminal Justice Act] obviously haven't helped matters either.

"With hindsight it may have been somewhat naïve to call ourselves 'anarchists'. We did try to live as alternative a lifestyle as possible, and still do, to varying degrees of commitment. We questioned and challenged what was handed to us as socially acceptable and tried to find alternatives, helping create yet another link in the chain that was the scene at the time..."

Sadly, Tears Of Destruction split prematurely in late 1983 due to personal reasons, after what was "possibly their best ever show" at the Portsmouth Wedgewood Rooms, a benefit for South East Animal Liberation with Flux Of Pink Indians, Omega Tribe, Andy T. and Polemic.

"The gig was rammed! About 300 people turned up (again, with very little publicity), everyone had a great time, and we raised a fair amount for the cause... although yes, it also turned out to be the last gig we did together.

"There was a bit of an issue between two of the members that saw Beki and myself (we were seeing each other at the time) being asked to leave whilst the other members tried to find another singer. I was gutted by this – it was my life – but a line had been crossed and there was no going back."

Ian went on to play in several bands, most notably Bliss The Pocket Opera (who toured with Poison Girls and released the album, 'Wisdom, Magick, Chaos') and Ye Fungus, who issued several cassettes and toured with the likes of Blyth Power and Citizen Fish.

"And Dave went on to gig in a prog rock band called Paradox down in Brighton, Mike played in some power punk band that occasionally used to get up to support Ye Fungus in Walsall – which was where I moved to after Fareham... I went up to visit Corny from The Sears, and never went home!

"Rob did some acoustic stuff, Chris was last seen playing the drums, for some pop band whose name I forget, on kids TV, and I don't think Beki did anything else musically; she's now a teacher in Portsmouth.

"I have since worked with various community schemes and helped set up different youth arts projects," explains Ian, on what else he has done since the heady heyday of anarcho punk. "I worked collectively for many years and set up various co-ops and organisations that had the community at heart. I also worked as a booking agent (a nice one... honest!), booking gigs for bands such as Blyth Power, R.D.F, and the Rhythmites etc. I have now landed in the niche of youth worker, working on an estate in Bath, trying to help the young people here make sense of it all and find their own voice. It feels like a worthwhile thing to do."

At A Glance:
The more intrepid reader ought to be able to locate a complete version of 'Death Of A Nation' on the internet, but for those not so inclined, the demo's title track recently appeared on Overground's 2006 'Anti-Capitalism: Anarcho-Punk Compilation Vol. 4' CD.

CHAPTER FOUR

One of the most powerful of the Eighties anarcho bands – musically, lyrically and visually – were the ICONS OF FILTH from Cardiff, who even kick-started themselves back into convincing active service again in the late Nineties with a storming new album, 'Nostradamnedus' for US label, Go-Kart, and several well-received tours that proved they were still a relevant force in underground music and not some opportunistic cashing-in on the punk nostalgia trip of recent years. Sadly though, their welcome return to the scene was cut tragically short when vocalist Andrew 'Stig' Sewell died, October 2004, outside a gig they were playing with The Varukers in Hackney, just minutes after walking offstage.

Originally conceived as Atomic Filth in 1980, the band comprised Stig on vocals, Simon 'Daffy' DeManuel on guitar, Tony 'Socket' Watts on bass, and Mark 'Harry' Wilson (real name 'Aitch') on drums, and they quickly recorded a decent enough demo in Cathays, Cardiff. It wasn't long however before Socket was replaced by Eddie Flemming and the band changed their name to the far more stimulating Icons Of Filth, playing their first show under the new moniker at Cardiff's Central Hotel with Conflict, Rubella Ballet and No Choice.

"Me and Stig were living together at the time," explains Ed. "And me and Aitch had always been drummers. Socket wouldn't turn up for practises and stuff, and the boys would be there jamming, and I'd jump on the drums and me and Daffy would do Discharge songs and MDC songs... but then somehow I ended up playing bass, basically!

"Socket had been one of the first black punks in Cardiff, and he used to get a lot of grief from the docks people and rastas and stuff 'cos he was black and he was a punk; he had a lot of shit, but fuck me, he

Icons Of Filth (left to right: Stig, Fish and Daffy), picture by Mick Slaughter.

was a great bass player… just unreliable. He was a big fucking lump, always handy when there were fights with skinheads – he had a cracking left hook!"

"He's now joined the police force… bastard!" interjects Aitch, with a sardonic chuckle. "Anyway, it was 1981 when we changed the name… Stig had been touring around the country, following Crass about…"

"That was when we first met Colin and Conflict, and the guys from Omega Tribe and stuff," adds Ed. "Everyone knew each other from the Crass gigs, and everyone splintered off and started their own bands. Me and Stig would get our giros, hitch around seeing bands, come home and get our next giro, have a wash and go back off and stuff. And he just got inspired and said, 'Right, we're the 'Icons Of Filth' from now on…!' "

Aitch: "And he changed his nickname to Stig – 'cos he was always 'Sid' up until then!"

"But it wasn't 'cos of drugs!" quips Ed. "He didn't have a 'Jesus moment' or anything, no 'moment of clarity'; he just came back, all fired up by Crass… well, we were all angry, weren't we? And the early Eighties were just getting bleaker and bleaker, especially for the working class, and Crass came along at the right time for us all really."

"They were a great inspiration; they were just so honest," reckons Aitch.

Ed: "They were saying, 'Open your fucking eyes and think for yourself.' And they were just brilliant live, and every fucking gig would be crawling with skinheads, and there'd be fucking fights all the time, despite their pacifistic message. Typical of skinheads really… 'Let's go and pick a fight with the pacifists!' But some of us were prepared to fight back, and Stig and Colin had some right battle tales."

"It was like one big happy family really, all mates together," reckons Aitch, of their relationship with Conflict. "They were like an extension of our band, and vice versa. And what a cracking drummer Paco was! But there were always rumours that skinheads would be along to smash the gig up, and in the end you just expected it. Daffy had a chair leg over his head in Ipswich… that was a bad one… until Colin got his 'bag of tricks' out… this old duffle bag full of baseball bats!"

"It was a shame it came to that really," sighs Ed, "But you had to defend yourself, didn't you? We had a police escort out of Glasgow once… 'cos we nicked a case of orange juice! Twelve little bottles of

Britvic... fuckin' hell! We never got paid in Preston... there were loads of people through the door, and both bands played a crackin' gig, but then the guy said he hadn't taken enough money on the door, and all this nonsense. So, allegedly me and a few of Conflict allegedly smashed all the venue windows... allegedly... which was a lot of fun – allegedly! That was when Socket was still in the band, and I was just a roadie for 'em, so that was early on..."

As a result of the growing friendship with Conflict, the first Icons Of Filth demo, 'Not On Her Majesty's Service', became the first official release on their label, Mortarhate.

"Initially Colin was only going to do cassettes," reveals Aitch. "Back then none of us had any money, and if one of you bought a cassette, you'd have all your mates saying, 'Oh, do us a copy.' It was just a good way to get our music out there, and we still give thanks to Colin for helping us out big time..."

"We did it at the Poison Girls house," recalls Ed. "Where we met Penny Rimbaud, who was a lovely chap. We sat chatting with him, and he seemed very warm and caring; it was like talking to a professor or something, he just had that nice warm tone to his voice... what a lovely fellow!

"Anyway, they [Icons Of Filth] were booked in to do this cassette, and Socket left, and they were in the shit really. So Daffy sat with me, and taught me the twelve songs the night before, and we went in the studio the next day! The girl from Rubella Ballet lent me her bass 'cos I didn't have one! I suppose, 'cos I was a drummer, I picked it up quite quickly; I had a natural sense of timing, and I'd already been mucking about with the band at practises and stuff. I think Daffy had to overdub two or three parts that I couldn't get... but I'd only been playing bass for, like, two days at that point!

"And that was my introduction to recording with the Icons. Although me and Aitch had been at junior school together; we've been friends since we were six! Then I met Stig when we went to Rummey High School, when we were thirteen or fourteen, when we first got into punk..."

Aitch: "We were going to gigs when we were fifteen, weren't we? Getting beaten up by doormen at the Rank..."

"Getting beaten up by people from Bristol..." laughs Ed, "Getting beaten up by people from Newport... and then even Cardiff people were fighting other people from Cardiff... and all we really cared about was the music at the end of the day. It was mad though, 'cos we'd been at school together and were then such good mates together, and then we ended up in this hurricane that became the Icons Of Filth..."

Unlike most other bands who turned in a spirited but fatally flawed debut recording they would later prefer to forget, the Icons Of Filth – possibly as a result of the learning curve begun whilst known as Atomic Filth – produced a genuinely striking collection of indignant punk songs that truly set the tone for the astounding works to follow.

"The best compliment we ever had was talking to Jerry A. from Poison Idea," says Ed proudly, "When he said that their whole sound came from Motörhead and that first Icons of Filth demo! So when they played in Newport, we all went along, just to say thank you back for all the inspiration they gave us, you know what I mean? I think I was drunk that night though, and ended up bear-hugging him and trying to pick him up! I nearly did...! I was kissing him and telling him I loved him too!"

Although fuzzed-out guitars and Mad Hatter tempos were the obligatory order of the day for 'Not On Her Majesty's Service', songs like 'Cut The Crap' actually managed to wring a few catchy hooks from all the gnashing of teeth, and Stig immediately established himself as a vocalist of palpable intensity. However, it wasn't until Corpus Christi asked the band to follow-up the success of the cassette with a vinyl single – 1983's stunning 'Used, Abused And Unamused' EP – that his lyrical aptitude really came to the fore, with the track 'Asking Too Much' in particular being an especially articulate condemnation of the system's stifling asphyxiation of people's personal freedoms.

"Yeah, I think Stig was a little bit embarrassed by some of the lyrics on the cassette," offers Aitch, "Because he grew really quickly as a writer... 'Your Military' was one that he never wanted to play again… so we didn't!"

"He really concentrated on his lyrics, didn't he?" agrees Ed. "And they did become a bit like essays on the first EP, so when we played live, everyone was like 'Bastard!' No one could believe how he fitted all the words in! It used to amaze me how he could get that many words in one sentence, let alone then sing it…

"He started writing lyrics even before he was in Atomic Filth, just these poems really, and the stuff on the first cassette was basically his poems set to music. But later on, he would get ideas and write them down, and he'd say, 'Right, what tunes have you got?' And we'd give him a riff… then a lot of times at practise, he'd just sit and listen, but he'd take the song away in his head, and then next practise, he'd start rolling off all these lyrics, and you'd think, 'Fuckin' hell…' It'd be amazing; he wrote like a professor!

Icons Of Filth, Stig at the 100 Club, April 1983, picture by Paul May.

"Anyway, we recorded it [the EP] all in one day. But then, one thing we've always prided ourselves on was getting ourselves well rehearsed. We used to practise in these old malt buildings, and it was scary as fuck up there, really eerie… just one light bulb… all the old wheat bins and stuff… and we used to chip in with three or four other bands, and we'd all share gear. But if there was a gig coming up, or some recording to be done, we were on the money with our practises… we really knew what we were doing when we hit the studio. We'd go in there ninja style! Set up the drums, Aitch would bang out his parts, then I'd bang out the bass… Daffy would bang down the rhythm and lead tracks just like that, and Stig would bang down his vocals… no fucking about. The passion was there; we were young and angry. But we've always practised hard, because we wanted to be tight."

"We were never blasé about recording, but we didn't overdo it either," clarifies Aitch. "We'd be like, 'Yeah, that's good enough!' There was never any pressure though, because we just had that natural drive to do our best anyway."

Recorded at Cave Studios in Bristol, 'Used, Abused And Unamused' remains a vitriolic slab of angsty hardcore thrash to this day; despite it's thin, trebly sound, it's still more than capable of knocking a copper's helmet off at a hundred paces, and it really put the Icons on the international punk map, making the Independent Top Ten upon its release in late 1983. Surprisingly Ed decided he'd had enough and quit the band soon after, playing briefly with Cardiff psychobillies Demented Are Go, before immersing himself in bodybuilding and martial arts. He even placed fifth in 1990's Mr. Wales, but was forced to give up the sport after a near-fatal motorbike accident ("I nearly lost my leg; I could've been the punk rock version of the Def Leppard guy… playing with one leg and biting the cymbals!"), and he eventually ended up opening a tattoo and piercing parlour and playing drums for the criminally-overlooked Newport band Cowboy Killers. He was replaced by Richard Trevor Edwards (aka Fish) from local act Corruption.

"Yeah, I was gone after that first single, but we still stayed friends; there was no animosity or anything. Aitch is like my brother, I've known him since I was six, you know what I mean? Why did I leave…? Well, everyone's got a fucking daft side to them… but I seem to have everyone else's as well! And deep down, I think I've always thought of myself as a drummer, to be honest… plus I thought everything was getting a bit too serious…"

Aitch: "If there were any expectations from outside though, we weren't aware of them. We were in our own little bubble really, riding our own little wave. We were just a poxy little band from South Wales who enjoyed gigging…"

"I did let the boys down one night, although not intentionally," continues Ed. "There was a gig at the Brixton Ace, and they went up to mix the single, but I didn't have any money, so I never went up. This guy I knew was going to hire me a van, and I was going to drive up with a load of friends. Anyway, he fucking stiffed me and gave me an old van, and it was pissing out oil everywhere. Stig's brother Kev was driving, and we got stopped by Swindon police, and when they saw all the people in the back of the van without seat belts, we had a police escort back to Wales. Kev had to drop everyone off, go home and get his car, and then go and pick them all up, 'cos they were stuck in London. So the boys were none too happy, 'cos I let 'em down like, so that was another reason…

"That's why I went with Demented who were completely off their tits all the time, you know? To do something totally the opposite… plus I've always had a warped sense of humour… to the point where I have no shame apparently! But I was the jester, y'know? They were down… I picked them up, it was my job! Stig and me hung around together for years, and he always said I was the funniest fucker he ever met; my sense of humour kept us going sometimes… even if deep down they wanted to kill me… bury me somewhere at the side of the road. My girlfriend now's on medication, if that's anything to go by…!"

The band's defining moment came in March 1984 when they released their album, 'Onward Christian Soldiers', which spent fourteen weeks in the Indies, peaking at No. 7. Recorded at London's Heart And Soul Studios and produced by Pete Fender of Omega Tribe, it was a perfect

fusion of intelligent lyrics, pounding punk rock and a striking gatefold sleeve blessed with yet more incredible, chilling artwork from the band's resident artist, Niall 'Squealer' James. Opening with the insistent thrust of 'Why So Limited?' and climaxing in spectacular fashion with the raging 'Power For Power', every track is an essential listen, with the highlight for this writer being 'Show Us You Care', surely one of the most potent – and poignant – anti-vivisection songs every penned.

"Chips and a bap, ha ha!" is the slightly less serious way that Aitch recalls the album. "I was sat in the drum booth, recording the drums, and they were all going to the chippy, and I thought they asked me what I wanted from over there, but actually they asked me what the title of

Daffy, guitarist with the Icons Of Filth, live at the Clarendon Ballroom, London, February 1986, picture by Paul May.

the next song was. I said 'Chips and a bap', and couldn't understand why they were all falling about fucking laughing!"

"Having not played on it, looking back now, I just wish I could've!" sighs Ed. "Every band has their moment, don't they? Like Motörhead and 'Ace Of Spades'... The Ramones' first album... The Dead Boys' first album... from the first listen it's a classic. And no one was playing that nasty and hard then, it was just so aggressive, and the lyrics were so brilliant... it's just one of them albums that, if you're going out, you put it on to fire you up and stuff. Especially the title track... I used to love playing that live... an absolutely banging song."

"Personally, I always thought we were a live band, to be honest with you," adds Aitch. "I never did like the studio that much. If only three people turned out for us, or three hundred, or whatever, we always went for it. That was where the fun was... the gigs were everything to us."

About this time, Icons Of Filth appeared on the awesome 'Welcome To 1984' compilation LP that was put together by the popular US fanzine 'Maximum Rock'n'roll' (it was reissued by Sonic Reducer Records in 2000 and remains a cracking snapshot of the international punk scene during the mid-Eighties). Although appearing alongside a formidable array of hardcore talent from around the world – including Rattus, Raw Power, BGK, Inferno and the UK's own aptly-named Mayhem – the band effortlessly stole the show with their most intense composition to date. With Stig bellowing out 'Fear fuels the mind-fuck, the consequence is grim, police control without, TV controls within' as if his life depended upon it, 'Evilspeak' was a formidable slice of intellectual angst warning against the dangers of totalitarian government.

Spring '85 saw the release of the 'Brain Death' EP, which actually achieved the band's highest placing in the Indies (No. 3). Sporting as its front cover Squealer's gruesome depiction of an evil skull exploding from the socket of a deformed foetus, 'Brain Death' pulled no punches musically either, with A-side 'Enough Is Enough' being an ambitiously arranged rant exploding from an atmospheric intro weighted with ominous hanging minor chords. The two B-side cuts were just as uncompromising, although the slightly forgettable title track was eclipsed by the relentlessly pissed-off anti-meat industry diatribe, 'Success On A Plate (For Who?)'.

"Well, Stig was really supportive of the Animal Liberation Front, and we were all hunt saboteurs and stuff," responds Aitch, when asked whether the band backed up their militant lyrics with personal action. "We used to do the Caerphilly and District hunt... we went to the Stop The City demos as well, and we always used to play Rock Against Racism gigs, and lots of other benefits."

"But we would still have gone hunt sabbing and on anti-war demos and stuff even if we hadn't been in the band," reckons Ed, "Because we all drank in the same pub and stuff. Everyone used to hang about together, and tag along to these things together..."

Aitch: "It was all an offshoot of our friendship really, just like the band was."

Ed: "Back then I was terrified of nuclear war... and it still scares me now... the thought of some fucking idiot being able to push a button and ruin everything. Nothing's changed, has it? We went through the Thatcher years and there was nothing for us, and there's still nothing for us now; it's like a depression again now – and the working class are still getting fucked."

There was no let-up for 1986's 'The Filth And The Fury' EP, which again managed a respectable chart placing despite being the least satisfying of all the Icons recordings thanks to an atrocious production and mastering job.

"It sounds like it was recorded at the back of a church hall," admits Aitch, before explaining the inspiration behind the track 'Sunk Rock': "It was just our comment on how fucking stupid the punk scene was becoming; there were a lot of shite bands about, and 'hunky punky' posters in glossy magazines and all this bollocks. It became a fucking fashion, a circus..."

"The whole point of punk was that it wasn't about a dress code," adds Ed. "It was about being yourself and enjoying it... but when the anarcho scene really kicked in, you had to wear black. And I didn't really like wearing black! Like when we were in America a few years ago, some guy came up to me and asked why I had a beard! He didn't think it was punk! So I said, 'Does it annoy you?'

And when he said, 'Yes', I said, 'Well, that's fucking punk enough for me! It's pissed you off anyway! I've grown a beard because I fucking can!' It was always supposed to be no uniforms, no rules, but it was quite the opposite…"

As well as 'Sunk Rock', the single also featured a re-recording of 'Evilspeak' and – stand-out cut – 'The Vivisector', complete with a haunting intro of plaintive animal cries and 'guest artwork' from Nick Blinko, guitarist and vocalist with the enigmatic Rudimentary Peni. However, it was to be the last of the band's Eighties recordings, with Fish leaving soon after its release, and being replaced by Tim Reed for a final bout of gigging commitments. Most importantly though, Daffy got married, whilst Stig and Aitch both became parents which changed their priorities and the zeal with which they had previously contemplated lengthy touring, and eventually the Icons Of Filth were put on a back burner indefinitely. And it was actually Ed that initiated their return to the fray once more during the tail-end of the Nineties.

"I was drumming for the Cowboy Killers at the time," he explains, "And we were in Seattle, where we were billed as 'The Cowboy Killers – the UK's answer to the Dead Kennedys, featuring an ex-Icons Of Filth member'! And every leather jacket I saw in the States had the Icons on it, and people were coming up with Icons tattoos on their arms – and that's the ultimate compliment you can pay a band, having their name tattooed on you. And I was like, 'What the fuck? Did we make that much of an impact?'

"And I just had it in my head then that I had to get the Icons back together. The Mortarhate compilation had just come out [a retrospective discography CD], and I tracked everyone down – it took me about ten minutes, to be honest – and we all met up and had a beer. Cowboy Killers had split, and I missed being in a band, and we all decided to give it a go… our kids were all growing up, and it was nice to have some 'boy time', you know? Stig could be Stig again, instead of 'Dad' or 'Andrew'! We could get away from work and all that shit, and vent it all again, 'cos we were all still angry.

"And it was literally like picking up where we'd left off. Although Daffy had actually improved his playing, it took me a few months to get back to feeling confident on the bass again, and Aitch hadn't played drums for fourteen years… we still share a drum kit now, we have done since '95 onwards…"

"I was a bit worried at first… you know, could I still play?" admits Aitch. "I was terrible, really paranoid… but once we got motivated and decided to do it, the old magic was soon there again…"

Ed: "And I'm not being big-headed, but I think the best line-up of the band was when I was playing with them, back around the time of the first single. So we had a few beers, and sat down to write some new songs really, just to see what would happen… and I think it was Daffy, who was originally the most reluctant to play live, that suggested we do some gigs again."

Work began on a new album, 'Nostradamnedus', at local studio, Strangedays, with Nick James at the production desk, during August 2001, and Pete Rose from Bristol band Spite joined on second guitar soon after.

"We did have Ada from No Choice to begin with," reveals Ed, "But it wasn't his cup of tea, and then No Choice got back together anyway. But Pete was with us when we played our first gig back [October 19th, 2001 at Bristol's Easton Community Centre, with Bug Central and Disruptive Element – a benefit for anti-G8 protestors arrested in Genoa and Gothenburg]. We wanted someone who was about the same age as us, with the same ideals as us… Stig said he wanted another guitarist to fill the sound out, but he had to be a veggie, anarchist punk… and I said, 'I have the very man for you!' Pete was a body piercer like me [he's since become a plumber], and we knew him from his other bands… and to this day he's gutted he never played on 'Nostradamnedus'. And we were actually writing a new record with him, but unfortunately never got to record any of it, because of what happened to Stig."

'Nostradamnedus' remains a fitting epitaph to the band though, and in particular to Stig's lyrical genius. Far more considered than previous writings, and steeped in deeply cynical humour, songs like 'Treadmill' ('Your capital's an 'ism', your pipe is just a dream; your fortress is a prison and your 'has' has never been…') revealed a sensitive, thoughtful man reconciling his anarchic ideals with the mundane realities of everyday life. The band had also matured gracefully, cannily working to their natural strengths rather than struggling to resurrect the thrashier moments of their salad days.

It's a genuine shame for all concerned that their 'comeback' was halted in its tracks by Stig's untimely death, as the last album – like the first – hinted at a band capable of truly great things.

"Icons Of Filth is finished," declares Aitch, before adding, "Although we all might play together again one day… just not as Icons. Not without Stig; we were never going to carry on with a new singer."

"At the end of the day, we were five strong-minded

Icons Of Filth, live at Eric's, Bournemouth, 1985, picture by Marc Freeman.

individuals, but it was Stig who gelled it all together," confirms Ed. "I mean, I can't even fucking spell, let alone write a lyric! And when we got back together, if Daffy hadn't wanted to do it, we weren't going to bother, 'cos it was always Stig and Daffy that wrote the stuff. Even in the early days, he and Stig used to joke that they were the Lennon and McCartney of the punk world…! But it was true in a way, 'cos they were a great team.

"People said about 'Nostradamnedus', 'Oh, it was a bit rockier…' But at the end of the day, it was right for us; we wrote the songs we wanted, arranged them how we wanted… we did it all ourselves, and coming back after fourteen years, I think we did a fucking good job."

Aitch: "We'd moved on anyway; we were sick of the same old, 'One, two, three, four!'…"

Ed: "And we didn't wanna come back and just play the old stuff… you know, expanding waistlines, going bald, trying to relive our youths… if other people wanna do that, that's fine. But everything has to be real for us, y'know?"

Aitch: "So we came back with a brand new album, all new material. We never did a cover song either – not ever…"

The band also never ever posed for a line-up photo, testament to their impressive modesty.

"Well, maybe once…" corrects Ed. "We went for a meal in LA [during their first US tour, March 2003, travelling up the West Coast with Defiance] with Jay Lee from Resist And Exist, who had an anarchist bookstore and a vegetarian café there. Anyway, a few of the anarchist punks he knew were locked up, doing time, so we all sat on the steps and had a photo done together, and then all wrote a personal message on it… Stig wrote something like, 'Stay strong, don't let the bastards grind you down…' And apparently it lifted their spirits when they got it, and that was the only time we ever had a line-up shot done – but it wasn't for a fucking album cover or a magazine

THE DAY THE COUNTRY DIED

article, it was a goodwill gesture for these guys in jail, to try and cheer them up… 'cos if you're an anarchist in the USA, you're basically regarded as 'a pinko commie fag'.

"It's very rare you'd get us all together anyway, unless it was onstage; it was all about the music… we're ugly fuckers, to be honest. We couldn't see the point in spending money on videos and stuff… Stig would much prefer to give any money we made to the Animal Liberation Front… that was a cause very close to his heart; he was 120% into that, so pretty much every gig we did was a benefit."

"Some people said we only got back together for the money," spits Aitch passionately, "That we'd tour America once and then split up again… what a load of shit!"

"We did get an advance from Go Kart," Ed readily admits, "$10, 000, but we put it all back into the band, into air fares and stuff. We never had any gear; I'd owed my mate £700 for eighteen months for my bass rig before we got that money. We didn't have a penny between us to start back with… if you've got kids, you know what it's like. The second US tour we did [this time up the East Coast with Thought Crime, during January/February, 2004], we lost over a grand… but we didn't care, because we enjoyed ourselves."

Aitch: "And people forget about all the behind-the-scenes costs like rehearsing and guitar strings and drum skins…"

"There were rumours going around that Daffy was a copper," laughs Ed. "That one of us had a fish farm, that Stig had a scrap iron business with a guy from The Mob… but there were no rumours going around that I was good-looking or a porn star or anything! That I was tall, dark and handsome… never any good rumours started about how fantastic I am!"

When pushed as to what may have set them apart from their peers, Aitch offers cautiously:

"Our aggression perhaps… us and Conflict really had that edge to our music… but hopefully we had our own sound as well. We didn't try to copy everybody else. And Stig was a very intense front-man; he was like Clark Kent offstage, but as soon as we started playing, we'd be waiting for the veins in his neck to explode. I remember one time, at the first 'Gathering…' gig that Conflict did after we came back, and this guy at the front kept shouting, 'Why are you here, Stig? Do you really mean it?' And he was like, 'We'll talk later…' As soon as we finished, he was straight off the stage to confront the guy. He'd always tell you what was on his mind, and he didn't suffer fools lightly."

SELECT DISCOGRAPHY

7"s:
'Used, Abused, Unamused' (Corpus Christi, 1983)
'Brain Death' EP (Mortarhate, 1985)
'The Filth And The Fury' (Mortarhate, 1986)

LPs:
'Onward Christian Soldiers' (Mortarhate, 1984)
'Nostradamnedus' (Go-Kart, 2002)

At A Glance:
Mortarhate's 1995 release, 'Icons Of Filth: The Mortarhate Projects', compiles the debut album, the three Eighties singles and the best tracks from the 'Not On Her Majesty's Service' demo onto one essential disc. It comes complete with much of Squealer's incredible artwork, but unfortunately with none of the lyrics reproduced.

No Choice, 1983, picture by Robert Power (left to right: Ada, Martin, Gagz, and Jake).

lso from Cardiff, **NO CHOICE** had a foot in both camps of punk philosophy. Their intelligent pacifist lyrics suggested that they were very much of the Crass school of thought; however, the 'Sadist Dream' EP, their only proper release of the early Eighties, was on Riot City, a label predominantly associated with – for want of a better description – the chaos faction of punk rock.

So, it's a tribute to the punk ideals of tolerance, experimentation and diversity that both band and label not only decided to work together, but also between them actually produced one of the more adventurous and memorable releases of the era.

No Choice were formed in early 1982 by vocalist Gary 'Gagz' Williams and guitarist Martin Owen. According to the 'Young Blood' section of Punk Lives magazine, they arrived at their moniker when, after several weeks arguing over a suitable name for their band, they eventually had no choice but to call themselves No Choice! In the liner notes of their recent 'Try And You Might…' discography CD on Grand Theft Audio however, the band attribute the name to feeling so frustrated with government policies of the time, they felt they had no choice but to retaliate somehow, if only through their music and lyrics.

"Personally I just loved music, and with Martin Owen being exactly the same, we just had to get some instruments and have a go at it ourselves," explains Gagz. "Then we met Terry (AKA Spike), Svend and Cid, and they were our mirror images too, and it went from there.

"I suppose we were products of our environment to an extent; we just loved the punk attitude of rebellion and hated Margaret Thatcher and her sycophantic party – and still do! But punk hit a chord with a hell of a lot of people, and we were just some of them."

Spike was recruited as drummer (he just needed to get himself a kit!), Svend as bassist, and Cid as a second vocalist. Local gigs soon followed, playing alongside the likes of Conflict, Icons Of Filth, Moira And The Mice, and Omega Tribe, as well as Chaos UK from nearby Bristol. It was actually Chaos from Chaos UK who passed the band's first demo onto Riot City boss, Simon Edwards – who liked it so much he agreed to release the 'Sadist's Dream' EP in 1983.

"The single's a documentation of how we felt at the time – angry and ignored. Personally I didn't like anything on that label all that much, but when you're young, you're a bit naïve and tend to jump at these chances, and some people have said we learnt more doing it that way… which is probably right."

'Sadist's Dream' was certainly unlike anything else unleashed by Riot City. The A-side was

No Choice, 1982, picture by Robert Power (left to right: Cid, Martin, Svend, Gagz, and Spike).

basically a subtly unsettling spoken word piece over a melancholy acoustic melody, with lead 'vocals' courtesy of Cid, and whilst the two tracks on the B-side were more standard punk fare, even they challenged the listener's preconceptions. 'Nuclear Disaster' was a frantic anti-war rant, that burst forth from yet another atmospheric intro, but it was 'Cream Of The Crop' that revealed No Choice's hidden potential, an infectious upbeat class war anthem that couldn't fail to inspire with its positive message of self-empowerment.

"Actually, Riot City would have preferred 'Cream Of The Crop' as the A-side, which would have sold more records, but we didn't want to be 'just another Riot City band', so stuck with 'Sadist Dream'…"

Sadly, soon after the single's release, the band split up ("Over a stupid argument about some money going missing," according to Gagz) before they'd had chance to even promote it properly. As a result, it was consigned to the ranks of 'also ran' before it had even found its feet. But Gagz and Martin soon resurrected No Choice, recruiting Adrian 'Ada' Williams on bass and Jake on drums, and recording the excellent 'Question Time' demo, which they sold themselves at shows, mainly anti-apartheid and miners benefits. The tape featured several songs from the first demo – this time enjoying a far superior production – and actually had Gagz playing the bass parts because Ada couldn't make the studio session. Four of these songs eventually appeared on Volumes 1 and 2 of the 'Have A Rotten Christmas' compilations on Rot Records.

When Jake moved away, another friend of the band called Steve filled his place, until that is Spike rejoined, and Martin moved to bass, with Ada getting promoted to guitar. More gigs were undertaken, but all the fun was rapidly leaving the band, so they decided to call it quits whilst they were still good friends.

Spike, Ada and Gagz turned up again in the early Nineties, alongside Tim from the Icons Of Filth, in S.A.N.D. ("The name came from Shallow Acts = No Depth, mocking the apathy that wins all too easily," says Gagz), who self-released the rather good 'Lever, Neurosis, Hysteria' 7". And after another long hiatus, the intrepid trio (with new bassist P.M., and most recently rhythm guitarist Kaney) gave birth to a revitalised No Choice in 2001 and the 'Dry River Fishing' CD for Cardiff label Newest Industry. By far their most accomplished work to date, it sees the band's original feel refined and updated, and sounding better than ever. It has its attitude and feel firmly rooted in the band's past as an early Eighties anarcho-punk band, but takes as its major musical influence melodic US hardcore, a hybrid that is both pleasing to the ear and vibrantly original, sonically residing somewhere between Dag Nasty and The Mob. With newest member Mowgli onboard (he replaced Kaney during late 2005), the band plan to release their new album, 'Vive Le Internationalist', dedicated entirely to the memory of their late friend, Stig, before the end of 2006.

"After S.A.N.D., Ada still kept coming up with riffs, and I still kept coming up with lyrics and melodies, so I suppose it was inevitable that at some point, we were going to find a practise room and try them out again with Terry and another bassist. But for a while there, we were too busy bringing up kids and playing footie!

"We wanted to go back to basics, leaving The Jam-type influence behind with S.A.N.D. No Choice challenged us and fuelled our emotions, which were screaming for a release again. And S.A.N.D. was something similar that was right for us at that particular time. But, at the end of the day, No Choice was, and is, just five guys who do what they do, and who still have a passion for justice – avante the people."

SELECT DISCOGRAPHY

7"s:
'Sadist's Dream' (Riot City, 1983)
'Split' (Newest Industry/No Idea, 2004) – split with Fifth Hero

CDs:
'Try And You Might... Don't And You Most Certainly Won't!' (Grand Theft Audio, 2001)
'Dry River Fishing' (Newest Industry, 2002)

At A Glance:
Grand Theft Audio's 'Try And You Might...' discography CD is the logical place to start for anyone specifically interested in the band's earlier recordings – it even includes the S.A.N.D. demo, 'Tape Of Two Halves' – but the best No Choice recording by far is the excellent 'Dry River Fishing' album.

Many great bands have slipped silently beneath the radar of the average punk rock fan, never gaining the kudos they rightly deserve; in the wrong place at the wrong time, they just never got the breaks afforded far lesser bands and remain criminally overlooked by all but a few die-hards. If a book like this can change anything at all for the better, bands like SHRAPNEL will finally be acknowledged as the fine song-writers they truly were and hordes of new adoring fans will run up and down the streets screaming 'Missile!' at bewildered passers-by…!

It seems as if the majority of early Eighties punk bands formed out of boredom, and Shrapnel, who got together during late 1981 in Briton Ferry, a drab small town just outside Neath, South Wales, were no exception.

"Well, Briton Ferry *is* a small place, with a population of about 8000," explains vocalist Stewart Summers, "And there's very little to do if you're in your early teens, other than sport… mainly hanging about on the streets, or up in the large woods nearby, drinking and having a laugh with your mates… so yes, boredom was a huge factor in the band forming. Plus, of course, a love of punk rock and its philosophy that anyone could do it… 'Here's a few chords, go out and start a band!'

"Paul [Stewart's twin brother] got a guitar from the catalogue, Geoff [James] was in the band because he was the only person we knew with a drum kit who was both a punk and a mate. [Original vocalist] Andrew Kingdom plugged his mike into Paul's amp at first, then we scrimped and saved to get a vocal PA from a local pub; it was a real struggle to begin with, all sorts of begging and borrowing going on just to do a gig. Rehearsing was easy as there was an old garage next to our house with a loft on top of it, so we practised there for years – pissing everybody off in the process – then we moved to a church hall, which only cost a few quid to rent out; we rehearsed like fuck 'cos there was nothing else to do…"

With Andrew, Paul and Geoff joined by Mark 'Hitla' Rees on bass, the band tentatively found its feet with a handful of local gigs, the first being in Briton Ferry's Hengwrt School Hall.

"It was just the one band playing, and from what I remember it was a chaotic affair and not very well attended, but it was just great to have a gig which we'd organised ourselves going on in our home town, so on that front it was a success."

Stewart joined in mid-1982 when Andrew Kingdom decided to call it a day, making his own live debut at the Cardiff Central Hotel supporting Riot Squad, the Mansfield-based band who had just released their 'Fuck The Tories' single on Rondelet.

"He left because he wasn't committed enough, to either the band or punk," explains Stewart of Kingdom's departure. "It became obvious that they needed another singer to continue, so he dropped out and it was all amicable enough, and they even kept a few of his lyrics.

"It wasn't so much a case of me being the first choice," he adds. "I was the *only* choice, there being so few punks in Briton Ferry. The boys said, 'You know most of the words, have a go!' So I did, albeit very nervously. And it was a pleasure to be in the band with Paul and Geoff 'cos we got on so well, and we were all roughly into the same music and liked getting pissed and having a laugh.

"We began organising gigs ourselves, in local school and church halls, playing on our own to start with (I think!), but then we bumped into people at the gigs who played in other bands and we got them to play with us. Bands like Reality Attack, Armistice, Nux Vomica and Skull Attack, all from Neath and Port Talbot, and a couple of bands from Ebbw Vale called The Secluded and Birth Trauma. It wasn't that easy to get gigs though, and when we did get a suitable venue, somebody would always do something to piss the owners off – fighting or vandalism usually – and we'd have to find a new place. The Rail And Transport Club in Port Talbot was one of the best places we used… we did a great gig there with the Subhumans and Organised Chaos; it was packed and everyone enjoyed themselves, a huge piss-up – of course!

"Later on, there was more of a scene, with other people getting together to put gigs on in Swansea and Neath; there were also people like Marv [who went on to play bass for Chaos UK and The Varukers] putting gigs on in Cardiff and, of course, Simon and everyone at the legendary TJ's in Newport. Sure, the scene could be competitive sometimes, but on the whole people helped each

Shrapnel vocalists Gaz and Stu live at the Blue Bell, Neath, September 1985, picture by Dai Joseph.

other out… saying that though, there were plenty of rumours flying around about our 'bad habits' – all completely untrue!"

The first demo was recorded during February 1983 at a four-track studio in Tonypandy, up in the Welsh Valleys, an eight-song cassette that really captured Shrapnel's raw, energetic sound. Much of the material was very obviously penned by a young, naïve band still coming to terms with their instruments, but several songs – namely the aforementioned 'Missile', the anthemic 'Let There Be Anarchy', and the impassioned 'Fight For Freedom' – still stand up to close scrutiny even today. And for such a modest recording, the production sounds remarkably fresh as well, especially Hitla's bass guitar, granted great prominence in the mix thanks to its lively top end frequencies.

"I remember having a lift up to the studio with my grandad," laughs Stew, "knocking the tracks out really quickly, before having a break in the local pub, then getting it all done 'n' dusted straight after; it must've taken about eight hours in all! I'm sure we had a laugh, but I honestly can't remember very much about it. We wrote off to Sounds, 'cos they had a section for unknown bands, bless 'em, giving our address and saying that we now had a demo available, and the following week we bought a copy and there it was, 'South Wales punk band Shrapnel have an eight-track demo for sale…' Next thing we knew we were getting three or four orders a day, it was bonkers; we had to get a tape-to-tape recorder to keep up with the demand… we ended up selling hundreds of the fuckers."

Soon after, and still riding on the back of the demo's success, Shrapnel made their London debut, supporting the Subhumans at the prestigious 100 Club.

"That came about through us knowing the Subhumans a bit and giving their roadie Pete a copy of our demo – not to mention nagging them every time we saw them as well! [Vocalist] Dick just phoned up out of the blue one day and asked if we'd like to play the 100 Club with them, and we jumped at the offer; not only was it a gig in London, but it was at one of the birthplaces of punk rock. It was billed as 'A night of bands beginning with 'S'!' There was us, the Smart Pils, the Sears and the Subhumans.

"We drove up with a van load of our mates; I remember being very nervous before going on and someone shouting out 'Welsh wankers!' at us, but we went down okay – the usual 'first band' sort of reaction – and made some useful contacts. Some people who saw us there offered us more gigs and started coming to our other London dates. After we played, we did the usual 'get pissed and enjoy the rest of the gig' thing, and one of the Smart Pils gave a few of us some acid, so the gig and journey home was a bit more interesting for some than others!"

Shrapnel guitarist Paul at the Blue Bell, Neath, September 1985, picture by Dai Joseph.

Although Shrapnel were also gigging with the likes of Broken Bones and even Guana Batz, the Subhumans show, and the contacts they made there at, saw them gravitating more towards the anarcho side of the punk scene, and before too long the band were asked to record an album, an ill-fated project that never saw the light of day.

"Yes, I suppose we did move towards the anarcho thing. To us, we were always just 'punks', but I'm sure if you read interviews we gave at the time we may have described ourselves as 'anarchists'. To be honest with you though, we never really gave it that much thought; we definitely weren't sitting around reading anarchist literature all day, that's for sure! Anarchy seems like a good idea in theory… but as to whether it would work in practice, who knows? It's still not something I give a great deal of thought to; I don't really envisage the population of Britain overthrowing the government and declaring it an anarchist state any time in the foreseeable future though, do you?

"As for the album that never was, we'd sent our tapes out to lots of labels with no joy, but some bloke – I can't even remember his name – got in touch with us and said he'd like to release an album on this label he was setting up. We went back into the studio and re-recorded the songs off the first demo, plus about four extra tracks; they sounded miles better too, because it was recorded onto eight-track tape instead of four-, so we were pleased with the results. We sent him the master tape – and that was the last that was ever heard of it! We made lots of phone calls etc. but no joy… in hindsight, I'm glad the album was never released though, because I think the same bloke released an album by the Cult Maniax, who we knew, and they were not pleased with it at all, and got completely ripped off by him. In true Shrapnel style, we only kept one cassette copy of the album which duly snapped in someone's car stereo, so the recording was eventually completely lost."

Disillusioned by the whole debacle, Hitla left in 1984 and was replaced by Richard 'Coley' Cole. A second demo, 'Restricted Existence', was recorded during late September '84, a four-track affair that showcased the band's rapidly evolving sound and competence, a subtle yet powerful understanding of melody beginning to assert itself on songs such as 'Fragments Of Hope'. One track, 'Unjustified Actions', was included on the Mortarhate compilation album, 'We Won't Be Your Fucking Poor', Shrapnel having by then played with Conflict in both Swansea and London.

The bassist situation remained unstable for the band, with Coley being replaced by Andy Bull, who himself was replaced by Dai Joseph… although during this time Shrapnel managed to play the length and breadth of the country, displaying a kind of work ethic unheard of even amongst many of the more established bands on the circuit. This turbulent period also saw the brief addition of a second vocalist, Gaz Landeg, a close friend of the band who helped up the visual intensity on several tours – including a stint with Organised Chaos during November '85 – but never entered a studio to record with the band.

"Most of the gigs we did were enjoyable for one reason or another," reckons Stewart. "Of our early ones, a gig in a place called 'The Alamo' in Carmarthen stands out; it was like an American roadside diner in the middle of nowhere, and on the night a load of hippies from the nearby teepee village turned up with carrier bags full of home-grown grass and just dished it out! We played – completely stoned – and looked out at a load of hippies dancing to this full-on punk music in a big cloud of smoke… it was pretty surreal, maaan!

"All the gigs we did with the Subhumans were great, 'cos we obviously got to see them after we played and they were really nice people as well; the tour we did with them in Ireland stands out (as does the later Irish tour we did on our own). We had a great time, the people over there were so friendly… plus it was just an experience being in Belfast at that time; it was pretty grim, but the punks just got on with putting on gigs and having a good time.

"The only two gigs I remember as being real duffers (though we had plenty of hard times on the road) were at Oddy's in Oldham; there was nobody there, and then all of us were freezing, trying to sleep in the van afterwards! And one at the Hereford Market Tavern; there was lots of trouble, a couple of our friends got seriously hurt and most of the crowd had no interest in the bands, but all went berserk when the DJ played 'Friggin' In The Riggin' by the Pistols after the gig! We had to flee that place for our lives…"

In September 1986, Shrapnel recorded two new songs (including their finest moment, 'They Are Wrong', with its vehement chorus refrain, 'They can hide in their shelters all day long… but the burns on the bodies will prove the bastards wrong!') for a split single with Symbol Of Freedom

Shrapnel drummer Geoff at the Blue Bell, Neath, September 1985, picture by Dai Joseph.

from Pontypridd. Steve Bluemer, vocalist with Symbol Of Freedom, who financed and released the EP on his own label, then joined the band on bass when Dai left – just as they also added a second guitarist to the line-up for the first time, in the shape of Ivor White of Bridgend band, Capital Gain (who later became the much heavier Life Cycle).

"Ah, yes, the mighty Ivor White," laughs Stew. "A great guitar player, by anyone's standards. When he joined the band we realised it was time to start from scratch and write a whole new set of songs; this was because the addition of Ivor had given our sound an extra dimension. Also, Steve Bluemer, our new bassist, was a prolific lyricist, so as a result we wrote a lot of new stuff very quickly. We became a new band overnight really, one that was very different to the punkier Shrapnel of old."

More gigs were undertaken with the likes of Chumbawamba, Generic and Culture Shock, and then in 1988, two new songs were recorded for yet another split single, this time pairing Shrapnel with Scotland's Toxik Ephex for the new, upcoming Welsh label, Words Of Warning. A tour of the UK supporting San Francisco thrashers Christ On Parade was booked to promote the release, but internal pressures tore the band apart before the dates could be completed.

"The first night of that tour in Bradford is the last gig that really stands out for me," remembers Stew fondly. "I remember looking out at a pretty packed crowd, all dancing, and then looking over at Paul and we were both just pissing ourselves laughing, as we've always done if we were playing and having a good time; to me that's what it was all about: the joy of playing.

"Anyway, Ivor had told us he was leaving the band after the dates with Christ On Parade, because he wasn't really cut out for the increased gigging we were doing, so we knew a change was in the air. This was disappointing news for us, 'cos Ivor was a lovely bloke and a great guitarist, but we respected his decision and wished him all the best. Unfortunately, it became obvious as the tour progressed that Steve Bluemer didn't want to be there either. I'm not going to go into detail, but Steve's behaviour and attitude became so bad that, by the time we got to Newcastle, about two-thirds of the way into the tour, we gave him his bus fare home and told him to fuck off. And because we lost both Ivor and Steve, we just decided to call it a day; it was just too much hassle to carry on. Some of us – all except for Steve, really – had a good time on that tour though; C.O.P. were great people and always up for a party which made it all the more frustrating having to bail out before the end. Luckily our friends Life Cycle stepped in and saved the day for the last couple of gigs."

Life Cycle also replaced Shrapnel for some dates they had booked across Germany, with Kettering-based anarchos The Next World, for December 1988. Shrapnel did play one final show though, at Swansea University's Nelson Mandela Hall, with Aardvark Generator, Life Cycle and The Abs.

"Steve Bluemer asked us to do it at the end of the C.O.P. tour as some sort of gesture. We went on first, and I remember being really pissed on stage, announcing it was our last gig, and that was the end of that. I still think it was a mistake doing it, but I probably enjoyed the rest of the night 'cos there were a lot of old mates there."

After Shrapnel, Stew and Paul played together in The Duvals, who released the well-received 'Beauty' album on Mother Stoat Records in 2001, before Paul went on to join Ten Benson, touring the UK twice as main support to The Darkness in the process! Both the twins are still involved with music, Stew selling T-shirts for bands and working at a rehearsal studio, Paul driving and tour managing bands for a living. Steve Bluemer played briefly with Crabladder, who released a split single with Slowjam in 1993 on Power Tool Records, whilst Dai Joseph now plays with Swansea noisecore outfit Black Eye Riot.

"In many respects, yes," responds Stew, when asked whether his mindset is still the same now as back then. "I still have no interest/faith in party politics, a healthy disrespect for authority and still get bothered by a lot of the shit that's happening on this planet of ours. I'm not walking around with red spiky hair anymore and have mellowed a bit, but, saying that, I was never a particularly 'angry young man' in the first place. Times change and so do your priorities as you get older; I'm not out on demonstrations week in, week out, but I know where I stand on certain issues and still feel comfortable with that."

SELECT DISCOGRAPHY

7"s:
'Untitled' (Hand In Hand, 1986) – split with Symbol Of Freedom
'Acts Of Desperation' (Words Of Warning, 1988) – split with Toxik Ephex

At A Glance:
Unfortunately there is no official retrospective Shrapnel CD available... but there should be!

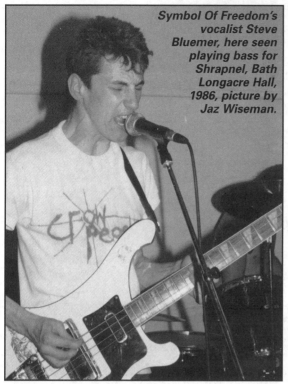

Symbol Of Freedom's vocalist Steve Bluemer, here seen playing bass for Shrapnel, Bath Longacre Hall, 1986, picture by Jaz Wiseman.

One of the 'smaller' names (but what a great name they chose!) when analysing the early Eighties anarcho-punk scene in retrospect, the aforementioned SYMBOL OF FREEDOM were still of tremendous importance on a local level, to the people they interacted with and influenced on a daily basis. Formed in Pontypridd in 1981, the original line-up was Lyndon 'Foxy' Fox – bass, Rodney 'Yan' Leyshon – guitar, John Jones – guitar and Steve Bluemer – drums/vocals, although Lyndon, John and Steve had previously played together as Drab Confusion.

"I can't really speak for anyone else, I guess, as things change in retrospect, and youthful agendas can be fickle things," begins Steve carefully, before cutting loose with a veritable stream of consciousness. "I would say though, that my influences were not that dissimilar to most folk that form punk bands, i.e. an innate desire to prove that capitalism is a fucking monstrous perversion, relevant and beneficial to only a possessed part of society that, through sly fingers and sharp practise, mangles others for sexual collection, international carnage, vulgar probabilities and fiscal return! To me, these deathly pale apparitions move nothing through this world but dead confederation and they should be named at all times.

"I don't personally think that we were any good at all," he adds, self-effacingly, "But it was an enjoyable part of my life, nonetheless. What stands out for me, however small, was the contribution, visually, financially or otherwise, to things we correctly called at the time. It isn't enough to say that rape is appalling, whilst watching crisis phone services collapse due to lack of funds – you have to take part in protecting what little communal partnership you have. Apart from providing the possibility of substantial support to others, good will can be infectious, and without sounding too daunted, it seems we need a whole heap of that right now.

"And I do believe that the rudiments of anarcho-punk were no bluff, but communal mettle is not exclusive to a musical genre. Townes Van Zandt's 'Rear View Mirror' is just as arresting as, say, The Mob's 'Let The Tribe Increase'… but the greatest single influence in my life was my grandfather, who worked most of his life down the [coal mining] pit and never once hit his wife."

Kevin 'Scottie' Hunt joined on vocals, about the same time as John Jones left, just as the band were starting to get a little more serious, gradually acquiring some real equipment… until this point, Steve was banging away on tins and bins, with bits of wood acquired en route to rehearsal!

"We all went to school [the Coed-y-Lan comprehensive] together," explains Scottie, of how the band members met, "And we were already good mates, with a shared love of punk rock, long before we did the band… although Foxy also had a fondness for Chas 'n' Dave as well! It was strange; we would be buying Crass records, and he would be buying 'Rabbit' and 'Gercha', ha ha!

"When we weren't practising, we used to go to the local YMCA, which was run by a woman called Mrs. Price, who encouraged us in what we were doing and offered us the use of the building every

Sunday, when it was not in use. By this time we were all out of school and out of work… the miners had been defeated, Thatcher and Reagan ruled the world, and there was the constant threat of nuclear war. We were skint, bored and angry, like most teenagers at the time, and we were listening to Conflict, Crass, Flux, and The Apostles, who were just my favourite band of all time, plus all the more mainstream punk bands like the Anti-Nowhere League and the Test Tube Babies…"

Symbol Of Freedom didn't actually play live until January 1983, when they made quite an impression at Pontypridd's Victoria Club, where they debuted with local acts, Rachael's Ravenous Offspring and All Teeth And Makeup.

"We played okay, mostly our own songs, but also a few covers of stuff like 'Pretty Vacant'. But twenty years on, people still come up to me and talk about that gig – not because we played a blistering set and our rabid energy onstage changed their lives forever or anything like that though… no, it was because the ceiling of the stage was very low, and in the middle of one of our songs, I jumped up and smashed my head on a strip light, cutting my head open and covering me and the stage with glass and blood! The rest of the band were laughing so much, they had to stop playing; Steve actually fell off the drum stool…"

During spring 1984, the band recorded their first demo, live at the YMCA where they rehearsed, and one of the tracks – 'What's Your Alternative?' – appeared on a compilation cassette of Welsh punk bands, entitled 'There's More To Wales Than Male Voice Choirs', which is how Symbol Of Freedom first became aware of Shrapnel, with whom they began gigging regularly around South Wales. Other gigs were undertaken with Liberty, The Astronauts, Political Asylum and Karma Sutra, and another live demo recording was undertaken at the YMCA, for sale at these shows.

"Unfortunately, it was about that time that violence at gigs started to rear its ugly head," sighs Scottie. "The worst I was involved in was at a gig near Merthyr Tydfil, when we were supported by Foreign Legion and this new romantic band, La Resistance. Most of the people in the venue took an immediate disliking to them and decided to have a mini-riot, smashing up the venue [the Hirwaun YMCA], two nearby pubs and a chip shop, as well as a few cars along the way. Several people got hurt, we had a police escort out of town, and were warned that, if we ever played there again, we would be arrested… that's the kind of thanks you get for offering to play for free to raise money for the community! Events like this made me write songs about the scene; there were loads of people pissing me off, because they were totally missing the point of it all."

"I categorically loathed the whole skinhead/Oi thing," spits Steve, with considerable venom. "Honestly, you would organise a benefit gig for, say, miners' families, or affordable housing schemes, or mental health self-support networks, and these gate-crashing, tongue-tied, hulken arseholes would turn up, smash the fucking windows, beat up the audience, and close down another potential venue, and the money we could've made would always end up paying for the damages. And all this from the idea that 'street punk' was an apparent antidote to the pose of the middle class...

Symbol Of Freedom, live in Swansea, November 1985, picture by Dai Joseph.

"Yeah, well, I don't like a pat on the back at dinner tables either, but just because some kid's wearing a Dead Kennedys shirt at a gig, you don't have to put a cigarette out on his naked eyeball. It was an awful, festering sore upon the punk scene at the time, and was without question riddled with an obvious, vicious racism and homophobia. Ideas we had no collusion with. And in the end, we got terribly sick of the debates it engendered. Why, in whoever's name, we ever allowed ourselves to lay an inviting table to this blatant bungle of conspicuous madness was beyond me. I come from the South Wales valleys, and being working class does matter here, because working class people must conjure up the will to disapprove of and disappoint these people who would drive abject aspirational poverty into our communities when they are overlooked by those who have agendas elsewhere..."

Towards the end of 1985, Scottie got a job and left the band after realising that he could no longer commit to it properly, which resulted in Steve moving to vocals and Mark 'Hitla' Rees, formerly the bassist of Shrapnel, joining on drums.

This line-up recorded the track, 'Suffering Persists', in Cardiff's Music Factory, for the 1986 four-band compilation EP on Words Of Warning, 'You Are Not Alone', that saw Symbol Of Freedom holding their own alongside Oi Polloi, Hex and Stalag 17. The band then also enlisted a female singer, Alison, the girlfriend of Shrapnel roadie 'Slag' (he was also the editor of the short-lived but riotously funny 'Smiling Faeces' fanzine), to lend their material some extra dynamics, and returned to the Music Factory to record two blisteringly fast songs, 'Against Our Wall' and 'Another Day', both reminiscent of Conflict at the height of their powers, for a split single with Shrapnel, on Steve's own label, Hand In Hand.

By this time, Steve had actually joined Shrapnel on bass anyway, and was expending most of his time and effort touring with them, effectively leaving Symbol Of Freedom high and dry. They split for good in 1987, but managed to remain friends, with Scottie and Foxy working together in the same furniture factory for a while.

"Steve moved on, I felt," offers Foxy. "He spent all his time with Shrapnel, until there was no interest left in our own band. The last gig was in Malvern [at the Herefordshire House, with the Amebix]; it started well enough, until Yan's twelve cans of Stella, and four pints in the bar half an hour before we were due to play, kicked in; he was on a planet all of his own! We did two songs before he broke into a load of his own riffs and solos... we all looked at him and walked off, and that was the end of that."

As detailed earlier, Steve went on to play with Crabladder, but still basically feels the same way he did then about the issues that were most important to the band, such as animal rights and pacifism.

"Obviously, as a teenager, you are aspirant, difficult, forthright, and illuminated by stupidity, yet convinced and strangely cantankerous," he muses. "But that doesn't detract from the fact that what you considered ethical is subject to change, just because you are involved and have more responsibilities. I don't have children, for example, but I guess that having them changes your priorities to a certain degree.

"Actually though, if I'm honest, I think that the animal rights movement has become too arbitrary these days. While I still consider fox-hunting to be detestable, and I commend those that try to highlight the bunkum of its advocates, I never found going sabbing to be a particularly enjoyable day out. I loathe violence, and hunt supporters can be a deranged bunch, but it seemed that, over the years, we tended to adopt the same strategy as them. I know that having the shit kicked out of you isn't much fun, but I grew depressed at having to approach the issue by the hunt's own standards. I don't have the answers, but I've never believed being a bully to be one of them. I still envisage a time and place when we will feel bored by the 'history makers' who would have us believe that we're destined to steer ourselves into catastrophe, calamity and repetition. Telling ourselves off now and again helps a little, I think!"

SELECT DISCOGRAPHY

7"s:
'You Are Not Alone' EP (Words Of Warning, 1986) – four-way-split single
'Untitled' (Hand In Hand, 1986) – split with Shrapnel

At A Glance:
As per the preceding Shrapnel chapter, some discerning label out there really needs to exhume the releases of these great Welsh bands and make them available for further examination by a whole new generation.

Vocalist Pig of Classified Protest, live in Swansea St. Phillips Community Centre, November 1985, picture by Dai Joseph.

CLASSIFIED PROTEST may never have released any vinyl in their own right, but they made several noteworthy compilation appearances, and, with their fiercely defiant working class background (growing up on rough council estates in Blaina and Nant-y-Glo), were another prime example of street punk sounds colliding with anarchist politics. Perhaps most importantly, they morphed into Rectify during the late Eighties, who were to prove one of the most intense and focused hardcore bands to emerge from South Wales.

"We were definitely a street punk band," reckons vocalist Wayne 'Pig' Cole, "But I'm not sure that we were anarchists. Because of our personal backgrounds, growing up in the Valleys, with the miners strike, we were obviously politically militant, but more Socialist than anarchist. Our lives could never really be geared up to be anarchist… that was a luxury that had to be paid for by mam and dad, and our mams and dads didn't have any money! My dad was really ill back then, and couldn't work, and he and my mother got divorced when I was fifteen, so I was the one bringing the money into the house when I was sixteen, topping my dad's income up. I didn't have time to think about being a fucking anarchist, do you know what I mean? I had to deal with the reality of every day life, right there and then.

"You had the Blaina riots in the Thirties, you had close connections with the iron works at Merthyr, you had the Chartists… the list is endless for political struggle in the Valleys of South Wales. But we weren't the kind of trendy anarchists that went on about Spanish revolutions, rubbing margarine into our jeans… that had nothing to do with our lives at the time. And punk is all about reality at the end of the day.

Classified Protest at Swansea St. Phillips, November 1985, picture by Dai Joseph.

"Crass understood though; their last gig was over in Aberdare, a benefit for the striking miners… but Penny and that were older guys, and it was a lot of the younger guys in these other anarcho bands that didn't make the connection.

"A load of us went to that [last Crass] gig; that was actually the first time we ever met [Bristol punk bands] Chaos UK and Lunatic Fringe, we sat in the pub with them before the gig. I remember everyone surging forward when Flux came on to do their sound-check, and all the cinema seats got flattened straight away before the gig had even started!

"Anyway, we were all hanging around outside drinking, and the local paper came along, and the headline was something like, 'Punks make pilgrimage to Aberdare for South Wales miners!' They were taking pictures of all the punks and that, and Craig from Political Reform had this big dog collar on with nails in it, and 'Classified Protest' painted on his leather jacket, and that was the photo that ended up on the front page of the local paper…"

Formed several years earlier, in 1982, from the remnants of The Unreal and Assault, and known briefly at first as State Of Mind, Classified Protest were Pig – vocals, Mark 'Wedge' Wedgebury – drums, Andrew 'Footy' Foot – bass, and Kirk Johnson – guitar. The first gig was at Blaina's old youth centre, The Legion, with Surrealist Dream, with members of the Soldier Dolls and Impact in the audience, the latter being so impressed with the band's performance, they offered them their first gig out of the Valleys early the following year, in nearby Newport.

Wedge departed the band briefly in 1983, and they recorded their first – self-titled – demo with stand-in drummer Mark 'Frankie' Fowler ("We actually nicked some artwork off the first Subhumans LP," chuckles Pig, "Just chopped it up and stuck it on our own tape cover!"). The disagreement with Wedge was just a spat though, and he was soon back behind the kit. 1983 also saw (most of) the members of Classified Protest awakening to the animal rights issue…

"I remember it was me, Wedge, Kirk, and my ex-girlfriend Linda, and we all went on this camping holiday to Tenby. Actually, it's really funny, 'cos there's some girl on myspace.com now, who's still into hardcore punk today, and there's a picture of me on her web space, with three mohicans all stuck up, taken over twenty years ago in Saundersfoot, with a little caption from this girl saying, 'This was the first punk rocker I ever met!'

"Anyway, we decided that it was going to be a vegetarian weekend, and our mate Maggsy came down, and he introduced us to Sosmix and things like that… the thing is, he was so fucking dirty, a real crusty little fucker, he was rolling the Sosmix into sausages, and it was making his hands clean! And we all sat in a circle in this tent, eating Sosmix, beans and rice, with tomato ketchup, and that was our first small step towards vegetarianism. One morning, we left Linda in the tent, headed off down the local shop, and she came down and caught us all, sat outside the corner shop scoffing steak and kidney pies! We all had a bollocking and had to throw them away, but a year or two later, me and Wedge were serious vegetarians… Footy went veggie for a while too, but as for Kirk? You couldn't get him to do anything he didn't want to… this was the man who ate frogs and spiders in school and stuff, you know? He looked like a typical skinhead, but was always more into the Dead Kennedys, and a lot of old metal, like Sabbath and Maiden. We'd do gigs where he'd turn up wearing these old trousers and boots covered in concrete, 'cos he'd come straight to the venue from work. A typical chat-up line from him would've been, 'Oi love, what football team do you support?' Whilst dribbling cider all down his chin! You know what I mean?"

By 1984, the band were gigging further afield, including a prestigious support slot to the UK Subs and Fifth Column at London's 100 Club. A second demo was recorded, the eleven-track 'Music For The Streets', the desperately melodic title track of which was included on the 1985 Mortarhate compilation, 'We Won't Be Your Fucking Poor'.

"Being naïve we sent the whole master tape down, 'cos we couldn't afford to get that one song put onto a separate tape, and we never had it back, which is a shame, because we had someone interested in putting all that old stuff out a few years back. But money was always an issue for us, 'cos we were only kids, all on the dole… for example, originally I was going to be the drummer, but when I decided I didn't want to do that, my dad still bought the band a drum-kit, for £150, off this old band called The Deep, and Wedge paid him back every fortnight out of his giro!"

"'Cos I couldn't afford a drum-kit," admits Wedge, "And if Pig's old man hadn't put the money up, I don't know what we would have done…"

"We did the demos in this studio up in Tonypandy, up the top of the Rhondda [Valley]," adds Pig. "And I'm sure it was the same studio that Foreign Legion did their early stuff in. Of course, they put this echo on some of the vocals, and we'd never heard nothing like it, had we? We were jumping for joy over a bit of reverb, it was mad."

An extra guitarist in the shape of Andrew 'Jammy' Rogers joined, in time for some high-profile gigs at the Newport Stowhill Labour Club in 1985, the first of which was with American hardcore legends Hüsker Dü.

"It was their first time over here," remembers Wedge fondly, "and they were something totally different to anything we'd ever seen before. We were still doing this fast street punk with political lyrics, and they were something else altogether; they blew everyone away that night. We took two or three mini-buses down with us, so we had great support, and that's still my favourite gig with the band."

Jammy was replaced by 'Ghandi' [real name Rhys Martin], but then Kirk left, so Classified Protest drafted in Dai 'Cheese', from the brilliantly-named Pork Pie Rabbis, and recorded the 'Out Of Sight, Out Of Mind' demo. One track, 'I Remember', was included on the six-band Welsh punk compilation EP, 'The First Cuts Are The Deepest' (the second release by Newport label, Words Of Warning), alongside I Mobster, The Bugs, Yr Anhrefn, Elfyn Presli and The Heretics (who would later become the awesome Cowboy Killers).

"It was about this time that the guy from 'Beyond The Grave' fanzine offered us a gig up in Presteigne, in some local sports hall place, an all-dayer which The Oppressed were meant to headline [they pulled out, due to illness], with loads of other bands, including Annex UK and Condemned 84… it was my 21st birthday, so it would've been 1986, and a Friday night. The next day we were due to play down in Portsmouth with Ad Nauseam, so we did the Presteigne gig, and it all went tits up; a huge punch-up kicked off between the Condemned 84 and Annex UK fans. Unfortunately, someone got really badly stabbed with a Stanley knife; it was complete chaos, one of the very worse gigs we ever did for violence.

"Anyway, on Sunday morning, just after we got back from a really good gig down in Portsmouth, my front door got kicked in by the Malvern and Worcestershire police, who arrested all of us 'cos the Presteigne promoter had apparently told them that our guitarist, with the Clockwork Orange symbol on his jacket, had been the one who stabbed this guy. That was a nightmare."

After enlisting the services of saxophonist John 'The Busker' for a brief period, in a brave attempt to spread their musical wings, Classified Protest decided that a change was as good as a rest and became the much faster, harder Rectify after recruiting new guitarist Michael 'Mudgey' Mudge from Political Reform in 1987. They had, after all, evolved by this time into something far removed from their earliest efforts at composing.

"We knew our sound was changing," concedes Pig, "To more metallic guitars, more anarchist lyrics, we were sounding more hardcore than street punk… and that was mainly from playing outside the Valleys, and just growing up a little bit in the process… so a name change was definitely in order.

"Classified Protest had a lot of punks and skinheads that followed us around, but here in the Valleys that never made a difference to anyone, 'cos we were all in it together; it was only when we went to places like London that it became a problem. But the main reason for the name change was that we had new members, and a lot of new songs."

In 1988, Rectify released the highly-recommended '20th Century' EP on their own Taffcore label, before issuing a split album with Bazzy (of 'Blown To Bits' fanzine) And The Budgies, the 'Ebullition' cassette, the 1999 'Manmade' CD, and, most recently, the 'Fall On Evil Days' disc, a veritable classic of Welsh hardcore if ever there was one. The band toured Europe many times during the Nineties (their first stint there being in 1991, a seven-week trek as support to Chaos UK), establishing themselves as a major underground force internationally, before splitting in 2000.

"As a Welsh band, we always struggled," reckons Pig, who now fronts This System Kills, alongside ex-members of In The Shit. "We never followed fashions within the punk scene, were never part of any cult… we were just ourselves, but I thought that was what it was all about anyway? The whole anarcho scene sometimes seemed a bit of a bluff for trendy boys, you know what I mean? I think it was another fashion within punk that we could've done without. All the sentiments and ideas were great, but it still had all that bollocks with certain people thinking they were better than everyone else. And the proof of the pudding is when you look at where some of those people are now… I mean, we're still here, still doing our thing, but where are they?"

SELECT DISCOGRAPHY

7"s:
'The First Cuts Are The Deepest' (Words Of Warning, 1986) – six-band compilation

At A Glance:
The band's first two demos are available as a bootleg CDR, but the curious would be best advised to track down 'Out Of Sight, Out Of Mind', or, better still, check out Rectify, who successfully delivered on the potential that Classified Protest always promised.

HE LIVING LEGENDS were a mischievous, albeit rather disposable, punk band from Swansea who released just one single before splitting up, but they managed to cause some memorable chaos during their brief time together, and – more importantly – band founder Ian Bone went on to head **CLASS WAR**, the outspoken and violent anarchist network who became inextricably linked with the anarcho-punk scene via their close ties to bands such as Conflict and The Apostles.

Formed in 1979 (bizarrely enough after a drunken night out to see Paul Young's Q-Tips at Swansea's Patti Pavilion!), the Living Legends were originally called Page Three, and courted controversy from the off.

"When we were choosing a name, someone stuck a pin in a book, and we decided we'd call ourselves whatever it said," admits Ian. "We played quite a few gigs around Swansea, but never anywhere else; we called it 'porno punk'… all the songs were about sex, and we had strippers… a bit like The Tubes really – but nowhere near as good! And we did these hugely shambolic gigs around Swansea… there was one club, Dirty Dora's, and we played there loads of times; we used to get really big crowds, seven or eight hundred people… but there were so many people in the band, and everyone knew everyone else, that by the end of the night, everyone was onstage with us. It was really chaotic, but always a good laugh.

"And then one day we had this idea, seeing as we were called Page Three, 'Why not get The Sun [newspaper] to sue us?' So, I wrote a letter to them, saying, oh, you know… 'I took my children out to see this band, thinking they were associated with The Sun because they were called Page Three, and I was disgusted by their filth!' That kind of tactic… and the very next gig a couple of odd-looking blokes turned up, obviously undercover Sun journalists, and we were summoned to appear in the High Court in London – the proper one, the one you see on TV!

"Keith Allen, the comedian [of 'Comic Strip' fame], drummed for the band for a bit, and he came along for a laugh, and there were about seventeen of us there, everybody looking as punky as fuck, apart from me. So, we all turned up in court, and The Sun had this high-paid lawyer, and idiotically I'd brought with me a copy of the original letter I'd sent to them complaining about us… in fact, I was sat there doodling on it, opposite the judge, and he said, 'Can I have a look at that?' And there he was, looking at the original letter, looking at my handwriting and all that, and I'm sat there thinking, 'We're dead! He's rumbled me!' But he looked up at me and handed it back, and didn't say a fuckin' dicky-bird…

"Eventually he found in favour of The Sun, and said that we had to change our name, and Keith had said earlier, 'Oh, they're living legends…', so he gave us our name really. The Sun asked for costs, like £20,000, but the judge asked us what our means were, and when we said we'd hitched up from Swansea 'cos we didn't have any money, he said, 'I think both sides will meet their own costs on this occasion.' Then he just sort of looked at me and walked out!"

The band dutifully hitched home to South Wales (but not before playing an impromptu set supporting Keith Allen at Raymond's Revue Bar, a strip club in Soho), where they then recorded their best material for posterity, played a notoriously troublesome gig with Crass, and split up.

"Yeah, we had a bit of a fall-out with Crass really," chuckles Ian, wickedly. "We put 'em on with the Poison Girls first, and the club was packed out, but then we got them back to play the St. Phillips Centre, a fucking awful place, and the Living Legends supported them and Dirt. And we completely fell out; they were pacifists and we were advocating violence in every song. I was pissed and ranting, and there were all these football hooligans there from Swansea that we all knew, and I was really winding them up. The whole thing went belly up, and a huge fight started; Crass pulled the plug on us, and to be fair to them, somehow managed to restore some order and went down a storm. Mick Sinclair reviewed it for Sounds, and described us as 'pedestrian pantomime punk', saying that I 'whipped the crowd into a mindless mob frenzy'! We fell out with Crass a bit after that, and I don't really blame them, because I was more at fault than they were, but it all percolated through a bit after Class War started, and we sorted it all out. Even though we still had

Living Legends vocalists Lisa Ambalu, Ian Bone, and Sarah and Amanda Bewara.

political differences over the pacifist thing, at least they realised that I wasn't some wind-up merchant just trying to get mileage out of attacking Crass like Special Duties or whatever.

"After that we staggered on a bit... played a gig with Conflict at the 100 Club... but that was really the end of the Living Legends. We never really had a punk following... none of us ever looked like punks really. We had a few periodic revivals, but it was just a good laugh really; we were more like a wind-up project than a proper band. It was fun to do, but we had other things going on in our lives as well... and besides, music as a force of change was something I was always pretty cynical about anyway. And it was just after the '81 riots all across England, and that's where Class War sprang from; the political ideas had always been more important than the music – the music was just a happy add-on for a few years."

However, a track from the Living Legend demo, 'The Pope Is A Dope', caught the ear of Bill Gilliam, who would later run the Alternative Tentacles label in the UK, but was then setting up his own – short-lived – Upright Records.

"He really liked it for some reason, and it was just before the Pope was due to visit this country so it seemed like the right time to release it. So, Bill called me over, and I think he thought he'd be meeting this punk-as-fuck kinda geezer, and I turned up with this camel-hair, Arthur Daley overcoat, and hair down to my waist 'n' all... and I can almost see him thinking, 'Jesus Christ, I really know how to pick 'em! Why can't anything ever be simple?' Ha!

"Anyway, he said he wanted to put it out, asked me if there was actually a band to promote it... he liked the idea of Keith Allen as well, and he knocked it out as a single on Upright. He pressed about 5000 of them... and I think he probably sold about 500! It crashed into the Indie charts the following week at No. 27... I was hanging around outside this place in Notting Hill that stocked Sounds on a Tuesday, a day earlier than anywhere else, to see where we got to. The following week, it crashed straight out again! He had loads of trouble flogging it... originally he wanted to make it more of a joke single and call it 'The Pope Smokes Dope', but we wanted to go for the more violent imagery, and then someone tried to assassinate the Pope... and we had the Pope on the front cover in a gun sight, and a lot of distributors weren't very happy with that at all. Still, we did a few gigs in London, which were quite a laugh, and that was about it...

"At least until I moved to Cardiff the following year, and the Living Legends were revived with possibly our best line-up: 'Doc' Whelan, Dean Poole, Gareth Joseph, Roland Cleaver, Nicky Evans and me. That was when we recorded a lot of our most offensive stuff – 'Tory Funerals', 'God Bless You, Queen Mum', 'Motherfuckers' and 'Trendy Leftie, Drop Dead' – and we did gigs with the Soldier Dolls, The Oppressed and Demented Are Go. One memorable night in Abergavenny, I threw a chair through the window of what I thought was an expensive antique shop window, hoping to start a riot after the gig, but I was so pissed I threw it through the local barber shop by mistake, and got banged up all weekend, with no rioters trying to liberate me! Legends gigs tended to be like that…"

Ian also began publishing his own revolutionary paper, 'The Scorcher', whilst living in Cardiff, but decided to overhaul his whole approach when he realised that a large percentage of the growing anarcho-punk movement were already sympathetic to his radical politics – if only he could reach them effectively… and hence the 'Class War' paper was borne, complete with a garish skull logo 'borrowed' wholesale from the aforementioned Soldier Dolls.

"It was 1982, and CND and Greenham Common were on the go. Me and my mate Jimmy went on this march in Burford, and we were a bit out of touch with the punk scene at the time, and there were all these dressed-in-black Crass punks running around going, 'Fight war, not wars', and, '2, 4, 6, 8, organise and smash the state', and all that. And we thought, 'Fuckin' hell, this is the kind of market we should tap into!' But they weren't interested in our stupid paper, so we went back home and thought about how to appeal to that faction, 'cos there was a lot of 'em, and they looked dead sexy, running around with their black flags and everything; it was quite exciting.

"We decided we were going to push violent anarchism, and we were gonna make it look like a punk fanzine, big and brash, loads of good graphics and funny little bits… and a lot of people loved it… but a lot of people hated it as well. Some people would only buy it because they thought it was like a comic! But it was meant to be fuckin' funny, it wasn't meant to be something that you took home and put on your mantle piece. When the first issue came out, a lot of older anarchists were saying, 'Well, where's the theory?' Fuck the theory, what's all that about? This was a deep appeal to the irrational!

"It was aimed specifically at the punk movement, at all those people we'd seen at Burford; we wanted to turn all those Crass punk pacifists into violent, street-rioting revolutionaries with a class analysis. And for all our efforts to get away from the punk image for years afterwards, all the people that came on all our actions were all punks! And we weren't, we were a lot older really. But we also 'inherited' a lot of existing anarchist groups that came over to us in London, a lot of really interesting people with a lot of political experience.

"It was only ever intended as a one-off paper, to be truthful; it wasn't meant to last. But we sold over two thousand of the first one, so we did a second one, and then people started taking bundles off us to sell in their own towns, and before we knew it, we had people fucking everywhere.

"By then, I'd moved to London, and we'd had contact with Crass, so in the very second issue of Class War we did this little analysis of them, of what they'd achieved and where we wanted to take it from there. It basically said that they'd made more people anarchists than Kropotkin, but we thought their politics were up shit creek, because of the pacifism issue. It was one of the few articles that we ever had in Class War about music really. There's a little quote from The Apostles down the bottom of that page as well; I liked Andy Martin, he was a really powerful force in the London punk scene. Ian Slaughter and Martin Wright of the London Autonomists were other influential characters about at that time, during the early days of Class War."

The paper quickly generated notoriety, with the tabloids dubbing Ian 'the most evil man in Britain', and full articles about the organisation smeared sensationally across the likes of the News Of The World, the journalists responsible completely missing the blackly humorous inspiration behind every issue.

"There's no doubt about it, my upbringing was weird!" chuckles Ian, when prompted as to just why he ended up fronting Class War. "My dad was a butler, and we lived on all sorts of country estates where he was in service. He was like a left-wing butler though, he wasn't a deferential

Class War turn up at the Henley Regatta, 1985.

one… he was a footman to start with, believe it or not, at this castle in Scotland, but his family were all miners, then after the war, he ended up being a butler. My abiding memory of childhood is of whizzing around the Southern English countryside in the back of a furniture removal van because my dad had been sacked again for being rude to his boss! He'd always pinch a bit of headed notepaper before he went though, to write himself a couple of good references!

"It was a total class background as well, because my dad had to call the people he was working for 'Master this' and 'Master that'. And they would call him by his surname, 'Bone', and it's not the kind of job you can leave behind. You can't walk out the factory gate and say, 'Fuck the boss!' You have to be deferential all the time; we had a tied cottage, so if he lost his job, he lost the house.

"I left home in '65, and went to Swansea University, which was a fucking great time to be at university! We were all hippies in '67 and it was all 'peace and love', and then in '68 it was all violent revolution and I got really politicised. I arrived at anarchism on my own really, but in '68 fuckin' everyone was an anarchist! Which mostly consisted of posing about with long hair and getting stared at… but it was going off in Paris, all over Europe, and we had our own little anarchist group that did loads of stuff. We started getting some national contacts, going up to London on demonstrations; we did the Grosvenor Square one in '68… we were the ones trying to push through. It was a really funny change – in '67 I was a real pacifist, but by '68, I was this crazed 'Citizen Smith' character! That was an important time for anyone who was around then…

"Yet Class War couldn't have happened during any other time but the Eighties, 'cos we had Thatcher – and she herself was waging class war… the miners, the dockers, the print workers at Wapping… it really was gloves off. And gradually people were getting into it, and there was that real change-over that even happened with Crass as well. I mean when the police were smashing the miners, where was the pacifist answer to that? And [the] Stop The City [demonstrations] had been mega too; windows were being smashed, bricks were thrown, vehicles overturned… and Class War was just reflective of that change that was going on, we might have even helped it along a bit.

"And by 1985, we'd virtually won the battle, as it were. There were still a lot of pacifists about, but even Crass had gone to the opposite extreme, almost advocating Angry Brigade-style terrorism! I think when Class War first came out, they probably thought, 'Oh no, it's Ian Bone, that cunt from Swansea!' They didn't think we would last, and we thought their politics were rubbish. But there's no denying that they reached a lot of people, and if it wasn't for Crass there would have been no Class War."

1985 did indeed see Class War at the height of its power, the heavy-handedness of the authorities in quashing all that opposed them attracting even regular folk to the garish, cocky publication.

"Yeah, the miner's were going nuts for the cover with Thatcher getting a cleaver in her head; they thought the Socialist Workers paper was a load of fucking rubbish! A lot of them came down to Stop The City, and our plan was to try and link up the inner city riots with the miners strike, and we decided to instigate a riot in Wood Green on Guy Fawkes night. All the cops were off with the miners, and we thought we could open up a second front in the inner cities... it was no good going on the fuckin' picket lines to support the miners, they didn't need a load of fucking idiots like us turning up telling them how to fight the coppers – they were doing a perfectly good job of that already! We decided the best way to show our support would be to riot, so we all decided to meet in Wood Green, get pissed up in the pubs, then all out come closing time to wreck the fuckin' place! So we get down to Wood Green at about 6.30pm, and there's all these punks wandering around... the most obvious-looking punks you could imagine... all walking about saying, 'Alright, mate, when does the riot start?' Our 'top secret plan' was out the window then, but we did it anyway: got pissed up and trashed Wood Green shopping centre at midnight. Trouble is, the idea was to lure the police in so we could have it out with them, but none of 'em turned up; they just let us get on with it. So in the papers the next day, the headlines were like, '200 punks run amok in shopping centre!' That sort of thing, nothing remotely related to the miners strike or anything.

"The other funny thing that happened in '85 was when we had a do at the Henley Regatta. The idea was, we'd go to them [the rich socialites], and we told everyone that they wouldn't get into Henley if they looked like an obvious punk, y'know? But when we got there, there were all these punks on the train, and then we met up with these punks from Swansea, who'd got there the night before. And two of them had been caught shagging in a shop doorway at 10.00 in the fucking morning... and this is meant to be low profile, y'know? And another of 'em had nicked a boat wheel from some yacht! And it was really funny, because there were all the cops, and all these punks... it was brilliant.

"Bizarrely, our original plan was to take the cops by surprise and launch an attack on Henley police station, but there were about 300 cops in riot vans outside, so we reverted to 'Plan B' – get pissed and storm the bridge to the Royal Enclosure!

"Our ultimate aim was to get away from the punk thing though, and we never did... and I'm not sorry that we didn't now... but we obviously wanted to be more than just a punk movement, we wanted all sorts on our side. We didn't want to dilute the politics, but we wanted to somehow crossover to the mainstream... of course we didn't, but fuck it, it was a really good time while it lasted. We were basically rent-a-mob; we went up to the big miners strike at Mansfield, and they were really pissed off with political papers, but when they saw us, they were like, 'Fuckin' Class War! Yaay!' And they were all like, 'When's the next Stop The City?' It was one of those magic moments, a dream come true, a revolutionary's wet dream.

"We really thought we were going to change the world for a moment back then! The reality of Class War though, there was no membership as such, and a lot of people thought they were in it... anyone could be in it, in fact... and we did have a few odd characters, fuckin' hell. We had a really brilliant conference in Caxton Hall in '85; it was fucking heaving in there, must have been about three hundred people turned up. And at most anarchist meetings, they're on about all these dead people from Spain, 1936... all totally irrelevant to most of us. All we had were different people getting up and saying what they thought about whatever they wanted! We had football hooligans, women cleaners, loads of blacks from Brixton, miners, punks of course... and all these older anarchists were saying, 'Where'd you fucking find all these people?'

"Needless to say, I was pissed up – alcohol always played a big part in Class War – and come mid-afternoon I had to make a speech. So I got up, and said, 'There's fucking old people dying of hypothermia, right...' And you could almost see my brain ticking over, wondering what to say next! 'There's fucking middle-aged people dying of hypothermia...' And a few people are saying, 'Yes, yes, that's right!' Then I say, after a big pause, 'And there's fucking young people dying of hypothermia!' And a few people are thinking, 'Alright, we've got the point now...' And then all I could think to say next was, 'Fuckin' everybody's dying of hypothermia!' And completely lost the plot!

"But it was great, right after the miners strike and Stop The City, there was the Battle of The Bean Field [the brutal police ambush in June 1985 of a peace convoy en route to the Stonehenge free festival]… then Henley Regatta was like the week after… we had a fucking force at our disposal. Then Joe Strummer did that 'Rock Against The Rich' tour for us in '87, which was brilliant. He paid all his own costs, to bring all his band over from the States, and he did about 30 dates in the end! The idea was, something was already going on in each place he played, some local struggle, so it wasn't just any old gig, not just an excuse to put Strummer on. Years later, he was being interviewed by someone, and he said, 'The best organised tour I've ever played was organised by anarchists!'

"It was brilliant. There was a great gig at the Brodsworth Miners Welfare Club, Doncaster, and I was nearly in fuckin' tears. All these miners who really respected The Clash and Joe, all stood there cheering him, like a mutual love fest… he was there for hours after the gig meeting them all. It just shows that my cynicism about music ever changing things isn't always true; it certainly had a beneficial effect that night."

In 1986, Ian teamed up with his mates in Conflict ("Colin and that lot were Eltham street boys, people who would sooner go down the boozer and get involved in a punch-up than hang around a commune…") to release a Class War single on their label, Mortarhate. Recorded at London's Alaska Studios during May of that year, 'Better Dead Than Wed' was a jovial tirade against the monarchy, in particular the excessive amount of tax-payer's money to be lavished on the [July '86] marriage between Prince Andrew and Sarah 'Fergie' Ferguson, the Duchess Of York.

Despite being a rather rock'n'roll affair compared to most releases on Mortarhate, it managed a respectable placing of No. 5 in the Independent Charts, although that was possibly more on the basis of the record's admirable intent than on any especial musical merit.

By 1987 though, Class War's momentum was stalling, with inevitable internal pressures fragmenting the group, and although there is still a Class War in existence even today, Ian Bone stepped down as its public figurehead long before the Eighties drew to a close. His politics haven't mellowed over the years though, as his recent 'Anarchist' novel demonstrates; a semi-autobiographical, part-wish-fulfilment stream of consciousness, it is as blackly humorous as it is sensationally shocking.

"People started falling out with each other," he says, of Class War's inevitable decline. "Other things came along… people realised the revolution wasn't about to happen… basically people had other things to do with their lives. And it was quite intense too, for us in London at least; it was your whole life really. Which was good, we wanted to be professional revolutionaries at the time, but it was wearing, and there were lots of not-so-funny moments. We had a lot of problems with fascists and Combat 18; we had three young kids, living in a tower block in Hackney, and we were having lighted stuff pushed through our letter box, threats from all these fascists.

"Once I'd been picked out as the leader, I was always in the papers, and then the Sunday People did that front cover with me as 'The most evil man in Britain'! 'Evil'? 'Most dangerous' would have been good, but 'evil'? Was I worse than the Yorkshire Ripper? And my mum didn't like that, her son being called evil in the papers, and all the neighbours were giving me funny looks, thinking I was going to kill them or something, and it sounds sad, but it's those little things that do get to you in the end.

"I can remember going out to get a Sunday paper one morning, and I saw this bloke leap out of the hedge about thirty yards away, and he adopted this sort of kneeling position… and I thought he was going to shoot me, but it was just a photographer for the Sunday People. And I dived for cover, just an instant reaction, and that was the photo they used in the paper, of me with this wonky look on my face diving for cover, looking like a fucking idiot…

"We didn't want to make ourselves rich or anything as simplistic as that," explains the perpetually misunderstood Bone, on the basically honourable principles behind Class War. "We wanted to get rid of the class system that kept us poor… get rid of the ruling classes. I had fairly traditional anarchist ideals of equality and liberty… still do, in fact, and I remain optimistic about radical social change, and do we ever need it! How can you have a world system where millions of people are starving and then you have a fortunate few poncing around with conspicuous wealth? But the big problem now is, that post-9/11, with everyone so concerned about terrorism, this sort of change is more or less off the agenda.

"There was a peculiar time in the Eighties though, when a very ideologically-driven Conservative government set out to destroy the working class. Anywhere where working class people congregated, they wanted to destroy… they wanted to destroy whole communities… they wanted to destroy Stonehenge, well the festival at least. They wanted to have police at Notting Hill Carnival, they wanted to get rid of standing terraces at football… just chipping away at any and every collective experience of working class people. There was a conscious effort made at gentrification of whole areas of London; turn the houses into yuppie flats, move all the artists in… policing by design really. You didn't have to worry about inner city riots if you'd sent all the working class people out to Basildon! When Thatcher said she was going to do something about the inner cities, she didn't mean make them better for the people living there; she intended to drive the potentially troublesome elements out and yuppify them.

"I certainly thought we'd get bigger and bigger until we had an uprising. It didn't seem too far off in '85, there were a lot of people prepared to fight with all their means; there were a lot of people who were very brave. There were a lot of very sound people in Class War; it represented all that was best in working class values. It was a stand against Thatcher constantly saying that everything was all about the individual, that there wasn't any such thing as society anymore; we had a real sense of class consciousness.

"We were doing 15,000 of each issue at our biggest, which doesn't sound that big, but when you compare it to the other anarchist papers like Freedom; they were only doing 2000 tops. People would say it was just a laugh – but it was meant to be! But it's satire and scandal-mongering that has always undermined the state here in England; we've got a brilliant tradition in this country of anonymous pamphleteers and people who really expose corruption, and we saw ourselves as part of that whole line going back to the Levellers and the Diggers in the Civil War. We didn't worship all the usual anarchist heroes, we were very much about the here and now, and couldn't see the relevance of peasant wars in the Ukraine… and if we could have produced a 30-page tabloid, we would have! We would've filled it with greyhounds, horse-racing, boxing, and wrestling, and nothing else – the rest of it was all middle class!"

SELECT DISCOGRAPHY

7"s:
'The Pope Is A Dope' (Upright, 1981) – as Living Legends
'Better Dead Than Wed' (Mortarhate, 1986) – as Class War

At A Glance:
No official retrospective of the Legends is likely to appear on CD in the foreseeable future, but the Class War EP, 'Better Dead Than Wed', appears in its entirety on Mortarhate's 'A Compilation Of Deleted Dialogue: The Singles'. Elsewhere, the BBP Records cassette, 'Living Legends: Greatest Hits 1980 – 1999' contains all the 'Cardiff recordings', as well as the Upright single and even several Page Three numbers. Ian Bone's much-anticipated book, 'Bash The Rich: True Life Confessions Of An Anarchist In The UK' is set for publication by Faragher Jones in October 2006; he is contactable at: localnews4us@yahoo.co.uk, whilst Class War can be found at PO Box 467, London, E8 3QX, England.

CHAPTER FIVE

Many may question the validity of including **THE CRAVATS** in a book about anarcho-punk (including The Cravats themselves, in typically contrary fashion), but Penny Rimbaud of Crass enjoyed the oddball forces at work in their music enough to volunteer to produce their fourth single, 'You're Driving Me' (backed by the brilliant 'I Am The Dreg'). And there's no doubting that their subsequent single for Crass remains one of the most memorable the label ever issued, if only for the sheer number of punk foreheads it provoked to be furrowed in complete confusion. Indeed, if anarchy was a musical entity, it might well sound just like The Cravats, an ever-shifting, uncompromising racket that means something uniquely personal and surprisingly enlightening to each individual that encounters it.

"We were cocooned in a small town," explains bassist/vocalist 'The Shend', of their humble origins in Redditch during 1977, "And I didn't really regard ourselves as punk… more as oddballs who had found a movement that we could awkwardly fit into with the help of a very large shoehorn. Yes, I had hair like the hero from [the David Lynch movie] 'Eraserhead' and wore orange boots, but I just liked the reaction that created… plus it saved me from ever becoming assistant manager of Tesco!

"As for anarcho punk, we were only really associated with that due to the fact that the awesome Crass boys and girls helped us reach a wider audience… we never played with any anarcho bands really, apart from the Poison Girls at Chat's Palace [and Honey Bane at the London Hope And Anchor]. In fact, we played gigs in the early days with such awful bands as Blind Owl and Speed Limit, who were about as anarchic as Barclays bank!"

"But it was punk that fired us up," adds guitarist/vocalist Robin Dallaway. "It seemed to allow for a whole variety of types of expression. Sadly that phase didn't last long and it soon got all narrow and codified, with a very recognisable uniform, but that first blast did spawn loads of great bands and creativity. We wandered off in our own direction pretty quickly too, drawing on wider influences like jazz and rockabilly. We grabbed music back for ourselves, made songs about all the stuff that interested and affected us. It was so incredibly exciting, it was a revelation.

"I have to disagree with your comment about our music though; I don't think that it was anarchic at all. It was highly structured and very rehearsed; I was amazed at the skill and discipline listening back to our stuff, when I was working on tracks for the forthcoming compilation CD…"

Joined by Mart E. Knee on second guitar and Ethos Yapp on drums ("None of us had ever played a note," laughs The Shend, "And we only had a pair of bongos and an acoustic guitar between us!"), The Cravats set out their unorthodox stall at the earliest opportunity, making their auspicious public debut at an Alcester Grammar School's open day for parents.

"Except the headmaster advised all parents to leave the room because we were about to play!" recalls Shend proudly. "We were excreting breeze blocks as we waited behind the giant red velvet curtains for the off, but had prepared four songs: 'Crash Barrier Dancer', 'Shut Up', 'Precinct' [which would eventually be recorded as the A-side of their third single] and 'I Hate The Universe' [later to appear as part of their second EP]. The curtains parted and the whole hall was stuffed with kids, and, as we started playing, they went bananas, screaming and yelling like banshees. We were slightly non-plussed at this dramatic show of manic affection, but made it to the end intact, and then the headmaster declared that no pop group would ever play in the school again!"

"I remember morosely sitting outside the hall because the friend of a friend, who we had

Cravats (from left to right: David Bennett, The Shend, Robin Dallaway, and Svoor Naan).

persuaded to lend us a PA, hadn't turned up," says Robin. "It wasn't going to be loud enough and there would be nothing to sing through. Then, at the last minute, he showed – yeah hey! – and we looked out through a window just before the gig, and could see loads of kids waiting to try and get in before we went on. We were so scared, but making such a big noise, especially at school, was just brilliant."

And how truly bizarre that 'big noise' was. Somewhere between Killing Joke, The Stranglers and Captain Beefheart, albeit filtered heavily through an eclectic vein of electronic, industrial and jazz influences (those wanting to hear an Eighties precursor to Primus and Mr. Bungle would be well advised to check out 'Daddy's Shoes' from 'The Colossal Tunes Out' LP), The Cravats remain to this day a 'love 'em or hate 'em' proposition.

After self-releasing their 'Gordon' (b/w 'Situations') 7" in 1978 (recorded at Outlaw Studios in Birmingham, using Judas Priest's drum kit… following which Svoor Naan and David Bennett took over on saxophone and drums, respectively), the band hooked up with Small Wonder, who released four singles (a further 7" was issued by Glass) and 'The Cravats… In Toy Town' album over the next four years, during which time they were also invited to record four sessions for John Peel, who always had an ear for the adventurous and unconventional.

"Not only did he give us four sessions," points out Shend, "But knowing how important the PRS payments were to us small bands, he used to even play two or three tracks a night in order to help us out financially. He was responsible for most good music even being heard in the first place, and I'd actually say he was the most influential person ever in British music; he gave everybody a chance. I always thought how this bloke had championed Jimi Hendrix and Roxy Music, and here he was, playing our discs with the same enthusiasm and joy. It was always personal to him and everybody felt he was their best chum... except golfers and U2, which was fine by me. He is one person I miss more than any other, if the truth be known."

"We got precious little positive feedback from elsewhere," offers Robin. "I don't think many people understood what we were up to, but Peel got it right away, and I was just so humbled to be in the company of all the other artists that he supported over the years, very often going against the grain of popular taste. Using the 'Beeb' [BBC] studios at Maida Vale was a fantastic experience for us, an opportunity to try out things whilst using the best engineers and equipment. Peel was extraordinary; his breadth of taste and generosity were unique. I'm proud to have known him."

As mentioned earlier though, John Peel wasn't the only one to pick up on the band's skewed potential; Penny Rimbaud produced the 'You're Driving Me' single, then invited the band to record a single for Crass, and an album for the closely affiliated Corpus Christi label.

"I never felt uncomfortable about anything to do with Crass," reckons Shend, "Because they were truly lovely people who did what they believed, and did it well. In a musical world of opportunist, jump-on-the-bandwagon ne'er-do-wells, we were very happy to be associated with folk of integrity and warmth. We too appealed to a wide variety of people who felt at odds with society, and the fact they had us on the label showed how open they actually were to new ideas and different styles. I loved them then and I love them now."

Robin: "And Penny has a great sense of fun, and of the absurd. We had a great time working with him. We didn't fit the profile of a typical Crass band, but I think it speaks of their generosity and breadth of taste that they wanted to work with us...

"Penny definitely has something too, when he describes us as 'freeform jazz meets German industrialism'... although it makes us sound a little serious and difficult. I would add that other important strands of our sound, especially for the later stuff, were rockabilly and be-bop. Some of it is very extreme, but I think it grooves too..."

"Well, my dad was Austrian and worked in the Bauhaus factory for a while, bending chrome pipes," comes the Shendian interjection. "But Rob has always been better at defining our sound, while I'm better at eating cakes."

During this time, The Cravats bemused audiences everywhere with their unpredictable live performances, a typical show usually involving chaotic performance art, not to mention vacuum cleaners and coffee percolators!

"Well, 'typical' was not a word in our musical vocabulary," scoffs Shend. "Yes, we were often suited in charity shop dress suits, white shirts and ties, and we had a TV set onstage being watched by Mr H. (a huge 50-year-old businessman from our hometown) who sat in a comfy chair, alternating his viewing with reading the paper. We had cassette players held up to microphones, and the various household appliances of which you make mention.

"Svoor Naan, the sax player, would rush about manically, turning on his various antiquated effects, and might even play clarinet and sax at the same time on occasion. A huge white 'C' in a circle hung behind us, and we would usually end with a blistering, ear-popping rendition of 'I Hate The Universe', which is when everything that could be broken would be, and Mr H. would attack his comfy chair with gusto. Due to the resulting carnage, encores tended to be few and far between...!"

The second album, which spent a month in the Independent charts upon its release in early 1984, peaking at No. 22, included a flexi-disc introducing the outfit's D.c.L. offshoot project: the Dada-Cravat Laboratories, through which they unveiled music as The Babymen, D.c.L Locomotive and The Very Things, who were especially prolific, releasing three albums and five singles, including 'Let's Go Out' for Derek Birkett's One Little Indian label in 1987.

They returned as The Cravats once again (with new drummer – and D.c.L. collaborator – Robin Holland replacing David Bennett, who had joined Poison Girls), for '85's curious 'The Land Of The Giants' 12" on Reflex Records.

"The Cravats never really split though," claims Shend (in fact, they've just released the 'Séance' single on Caroline True Records, working in conjunction with Paul Hartnoll of Orbital fame). "We just went and played in the garden for twenty years until tea was ready! I also had a psycho-grunge-biker band called Grimetime, who did an LP called 'Spirit Of Disgust' [Kill City Records, 1994], and then I became a thug on the telly, acting in stuff such as Guy Richie's 'Revolver' film, 'Red Dwarf', 'Men Behaving Badly' and loads of other jolly televisual and cinematic fare – which suits my cartoon world down to the ground. I also run a suave Vegas Lounge Club in Brighton called The Kroon Kat Lounge [www.kroonkat.com].

"As for modern day punk rock…? There are still some like-minded souls making good music but I don't see a musical threat to the establishment anymore, although bands like Coldplay may unwittingly cause people to give up their reason to live. The threat to the establishment, as far as I can see, comes from the actions of that establishment against those they do not think are a part of it.

"I can honestly say I still hold most of the views I had then, as that was the time I formulated many opinions due to my constant yearning to learn. As you get older, it is suggested your anger begins to mellow, but I would dispute this as, if anything, the older I become the more I understand why I was angry in the first place."

SELECT DISCOGRAPHY

7"s:
'Gordon' (self-released, 1978) – although later copies re-labelled 'Small Wonder'
'Burning Bridges' (Small Wonder, 1979)
'Precinct' (Small Wonder, 1980)
'You're Driving Me' (Small Wonder, 1981)
'Off The Beach' (Small Wonder, 1981)
'Terminus' (Glass, 1982)
'Rub Me Out' (Crass, 1982)

12"s:
'The Land Of The Giants' (Reflex, 1985)

LPs:
'The Cravats… In Toytown' (Small Wonder, 1980)
'The Colossal Tunes Out' (Corpus Christi, 1982)

At A Glance:
Robin Dallaway (who is also working on the jazzy dance music project, Silverlake: www.silverlake.ukgo.com) is currently compiling a double retrospective Cravats CD for release by Overground during late 2006.

Wolverhampton-based **CONTEMPT** became quite a strong draw on the Midlands punk circuit in the mid- to late-Eighties, but the politically charged band actually emerged from the ashes of a far more obscure Black Country act, Vendetta.

"I'd been trying to get a band together since about 1979, mainly with some mates from school in Telford," recalls guitarist Martin Shaw. "We'd come up with some embryonic names for the band such as The Dissidents and The Stapes and even written a few songs. We had a few attempted rehearsals at my parents' house and a local youth club, but didn't get very far.

"There was a very healthy scene in Telford back then; St. Mick's, the aforementioned youth club, was a hive of activity in terms of the local punk scene. As well as providing rehearsal space for many local bands, it was home to the infamous 'Guttersnipe' fanzine, which achieved notoriety on a national as well as local level and was even featured on a BBC2 'Arena' programme!

"I remember going there when I first started to play guitar and being taught how to play bar chords by a French punk called Bruno who was on the run from his national service back in France and living with some of the locals!

"I suppose it was the music and its anti-establishment nature that drew me to punk rock in the first place. Like all my mates from school, I'd started listening to punk in 1977, but at the time I was also getting interested in politics and became involved in the Anti-Nazi League and going to Rock Against Racism gigs. To me punk was always more than just a fashion or a musical style, it was a way of life; a way of channelling and vocalising my political views. I suppose that's why I'm still playing it all these years later.

"And the second wave became even more political, which I personally felt was a good thing. Bands were very much into the anti-war message, were pro-CND, pro-animal rights and stuff. As well as playing music, we were very active in other ways, going hunt-sabbing, attending Stop The City marches and various other demonstrations, and there were always loads of punks at these events, which was great to see. To me, that side of it was just as important as the music. Bands like Crass were promoting an alternative, anarchist lifestyle, which we had a lot of sympathy for at the time...

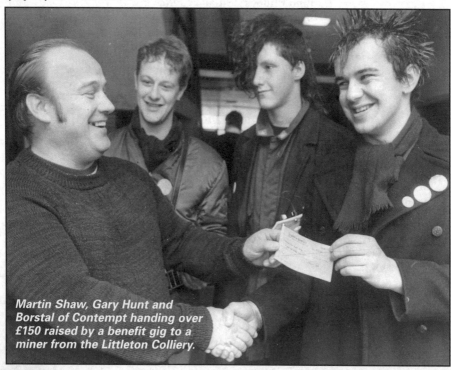

Martin Shaw, Gary Hunt and Borstal of Contempt handing over £150 raised by a benefit gig to a miner from the Littleton Colliery.

"And we had loads of bands in our area: Limited Talent, Platinum Needles, Orinj and Yella Curtain Raylz, Misurabul Barstewards and The Bored, to name but a few... the latter even featured on one of the 'Bullshit Detector' albums put out by Crass ['Volume Two', with the track, 'Riot Style']...

"Anyway, I left home at eighteen, in 1981, and went to live in Wolverhampton," he continues, on the actual origins of Vendetta. "Whilst I was there I linked up with some lads from the local Polytechnic who were into punk, and a few of us shared a house in Chapel Ash known locally as 'The Squat'. It wasn't a squat really, though; we rented it off a private landlord, but it sounded good for the street cred! Anyway, a couple of us could play a bit, so we decided to try and get a band together."

As well as Martin on guitar, that very first incarnation also included Jimmy 'Jazz' Lawton on bass, 'Junkie' John Cartmell on drums, and 'a lad called Pete from Brum' ("A bit of a strange character really; obsessed with doom and gloom, more of a goth than a punk...") on vocals. He only played one gig with the band, their first, which took place during September 1982, at The Crown in Dudley.

"We were supporting a band from Shropshire called the Stoned Rayzens. I shit myself big style; I can remember standing there playing and me knees were literally knocking! I think we'd only been together about six weeks and had a very short set, but somehow we bluffed our way through it. People said we sounded okay, but whether they were just being polite or not, who knows?"

Vocal duties were then taken over by fellow 'Telfordian' Pete Cowley, who had also moved to Wolverhampton, and the band began to gig locally in earnest. The Squat's cellar provided a useful rehearsal space, and was shared by several other local bands, including In Sex, whose drummer Martin Gilkes went on to find fame and fortune with The Wonder Stuff.

"Eventually Pete and John left the area and arch-anarchist Carlton [Griffiths] took over vocal duties, and Rick [Hermolle] came in on drums... Carlton was actually related to Stu 'Pid' [Jones, who would later end up fronting Contempt in the mid-Nineties]. It was this line up that recorded the Vendetta tracks for the 'Aristocrap' EP."

Funded by Nick Moss (who himself would also later turn up in Contempt), the EP was a showcase for several upcoming Wolverhampton punk outfits, and, as well as Vendetta, featured Seventh Plague and Nick's own band at the time, Pulex Irritans. He not only funded the pressing of the single, but also the recording, and named his label Relegated in honour of local football team, Wolverhampton Wanderers, who had fallen four divisions in consecutive seasons. The powerful, brooding 'Painful Death' by Seventh Plague remains the stand-out track, although Vendetta fare competently enough, especially with 'How Much Longer?' (their other contribution, 'Underground', is a tad generic).

Although a decent – admittedly rough and ready – snapshot of three enthusiastic young bands struggling to find their own style and direction (not to mention their feet in the recording studio), Martin holds little love for the release with the benefit of hindsight.

"The session for the EP was a nightmare; we were all pretty nervous about it, to be honest. I don't think the engineer helped, as he wasn't really into our music at all. We had to do take after take, but couldn't get it right; we gave up in the end, and we weren't happy with the final product. We wanted to go back and re-record the tracks really, but couldn't afford it."

Vendetta only played twenty shows in total, including a memorable date at Wolverhampton Polytechnic in March 1983 supporting The Lurkers, and a date in Northern Ireland with Seventh Plague.

"That was an experience! Borstal [real name Mark Shaw], who was singing for Seventh Plague at the time, had made contact with a couple of girls over there via the 'Punk Lives' magazine. We'd got this vision of Northern Ireland, because of how the troubles were portrayed in the media, as being some kind of war-ravaged country and we ended up playing a quiet picturesque little seaside town [Port Stewart], which was an eye opener. Despite everything that was happening over there,

Contempt, Borstal (left) and Martin (right), lost in London, Stop The City.

most people were quietly getting on with their lives."

Soon after the release of 'Aristocrap' however, all three bands that appeared promptly split up.

"I'm not sure why really," ponders Martin. "I suppose people wanted to go off in different musical directions and form new bands. As well as Contempt, a band called The Innocent were formed who were a bit more arty in their approach, and also Primal Trash who were more glam punk, both with members of the various bands who were on the EP. As far as Vendetta were concerned though, we'd gone as far as we could with that line-up, and the time was right to move on."

Contempt came into being in early 1984, originally a three-piece with Martin being joined by Rick from Vendetta and Nick from Pulex Irritans. Eventually Borstal from Seventh Plague joined on vocals.

"We didn't differ that much from Vendetta, although musically we were harder, I suppose. In fact we even carried on playing a couple of Vendetta songs in the set. We also did an old fave from the Seventh Plague set, 'Frank Sinatra Is A Bastard'. And a version of the Pulex song from 'Aristocrap', 'I Hate Tories', with new lyrics."

Contempt's vinyl debut came in 1986 with the 'Familiarity Breeds...' 7" on their own label, Insurrection ("Again the recording was a bit naff... too much reverb and just weak overall... I don't think the engineer was that interested in what we were doing, to be honest!"). And with circumstances conspiring against them, it would be another six long years before any further vinyl bearing the Contempt name would see the light of day.

"Yeah, the late Eighties and early Nineties was a tough time for us with a myriad of line-up changes affecting our progress. We recorded three or four demos, and had tracks on various compilation tapes, and we were still gigging regularly, then Borstal left the band and went to live in Exeter. There was a big [hunt] sabbing scene down there, and he went to live with some old mates of ours."

Mark Maher joined the fold as both vocalist and rhythm guitarist, but didn't reign for long, lasting just a few gigs, one of which was supporting the Subhumans at the Sugarhill Club in Dudley. The nomadic Borstal was enticed back soon after, only to depart again in 1987. Predictably enough, that wasn't the last to be heard of him though...

"So, we went down to a three piece with me on vocals, Rick on drums and Phil 'The Hippy' on bass. Then the original line-up got back together again... just as a celebration of Wolves winning the Sherpa Van trophy and the old Fourth Division championship in 1988, but we decided to carry on. Stu [Pid] joined in April 1991, with Borstal's last gig before then supporting Conflict at the Moseley Dance Centre in Brum. He later rejoined the band for his fourth stint in 1995 when Stu left to join the English Dogs. This was under his new guise as 'Stan'... due to his striking resemblance to Stan Ogden of 'Coronation Street' fame!

"All these line-up changes over the years have really held us back. We'd just get settled together, work up a decent set and then all of sudden somebody would decide to leave and we'd have to start again. I worked it out the other day that since we started we've had six lead singers (including myself), seven bassists, eight drummers, six rhythm guitarists and one lead guitarist... me! Very frustrating!"

The 'Still Fighting On' album was 'nearly' released in 1990 [it eventually emerged through Retch in 1994] by Paul 'Percy' Perciville ("An old mate of ours from Walsall!") of Duck Pond Records, who had previously released 'Wisdom, Magick, Chaos' by Walsall band, Bliss The Pocket Opera. A Contempt LP was the next release planned, but unfortunately never happened.

"And the scene just generally changed at that time," sighs Martin. "The harder thrash stuff and American influenced hardcore came to the fore and perhaps our style of singalong punk wasn't as popular as it used to be. We were still active politically though, and got heavily involved in the local anti-poll tax campaign, doing loads of benefits etc."

Their perseverance eventually paid off though, and Contempt have become a well-known act on the European touring circuit, with several EPs and LPs released to much critical acclaim during the late Nineties. The 'Frantic' EP on Angry Scenes is the band's latest offering, and they are currently working on a brand new album.

"Definitely for the worse," laughs Martin, when asked whether he feels his involvement with punk has changed him for better or worse. "I've become a boring old middle-aged fart still ranting and raging like some punk version of Victor Meldrew! Seriously though, I do think it's had a positive effect on me. I turned vegetarian at nineteen, largely as a result of listening to bands like Crass, Flux and Conflict, and have been a veggie ever since. Many of the principles I held dear in my early punk days I still hold true to now, even though I'm probably not as active as I used to be. Sounds corny, but I think punk has definitely played a major part in making me the man I am today."

Adding on the thorny subject of modern-day punk rock: "Very bland and inane, sugar-coated and sanitised... MTV fodder, basically. I look at some of these younger bands and think they're missing the point. They've taken what I see as the more frivolous elements of punk, mainly the image, and packaged it with unchallenging 'pop' lyrics to create a very weak – and ultimately impotent – hybrid. It's a shame really, because musically some of the bands do sound really good."

SELECT DISCOGRAPHY

7"s:
'Familiarity Breeds....' (Insurrection, 1986)
'12 Years On' (Insurrection, 1992)
'ACAB' (Barbaren, 1994)
'War On The Poor' (Harmony, 1997)
'Justice For Who?' (Data, 2000)
'Frantic' (Angry Scenes, 2006)

LPs:
'Still Fighting On' (Retch, 1994)
'Fuck Off Royal Parasite – Live' (Red Rossetten, 1995)
'Shouting The Odds' (Bomb Factory, 1998)

At A Glance:
German label, Not Clever Records, has the twenty-track 'Best Before 2005' CDR retrospective available as an official bootleg, but Martin has no hesitation in nominating Bomb Factory's 'Shouting The Odds' disc as the band's best release. "No offence to the other singers we've had, but Stan/Borstal had the voice most suited to our material, and I think a lot of our better stuff was written with him in the band."

The Sears in their practice space, 1983, left to right: Aleric [not a band member!], Taffy [on shoulders], Corny, Nick, and Alan [on shoulders].

Hailing from Wednesbury in the Midlands, a stone's throw from junction 9 of the M6, **THE SEARS** are one of anarcho-punk's best-kept secrets. Effortlessly tuneful, and with striking female vocals far removed from the screech'n'scratch school of yelling that many a punkette seemed to graduate from, they tragically only have one official release to their name, the brilliant 'If Only…' 12" for Bluurg, but it's more than enough to ensure they'll not soon be forgotten by fans of the genre.

Formed in January 1981, The Sears (who were actually known as The Wait, for a few short weeks, after the Killing Joke song) originally comprised guitarist Dave Nicholls, bassist Nick Jardine, vocalist Clare 'Corny' Taylor (who was then Nick's girlfriend), with Kevin Thickett being the first in a Spinal Tap-esque string of drummers.

"We were all at school together, and we started out practising in Nick's mum's loft," explains Dave. "The funny thing was, the drummer used to play plastic dustbins, and after a while, when you went up the stairs and looked up at the roof, all the plaster had cracked – the ceiling was coming down – because we were rocking out, dude!

"I remember the first time I met Corny – and she scared the shit out of me! Just the way she looked, the way she acted… but I was really into music and just wanted to play guitar. I bought this old electric thing, but couldn't play that to start with, 'cos I never practised, and we eventually turned that into a bass for Nick! Took the strings off, put a new bridge on it, and some bass strings; it sounded good 'n' all… the best bass he ever had!"

"The only one I could play anyway!" laughs Nick. "It was a Gibson SG copy, ha!"

Taking great inspiration from the nearby Birmingham punk scene, where the band would travel every weekend to see bands such as GBH, Dead Wretched and Drongos For Europe in venues like the Cedar Club and the Golden Eagle, The Sears were soon making their own live debut. At the Holyhead Youth Centre in Wednesbury on May 11th, 1981, where, as well as a clutch of original compositions, they even performed covers of Penetration ('Free Money') and Crass ('Shaved Women'). "It was just us and all our mates, and our little 50 watt PA!" reckons Nick. "We had people from Walsall and Birmingham, all these scruffy punks descending on this little youth club… but it was really good."

"I can remember plugging in these lights we'd borrowed," chuckles Dave, "Just a basic red light with an on/off switch… and I got a savage electric shock. I remember that to this day, what a pisser…"

A little known fact about The Sears is that they weren't always a purely female-fronted band… they briefly had a second – male – vocalist, 'Gnasher', but he only played one gig with them, at the Roebuck pub, Erdington, Birmingham, on November 19th, 1981.

"He answered an ad we placed in Sounds," elaborates Dave. "We only did the one gig with him 'cos he ripped us off a load of money – and that was the end of that!"

It was also about this time that the band began to demonstrate their severe inability to keep a regular drummer. Kevin Thickett was the first to go.

"He lasted about six months, 'cos he was crap!" reveals Nick, with a complete lack of malice. "He only had a bin to play on, mind you… we even had a bin with a snare taped underneath it… that was our best drum! And it was my dad's bin, for fermenting wine in… he was well pissed off, 'cos it was all fucked, with holes drilled in the bottom! We'd just covered them all in fucking brown tape… brilliant!"

He was replaced by Chris Boot, the band's "first proper drummer" ("Well, he had a drum kit anyway!"), who himself was replaced by Allan Higginson. By this time however, Dave had temporarily left the band over what can only be described as a trivial misunderstanding, leaving them to record their first demo – a rather impressive three-song affair, committed to tape in a local eight-track studio during July 1982 – without him.

"I got us a gig at the Cedar Club," says Nick. "I spent six months trying to get us a gig there, I begged and begged and begged… and then Dave decided he didn't wanna do it! I absolutely loved that club; my whole ambition in life was to play a gig there, and when I finally got us on one, after creeping around the manager for god knows how long – it was supporting the UK Subs 'n' all – he wouldn't do it. We had a big fight about it, didn't we? Proper fisticuffs!"

"Well, it was Chris really, wasn't it?" claims Dave. "He decided he wanted to go out and get pissed the same night as the gig… and I went with him – what a fuckin' idiot! So, I left the band for about eight months, or a year or something; it was during '82 anyway. And when I came back, Allan was the drummer and Taffy was the guitar player, so it was back to two guitarists. And Allan was a proper drummer, he could really play…"

"But Taffy as a guitarist? He made a better football player!" guffaws Nick. "But don't put that in your book! He was a really nice chap… but couldn't tune up! I had to ask him to leave in the end, which was a shame, but he just shrugged his shoulders and took it in his stride…"

Dave: "When I look back at The Sears, I always look back to Allan, and think that was when

The Sears, Bristol, July 1985 (left to right: Corny, Dave, and Faz).

The Sears, live at the Digbeth Civic Hall, Birmingham, April 1984, picture by Paul May (left to right: Dave, Corny, and Nick).

we first started playing properly; I always liked that line-up."

"But he went mental, didn't he?" interjects Nick. "Coming out with all this bollocks about his mum being dead, and she wasn't… we used to knock his door and she'd answer it! He'd come to practise with bandages on his arms, saying he'd slit his wrists… in the end, he just pissed off somewhere and never came back."

Meanwhile, The Sears made their London debut, supporting Conflict and Anthrax at The Moonlight Club in West Hampstead on September 26th, 1982, a benefit gig for the ALF. Another London date with Conflict (and the Icons Of Filth) resulted, this time to raise money for the Anti-Whaling League, at the 100 Club on April 21st, 1983.

Back at home though, the drummer soap opera continued unabated, with local thrasher James 'Bradda' Bradley replacing Allan ("He was so fast, he had to go," sighs Dave, "And that was hard for me, 'cos he was a good mate of mine…") before the band recruited Ian 'Batesy' Bates. It was this line-up that recorded the aforementioned 'If Only…'12" for Bluurg. Prior to that there was talk of a 7" for Mortarhate, which never progressed past the initial negotiation stages.

"We were really, really disappointed with the record, though," groans Nick. "It's fucking terrible! We were there for nearly a week [during early June, 1984], put a lot of time and effort into it, and when we played it back… well, it was shite. The timing's out, the tuning's out… Batesy was a bit of a nightmare, in that respect… I just can't listen to it, 'cos of all the mistakes we made. Everything was rushed from the minute we got there; we even had to go and hire drums and amps and stuff… it was just a big fuck-up from day one.

"And we'd done a load of artwork to take down with us, but none of that was used, 'cos Dick didn't really like it. At the last minute on the last day, it was like, 'Right, let's pop upstairs 'cos we gotta get the cover done!' I'm really glad we did it, but I look at it now, and think, 'Fuckin' hell…' We'd all been looking forward to it so much, and it turned out a bag of shit in the end; we were really despondent afterwards…"

"Dick and Bruce produced it," adds Dave. "And, not being disrespectful towards anybody or anything, but it seemed like a case of, 'Let's record a band because we wanna learn how to do it ourselves…' You know what I mean? We ain't knocking 'em; they were only trying to help us, and I wouldn't change a thing if I could go back and do it all over again. But I remember losing whole songs, and we had to go back and record them again 'cos tapes got wiped and stuff…"

Despite the band's low opinion of 'If Only', it remains a definite highlight of the genre for many connoisseurs of anarcho punk, and a very distinctive and passionate offering, albeit carried to an extent by Corny's rich, powerful voice.

Unfortunately, Batesy was forced to quit the band due to illness (he'd contracted leukaemia and later died, tragically aged just 21), and was replaced by 'Faz' (real name Sean O'Farrell from Winsford)… but the band split six months later – after completing a mini-tour of the UK with Norway's Bannlyst during early July 1985 – when Corny decided she'd had enough.

"Faz was a great drummer," reckons Dave. "And the two songs we wrote with him were definitely moving in a new direction, more structured, a lot harder, more up-tempo… not exactly 'rock' as such…"

Nick: "That's what pissed me off about our group; we split up just as we were getting good! Corny decided she didn't wanna carry on… she wanted to become a hairdresser, and we couldn't really replace her 'cos of her voice. We'd [Corny and Nick] fell out by then anyway, so the last year had been quite hard, being in the same band together, but I was devastated when we split up, 'cos I absolutely loved the band to bits…"

The Sears played their 'official' last gig at the Sunderland Bunker on September 14th, 1985, supporting DOA and the Instigators ("Corny decided to make a political statement between each song," laughs Nick, "and we got pulled off about halfway through our set… we only played five numbers!"), although they reformed for one final show at the Anchor in Wednesbury on July 19th, 1986, a benefit gig for the young widow of Ian Bates, their old drummer.

Dave went on to drum with Grimlock, who only played a handful of gigs before vanishing without trace, while Nick ended up playing with a busy R&B band before – much to his own eternal chagrin – he briefly joined The Next Pistols, a Sex Pistols tribute band.

"They were fuckin' brilliant," chortles Dave, enjoying the bassist's discomfort. "Don't let him tell you different!"

Nowadays Nick regrinds cutting tools, Corny works for the council, doing music courses for underprivileged kids, and Dave is a sought-after soundman, having worked with such massive-selling metal bands as Slipknot, Slayer, Obituary, and Fear Factory. The three of them are in contact with each other again, and last year even re-recorded the songs from the 12" in Dave's home studio ("Just to see what they might have sounded like… and they sound great!").

"That's a fucking good question!" ponders Nick when pressed for how he might like the band to be remembered. "I think we were slightly different really… there were hundreds of bands out there, and a lot of them were doing exactly the same thing, but we were a bit more musical…"

Dave: "I'd like to think that we will be remembered as a live band, rather than be judged solely on the 12". We always used to play the best gig we could, and towards the end we started to take a real pride in what we were doing.

"I always thought punk was about doing what you wanted to do, being who you wanted to be… and to a certain extent, I'm still exactly like that now. I still don't give a toss in that sense."

Nick: "Well, you look at the photos of yourself from back then and think what a dickhead you looked, but at least that was how you wanted to look…"

Dave: "And I still think I look like a dickhead now!"

SELECT DISCOGRAPHY

12"s:
'If Only…' (Bluurg, 1984)

At A Glance:
No such luck, The Sears are yet to be immortalised in their own right on CD, although they have one track ('Not Prepared') on Volume Three ('Anti-Society') of Overground's excellent Anarcho-punk series.

The name **INDECENT ASSAULT** suggests that these Midlands-based punkers should have actually been featured in this author's 'Burning Britain' book, but a closer inspection of their lyrics reveals a socially aware band with a great deal of political savvy. They only released two EPs – and one of those was a split with Birmingham's Anorexia – but they certainly made their mark on the Black Country's underground music scene, and they're back together today, hopefully soon to pick up where they left off.

"As much as I wanted the band to be political and have this Discharge/Crass mentality…" ponders vocalist Darren 'Rat' Radburn, on their not-exactly-anarcho-punk moniker, "As much as I wanted it to be anti-war and all that, 'cos the Falklands was just round the corner, and I was very preoccupied with that, at the same time I wanted a punk name more akin to, say, GBH. I remember there was a girl at school and she was into The Damned, but she wasn't allowed to go to see them play because her mum wouldn't let her see a band called 'The Damned'… and I thought that was an achievement in itself, that it had pissed off the next generation just because it sounded wrong. And that was the mentality of our name, to be honest, and we joke even now about how crap it is! But we wanted something a bit punk, a bit violent… even though we weren't like that at all…

"Actually, whilst talking about dodgy names, there was a band from [nearby] Halesowen called Another Rapist, and they had a helluva lot of trouble with the local Rape Crisis Centre, who obviously thought their name was one big insult."

Formed by Rat and Michael 'Rich' Richards in 1981 after the pair were privy to an inspirational Crass, Flux Of Pink Indians and Dirt performance at the Digbeth Civic Hall, Indecent Assault got off to what can only be described as a shaky start.

"Between us, we had a basic backline," recalls Rat. "Rich bought a second-hand drum-kit, and he had his bass; I had a guitar, and we had a few schoolmates with us, who shall remain nameless, because they never lasted more than one practise. We had a pub to practise in, but stuff was getting thrown out of top-floor windows and stuff… the results were pathetic, to be honest; it wasn't going anywhere fast.

"And, actually, if I had to pick one band that prompted me to start a band of my own, as opposed to picking a band that influenced me and changed my thought process (which would be Crass), I'd say Dirt… just the fact that they could release 'Object, Refuse, Reject, Abuse' and communicate their ideas to so many people in such a short space of time. The EP hadn't been out more than five minutes when I saw them at Digbeth, and they had several hundred people singing along to the chorus, and all of them as if it really meant something. It seemed that these bands were really connecting in a way that nothing else had managed to previously. I came away from that gig and

Indecent Assault, live at The Swan, Dudley, 1983 (left to right: Shake, Morg, Pete, and Rat).

decided that I wanted to do the same – not just be onstage and in the spotlight, but speak my mind and convey views that other people might relate to."

Indecent Assault didn't really get into first gear until 1982, when Carl 'Morg' Morgan and David 'Jake' Jackson joined, on drums and guitar respectively (the latter leaving Rat to concentrate on the vocals), and they began rehearsing at Different Disguises in Cradley Heath. Jake only played one gig with the band though, at Stourbridge Youth Centre, supporting Overdose, before leaving in search of something poppier.

"They were like the local Blitz," smiles Rat of Overdose. "The singer and drummer had six-foot spiky hair, whilst the guitarist and bassist were a couple of skinheads, but they were quite good, to be fair. We just turned up on the day of their gig and asked if we could support them! So we got up and did our six songs, and one of those was 'Bela Lugosi's Dead' by Bauhaus; it went pretty disastrously really, but – and this is no word of a lie – a few of the songs were very stop/start even then, and we had a few folk heckling us in the crowd, comparing us to the Subhumans. 'If only…' was all I could say!"

Andrew 'Earpy' Earp joined, in response to an ad that Rat placed in Sounds, but after several further gigs and an extremely poor three-track demo, it was apparent that Indecent Assault were yet to find the right members to fully realise the vision of the band that Rat was by then carrying around in his head.

"Rich was a nice lad, but no matter how serious we were about the band, he was always more into just jumping about at the front; he wasn't concerned with input, and that sort of attitude stalled all our momentum at a very early stage, so he had to go. And there were a couple of the 'Crass type' bands back then who had this dual vocal attack, and we were considering that route, so Shake [real name Paul Shakespeare] was drafted in, because we'd seen him about at gigs and knew he could play bass; in fact, I think he was the only member that had had any proper musical training… he'd actually had some bass lessons! He turned up with lyrics and songs and everything, and we thought, 'Right, we've got to give this a go…' So we suggested to Rich that he switch to being second vocalist, but by then he had other interests – namely, he was seeing this girl – and he packed it in. And that was the end of that… although some of the lyrics he contributed to, made it as far as the first EP…"

August 1983 saw the band recording the five-track 'Rebellious Rantings: Certified Insane By The US Government' demo at Different Disguises, which they released through their own Toxic Tapes (a label they billed as being 'The poison in the machine!') A good effort all round despite some dubious tuning, it married anarcho sentiments to strong street punk tunes, yet Earpy left soon afterwards, in the strangest of circumstances.

"Well, we had this letter through the post off Earpy's pretend music management company," laughs Rat, "Saying that he wasn't going to be in the band any more, that he thought Indecent Assault were great… well, apart from the music and the lyrics and the bassist and the singer! He basically wished Carl all the best and left! And started up his own band [The End], who we actually played with later on.

"There was another local band, Subterfuge [from Kingswinford, one of their founding members was Rob 'The Bass Thing' Jones, who would later join The Wonder Stuff as well!], and Pete [Murphy], their guitarist, wasn't happy with them, so when Earpy left us, he

Rat of Indecent Assault, live Dudley 1983.

joined straight away. We did an eight-song demo, a selection of our sixteen-track recordings basically ['Welcome To The Service'], that was never officially released, and we touted it, along with 'Rebellious Rantings', round a few labels… like Riot City, who wrote back and said they were short of funds. No Future said a similar thing, that they had no money… we sent it to Crass as well, I think, to be considered for 'Bullshit Detector 3' and they wrote back saying they already had enough of that type of band for the album; basically, 'Thanks but no thanks!' So, we were probably about twelve months too late, I guess…"

Indecent Assault were by now playing regularly at popular Midlands venues such as The Swan in Dudley and The Mermaid in Birmingham, as well as further a-field, with the likes of Napalm Death, The Sears and Contempt, although by late '84 Pete was proving a liability, not showing for rehearsals and generally hindering the band's progress. He was promptly replaced by Gary Dicken from Gornal-based Pure Mania ("Who were terrible!" guffaws Rat), the band finally arriving at the line-up that would record the two singles.

The anti-vivisection song, 'They're The Murderers', was recorded at Different Disguises, for possible inclusion – via a competition ran by Beacon Radio – on an album of local bands, but when Indecent Assault "got bloody nowhere" with that, they submitted the track to Mortarhate to be considered for one of their various compilations. However, the tape got lost somewhere in transit, and, frustrated at yet another missed opportunity to be immortalised on vinyl, the band took the plunge and released the 'Dawn Of The Android Workers' EP on their own Reaganstein Records. As well as finally utilising the 'They're The Murderers' track, they entered Barn Studios in Hatton, with their mates from Leamington Spa, The Depraved, on hand to lend production advice and assistance, and recorded 'Nation's Prisoners', '(I Can't Stand) Top Of The Pops' and 'Have You Ceased To Function?' Although Rat feels the single turned out too polished and so didn't quite capture the rawness of Indecent Assault's live attack, there's no stopping the huge choruses in 'Have You Ceased To Function?' and 'Nation's Prisoners', both boisterous numbers more akin to the likes of Court Martial than your typical peace punk act. The striking cover art was adeptly inked by Rat himself, making for a memorable release of which the band remain cautiously proud, and with no distribution deal in place, they resorted to the time-honoured tradition of selling them at gigs up and down the country, some of the more memorable of which were supporting Conflict in Leeds and Antisect in Nottingham.

Late 1987 saw the release on Reaganstein of the 'United We Stand… But So Do They!' EP, a split single with Birmingham's Anorexia, who had just issued their 'Radical Riot' demo tape.

"We'd previously spoken to The Depraved and Decadence Within, about possibly doing a track each and making it a four-way split, but The Depraved got signed to COR, and Decadence to Floating Gerbil, so we were left with Anorexia. And one rather inebriated night after a gig at the Mermaid, I went over to [Anorexia drummer] Scott's car and listened to their latest recording, and I must have been really pissed, because I thought it was fantastic, one of the best things I'd ever heard! Then, when it came back from the pressing plant, no matter how well they'd mixed it, it wasn't very good at all. I got on well with Anorexia as people… Scott's a smashing chap, and I always got on with [vocalist] Dave – he was a very committed individual – but I wish we'd never saddled ourselves with them on a split single."

The Indecent Assault tracks stand up to (relatively) close scrutiny though, especially the highly-infectious 'High-Tech' with its simple-yet-inspired chorus hook.

"I wasn't really happy with our stuff either, to be honest," sighs Rat. "Mainly 'cos we'd gone back to Different Disguises, in an effort to get a thrashier sound, and it came out too trebly. Plus we used all new songs, when I think we had stronger songs that we'd already recorded previously, but we were just trying to push ourselves, trying to evolve… and we thought if we could just get the second EP out, someone, somewhere, might pick up on us…"

It wasn't to be however, and Indecent Assault folded under the weight of internal apathy before 1987 drew to a close. Keen to continue writing and performing, Rat formed the short-lived Trademark Go before joining Birmingham's Depth Charge, helping pen the songs that appeared on their debut demo, 'Let The Killing Start!' He then teamed up with members of Genital Deformities in Semtex, before forming Excrement Of War alongside his old friend Tom Croft, with whom he recorded two EPs (a split with Dischange on Finn Records and 'The Waste And The Greed' on RTP) before leaving in 1992.

Then, over a decade later – 2003, to be precise – Indecent Assault re-grouped for sporadic rehearsals, that saw Shake back on guitar, Rat on both bass and vocals, and Ade Jones of The Cudgels now on drums. During 2005, it was decided to commit to a regular weekly rehearsal and begin writing again, and a new five-track EP, 'Still Burning', was being recorded as this book went to press.

"I look back in disbelief at all the hours we put in back then," muses Rat in conclusion. "Because the anarcho mentality was totally DIY, we really did everything for ourselves: rehearse, write stuff, answer mail, sort out the gigs, do our own zines or contribute to others, hook up with like-minded friends around the country and get organised… I'm at a loss as to where I'd fit all that in now, even on a casual basis. But I do think that, at the time, all the effort paid off, and anyone that saw us got something out of it. I look at Dudley now and can't think of anything comparable to that period, and some days I really yearn to give the whole thing the good kick up the arse it desperately deserves!"

SELECT DISCOGRAPHY

7"s:
'Dawn Of The Android Workers' (Reaganstein, 1986)
'United We Stand… But So Do They!' (Reaganstein, 1987) – split with Anorexia

At A Glance:
A welcome retrospective CD – provisionally entitled 'Previous Convictions' – is still in the planning stages.

'One, two, three, go, I've got an ego… it won't let me go, what am I going to do? A, B, C, D, paranoia's killing me… I'm dying on my aching feet, what a way to go!' Hardly a typical approach for an anarcho-punk lyric, but then **ZOUNDS** were never a typical anarcho-punk band, their infectious quirky style just as eccentric as the mischievous words they often set to them might suggest.

Playing their first gigs as Zounds in 1978 – one of which, at the Mayfly Festival, actually got reviewed in the NME "totally by accident!" – the band started life in Oxford, but soon relocated to the much more radical climes of London.

"Yeah, it all kinda evolved out of this scene I was in, in Oxford," explains band mainstay, bassist/vocalist Steve Lake, "Myself and some friends of mine; we were all on the dole, feeling kinda dislocated from what was going on at the time, and we just used to hang out, jamming… but at that time, everybody was forming bands. We'd probably been playing together since about '76, just not called 'Zounds', and we were a bit of a weird band from the start, to be honest, but as we progressed, and different people came and went from it, and I began to write most of the songs,

we grew more political… I mean, I used to say that we weren't a political band, but obviously we were. But the politics of the band came out of how we lived, not from reading books. We were living a pretty free-form lifestyle up in Oxford – none of us working… all of us actually, actively, against the notion of working.

Zounds circa 1980 (Steve, Josef and Lawrence), pictures taken during first Dutch tour.

"We'd all been at school in the Sixties, and you'd see all these older people and all the liberating things that were going on, and that had quite a deep effect on everyone; we were influenced by a lot of the fringe hippy stuff… especially people like Mick Farren and the Pink Fairies. They lived over in Ladbroke Grove, and they put on free gigs and supported the free festival scene. We were a bit young for it, to be honest, but we were aware of it, and I always found that all quite appealing – loads of young people living together in houses, free to do what they wanted. You know the kind of jobs we were being offered… especially someone like myself who'd been to a secondary modern school… I left school and seemed completely incapable of handling anything really… it came up on me so fast; one day I just didn't have to go to school! I got a succession of dead-end jobs, in factories and what-not, and it was fucking destroying me... which is why I say, our politics didn't come from meetings, or reading political pamphlets, or anything... it was just that, I'd been at school until I was sixteen, forever attending double maths, and double this and that, and doing my homework, and there I was, in a factory, and that was all I could see, stretching ahead of me forever. And that was such a depressing thought, so as soon as I met like-minded people, who liked hanging out, playing the guitar, smoking dope, going to gigs... you know, I drifted in with the wrong crowd! And somehow I ended up homeless, and a group of us gathered in Oxford, and the band evolved from that. We liked the idea that life was about playing, not working.

"I remember seeing posters from the Socialist Workers' Party – well, it was before the SWP, but it was one of those type of organisations – saying, 'Fight for the right to work!' And I thought, 'Fuckin' hell, fight for the right to go back to the factory... no thanks!' So we started up this graffiti campaign, 'Fight for the right NOT to work!'

And once you get out of that whole working situation, especially if – like us – you're a heavy

dope smoker, you quickly find yourself completely disassociated from everything going on around you. We lived in this old house, and we all hated everything, and we got into arrears and all sorts."

Inspired by the free festival scene of the Seventies ("This whole notion that people could get together and organise themselves… and this was long before I'd ever heard the word 'anarchy'…"), Zounds played several gigs with 'Gong understudies' Here And Now, their free-form jams developing into something more subversive about the same time they formed a strong allegiance with two of Here And Now's other touring partners, The Mob and The Astronauts.

"The thing is, throughout '78 and '79 the political situation was getting harder and harder, and whereas we'd been living on this marijuana cloud of 'Let's all be free and ignore all the straights and go away somewhere to play by ourselves…', lines were now being drawn up in society… the National Front were marching… people were on strike… you know all the clichés from all the documentaries – the country in chaos, the dead unburied, all that 'winter of discontent' crap. And we had an idea of what Thatcher was going to be like, but none of us knew how bad it was going to get. So, as the political situation was getting harder, my writing was becoming much more pointed… and I moved to London at about that point too, and there was nowhere to live, so I started squatting, and there was the Special Patrol Group of the time, who were fucking notorious for being thugs. You constantly felt under threat from all that, and the only 'advantage' of moving to London, as opposed to staying in Oxford where we were hassled by the police all the time as well, was that there was such a racist vibe in the Metropolitan police, you weren't that bothered by them because they were too busy terrorising gangs of West Indian youths.

"Anyway, my writing became a lot more focussed on what we were experiencing, the music became a lot harder… what started off as this sort of formless stream of consciousness became much angrier, in direct relation to how much more we were feeling under threat as individuals."

With rhythm guitarist Nick Godwin and drummer Judge (real name unknown, "But he was from Essex and ended up doing the light show for Wham at the peak of their popularity!") joining Steve and co-founding guitarist Laurence Wood, Zounds roamed the UK alongside The Mob as part of The Weird Tales Tour, but found themselves in disarray by the end of it, with what everyone considers the band's classic line-up emerging from the resultant chaos.

"That was in '79, and it was a nightmare," sighs Steve. "It really taught me a lot of lessons, and there was this big fuckin' bust-up between us and The Mob… me and [their bassist] Curtis actually had a fist-fight at the time, and that was the only fight I've ever had in my fuckin' life!

"Anyway, at the end of all that, it was just me and Lawrence left, and we'd met Crass by this point, and we got Josef [Porta] in, who'd followed The Mob up from Yeovil; he was playing in some terrible mod band, but was basically biding his time until he could get into The Mob himself, which was always his ambition. And eventually he did, which was great for him.

"We'd already done this demo with Judge on drums, to give to Crass [recorded at Here And Now's Street Level Studios in Bristol Gardens, London, it comprised early versions of 'Subvert', 'War' and 'I Just Wanna Be Loved'], but he didn't really fit in with us personally, whilst Josef was this really fantastic, colourful character, who could also play the drums."

Crass producer Penny Rimbaud didn't think so however, persuading the band to employ the services of a session drummer for the first Zounds single, 'Can't Cheat Karma'. Recorded at Southern Studios by John Loder during early July 1980, the three-track EP was an invigorating slice of rhythmic punk rock, the title track in particular something unique and compelling and unlike anything heard before or since. It rightfully shot straight to the top of the Independent Charts, although Steve remains happily cynical of the reasons for its success.

"Yeah, of course, we had no illusions as regards that. There we were, these weird, punkified hippy squatters, who'd done a few gigs with the Poison Girls, and our record went straight to No. 1? Well, you know… we'd done a few gigs around West London, but I don't know that we were that well liked! It wasn't because the Zounds name was on it – it was because the Crass name was on the label! Of course it was! And there's two ways of looking at that, isn't there? It was either blind fan worship… just like some people will buy everything that bloody Robbie Williams puts out… or, it was more a case that, you knew what you were getting from Crass, a particular type of thing. And I've done it myself… bought records that were on a label, or by an artist that is associated with something I already like… that's how you find out about stuff, isn't it?

"But I really hate those things on e-bay that say, 'If you bought this, you'll like this, this and this…' And I go, 'Yeah, right, I'm not that predictable…' But they're often right! And that's the cruel thing – now I'm just a cog in some advertising jerk's idea of a profile, and he's bloody right, and I'm really that shallow!

"We kinda met Crass before I'd even heard them," he adds. "We broke down near their house when we were on tour with The Mob, and then we went to see them, with their banks of video monitors and banners, the whole fucking bit, and I thought, 'Fuckin' hell, what is this?' We were a little bit older than most of the audience – mind you, Crass were *much* older than most of the audience – and I appreciated it more as some kind of theatrical, Brechtian presentation. I found it very, very compelling… but they, and the Poison Girls, were from an arty Sixties background. Then again, a lot of the main movers in early punk, like Malcolm McLaren, Bernie Rhodes and Vivienne Westwood, were all at university in 1968 and never got over it really.

"A lot of people had Crass down as some sort of rudimentary lowest common denominator musically, but like a lot of successful artists, they recognised their limitations and worked well within them, and created this very minimalist sorta vibe. They were truly a phenomenon, whereas the rest of us were just little cult bands; their potential reach was more than the rest of us put together."

Still, topping the Indies with your debut single is no mean feat by anyone's standards, and whilst it's absolutely true that much of what was released on Crass sold well by association, there's no denying that 'Can't Cheat Karma' is such a deliciously odd little number it was always destined for greatness.

"I don't know what it was," shrugs Steve, nonplussed, "Just a combination of all our influences, I guess; we were a very idiosyncratic band anyway, in our whole approach, and that single was very much a fusion of what we were doing and how Penny and John Loder saw it. We weren't actually that happy with the recording, to be honest – we thought it sounded very thin and weedy, but a lot of people really liked that tight, compressed sound. And for a lot of people, it's probably the only record of ours that they do like!

"But it is a strange song, and it was one of the first songs that I ever wrote seriously for the band. It came to me one day when I was walking down the street, which is very unusual for me anyway. And I was living in this house with all these people who were really into Frank Zappa, and he has this thing where he does a line, and then there's a riff, and then he sings another line, which I thought was quite an interesting way to write. But I always thought it was a terrible song, thought the lyrics were very wishy-washy… I was just feeling a bit hopeless, and wondering what the hell I could do about that, and people just responded to it. I've grown to like it for what it is over the years…"

Much more obvious, but no less striking, is 'War', one of the songs on the flip-side of the EP.

"I'm surprised that no one else has seen the connection, but I heard this Bob Marley song that was going on about 'War!' and I thought it was great, very direct. And I was also very into a lot of weird German Seventies music, with all these choppy rhythms and insistent drums… so it was a mixture of all that really.

"It's funny too, 'cos we might never have done it. I showed it to Lawrence one time and he really liked it, and then we were playing this gig, and we'd gone down really well, but we had no more songs, and he said, 'Let's play that thing you showed me!' And he'd only learnt it that afternoon or something, and I said, 'No, I don't wanna do it, I'm not even sure I like it…' but he just started playing it, and we had no choice but to play along. And I thought, 'Actually, this really fucking works!'"

Zoundz, Steve Lake at Solfest 2005, picture by Trunt.

Despite the single's success, Zounds weren't invited to record again for Crass, the label preferring to release one-offs by bands, encouraging them to start up their own labels, thus propagating the scene rather than dominating it.

"I'm not sure if that was a policy or what, but we did the record and it went to the top of the charts, and we went to see them and they were like, 'Oh, hello boys, saw your record in the charts…!' But they were never interested in rock'n'roll, and that's where Zounds differed from them, because we were! I mean, we were into the politics and all that, but we were also into having a laugh, getting out of it, and all the rest of it. They were like adults, and we were like big kids really. We still wanted to change the world into some giant, lovely, ecologically sound, anarcho… thing… but we also liked playing rock'n'roll and having fun!

"But Penny was saying, 'Oh yeah, we'll do another single, and we'll do an album…' and we were like, 'Yeah, great!' But then when we went round there next, he was much more sombre, and he said, 'Well, we've been discussing what we're doing, and we've decided that we don't want to be like just another record label, so we're just going to do the one record by each band… so thanks a lot, boys…!' and that was it really. I mean, they worked with the Poison Girls on more than one record, but they had a totally different relationship with them to anybody else, and there was a very definite hierarchy in that scene, despite what some people might tell you otherwise.

"But after having a No. 1 single, there's only one way to go and that's down!" guffaws Steve. "When Crass told us they didn't want to do anything else with us, we knew absolutely nothing about the music industry, and Rough Trade seemed like nice people, so we thought, 'We'll go down there and ask them how you make a record…' When we got there and met Geoff Travis, he said, 'Loved the single, lads, you can make a record for Rough Trade, if you want!' And I thought, 'This all seems very easy!' And I knew we were destined for greatness… but it was all downhill from there!

"And we were so very, very naïve. The thing is, we were always fucking out of place in any scene. We'd always felt awkward and out of place when amongst straight mainstream society, but we also felt a bit out of place with Crass and the Poison Girls because they seemed to know much more than us, they were so much more older than us… then we went to Rough Trade, and Geoff, who had the shop and started up the label, is such a lovely, lovely guy… and there were a few other people at Rough Trade who were very nice to us, a guy called Pete Walmesley especially… but we'd go down there, and all the other people working there were all so painfully hip and trendy… with that week's haircut and the grooviest record as seen in the latest New Musical Express. And they didn't really seem to like us.

"I've never put much of a class analysis on these things, but we weren't grammar school kids; we were working class people, punk rock squatters, and we weren't highly regarded by those people, but thankfully Geoff and Pete were great. But we very naïve, and Geoff said he'd put us in a studio for four days to do the album, to do what we could, and we thought that was great: we had four days to prove we were the anarcho Beatles! Like all bands, we thought we were the best thing ever… or at least we thought we had the potential to be… if only people could see it the way we saw it! 'If only you were here, in my head with me, you'd realise how fucking fantastic we are…'

"Funnily enough, when we went to Rough Trade to see about making another record, Geoff Travis, who was very welcoming, asked us, 'How do you see yourself sounding?' And Josef said, 'Like the Dead Kennedys!' And I suppose that was what we did want to sound like, with a much bigger kind of sound, but the Crass approach to production was very trebly, and sounds very compressed. I mean, we weren't in the studio when they mixed it anyway – god forbid, they wouldn't allow that! They kept very tight control over absolutely everything they were involved in, which some people might criticise them for, but personally I never had a problem with. It kept it focused… and it was their thing, after all… they'd say, 'We've got this thing, it's Crass, and we do things like this… if you want to do something with us, we work with people on our terms…' They never forced anyone to do it, y'know? Either you were prepared to do that, or you weren't… and whenever you do something with somebody else, there's going to be a bit of you and a bit of them, and if you want it to be all you, go and start your own record label… they did! I've never really had a problem with the fact that they wanted things to sound a certain way, look a certain way… that was their trip, and that was fine by me."

Ensconcing themselves in London's Berry Street Studios during March 1981, Zounds recorded 'The Curse Of Zounds' album and the 'Demystification' single back-to-back in record time, with producer Adam Kidron – "the charismatic son of a socialist millionaire!" – at the helm.

"He was actually meant to be up in Oxford doing a degree in maths, but had decided he was going to be a record producer," recalls Steve. "We were all really fucking stoned when we went in there… and the first thing he said when we met him was, 'I don't like guitars!' And we still had all these visions of ourselves as a big guitar band! You actually got the impression that he didn't like rock music full-stop, but he was very funny; he had that kind of confidence that being the son of a millionaire might give you. And he'd travelled all over… he was twenty-fucking-one and he'd say things like, 'Oh, my two favourite places are Los Angeles and Moscow!' We were used to hanging around the Cowley Road in Oxford!

"At one point he said, 'So, has Geoff discussed the deal with you?' And we were like, 'Deal? What fuckin' deal?' It hadn't even crossed our minds; we thought someone was just letting us make a record! And he told us that all the records he worked on, he got a producer's credit and so many royalty points… we'd never even heard of 'points'! So we said, 'Whatever!'

"And I think that's one of the reasons we did it all so quickly too; his opinion was that he was dealing with a bunch of giggling, stoned children, and he wanted it over with as soon as possible… just make sure he got a few points of it and move onto the next Scritti Politti record!

"Essentially that album was all recorded live; the drums, bass and rhythm guitars went down, then the vocals, and then Lawrence put some extra guitars on, and then we put some Hammond organ on 'Demystification'… and some tambourine! By which time, after being in the studio for four days, we thought we were fuckin' Tamla Motown! We weren't that stupid, but at least we were trying to make a good record…"

And they succeeded, both the album and single being exceptionally memorable slices of cerebral punk, Steve's dreamy floating bass lines combining with Josef's powerful understated rhythms to provide the perfect ambient canvas for Lawrence's unpredictable jangling guitars to seduce the listener at every daring twist and turn. On tracks such as 'Dirty Squatters' and 'Did He Jump (Or Was He Pushed)?', the insistent combination of subtly driving sounds and Steve's inimitable vocals even generates an insidious atmosphere of oppression.

"That's one song that people have really connected with," comments Steve on the latter, "and although it's a bit clumsy in places, it's… well, the inspiration came from several places. When I was about fifteen, I played bass in some band with this guy, and he read me this poem, and it was something like… 'When I was five, I came home from school, and I did a drawing of this aeroplane, and the teacher put a star on it, and I took it home to put it on the fridge, but my mum wouldn't let me…' Something really affecting like that anyway, and he said to me, 'What do you think?' And it turned out it was written by a kid who later killed himself when he was fifteen. And that was years before I wrote that song, but it always stayed with me… something about the loneliness and the isolation.

"And then there was another time when I was hitching to a free festival somewhere, and I'd been waiting for ages to get a lift. I'd rolled this joint and was smoking it while I was waiting, and then this car stopped, with a very nice middle class lady in it, and I got in, and forgot that I was even smoking this joint! And she laughed and said, 'When did you drop out?' And I said, 'I don't think I ever dropped in!' And although it was said humorously, that phrase stayed with me, and the more I thought about it, I realised that I felt like I'd never fitted in. I don't think I dropped out, I was pushed out. I wrote it more as a poem, rather than a song, and one day we were just jamming, the words came back to me… and it proved to be a song that really resonated with a lot of people. Because as we've got older, we've all known people who haven't been able to fucking handle the alienation."

Three strong singles followed, 'Dancing', 'La Vache Qui Rit' and 'More Trouble Coming Every Day', all of them assaulting the Indie charts with a diminishing amount of commercial success, the latter – and its B-side 'Knife' – being an especially potent pop-punk gem in the vein of classic Buzzcocks. However, disillusioned by the music industry and with real life increasingly encroaching on their rock'n'roll fantasies, Zounds split in late 1982, before they could complete work on a proposed second album, 'The Wounds Of Zounds'.

"Well, there were a lot of reasons for splitting… Mandy was pregnant, and I couldn't afford to go swanning off making no fucking money every night… but also relationships were becoming strained… not just within the band, but in and around the house we lived in, in this street full of squats in Hackney. You'd be in the house and there'd be a knock at the door, and it would be this fifteen-year-old punk from Belgium asking to live with you. And you'd say, 'No, not really…' And they'd be like, 'But I thought you were anarchists?' 'We are, and that means we can do what we want, so fuck off!'"

"But loads of people moved in, and there were all these petty rivalries, and I was unaware of a lot of it; I always thought it was this spirit of cooperation, but there were so many jealousies and stuff. We were meant to be free, but we were far from it… it had worked all right for Crass, but we were full of all these little complexes.

"And Josef was a bit unhappy with some of the things we were recording, and he flounced out of the studio when we were dong 'Dancing'. And The Mob had come up with this guy Tim on drums, a brilliant musician, a real natural, and he'd replaced their original drummer Graham, who himself was a great drummer but idolised Keith Moon and basically wanted to drive round in a Rolls Royce and marry a model – and by then, The Mob had become somewhat more serious than that... well, Mark had, and Curtis idolised Mark.

"So, anyway, Tim came down to the studio and played the drums on 'Dancing', played some stuff on [its B-side] 'True Love'... and Josef said, 'Look, why don't we get Tim on bass and Steve, you could move over to guitar, and we'd have a bigger sound...' We were still after that 'big sound', and it never happened...

"Then Tim announced to The Mob that he was playing bass for us as well as drums for them, and they said, 'No, you can't, it's not possible, it's too much, playing in Zounds and The Mob, it'll never work...' Even though we hardly ever played live unless it was with them! So, Tim said, 'Well, I'll go and play bass with Zounds then, 'cos I'd rather be a guitarist than a drummer...' And after saying all that, about not wanting Tim on drums if he was in two bands, they said, 'Well, we'll have to have Josef on drums!' Hold on a minute... we'd go to gigs and play with about five other bands, and Josef would be the only drummer there... and we'd be on last 'cos we had a bit of a name by then, and he'd be fucking knackered!

"Just before Tim came in, we toured Scotland for Scottish CND, and on the way up, we did a gig in Doncaster, and afterwards, as we were packing up, all these beer monsters broke into the venue and started going crazy, beating people up... and Lawrence got beaten really badly, the bastards. The police came and he got taken to hospital...

"And then when we got to Scotland, the National Front turned up at some of the gigs and were seig-heiling in front of the stage... and we had this really weird band supporting us in Aberdeen, and the audience invaded the stage and nicked loads of equipment. The place was packed with all these glue-sniffing, young punk rockers, and I had to go onstage and say, 'Right, we're not fucking playing until you give us back all our gear!' Everything was passed back up to us apart from the microphone, and everyone's chanting, 'Bring back the microphone!' It was fucking weird!

"And then there was a riot at a gig in Huddersfield on the way home, and I was just thinking, 'This isn't fun anymore!' And that was the whole reason we were doing it... we didn't want to have jobs and wanted to have some fun.

"All that happened, and then we got Tim in, and Josef joined The Mob, and then we went to Belgium and Holland, and the van kept breaking down, and it was the middle of winter... and everything just seemed really fucking bleak. I just had to get away from the whole fucking scene in the end... it was just becoming unworkable, so we split the band up, and I moved out of Brougham Road and had nothing to do with anyone from that scene for years and years. I remember we had a gig booked in Colchester, and we phoned up on the day of the gig and said, 'We're not coming – there is no band!' "

After working with Lawrence for a few years in video production, Steve took a degree in cultural studies, finding time to record several solo albums for the Dutch label that became Play It Again Sam ("But they're shit records, and I wouldn't bother searching them out!"), and now lectures at further education colleges. In recent years though, he has been involved in various Zounds resurrections, issuing two new singles ('This Land' and 'Go All The Way', the latter a self-released CDEP, the title track being resurrected from the demo sessions for the aborted second album) and touring Europe quite extensively in the process, but seems adamant now that he's finally got it out of his system, that the book has been closed on the band for good.

"It was just people constantly saying that we ought to get together and do another Zounds gig," he explains of the initial comeback. "We played for Vi [Subversa]'s birthday... we did one with the Poison Girls, and some members of Crass came along and did their avant-garde thing... then we did an anti-McDonalds gig... just things that were quite close to our hearts really. However I'm not a fucking prostitute, and if I couldn't sing the words with any real passion, I didn't want to sing them at all. But suddenly I felt a lot closer to these songs as the whole war situation built up in Iraq, so I did a few acoustic solo gigs and I played some Zounds songs.

"At the one gig I plugged into this fucking big Marshall amp, and even though it was my acoustic guitar, it made a fucking great noise, and I thought, 'This is alright…'

"So I hooked up with Stick from Doom and Protag from Blyth Power and ATV, and we played a few gigs and people started calling us 'Zounds'… and I was really feeling it again, so I thought, 'Fuck it!' and we did it for about three years, and it was very nice while it lasted, 'cos a lot of people out there still really loved the material and wanted to see it performed. But eventually I felt myself growing distant from it all again, and I didn't want to end up just another fucking band… I know every band in the world has reformed, even the dead ones, filling in the gaps with roadies and old girlfriends. I felt like doing it, so I did it, but now I don't feel like doing it, so I'm not, y'know? It was great to be a part of the whole crusade, and play some electric guitar on the way, but when it's over, it's over…

"We were never really a punk band as such," he ponders, trying to decide just where they fit into the grand scheme of anarcho punk. "I certainly didn't regard us as such anyway. I was really into the whole punk thing – but then again, I was really into a lot of other things as well. The thing I liked about the punk explosion, as well as a lot of the music, was that people could do stuff for themselves… you didn't have to go to music college for a hundred years, you didn't need the best equipment and all that. The Pink Fairies had this song called 'Do It', which went, 'You don't have to think about it, just do it,' and there seemed a direct link between that and punk rock, y'know? That was what it was all about, and it didn't matter if you were weird or trying something completely different.

"We weren't great musicians, we were naïve and clumsy, but I've always stood by the songs. And it's weird, doing these gigs recently, sometimes you feel they connect, and other times you feel like it's just a bit of nostalgia. I always say, 'I'm never going to reform the band,' and all that, but that in itself is a little bit of show biz… that rock'n'roll mythologizing… that you can only play rock'n'roll when you're young and good-looking… well, comparatively speaking, of course, compared to what we're like when we're old, ha ha! But actually that's bollocks, isn't it? The thing is with punk rock, you're never too old, never too young… it doesn't matter if you're black or white, or disabled… if you've got something to say, fucking say it…"

SELECT DISCOGRAPHY

7"s:
'Can't Cheat Karma' (Crass, 1980)
'Demystification' (Rough Trade, 1981)
'Dancing' (Rough Trade, 1982)
'La Vache Qui Rit' (Not So Brave, 1982)
'More Trouble Coming Every Day' (Rough Trade, 1982)
'This Land' (Active/Rugger Bugger, 2002)

LPs:
'The Curse Of Zounds' (Rough Trade, 1981)

At A Glance:
The superb Broken Rekids CD reissue of 'The Curse Of Zounds' (originally released in 1993 by Rugger Bugger/Gap) also includes all the (Eighties) singles, plus artwork, lyrics, fliers and press cuttings, making it the only Zounds disc you'll ever need.

THE SNIPERS, who hailed from the wilds of rural Oxfordshire, were bona fide 'one hit wonders', releasing just the one single on Crass before vanishing back into obscurity. But 'Three Peace Suite' is such a great single, its creepy A-side, 'Parents Of God', effectively reverberating with the accumulated anguished echoes of centuries of religious persecution, it's well worth the reader's investigation.

Dave Hounslow of The Snipers, with guitar, 2006.

Formed in Spring 1979, and comprising Russell Bowers on vocals, Dave Hounslow on guitar, Steve 'Wacker' Harris on bass, and Mark Taplin on drums, The Snipers were spread across three sleepy Oxfordshire villages, Shipton-Under-Wychwood, Burford and Brize Norton, but punk rock has a knack of finding those susceptible to its charms no matter where they might be secreted away.

"Some of us had seen Crass a couple of times, and thought they sounded good, and that maybe we could do something similar," reveals Dave of their inspirations for forming. "A few of us went to see them at Stonehenge… they played there twice, I think; the second time, when we actually played with them, was the time the bikers smashed the place up… but a few of us saw them the previous year as well. I first saw them in a little club in Swindon, and from then on we followed them around a bit; we'd always go and see them if they played anywhere locally. They had this ambience about them, this DIY ethic, and it became apparent that you could make music and convey a message without actually being particularly good musicians… and seeing as none of us were musicians at all, it was quite inspirational. None of us had any musical inclinations before that whatsoever…

"We were going to call ourselves The Sinyx," he adds. "But then we heard that there was already another band called that. We had access to some loft space above Russell's parents' garage, which was where we used to practise. Personally, I bought a guitar for £5.00, which was horrible and really difficult to play… and we collected together various instruments, half a drum-kit… I think the best bit of equipment we had was a microphone for Russell. So, anyway, once we'd decided to form this band, we assembled one Sunday afternoon and tried to work out who was going to play what! I only ended up playing guitar because years and years before that, when I was about twelve, I'd been bought a guitar and learnt to play along to this tape, so, seeing as it was probably the most difficult instrument to play, I didn't mind having a go at it. The rest of them had to fight over bass, drums and who was singing, but it worked out alright."

After spending most of 1979 slowly getting to grips with their chosen instruments and writing a set of songs, The Snipers made their public debut, at a Christmas party in the Victory Hut, a community centre in Brize Norton.

"It was just this little hut left over from the Second World War; it had been used as a makeshift hospital once upon a time. We packed the place out and had a bloody great laugh… and, of course, we had to play our set twice, because we didn't have enough songs!"

Bolstered by their success, they entered Hugh Shewring's Windrush Recording Studios in the High Street of Bourton-On-The-Water, where they recorded their eleven-song set for posterity. The resulting demo was basic to the point of being primitive, the band's overly simplistic tunes reminiscent of The Destructors at their least inspired, but certain tracks, especially an early version of 'Parents Of God', hinted that The Snipers had at least one great record in them.

"Yes, it's a bit rough and ready!" laughs Dave amicably. "We'd never been in a studio before, so we just played it all as we would if we were doing a gig, straight through… the only thing was we'd started going out of tune before we got to the end! And yes, 'Parents Of God' turned out particularly well, considering it was the only song that we'd hardly practised at that point, and had never played live.

"Although it was the engineer's own studio, it was the first time he'd ever recorded a band there; he usually hired an engineer in normally, but he ended up doing this session for us, and we were the first proper band he'd ever done apart from a local school choir! And I think his inexperience shows through in the quality of the recording… or lack thereof!"

Originally the demo was recorded purely for the pleasure of the band and their closest friends, but The Snipers couldn't resist giving one to Crass at the earliest opportunity, who asked them to re-record three or four of the best songs with a view to releasing something on their label. Suitably impressed, Penny Rimbaud then invited the band down to Southern Studios for a session that produced the aforementioned 'Three Peace Suite' EP, which appeared in December 1981 and actually spent two months in the Independent Charts, managing a very respectable No. 16 placing.

Just prior to the release of the EP, Crass also included The Snipers on the first instalment of their 'Bullshit Detector' compilations, although the unimaginative dirge 'War Song' was lifted from the band's first demo and paled alongside the infinitely more competent 'Three Peace Suite'.

"When we did the single, we had a whole weekend to record," recalls Dave, of the artistic heights that Penny and engineer John Loder helped the band attain. "And we tracked all the instruments separately, which was a much more technical process than what we were used to doing, but we really enjoyed it. We tried out lots of effects and even some 'proper production techniques', and messed about with the tuning a bit on 'Parents Of God', and it turned out really well.

"And we were totally made up that we'd done this single for Crass, and sold eight thousand copies, but it didn't make much difference to our profile locally or anything. We carried on booking our own shows and stuff… although we did go to Stevenage and played with Crass at the Bowes Lyon House. That was a really big show for us, and we seemed to go down well enough with the Crass fans…"

Proof of the local scene's ignorance that The Snipers had just issued a single on one of the most respected punk labels in the world came with what Dave still remembers as their worst show ever; it even coincided cruelly with when the band were flying high in the Indies.

"It was Christmas Eve 1981, in a village hall in Taynton, this tiny little village just outside Burford. It was freezing cold, and there were only eight people there... including the band! We just misjudged how many people would want to go somewhere like Taynton on Christmas Eve, when they didn't have any transport and they'd want to get drunk and then not be able to get home. So we just treated it like a rehearsal, had a few beers and a bit of a jam."

The beginning of the end came during spring 1982 when drummer Mark moved to Telford; although his new location helped precipitate a short tour of Shropshire, it was hardly conducive to regular rehearsals. After soldiering on gamely for a year, and playing the Banbury Peace Festival, The Snipers played their last show at the Wapping Anarchy Centre with The Failing Parachutes in support, a local band that Dave had included on his [compilation of Oxfordshire punk bands] 'Spirit Of An Age-Old Anthem' cassette.

"We weren't really that interested in replacing Mark or anything, because we'd only ever formed the band out of friendship anyway, not to be proper musicians or anything; we were just entering into the spirit of the time. And we were never an ambitious band as far as wanting to make a career out of music; we were just lucky enough to know Crass and put out a decent record. Apart from Mark, we all carried on going to punk gigs, following Crass about and seeing them play, but eventually we all went our separate ways."

And Dave, who sadly developed schizophrenia during the late Eighties and has since been right through the mental health system ("It hasn't been easy, but the illness is in remission right now, and has been for a couple of years, so it could be worse..."), still remembers his time with The Snipers most fondly.

"I honestly didn't think anyone cared about us anymore, so it was a nice surprise that people are still interested. It was a powerful movement we were involved in, that evolved and survived, so as long as people are taking that same feeling and applying it to their own situation and today's political climate, I think it's still relevant. It seemed hugely important to me at the time, of course, but how important it actually was is almost impossible to measure. I do know that I met a lot of very interesting, enthusiastic people who were on the same wavelength as me, and when you are a teenager, that in itself is a rarity."

SELECT DISCOGRAPHY

7"s:
'Three Peace Suite' (Crass, 1981)

At A Glance:
The band's finest moment, 'Parents Of God', appears on the 'A Sides' compilation CD (Crass Records, 1992), whilst the endearingly generic 'I Know' (from the band's first demo) was re-mastered and included on Overground's 2005 CD, 'Anti-War: Anarcho-punk Compilation, Volume One'.

Antisect at the Bierkeller, Leeds March 1984, picture by Paul May.

ANTISECT were one of the most sonically formidable of all the acts in the anarcho-punk scene; a genuine force to be reckoned with live, such was the power generated by their presence and sound, their sole album, 'In Darkness, There Is No Choice', still shines as one of the most furious and potent releases of the whole period.

Formed in Daventry in 1981, the band began life as a four-piece, comprising Pete 'Lippy' Lyons on guitar, Pete Boyce on vocals, Pete 'Polly' Paluskiewicz on drums, and 'Wink' (real name Renusze Rokicki) on bass, thrashing out raw, fast hardcore punk, justified by some simplistic anarcho lyrics.

"Where we lived, Saturday afternoons after pub kicking-out time became a game of hide-and-seek between us and the local pissed-up, knob-end, beer-boy fraternity," laughs Pete Lyons. "It'd usually end up with someone getting a kicking; they didn't like us 'cos our clothes were fucked-up and our hair was a bit weird. I remember, and still have the scars from, ten or so blokes kicking the shit out of me after a UK Subs gig in Nuneaton...

"I never really felt comfortable calling myself a 'punk' though. It was bollocks really... in one sense, it helped form a sense of identity, but then I'd see bands and people that I thought were just the same as the sort of wankers that I was trying to get away from – the only difference was that they had a studded belt and a mohican!

"We didn't really fit in anywhere properly as a band either. Although we had roots in the earlier generation of punk, coming as we did from the cultural backwater that was Daventry, we were never really part of the London scene. We'd find ourselves hitching to gigs up and down the country, regularly waking up in some pissy bus shelter or train station, the morning after the night before. We did meet a lot of absolutely fucking mental people along the way though, some of whom would later show up at our own gigs. At the time, to be honest, we were probably more into Motörhead and stuff than a lot of the newer punk bands that were out there, and I never really felt the second wave of punk was that inspiring. There were bands like Killing Joke, who, despite being to this day one of the most powerful live bands I've ever seen, were just so obviously fucking mad that, although the music was awesome, it was kind of hard to truly relate to them. When Crass came along, it was kind of the other way round; we thought the politics were great, but felt that for the most part the music was just a bit too tinny and shit-sounding..."

After playing their first gig supporting The Barkers in Preston, during early 1982 ("We hired a high-top Luton van, all piled in the back with the gear, consumed far too much alcohol and cheap drugs, and ended up going arse over tit as the wind blew the van over, whilst going round a corner in Southam on the way home!" laughs Pete), Antisect recorded three formative demos (the first of which was tracked in Iron Maiden's old rehearsal room in Covent Garden) that captured well enough their youthful speed and energy, but merely hinted at the glorious album to come.

A big break came when they landed the support slot to Discharge, who were promoting their seminal 'Hear Nothing, See Nothing, Say Nothing' album, on their UK tour, but it was a double-edged sword in many respects. On the one hand, the band really hit it off with the headliners and played some incredible gigs (not least of all at the Zig Zag and the 100 Club); on the other, they often found themselves increasingly at odds with the mainstream venues they were playing, whose very 'un-punk' attitudes to door prices and security they were effectively condoning by their appearance.

"Yeah, after that tour, we began to seek out more independent local promoters, who actually might want to put the bands on so people could see them, rather than simply use the opportunity to make money out of everyone. We were starting to grow up a little bit, becoming more aware of how certain things shaped up in the big, wide world, and, as our opinions and ideas began to harden, the band began to take on a much more political edge.

"I think we just came down to feeling that, whilst it was fine for us to scream and shout about whatever we may have thought was fucked with it all out there, unless we were actually prepared to get stuck in on a practical level, anything we ranted on about as a band would always feel a bit hollow. At the time, we were living under one of the most repressive UK governments for generations, that seemed intent on obliterating anything that didn't fit in with its way of thinking, sound in the knowledge that those they were squeezing were not the ones who were ever likely to vote for or against them: the disenfranchised... the great unwashed. So, we started to attend some of the direct action protests of the time...

"In the dying days of the cold war, cruise missiles containing nuclear warheads were being delivered to both British and American air force bases up and down the country, and, because of where we lived, we were surrounded by the fuckers. We didn't like it, and there were thousands of people from all backgrounds who felt the same way. We became experts at the old 'sitting down in front of the missile transporters' routine, and we all made some fantastic, and often unlikely, friends.

"For some reason though, my two overriding memories are of being arrested by the military police, after waking up in the middle of the night in a sleeping bag full of rain water, in a shitty communal tent outside the Upper Hanford air base; and having a severely fucked-up conversation about Plymouth Argyle [football club], whilst coming down off acid, with former Labour Party leader Michael Foot at Greenham Common. I was coming down off acid, at least, not him... well, he might have been for all I know – he was shaking a bit!"

About this time, the band expanded to a six-piece, with the addition of two more vocalists, Richard Hill and Caroline Wallis. They also relocated to nearby Northampton ("We rented a house almost directly behind the police station from a woman who literally creaked when she walked; we co-ran an organic food co-op, which was almost unheard of back then, and sampled the delights of hunt saboteuring... momentum was building and things felt good..."), and, after a gig with Flux Of Pink Indians at the Greyhound in London during late summer 1982, were approached by them about doing an album for their Spiderleg label. The aforementioned 'In Darkness, There Is No Choice' was committed to tape at Southern Studios during September 1983, and crashed into the upper echelons of the Indie chart when it was released in January 1984, only kept from the No. 1 spot by The Smiths' self-titled debut. It was a truly ferocious offering, imbibed with an almost tangible intensity that has been oft copied but never quite equalled ever since.

"We spent fucking weeks writing and re-writing the material for the LP," recalls Pete. "We ditched or reworked old stuff, wrote plenty of new stuff, and basically worked our fucking arses off to try and ensure that we would end up with something that would have as few contradictions as we were capable of having. We probably didn't succeed as well as we thought at the time, but thankfully, twenty-odd years later, I can read most of the lyrics and all the album blurb without flinching, and I think I can honestly say that, despite the ravages and cynicism of time, I still believe in most of it, too.

"Looking back at the album now, there are all kinds of references to other people's stuff, both musically and lyrically; it's probably fair to say that we were nicking the best bits from a few different bands along the way. The thing was though, as I've been repeatedly told through the years, we came across as a bit dirtier and 'punkier' than the likes of Crass and Flux, and a bit more serious than the likes of Discharge, who by then had gone just that little bit too 'rawk' [i.e. rock].

"We really wanted to make something that was a bit more interesting than the usual 'twelve, three-minute songs, bunged on a bit of vinyl'-type release and came up with the (somewhat less than) revolutionary idea of joining all the tracks together. John Peel later complained that he couldn't cue the track he wanted to play, because he couldn't see the grooves in the vinyl properly...

"The studio sessions at Southern were great. Inspired by the enthusiastic engineering skills of Barry Sage, helped along by the downright weirdness of one Annie 'Anxiety' Bandez, and loosely kept in line by Colin from Flux, we had tape machines on either side of the control room, throwing guitar feedback loops back into the mixes. All manner of things were fed in and out of various effects units... double-

tracking? That's for wankers! We wanted sextuple-ultimate-bollocks-tracking, or we were fucking going home!

"The track 'A Midsummer Night's Dream' came out of a lull in the proceedings, when Rich started dicking around on the piano and Barry craftily recorded it through one of the ambient mikes that were set up in the live room. 'Go on, Rich, mate; it's beautiful, son!'

"The sessions weren't without their minor rumblings though. There was a subtle battle going on between the band and 'co-producer' Colin over how heavy the album should sound. Most of us, by this time, were leaning towards a heavier, darker sound than we had previously had, whereas Colin had wanted to keep things a little more punky-sounding. I remember leaving the studio at 6.00 am one morning, after we had completed the mixes with Colin and Barry, and feeling slightly pissed off that, somehow, it didn't sound as menacing as I had hoped it would..."

A short UK tour was undertaken with Crucifix and Dirt (MDC were meant to headline, but didn't made it past UK customs), and the NME music paper reviewed one of the shows, describing Antisect as 'sounding like an angry fighter jet crashing through an aircraft hangar'!

"That'll do nicely, thank you very much," laughs Pete, before adding of another memorable show, "We did a 'Bring A Toy' benefit for one-parent families and Women's Aid at the Marples in Sheffield, and it was as funny as fuck to see the multi-coloured, spiky-topped hordes outside the venue on the night, holding various teddy bears and giant fluffy rabbits as they queued to be let in.

"Golden Voice, who at the time were a fledgling US 'rock bollocks' tour promoter, wanted us to go and tour America. We eventually declined, deciding that if we did go to the States we would prefer to at least try to organise things ourselves, through local promoters. But did we

Antisect (Caroline Wallis and Pete Lyons) at the Interaction, Kentish Town, 1985, picture by Paul May.

ever get around to playing there? Did we fuck!"

Touring continued throughout 1984, towards the end of which, the band parted company with vocalist Rich, and bassist Wink was replaced, first by Tom Lowe, formerly of The Varukers, and then by John Bryson. Dates were undertaken across Europe, as well as the length and breadth of the UK.

"We especially liked Italy," reveals Pete. "The scene there was very militant at that time, and there were loads of very well-organised squat venues. Not least of which was the Virus Diffusioni in Milan. We toured with some great Italian hardcore bands, including Wretched and Negazione, and generally made some very good friends over there. Of course, we were chased, beaten up, and eventually held at machine-gun point, by the Carabinieri for stealing a family-sized Toblerone, but overall we had some great times.

"Back home, inspired by the enthusiasm for the squat scene that we had found in Italy, we began to organise and play at more and more of that type of event."

By this time, Antisect were widely regarded as one of the premier bands the anarcho-punk scene had to offer, and alongside Amebix, they probably pioneered, albeit unwittingly, the whole 'crust punk' debacle, where greasy clothes and even greasier hair reigned supreme.

"As time wore on, our previously spiky hair gave way to dreadlocks, and our clothes became tattier and tattier, and less… er… washed," explains Pete. "Not a fashion statement as such, just more of a reflection of the lifestyle that we were living… and if you've ever tried spiking your hair up at 6.30 in the morning in a bus shelter in Winslow after a night of class-A amphetamines, you'll probably know what I mean!

"One or two of us became more involved with various animal rights organisations, and we were starting to get a reputation for being weird, humourless, veggie, anarchist types… though it was fucking hard work being a weird, humourless, veggie, anarchist type in those days. A couple of us were vegan and that was just fucking stupid; soya milk and dairy-free margarine were only available from odd-looking people in kosher shops or through the outlets of a very sinister group of individuals that later became The Jesus Army. We seemed to spend a ridiculous amount of time wading through books, trying to figure out how to make stuff that was actually nice to eat. We even tried to make our own non-leather DMs [i.e. Doctor Marten boots], but they were just fucking shit, so we had to put up with the somewhat-less-than-substantial black plimsolls of the

Antisect drummer Pete Paluskiewicz at the Old Arts Centre, London, November 1985, picture by Paul May.

time: stinking in the summer, soaking in the winter.

"I even went to the extreme of buying job lots of ex-army rubber galoshes from my folks' home town in Ireland but, whilst they looked kind of cool in a 'What the fuck is that twat wearing?' kinda way, they had the plimsoll stink times ten which, let's face it, is not going to make you many new friends, and will probably lose you a few of your old ones along the way. Funny as fuck, looking back on it all really…"

Disaster struck though, when remaining vocalist Pete announced he was leaving the band on the very morning of the first day of a UK tour. Rather than pull the whole trip, the remaining members did the dates as a three-piece, with Pete (Lippy) and John handling vocals – despite not being able to remember all the lyrics!

"Pete had been through quite a lot in the preceding years and, in particular, one of Her Majesty's 'short, sharp shocks' in a young offenders institute had definitely left its mark on him; in fact, we all thought that the person that came out was somehow not the same person that went in. He became a much more serious individual in his outlook, and, in truth, his leaving the band had probably been on the cards for a while. It was however, the worst moment he could choose to tell us, and at the time we all wanted to kick his fucking teeth in. But we did the tour as a three-piece, and somehow contrived to do some of our best shows in a long while, even though none of us knew all the words properly. 'Fuck it!' we thought, 'We ain't gonna be able to do it all instrumentally, are we?' And there have been fewer lousier ways to illustrate the phrase 'necessity is the mother of invention' than our decision to replace any words we couldn't remember with the names of the 1966 England world cup squad! There's a certain risqué elation to be had, trying disguise the words 'Nobby Stiles' and 'Jackie Charlton' in a four-chord punk/metal thrash-out that I've struggled to rekindle ever since, even in times of occasional tantric sex.

"Meanwhile, back in Northampton, things were starting to look a bit grim. We were beginning to feel that a lot of the new acquaintances that we had met since moving there were turning out to be something other than the people they were making themselves out to be. Various pretentious little scenes were forming, and, on top of that, our house had now become known by the police as a meeting point for a lot of people they didn't like very much, and we were beginning to receive regular visits. One of the final straws came when I had just returned from court in London for an alleged offence during one of the Stop The City demonstrations, to be arrested for 'not attending' the court case I had just got back from. I guess it was the two microdots I'd done about half an hour before they came for me that at least made the mould on the cell walls appear more interesting."

By Pete's own admission then, the band were getting a name for themselves as heavy drug users, and were finding it increasingly difficult to maintain a balanced focus on their identity, purpose and direction.

"Yeah, and this all came to a head during a disastrous Dutch tour. In all fairness, Amsterdam was not really the best place for us to be based at that precise period in our history. Basically, we all metamorphosed into wanton, hairy, slavering, drug-crazed beasts. The problem was that we all seemed to be on different drugs at different times, and communication therefore became a mixture of nods, grunts and infantile burbling, as the various mixtures of acid, smack, coke, speed, hash and whatever-the-fuck-else-was-out-there had their desired (and sometimes undesired) effect. A somewhat typical instance was when our drummer, in his infinite wisdom decided to bring along an aging hippy friend of his as a roadie. The 'friend', who for his own safety shall only be referred to as 'Big G.', duly turned out to be an ex-junkie who, unbeknown to us, began 'borrowing' money from the tour promoter on the strength that we would pay it back at the end of the tour! Upon obtaining his small wad, he would then disappear into the smack quarter of Amsterdam and return, shivering, every couple of days or so, to blag some more money. I don't recall seeing him lift any gear (of the musical kind, at least) for the duration of the time we were out there, and indeed, the only 'humping' any of us saw him perform was one night when a certain band member, awoken by a series of guttural grunts, found him stumbling around, wanking off into his pants in the middle of the room. 'Nuff said…"

When safely back in the UK, Antisect moved operations to London, and released the two-track 'Out From The Void' single on Endangered Musik in early 1986. Both tracks were classic 'metallic period' Antisect, snarling guitars and pummelling rhythms, but a thin production leeched much of the requisite power from the recording, although the 7" still made No. 7 in the Indies. It was, however, to be the band's final studio release.

"At a squat gig at The Hope And Anchor, Mortarhate asked us to record an LP for them," explains Pete. "We agreed, and tracking began in Greenhouse Studios, near London's Old Street. There was something mildly surreal about speeding off our heads whilst playing pool with Katrina And The Waves, who were doing their follow-up to 'Walking On Sunshine' in the studio next door. The sessions were a struggle though, not aided by having an engineer that, great as he was at helping us get the sounds we wanted, was even more willing to slide out to the pub at every opportunity.

"Musically, we had reached a bit of a crossroads where the more 'metal' side of our music was coming to the fore. The punk thing was beginning to feel a bit alien as the politics had been pushed aside by more and more people turning to the 'brew crew' culture, and we ourselves began to feel more and more disillusioned with what was left of the more politicised end of things. We were also beginning to notice that a lot of the people who were talking the talk, weren't, shall we say, exactly walking the walk. It was a weird time; whilst we were questioning our faith in many of those around us, we also began to question ourselves. The lyrics became darker and harder to write. Our beliefs had hardly changed, but we were conscious of not spouting the same old shit and repeating ourselves, and, in trying to write about what we were feeling at the time, we found ourselves railing against a lot of

Antisect's John Bryson and Pete Boyce live at the Interaction, October 1985, picture by Paul May.

Antisect, whilst touring as a three-piece, live in Bristol, 1985.

the people who were now coming to our shows. The people that just didn't seem to give a shit anymore, or perhaps worse, the people that appeared to give a shit but who, deep down, were just as selfish and self-centred as those they would appear to be criticising.

"Anyway, we laid down most of the backing tracks for the album [working title: 'Welcome To The New Dark Ages'] and, although we liked the way it was going musically, looking back on it, I think that subconsciously, we didn't feel quite right in our relationship with the label and I think that it was that, along with our growing disillusionment with the scene in general, that made us unable to complete the sessions. We'd come full circle, and it felt like we didn't fit in again."

The band's final line-up was arrived at when John was replaced on bass by Lawrence Windle, who had formerly played with The X-Cretas and Anthrax, and Tim Andrews was recruited on vocals. Although the band were welcomed with open arms by the then-thriving traveller scene, Antisect still found themselves disgruntled with the audience they were attracting.

"Most of them seemed content to use our shows as an opportunity to get as fucked up as possible... which was fine to an extent, but the problem for us was that we felt like we could've been playing any old shite, and it would've still been lapped up down the front no matter what it was. The gap between us and a lot of our audience was widening, and more and more things were just starting to feel fundamentally wrong; the optimism of previous years had finally given way to a brooding nihilism as people appeared to have simply lost their way. And as time wore on, without a new release, we began to find it harder to define to people where we were going, and although most seemed to like the direction the music was taking, it was getting increasingly difficult to articulate our thoughts to an audience that for the most part seemed hell-bent on getting wasted.

"To be honest, I think that we were all losing our way. Although we still believed in it, we now weren't quite the same band that had released 'In Darkness...' We'd all been through so many personal, and not-so-personal, ups and downs and ins and outs since then, that we had turned kind of inward. The outright political edge that was there in the earlier years had slowly developed into a much more personal set of values. Just as relevant we felt, but much more difficult to put into words."

One last chance to unleash that elusive second album, and, more importantly, pull themselves out of the rut they were floundering in, came via some unexpected attention from Genesis P. Orridge and his Temple Records, although negotiations quickly ground to a halt when the label presented the band with an impenetrable 30-page contract.

"Actually, it was fairly standard music biz bollocks, to be honest," admits an older, wiser Pete, "But we just didn't like it, and they weren't into changing it, so the relationship and the record soon bit the dust. Meanwhile, the shows were becoming ever more crazed and shambolic, and perhaps the first nail in the band's coffin came when, slap, bang in the middle of a UK tour, we had a show in Brixton cancelled on the night. A whole load of shit went down between disgruntled punters and the police, and, after returning home to crash for the night, we awoke the following morning to find the back doors of the tour bus wide open and every single item of our gear gone: the guitars that we had had for years, amps, drums, pedals, lighting rig, backdrops… the fucking lot. Astounding!

"We scraped through the rest of the tour with a mixture of borrowed gear and hastily bought replacement stuff, but, despite managing to hold the shows together, there was a slightly ominous and withered tone to the remainder of the dates. A few weeks after the end of the tour, a benefit show, to try and recoup some of the costs of buying new gear, was arranged for us at the Mermaid in Birmingham. It was an insanely hot night, the venue was packed out with various bodies from past and present, and we played probably one of the best shows we had done for ages. It was also the last show that I can remember doing…

"Soon after that, a couple of us moved into the infamous Laura Place, an old Salvation Army property in Hackney that had been turned into a giant squat. It was almost a self-contained community; arranged over two buildings, joined together by a pair of wrought iron walkways, we had a rehearsal room, motorcycle workshop, communal kitchen, two resident drug-dealers, and a rickety tree-house to disappear up to, when the other twenty-odd people that lived there became a bit too much. It was a superb place and, despite the squalor, the sheer mix of people and personalities that co-existed there, gave it the unpredictability of some kind of crazed inner-London psycho punk rock fortress!

"That summer we took off to a mixture of custom bike shows and free festivals, occasionally bumping into Rob and Chris from Amebix, and various ex-Londonites who were now down in the West Country… Brad Caddis and Monty Bagpipes, we salute you! It was a hot summer, and the last one for a while that there would be any attempt to stage a free festival at Stonehenge. The Wiltshire police and the army were out in full force, splitting up the various convoys of people who had converged on the area, and we spent a lot of the time blatting round the countryside on our motorcycles, trying to keep people informed of what was going on and where. It was the year after the infamous Battle of the Beanfield, where police riot squads had directed hundreds of travellers into Savernake Forest, and then proceeded to beat the shit out of them and destroy their homes and vehicles, before arresting them on various trumped-up charges. The tension was there again that year, but aside from a few minor skirmishes, no-one really wanted to push it; people were tired, wary of what might happen, and just didn't seem to have the heart for another fight where there was only ever going to be one winner anyway. We pretty much felt the same, and I think that was probably when Antisect ceased to function.

"Lawrence and Tim took to the road, whilst Pete the drummer and I came back to our pirate squat in London. It had become just too fucking difficult to arrange stuff around the way that we were now living, and try as we might, I think we just ran out of steam. We all still got along on various levels, but somehow it just seemed like the natural time for us to let go of it all. We never actually sat down together and made a conscious decision to call it a day; our lives just simply went off in different directions."

Pete and Lawrence went on to play in Kulturo during the late Eighties, but, despite high expectations following some well-received live shows and a 45-minute-long demo produced by Blockheads drummer Charley Charles, the band never officially released anything and split after a year and a half.

"We had an absolute fucking blast of a time whilst it was all going on though," he smiles, in closing, of Antisect. "We met some astounding people, forged some really deep, lasting friendships, and experienced things that we just simply never would have, were it not for the band. We were only together for five years or so, but in that time we lived our lives just about exactly how we wanted to. Whenever we would occasionally return to Daventry to see our old friends and acquaintances there, it would never fail to shock me how old, tired and resigned they all seemed to be; most had 2.4 kids, were either living in council flats or mortgaged up to hilt, and I thank fuck that we took another route in life. We never made pots of money, but that wasn't the important thing.

"Nowadays, I work in a recording studio and make records for other bands, yet I still meet people all the fucking time who want to talk to me about this band whose last record came out over twenty years ago. I see the people selling the dodgy T-shirts, DVDs and CDs on the internet and I have to admit that, as much as it fucks me off to see people making money out of us, I'm not so fucking modest that there's not a part of me that's proud to have been involved in something that, however warped and twisted it may have been at times, still managed to affect a few other lives in a positive way, and maybe even made a little bit of a difference. Whilst I still don't fit in comfortably with society's 'norms', time has probably allowed me to temper the way I express my thoughts... I'm still prone to the occasional forthright outburst from time to time though!

"And people ask me all the time if we will ever get back together in some form or other to do a tour, and, although we have at various times been offered pretty good money to do so, it just seems a bit naff to me. In this instance, I don't feel that nostalgia is a valid enough reason to do it. Antisect were a band of a time, and whilst I'm sure that the majority of the politics still stand up today, the world is a slightly different place now, and I think the only way I could possibly justify doing something like that would be if we could come up with something suitably relevant and imaginative... which, to be honest, isn't exactly on the immediate horizon."

SELECT DISCOGRAPHY

7"s:

'Out From The Void' (Endangered Musik, 1986)

LPs:
'In Darkness, There Is No Choice' (Spiderleg, 1984)
'Hallo There, How's Life?' (Graven Images, 1991) – live
'Peace Is Better Than A Place In History' (Vinyl Japan, 1994) – live

At A Glance:
There is a CD version of the – utterly essential – 'In Darkness...' album still available through Southern, the booklet of which even features all the lyrics and liner notes that came with the original gatefold vinyl.

Milton Keyne's **EXIT-STANCE** were also one of the heavier anarcho bands, their powerful sound propelled by thundering tribal toms and edgy minor chord progressions, and they enjoyed a modest profile mainly thanks to the endorsement of their friends in Conflict, who not only released their records but took them out on the road more than once. They were formed in 1982 from the ashes of fledgling punk band Fuck Authority who themselves were originally known as Ethnic Minority.

When Ethnic Minority's guitarist Dave Bancroft and vocalist Alison Wyn-De-Bank left the band to get married, bassist Mark 'Jevs' Jeavons, lead guitarist Dave Paul and drummer Sean Finnis started up Fuck Authority, with Sean taking on the vocal duties and Mark Donaghey filling the drum stool. They played several shows in and around Milton Keynes, including one as support to Flux Of Pink Indians, and quickly rose to local notoriety because of their less-than-subtle name.

"We wanted to create a noise, use our voice to provoke change," reckons Jevs. "To confront the wrongs we saw around us, and seeing as most of this was caused by the profiteers, the using politicians, the powers that be basically, we opted to call ourselves Fuck Authority. I painted the name on the back of my jacket, as you did in them days... and was arrested by the police within 24 hours! For displaying offensive material in a public place! I was charged and released after confiscation of the jacket (to be used as evidence), and a court case ensued at which the prosecution could only find an ancient by-law to convict on – at which even the magistrates laughed. I agreed a compromise with the court of no conviction as long as our band changed its name; they stressed that the new one would have to be inoffensive, and, just to make sure, I was 'bound over' for a year!"

"The name Exit-stance is basically a corruption of the word 'existentialism', a philosophy that places discipline and responsibility on the individual," explains Sean. "A good state of mind to have, I believe, though I must admit that I stole it from a Poison Girls poster!

"The Clash were my earliest influence," he adds. "I like my bands not only to have something to say but also to look good and sound good, so they always seemed a lot more relevant than the Sex Pistols. The lyrics meant something to me at the time; they seemed more real, more personal, I suppose. I could actually relate to what they were saying, the street politics were very appealing, whereas the Pistols were more of a 'shock band.'

"Mind you, the Pistols did give the banal music industry a good kick up the arse and we should all be thankful for what they set in motion. So much of today's music owes a huge debt to those early punk bands; they swept away the inane and encouraged people to create, to break down barriers and discover freedom of expression. Unfortunately though, punk eventually created new barriers, brand new rules for itself, and any band that tried to be different was deemed to have sold out."

Mark was soon replaced behind the kit by sixteen-year-old Andy Williams, who despite his tender years had an aggressive style that took the band to a whole new level.

"It was like we'd found the missing link in our sound," agrees Jevs. "He was a really powerful drummer, influenced more by the likes of Killing Joke. That was a very positive time for us, as we now had the confidence and power of delivery we needed to support the serious lyrical content.

"Due to the lack of venues and support from local bands at this point, the only place to practice was in an art room in the grounds of an old rectory, and we decided we would have to broaden our horizons and get out of Milton Keynes. So we finished writing a set and recorded it at a small local studio and, with the help of a friend [Tom Dallyn] in Sussex, set up a small tour down there. It was really good as well – but short-lived! All the local parish councils took offence to the religious imagery in our name on the posters [a broken crucifix, complete with a forlorn hanging Christ, doubling as the 'T' in 'Exit'] and banned us from playing, so after doing the Brighton Alhambra, and gigs in Billingshurst and – I think – Worthing, we had to return home. But the gigs we did do were really good, and so was the response we got, which all helped build our confidence."

*Exit-stance live at the
Gateshead Station 1985,
picture by Scotty.*

Tom Dallyn invited Exit-stance to accompany him on a Stop The City march through London, an experience that helped reinforce certain ideals about authority the band were already nurturing and where they met many like-minded individuals who offered support and encouragement.

Jevs: "We gathered to try and stop the city centre from functioning, to bring attention to the plight of the Third World. The money the City lost in trading on that day was all that was needed to clear Third World debt, the interest they owed on the loans we created for them; the money spent on arms on that same day would also be enough to solve the same problem, so we could change the world in one day – if it wasn't for greed and paranoia! Anyway, those demos were a turning point in the 'peaceful protest' movement. The police were very heavy-handed; in my view they were the ones rioting, abusing many a peaceful protester just going about a legal protest. After a lot of aggro and provocation the people eventually started to fight back, and it soon became like a battle ground.

"This is when I met the Vauxhall squatters, a whole street of squatters, who had come together, living in these derelict terraced houses [in Bonnington Square] that had belonged to the Prince Charles Trust. They had all learnt different trades and skills – plumbing, electrics etc. – and off one of the houses, where a mother and child lived, so by law they couldn't be denied the right to such supplies, they had linked to all the other houses and shared the bills. This is were I met Tracey and her friends, Dave Tibet [formerly of Current 93, who wrote for Sounds], Annie Anxiety and many others who lived there; they were all great people, very helpful and encouraging. They explained how to set up an independent label and how to release your own material and that of others, get distribution etc. and how much it would cost to fund it all. And with their support we felt confident enough to try and set it up, even though it would take some time to raise the necessary cash through gigging."

However before the band could undertake their ambitious venture, they had a call from Conflict's Colin Jerwood, to whom they had given a copy of their demo at a recent gig, offering them a space on the Mortarhate compilation, 'Who? What? Why? When? Where?' He booked them five hours in Waterloo's Alaska Studios with engineer Ian O' Higgins, who had just finished work on New Model Army's 'Vengeance' album, where they quickly laid down the anti-vivisection rant, 'Operation Successful'. There was ample time left to also record 'Ballykelly Disco', 'Mankind's Hand', and 'Blinded By Fear', which would later be released as an EP by Mortarhate.

'Who? What? Why? When? Where?' was released to great acclaim in March 1984 and spent four months in the Indie Charts, peaking at No. 3, its success greatly benefiting the profile of all the bands involved. The three 'spare' tracks from the 'Operation Successful' session then emerged as the 'Crimes Against Humanity' EP, a gratuitously heavy single whose A-side, 'Ballykelly Disco', became one of the band's most popular songs. Thickly produced and based around a heaving, insistent bass lick, it featured a super-intense vocal turn from Sean that encapsulated the frustration and anger he felt at the religious and political impasse in Northern Ireland and the many innocent lives it had claimed. On December 6th, 1982, a bomb planted by the Irish National Liberation Army had exploded at the Razzamatazz disco in a pub in Ballykelly, Northern Ireland, killing eleven soldiers and six civilians. The song was a reaction to such callous slaughter, not taking sides as such but merely imploring, 'Irish or English, we are all human beings…'

"I actually wrote it as a personal observation on not only the events as they were in Northern Ireland, but also about political groups like the Red Brigade and the Angry Brigade etc," Sean elaborates. "I'm not a pacifist, but so much political violence is just self-defeating. It always seems that it is the innocent shopper or drinker etc. that gets killed and maimed… does the end justify the means? Sometimes maybe, but certainly not always. 'Ballykelly…' wasn't a 'for or against' song though; it was trying to say that violence for violence's sake is completely un-productive. Much of the IRA's bombing in this country served only to steel the population against them, to harden attitudes against the Republican movement in Ulster and any grievances it had, justified or not. Lessons from history, like the bombing of Britain, and indeed Germany, during the Second World War, proved that killing civilians doesn't lead to a collapsing morale or a decline in the will to fight… just the opposite in fact; it unifies a nation and hardens their attitude."

To launch the single, the band did a triumphant gig at the Richmond in North London supporting the Subhumans, the same day that Dave Tibet nominated 'Crimes…' as his 'Record Of The Week' in Sounds and Conflict invited them to join the bill of their imminent UK tour. However, disaster was but minutes away.

"I had just got my VW tour bus sorted, what could go wrong?" says Jevs, with a wry chuckle. "I'd used it to get to the gig, full of band members, equipment and anyone else who could fit in, same on the way back, but unfortunately we had an accident on the way home, with some boy racers. It was all a bit surreal – lights, sparks and screeches; crash and bang, screams and shouts… and a reverberating street light I'd run into which shattered as we got out of the van, showering glass down on us all. Then through all of this walked a Queens Guard, with spurs and sword still on (he was just coming back from parade duty), who picked Andy up out of the van and walked off to the roadside with him draped unconscious over his shoulder! Checking that he was okay and arguing with two Turkish boy racers, one of whom had hit the van. The police and ambulance turned up, and took Andy off to hospital, whilst the police took my details and got the van taken away. The next I know we're stuck in London with no money, van or equipment, so we headed off to the hospital to check on Andy and ended up kipping on the hospital corridor floor, 'til the next morning when we proceeded to bunk our way back to Milton Keynes.

"The van being written off meant we had to go on tour without a vehicle, so we borrowed a car and set off down south to support Conflict in Plymouth, but that blew up just outside Exeter, so yet again we were jumping trains. We got there in time to start the tour, and it was another good gig, then we tried following Conflict by rail to Portsmouth, then on the boat to the Isle of Wight... where we all got nicked for vagrancy and possession! I still think it was a plant though... just so the cops had an excuse to strip-search a couple of us!

"So from then on it was us and Conflict, with all the two bands' gear, crammed in an old Transit, off around the UK, kipping in the van, or on people's floors; as you can imagine, we had to get along! And we got to know each other pretty well... you get to know yourself a bit better as well, under such circumstances. It wasn't the easiest of tours; not only was it cramped, but it was also the middle of the miners' strike, and the country seemed to be in the middle of a civil war! Most of our gigs were benefit gigs for the miners, but most people at the northern gigs didn't have the money to pay to get in... and, seeing as they were the ones we were doing it for we just let them in anyway. I can assure you, no money was made on that tour; we survived on good people's generosity... and plenty of speed! Which was given to us, not paid for! I know it all sounds bad, but these were actually really good times; it made you feel that you were part of something that could end up a positive out of a negative... that this could really change the course of history. But it did take its toll, eventually contributing to our own demise as well as the miners..."

After that back-breaking stint around the UK, Andy – who had been suffering (quite unsurprisingly really) from ill health – decided he'd had enough and quit, leaving the band to recruit old friend Darren 'Daz' Pugh for yet more gigs with Conflict. Who himself soon walked out on them right before a gig in Worthing, where Conflict's Paco was coerced into saving the day by standing in behind the kit. Jevs called a recovering Andy up ("We literally begged him to rejoin!") and things were back on track, just in time to record the formidably vicious 'While Backs Are Turned' 12", which Mortarhate issued in 1986. A seven-song MLP, with a strong animal rights theme to many of the tracks, it rumbled through the listener like a tank, relying on brute static strength over any pretence at speed or dexterity for its quite profound impact. To promote it, the band embarked upon another national tour with Conflict, the dates just as eventful as before.

"Conflict were controversial," admits Jevs. "At the time, peaceful protest had been crushed by the powers that be, yet most people felt peaceful protest would eventually win over, but it did seem the only way was to fight back. Conflict always seemed to promote this, and you could see why. Many a gig I went to would be smashed up by right wing fascists, local gangs, or football hooligans, picking on – as they do – people who won't fight back. I once witnessed an Italian girl saying this to another girl, as she rammed a broken glass bottle into her face at a London gig; we broke it up and when the bleeding 'peace punk' girl turned and beat the crap out of her, all the Italian could say through her tears was, 'Why did she beat me up? Is she not a pacifist? She shouldn't fight back!' This is just one of many events I witnessed that caused me to question myself... but Conflict would fight back, take on a confrontation, whoever it was.

"I remember an incident in Oxford; a group of male and female skinheads turned up early before Colin and Big John had arrived. They just went around hitting people, threatening everyone; eventually we all stood our ground just as Colin and John walked in. John asked what was up, summed it all up without a word and went straight up to the biggest bloke and offered him out; he shied away and his girlfriend (who had already beaten two girls up) started crying and pleading with John to leave him alone. So John turned on the whole group and said, 'Okay, I'll have the lot of you! Come on then!' To which they all looked like little schoolboys being told off, shaking their heads as they single-filed it out of the door. We all followed them out and they ran off up the road... but they later returned and threw bricks through the windows, yet again running off, this time not to return, as we all ran out to confront them. No-one was hurt much that night – not one punch was thrown from any of us (Conflict included) – but it does show that, if you stand strong, then sometimes these people do back down, as they too feel pain and don't like getting hurt. People only have as much power as you let them have!

"I know there are many worse stories, and sometimes they get blown out of proportion, but I

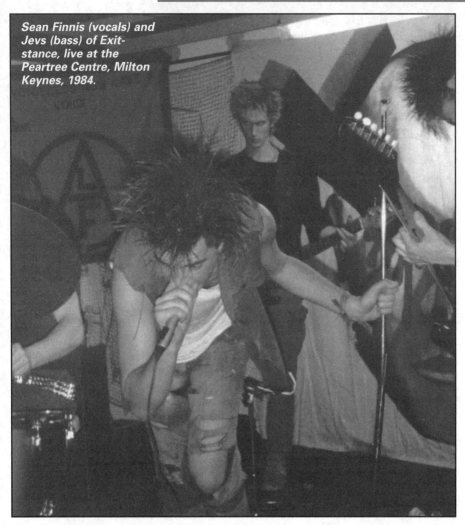

Sean Finnis (vocals) and Jevs (bass) of Exit-stance, live at the Peartree Centre, Milton Keynes, 1984.

always knew that, when we were with Conflict, if the trouble started they would be there to back us up, where as at many a peace gig, the fascists would freely roam, beating the crap out of anyone, cutting and bottling whoever they pleased, and no-one would stand up to them; they'd all just back off and watch, acting afterwards like it didn't happen.

"I've also seen the police act like this, on the second Stop The City event… not cutting people, but beating them with truncheons and stamping their horses' hooves down on protesters who were just sitting in peaceful protest outside a bank, breaking their ankles! As the people ran the foot police grabbed them, and I witnessed one officer grabbing a girl and ramming her head into the side of an open van door, then chucking her in the back and jumping on her head as she lay half conscious on the floor. I know I can't just stand and watch; I did then and have regretted it ever since. After witnessing that event, a short time later, I got caught in an alley full of police, all beating people up; one of them had a young lad by the throat, who was turning blue, and was smiling as he did it, so I ran over and gave him a dead arm. I hit his other arm as well, and shouted at him to let go; he turned, looking shocked, looked over his shoulder for back up, but he had none so he let go and ran off. No-one's perfect and I don't condone violence, but I do believe strength only respects strength; whatever your beliefs, people find power in hurting the weak and thrive on it. Why is it that in our society we are encouraged to seek out others' weaknesses to exploit them? Rather than looking for their strengths and encouraging them!"

After such a strong 12", Exit-stance looked all set to deliver a truly devastating album, but sadly split before they could finish writing it, the extensive touring taking its inevitable toll on the band and the relationships therein. Jevs also cites the cliquey nature of the punk scene as a major factor in their decision to disband.

"We did get disillusioned with the movement – the constant criticism… being judged all the time, attacked for not being perfect… people always wondering if we were conforming to the 'anarchist rule book'! That wasn't what I got into all this for; in fact, that kind of attitude was what I wanted to change!

"And to be honest, we did hold Conflict partly responsible at the time," he continues on the subject of their premature split. "Because although they funded the recordings, put out the records, and set up the tours, they would only pay us a tenner – if that – to do a gig, and that didn't even cover the cost of our travel etc., so we would always have to bunk trains and stuff to get home. The obvious answer would have been, 'So don't let's do the gig', but that was what it was all about, gigging and spreading the word. But Conflict had such a heavy schedule; it became more like a job… with no pay! And we couldn't afford to eat, let alone travel; we basically lived on meagre dole cheques and charity, but at the end of the day they did nothing more than what we didn't do for ourselves. Colin had more energy and drive than any of us; every band needs its leader, a driving force, and I suppose we were all reluctant as individuals in the band to lead. In some ways you have to force your opinions, your ideals, you have to motivate and make the decisions, but when each ideal is similar but the ways to achieve them so different, how can you do it jointly? How can you dictate to others you respect, to force them into doing what you want? That wasn't us, but we also just weren't functioning as a team any more. Expectations were high, enthusiasm low, everyone ended up compromising, suddenly feeling restricted by our own convictions and others' expectations. As a band we had never been that ambitious anyway, and we had achieved more than we had ever expected, so we split to start a-new…"

After a brief stint in Brighton, Jevs returned to Milton Keynes where he served time with various alternative acts, including The Art Vandal, Jumblehead, Phobics, and even an act called The Blues Collective, a group of local musicians who planned to fund their own independent ventures by coining in lots of cash doing covers from the popular 'Blues Brothers' movie. However they became so popular on the local college circuit, most of their other projects folded anyway, which had an adverse effect on the underground scene they sought to propagate, so he left ("We were just another rock'n'roll band chasing fame and fortune, which defeated the object…").

Andy meanwhile joined Indie rockers Clare, who became firm favourites with John Peel, and spent time in both London and Canada before returning to Milton Keynes. Jevs, Sean and Dave all became fathers as well, and in 2003 even briefly reformed Exit-stance, "to finish what we started," although it turned out to be a short-lived reunion.

"If we are to be remembered at all then, let's hope it's for our good looks, good music, our passion, our sense of life's worth. We never made a penny out of all of this, we never thought we would; we didn't do it for fame, we just did it because we cared – it felt right – and because we could. Not everything is done for a profit; we just did our bit to try and make the world a better place, and have some fun on the way.

"We used to say 'If you can change one person, to steer them in the right direction, to help make the world a better place, so that our children can inherit what's rightfully theirs (life without too much suffering, and a safe world to live it in… haven't done a very good job of that though, have we?), then we will have done something worthwhile.' In a small way I think we may have helped some people change; mainly because they could relate to the music and the songs, so they knew they weren't alone. Just as I did as a youth when I found punk, which at last made me realise that there were others like me dreaming of a better life; that I wasn't strange or abnormal because I cared. It seems that to care is seen as a sign of weakness, I see it as a sign of strength."

"The term 'anarcho punk' was coined by the music press who've always wanted to safely

Exit-stance bassist and band backdrop.

pigeonhole any form of musical movement to satisfy the lazy," concludes Sean, on a serious note. "Personally I would prefer to avoid any such labels... why be confined or limit yourself to one form of expression? Surely it's better to experiment and keep things interesting, to keep confronting? Standing still just invites stagnation to set in, which is surely against the whole ethos of punk.

"Pure anarchy is a pipe dream though, totally unworkable. The only form of anarchism I believe could work is anarcho-syndicalism; some form of organisation and leadership is always needed, no matter how libertarian it is. My greatest inspiration in this respect were the 1936 events in Barcelona, during the Spanish civil war, when the anarcho-syndicalist trade union, the CNT, literally took control of the city and ran it themselves. One good example was the city's tram workers, who decided to run the tram system as they saw fit; a committee was elected and within a week, 700 trams were running. Fares were slashed, yet profits increased! The workers' wages were standardised, which gave most a pay rise, and free medical care was provided. And this isn't theory or sloganeering, just an example of ordinary people changing their lives for the better and giving all a decent living, not just the privileged few."

SELECT DISCOGRAPHY

7"s:
'Crimes Against Humanity' (Mortarhate, 1984)

12"s:
'While Backs Are Turned' (Mortarhate, 1985)

At A Glance:
In 2004 Mortarhate released the 'While Backs Are Turned' MLP as a CD with sixteen bonus tracks, including the 7" and the band's demos; it contains all the lyrics and artwork as they appeared on the original vinyl releases and is easily the best place to check out Exit-stance at their juddering, foul-tempered best.

Far less acknowledged than their peers in chapter one, Rudimentary Peni, yet equally esoteric, and mining a similar vein aesthetically, **PART 1** were with the early 'death rock' scene that skirted uneasily around the edges of the anarcho-punk movement that helped spawn it before making a break towards gothdom.

"Well, I think it was in '76 or early '77," muses guitarist Mark Farrelly about when he was first bitten by the punk rock bug. "I was thirteen, and I saw that Janet Street-Porter interview with the Sex Pistols some Sunday afternoon... I was on the verge of getting into Kiss when the Pistols came along, but I was a bit too young to go to any of the gigs or anything. I was going to secondary school [The Lord Gray Comprehensive in Bletchley], and there was this deluge of first wave, first generation, punk bands. I knew Bob [Leith], who was eventually our drummer, going way back... and he started

Part 1 at the Wapping Autonomy Centre, January 1982, picture by Paul May.

up this band at school called The Bleeding Lips, and he brought this tape he'd done round to my house one night... and it was amazing to hear somebody who'd done something off their own back really, because music was something you bought on a vinyl album until then. And you just didn't question it really... but I was, like, 'Wow, he's actually done something for himself!'

"So I hooked up with this guy called Sean Finnis [yes, who ended up in Exit-stance], and we had this very basic, little school band going, The Urban Guerrillas. By the end of 1978, me and Sean joined up with Bob and another guy, to form a school 'super-group'! Like so many other kids up and down the country, we were just inspired by the whole punk ethos, of getting hold of an old instrument and doing it, just the energy of it all... it was so exciting to make your own cassettes and swap them with each other... and all us school bands were following along with all the changes that were happening. After the Pistols' American tour and all that, a lot of the media lost interest, and then you had that UK Subs-type period, and then the Crass thing came along...

"I remember reading about them in the Garry Bushell column in Sounds, and then I heard 'Reality Asylum', and I'd never heard anything like it before. Just the sheer ferocity of it, just the volume of expletives in there, and it was so militant – all the other bands seemed to pale into insignificance. Bands like The Clash, as far as we were concerned, had just sold out..."

This short-lived 'super-group' was hilariously named Matt Vinyl And The Emulsions, and played their first gig in the school hall, a benefit for a science teacher who'd been killed in a car accident (mysteriously, yet hardly unsurprisingly, most of the proceeds raised went missing). Mark and Sean then went on to be in several other bands together, including one called The Snipers (not to be confused with the Oxfordshire band of the same name) before Mark formed Part 1 with Bob, Chris Baker and Chris Pascoe.

"Chris [Pascoe] loved Santana! Which was kinda nice, because the people I'd been in bands with up until that point had been extremely dogmatic about what was and wasn't acceptable in punk rock. Chris shared our love of Public Image too; this was about the time that 'Metal Box' came out, and that was a real big influence on us. Their attitude as well as their music; 'cos they were Johnny Lydon and Jah Wobble, they had this real biting cynicism towards everything, yet they were doing this very odd, experimental music... I mean, we hadn't heard bands like Can, we didn't know of anything that had gone before, having been raised on a diet of first generation punk rock'n'roll, so hearing experimental twelve-minute-long songs was really pretty exciting.

"Another major influence was when me and Chris Pascoe attended the now-legendary UK Decay/Bauhaus double-header at Luton Technical College in January 1980. We totally missed the last bus back to Bletchley and were walking back along the A5 in the snow, trying to thumb a lift at 2 am, but we were really buzzing from that one.

"I'd made a kind of school boy pilgrimage the summer before, to Wellington Street, Luton, home of Plastic Records, to pick up the 'Split Single' that UK Decay did with Pneumania. I was obsessed with the 'Join Hands'-era sound of the Banshees as well, of John McKay and his flanger, so when [Steve] Spon joined Decay, I tried to get to all those gigs, and my own ideas for the sound of our band were set to follow a similar path.

"But as far back as I can remember, I was always into horror and death, stuff that's just goth cliché now: morbid, gruesome stuff. That's really how I met Bob… when we were about nine years old, and his dad managed the local cinema; he was really into films and everything, and me and him were always swapping horror magazines and plastic monster models… this was about 1975, and we were really into that sort of thing.

"So, when we got the band together, I was already a very morbid person, and mixed that with the anti-religious stance that I found so appealing about Crass; we were into that whole imagery of Christ bleeding, all the mourning and the death… graveyards… all the cliché stuff, but it was kinda pre-goth in our defence. There was a lot of that imagery around, but you didn't have the goth label yet."

Part One made their live debut during October 1980, at Bletchley's Compass Club, supporting local band, The Flying Ducks.

"We were really happy with that first gig, but the second one at the Peartree Bridge Centre, home to bands like Ethnic Minority and The Fictitious, was terrible. We had our own little clique, they had theirs, and we kind of ventured onto their turf to play the gig, which just went down so badly. But no one wanted to like it anyway, and that was kind of a turning point for us, when we decided to look beyond the confines of Milton Keynes, because the whole punk scene there seemed to be this jolly little mafia ran by people we didn't like, or people we didn't get on with at school at the time – which sounds really daft now, I know!"

January 1981, and Part 1 recorded their first demo at The Crypt in Stevenage, an eight-track studio situated in the basement of an abandoned church – an ideal location, in fact, to commit to tape such tracks as 'Tomb' and 'The Graveyard Song' (with lyrics the like of, 'Christian believer, you've filled your head with shit, there's nothing left for you, save the slime of the death pit!'); the latter number especially being a pivotal one in the evolution of the band's sound.

"Oh yeah, it was, absolutely. That changed everything for us. It was a long song, which was quite unfashionable at the time, and had all the death and horror elements we went on to cultivate; it was about someone being buried alive. It had all this stuff about how rotten Christianity was, and how we were all being buried alive under this heap of shit… that song set the tone for everything that was to follow. We stopped doing stuff like 'Atomic Age' about then… although there was a song on that demo called 'Marching Orders', the only track which I hadn't used my flanger on; it was a straight UK Subs strummy, thrashy-type thing, and later on, people would annoy us, especially at places like the Anarchy Centre, because they would shout out for 'Marching Orders', knowing we'd never ever play it again 'cos we were deep in the realm of the 'Graveyard Song' by then."

In fact, so much did Mark hate 'Marching Orders', when Crass short-listed the song for inclusion on volume two of their 'Bullshit Detector' compilation, he rang them and politely requested they not use it.

Another demo was recorded, 'In The Shadow Of The Cross', again at The Crypt, during Spring 1981, a competent seven-track affair that captured their sinister, atmospheric meanderings perfectly and garnered them much attention from the then-thriving underground network of zines and like-minded individuals, not least of all Andy Martin of The Apostles who invited them to play the squatted church in Pentonville Road, Kings Cross, with Dirt, The Sinyx and The Chronic Outbursts (from Leighton Buzzard). However, despite travelling down there, Part 1 didn't end up playing… in fact, they didn't actually play any of the first three London shows they had booked!

"I just thought Dirt were Crass clones," says Mark. "I'm not dissing them or anything, but there were so many bands around at that time who were bad photocopies of Crass… and who could blame them? Crass were A-list… 'A' with a circle around it, of course! But we had our own kind of slow dirges; the flanger on the guitar, our bassist obsessed with Jah Wobble, always trying to get his bass sound deeper and deeper, more dubby. We were on a totally different trip; we felt like outsiders to it all, but we also felt that that was our realm, as it were.

"Anyway, I'd spoken to Andy Martin on the phone, and he just told us to turn up with our guitars, so we rolled up there and it looked like complete chaos. We tried to play there twice, in fact, but it was like something out of a 'Keystone Cops' movie. It wasn't like we were that naïve, but it wasn't what we wanted for our first London gig… it was just fucking awful… drunken tramps sprawled out everywhere, vomiting… and we just thought, 'We can't play here!' So we sat around for a bit, getting pissed, and went home… just didn't bother playing – quite odd!

"Then, after the two Kings Cross no-shows, there was one that got really nasty in Walthamstow. That was really scary… I think the gig was on Halloween, October 31st [1981], and we turned up; we'd driven all the way from Milton Keynes, in a hired van, driven by a friend of a friend, 'cos none of us could drive… with all our own gear, thinking that if we were actually going to play, we'd take all our own stuff, get our own sound… right prima donnas we were, ha! So, we roll up at this youth centre, and there's The Apostles playing – I really loved The Apostles – but there was the usual sort of chaos, and a quite nasty kinda atmosphere in there, y'know? There was a sense of vulnerability, that it was all going to blow up into something unpleasant…

"And someone came running into the hall, shouting and screaming, and, the next thing we knew, Andy Martin and a few others had thrown themselves up against the doors, slammed them shut, and there were these fucking shovels and pick axes coming through the wood! We've got all our stuff still outside in the van, and we're stuck inside the hall… suddenly we're not worried about playing our first London gig anymore; we just wanna get home to Milton Keynes!

"Apparently a punk had pissed some football fan off outside in the High Street, and it had escalated out of control, and these guys had gone home and got their shovels and pick axes and decided to fucking do everybody. We were holding these doors closed, and everybody was smashing up these little wooden chairs to use as weapons. So, we didn't play yet again; we managed to get out, jumped in the van, and roared away. Andy Martin didn't even know we'd arrived at the gig!"

Finally though, Part 1 played a show in London, on January 27th, 1982, at the Wapping Anarchy Centre with The Apostles, Blood And Roses and Witches.

"Oh yeah, that was one of the very best gigs we ever played. The Anarchy Centre had only just opened really… that place became a Sunday night haven for the Scum Collective: Andy Martin and all his kind of associated bands… they sort of monopolised the place, in a very positive way. He had a lot of energy, he was doing a fanzine, a tape label; he's an extremely creative guy, and someone that you could have an intelligent conversation with. He didn't do glue or drugs or drink or whatever… you'd go to a gig and there was this guy who you could actually sit down and talk with.

"Witches were Bob from Blood And Roses' girlfriend, Ann-Gee Zoff, and a few of her Scum friends. It was all pretty ad hoc, just get up and do it, but they had a few decent tunes. And that gig couldn't have gone any better for us, it was a really great night."

So good in fact, a recording of it appeared as a bonus live side on all subsequent cassette copies of 'In The Shadow Of The Cross'. Then, in early 1982, as mentioned previously, Mark met Nick Blinko from Rudimentary Peni ("A pretty twisted meeting of minds – centring around morbidity of outlook and very dark humour," he admits), and the two bands played four gigs together during

Mark Farrelly of Part 1.

the first half of the year, two at the Anarchy Centre and two at the Centro Iberico.

"The first time [at the Iberico] was just after Peni did their record for Crass, and that pulled everyone in; it was fucking packed out, but for some idiotic reason we decided we were going to go on after them... and, of course, everyone fucked off! There was about fifteen people left there... whereas if we'd gone on before them, we would've played to a reasonably-sized audience and maybe the people reading your book would have a better idea just who we are!

"The second time was upstairs; it was a cold winter's evening, and there was a big fireplace up there, and people started breaking up chairs to burn... but the chairs were all spilling out, and the fire was spreading more and more. And Peni were just starting (we'd learnt our lesson and had already played before them); they opened with 'Dutch Men' off 'Death Church', but Nick introduced it as 'This one's called 'I'm On Fire...' or something like that. He was glancing nervously at these skinheads throwing all these chairs on the fire, which was getting higher and higher... and then... well, it all gets a bit misty... or rather smoky..."

In May 1982, with a kind donation off Nick and Grant from Peni ("They'd just had some money off the Crass single and offered to help us out; they lent us £150... which they never got back!"), Part 1 entered the sixteen-track Octopus Studios in Cambridge to record their 'Funeral Parade' EP, which they released on their own Paraworm Records in October 1982. Sombre and oppressively gloomy, it featured re-recorded (and far superior) versions of 'The Graveyard Song' and 'Tomb' from the first demo, and 'Ghost' from 'In The Shadow Of The Cross', plus a new number, 'Salem', and an instrumental intro/outro; it captured the dour, measured energy of the band to a tee, but is now an incredibly elusive release to track down.

"I only know of one copy myself, and that belongs to my mother!" laughs Mark. "A shame really, because that was easily the best thing we ever recorded. The thing is, by then, I was more and more into art, and really wasn't that bothered about making music. We took some copies to Small Wonder and they had quite a few off us, and Rough Trade took some as well... but this was all through Grant and Nick. I was really very lazy about it all, whilst they were making all these phone calls on our behalf, ringing around, trying to drum up interest."

Nick even passed a copy onto Brian 'Pushead' Schroeder, vocalist with frenzied US thrashcore band, Septic Death, who in 1984 released 'In The Shadow Of The Cross' as the 'Pictures Of Pain' LP on his own Pusmort Records (he also included one song, 'The Black Mass', on his 'Cleanse The Bacteria' compilation). Sadly it was purely a posthumous release, as vocalist Chris Baker left Part 1 in December 1982, and although the band continued as a three-piece with Mark handling vocal duties for a short while, they played their final show in April 1983, supporting the Subhumans at Oxford Street's famous 100 Club.

"A really shit gig... but not a bad place to plant your tombstone!" says Mark wryly. "The thing is, we were having longer and longer breaks between rehearsals at that point. We weren't moving away from punk or anything, but we were starting to indulge some of our earlier, more 'proggy' [i.e. progressive rock] Seventies influences, stuff that we had grown up with. We were always sniggering about it, like naughty schoolboys really, because we were still caught up in this web of anarcho punk. Basically we were growing more comfortable with ourselves and wanted to push it out a bit, do whatever we wanted.

"We were seeing less and less of Chris and eventually he left, just disappeared; there was no great drama or anything. I started taking over the vocals and the guitar, and it was a really great period, we wrote some good material. We didn't play any gigs for three or four months, and we'd built up this set of new songs, and then I had a call off Bruce from the Subhumans. We'd played with them before, in '82, at the Bowes Lyon House in Stevenage, and we'd gone down like a lead balloon. Everyone went to the bar when we were on, and then when the Subhumans started, everybody piled back in and had a fantastic time. And I felt incredibly jealous; they were playing such great punk rock'n'roll, y'know? They were brilliant live and had everyone just bouncing around the place, and I was left thinking, 'Why can't we be doing something like this, instead of these slow, morbid dirges?' But we knew that that was all we could do, and that was the kinda stuff that, if I went to a record store to buy some new music, I'd buy to listen to. I wouldn't buy the Subhumans, even though I respected what they were doing.

"But Bruce, who was a lovely guy, really enjoyed what we were doing too, and he kept in touch, and then invited us to play the 100 Club with them, and everything that could go wrong, went wrong. Bob even split his bass drum skin – and that hardly happens to any drummer!

"We actually broke down on the way home as well, and spent hours bickering with each other sat in the middle of the Buckinghamshire countryside, and when we got back to Bletchley the next morning, we were, like, 'Yeah, see ya…' There was a feeling that we wouldn't see each other personally too much after that, but nothing to suggest that the band was almost over. I mean, we took copies of our single along to that gig, so there was still some degree of optimism; we had no idea that it was going to be our last show."

Bob left soon afterwards to join London band, The Snails, but went on to play with the reformed A.T.V. and eventually The Cardiacs, whilst Mark retired from music altogether, attending instead St. Martin's School Of Art. Nowadays he works in a second-hand bookshop, enjoys restoring antique automata, and performs Victorian magic lantern shows.

"I have very few regrets as far as Part 1," he reckons. "I'm not worried about screwing up the letter from [Dead Kennedys vocalist] Jello Biafra when he asked us to record for Alternative Tentacles, and I'm even not bothered that I didn't try to get the band back together to take advantage of the Pusmort release… we could have probably toured the States with Septic Death!

"No, the only thing that gets under my skin is that we never made the studio to record that last batch of material we wrote. There was one song that was twenty-five minutes long, called 'Kill The Converts', which was really over the top and very bloodthirsty. It was still very dark, and it was like thumbing our nose at all the established anarcho-punk conventions. We seemed at our strongest once we became a three-piece… that's my only regret; that we never recorded and released any of that material."

SELECT DISCOGRAPHY

7"s:
'Funeral Parade' (Paraworm, 1983)

LPs:
'Pictures Of Pain' (Pusmort, 1984)

At A Glance:
A retrospective Part 1 CD may yet be on the cards if only Mark can locate all the relevant master tapes...

Legion Of Parasites at the Newcastle AA Club, February 1987.

In stark contrast, Bedford's **LEGION OF PARASITES** were one of the thrashier anarcho bands, their music generally delivered at an even greater velocity than the likes of Conflict and Antisect, and owing more to early C.O.C. and the rest of the USHC scene than UK bands such as Crass and Flux. However, despite their noisier compositions being reminiscent of the 'studs 'n' leather' brigade, their lyrical stance placed them firmly in the anarcho camp, as guitarist Sean Houchin confirms.

"Yeah, I was very into the anarchist ideology, very into the vegetarian aspect of that scene (and have been for 24 years now)… it's a lifestyle, a whole attitude. We weren't happy with stuff at all, didn't like the Falklands War… our first demo had a picture of the Belgrano blowing up on the front cover… but it was all a complete mess at the time, with the miners' strike, rioting… and we were very influenced by everything that was going on around us; we definitely had an opinion and wanted to voice it.

"I remember buying 'Feeding Of The 5000' by Crass and playing it over and over again; it really helped focus some of the attitude and angst we had into something constructive. The punk scene had started to cross over and go all glam at the end of the Seventies, it didn't have the same anger and underground appeal, and Crass and the other anarcho bands like Flux, took it to a completely different place, a new level. They saw the door opening and just kicked it in, and it was like a rocket going off in everyone's head. There was a big blast, and repercussions, and after the dust had settled, we were just left with… this impression… I really embraced all that, read all the gatefold sleeves over and over; it really gave me something to believe in.

"We'd been fucking about in school bands with no name and stuff since about '78 or '79, and then me and my brother Cian moved from Hemel Hempstead up to Paven, this village in Bedfordshire, where we hooked up with Wag [real name Simon Wagstaff] in about '82. We were the village noise merchants and ended up taking advantage of the local village hall every Sunday… we had a few mates in the village and after we formed, this little punk scene started. Then we made a few friends in Bedford, where there were also few bands at the time, like Government Lies… and we were up and running."

With Sean on guitar, Cian handling vocals and Wag the drums, the Legion Of Parasites also comprised – initially – Steve 'Gibbo' Gibbs on second guitar and Scott Hickman on bass, but they soon pared down to a four-piece with the departure of Gibbo, which was how they remained until 1985, when Scott left and Cian took over the bass as well as the vocals. Not before Gibbo played on the band's first demo though, several tracks from which even appeared several years later (1986) on the US compilation LP, 'Empty Skulls', that saw LOP rubbing shoulders with such international hardcore luminaries as the aforementioned C.O.C., Half Life, Justice League and Crude SS.

"We just wanted something that stood out," explains Sean of their striking choice of name. "And personally I felt that we – everybody – were just this legion of parasites on the face of the earth really. If you look at the nitty gritty of the name, everybody is a parasite on something, and it just represented how we felt about the world in general, including ourselves. We knew we were parasites as well, but we were trying to change that, trying to put something positive back in…"

After an eventful first show at Sharnbrook Mill Theatre – a 21st birthday party that got trashed by the over-excited, drunken audience – the band entered Hero Studios in Luton to hammer out their first demo, 'Another Disaster'. Primitive though it was, it adequately captured their hyperactive, pacey intensity.

"It was a right dive," laughs Sean. "Only cost about £60 a day, and we just played all our songs,

Legion Of Parasites at the 100 Club, September 1984, picture by Paul May.

about ten or twelve tracks; did it all live, like it was a practise. 'Right… ready? Okay… go!' And then onto the next track! It was only later when we got into bigger studios that we started to want to do overdubs and stuff, but the first demo was all about getting the songs down, getting the energy on tape… the first takes are normally the best anyway. And it captured the moment… we played the best we could at the time… and most importantly we got our message across. The lyrics were a big part of it all, they weren't just there to accompany the music; we really stood for something, we weren't just a rock'n'roll band."

A copy of the demo found its way into the hands of Marcus Featherby, who ran Sheffield label Pax; he consequently included two tracks from LOP's second demo (recorded at Rock Snake Studios, Rushdon) – 'Death Watch' and 'Dying World' – on his hugely successful 'Bollox To The Gonads, Here's The Testicles' compilation. It spent over three months in the Indies upon its release during autumn 1983, peaking at No. 6.

"We couldn't believe the amount of mail we got off that, from almost every country around the world. We were then going to do this single for Pax, but we broke down on the way to the studio, blew the van up en route, and Marcus didn't like that 'cos he'd already paid for the studio time, and we never made it. But it cost us £300 or £400 to get towed off the motorway, get a new engine put in the van… my mate's dad's van that I'd borrowed! So, that was a bit of a nightmare…"

Thankfully Colin Jerwood of Conflict was waiting in the wings to sign the band to Fight Back, an offshoot of his Mortarhate label. The resultant 'Undesirable Guests' 12" featured six tracks of thrashy metallic punk, and although not brilliantly produced was a terrific stand-alone debut for the band that more than captured their rough-hewn ferocity.

'Sea Of Desecration', a superb track built around a startlingly effective high-speed bass run ("It was 'Tube Disasters' by Flux Of Pink Indians speeded up," admits Sean with a smile), was then included on Mortarhate's 'We Don't Want Your Fucking War' compilation in early 1985.

"We were playing two or three times a month by then, all over the place. We went as far north as Newcastle, the Sunderland Bunker… and we seemed to play London a lot… so much in fact that most people thought we were actually based there!

"We played a lot of benefit gigs as well; it seemed that every show we did was a benefit, in fact… for the Anarchist Bust Fund and stuff. We were quite involved with Conflict and played a lot of shows with them… including a great one at the 100 Club, which still rates as one of my favourite shows we ever played. We played with the Subhumans there as well, and with the Subhumans down in Bedford… it was great to meet these bands and be taken seriously; it was all about networking with likeminded people. As long as everyone got their petrol costs covered, we'd play benefits anywhere we could; it was all about the movement really… wanting to be a part of it all was really important to us."

As mentioned earlier, Scott left in early 1985 ("He wasn't as into it as the rest of us really, and moved on; it was one of those things…"), just before the band recorded the rather raging 'Prison Of Life' album, that really saw their US hardcore influences coming to the fore and was issued through their own Thrash Records.

"That ended up as a one-off release for 'our label' though," admits Sean. "Just to get us out of the shit, and then the [distributors] Cartel started going through a bit of a wobbly time, and we wanted to see if we could get more pressed of the next release, because we thought we could sell more. We just wanted to raise our profile really, and see where we could go, and we ended up applying to an ad in Sounds for S.T.U.D. Records, ran by this guy called John Sherry, who signed us for our second album [1987's 'Dawn To Dust']. The other bands on the label were shite really, all these crappy rock bands, but he put us in this big studio in Belgravia where they had recorded Eurovision Song Contest entries and stuff! It was quite a step up from what we were used to, but the cover of that release let it down really… it was a bit crap basically, but we didn't really give a fuck, did we? We told one of our mates, 'Yeah, yeah, we'll put your artwork on our next album…' But then you have to live with it!"

"There are not many fourteen-year-old kids that get to be A&R men," recalls James Sherry, John's son, who was responsible for signing the band to S.T.U.D., and is nowadays a successful journalist and press agent. "But for one brief moment there, I was one! My father, John, who sadly died of cancer in 1994, had been in the music business since the late Sixties; he played drums for a mod-ish beat band called The Bunch, and then went into live agency work and management. By 1986 I was firmly entrenched in the blossoming UK hardcore underground, doing fanzines, trading tapes and loving the scene at the time. My dad wanted to start this metal/punk record label called S.T.U.D. – which stood for Soon Turns You Deaf… that was my mum's idea! – and he decided to let his fourteen-year-old son who was actually into the music help pick the bands…

"So he placed adverts in all of the music press and soon enough hundreds of demos started coming in; I used to rush home from school and spend hours playing through them all, passing the good ones on to my dad. Most of them were crap, of course… bog-standard thrash metal bands, for the most part, but amongst one particular batch was this demo from Legion Of Parasites. I was already a fan of the band from their previous records on Mortarhate and loved the brutal, raw energy of the new songs, and somehow I managed to convince my dad to release their next record.

"They were due to play an all-dayer at the Sir George Robey in London, Finsbury Park, and we went to see them. My main memory of the night is that the venue owner's dog had crapped all over the stage, so the bands had to clean the stage of dog shit before they could set up their gear! But the Robey was famous for being one of London's scummiest venues so this was no surprise. Of course, LOP were great and soon after that my dad went to talk to them about the record and go through the contract. I remember him telling me later how he met them at one of their parents' houses and they all had tea and biscuits! I think he found this funny because he was half expecting a filthy squat and people passed out on cider and hot knives…"

Misfortune struck yet again though, when the Legion Of Parasites' proposed second album for S.T.U.D. never made it past the mastering stages of recording (although it did eventually appear through Plastic Head subsidiary, Rhythm Vicar, albeit after the band had split), and it was pent-up frustration at such constant setbacks that ultimately led to their demise.

"John Sherry really believed in us, and was sure our next album for him would sell shit-loads, but none of the big distributors knew how to handle it, so it ended up being shelved and the whole thing fell apart. We'd known Steve [Beatty, head of Plastic Head] for a while, and he was into our stuff, and when he offered to put this 'lost album' out for us, we jumped at the chance, even though we'd actually called it a day by then…

"It kinda just lost its momentum," he adds, on how Legion Of Parasites ground to an inglorious halt. "We really just questioned whether it was worth going on… the scene had changed so drastically, and it just seemed the right time to call it a day. Drugs killed it off really… not so much speed, but too much E… everyone was so 'loved up', and youngsters were more into the techno and rave scenes; people just weren't into it anymore. They became complacent, just accepted things at face value, were content to grow up not really knowing the struggles people had been through in the Eighties. The Miners Strike became just another piece of topical information… and the Falklands seemed as long ago as WWII! It was all ancient history.

"There was a real sense of finality to the last gig we did, and I didn't enjoy it much at all. There was such a degree of despondency and apathy, we really weren't into it, and we knew it was time to move on. It was in Bedford somewhere [where the band had logically relocated in the mid-Eighties], probably at The Horse And Groom, which was where we did a lot of our early gigs, so we ended up back where we started – and life is full of those little cycles, isn't it?"

Sean and Wag went on to form a dub reggae band called Franticise ("Because that scene seemed a lot more threatening than what punk was turning into… and we were still singing about the same kind of stuff as before, but putting it to a happier, more dubbed-out kinda vibe…"), whilst Cian joined Stevenage's dark gothic rockers, The Nephilim. He then went on to do another gothic band, Saints Of Eden, whilst Wag ended up in much-loved chaotic punk outfit Sick On The Bus (whom he left in 2004, due to increasing family commitments), and Sean's attention was captured by the drum 'n' bass scene.

"First I got into computers, DJ'd a bit, then did some drum 'n' bass… 'cos that's still right 'on it', still a bit angry. It's fast, it's got attitude, and it's singing about real issues, problems on the street; it reminds me of the punk scene really, because it's still very true to itself.

"It's inevitable though really, isn't it?" he sighs, when pressed about the state of modern punk rock. "It's just recycling your mother's record collection, y'know? It's very cyclic. I see these bands on TV now and think, 'Fuckin' hell, fifteen years ago, that would have been so underground, it would never have been shown!' Look at Green Day, who are fucking wicked, but really they're only like those old American hardcore bands, just that they've kept at it. And they're still political lyrically, but it's lost all its bite because no one's really interested in what they have to say.

"People like to put other people in boxes, everything's safely packaged away. And anarcho-punk was put in 'the scary box' that no one wanted to open… Pandora's box in a way. These days it's quite the opposite, it's all gift-wrapped and very acceptable to be a punk now… which makes you not want to be a punk in many ways. The reggae scene today is still dangerous though, and that's what makes it exciting for me; it's about the street, about what's going on in real people's lives, not about some fantasy on MTV. Most of these new US punk bands are rich kids, and if they can't make a hundred grand a year off it, they'll pack it in."

Pausing for thought, and breath, he ponders the musical legacy he himself has left behind.

"I suppose I'd like to be remembered as having attitude? And helping bring a level of awareness to people, supporting worthy causes like the bust funds, the hunt sabs… in fact, maybe that's part of our legacy… the fact that those hoity-toity tossers on their horses are at last having a hard time of it themselves! And that's today, the law is changing right now, but we were singing about it twenty years ago. But we were all singing about global warning too, all the environmental issues, about multinationals taking over the world… only no fucker was listening back then – they are now! It's all come to pass.

"The music was just a personal journey for me, but the lyrics are where we really wanted to make a change. If you've got something worth saying, then say it; if you haven't, then don't! Simple as that; I've never been into singing about relationships breaking up and shit like that… it's just so banal; it breaks you up and stuff, but it makes you a stronger person in the end. The dark side of life is the scariest, where people would rather not look; most people don't give a fuck unless it affects them directly. If it impacts upon how much money they have in their pockets at the end of the month, then they worry about it; if not, they don't give a shit."

SELECT DISCOGRAPHY

12"s:
'Undesirable Guests' (Fight Back, 1984)

LPs:
'Prison Of Life' (Thrash, 1985)
'Dawn To Dust' (S.T.U.D., 1987)
'Manmade Filth' (Rhythm Vicar, 1991)

At A Glance:
A thorough Legion Of Parasites retrospective CD is well overdue, although the Mortarhate compilation, 'We Don't Want Your Fucking War', featuring what is probably the band's best track, 'Sea Of Desecration', was reissued on disc in 2004.

Not strictly an anarcho band as such, East Anglia's REALITY (apparently named after the Chron Gen song) did however gig extensively with the likes of Flux Of Pink Indians, Subhumans and Conflict, and eventually released their second single through the latter's own Mortarhate Records. They were formed during the summer of 1981 by guitarist/vocalist Hedley 'Veng' Harnett, following the demise of his previous band, The Alternative Imbeciles.

"Reality grew out of a few school friends with some very dubious equipment," laughs Veng. "Such as a guitar plugged into the ageing family stereo and the worst drum kit you've ever seen; we'd lie around at the weekends playing Pistols and Subs covers. I remember an early 'rehearsal' which consisted of me (with my 'new' second-hand guitar and 30-watt practise amp) and Gullet [real name Steven Miller] on his first ever drum kit, bashing away on the front lawn down on the farm – well, this was Norfolk, after all! Whilst Gullet's mum and aunts were all inside watching the Royal Wedding on the TV… they came out to complain about the racket and asked if we knew any Jim Reeves numbers…!

"Our equipment was always limited – my first guitar had a bridge height of at least an inch! – but we did odd bits of part-time work here and there, and eventually graduated to Marshall amplification… but I never did make it as far as owning a Gibson!"

Veng and Gullet were joined by vocalist Louise Gould, additional guitarist Dick (real name Kevin Mummery), and Chris 'Neut' Gee on bass, and they quickly played their first show at – in time-honoured tradition – their local youth club. It was a shambolic, noisy affair, but Reality struck a chord with the local punks, who followed them enthusiastically as they graduated from 'headlining' village halls to supporting Chelsea in Kings Lynn in early 1982.

"Neut blagged that first gig for us, and the organisers weren't too pleased when they discovered that we'd advertised it heavily around town and about 50 punks turned up. We blasted through our set using a borrowed guitar amp and all three of our small amps plugged in a row for the bass. I can't remember what the vocals came out of, but it was still loud enough for complaints around the village to cause the police to turn up, join us onstage and cut the power. Luckily we were into our encore by then!

"But punk rock was always about raw energy, wasn't it? A complete absence of compromise," reckons Veng. "It was angry but creative, and tapped into all the energy that rural youth had little means of releasing. Dick liked the Subs and The Damned; I liked The Ruts and even, later on, a bit of early U2. We were influenced by all the early bands really, and a few of the second wave; we did a couple of thrashier songs, but they were never really where we were coming from. We were strongly influenced politically though by the likes of Flux Of Pink Indians and the attitude of the Dead Kennedys."

Inspired by their successes on the live front, Reality entered Stix Studio, Peterborough on June 20th, 1982, to record the 'Blind To The Truth' EP with Dave Colton. It was released that November by Subversive Records, a Kings Lynn label ran by The Nuclear Socketts; as well as Reality and themselves, they also did singles by Section A and the European Toys, and, although a small concern, got the band in select shops and played on John Peel.

"The first studio we went in was literally just someone's back room," recalls Veng. "We were so excited just to be there, it was a big buzz, but it was only really much later on that we developed enough to do some good studio stuff. That first single, paid for with a loan from a friend who'd had a work injury compensation pay-out, sounds exactly like what it was… a bunch of fourteen-year-olds learning how to play! But just a year or so later, our sound really came on."

But not before they had endured a brief hiatus and major line-up overhaul, that robbed the single of any real momentum.

"Louise left, bless her, because she couldn't sing and the novelty had worn off for her. Neut bought some dubious equipment from a friend of my brother Steve [Harnett, the band's manager] and got pissed off with us when he realised that it wasn't quite as he had been led to believe. He left to make a point, but we thought he meant it, and Sam [McCleary] had just left another local

Reality (left to right: Steven Miller, Veng Harnett, Pete McGregor).

band and asked to join, and we were off. It was only some years later that I found out from Neut that he would have come back, if only we'd asked.

"Dick had trouble getting the long nights and general disruption past his family and he had to pack it in. A shame really because it was him and me who started it all originally, and he wrote some great stuff. So then it was just me on guitar for a few years after that, until Jon [Waugh] joined us [in 1984]."

Sam was fired after a short UK tour (Veng cites the inevitable 'personality clashes'), and was replaced by Peter McGregor, who made his live debut supporting The Toy Dolls in Leeds. With Veng taking over the role of main vocalist as well as handling guitar duties, the new, improved Reality recorded the 'Who Killed The Golden Goose?' 7" (b/w 'Lonely Shadow') at Elephant Studios, Wapping, for Mortarhate on New Years Eve 1983. Frustratingly for all concerned, it didn't appear until July '84, but highlighted the considerably more melodic direction the band were keen to pursue.

"We never believed in noise for noise's sake; we liked 999, X-Ray Spex and Penetration, and we were also, I guess, influenced by some of the non-punk bands of the Eighties, so as our sound developed, it was becoming more sophisticated. When we reached the point where we were really progressing, the scene, which had shrunk at that stage, was turning more towards thrash metal and crossover, so the audiences weren't getting into us so much. Which was frustrating really, as only a few years later, I think we would have gone down a treat. I'd like to think that if we carried on, we might have ended up making an album like 'Youth And Young Manhood' by the Kings Of Leon, or maybe '1234' by The Jeevas."

Diminishing interest in Reality never stopped the band enjoying themselves whilst on the road though, as manager Steve recalls.

"There are loads of stories," he chuckles. "I remember them all going for a paddle in the fountains of Peterborough shopping precinct, to pick out the pennies at the bottom for extra beer money; the security guard went mad and kicked them out, and lots of colourful language was exchanged between both parties.

"And when Gullet the drummer went out, he always made sure he ended up vomiting; his favourite one was leaving a pavement pizza on the bonnet of people's expensive sports cars… or urinating on pub seats in front of people. And when supporting Flux Of Pink Indians once, in a venue above a disco, the band got their dicks out to show all the disco girls. They even played a gig in Ipswich in their underpants once, for some reason…"

As mentioned earlier, Johnny Waugh joined as second guitarist during autumn 1984 (he would later audition for The Wildhearts, and after a brief stint working for Ash is now sound man for Aswad), and although he barely lasted the year out, he played on the August '84 demo (recorded at Blumberg Studios, Cambridge, with Tony Leonard, who played drums for the Glitter Band). All three of the tracks from that session appeared on various compilation albums; 'Sign Of The Times' on Mortarhate's 'We Don't Want Your Fucking Law', 'To Know Her' and 'Ballad Of Mad Harry' on Rot Records' 'A Kick Up The Arse, Volume One'.

Back to a three-piece again, Reality soldiered on in the face of increasing disillusionment, even beginning tentative work on their debut LP (with a working title of 'Swimming Against The Tide'). But they threw in the towel once and for all following a local 'village extravaganza' where they supported Lene Lovich, on the same day as Live Aid during summer of 1985.

"The village me and Veng lived in at the time was Crimplesham," explains Steve. "And, yes, Lene Lovich was our next-door neighbour! I think that gig was to raise money for children's climbing frames or something? Anyway, we kept seeing this strange woman around the village… we couldn't believe it when we found out who she was. Veng blasted 'Lucky Number' out down the village, but it kept slowing down because he would keep putting his dick on the record…!"

"But the best show might have been one of our Ipswich gigs, where there was always a good atmosphere and we were always well received," adds Veng, now a clinical psychologist, remembering his time with the band philosophically. "Or maybe supporting the UK Subs at the Gala Ballroom in Norwich? The worst one was in Portsmouth, where we'd driven for hours to play, only to have half the audience leave as soon as the local bands had finished, without bothering to see what the East Anglians had to offer. Parochialism at its worse but also, or so it seemed to me, symptomatic that the energy (at that stage) was fast draining out of the whole punk scene.

"I'd like to be remembered though, not only as a moderately successful young punk band from the rural back of beyond where nothing ever got going normally, but also for the political voice we articulated… oh, and for the fact that we didn't take ourselves too seriously! Sometimes I tell people that I'm still a punk… mostly they just laugh, but the people in the know understand what I mean."

SELECT DISCOGRAPHY

7"s:
'Blind To The Truth' (Subversive, 1982)
'Who Killed The Golden Goose?' (Mortarhate, 1984)

At A Glance:
Overground's excellent 'Young Drunk Punks' discography CD compiles virtually everything the band recorded (bar 'To Know Her' from the '84 demo), plus various live tracks and informative liner notes, making it the definitive Reality overview. An abridged version has also been issued on 'puke coloured' vinyl by Italian label, Rockin' Bones, limited to just 300 copies. And there's now a Reality website at: www.steveharnett.com

One band that were due to appear in the 'Burning Britain' book yet were 'held over' for this anarcho volume, because they're genuinely difficult to categorise as either 'peace punks' or 'chaos punks' (a crude division of the genres, at best, admittedly) are **THE DISRUPTERS** from Norwich. They had a track on Crass's 'Bullshit Detector' compilation, yet possibly their best-known track, 'Young Offender', actually appeared on Anagram's hugely successful 'Punk And Disorderly' album.

Kev Wymer of The Disrupters live at the Jacquard, Norwich.

The first version of the band appeared in late 1980, featuring vocalist Steve Hansell, guitarist Andrew 'Gibbon' Gibson, bassist Dave Howard and drummer Kevin Wymer (who had previously played for The Aborts). It was this line-up that recorded the track 'Napalm' for 'Bullshit Detector', but Dave only lasted two gigs, before being replaced on bass by Tim Perkins.

"I was about fourteen when the whole punk thing exploded," recalls Steve. "Before that I was into those Seventies glam bands like T. Rex and Alice Cooper. Then someone played me some Ramones and Sex Pistols… and, at risk of sounding corny, 'Anarchy In The UK' was like a battle cry! I was, like, 'Yeah man! That's exactly how I fucking feel!' I was instantly hooked. I loved all those early bands, like The Clash, New York Dolls, and Generation X, and some of them were breaking out of London at the time and playing at a Norwich club called Peoples, or the West Runton Pavilion. I would spend every penny I could lay my hands on going to watch these bands and buying their records. Suddenly those dickheads and teachers at school didn't look so intimidating anymore!

"Locally, we had The Right Hand Lovers [featuring Paul Whitehouse and Charlie Higson from 'The Fast Show' fame] and Der Kitsch who had a great frontman called John Vince. I did eventually get drawn to the anarcho scene though, Crass in particular. 'The Feeding Of The 5000' had a big effect on me, and I still really admire Crass, even today; they were completely unique."

The Disrupters played their first show at the University of East Anglia in Norwich with The Torpedoes, a local covers band, and The Intensive Breeders; they gate-crashed the gig unannounced and basically forced their way onto the bill!

"We just turned up as arrogant as anything with our guitars and demanded to play," laughs Steve. "The Breeders let us use their amps and kit, and we did a twenty minute set. We were probably awful, but loved it anyway. Little did I know then what lay ahead for the next eight years!"

Other early shows were often eventful, one ending up in a mass ruck between punks and 'headbangers', another had someone throwing dog excrement at Steve ("I mean who the fuck takes dogshit along to a gig?" he asks incredulously). They took a step up to the next level when they entered the now-long-gone Whitehouse Studio ("just outside Norwich") and recorded their 'Young Offender' single, which they produced with the help of John Ward and released on their own Radical Change label. Although Steve admits they "stumbled through the session" and holds little regard for the recording now, the single did extremely well for the band, reaching No. 12 in the Indie charts. Fanzine interviews and offers of gigs came flooding in from all over the country.

"We were completely overwhelmed by its success," admits Steve. "To be honest, we never even thought about sending out any demos to record companies; that's why we just saved up some cash and had it pressed ourselves. When we released it, we were not really looking any further than that initial pressing of 1000. We gave most of those first copies to Backs Records for distribution, and within a week they were all sold and Backs wanted more. We were all skint so, from then on, Backs [ran by Johnny Appel] became the financial backbone of Radical Change.

"I didn't think we'd be able to even give our first single away," he adds laughing. "And suddenly there we were, discussing a follow-up single and an album!"

As mentioned previously, 'Young Offender' also appeared on the aforementioned 'Punk And Disorderly' compilation, which didn't do the band's profile any harm at all. And they were the only anarcho punks included.

"It's a great record," concedes Steve. "And I figured being on the same album as the Dead Kennedys had to be cool. Actually I like all the bands on there and in terms of exposure it was very good for us. The

royalties came in handy as well! They bought us some much-needed new equipment.

"I guess we did have more in common with the anarchist bands in that we wrote politically motivated songs, but I think it was a shame that these divisions within the scene arose in the first place; there was a lot of snobbery in both camps. Personally I was just as happy listening to GBH and the UK Subs as I was The Mob or Crass. The anarchist scene got a little too po-faced at times, which kind of threatened to take the whole rock'n'roll element out of punk; it was getting so conservative, just replacing old rules with new ones… that said, I detested the Oi movement that crept in too, and all the thuggish, right wing arseholes it brought with it. I wanted to put Garry Bushell against a wall and shoot the cunt!"

Gibbon was replaced by Paul Greener on guitar, and The Disrupters entered Spaceward Studios, where SLF recorded their 'Inflammable Material' opus ("It felt a bit like entering hallowed ground…!"), to record their second single, 'Shelters For The Rich', which appeared during August 1982. Both more urgent and more musically mature than its predecessor, with the title track being ushered in by a mournful acoustic intro, 'Shelters…' spent almost two months in the Indies, peaking at No. 21.

The third single though, 1983's 'Bomb Heaven', remains one of the band's least memorable moments, two rather throwaway, obvious tracks and a spoken word piece, the bleak, depressing poem 'Make A Baby'. Not surprisingly, it failed to chart.

By the time they recorded their debut album, which has aged far more gracefully than 'Bomb Heaven', The Disrupters had replaced Tim Perkins with Steve Hough on bass, and had recruited Prem Nick (real name Nicholas Lake, who still performs poetry to this day, usually at Blyth Power gigs) to perform their spoken word tracks. They maintained this line-up until they split in late 1988.

'Unrehearsed Wrongs' was a forceful distorted bludgeon, and a great success for the band, achieving their best Indie placing, No. 7, upon its release in June 1983. It remained in the chart for eight weeks.

The Disrupters 1985 (left to right: Steve Hough, Kev Wymer, Steve Hansell, and Paul Greener).

"I'm very critical of much of our stuff but I am proud of 'Unrehearsed Wrongs'," says Steve. "We used Flying Pig Studio, with an engineer called J.B. who was a pleasure to work with. I actually think that album has some of our best songs on it… 'Gas The Punx', 'Pigs In Blue', 'Napalm'… it certainly pisses on our second LP. Admittedly, there are a couple of dodgy tracks, like 'Obscene', but I stand by it all and wouldn't change anything on it, even if I could. We were never under the illusion that we were master musicians; that was never the point. We just wanted to give a big fuck off to the corporate machine and all the flag-waving arseholes that reinforce it."

As well as gigging with The Disrupters, Steve and Kevin were busy with Radical Change Records, who were signing and releasing other bands such as Revulsion, Icon AD and Self Abuse.

"Revulsion were good mates of ours, we used to go on the road with them a lot, so anyone booking us got both bands for the price of one. We shared a van and equipment with them, so it seemed obvious to help them put their records out too. Actually, we knew most of the bands we put out personally, or had been sent demos by them. I still think the Icon AD EPs are well cool. I liked their track ['Cancer'] on the first 'Bullshit Detector' album and contacted them to see if they wanted to release anything on Radical Change; it's still a mystery to me why they didn't sell better…"

Possibly as a result of these other commitments, or maybe due to the onset of complacency, the second Disrupters album, 1984's 'Playing With Fire', sounded rushed and unconvincing, and was a disappointment compared to the first one. It opens well enough with 'Evil Dead', but soon deteriorates into something quite generic and dull – even the title track is plodding and stiff.

"I don't really like any of our singles or the 'Playing With Fire' LP," agrees Steve. "I think that album sounds lazy and weak; it was a shame we didn't spend more time on it because some of those songs had potential.

"After that album we knew we had to do better, and we followed it up with the 'Alive In The Electric Chair' 12" [1985]; that's my favourite of all our releases. We worked hard on that record."

Steve is right to be proud of 'Alive…' which positively emanates energy, especially the driving opener, 'Give Me A Rush', which chugs along with a vengeance; other highlights are the desperately vehement 'Rot In Hell' and the surprisingly melodic 'Tearing Apart'. It was to be the last official release by the band (apart from two tracks, 'Arse End Of The Establishment' and 'Dead In The Head', contributed to the 1986 'Words Worth Shouting' compilation) and it serves as a fitting epitaph.

Always ones to 'put their money where their mouths were', The Disrupters became increasingly embroiled with political activism, attending and helping organise anti-vivisection protests and the Stop Norwich demonstrations, and they paid the price for such direct action, finding themselves hauled before the law courts on several occasions.

They also grew disillusioned with the small-minded trials and tribulations of the music scene they were involved in, so for the latter part of 1986 and most of '87, the band went into a self-enforced hiatus.

"We don't have a rose-tinted view of that period; we encountered plenty of bitching, dodgy promoters, petty rivalries and I personally got a bit sick of the whole circus. That's why we hibernated when we did."

They reformed briefly in 1988 for a flurry of shows, some of which were filmed and released posthumously as the 'Anarchy, Peace And Chips' video. Not only is this thirty-three minute film an excellent – not to mention, thoroughly professional – visual document of the band, but with its footage of Margaret Thatcher, pompous royals, police brutality, raids on vivisection laboratories and gas-masked punks 'nailed' to crosses, it's also an evocative snapshot of the political climate of the time.

"The 'Anarchy, Peace And Chips' thing was done by an old mate of mine, Derek Williams, who had access to all the gear... he filmed and edited the whole thing in exchange for a case of Budweiser!"

The Disrupters then did their final gig at Jacquard's in Norwich, a venue that had been at the hub of the city's alternative music scene for many years, supporting the UK Subs.

"I never expected The Disrupters to last eight months, let alone eight years," admits Steve, who currently sings for a Ramones tribute band, The New York Scumhaters. "I felt the scene was crumbling around me at the time. I just couldn't work up any enthusiasm for it anymore, so I quit and the others followed suit.

"I would like us to be remembered as a band that tried to do things our way and on our own terms; whether you like our music or not, it was always heartfelt and honest. There's a piece of us all in those songs we recorded.

"Our farewell gig was cool though; we went out with a bang that night! It was a great gig, one of our best. Backstage, Charlie Harper [UK Subs vocalist] was disgusted that we were jacking it in. 'You'll miss it', he said, and on reflection, eighteen years later, I think he was probably right!"

Kevin Wymers now sings for Saigon Kiss, whilst the New York Scumhaters still gig around the country, most recently with Blyth Power, and have even released (completely unofficially) a CD of Ramones covers entitled 'Rocket To Bangkok'.

SELECT DISCOGRAPHY

7"s:
'Young Offender' (Radical Change, 1981)
'Shelters For The Rich' (Radical Change, 1982)
'Bomb Heaven' (Radical Change, 1983)

12"s:
'Alive In The Electric Chair' (Radical Change, 1985)

LPs:
'Unrehearsed Wrongs' (Radical Change, 1983)
'Playing With Fire (Radical Change, 1984)

At A Glance:
In early 2006, Overground released the definitive Disrupters retrospective CD, 'Gas The Punx', complete with liner notes from the band and previously unreleased material. Anagram's excellent 'Punk And Disorderly' compilation featuring 'Young Offender' is also available. You might even be able to get a copy of the highly recommended 'Anarchy, Peace And Chips' video documentary by e-mailing Steve at disrupters@btinternet.com

CHAPTER SIX

Hailing from Wigan, **THE SYSTEM** produced one of the most immediate and listenable of all the anarcho-punk singles in the guise of 1983's superb 'The System… Is Murder' EP. Signed to Flux Of Pink Indians' Spiderleg label, they possessed similarly harsh guitar tones and staccato rhythms, but also blended their aggressive libertarian politics with infectious tunes and accessible arrangements, most of their material throbbing with the same sort of gutsy street punk melodies as Anti Pasti or latter-period Blitz.

"I'd been messing about with a guitar for a few years anyway, but then I saw The Damned supporting T-Rex at the Apollo in Manchester – it was '77, the last T-Rex tour – and it blew me away," recollects The System guitarist, Andy Coward. "I thought it was really brave of Marc Bolan to take someone like The Damned out on tour… when he could have just gotten some crappy band or other to buy onto the gigs.

"Anyway, I started taping John Peel's shows and really started thinking about forming a band after that. It was the energy of it all, and the style… just daring to do something different.

"There was already a bit of a scene here in Wigan; this tiny little bar used to have punk nights, and they'd play all the latest stuff… although obviously mixed with a bit of reggae as well, 'cos this was late '77 or early '78, so they were a bit limited as to what they could find to play. I was still at school at the time, but we all used to pile down there, and it was a good introduction to it all: there were all these people a few years older than us, who'd come from the Roxy scene and the Bowie scene, and we just elaborated on their style really.

"Then the next thing after that was Wigan Casino, where Slaughter And The Dogs played a

Andy Coward of The System, picture by Trunt.

few times, and then Eric's Club, in Liverpool; we'd be there every Saturday... we'd get the train over, and they'd have matinee shows, so we could get a train home again after as well. I saw The Damned, Rezillos, 999, Ultravox, Japan, Lurkers... loads of great bands... and there was never any trouble."

After a short-lived outfit called The Condemned ("Just messing about really, playing Wire covers and stuff!"), Andy, then on bass, formed The Atomz with former Condemned members, Jimi on vocals and Steven 'Maki' McCallum on guitar, plus Paul White on drums.

"We were all just school friends," explains Andy. "Apart from Maki, who we knew from going to gigs. We used to rehearse in the drummer's cellar, and on the way home, we always used to call in this pub, the Derby Arms, with our guitars... and one day, the landlord said, 'Oh, you in a band, lads? Why don't you practise here, upstairs?' And that's where we ended up doing our first gig, 'cos he let us put it on for free.

"Getting gigs was always hard though, 'cos we didn't have any equipment really. I always remember practising with the drummer playing a steel fan heater! He'd just keep a beat on that! Money was short... I had to wait for my birthday to get a Hondo 2 [guitar] from the Freeman's catalogue!"

Despite the logistical problems entailed, The Atomz clocked up numerous shows in and around Wigan, and even one 'out of town' foray to Southport to play a punk festival at the Scarborough Hotel. They also recorded a demo, at Graveyard Sounds in Manchester in July 1979, a studio they would return to the following year as The System.

The metamorphosis from Atomz to System was precipitated by a growing friendship with local band The Lethal Objects. Their vocalist Ian Millington ("Or 'Jan Comode' as he sometimes called himself," laughs Andy) and drummer Jimmy 'Spider' Brown joined Andy, now also on guitar, Maki, and Jimi (now stepping into Andy's former role of bassist) to form The System... who controversially made one of their earliest public appearances in the car park of Wigan's Blue Bell pub – on Royal Wedding Day, July 29th, 1981.

"What happened at the Blue Bell was, we all started going in there, and eventually we took over the juke box, filled it with all our records, and on Friday nights, it was a major meeting place for all the Wigan punks. It was great really, the place virtually ended up a punk bar, y'know? And we thought, 'Why not go all the way, and have a gig in their car park?' And the landlord didn't mind, so we did!

"And it was probably the most political thing the band ever did, to be honest. We might have been 'political' when we were gigging with Crass, but who were we being political to? People who already agreed with most of what we were saying! Are you actually gaining anything, other than entertaining yourself and the audience? But playing on that car park, we had normal folk just passing by, watching us and wondering what we were doing. Perhaps it triggered a question or two in somebody's head...?

"Anyway, before we could finish our set, the local vicar phoned the police, and they turned the power off on us. We started playing 'Police Oppression' by the [Angelic] Upstarts as they were trying to pull the plug... which went down well, as you can imagine.

"But punk had started off with the Pistols talking about anarchy and rebellion, and being anti-state, but that sort of went into a lull, and a lot of second wave punk bands were just singing about being in love and stuff. Then Crass picked it up again, but about ten times more serious, and that anti-authority vibe was one of the things that drew me to punk in the first place, so it was natural we'd express it with our own band."

Maki soon left though, moving away from the area to get married, and The System entered Graveyard Sounds to track their first demo, sometime during 1980.

"We basically just banged out four or five songs live in the studio... not to send out to labels or anything; we just did them for ourselves, to see what our songs actually sounded like. And when we heard them, we decided they were a bit slow and needed speeding up a bit! To be honest though, we weren't that interested in getting on a record label or anything, we were more excited about playing live and having a laugh."

Travelling to see Crass play one of their first shows in the Northwest at the Preston Warehouse during May 1981 was to prove another milestone in the band's development, and The System subsequently organised Crass a Wigan show, at the much-loved Trucks venue ("It was one of the best clubs you could ever go to, always absolute chaos!"), that summer. Support came from the Poison Girls, who The System had previously opened for in Manchester.

Despite not shopping themselves to record companies, the band's inherent potential was shining like a beacon for all to see by this time, and they received offers from not one label, but two, the very first time they played outside Wigan town limits, as support to Flux Of Pink Indians in Sheffield.

"Well, they [Flux] were in a bit of a mess, weren't they?" says Andy. "They didn't even have a full band, and Simon and Dave from The Insane, this Wigan band that we knew, joined them on guitar and drums, and they asked us to come and play this gig with them in Sheffield [at The Marples, September 7th, 1981]. And it was really good, Flux liked us a lot, and asked us to do a single on Spiderleg there and then. Before that, we'd spoken to Crass quite a bit about doing something with them, but they were very busy with all these other bands, and Flux were really enthusiastic, so we went with them."

Ian and Jimi of The System live at the Sunderland Bunker, picture by Trunt.

Also at the same show was Marcus Featherby from Pax, who was so impressed with The System that night, he asked them to contribute a track to his anti-war compilation LP, 'Wargasm'. They contributed the insistent 'Their Decisions' to an eclectic line-up that saw the likes of Infa Riot, Captain Sensible and [Sheffield goths] Danse Society appearing alongside such luminaries as Dead Kennedys, Flux Of Pink Indians and Poison Girls.

The LP was well received, and paved the way nicely for The System's own 'Dogs Of War' 7". Recorded at Southern Studios by John Loder and Penny Rimbaud, the single saw the band's inherent '77-style tunefulness loaded with the snarling invective of anarcho-punk to great effect, and it justifiably made the Indie Top Twenty when released by Spiderleg during spring 1982. Many gigs were undertaken to promote it, most memorably several shows with Crass... some of them planned, some of them not.

"One time, we were playing the Triad in Bishops Stortford, and we visited Crass at Dial House beforehand and said, 'Come down to the gig...' They came along and ended up playing an impromptu set... it was about 50p to get in, and all these people were sat around on the floor – and suddenly Crass came on! They did loads of stuff off 'Christ The Album', and they really enjoyed themselves; it wasn't deadly serious or anything... in fact, it was the only time I ever saw Pete Wright drinking! He even wrote me a postcard a few days later, saying, 'Thanks for letting me use your amp!' They were really decent people to deal with.

"The second time they played Wigan, we supported them ourselves, and they asked us if we wanted to go along and finish off the tour that they were doing with them! They even gave us the money there and then to go and hire a van and said, 'Come down to Reading Town Hall tomorrow night!' I'd been down there the year before to see them, just to watch the gig, and that was actually the first time I met Andy T.

"It was all about networking, wasn't it? There were times when we'd be playing down in London and Flux would be playing the Northwest, and we'd stay round their house, and they'd stay round ours! We really trusted each other... and then we might meet up the next day for a gig together somewhere in the middle, as we were both travelling home...

"I think the most memorable gig for me though was at the Leadmill in Sheffield, sometime in '82, mainly 'cos it was such a great turn-out. It was a charity gig, with Dirt and Flux and Annie Anxiety, and we played in front of over a thousand people, which was a big crowd in those days. It was free to get in, but you had to bring along a child's toy, which they then gave to this kids' charity. Something like that's worth doing, isn't it?

"And the gigs up at the Bunker in Sunderland were always really good, 'cos it was a collective; it wasn't like when you turned up at most venues... 'Hello, I'm the manager of the club...!' It was more like, 'This is our place... let us know if you need anything!' We even got fed, which was definitely a rare treat!"

A Scottish tour undertaken with Flux, Andy T. and Alternative holds less fond memories for Andy however: "The gig in Dunfermline was pretty memorable – for being bad! Loads of skinheads there, threatening people with knives and stuff like that, it was horrible... a huge fight broke out in Inverness as well, in the entrance hall to the venue, and the place emptied whilst everyone went outside to watch the fight! What's the point in that?

"The other shows on that Scottish mini-tour were in Aberdeen and Glasgow, and thankfully went much better. We were going to go to Europe with Subhumans at one point as well, seeing as we were on the same label as each other, but it never happened. Dick had an accident or something, and they had to cancel the tour... and that was as close as we came to playing outside the UK! Oh well..."

Material was written and demoed for a proposed System album, and a second single – the aforementioned '... Is Murder' EP, featuring four of the best songs already penned for the LP – was issued in late summer 1983, by which time the band were already in the throes of self-destruction. A tremendous shame for all concerned, because such was the strength of the new compositions, one feels certain that with a strong full-length release in the racks, The System could well have emerged as a leading light of the genre.

As it was though, Ian left in late 1983 ("He had other ideas about what he wanted to do, and he was getting a lot more serious politically... he lives in New Zealand now..."), and the band decided to call it a day rather than try to find someone suitable to replace him.

After The System, Andy played with Wartoys for a short time, and then reunited with Jimi and Spider in the 'high energy rock band', Fear Of Music, who played several shows but never recorded a proper demo. The System later enjoyed a posthumous release of their missing-in-action album in 1998, when German label Skuld teamed up with Profane Existence in the States to release 'Thought Control', collecting together various unreleased System demos, of material originally intended for the LP, in an attractive gatefold sleeve.

Soon after its release, a version of The System appeared at the McLibel benefit show organised during June '98 at London University by Dick Lucas of the Subhumans and Jon Active. Unable to persuade Ian to participate, Jimi handled vocals, whilst Maki returned on bass, and Andy played guitar alongside second guitarist Simon and drummer Bri, both from the Wigan-based ACAB.

"Jon was distributing the 'Thought Control' album at the time, and asked me if we'd like to get together to play for a good cause," explains Andy. "It was an okay show too, I suppose; I didn't enjoy it all that much... it was a lot of time spent rehearsing for a short time onstage, but it was good to see all the other bands play and meet a lot of old friends.

"The only difference between The System and most of the other bands was, because we came from the early punk scene, we had much more diverse influences to draw upon," he adds thoughtfully, on what may have helped set the band apart from their peers, "Whereas a much younger band who started in, say '82 or '83, might only be influenced by Crass and all the subsequent bands that sounded like Crass anyway. We had that early punk attitude, with some politics thrown in. We were very aware that it was possible to politicise too much as well, so we made sure we entertained with a good tune or two.

"But were we anarchists? Well, that was our frame of mind, and I don't think it's changed really. It's a personal thing, there's no such thing as an Anarchist Rule Book, is there? It would defeat the object... but how can you be a 100% practising anarchist? Where in the world are you going to go to do that? It's more like, when a situation comes up, you look at it and deal with it in a different way to how a regular thinker might... that's all it is. It was never about freeing ourselves completely from society, more like freeing your mind of all their indoctrination. The system wants you to toe the line all the way 'til retirement, but we're all free to walk down several different paths along the way..."

SELECT DISCOGRAPHY

7"s:
'Dogs Of War' (Spiderleg, 1982)
'The System... Is Murder' (Spiderleg, 1983)

LPs:
'Thought Control' (Skuld/Profane Existence, 1998)

At A Glance:
In view of the scarcity of the beautifully-presented 'Thought Control' LP, Overground's 'The System Is Still Murder' is the most comprehensive System offering currently available, which features both singles and most of the demos, complete with a twelve-page booklet that thoroughly documents the band's all-too-brief career.

Wartoys live in Preston, 1982: Paul - vocals, Mick – bass.

THE WARTOYS were a Wigan band whose close ties to The System have already been discussed; a politically motivated and sincere young troupe, they never released anything on vinyl yet managed to make a lasting impression on their local scene with a strong cassette, 'Indoctrination Is The System, Indoctrination Is Death'.

Originally formed in Ashton-in-Makerfield sometime during 1978, Wartoys were vocalist Kevin Staunton and bassist Jason Walsh, with guitars and drums being handled – respectively – by brothers Tony and John Preston. When Kev left to attend college the following year, Wartoys asked Paul Haunch who sang with the experimental punk band, Pax Vobiscum, to take over the vacant vocal slot.

"They knew me from the local punk scene, especially punk nights at Trucks," explains Paul. "My own band never got off the ground, but we had rehearsed with Wartoys at the Ashton YMCA where they used to practice on Sundays. The System also used the YMCA venue for practicing from time to time, and there was much sharing of experiences between the bands. We also had a joint friend, Mike Ripley, who had a four channel reel-to-reel tape recorder, and he used to come and record us and allow us to go and hang out and practice at his house when his Dad worked away in Saudi.

"He actually challenged the Wartoys, albeit humorously, on my appointment as the new singer, because he believed he would've done a better job himself, and the band squirmed and tried to avoid the question. He then offered to join us as a poet; he liked winding the Wartoys up and offered to do some alternative verse about gay rights... he was quickly told that we were about anarchism, opposing war and animal rights, but not gay issues.

"Musically, the band's influences were a combination of Crass, The System, Crisis and Fallout," he adds. "We wanted to create a more musical, melodic and lyrically focused sound than some of the other bands at the time, and consequently the material was much slower than most of the ranting sounds of that era. Our tracks also tended to be longer than the average punk band... in fact, we considered ourselves to be anarchists rather than punks, and felt a separation from some of the other punk bands of the day, especially the Oi! scene. We defined anarchy as being anti-system and anti-authority; we wanted to be free and outside of all state control and religion... ironically, Tony, the guitarist, would eventually return to Catholicism years later."

Paul played his first gig with the band from the back of a wagon at a free music festival outside the John Bull in Wigan ("We played some pretty innovative gigs; they were a rare opportunity to reach the unconverted..."), but then Jason Walsh left, when his girlfriend Dot dumped him to go out with the new singer ("By the way, I'm still with Dot, and we have two grown-up children, Liberty (22) and Alex (20)!"); he was replaced by Mick 'Slick' McKevitt, who was several years older than his band mates.

"Yeah, he was ancient... 20-plus!" laughs Paul. "But he brought some maturity and some damn good ideas and bass lines into the band. To be honest, the Wartoys were never really (and quite unfairly) taken seriously within the local punk scene because they were youngsters and perceived as just kids messing around. Although I was a bit older than the rest of them, by about a year, I certainly encountered the same prejudices as well, because I was only just eighteen when I joined."

With a settled line-up and a firm idea of their musical direction, Wartoys embarked on the gig trail, embroiling themselves in the anarcho-punk scene, playing with the likes of Poison Girls, Anarka And Poppy, Andy T. and the Subhumans in the process.

"We were well connected with the local anarchist scene in Liverpool and played numerous gigs there – mainly at the Old Police Station on Lark Road. Interestingly enough, the gig we did with the Subhumans was at a venue called Pickwicks, and it was so poorly attended that the club management locked us in and we had to empty our pockets to cover the costs of the gig! So all the bands made a loss, but we had a great time anyway.

"The scariest gig in Liverpool was an afternoon and evening session at the Christian Steer Community Centre; there were a load of punk bands on but the local youth didn't take too kindly to our presence. They started throwing bottles at the building and, halfway through our set, they climbed on the roof and were throwing bottles through the glass windows on the roof. No-one got hurt, but as soon as we did our set, we sneaked out and ran all the way back to the station to escape! The latter was our worst ever gig actually, which wasn't helped when Jason, our bass player at the time, didn't turn up because he thought there would be trouble (how right he was); the end result being that, at my second gig with Wartoys, I was taxed with trying to sing, even though I couldn't remember all the lyrics, as well as trying to play bass (very badly) to cover for Jason!"

Two demos were recorded in 1981, with members of The System helping the band out with advice and encouragement – the first at Twilight Studios in Manchester on January 8th, the other locally in Wigan on July 24th ("I can't remember what the studio was called, but it's closed now...") – and the two sessions were combined as the aforementioned 'Indoctrination Is The System, Indoctrination Is Death' tape, which captured the band's powerful surging melodic style more than adequately. It also highlighted the gravitas they afforded their libertarian politics.

"We were very close in our shared values, and spent so much time together that we would talk about setting up our own commune," reckons Paul. "We did wonder whether our bassist Mick took vegetarianism seriously though, as it was rumoured he was once caught by a band member eating a meat pie, and when challenged on it he allegedly said, 'They don't put meat in them any more!'

"The rest of us got more and more into animal rights and joined a Wigan branch of the ALF and started to go on raids of turkey farms (but never knew what to do with the liberated turkeys!), demonstrations at pig farms, and city centre marches protesting against animal abuse. We started to regularly participate in hunt sabotage, and spent many an hour running round after dogs and horses with garlic spray... and then running for our lives as the bouncers or 'hunt heavies' tried to beat us up! This violence increased to the point where some of my fellow saboteurs were arming themselves, for their own protection, but the number of fights I saw threatened my own strong views on pacifism and eventually I felt I could not participate in this venture any longer, due to the levels of violence I was witnessing.

"Our excitement about anarchism and the brave new world that we were going to create was further developed when Dot got pregnant and we had our first baby – a girl whom we named Liberty, 'cos we wanted her to grow up in a free world. She became a kind of Wartoys mascot, and I have a photo of her in a Wartoys T-shirt at just a few months old.

"The anarcho-punk scene in Wigan was good," he adds, getting to the premature demise of the band. "We had Trucks to go to on a Saturday night, where many local bands performed, but it closed before Wartoys were even old enough to perform there. The System were a good inspiration locally, although they were in a different league and left Wartoys behind to some extent. After they split up, [their guitarist] Andy Coward came and played with Wartoys for a short time, and with his input we started to reach a whole new level... unfortunately we never recorded any of the songs we wrote with Andy, which is a pity as the musical content was getting better and better.

"But our lives were starting to take us in different directions – we were getting frustrated with each other and commitment to the band was dwindling – and not long after that we split up. We did a few more gigs, the last being at a mini-festival at the Burtonwood peace camp, which was a brilliant experience, playing outdoors on a makeshift stage, directly opposite the mighty US airbase against which we were protesting."

The Wartoys have since lost contact with each other, although – at the time of writing – Paul (who is now a director of an environmental charity) is actually putting together a new band with none other than Andy Coward. Watch this space.

At A Glance:
There's nothing official out there on CD, so get searching for the two demos...

Spider from The System, who sadly died in 2005, pictured holding Paul from Wartoys' daughter, Liberty.

Many bands in this book are featured because they helped shape the scene with a whole slew of wonderful releases… others because they managed to make an impression with just a single or two. A few others, such as Preston's **ANARKA AND POPPY**, who never actually released any vinyl in their own right, because their passion and commitment to anarcho-punk and all its libertarian trappings were so great, they were an inspiration to all who met and played with them. Thankfully, by the very nature of the scene, the importance of any band within it cannot merely be measured against any standard template of 'a successful musical career'.

Emerging from the ruins of a haphazard high school band Nihilist Insurrection, guitarist Sean Kirtley and vocalist Jane Mason decided to form Anarka And Poppy in late 1981, at the tender age of seventeen, originally as just a guitar/vocals duo.

"We had opened a squat up in Preston which always had floods of interesting people coming through it – and lots of mayhem too! We soon met Neil [Abercromby – drums] at the squat, and we all had plenty of personal politics we wanted to convey. Plus all three of us were veggies who did animal rights actions together, so we decided to start the band as yet another way to channel what we wanted to say."

After a debut gig in Manchester in 1981 ("It was shit," spits Sean contemptuously), Anarka And Poppy began gigging in and around Preston, usually to be showered by a hail of gob and have the police pull the plug on them mid-set. Unsurprisingly, considering the circumstances, it wasn't long before they underwent an extensive line-up shuffle.

"For the first year we played without a bassist, which really didn't matter to us; the sound we had sounded good enough, and Stoko [real name Michael Stokes, who replaced Neil behind the kit in early '82] made up for the lack of bass, or so it seemed, with his bass drum! We eventually hooked up with Paul 'Staby' Stableforth, but he wasn't with us long and was replaced by Ian [Rothwell], who we also met through the squat."

The expanded A&P also included Shaun Ellis on keyboards and a young lady name of Christine on tambourine and backing vocals.

"Originally we used to practice in Neil's dad's workshop in Leyland, near Preston, so we had no problem with practising when we needed to. Finding gear was hard though, as we had little money and most of us were on the dole. Neil provided most of the equipment, and we scrimped and saved for the rest. I remember we used to rely on any other bands that we were playing with to provide the bulk of the gear!

"The punk scene was pretty big in Preston about then. We tended to stick and work with the punks that had summat to say though, rather than with the poseurs. So, a good, co-operative, little ghetto was born in the heart of Preston; full of activity, never a dull moment, everyone was welcome… the 'other' punk bands all seemed to sound and look exactly like Discharge, and that was the more popular scene, to be honest. Jackets with studs on and all that; fashionable cheese cloths, bum-flaps and bondage straps; we didn't look like that, so we never got too much attention from the 'hardcore'. We didn't really care though; they could all go to hell as far as we were concerned at that time. That was our general attitude."

An excellent demo, 'All That Is Shattered', was recorded in 1982, at Twilight Studios in Salford, which the band sold in the time-honoured tradition at whatever gigs they could manage to blag onto. Another, slightly less convincing, cassette, 'Take It For Life', was recorded straight onto a four-track in '83, and released by Happy Apple Tapes.

"The best show we ever did was at Lark Lane Community Centre in Liverpool, with the Wartoys. We got a great sound and reception… but it was the sound that really makes that gig stand out in my memory. Usually our volumes were all over the bloody place, and it too often sounded like a cacophony, but that night it felt near perfect… we should have split up after that really!

"As for the worst gig we ever played? That was with New Model Army and Here And Now at the Bier Keller in Blackpool. We forgot that we needed our own drum kit and New Model Army wouldn't lend us theirs. We didn't like the idea of playing with them anyway, so it was off to a strange start from the beginning. Then when the bastards wouldn't lend us their drums, it turned into a right arse of a night. Someone eventually persuaded them, but it was like, 'For Christ's sake, you pricks! They're only bloody drums!' Here And Now were a sound bunch though, and they played an excellent set."

In 1984, after corresponding with Josef Porta of The Mob, Anarka And Poppy were eventually offered the chance to record a single for All The Madmen, The Mob's own label.

"Yeah, we got to know a few people who lived in their squat at Brougham Rd. in Hackney through a friend in Manchester called Richard. They included members of Faction, and the people who ran 96 Tapes; Paul-az and Rob Challice asked us if we'd like to get this single together for them."

Recording was undertaken in Hackney and three tracks of stirring, melodic punk rock were the result. The stand-out track, 'If It Dies, We Die' ('it' being planet Earth, of course), was a superbly-crafted environmental ballad (of sorts!); an upbeat, simple arrangement giving way to an instantly infectious, poppy hook-line. If the latter-period Mob had had a female singer, they would have sounded just like this, and put simply, the song is an unsung classic that would have almost certainly broken the band over to a far greater audience if it had ever been heard outside of their immediate circle of friends. Unfortunately All The Madmen changed hands before it could ever be pressed (eventually going under in 1989), condemning a truly great song to obscurity.

"I can remember thinking, 'Shit! What's going to happen to The Mob (who were a fave band of ours)?" sighs Sean, before adding gamely: "Then, of course, it sunk in that the single we'd recorded wasn't going to happen either. That was a real downer for us all – but at least we had fun creating it!"

Possibly disillusioned with their misfortune over the single, and under the influence of whatever chemicals they could lay their hands on, Anarka And Poppy then vanished without a trace in late 1984.

"Drugs hit the squats that we were living in big time around then, and that started to divide us greatly. Some of us were just tripped out, having adventures every day; others got pissed off at the inactivity. We also started going to the free festivals and getting sucked in by all that, which was nice 'cos it was like a break from three solid years of activism. We ended up going our separate ways eventually, but are still friends today... although most of the time, we don't

Anarka And Poppy (left to right: Ian Rothwell, Jane Mason, Michael Stokes, Sean Kirtley, and Christine).

even know which part of the country the others are in!"

Despite the lack of recorded output, and all the frustrations that entailed, Sean remains more than positive about what he achieved with A&P, and proudly maintains the exact same demanding principles he stumbled upon over twenty years ago, whilst still an enthusiastic, impressionable teenager.

"Admittedly they have warped and fluctuated, but never really been far away, and now they've settled back to exactly how they were during the band's existence… except for the old ideals being more refined and realistic than they may have been back then. After having an eighteen-year break from full-on activism to raise three children, it's back on the streets again, megaphone in hand on a very regular basis – for the animals! I guess this is it 'til I'm dead now, the passion is so strong.

"And I still firmly believe in anarchism as a principle that we can base our lives around for the good of the community and the world. Animal liberation first (because the animals have it the worst), then human liberation!

"I can't speak for the present day belief systems of the others as I haven't seen them for years (except for Jane who now has two children and lives very happily in a virtually self-sufficient traveller settlement in the middle of Wales), but personally my involvement with anarcho-punk opened my eyes tremendously, changed my vision, my heart and perception. Never has there been another time in my life that was as colourful, active, positive and full of energy as during the Eighties underground punk scene. What more can I say? Bring it back!"

At A Glance:

There's no official Anarka And Poppy retrospective available, but the brilliant 'If It Dies, We Die' track is included on volume four of Overground's anarcho-punk series, 'Anti-Capitalism'.

The beauty of punk rock really was that anyone could do it, and anarcho-punk furthered that whole mentality of self-empowerment to even greater heights. And as punk poets such as the Rochdale-based **ANDY T.** (real name Andrew Thorley) demonstrated, you didn't necessarily have to have a band to get up on stage and express yourself, although even Andy himself started his performing career fronting primitive punks, Reputations In Jeopardy.

"I've been into music ever since I could crawl, having two older sisters who brought music into the house," explains Andy. "Listened to anything and everything… The Who, Beatles, Stones, Small Faces, Elvis, Little Richard, Chuck Berry etc., soaked it up like the proverbial sponge. I began buying stuff myself in the early Seventies, spent all my Saturday afternoons rooting round in dusty shops in Manchester and Rochdale. T-Rex, Bowie, Velvets, Stooges, Mott, Zappa, and loads of other obscure stuff.

"I used to go to a club in Manchester called Pips, which had Bowie and Roxy rooms; a lot of the people who later formed punk bands also went there. And I had a girlfriend who worked in a record shop and was able to borrow LPs to tape. It was a chart return shop and they got all the latest releases; I picked up the Ramones' first album, mainly due to liking the cover, just as I had done with the New York Dolls a few years before. Like so many others who heard that album, something primal clicked inside…

"When punk came along it seemed like a natural progression. Bands suddenly seemed younger and more like the audience. It was a very exciting time, with new bands springing up every week – some better than others, of course, but all worthwhile in their own way. There was suddenly a lot more gigs to go to every week. Manchester had such a vibrant scene; I went to gigs in London as well, but they didn't seem as exciting as 'up north'… possibly because they were saturated with music down there?

"Anarcho-punk seemed like another inevitable progression," he adds, on the sub-genre where he made his own modest mark. "I followed The Clash round the country on their early tours, and it really felt like a cultural revolution. Things gradually changed as they played bigger places and they became distant, more removed from the fans; they'd always been so approachable and enthusiastic, but I suppose that's hard to maintain. They made promises they couldn't keep; maybe they should have known they'd get hung out to dry in the media glare. They continued to make excellent music but ceased to be 'a people's band', which they always purported to be. Hawkwind and the Pink Fairies managed to stay truer to their ideals than the Clash. And no one ever expected bands such as the Buzzcocks to do anything except make great music. So, I think anarcho-punk evolved out of that feeling of being let down by others, coupled with the need to do something ourselves, which had been brewing for years."

So, Andy formed Reputations In Jeopardy in late 1977, with bassist Chris, guitarist Siobhan and drummer Jane, the line-up being completed a few months later by the addition of a second guitarist, Chris 'The Joiner'.

"We played quite a lot of gigs in and around the Manchester area. The first time we used a PA was a bit of a shock, as I was used to shouting to be heard above the others, then a singer from one of the other bands on the bill advised me not to shout so much. I hadn't even realised I was doing it, and after that everything sounded so much better, as we got used to the equipment etc.

"I used to record most things we did, on a little portable cassette player, and send them to people with a view to getting gigs. I don't have any of these anymore, which is a shame. We never went into a proper recording studio; I don't think it ever occurred to us to try.

"The girls left the band to finish their A-levels and we got a new drummer, Pete; he used to complain his drum kit was rubbish all the time, so I invited a friend of mine from Manchester to come down and listen to us rehearse… John Maher, the drummer from the Buzzcocks! He liked us and had a go on Pete's kit with us… of course, it sounded really good, and I wish I had a tape of it. And Pete never mentioned his rubbish kit again after that night!"

It was this line-up that contributed the – rather poor – 'Girls Love Popstars' to the first 'Bullshit

Andy T. at the Sunderland Bunker, April 1983, picture by Trunt.

Detector' compilation, by which time Andy had decided to go it alone as a solo performer, his first appearances on vinyl in his own right, 'Jazz On A Summer's Day' and 'Nagasaki Mon Amour', on the very same album his old band also appeared on. He even had another cut on the album, 'Right Or Wrong', under the guise of Fuck The CIA!

"I can't remember where I first met Crass exactly," ponders Andy. "I think it was through my friendship with the Poison Girls, who lived just down the road from them. I found we had very similar ideas, and Penny, Gee and Steve have been lifelong friends ever since, and are still very dear to me. Sometimes people said they felt intimidated in their presence, although I never felt this; we always had lots of fun. They pioneered the whole 'playing in very out of the way places' (i.e. not on the usual rock'n'roll circuit) approach. We went places together that bands didn't normally play, and always met enthusiastic audiences.

"Crass chose five tracks from a pile of tapes I sent them for 'Bullshit Detector'. They asked for artwork of a certain size, so I crammed the info for all five tracks into that sized space, but when the sleeve was printed, they had blown the writing up large. I didn't realise that I had five such spaces to fill up… a bit of a missed opportunity.

"I used to record loads of poems and songs in my bedroom. The Fuck The CIA track was me and my younger brother Jerry. When Crass chose the track for the album, I had to think of a name and chose it from an old Sixties poster… I used to use anything that came to hand to make a sound or a point!"

The developing friendship with Crass led to Andy being invited to record a single for their label, and in late 1982, the 'Weary Of The Flesh' EP was borne, a bold, striking statement that challenged the listener on an aesthetic level as well as an ethical one.

"Penny wanted to record me for posterity," reckons Andy, "Which he did during yet another nice weekend up at Dial House. My friend Ian [credited on the sleeve as 'E'] made some noises with his mouth, and we had loads of fun doing the backing tracks, which were then mixed at Southern Studios in Wood Green. I thought it came out well… we aimed to cram as much as possible into those grooves and I think we filled about fifteen minutes, quite good for a 7" single. I don't even have a copy of that these days; I had to borrow one off a dear friend to put into an exhibition recently.

"The inside cover photo was from another fun session involving Phil Free, Annie Anxiety and Steve Ignorant, all wearing animal masks. They were photographed in one of the garden sheds and we utilised a lot of printing ink – not blood!

"I was quite proud of the finished article and wanted to give John Peel a copy to play on his show. Rather than post it, I chose to wait for hours outside the BBC to give it him in person; I'd been listening to his radio programmes since the early Seventies and he'd introduced me to a lot of good music. I told him a little bit about it and he seemed interested, but unfortunately he never played it on his show. A friend of mine asked John about it at one of his University gigs in Suffolk a few years later, and he said he thought it was a bit too extreme for the radio. That made me very proud indeed, to be thought too extreme for John Peel's listeners! I think it still stands up these days, and is still an unusual approach in today's climate where anything is possible and sometimes easier to achieve."

With fourteen tracks in all, the EP takes in many thorny topics, from sexism ('Exploitation') to pointless violence at gigs ('Big Boys'), via the horror of the meat industry (the title track) and the self-destructive lifestyles favoured by the less intellectual punk rocker ('Wasted Life'); all tackled by Andy with his endearingly deadpan Northern earthiness.

"Yes, my background was strong Northern working class, we never had a great deal of anything. I used to go to work with my Dad, plumbing, from a very early age; had paper rounds before and after school, used to collect pop and beer bottles from the bin rooms, in the flats where we lived, then take them back to the off-license – anything for a bit of extra money. Our playground was the rows and rows of derelict buildings lying empty after the occupants had left for 'better' housing. We found all sorts of things to play with: guns hidden under floorboards, loads of old pianos to play on. We got a shock one day playing in an old gas works gatehouse though; they were knocking the place down, but we didn't realise they'd started on the bit we were in – 'til we opened an upstairs door and saw a big iron ball swinging towards us! Hours of fun in the sun…

"My dad wanted me to go into the army, and I received plenty of training from him in the techniques necessary for protection and survival. This was a time when the Cold War was at its height, and there was a strong sense of a nuclear threat, a feeling that war could break out at any time. I don't think the army would have been the place for me though; I would never have been any good at subservience! I didn't like authority in any of its forms; I was quite happy to do anything to protect my loved ones, but wouldn't follow the orders of the 'Ruperts'!"

Musically the EP confused many of its listeners, with its out-of-tune guitar 'accompaniment', and the myriad voices wailing in the background, the discordant cacophony sometimes detracting from the message it was probably intended to enhance. It was no wonder the EP didn't chart, it being far too avant-garde for even hardened fans of the Crass label roster.

"My musical tastes have always been very eclectic," admits Andy. "I'm usually drawn to unusual sounds and voices and mavericks. I've always liked lyrics in songs as opposed to straight poetry, though I read a lot when I was younger. I had a nervous breakdown during my adolescence and was given E.C.T [the controversial psychiatric therapy, Electro-Convulsive Treatment], which fried a lot of early memories. I spent about six months in the hospital after being sectioned. I squirreled myself away in a small library room with a stack of cassettes and paper, and read and wrote loads of stuff.

"I don't know if I could put a name to any particular influences as such. There were plenty of writers I admired and enjoyed: Bob Dylan, Lennon, Townsend, Zappa, Roy Harper, Patti Smith, Howard Devoto, Burroughs, Kerouac, Hunter S. Thompson etc. Although, apart from awakening my love of language, none of them directly influenced the way I wrote myself. I think everything we see or hear somehow gets lodged in our heads for future reference.

"I do think there was a strong feeling around that the generations before had really messed things up. When punk came along, it spoke to a lot of young people with a similar mindset, those wanting more from life than our parents had. I don't mean material things, but more a different way of living, with our own set of rules, rather than those handed down to us. A small example was my choice to be vegan, which is much easier to do these days. There is so much choice around in shops, supermarkets, and restaurants now: organic/non-G.M., free-range etc. In the Seventies, choice was very limited and there was no help whatsoever, save some leaflets from the Vegetarian Society. Aye lad, it were proper grim…!"

The confusion Andy caused in the punk scene predictably extended to live performances. He toured the UK extensively with the likes of Crass, Poison Girls, Flux Of Pink Indians and Dirt, and climbing up onstage in front of a thousand hardcore punk rockers baying to see the headline band and reciting provocative verse must have been incredibly daunting.

"I used to record most things and often taped backing tracks for use in my live show," explains Andy. "I did a tour with a guitarist friend improvising once, which went down very well indeed. I also had a tendency to get anyone who happened to be about to improvise behind me. Often I liked to get people to use instruments they weren't familiar with… I always liked to experiment with ideas and subvert expectations.

"I used to get friends from other bands to back me sometimes, just improvising in the background. Mostly we used a backing tape, but not every PA had a tape deck we could use. I also had a poem in the middle of the set, which needed drums and it served to break things up a bit. I'd often get a drummer from one of the other bands to play; Martin from Flux, Spider from The System, Penny from Crass, and Sid from Rubella Ballet all had a bash at some point, and very good they were too.

"The message was fairly clear and direct, and not buried within music. People tended to stop pogo-ing and listen, and they usually responded in a positive way. Sometimes they would throw bottles, but I saw this as a sign of affection! Also, drunks aren't particularly good shots. One time in Manchester, my mate Dave was playing drums for me in the middle of my set, waiting on the kit for his cue. This crowd was a bit rowdy, with a lot of heckling going on. Someone threw a bottle, which sailed a couple of inches past my head and smashed in front of the kit. Dave was shocked but impressed by my ability to not miss a beat, as were the audience who were all ours after that. When we came off, Dave remarked on my nerve, to which I replied 'What bottle?'

"I suppose the tendency is to remember the bad gigs, where various factions tried to spoil it. Sometimes right-wing, sometimes left-wing, but mostly idiots. I wrote about the 1981 Perth gig in the liner notes to the live Crass CD that Pomona released; that's a fairly vivid memory for a lot of us. Then there was Stonehenge, where the [Hell's] Angels took exception to the punks. As I never looked particularly 'punky' myself, I wasn't their first choice for attack, but ended up hiding this young lass from Birmingham who was a definite target with her bright pink hair. I had helped a biker stranded on the roadside a day or two before, with a spare jubilee clip I had in my rucksack. He stuck up for me with his mates and probably saved my skull.

"Having been brought up to be able to defend myself, I've never been afraid of violence, seen too much of it for that. But I've always stuck up for the underdog and have always considered myself a pacifist. I remember a gig in London – I think it was the Conway Hall – when a London anarchist group was berating a few of us for being pacifists. They were threatening to beat us up with karate and kung fu… until I offered to propel the loudest and biggest one through a window of his own choice. This had the desired effect of stopping them in their tracks, as they changed tack and started berating me for not being a proper pacifist. I had to explain that my personal interpretation of pacifism didn't involve putting up with dickheads. And after that we became friends!

"There were loads of brilliant gigs as well, of course, the best being in some very out of the way places. The whole village would turn out, as nothing exciting ever happened normally. There were some great venues set up in those days, which still operate with similar values, such as the 1 In

12 Club in Bradford and the Bunker in Sunderland. The thing that made it special was always the people, rather than anything to do with the music. I know there is still a scene out there these days, but I admit that I know very little about it."

Because, feeling increasingly jaded with the dead end ghetto that anarcho-punk seemed content to drink and smoke itself into, Andy stopped performing in late 1983, and has done little creatively since.

"I've been too busy bringing up kids and working," he laughs. "Plus I had another breakdown in the early Nineties, when the doctors filled me up with more medication, none of which made me better – some of which made me worse. After talking to a drugs worker that I trusted, I decided to try another bout of E.C.T. which he assured me wasn't as barbaric as when I first had it. After a few courses I began to come back to life, but I found that the treatment had destroyed chunks of my memory, so I have a lot of blank spaces yet to be filled in, though this doesn't bother me like it used to.

"Then, about three years ago, I had a brain haemorrhage, followed six months later by a diagnosis of cancer! I'm fine now, but all that was a bit time-consuming! I don't feel the need to shout at audiences anymore, but still believe in the vast majority of ideas and beliefs I held then.

"I was actually interested in anarchism before the punk thing," adds Andy. "I was a member of a political group called Direct Action Movement. We met in a pub every week and talked endlessly, and that was about as direct and active as it got!

"I always believed – still do – in a personal form of anarchy, which influences the way I live my life. Simple things like not treating others badly for gain, and not allowing others to do the same to me. Anarchy for me is like any belief system; it's always there, switched on in the background. Complacency is the thing that kills free thought.

"And the politics almost seem more relevant now than they did then, with political lies for personal advancement, warfare, ID cards, corporate greed and corruption, and environmental destruction all being the norm. Nothing's really changed much on a worldwide scale. At the time, we had Thatcher and Reagan in power, not to mention each other's pockets. Now we have Bush and Blair, still treating us all like fools and getting away with it.

"In the Seventies, all you needed to get locked up by the police was an Irish accent. These days the targets are Muslims, and the authorities are calling for stricter detention laws all the time. But kids these days don't seem as angry or politicised as we were, my own kids and their friends included. There are so many distractions for them readily available. All we had was a couple of TV channels, which closed down around midnight, Uncle John Peel on the radio, and some gigs to go to.

"If I'm to be remembered at all, it'll be as a loud Northern lunatic in a scruffy cardigan," he smiles. "And to that charge I must plead guilty, but I know for certain that I helped a few people along the way to try and live life as they wanted to, rather than as they were conditioned to. I can't ask for any more than that."

SELECT DISCOGRAPHY

7"s:
'Weary Of The Flesh' (Crass, 1982)

At A Glance:
No comprehensive CD retrospective yet exists from Andy T., although one side of his EP was included on the Crass singles CD, 'A-Sides, Part Two, 1982 – 1984', and one live track also featured on Overground's 'Anti-Society: Anarcho-punk Compilation Volume Three'.

So, the anarcho-punk scene was rife with bands that never officially 'made it', but does that make their creative efforts any less important than those of bands that did? Of course not, and by the very nature of the scene that nurtured them, acts such as Rochdale's UNTERMENSCH can be assured that they played as big a role in the creation of anarcho-punk as the next man… and with songs as good as 'Ashfield Valley Headkick' and 'The Sociology Man' in their arsenal, it was just bad luck for the national punk scene that they didn't reach more people than they did.

"I'm not even sure we were punk rock," ponders guitarist Mark Hodkinson. "We were always a bit too clever and arty to say, 'Right, we're this or that.' We loved the energy of punk, but also the free-for-all, more experimental edge of new wave, and there were very few bands that we were all unanimous about liking. When we later evolved into The Monkey Run, playing gigs with the likes of The Chameleons and The Stone Roses, we were even less definable as punk-influenced, but the philosophy of the whole thing never left us.

"We were basically a bunch of quiet kids really, the type that weren't let into any gangs at school, so we formed our own. We were mostly from traditional working-class backgrounds, so the whole idea of a band was our big chance to use our imaginations. At school if you did any homework or showed any interest in learning, you were automatically assumed to be a creep or, more likely, gay. All our energy was put into being creative, without us ever trying to be high-minded. We did our music, put on gigs, published a fanzine…

"And we wanted the band to be a 'floating zoo' (yes, really!), so the line-up was incredibly fluid; no one was ever turned away or judged by any other criteria apart from their wanting to be involved."

The core of the band was always Mark on guitar, with his best mate Dave Taylor on bass, and, in January 1981, they were joined for the first incarnation of Untermensch by drummer Shaun Moseley and singer Steven Bridge, who actually thought of the name ("He'd been reading a Sven Hassall novel; it means 'sub-human' or 'scum' in German, but no one ever spelled it right, and I think it sounded pretentious – which we definitely weren't…"). When Shaun and Steven left, they were replaced – respectively – by Robert Taylor and Chris Griffiths, the latter of whom was himself superseded by Jim Stringer in early '82, but not before the band had recorded a live rehearsal demo to give to Crass when they played at the Manchester Mayflower on October 30th, 1981. By this time, Terry Eves, formerly of The Pranksters, a Rochdale band who played several gigs supporting The Fall, had also joined on keyboards.

"The only label we ever approached was Crass Records, and we 'nearly' made it onto a 'Bullshit Detector' – but didn't everyone? They said we sounded like another band that was already on there though… we hated them forever after that, being bitter buggers that had no idea how the record industry worked…"

In an additional bid to publicise their efforts, and help promote the burgeoning Rochdale music scene, the intrepid youths produced a Xeroxed fanzine (called Untermensch, of course), the first issue of which featured a live review of the above-mentioned Crass gig, and a rather negative editorial about how it had been planned to include an interview with the band themselves but Crass hadn't deemed to grant them one.

"The fanzine was brilliant; it just kept trawling in more and more kids who wanted to be part of it – doing poems, organising their own gigs… it was a real catalyst and great fun to do. That bit about Crass was dumb of us… well, me really. We went to see them in Manchester and, about half an hour before they were due to go on, we spoke to Andy Palmer and expected him to drop everything and speak to us there and then, without any forewarning or anything. We were extremely naïve…

"We all liked Crass though, the idea of them if not the music (though I liked that too). They were, and I hate this word normally because it's become over-used, awesome. You were sort of rinsed out after seeing them. I think at the age we were, we were susceptible to the message they

Untermensch (left to right: Mark, Terry, Jim, Robert, and Dave).

carried. I'd be much more questioning and cynical now, though I was a bit then too."

Having finally settled on a steady line-up, Untermensch made their live debut at a Rochdale open air festival during spring 1982.

"I completely freaked out and couldn't remember any of the songs," laughs Mark. "Dave turned my fuzz pedal up full and said, 'Fuck 'em, play anything!' So I did. Cyril Smith, the rotund Liberal MP, was in attendance and from the stage our singer Jim announced that, 'This track is dedicated to the Member of Parliament on the front row sitting in seats two, three, four and five!' I'm sure we sounded bloody awful…"

Entering Vic's Place, a studio in Belfield Mill ran by another Rochdale band, Local Heroes, Untermensch tracked eight of their compositions in just one day; a powerful, solid recording that thankfully captured the band's expansive, eclectic influences for posterity's sake, as they then split, long before they could begin to break out of Lancashire.

"By absolute chance, we had our own distinctive sound," offers Mark on their unique flavour. "We couldn't play very well, but we pushed ourselves to the limit. Jim had a very strong voice, so that gave us an edge. Another thing was that we were all totally obsessive about music, so we would try and mix up Talking Heads, (early) Ants, Hawkwind, Joy Division, Dead Kennedys, and someone else – usually in the same song!"

When pressed for an explanation behind the aforementioned, and irresistibly boisterous, 'Ashfield Valley Headkick', the band's best song by a mile (although the measured melodrama of 'The Sociology Man' comes a close second), he adds:

"Well, me, Dave and Terry went out for a takeaway one night, and we were walking home through the notorious Ashfield Valley estate, when a bunch of lads came behind us, about fifteen in total – just as we describe in the song – all of them skinheads. They attacked us; Dave and Terry got a good kicking, but I managed to escape. I remember looking across and seeing Dave

slip – it was a snowy night – and this bastard setting on him. I ran to get help and, weirdly, bumped into a black kid from our school, Mick Harper, walking home on his own. I told him to take a detour... but I often wonder what would have happened to Mick if they'd seen him first. A horrible night..."

Whilst having all the band members pulling in such dizzyingly disparate directions makes for some terrific creative tension, it doesn't make a particularly stable foundation on which to base a lengthy career as musicians together, and sure enough, after a great gig at the Dale Club (the social club attached to Rochdale FC) with The System in December 1983, Untermensch went their separate ways. Mark headed off to journalism college, and is still writing today, his company Pomona having recently published 'Love Songs', a superb anthology of Crass lyrics presented, for the first time ever, as stand-alone poetry.

Dave and Terry meanwhile "went all electronic" with Incubus Succubus (not to be confused with the Cheltenham goths, Inkubus Sukkubus), before Dave joined Black Alsatian, who released the 'Something' single on Intense Records. Mark, Terry and Jim then became The Monkey Run, who recorded a session for Radio One (coming "fairly close to signing with various major labels...") and have a retrospective album, 'Escape From The Rake', available from Pomona.

"But I think we're all pretty much the same now as we were then," reckons Mark. "We're considerate, honest people that respect others. I don't think we're quite as earnest as we used to be – me especially – but we probably over-did that a bit anyway. We had some fantastic laughs though, and had that sort of telepathy that makes for great bands.

"And I'm not really bothered if anyone remembers us... though it's nice if they do. I still see people in Rochdale or thereabouts who say, 'Weren't you in that band?' and I'm still proud to say, 'I was!' But it was done for ourselves really, and everyone should do it – invest time and effort into something that is all your own. I can't think of a better way to spend your time. I've got two lads of my own now, and I'd love it if they got into music; after all, there's still a drum kit in the house, and plenty of guitars and amps..."

At A Glance:
The curious reader might wish to contact Mark for a copy of the band's sole studio demo (mark@pomonauk.co.uk), and everyone else would be well advised to visit the Pomona website to pick up a copy of the beautifully-presented Crass lyric book, 'Love Songs'. Meanwhile, 'Ashfield Valley Headkick' is one of the many highlights on Overground's 'Anti-Society: Anarcho-punk Compilation, Vol. 3' CD.

Cumbria's **PSYCHO FACTION** are another classic example of an anarcho-punk band that never recorded a thing, yet by virtue of their untiring, selfless commitment to the scene, are still remembered fondly by anyone that ever encountered them, either as a band or as individuals. Indeed, they were one of only eight bands thanked by Crass on 'Christ The Album', and for a brief moment were even slated to have a record released on the Crass label.

"We actually booked them in our hometown of Cleator Moor in October 1980," explains vocalist Sean McGhee, "And after the gig, Penny [from Crass] suggested a split single between ourselves and Counter Attack, the band that had supported them at their previous Cumbria gig [in nearby Maryport, summer '79]. Because the Sellafield nuclear plant is nearby, he thought it would be both interesting and topical to make it on an anti-nuclear theme, but for reasons that I can't remember now, it never happened. It would have certainly made a difference to the band, and I guess would have propelled us overnight to some sort of 'fame' in the punk world… it's quite funny looking back and thinking about that now."

Formed in early 1979, following the demise of Whitehaven-area punk band, Anti-Climax, Psycho Faction comprised Sean on vocals, with his brothers Kieran and Brendan on guitars and drums respectively (although Kieran was replaced by Wayne 'Nelly' Stevens in early '82), and Edmund 'Butty' Butler on bass. They made their public debut at the Whitehaven grammar school, alongside fellow Cumbrians, the Renwick Bats and the Chevettes, and it was, of course, an absolute shambles.

Psycho Faction live October 1983 (left to right: Edmund Butler, Sean McGhee, and Wayne Stevens), picture by Chris Morrison.

"Well, the early days were all pretty chaotic," admits Sean. "We played very rarely 'cos, at that time, all punk gigs for local bands were self-run affairs, so we had to find/hire venues, then convince the owners that the audience wasn't going to destroy the building, and then learn about promotion and actually getting people to come along.

"We had so little gear it was embarrassing... I remember playing in a village hall in Staveley, near Kendal, in late 1980, and the support band were so shocked with our gear, they actually drove home and brought back their own amps and drums. We had so little money back then that it wasn't rare for us to do gigs with a five-string lead guitar and a three-string bass. And transport was practically non-existent; I can remember us wheeling amps two or three miles to where we practiced on skateboards, while it was snowing heavily! It was all a struggle. The drum kit especially was a real mongrel, with parts added from everywhere and anywhere, and the guitars were the cheapest you could get. But we were still very young around 1980; all aged between thirteen and sixteen.

"I often say 'The Three Cs – Clash, Crisis and Crass'," adds Sean, on the band's initial influences, "But we were influenced by so many of the early punk bands, and used to attempt covers like 'Teenage Kicks' by The Undertones, and 'Warhead' or 'Telephone Numbers' by the UK Subs. We were into many different bands collectively, and probably had in all our heads an idea of what we each thought we should sound like, but apart from me adding an American hardcore element to the sound later on, I can't honestly remember anybody suggesting we should try to sound like someone in particular. I think we found it hard enough playing our own stuff, yet alone trying to sound like anyone else.

"Lyrically, there was a definite Crass influence; I really liked the way their lyrics were unambiguous and didn't mess around, and, although not consciously trying to ape them, I often used their words as a starting point."

Whilst they may not have sounded like a typical anarcho band (most of their numbers combined the frantic tempos of punk's second wave with the pleasingly simple tunes of the first wave), the obvious anger inherent in songs such as 'Attack The System', 'Right To Live' and 'Question Everything' placed Psycho Faction firmly in that camp philosophically. Their song 'Windscale Is Deathscale', aimed unflinchingly at the Sellafield nuclear power complex, even earned them numerous death threats from the local community, who short-sightedly refused to look beyond the thousands of jobs the plant had created in the vicinity.

"The anarcho-punk scene opened my eyes to a lot of things I might never have seen otherwise, and gave the punk scene and myself a lot more focus and direction... although, looking back, there were certainly lots of things I might have done better. But the political situation today is probably far worse now than it was back then, and my own beliefs have not softened with time; I still believe that the vast majority of the problems we face as people come down to the greed and inhumanity of a ruling elite obsessed with power, wealth and control. Yet I still believe that people are generally good at their core...

"We played various CND/peace movement shows and were fairly active in our local group, Cumbrians For Peace. We also played benefits for everyone from local musicians collectives to animal rights organizations. We produced a lot of anarchist and anti-state literature and handouts, and were involved in other activities targeted at the war machine and nuclear power. I was later involved in the Troops Out movement and the Birmingham Six/Guildford Four campaigns.

"And I do think that the organizational skills I learned in the band have helped me be a little more organized in my life since. That said, I don't feel better than someone else because I happen to read Bakunin or John Pilger or Noam Chomsky..."

As well as with Crass, Psycho Faction played with many of the scene's other 'big names', including one gig supporting Poison Girls and Rubella Ballet at the Carlisle City Hall in November 1982, which was trashed by Nazi skinheads and ended in appalling violence, Sean himself walking offstage after being hit square in the face by a beer can hurled at the band. A much more enjoyable

Psycho Faction live November 1983 (left to right: Glen Hurst, Wayne Stevens, and Sean McGhee), picture by Trunt.

show for all concerned was the opening night of the Gateshead Station, a prestigious event in hindsight that saw Psycho Faction appearing alongside Alternative, Reality Control and Blood Robots. Despite regular gigs though, the band never made it into a proper recording studio to document their set for posterity.

"The reasons were financial, of course... we couldn't afford to!" explains Sean. "And when we were actually paid for something – an appearance on a TV programme [BBC North's youth culture show, 'Off The Peg', aired in March 1984] – the money was frittered away on drink, and the planned recordings that were to lead to a split single on Scrobe Records with The Dead never happened [the Famous Imposters eventually took the place of Psycho Faction on the 7"]. The nearest we came to a studio was a live practice recording on a four-track which is pretty poor, as everything was turned down and it lacks presence and bite. It didn't seem too important then, but nowadays I regret never getting into the studio as we had some decent songs and I think they would have scrubbed up quite well if we'd made the effort..."

The gig at which the band was filmed for 'Off The Peg' actually transpired to be one of the last Psycho Faction performances anyway, by which time Glen Hurst had joined on additional guitar (although original guitarist Kieran had to be reenlisted for the TV recording as Glen "got cold feet"

and vanished off to Greece for several months!), allowing them some extra scope to do further justice to the material.

"We didn't so much 'split' as fall apart," recounts Sean ruefully. "As we all grew up, we got jobs, had girlfriends and children began appearing. Time, financial concerns, widening musical tastes, and other interests all played their part. After our bassist left, the heart really went out of it, although we limped along for a few half-hearted practices with a bassist who couldn't really play, which almost took us back to our humble origins. Our last gig was in November 1984, in Cleator Moor, in the same venue where we'd played some of our first gigs back in 1980. We shared the stage with three local acts, The Dead, Anarchism and A Touch Of Hysteria, and unfortunately, the gig was marred yet again by violence, which was almost par for the course by then.

"I've lost count of the times I've been asked about reforming since, so we seem to have been remembered well enough by the people who used to 'follow us' round. That's good enough for me, but if we made people think about things as well, then that's even better. As for reforming, my response is often along the lines that, 'We couldn't play then, so I doubt we'd be able to now!' That said, I wouldn't mind recording some of the songs today in a decent studio scenario, as I do really regret the fact that they never got the chance to be presented in such a way."

Psycho Faction, live in Whitehaven, 1983 (left to right: Brendan McGhee, Sean McGhee, Edmund Butler, and Glen Hurst), picture by Chris Morrison.

After Psycho Faction's demise, Sean's musical tastes widened considerably, and in 1988 he launched the popular 'Rock 'N' Reel' fanzine, which focused more on folk-related sounds and ran for fifteen years, reaching an impressively hefty 148 glossy pages per issue by the time it folded in 2003. More recently, he has been responsible for overseeing and compiling the series of anarcho-punk compilation CDs that Overground Records released in 2005 and 2006. And Psycho Faction themselves, whilst not likely to reform for live performances, have finally had the official release they never enjoyed whilst they were in existence over twenty years ago. The aptly-titled 'Twenty Two Years Too Late' single was released by Californian label, Shock Horror Records, in 2006, and features six songs culled from old gig and rehearsal tapes.

"I'm still proud to call myself an anarchist, and do see it as a sensible and understandable reaction to the vagaries of organized politics… especially the lies, mass murder, and war obsession of the state. That said, I also support other movements on the broad left. I don't try to define anarchy though, as I think the freedom of the idea means that it can define itself for each person, but a basic concept of respect and love for people, and believing that we can all exist beyond control and patronizing attitudes, is a good starting point."

SELECT DISCOGRAPHY

7"s:
'Twenty Two Years Too Late' (Shock Horror, 2006)

At A Glance:
Psycho Faction appeared on Overground's first anarcho-punk compilation, 'Anti-War', with 'Threat', a version lifted from the live set they recorded for 'Off The Peg'.

CHAPTER SEVEN

Although they only released the one split flexi-single ('Within These Walls', with Reality Control) whilst they were together (several other tracks appeared 'posthumously' on various compilation albums), Newcastle-Upon-Tyne's **BLOOD ROBOTS** were an important part of the fabric of the Northeast anarcho-punk scene, whose members went on to play with such influential hardcore bands as Generic and One By One. Their music was joyously eclectic, sometimes up-tempo and melodic, at other times painfully introspective and discordant, but always charged and loaded with a sincere, provocative message.

"The name was lifted straight from the Androids Of Mu LP title," explains guitarist/vocalist, Sned. "Staring us in the face from the front of my record collection! We attached our own meaning to it in that people are treated as machines, or as a part of a machine, so to put the two together, 'blood' and 'robots', seemed obvious.

"And being thirteen years old in 1977, this new 'punk rock' thing was exciting! Controversial and full of energy; I liked the swearing, saying 'Fuck you!' to the establishment, especially the royal family, via the Sex Pistols' 'God Save The Queen' and so on. There were awesome new records with picture covers coming out every week; it was just a wave that hit everywhere... of course, most people moved on into 'post punk' and futurism, or became mods or whatever, but the excitement of punk rock stuck with me a good while longer than most of my friends at school.

"By the time of Crass and anarcho-punk though, there were just such a small number of people left taking notice; I mean, anarcho-punk was huge, don't get me wrong, but not completely overground like the first wave. It's still funny to me when out on tour, getting pulled over by the 'long arm of the law', the cops asking what kind of band you are and then saying, 'Yeah, I used to be into punk when I was a lad...'!"

"I got into punk through a combination of John Peel and my mates, some of whom had older brothers who were punk," adds guitarist/vocalist Micky. "It was 1978 for me... being a few months younger than old man Sned and not actually having a record player in the house until then are my excuses. My dad won our first record player as a third prize in the local leek club show!"

Sned originally got Blood Robots together with drummer Hec in early 1982, Micky joining after responding to an ad placed in the local record shop, Listen Ear, and bringing his mate Andy along to play bass.

"For all of us it was our first even remotely serious band, the 'pre-proper' line-up just doesn't count," reckons Sned. "And neither do real names... bands always go downhill when their real names are used. Fuck that! 'Sned', 'Hec', 'Micky' and 'Andy' is all you need to know, pal!"

The band were lucky enough to align themselves with the Gateshead Music Collective, an organisation that helped build a thriving alternative scene in and around Newcastle, providing bands that had little or no equipment with the opportunity to rehearse, play gigs and – most importantly – express themselves freely.

"Ah, the 'good old days'!" laughs Sned. "We didn't have real amps or drums, only guitars and sticks; no wheels either, so it was all about public transport. We were very lucky in terms of rehearsal space as the Gateshead Music Collective's venue, the Station, was up and running by then; there were at least twenty bands using the place for practice, all through the same collective backline, which is hard to imagine as being operable nowadays! The GMC would meet up on Thursdays at the library, and practices would be booked; there was also a key rota... i.e. you would be responsible for the place while another band was practicing, and vice versa, so a lot of cold nights were spent down there waiting for a band to finish practicing, then the long trudge home. The GMC brought together bands from different parts of the city; I have fond memories of some of the characters from there. I don't think we'd have got nearly as much done without the GMC/Station. Two of us lived in north Newcastle, and two in the south, so Gateshead was conveniently halfway; most of our local gigs were at the Station or nearby, so it wasn't a big problem us having no transport. We did organise a gig in Jesmond one time though, hauling big speaker cabinets and everything some three miles via shopping trolleys or on the metro train! Pretty ridiculous, even back then."

Micky: "Apart from the lack of transport, access to equipment was for us perhaps

Sned of the Blood Robots, picture by Andrew Medcalf.

easier than for a lot of other bands elsewhere in the country, but without the GMC we would have been fucked. In fact, there were a couple of times when there was no working backline at the collective and we had to practice elsewhere. I seem to remember a couple of times we practiced on The Abductors' gear at Allendale Road Community Centre. Essentially though, when the GMC's backline fucked up, most of the twenty bands couldn't practice, as no one had their own stuff."

Blood Robots played their first gig at the city's Spectro Arts Centre during February 1983 (Sned: "We were terrified but got away with it, I think… after a year or so of being utterly crap, we were finally an okay band!"); it was with Reality Control, a local act with whom they quickly established a strong allegiance.

"I went to the same school as the Reality Controls," elaborates Sned. "It was great to discover this incredible band these kids had got together; a couple of years later, we left home and lived in various shared house set-ups from '83 to '86, and we worked together closely on a lot of stuff, music and otherwise… I miss them.

"I went to see Crass a few times with the two Michaels from Reality Control, the only others from school keen enough to spend the night in Carlisle or Middlesbrough train station and skive off school/college the next day. This is when we started hanging out and how we got to know each other. Looking back, I'd say Reality Control were a hell of a big influence and we were in some ways their 'little brother band' – despite us being two years older than them!

"Crass were a revelation too; on record, through their lyrics, packaging, art, literature… just the whole live experience, but they never played in the Newcastle area, so we had to travel. The fact that some other people from our area 'got it' as well meant we were not so alone; through the 'zine ['Stepping Out'] and the bands we were finding other like-minded people and a scene was developing. A lot of influence came from those contacts and interaction; Crass passed us the ball and we ran with it, if that's a cheesy enough analogy for you!"

"I really liked a lot of the better Oi bands as well," interjects Micky. "Like Blitz and The Violators, and more avant-garde bands such as Cabaret Voltaire, The Virgin Prunes, Pere Ubu, Crispy Ambulance, Joy Division, The Residents, and some older non-punk avant-garde stuff like Red Crayola and The Velvet Underground etc. Lyrically though, Crass struck a chord with all of us and helped put a name to the feelings that we felt. I saw them at [Birmingham's] Digbeth Civic Hall, which was a night of dodging maniac skinheads both inside and outside the venue. And getting chased through the Bullring [shopping centre] by skins, before finding relative safety overnight in the train station. Oh, and did I mention, it was fucking cold?"

"The second time I saw them involved a coach trip up to Cleator Moor, not long before Crass split, and they were on fire. There was bit of bother with some skins hanging round in the bogs that night as well, but they fucked off after a little chat."

Indeed it was Michael Barlow from Reality Control that engineered and mixed the Blood Robots' first demo, 'You Fuel The Fire And Fan The Flames', recorded at the Spectro Arts Centre's eight-track studio during July 1983. An impressive six-track debut that ranges from the generically obvious opener 'Pawns', through some well-realised melodic punk ('The Valley' and 'Poppies') to the moody rock overtones of 'Poetry Competition'. By far the most potent track though is 'Where's The Blood?', an emotive questioning of the meat industry's ethics (or lack thereof) set to a compelling chord progression laden with swirling guitar harmonics.

"We were singing about war, death, unemployment… wasn't everybody at that time?" offers Sned. "Crass had a profound effect on us but it was only a part of a bigger picture; there was depth to what we were writing/saying/doing… through our zine as much as the band… we were most definitely involved with anarchism in the broader sense. We didn't look how you would imagine an anarcho-punk band would look, but well, who gave a shit? Only in hindsight could I label us 'anarcho punk'; that term wasn't even around then, and once 'punk' and 'anarcho' have reached their limits and been defined then the shit is dead in the water. Time to move on; it's all about moving forward, and we all have our own ways of defining that."

"Even now when I go into the studio, I'm still learning how best to translate the power and energy of the live environment into a studio recording," admits Micky, on the subject of their first studio session. "The main difference was that back then we didn't really know what we wanted to sound like, or how to achieve it. Turning up at the studio with equipment you've hardly used before, with not much clue how to get the best sound from it, doesn't really help you feel at ease. Now it's easy; we all turn up with our own back-line and just turn on. The engineer sets up the mikes and we're away! The music goes down first take and it's all done, bar the overdubs and vocals, before lunch. Back then it took us most of the morning to set up."

With the tape to sell at gigs, Blood Robots began gigging in earnest, including lending their support to squat gigs in Leeds, with Chumbawamba, in Dunfermline with Alternative (Micky: "I seem to recall it got stopped before we actually played but it was as much about being there and taking part as it was about playing anyway!"), and even one in Gateshead, during April 1984 ("That was a high point and most inspiring," laughs Sned. "The noise and smell of the generator… then slicing up carrots for the stew by candlelight when the power cut out!")

They also added another vocalist, Richard, in late '83 (Sned: "He wasn't in a band before he joined us, but he used to do a 'rant' thing called Edible; I wish I still had that tape – angry young man!"), which allowed Micky and Sned to concentrate on their playing a little more, but he left in mid-'84, meaning the band had to rework the new material they were writing to make it suitable for a four-piece again.

March 1984, and Blood Robots were back in Spectro with Michael Barlow, recording four new songs, one of which, 'Loaded Guns', appeared as part of the aforementioned split flexi with Reality Control.

"It was self-released between the members of the bands, with money borrowed off our mate Slob," says Sned. "It originally should have been a one-sided effort, which would've been a lot cheaper, but we fucked up as the songs were too long; there was a delay while we had to pay for extra mastering. Although I wish now it had been on hard vinyl, it was still great to take DIY to the next level beyond tape copying, just to show that if we could do it then anyone could! We also included all the contact details for the pressing and printing, along with a cost breakdown to demonstrate this, something we repeated later with the first Flat Earth release. There wasn't the network you have now of established distro people who'll trade with you and so on; it sold via gigs and friends from other places taking copies. This was at the very beginning of the DIY record network... I remember one of the first international trades I did with someone in Italy – from that we picked up EPs by Declino, Wretched, Peggio Punx and loads more... yes!"

Unfortunately, soon after the release of the flexi, Blood Robots played their last show together during August 1984, at the Nottingham Narrowboat – the furthest they'd ever travelled for a gig – with Famous Imposters, The Sears, Kulturkampf and Idiot Clone, and, apparently still struggling to come to terms with Richard's ill-timed departure, split soon after. Hec went on to play with Rhombus Of Doom, whilst Sned and Micky formed Generic, one of the UK's earliest political hardcore bands, and founded Flat Earth Records (that Sned has ran until this day); they later wound up together again in One By One during the early Nineties. Nowadays, Sned drums for various bands, most recently War All The Time and Threads, and Micky guitars for Jinn, both of them remaining cautiously optimistic, far more interested in creating brand new challenging music than rehashing past glories.

Sned: "The years have knocked the stuffing out of me, but I still think the planet would be better off without the shitty human race fucking it up. Andy clearly never got what we were about though, as he's a fuckin' copper now! Hec has a somewhat less bleak outlook than my own, and it was refreshing and inspiring to hang out with him recently, and to discover that we're actually not all that different to how we were twenty-plus years ago!"

"I guess I'm not as despondent as Sned," laughs Micky. "I do at times feel a bit more misanthropic than is healthy, but I think that having a child has helped give me a much more positive outlook on the world. Also my perspective is different, having worked all of my life; in some ways I'm more idealistic than Sned, and in others I have more of a real-world view... I think essentially we are both the same people, just older, fatter and less fit! And maybe a bit less intense about everything... only a bit, mind you! Neither of us is ready to join the 'pipe and slipper brigade' just yet."

"Yeah, it's nice to reminisce a bit," agrees Sned. "But I'm still alive and living in the present day and that's what is important; to live in the past all the time is to be dead already. We were an awkward bunch of geeks in a crap band, who learned a lot from each other and our friends during our short time together... and you can put that on our tombstone."

SELECT DISCOGRAPHY

7"s:
'Within These Walls' (self-released, 1984) – split flexi-disc with Reality Control

At A Glance:
Two other tracks from the band's final recording actually appeared on vinyl after they'd split – 'Dust' on the late '84 'Tracks From The Station' collection (GMC Records), 'Black' on an American compilation, 'Compulsory Overtime' in 1985 – but the only Blood Robots material available on CD at the time of writing is the track 'The Valley', that appeared on Overground's excellent 'Anti-War: Anarcho-punk Compilation, Volume One' in 2005.

et's face it, there was a lot of dross padding out the 'Bullshit Detector' compilations, but each album was thankfully salvaged from complete anonymity by at least one or two strong tracks, and the undisputed highlight of 'Volume Three' (issued during November 1984) was 'The War Is Over' by the aforementioned **REALITY CONTROL**, a staggeringly heavy and intense offering that utterly belied the sonic limits placed upon it by the paltry budget under which it was committed to tape. Loaded with twisted guitar noise and profound metaphor (perfectly demonstrated by the visceral opening couplet, 'Lies spew forth from their mouths, like a jet of blood from punctured flesh...'), it hinted at a considerable well of musical and lyrical potential that largely went untapped.

Reality Control, Leeds 1985, picture by Andrew Medcalf.

Formed in late 1980 and comprising Michael Barlow on vocals (who would later take up the rhythm guitar as well), Michael Scott on guitar (who would graduate to providing additional vocals when Michael B. took up second guitar duties), Ken Fawcett on bass and Paul 'Rid' Ridley on drums, the band played their first show in Heaton, Newcastle-upon-Tyne, during April 1981.

"It was at some church/community hall with two other bands from school," recalls Michael Barlow, "namely No Sweat, who were a Pink Fairies/Motörhead-influenced outfit, and Totally Innocent, this New Wave-ish band who Paul Ridley, our drummer, also played guitar for. It didn't go too badly either, with us playing all our own stuff... apart from a cover of 'Blockbuster' by The Sweet – but our version was more akin to how the Cockney Rejects did it!

"We used to practice in bedrooms, garages and church halls, annoying the hell out of people in the process! It was always really hard to be able to afford equipment and we had to rely on the generosity and good will of other bands and the patience of our parents, until we later discovered music co-ops. A couple of years on, we became involved with the Gateshead Music Collective who provided much-needed rehearsal space and shared equipment. Without them, many bands in the area just wouldn't have existed. The rehearsal space also doubled as a venue, The Station, which we helped with initially, putting on gigs for local bands with more nationally-known ones.

"At first we were all influenced by the likes of the Damned, UK Subs, Fall, early Cure, Joy Division and PIL, to name but a few," he adds. "But we basically listened to quite a broad spectrum of music from Discharge to The Doors. Increasingly though, we were all listening to Crass and the music produced by bands on their own – or associated – labels, which politicised and influenced our views. This increased political awareness was consequently reflected in our songs, alongside our own experiences and viewpoints.

"But I don't think we walked about pigeon-holing ourselves with that 'anarcho punk' label as it did become restrictive, although we certainly identified greatly with that scene. I suppose at the time we regarded ourselves as being within the anarchist political spectrum, but to us it was just about fairness and equality. It was an experience which politicised us all and, ultimately, I think it was about being a good human being. A healthy sense of humour and cynicism also helped us, I think…"

As detailed previously, Reality Control quickly hooked up with the Blood Robots, with whom they produced a fanzine and played many a gig. In early 1983, they recorded their debut seven-track demo, 'The Happy Face' (from which Crass lifted 'The War Is Over' for 'Bullshit Detector 3') at Newcastle's Spectro Arts Centre, with Michael himself overseeing the session.

"We were fortunate in that when I left school I got a job as a trainee sound engineer at Spectro, where

they had an eight-track recording studio. This meant that we could record all our demos there, plus those of the Blood Robots and a few other local bands, as it was affordable and I could do all the engineering and production work for free. The centre was much cheaper than commercial outfits because it was publicly funded as a community arts resource… but inevitably it closed.

"Anyway, we just recorded what we thought was our strongest material, which was the bulk of our live set. The title of the demo reflected how we saw people putting on a happy face, no matter what miserable life mainstream society dealt them. We wanted to encourage people to question things instead of blindly accepting them. I'm still reasonably pleased with it now as well, apart from my questionable singing abilities!"

'The Happy Face' tape sold very well through the local independent record shop, Volume, and as a consequence, the owner offered Reality Control the opportunity of doing an EP for Volume Records, who had already successfully released singles by the likes of such Northeastern luminaries as the Toy Dolls and Total Chaos. Three-track 7", 'The Reproduction Of Hate', was the rather glorious result, with the brooding, sombre 'Another Sunrise' (a vastly superior version to that on the first demo) being the definite highlight of the cuts on offer.

Ken and Michael B. of Reality Control.

"We recorded it at Impulse Studios in Wallsend, Tyne And Wear, and it was principally an anti-war record, in particular against the British war with Argentina over the Falkland Islands around 1982. Although we were only sixteen at the time, we felt very strongly about not only the futility and horror of war, but in particular the way thousands were sacrificed by Margaret Thatcher in an (ultimately successful) attempt to whip up this ridiculously nationalistic support for the war, which in turn cynically resulted in her flagging Conservative government being returned to office on the back of it. Not only that, but the jingoistic 'our boys'-type support pushed by the British gutter press was particularly objectionable. I'm still pretty proud of it even now; I think the sentiment still holds very true... the only regret being a slightly out-of-tune bass on 'Man Reproduce'!"

After the EP, bassist Ken left "to pursue other things", and was replaced by Carl Craig from local punkers, The Abductors, in time for the early '84 recording of the band's second cassette release, a nine-track affair entitled 'While We Live In Cages', that took their trademark gloom into surprisingly tuneful territories. Two tracks – 'The Law' and 'Sugar And Spice' – were even included the following year on 'Compulsory Overtime', the compilation album issued by an American label, Dasein, that also featured the Blood Robots.

Then, in March 1984, Reality Control recorded 'Tears Of Blood' at Newcastle Media Workshops, where Michael was then working as a sound engineer, for their side of 'Within These Walls', a split flexi-disc with Blood Robots that the two bands financed and released themselves. However the record was hardly out before Rid left and was replaced by Alistair, who drummed on the band's third – never released – demo. He then departed himself for pastures new and was superseded by [James] Murphy, formerly with Scottish anarcho punks, Alternative.

"We had played in Bristol with the Alternative and, I think, Flowers In The Dustbin, a gig which sticks in the mind as it went very well and we had a proper PA so we got a really good sound, which we taped through the mixing desk. Another good gig I have fond memories of was in Leeds... can't remember who it was with or even where it was... I think it was late '84 or early '85... but we just had a really good night where we played particularly passionately.

"A gig in Edinburgh sticks in the mind as well... for all the wrong reasons though!" laughs Michael. "I'd bought a new guitar with a locking nut and 'wangy bar' [tremolo arm], which would in theory keep the guitar in tune for ages. However, the down side was, when a string broke the tension would go and send the whole guitar out of tune. Of course, this is what happened less than halfway into our set and it was such a long, drawn-out faff to put a new string on, retune the thing and lock it up again with Allen keys, that we just abandoned the gig! Dreadful! And I'm sure there were a few more like that too, which thankfully escape me now!"

Reality Control played their final show at the Nottingham Narrowboat on October 10th, 1985, with Chumbawamba and No Defences.

"It wasn't a bad gig as far as I can recall but after we just kind of fizzled out and were no more... no specific reason as such; I think in hindsight we were just growing a bit older and getting into different things, and the band came to its natural end. Also, Carl and Murphy were living in Scotland, which made practicing less frequent and more difficult, so perhaps the desire to get together and make music waned a bit.

"I really haven't got a clue if anyone joined any other bands afterwards," offers Michael, when quizzed as to what happened next. "I'm sure they did! Ken, our original bassist who has moved back to the Northeast of England in the past year, later became a teacher. I'm now a graphic designer and photographer in the Health Service. And last I heard, Michael [Scott] was living on the South coast of England, Carl was a football [soccer] coach at a school in the US, Rid was living and working in France... and I don't know about Alistair or Murphy!

"But the band was an experience which both politicised and enthused me. Okay, we were young and naïve to think we could change the world, but I think at least some of the values will have stayed with a lot of people involved in that scene in one way or another. As I've said earlier, ultimately it was about being a good human being; I know I still try!

"My only regret was that we didn't release anything more on vinyl, as I think we had something a bit different to many bands, and that might have got us out to a wider audience. If anyone was to remember what we did, I think that would hopefully be it: that we had something a little bit different to offer..."

SELECT DISCOGRAPHY

7"s:
'The Reproduction Of Hate' (Volume, 1983)
'Within These Walls' (self-released, 1984) – split flexi-disc with Blood Robots

At A Glance:
Unfortunately there has not yet been a Reality Control compilation CD (note to any labels reading this: what the hell are you waiting for?)

he **FAMOUS IMPOSTERS** were one of many fiercely independent bands that sprung up in the Northeast as a direct result of the Sunderland Musicians Collective and the alternative venue they founded, the Sunderland Bunker, a genuine focal point for the scene both musically and socially that still hosts live events to this day. They weren't the biggest band from the area, nor the fastest, nor the heaviest, but in terms of passion and sincerity, they were up there with the best of them.

"Punk had energy, ideas and purpose," exclaims bassist Raf Mulla (also co-author of the much-respected Acts Of Defiance fanzine), who replaced the original bass player Tony in 1983, about a year after the band formed. "You didn't have to conform, and it was the one form of music to really have something to offer that said it was okay to be an outsider... and I certainly was an outsider. At that time in Sunderland there were a few really distinct groups that you could fall into: the 'townies'... beer, disco, Ford Capris, fighting and more beer; the 'rockers'.... beer, heavy metal, bikes, fighting and drugs; or the 'skinheads'.... beer, fighting and NF meetings! Above all, they were so very rigid – you had to fit in to be a part of the crowd – and as that wasn't going to happen for me, punk was really the only place that I had to go. Where you didn't expect to get the crap kicked out of you for daring to be different... in fact the challenge was to be different."

Alongside Raf, the Famous Imposters were guitarist/vocalist Anth Irwin, drummer Andy 'Hardcore' Burden (formerly with Barnsley's Societies Vultures) and second guitarist 'Teaser', although the latter left about a year after Raf joined, resulting in the three-piece line-up with which the Imposters made most of their live appearances. They quickly cultivated a fairly unique sound for themselves, based on driving rhythms and fragile thoughtful melodies that owed as much to the likes of Killing Joke, Southern Death Cult and Joy Division as they did Crass or Flux Of Pink Indians. Raf even cites personal influences as eclectic as The Cure, Gang Of Four and The Beatles – hardly the norm for the anarcho-punk genre.

"I don't think that we actually ever regarded ourselves as anarcho-punk anyway, but that is how we were regarded by others, partly because of the lyrics, but probably as much because of who was in the band. Both Andy and myself had been active in other areas of what was then the anarcho-punk movement, and because of this we spent a lot of time playing with other bands on that circuit and were categorised alongside them. If we had bothered to analyse it (which we didn't), not everyone agreed politically – not even close on some issues – but close enough generally to agree on what we said as a band."

They soon set about gigging enthusiastically around the Northeast ("The biggest was probably at an all-day punk festival in Leeds to a few hundred people; the smallest to five lads and a stray dog in a youth club in Peterlee one cold winter night... but we had a laugh anyway!"), even supporting Conflict at the Newcastle Guild Hall. Yet they built the majority of their grass-roots following with regular shows at the Bunker.

"I don't think that I can overstate how important the Bunker was to many people in Sunderland. The Musicians Collective had formed a few years earlier, releasing a compilation LP of local bands in the collective, and that really set the tone. Through a lot of hard work and lateral thinking, the collective somehow managed to persuade the local council to have the use of an empty school right in the middle of town; the deal was done before I became involved, but as the place had to be done up, etc. with no money, I started to help out about then. And there was this real big contrast as the next building to us was this huge leisure centre that the Council had spent literally millions on, and there in its shadow was us, with no money but huge determination; I remember the Guardian newspaper came down and interviewed some of us, highlighting the contrast between our do-it-yourself attitude and the council-funded centre. I think it all kind of embarrassed the council because, after about eighteen months, they decided to knock our building down and build a car park there instead! But there was such support for the Bunker that they couldn't just put us on the streets... remember, this was in the days of Thatcher's reign and the local Labour council had to at least be seen supporting some kind of alternative.

"Anyway, after more campaigning and work we got a much bigger building; well, it was the shell of a building, an old arts centre so we had to build the stage, practice rooms, café, everything, from scratch. I can remember sending off literally thousands of letters asking for money from all sorts of places… we had so many rejections that we papered the first floor with all the 'No' letters! Still, we managed to get enough to survive on for a good while. And once it was established, it was brilliant; here was an example of how we could work together collectively and build something good and worthwhile for ourselves. In my mind it was a kind of model for the future, of what we could achieve through cooperation; maybe I had my rose-tinted glasses on, but that was how it

felt, for a while at least. For the Famous Imposters, it was our spiritual home; we met there, we practised there, we played there, we went every Friday night to see who was on, and, as me and Andy were on the dole, we spent a lot of our days there as well…"

Entering Felling Studios, the Famous Imposters recorded their cassette debut, 'Cradle To The Grave', which brought them to the attention of Whitehaven-based label, Scrobe, ran by Martyn 'Trunt' Cockbain, who also did a fanzine of the same name. Scrobe released a split single between the Famous Imposters and The Dead in 1984.

"After seeing the Imposters play with Flux, The System, Alternative, Psycho Faction and Dirt at the Bunker, I thought they had something different," reckons Trunt. "Really catchy songs, lyrics you could listen to instead of them just being yelled at you, and a great name. I saw them loads of times after that, even travelled to Leeds to see them play the Bier Keller. I had previously said in an interview with the BBC [for an episode of 'Off The Peg', focussing on the Cumbrian music scene] that all profits from the zine and tape releases would be fed into a split single, and, true to my word, I started the ball rolling with The Dead, a local band that I hung out with, and thought needed that extra boost to get them noticed a little bit more. The other group was originally going to be Psycho Faction, as I knocked about with them as well and had been to many gigs with them; I loved their sound and their lyrics, which were really from the heart. They had some great tunes, and I think they could have gone onto better things, but they sadly split – and I didn't want to put a group onto vinyl that wasn't going to gig, because at the time bands seemed to sell most records at gigs... especially those bands with no record company behind them.

"So, there was only one group who I thought were worth the other side of the vinyl, the Famous Imposters, and they jumped at the chance; I think they thought it wouldn't come off at first, and were a little shocked to even be asked by me. Scrobe paid £307, The Dead paid £150 and the Famous Imposters got the covers done, then the Imposters got 500 copies to sell, The Dead got 200, and I got 300. I know that F.I. sold all theirs, and I was left with only four copies, but I'm not too sure whether the Dead

Famous Imposters (left to right: Raf Mulla, Anth Irwin and Teaser) live at Sunderland Bunker, 1984, picture by Trunt.

sold all theirs? I wasn't too sure about the cover either, as The Dead only got a little bit on the back, and I've even seen it advertised as the 'Famous Imposters' 'Open Your Eyes' 7'' when really it's a split single. I wanted to release a compilation LP of Cumbria bands after that, but it never got off the ground, 'cos the scene was slowly dying..."

The two Imposters tracks on the split single ably demonstrated the daring diversity creeping into their music (like kindred spirits The Mob, they were totally unafraid of revealing their deepest emotions through their writing, no matter how vulnerable it left them), whilst on the flip [Whitehaven five-piece] The Dead didn't let the side down either, with two tracks of well-executed pop-punk powered by classy female vocals and subtle keyboards.

As mentioned earlier though, Raf left in 1985, just before the release of the band's second – and final – release, a self-titled 12'' courtesy of Bristol label, Children Of The Revolution. A five-track affair that had Raf playing bass on the three songs on Side A, and his replacement, Anth's brother, David, playing on the two B-side cuts, the 12'' was another confident display from the band, although by then their sound had practically nothing in common with the punk scene of the time; Anth's moody vocals and delicate guitar work (much of it acoustic) were actually more reminiscent of the darker elements of Eighties pop music.

"The last gig I played was at Sunderland Poly," ponders Raf. "I think it was a benefit for CND, but everyone knew it was my last gig, so we went out and had a good time of it; it was a great night, no animosity or anything like that. I don't know about the final gig for the band without me, but, to be honest, I hope that somewhere out there Anth is still playing; he was a bloody good guitarist with too much talent to let go to waste."

Sadly the Famous Imposters ground to an inglorious halt not long after the 12", and, after an ill-advised solo spot at an open air show in Yorkshire, Raf retired from music completely, relocating to Newcastle-upon-Tyne and concentrating his efforts on political endeavours for several years, before settling down and having "two beautiful kids."

"It's questionable that we were even a threat back then," he responds, when asked how he views modern-day punk rock. "I don't know if there is that same sense of belief in the need for radical change, or the ability to bring about that change. They were very different times politically back then; all kinds of different movements were challenging the status quo and, while we didn't usually agree with their aims, we did have a common cause in what we were fighting against. That backdrop doesn't exist anymore; there is much more cynicism than idealism these days, and cynicism breeds inaction and contempt, which is how I see most of the current punk movement.

"The passing of the years has proved three things to me. That (a), we were right! I still believe in those ideals; they still matter and, whilst the expression and manifestation has changed (I've got more shoes than just a pair of Doc Martens now), that core is still there. (b) We were wrong to be so sectarian and holier-than-thou; that's what really killed off the momentum – so many people, myself included, thought that we had the only answers and every other movement was to be attacked, and anyone who didn't match our standards was to be sneered at. If only we had made a stronger common cause with other groups, then we would have made so much more progress. (c) It was so much more difficult than I could have ever imagined… and I think that our underestimation was also fatal. Instead of getting ready for a long haul, we all got despondent 'cos the world didn't stop when we shouted 'Anarchy!'"

SELECT DISCOGRAPHY

7"s:
'Open Your Eyes' (Scrobe, 1984) – split with The Dead

12"s:
'Famous Imposters' (Children Of The Revolution, 1985)

At A Glance:
Although the Imposters have enjoyed one official CD release with the track 'Fighting Again' on Sean McGhee's excellent 'Anti-State' compilation for Overground Records (2005), any reader wishing to purchase a CDR of all their recordings ought to initially contact Trunt of Scrobe Records:
trunt@btopenworld.com

Ⓞne of the more controversial bands in this book, many readers may not even regard CHUMBAWAMBA as a genuine 'anarcho punk' band in the first place, partly because it's been a long, long time since they produced anything sonically resembling hardcore punk, but mainly because they committed the cardinal sin of signing to the very same major label they had previously vociferated so vehemently. However, any band that caused such a furore is obviously full of good-natured agitators, and besides, nothing is as black-and-white as it at first seems, especially in the complicated soap opera of musical subcultures.

"Chumbawamba, and you can ask several different members of the group, both now and from the past and get the same answer, were grounded in the fundamental ideas of fun, first, and anarchism, second," reckons guitarist Allan 'Boff' Whalley. "Of course we all lived together and took the piss out of everything, and laughed the days away, etc., but that basic idea of anarchism rooted us all, and kept us talking, kept us questioning things. We loved it! Anarchism even taught us how to share the bloody washing up! Anarchism taught us how to be on tour in a small van in Europe for five weeks and still come out of it loving each other.

"And it wasn't that we were disillusioned with punk, just that we wanted to do something different," he adds, with appropriate disdain for their irrelevance, on the dubious nature of his band's punk credentials. "There were things like... uh, that bloke John The Postman from Manchester... he was fantastic, even though he couldn't sing! He was just a postman, but he cut two albums, on which he just moans and groans. There were all these amazing people, who all came under the banner of punk; John Peel played it, and we heard it, and we wanted to do something just as strange. So, we were still really excited by it all, even if we didn't sound like everybody else; I was saving up to buy records all the time, it was like a religion."

Chumbawamba, then based in Burnley, made their vinyl debut, as did so many other bands of the time, in late 1982, via Crass and their celebrated 'Bullshit Detector' compilations, appearing with the track 'Three Years Later' on 'Volume Two'. Instantly recognisable amongst the other acts included thanks to its unorthodox a cappella intro, it set out the band's ambitious musical stall very early on. At the time, Chumbawamba were merely a three-piece, Boff being joined by Danbert Nobacon (real name Nigel Hunter) and Midge, both of whom he had previously played with as Chimp Eats Banana.

"We sent the track to Crass without any idea that they were putting together another 'Bullshit Detector'; we just thought it a good idea to send them our music. When we got a letter from them saying they'd be using two bits from the songs on an actual record, we were gobsmacked, amused, happy, and confused – but proud and chuffed, nonetheless.

"We recorded 'Three Years Later' long before we even did our first demo, in the basement of a terraced house in Leeds. Which was owned by a bloke called Mr ComeInLads! Who lived next door to three nurses. One of which was an obsessive Beatles fan. What year was that? I really, really don't know... some time between dropping out of full-time education and wondering whether or not to get a proper job!"

Boff himself also made a 'solo appearance' – as 'Boffo' – on the same 'Bullshit Detector' album that introduced the world to Chumbawamba, with a pointed, yet humorous, attack on The Clash and the empty promises with which they clawed themselves up out of the punk scene to international stardom.

"The Boffo track was from a spoof of the 'Clash On 45' thing which I recorded onto cassette. I'd been a big Clash fan and was sad to see them getting into the whole cocaine/USA rock'n'roll lifestyle. The full recording I did went through a series of parodies of Clash songs where I vented my bitter spleen in a very angsty way against these rotters who seemed to be selling out my dream.

"Actually, as well, when 'Bullshit Detector 2' came out, we wrote a personal letter to every other band on that album and encouraged them to somehow be involved in something else, without Crass helping us. We only got about five or six replies, and were a bit disillusioned by this aspect of anarcho punk. But Daz and Dave from Passion Killers, who were also on that comp, came up to

Chumbawamba busking in Paris, 1980.

visit us, and ended up staying – and joining our band! So, at least some good came of it all…

"I'd always been interested in music but had never played an instrument," adds Boff, on his taking-up of the guitar. "I wasn't even vaguely musical, but just thought it would be a great thing to do. And there was this musicians collective in Burnley – basically all these punk and heavy metal bands – and at their very first meeting, they asked who was in a band, and you had to write the name of your band down on this sheet of paper. We'd always had this joke about one day forming a band called Chimp Eats Banana, so of course we wrote 'Chimp Eats Banana' down, thinking we were being really funny, and about two weeks later, one of the people from the collective rang up and said, 'We've got you a gig!' And we went, 'Shit!' I literally sat down and said to Dan, 'Right, okay, I'll play guitar, and you'll have to sing…' He was like, 'But I've never sang before in my life!' And we thought, 'Well, we'll just try it!' And that was it; we had our own band together! It was mad, and no other kind of music ever let you do that sort of thing before punk… and it meant that we were trying all these different things, because we didn't know what 'the rules' were. It was never like, 'Right, this is what we do: play these chords like this, and the drums like this…' We just looked at what other people were doing and tried to do it ourselves… and we were into John Cooper Clarke as well, so we wanted all this poetry and general weirdness going on…

"Plus the whole fact that I was supposed to be a Mormon gave me a very good reason to say, 'Right, I'm going to start doing this right now!' And it just blew everything away, and filled me with the idea that I didn't want to go to school anymore…

"After the initial thing with the Pistols and The Clash, it was more The Fall and Wire, and PiL and Adam And The Ants… and that was when I got really obsessed with punk music. Even now, I can listen to 'Dirk Wears White Sox' [by The Ants] over and over again; it was so peculiar, they were so different to anything else. Great album that, really great, and it was a shame that their music lost that strange, quirky, angular quality after that. I saw them just after they bought out 'Dog Eat Dog', and there were all these old, die-hard Ants fans there who couldn't decide whether to desert them or not… I had a few friends who even had Ants tattoos, and did they ever live to regret getting those!"

Chimp Eats Banana quickly morphed into Chumbawamba though, and were joined by Lou Watts before they made their public debut on January 8th 1982 at the Hendly Hotel in nearby Colne.

"I think it was probably a really interesting evening… because we were aware that we were playing to the Burnley punk crowd who had sort of moved into other things. We grew up in that area, and all the bands knew each other, and there was a sense of punk community, which was great, but by 1982… maybe 1981 or even 1980, in fact… a lot of drugs got involved in the Burnley scene, and we'd tried to do other things, and that gig was a bit of a reaction to all that. We were playing some really strange music, and had all these different people getting up to do different songs… it was very purposely un-punk!

"Right from that first gig, we had people dressing up, and we weren't afraid to stop the gig to show a film… we had two drum kits, and we had these flip charts, to do the Bob Dylan thing where we'd show the people the words as we sang them… that sort of stuff! We just tried to cram as much in as possible, so people had lots to look at, as well as listen to… we were desperate, right from the start, not to just be four people in a band playing rock'n'roll music. We were fans of early Frank Zappa and things like that, who – even though they were from a different era – really tried to challenge their audience with what they did onstage, the way they presented their music, the way they chopped and changed all the time…"

Of course, Crass also had a very definite concept of how they wanted to present themselves onstage, although they were never as gleefully theatrical as Chumbawamba.

"Oh yeah, the first time I saw them [Crass], I'd only heard their first album, and I was gob-smacked by their whole performance. I thought, 'Wow! They've really thought about what they wear, what they say… the lighting… everything about it…' They were trying to reach people in different ways, playing all these weird venues…

"And all these new bands were watching them, thinking, 'What a great idea! We'll all wear black from now on!' And it's just a shame that someone didn't watch them and think, 'What a great idea! We'll all wear… pink! And recite poetry…' But instead everybody got out their stencils and did their anarcho fanzines…

"The thing is, when Crass came along, they were unique; they didn't sound like anybody else I'd ever heard before. And not just with what they were saying, and playing, but the way they did it… like the production – it was really weird, but I loved it. But it quickly became obvious that they were setting up a kind of blueprint, and a lot of people just followed that blueprint blindly… we did, to a certain extent, as well. You didn't have to be good musicians to play music like that… even though Crass were really, really good musicians, as it happens, but you know what I mean… they really showed you that you could do it, and a lot of people did do it. When I saw bands like Dirt, they were good, really good, and as it turned out, I was really into them, but I couldn't help thinking, 'They're so similar to Crass… but Crass do it better!' I much preferred stuff like Annie Anxiety, because she was taking what they did some place new.

"But no matter how much people like Penny Rimbaud slag off Johnny Rotten, saying that they were no influence on Crass or anything, and no matter how much that changed the whole way I thought about music, Crass 'came' from the Sex Pistols for me, and I can't change that, because they completely turned my life on its head. Even when Sid Vicious did 'My Way', even though it was all Malcolm [McLaren]'s idea, and he didn't know what he was doing – he was just doing it for the money – and even though Steve Jones did all the music for it… whatever… for sheer shock value, for pure emotional impact, I was absolutely gob-smacked by it."

Chumbawamba's mischievous nature was further demonstrated by their inclusion on the 'Back On The Streets' EP, for which various members contributed the track, 'I'm Thick', masquerading as a street punk band called Skin Disease to highlight what they regarded as an inherently stupid offshoot of punk.

"That was when there was all that Oi thing going on, and we wrote to [Sounds journalist] Garry Bushell [who popularised the whole Oi genre in his weekly column], just as a joke really, because we thought the name was funny, saying 'We're a Burnley-based Oi band called Skin Disease, and this is what we're doing, and this is what we think…' And a few weeks later in Sounds, we were mentioned in his round-up of new punk and Oi bands! So then we wrote a few songs, just parodying what we thought most of the Oi bands sounded like, and sent them to him, and he wrote back asking us to go on the next Oi album! And there we were thinking, 'What's the most we can get away with here? How about shouting 'I'm thick!' sixty-four times?' It was really funny, because the producer couldn't quite tell whether we were serious or not… it was great to do anyway, looking back; it was by far the biggest, poshest studio I've ever been in, in my whole life. We were sitting in the foyer with this other band who were recording on the same day; I can't remember what they were called, but they were quite young, all skinheads… and they were really nervous, 'cos it really meant a lot to 'em being asked to record for this single, and I felt a bit bad for them, 'cos we were just there taking the piss!

"When I grew up though, in the Seventies, there used to be a lot of humour in music… you'd get records in the charts that were parodies of other records, taking the piss out of bands that were No. 1 and stuff, and that just doesn't happen anymore – no one gets onstage and tries to get people to laugh at them."

By late 1982, Boff, Dan, Midge and Lou had been joined by Alice Nutter, of Ow, My Hair's On Fire, and Dunstan 'Dunst' Bruce of Men In A Suitcase, and were squatting a house in Leeds, which would become their band HQ as well as their communal residence. They were joined in their venture by Harry 'Daz' Hamer and Dave 'Mavis' Dillon from the Passion Killers, and soon after recorded their first official demo, 'Be Happy Despite It All' in early 1983.

"We basically did a lot of growing up," begins Boff's stream of consciousness rant on this extremely important, memorable time of his life, "Met a lot of people, got a sense of sociability, learned how to live with others, had relationships, squatted this large Victorian house, encouraged people to move into it, and created the idea of working and living as a co-operative. The band doubled in size by dent of those relationships and empty rooms. 'Look at this huge house we've squatted! Come and grab a room!'

"So, we practised a lot, got involved in many political things, got involved in the local music scene, involved in growing vegetables and learning about plumbing and electrics, and eventually ended up deciding to make a single. We were such music fans then, and such political activists, avidly reading about Dead Kennedys and Crass and all the British punk bands. No-one was offering to help us put a record out, so we eventually made our own. Flux, who we'd met after a gig a year earlier, half-promised to put something out by us on Spiderleg… but we waited and waited, and nothing happened, so we gave up on them. We saved up the money ourselves, booked a studio, rehearsed the songs and went and recorded it all in two days."

The resultant 'Revolution' EP was released on the band's own label, Agit-Prop, in 1985, and quickly sold out of its initial pressing. When it was repressed, it sold in sufficient numbers to bother the Independent Charts for over thirty weeks, peaking at No. 4.

"It was very DIY to start with," Boff recalls proudly. "We had a little production line going, putting the records in their sleeves and stuff… and then we got a distribution deal with Red Rhino from York, because we were getting a bit disillusioned with all the London-based people not being remotely interested in our record, and John Peel started playing it loads and loads, and it took off from there… and whereas most people feel it's a huge thrill to hold your very first record in your hands – and it is – hearing it played on John Peel was even better for me. And I'm not saying that because he isn't around anymore, but because I idolised his show when I was a kid."

Chumbawamba at Sion Hill Art College, Bath 1986, picture by Jaz Wiseman.

Chumbawamba, Bath 1986, picture by Jaz Wiseman.

The second release on Agit-Prop was a split EP with San Franciscan punkers, A State Of Mind, entitled 'We Are The World?', but it was with their debut album, 'Pictures Of Starving Children', that the band made their most enduring and potent statement against the corporate rape of Third World economies. Its scathing condemnation of most charities as mere salves of public conscience (not to mention springboards for kick-starting ailing careers!) was inspired by Live Aid, the 'Band Aid' event held on July 13th, 1985, and apparently watched by 1.5 billion people around the world.

"We'd already written most of the music for the album – we had about ten songs finished – and then Live Aid happened, literally a few weeks before we were due to record. We only had a month to go, but we scrapped all the original lyrics for the album and started from scratch, and it was really scary actually, because it was our first ever album and we had been rehearsing the songs and they were getting better and better – and now we were scrapping all the lyrics! But it was also great, to just be able to do that and say what we wanted.

"It was all such an incredible smokescreen really, even though I'm sure that a lot of people behind it had very genuine motives, and all the people who bought the record meant well – they were just naïve about what was really being achieved. And when people really want to change something for the better, when they've got their hearts in the right place, it's hard to convince them that there's a big difference between charity and real, meaningful change, that they're only buying all these records to make themselves feel better…"

Recorded at Woodlands in Castleford, 'Pictures Of Starving Children' remains for many the definitive Chumbas record; effortlessly tuneful, daringly innovative, and thoroughly provocative throughout, it was the essence of anarcho-punk in a cocky new disguise.

European dates with Dutch band The Ex on the back of the album led to the formation of Antidote, a brief collaboration between various members of the two bands that released the

'Destroy Fascism!' EP on Looney Tunes, a label ran by members of Active Minds, the fiercely political and independent hardcore punk band from Scarborough.

"We'd been playing a bit with Heresy in Europe," admits Boff, of the inspiration behind Antidote, "a couple of little tours here and there, and we were really into them, and so some of us decided to do some really out-and-out fast stuff. We did this demo of about fifteen songs, all about a minute long, and Looney Tunes really liked it; they wanted to put the demo out as a single, but then, to be a bit contrary, we decided not to use any of the songs off it. We had this idea to do an anti-fascist record, and we'd been doing some stuff with The Ex, so we asked them to join us, and Looney Tunes were a little bit miffed, because what we recorded for the single wasn't really like the demo that they had liked in the first place… but it came out alright in the end."

Summer 1987 saw the release on Agit-Prop of 'Never Mind The Ballots… Here's The Rest Of Your Lives', another 'concept-like' album; a response to the general elections being held in the UK, it questioned the validity of the democratic system that allows the average person on the street the luxury of at least feeling in control of their own lives for the length of time it takes them to decide where they're going to place their 'X' come polling day. Opening with the brilliantly bonkers 'Always Tell The Voter What The Voter Wants To Hear', that borders on deranged Country and Western, it was another spectacularly eclectic outing for the band.

"Not really that keen on 'Never Mind The Ballots' actually! I think we got caught on the hop too much, and left it a bit late to write some of the material. It's hard to be objective about the things you create, but as far as we were concerned, it was like, 'Okay, this is happening in the world, let's react to it, let's put a record out!' It seemed the right thing to do, but looking back at it, you can see that some of it worked better than others. I'm not sure we changed the lives of anyone with our records anyway, but we certainly changed their lives for the hour that we were onstage if they came to see us play live, and then we always tried to give out leaflets and booklets and stuff for some added focus."

Another scathing undercover attack was launched when Chumbawamba became Scab Aid and released 'Let It Be', mocking the motives behind Ferry Aid, a popstar-powered super-group a la Live Aid who had also just released a version of the old Beatles chestnut, to benefit the families of those lost when the Herald Of Free Enterprise ferry capsized off Zeebrugge in 1987. Chumbawamba took particular offence that the single was backed by Tory newspaper The Sun, a low-brow right-wing publication they referred to as The Scum. The single went Top Ten in the Indie Charts and was nominated as Single Of The Week in the NME (New Musical Express) before anyone actually realised that Scab Aid was the Chumbas in disguise.

Although furthering their reputation within anarcho-punk circles by appearing on compilation albums such as 'A Vile Peace' (Peaceville Records), 'Mindless Slaughter' (Anhrefn) and 'The ALF Is Watching' during 1987 and '88, Chumbawamba made a concerted effort to distance themselves from their restrictive punk roots in 1989 with the release of the 'English Rebel Songs, 1381 – 1914' 10", a collection of a cappella protest songs that sent ripples of outrage through the frustratingly conservative punk community. By the time of 1990's 'Slap', with its heavy dance vibe, Chumbawamba weren't just on a different playing field but in a totally different ball park to their former peers from the anarcho-punk scene, but at least they were taking a credible revolutionary message to an uninformed mainstream audience.

"Actually, it wasn't that we wanted to take our music to a bigger audience, but rather that we wanted to take our music somewhere where it would challenge the audience we already had. About the time we recorded 'Slap', we went to America for the first time, touring up and down the West coast, and by that time [influential punk fanzine] Maximum Rock'n'roll, who had always been champions of the band up until that point, refused to review anything we did after 'English Rebel Songs', because they decided 'it wasn't punk!' They actually sat around and had a meeting about this Chumbawamba record, and decided that it was just going too far to have a punk band playing a cappella folk songs. On the one hand we thought it was ridiculous, and on the other we thought it was quite funny! Some of those people were just gob-smacked that we were using these dance beats, but for us, that was what it was all about, not to get stuck in one style. And it's no good getting all upset about it; we never said anyone had to like it; we just wanted to provoke them, to get them to try something different for once…"

After contributing to the 'Fuck EMI' compilation album (an appearance that would transpire as being rather ironic two years later), the band almost released the album, 'Jesus H. Christ', which was reworked and re-recorded as 1992's 'Shhh!'

The sabre-rattling generated by that being the band's first CD release, a business move greatly frowned upon by puritanical DIY advocates (more controversy was duly courted following the release of 'Anarchy' on One Little Indian in '94, because of its 'offensive' sleeve – a baby being born, oh horror of horrors!), was nothing compared to the shit storm that descended when Chumbawamba reneged on their word, thus losing much of their ethical integrity for many, by signing to EMI for the release of 1997's 'Tubthumper' album. The hideously catchy 'Tubthumping' single itself sold over five million copies worldwide. One would like to think they sought to subvert the evil corporate music industry from within, but alas, one of the main considerations was fiscal.

"Uh, that should've been our motive, I guess, but it wasn't; it was the culmination of several things. The first thing, and the main thing really, was that the corporate music industry had changed… EMI had ceased their involvement in the manufacture of arms and weapons. So, at least we had a clear conscience as far as that was concerned. We'd already recorded the 'Tubthumper' album, and without any thought about selling a lot of records and all that, we were wondering what to do with it, and we were getting a bit pissed off with it all, to be honest, and some of us got part-time jobs and stuff. Some bloke in Germany had a copy of the recording and really liked it, and then the German EMI got in touch with us, and we had a meeting with them, and we said, 'You do know who we are, don't you?' And we gave them a copy of the 'Fuck EMI' album, just to make it clear to them what they were dealing with, but they were still really into it, and offered us a £100,000 advance. And we thought, 'Shit…!' With that sort of money we could put out whatever records we wanted, and play whatever gigs we wanted, for the next five years!

"But the biggest argument for signing was that we were in a rut, and we had this audience that expected us to do a certain thing; we played to the same people all the time, and we weren't really going anywhere fast. We knew that signing with EMI would upset a lot of people, but we thought that would be really interesting as well, so we got this fantastic legal document drawn up that covered us for virtually everything and signed. It only lasted a couple of years, but it went fine and I've got no regrets whatsoever; we got what we wanted out of the deal… we released some great records, we travelled all over the world, appeared on all these TV programmes, and we made loads of money, a lot of which we gave away or ploughed into worthwhile causes."

During the year-long whirlwind that followed the stratospheric sales of 'Tubthumping', Chumbawamba found themselves performing at the 1998 Brit Awards, and an opportunity arose for yet more well-timed mischief. Labour MP John Prescott was in attendance, and after changing the words to 'Tubthumping' to include, 'New Labour sold out the dockers, just like they'll sell out the rest of us', Danbert doused the lumpy minister with a bucket of ice water, declaring loudly, 'This is for the Liverpool dockers!'

"Well, we had to do it, didn't we?" laughs Boff. "You get an opportunity like that, you have to do something with it."

In 2000, the band released the 'What You See Is What You Get' album through EMI, before starting up their own label, Mutt, in 2002. They continue to record and perform regularly, their latest album being 2006's 'A Singsong And A Scrap', with songs such as 'Walking Into Battle With The Lord' and 'The Land Of Do What You're Told' ably demonstrating that they've lost none of their political invective. Indeed, in recent years, they have contributed tracks to various releases to benefit the women of Afghanistan, the Trafalgar Square Defence Campaign, the Medical Foundation For Victims Of Torture and the Prison Literature Project. So, as you can see, Chumbawamba may not sound like an anarcho-punk band anymore – in fact, may not have ever sounded like an anarcho-punk band – but, just as words are no substitute for actions, neither is sound, and it would appear that the Chumbas have always put their money where their mouths purported to be.

"Yes, we are still avowedly anarchist. We weren't ever in a band to rock and to roll, and make it big some day. We were in a band to change the way people thought about things. That didn't mean it couldn't be fun – it was, and still is – but we really were different to a lot of the bands we 'graduated' with; we wanted fun and we wanted revolution, seriously. And we all believed it, every last word."

SELECT DISCOGRAPHY

7"s:
'Revolution' (Agit-Prop, 1985)
'We Are The World?' (Agit-Prop, 1986) – split with A State Of Mind
'Smash Clause 28' (Agit-Prop, 1988)
'Ugh! Your Ugly Houses!' (One Little Indian, 1995)
'Tubthumping' (EMI, 1997)

12"s:
'I Never Gave Up' (Agit-Prop, 1992)
'Behave' (Agit-Prop, 1992)
'Enough Is Enough' (One Little Indian, 1992) – split with Credit To The Nation
'Timebomb' (One Little Indian, 1993)
'Homophobia' (One Little Indian, 1994)

LPs:
'Pictures Of Starving Children Sell Records' (Agit-Prop, 1986)
'Never Mind The Ballots' (Agit-Prop, 1987)
'English Rebel Songs' (Agit-Prop, 1988)
'Slap' (Agit-Prop, 1990)
'Shhh' (Agit-Prop, 1992)
'Anarchy' (One Little Indian, 1994)
'Showbusiness' (One Little Indian, 1995)
'Swingin' With Raymond' (One Little Indian, 1995)
'Tubthumper' (EMI, 1997)
'WYSIWYG' (EMI, 2000)
'Readymades' (Mutt, 2002)
'A Singsong And A Scrap' (Mutt, 2006)

At A Glance:
EMI's 1999 'Uneasy Listening' compiles 23 tracks from the whole of the band's history, but those wanting to hear the band at their best would be well advised to pick up Agit-Prop's 'First Two' CD (1992), which features the first two brilliant albums for a budget price. Similarly, the far less convincing albums, 'Shhh!' and 'Slap!' were packaged together onto one CD, 'Shhhlap!', by Mutt in 2003.

ICON A.D. from Leeds were only together but a couple of years, yet in that short time released two very credible singles and recorded a well-received John Peel session. They were widely regarded as an anarcho-punk band, mainly because of their deal with Radical Change, the label ran by members of The Disrupters, but when they formed in 1979, as simply Icon, their primary influence was right on their doorstep and anything but 'anarcho'.

Icon AD's Craig Sharp-Weir live in Leeds, March 1984, picture by Paul May.

"I was weaned on the [anthemic street punk band] Abrasive Wheels," admits guitarist, Craig Sharp-Weir. "Hearing them was what made me first pick a guitar up, although I also liked The Clash, The Jam and the Pistols. I was into The Ruts and Penetration a lot too... those bands were good writers, they weren't three chord wonders.

"Our drummer [Mark Holmes] was more into the Crass stuff, but he was into some of the weirder, more tribal, stuff as well, like Siouxsie And The Banshees and Killing Joke. The bassist [Phil Smith] was into The Ramones, AC/DC and Motörhead, a bit of a mismatch. Our first singer was Dicky Walton; he was the John Lydon of the band, and liked anything punk!

"When the Abrasive Wheels started, we thought, 'We can do this!' My brother liked 'cock rock', so I grew up with a lot of that; I always liked Slade, The Sweet, and early Bowie and stuff as well, anything with a bit of balls. Without sounding conceited though, I always thought we were better than the Wheels; our songs were more thought-out, but they fit the bill, they had the right image... they were the street kids who just bought a van and went off and did it. And they did what they did well... Dave [Ryan, the Wheels guitarist] had a knack for catchy tunes you just couldn't help singing."

The four original band members were all friends in the sixth form of Templemoor High School; Craig and Mark had previously played together as The Jackets and Terminal Boredom, but neither band actually did anything of any significance. Icon though cut their teeth playing the local Methodist church, lovingly referred to as 'The Mef', where the Wheels were hailed as local heroes, and soon began landing bigger support slots at The F-Club (i.e. The Fan Club, below Brannigans in Leeds town centre) and Tiffany's.

Mark sent a home recording of the band to Crass, hoping to be considered for inclusion on their first 'Bullshit Detector' compilation, and, before they knew it, their ludicrously catchy track 'Cancer' was immortalised on plastic.

"I never really liked Crass musically though," laughs Craig. "It was all that military drumming

Icon AD, at the Leeds Bierkeller, picture by Trunt.

and those shitty guitar sounds that put me off, but I listened to them through Mark, and I knew that it was more about their attitude than their music. I always saw us as just a punk band, to be honest, but I'm sure Mark regarded us as anarcho punks. We did get involved in the CND thing quite a lot later on... we played on picket lines, from the back of a van with a generator, which I'm glad we did. It wasn't to be fashionable either; it was something we really did believe in... I can remember shitting myself when we went to war in the Falklands. I'm no coward, but I would've been taking my white feather, for sure!

"Anyway, 'Cancer' wasn't a bad recording seeing as it was done through a little condenser mike on a 'press play' recorder in a bedroom! Crass were adamant that if it was a proper recording in a real studio, they didn't want it... which is quite ironic now, seeing as a lot of professional albums are recorded in bedrooms, because of how technology has come on.

"So, Mark just sent it off, and when it came back, we were like, 'Wow!' It sounded the same as on your cassette player really, but because it was vinyl, and you could see the needle going round, it was ace. We never had any ideas of grandeur though... in fact, the whole idea of us being called Icon was that we didn't want to be icons, it was a tongue-in-cheek reference."

Icon fizzled out in early 1981 though, when the band members left school and were compelled to search for gainful employment.

"Dicky got a bit unreliable as well, dabbling with a few drugs 'n' that. There was a few times he didn't turn up and I had to sing, and we'd dedicate the song 'Overdose' to him! But I loved playing, and so did Mark, so we kept writing, sometimes rehearsing with just the two of us... but it sounded shite, like the fucking White Stripes or something! I hate them, yet they're so popular – she can't drum to save her life... it's total shit, like The Carpenters on acid.

"Anyway, when Icon finished, I kept writing, and for my birthday, my wife at the time paid for some studio time for me. It wasn't even going to be a band! I said to Mark, who was my brother-in-law by then, 'Just come in the studio with us and we'll have a few rehearsals prior…' We went in and laid it all down live, eight hours in an eight-track studio [Woodlands, Normanton], then I dubbed the bass, did a bit more double-tracking of the guitar parts… and my wife of the time [Caroline Sharp, nee Smith], and her sister [Bev], sang. And even with the modern technology available today, I still reckon that's a good recording. It was never meant to be a band though; we just thought it would be a laugh…

"And Mark sent it off, 'cos all these people were saying they thought it was pretty good. He sent it to Radical Change, who were part of Backs Records in Norwich, and they really wanted to release it. It hadn't cost us anything… well, £150 of my birthday money… so I said, 'Why not?' We got ripped off, of course; I don't know how many copies we sold, but we got in the Indie charts, and the fact that they even wanted to do a second single with us suggests that they knew they had some sales there!"

The 'Don't Feed Us Shit' EP (its title lifted from the chorus of the 'Bullshit Detector' track, 'Cancer') came out on Radical Change, with the band now using the name Icon A.D., and made the Indie Top Twenty upon its release during September 1982, remaining to this day a near-perfect punk record. Still eminently listenable thanks to their raw melodies and obviously unbridled energy, it's hard to find fault with such well-rounded songs as 'Face The Facts' and 'Fight For Peace'.

Recruiting new bassist Roger Turnbull from F-3 ("Another Leeds band, very underground and very much like the Banshees or The Fall… not really my cup of tea, but he was reliable, liked what we were doing, and was a good player…"), the new-look band started playing out with great success, although Caroline quickly decided she wasn't cut out as a punk rock singer and stepped down, leaving Bev to front the band on her own.

"That was a shame, 'cos the two girls always looked good onstage together, with their spiky hair, skin-tight trousers, studded belts and all that… we had the 'two Beki Bondages at the same time' thing going on, ha ha! There'd be shouts of 'Get your tits out' or whatever, but so what? It didn't really faze us.

"The best thing we ever did though was going down to Maida Vale Studios and recording the John Peel session [in October '82]. That was after the first single, and it was just so great to hear it on the radio. We had a 'Beverley' drum kit, smashed-up cymbals… I had a Les Paul copy that kept going out of tune every other verse… we were in a state-of-the-art studio, yet it was a crap recording because of the equipment we had. But despite all that, the recording really captured the energy of these seventeen- and eighteen-year-old kids playing their hearts out, going, 'Fuckin' have some of that!' You know? And if you set out to try and record that, you can't, can you? It just happens, and you're lucky if you capture it. So, I'm quite proud of that now."

The second Icon A.D. single, 'Let The Vultures Fly', came out in June '83, again for Radical Change, and this one spent seven weeks in the Indie charts, peaking at No. 7, even though it was a less convincing offering than its predecessor.

"The title was our way of saying, 'No! Stand up for what you believe in!' It was a plea for peace, an anti-war message, against all the senseless killing which we regarded as little more than 'legal murder' authorized by selfish world leaders.

"Backs actually paid for us to record that second single, and it was done in Ric Rac Studios in Leeds, which was a more high-tech studio, and to be honest, I don't think it sounded as good. It was too polished, all this reverb on everything… but it happens to bands, doesn't it? Like The Clash – the first album's rough, but with great material; the second album's much better, then the third album has excellent content but sounds over-produced! There was a fuck-up in the pressing too; a song called 'Medals For The Dead', this reggae song, got left off by accident."

It was also to be the band's final release, as a proposed third single never materialised, following disagreements over commercial direction between the band and their label.

"We actually wrote a song for the next single, called 'Backs To The Wall', which was a subtle, pointed comment towards Backs Records, but we think they saw through it and decided to pull the plug on us. It was our way of telling them that we knew they'd fucked us over, and we thought it would be funny if they released it, thinking they were doing us a favour, and then we could tell them to fuck off! 'Cos we weren't bothered about making money or getting big, we really weren't.

"And it just fizzled out really; I got bored of it all, and, if I'm honest, family life played a big part. I had two babies in the house, and you know what it's like, getting in from a gig at 2 o'clock in the morning, trying to get your 4 x 12 [speaker cabinet] up the stairs and waking everyone up...! It can be a strain. I enjoyed it, but I wasn't too bothered when it finished – like I said, it was only meant to be a bit of fun, and it just so happened that someone was interested in it."

After dabbling further in music with White Feather, Blood Brothers, and – much later in the Nineties – Snitch, Craig now manages a busy bar in the centre of Derby, content to let his son, Danny, carry the punk baton for the Sharp-Weir family with his exciting young band, Guns On The Roof... who are now managed by none other than Dave Ryan of the Abrasive Wheels. Well, who else?

"They've come on in leaps and bounds since Dave got behind them," beams Craig. "He doesn't need the money or anything; he's such a genuine guy... he's had a bit of the high life, touring America and stuff, and now just wants to hopefully see my lad's band make it, by helping them avoid the many pitfalls and 'snake in the grass' characters that are so rife in the music industry; he would feel good if he can help them up that ladder...

"I'm so proud of my lads, 'cos they could've gone down the fuckin' 'Westlife/Boyzone route', you know what I mean? That always worried me! My eldest lad plays drums as well, y'see, but Danny especially loves punk! And it's not like I've made him that way, 'cos I've not been living with him since he was eight, although I see him at least every weekend. I even stood in for the Guns On The Roof bassist at a few gigs, when he was too ill to play, and I was dead flattered to be asked, 'cos it meant my son had some respect and faith in me, and I really enjoyed it. Punk may have destroyed itself, but I still feel the same as I ever did deep down."

SELECT DISCOGRAPHY

7"s:
'Don't Feed Us Shit' (Radical Change, 1982)
'Let The Vultures Fly' (Radical Change, 1983)

At A Glance:
In 2006, Overground released the highly-recommended Icon A.D. retrospective, 'Lest We Forget'; it features not only the two singles, but the also preceding demos and the fantastic (until now unreleased) third single, and comes complete with extensive liner notes, rare pictures and original artwork. Craig's son's band are also well worth checking out: www.gunsontheroof.com

One of the most ferocious of all the anarcho bands, Bradford's **ANTI-SYSTEM** had a live power the equal of Conflict and Antisect, although it has to be said they never quite reproduced that heaving intensity in their recorded works. Despite its sonic limitations however, their sole album, 'No Laughing Matter', remains a truly raging and overlooked classic of the anarcho-punk canon.

"Apart from hearing music on the radio, my initial introduction to sounds that existed outside of the mainstream came via an elder brother," begins original Anti-System vocalist, Simon 'Nogsy' Nolan, eloquently describing his introduction to punk and subsequent conversion to the Crass train of thought. "I liked all the usual suspects: the Sex

Nogsy of Anti-System.

Pistols, Clash, and Damned… even daft stuff such as The Jerks and 'Get Your Woofing Dog Off Me' got a look-in at our house. However, the growing preponderance of people adorning their clothes with the enigmatic Crass symbol began to catch my eye sometime around 1979.

"I was in the queue for The Clash at St. George's Hall, on their 1980 'Armageddon Times' tour, eavesdropping on some lads ahead off us who were discussing the likelihood of Crass being the support band that night. Not being au-fait with Crass's politics, let alone their derisive view of The Clash, I enquired of the lads if they really thought Crass might be playing. Imagine my chagrin at the guffaws that ensued; I resolved to buy some Crass records immediately.

"The next day, in the HMV shop on Petergate, Bradford, the assistant Danny narrowed his eyes and looked me up and down, noting my school uniform and less-than-advanced years (I was fourteen); I walked out of the shop that day not quite knowing what the hell I had bought. To begin with, the record was sold to me from under the counter; it was housed in a plain white paper bag and I was told that no receipt could be issued for a record such as this. To cap it all off, Danny had told me that should the police stop me and ask where I got it from, under no circumstances was I to lead them back to HMV! What I had in fact bought was a copy of 'Feeding Of The 5000'…

"The bus ride home I don't remember; so unforgettable was Gee's artwork, it completely absorbed me… just looking at the cover aroused in me a sense of dread, shock, horror, outrage and awe. And on first hearing 'Feeding…' I was staggered at how well the music – and the sentiments expressed therein – was complimented by the sleeve and lyric sheet; I loved the whole package instantly. My affair intensified when I first copped hold of 'Reality Asylum'; the note explaining its omission from 'Feeding…' really pricked my curiosity. Again it came from under the counter, and again I was knocked sideways. The fold-out sleeve was revelatory, the inner collage mesmerizing; it had the profoundest of effects on me.

Anti-System drummer Phil Dean.

"Raised as a Catholic, my disgruntlement with religion had a much earlier root. As seven- and eight-year-olds, Mick Teale, Paul Flaherty and I formed a rebellious coterie, and with infantile terminology we shared our misgivings about the so-called benevolence of God. I know Mick had difficulty reconciling the notion of an omnipresent and omniscient kindly God with the real world in which his mother had suddenly been taken away from him. I'm not so sure about my own reasons for being suspicious of the whole church business; maybe it was merely the cruddy hand-me-downs that I was forced to wear to school? Whatever, hearing 'Reality Asylum' scared me; I was stunned by the measured delivery of its unrestrained attack. Offering no comfort zone of a familiar song structure, the potency of its ability to move those indoctrinated within a Christ cult is still overwhelming. I once witnessed an otherwise rational person wrenching 'Reality Asylum' from a turntable and snapping it in half, his last vestiges of God-fear impelling him on his crusade, the flash fire of realisation. The remainder of my school days would be marked by frequent run-ins with deceitful authority figures..."

Forming "an imaginary band with no instruments" called Crust Crucible Crucifix And Varik, with Mark Keane and Mark Teale [AKA 'Varik' himself!] and being banned from playing even secret gigs at their school because of song titles such as 'Nuns On Toast', Nogsy soon found himself incurring the wrath of the teaching establishment.

"On one particular occasion I was hauled up in front of the deputy headmaster because he disapproved of an article I had written in my fanzine, Creation, about bully-boy teachers," recalls Nogsy. "To make me see the error of my ways, the aptly-named Mr Wilde offered me the rough end of his leather strap across my arse. The fool, could he not see the irony of his actions and the manner in which he unwittingly confirmed the very essence of the article he so cack-handedly attempted to dismiss as 'schoolboy twaddle'? Incidents such as this go some way to explaining how I so readily lent my hand to any project that went by the name of Anti-System!"

Anti-System actually materialised from the remnants of another Bradford band, The Insane (not to be confused with the Wigan-based band featured in 'Burning Britain'). Featuring 'Paki' Kenny Thomas on vocals, Nev Cartledge on guitar, Phil Smith on bass, and Phil Dean on drums, they had previously been known as Complete Disorder, and soon Kenny, Nev and Phil were replaced by – respectively – Dave Damned, Dominic Watts and George Clarke, a line-up reshuffle that also coincided with the name change to Anti-System.

"Kenny was, and remains, a legend in Bradford folklore," laughs Nogsy. "The epitome of the 'peacock punk', not a spike out of place and every stud applied with millimetre perfection, he was a total sweetheart. The Insane were a good band; I would watch them rehearse at Low Moor Working Men's Club or sometimes at Shearbridge Mill. I can recall a seminal gig at The Mayflower Club on Manningham Lane featuring the Insane, [Bradford's own] Southern Death Cult [originally known as Violation] and Abrasive Wheels. The event was to be filmed for some local T.V. show, but apparently the film crew were freaked out by the rowdy behaviour of the Abrasive Wheels fans and scooted early. Tensions aside, it was a great gig that.

"At this time I was drumming and singing in a band myself, a loose collective of Wibsey boys, including Shaun 'Bod' Kelly [who would later play one show with Anti-System, when George failed to turn up]; without the slightest sense of irony we would perform the craziest mix of songs. We had no static name but a typical set would include 'Green Onions', 'Tomorrow's Girl', 'I Saw Her Standing There' and 'Tube Disasters'… you get the picture! Independently, Mick and the two Marks, along with Eddie Noonan on drums, had formed Subvert; I enjoyed that band too, but they never did any gigs."

Anti-System played just one gig fronted by Dave Damned, at the Palm Cove in Bradford, before the erstwhile singer's infrequent attendance at practise precipitated Nogsy taking over as vocalist in 1982.

"There was a commitment problem with Dave; an otherwise splendid bloke, he would go walkabout during rehearsals or simply fail to show up. It was on just such an occasion that I called into Shearbridge Mill to check them out… it required very little pressing to get me onto the microphone, and we ran through their set. I particularly remember doing 'Why Should It Happen?' and 'Government Lies', but I also recited 'Service', a poem I'd had kicking around for a while. I left Shearbridge that night feeling utterly exhilarated by the experience. A few weeks later Phil, Dom and George paid me a visit at the Windmill in Wibsey; they wanted me to join the band and told me that a recording session had been booked for the following week!"

Entering Lion Studios in Leeds, Anti-System tracked their debut demo, and, with opinion divided over the results ("Whilst it clearly showcased Phil's incredible drumming and the lo-fi production helped to accentuate Dom's wonderfully idiosyncratic guitar style, I felt that my vocals sounded weedy and ineffectual…"), they sent the tape to several labels hoping for a deal, eventually choosing Marcus Featherby's Pax Records over Norwich-based Backs…

"I have seen a lot of things written about Marcus and how untrustworthy he was meant to be, but I never saw him in that way at all. The body of work that he was able to help make available is testament enough to the fact that he 'meant it, maan!' Those people that attended the memorable gigs at The Marples in Sheffield know full well his good intentions. Also, it should be remarked that much of Marcus's output clearly had no mass commercial potential anyway, and he knew it. From our first meeting onwards, I always considered him to be straight-up. Sure he had pretensions – such as tossing over a dictionary and offering to give the correct definition of any word put to him – but from day one he told us that if we wanted to make sacks full of money we had come to the wrong place. It may be my naiveté, but I think the 'Marcus is a rip-off' stories emanate from those factions that had no interest other than lining their own pockets by flogging tired and sagging product. The fact is that none of us cared a hoot for the money; our main concern was getting the material out there in as palatable a manner as was possible. Personally, I was also a bit thrilled at the prospect of being on a record with The Xpozez. I loved that band!"

Said record being Anti-System's vinyl debut, two tracks ('Break Out' and 'Man's World') featured on Pax's 1982 'Punk's Dead? Nah, Mate, The Smell Is Jus Summink In Yer Underpants' compilation 12". Meanwhile the band made their first live appearance in Bradford, where they soon began amassing a sizeable following.

"It was at the Cathedral Centre, which was a crucial muster point for much of the emergent second wave of punk in Bradford," reckons Nogsy. "It was ostensibly a government-funded scheme that offered Youth Opportunity Programmes in various skills. We now know that these schemes were little more than a method for the useless Tories to cook the books regarding unemployment figures. However, at the time there was a waiting list of young punks trying to get onto the screen-printing course. It was brilliant; we may have only been paid £25 a week but were able to print T-shirts, fanzines and gig posters free of charge. Matt 'Perfect Pete' Webster, drummer with the delightful Convulsions, particularly excelled as a publicist and was adopted as court promoter, churning out superb posters for bands of all descriptions.

"The DIY ethic was particularly strong in Bradford at the time. Andy Ashton and Andy Farrow of Apathy Productions are due credit for their efforts; they each had an excellent band – Chronic and Living Dead – and put out their own flexi featuring 'Procession' and 'No Time', which, for me, still ranks as one Bradford's greatest releases."

Anti-System bassist Mickey Knowles.

Unhappy with the weak mix of their first demo, the band decided to record their first single at Rochdale's Cargo Studios, and whilst the resulting 'Defence Of The Realm' 7" was a tense, aggressive offering, drenched in howling feedback, the trebly tones leeched much of the band's live power from the production.

"We only chose that studio because Discharge, who were always my favourite band, had used it," explains Phil. "We wanted to get a good, heavy sound, just like they had, but it turned out terrible. My hi-hats were too loud, and they made me track them again separately, with all the drums covered up, just playing the hi-hats! It was really hard work, sat there recording the hats and just bashing away in mid air for the rest of the kit. We recorded it through the night as well, 'cos it was cheaper, so we were all knackered…"

During the recording of the single, George left and was replaced by Mickey Knowles, although both bassists actually feature on the record itself, George playing on '1000 Rifles' and 'Bomb Threat', Mickey on the other three tracks (including the record's vehement highlight, 'Animal Welfare'). It was a turbulent time for the band, because Nogsy left soon after ("There was no big falling out; there just came a point when I no longer felt that I could contribute to Anti-System…"), eventually turning up in Zed who released the 'A Dollar And A Dream' 12" on Wild Willy Beckett's Q.T.A. label and toured Europe several times with the likes of The Levellers and Radical Dance Faction. He was replaced – at first, anyway – by Liam Sheeran from Bradford-based noise-mongers Raw. Then Dom departed and was superseded on guitar by old friend Varik, a personnel change that helped usher in a much heavier, gnarlier direction for the band.

"I'd been to see Discharge at the Palm Cove in Bradford, and Antisect were supporting them," says Phil, of where he's always regarded Anti-System's single biggest inspiration as lying. "And even though I loved Discharge, Antisect blew them offstage; I was very impressed with them. They stopped over at my house after the gig, and we sat up all night, smoking and talking; I just liked what they were about, and I knew that the next band I was in, I wanted them to be like Antisect… seeing them that night was definitely a turning point for me.

"I lived here [in Low Moor] with my mum, and she freaked out when I bought all these people back to sleep! There were fifteen or twenty people stretched out on the living room floor. In the morning, she was like, 'Have you seen the state of the soap?' And it was covered in black hair where they'd all been spiking their hair up."

Although two songs recorded by the old line-up – 'Why Should It Happen?' and 'Schoolboy' (the William Blake poem set to high-speed punk rock!) – appeared on the 'Bollox To The Gonads, Here's The Testicles' compilation in late '83, by the end of that year, the Anti-System transformation was complete, with Mark Keane replacing Mickey on bass, and Liam Sheeran being replaced on the microphone by not one but two singers, Mick Teale and Kev Haste ("It was great having two singers live, but even that was a bit of a rip on Antisect," confesses Phil).

This expanded version of Anti-System recorded the brutally heavy 'No Laughing Matter' album during October 1984 at Woodlands Studio in Castleford, with Neil Ferguson at the desk, for their own, newly-formed label, Reconciliation.

"We went to Woodlands because we loved the sound of the Instigators records they'd done," explains Phil. "But again, it didn't really turn out as planned. The thing is, although the album's heavy, you can't hear the drums at all! We got carried away with the guitars.

"My ex-wife, Paula, who used to do all the artwork, talks on one of the songs ['No Laughing Matter'], this acoustic track we did to break the album up a bit… but to be totally honest again, it was another nod towards Antisect, who had done that 'Tubular Bells' bit on their album; we were really impressed with that and wanted to try something similar…

"And it was actually Neil Ferguson who played keyboards on that track; he used to be in Black Lace, the band that did 'Agadoo'!" chuckles Phil, incredulously. "They were just finishing recording when we were arriving to start our album, and he said, 'I'll play a bit of keyboards, if you want?' And we thought, 'Why not?' "

Before the album was released in early March 1985, Reconciliation issued two of its tracks – 'So Long As' and 'Strange Love' – as one side of a split EP with Morbid Humour, a short-lived Bradford-based band with a uniquely morose style and close connections to Anti-System.

"I even played a few gigs with them, when they reformed briefly after Anti-System split," says Phil, of the enigmatic Morbid Humour, "But the band that appeared on the split single was Mark 'Mugsy' Muller on vocals, Nogsy, Phil Hobson, Varik, Darren MacKenzie on bass [who was later imprisoned for stabbing his ex-girlfriend to death], and a lad called Kevin Granger on drums. They

Morbid Humour: Nogsy and Mugsy.

didn't do many gigs, and only the one recording... I think they recorded four songs, and the split EP was lifted from that... they just fizzled out really, before Anti-System finished, and then when we split up, they reformed and did a few gigs, which is when I joined them on drums."

A two-week UK tour was undertaken, supporting the Icons Of Filth, before Kev Haste left, leaving Mick to handle vocals on his own, and Phil Hobson joined on second guitar. Anti-System then recorded their parting shot, the 'A Look At Life' 12", at Bradford's Flexible Response Studios (where they also rehearsed, alongside the likes of New Model Army) with Mike Banks. A thoroughly enjoyable, but altogether more polished, metallic affair, it saw them parting ways with some of the hardcore punks who had followed them since their inception.

"We were hoping to get a heavier sound when we played live," reckons Phil, of the thrashier edge the additional guitarist gave the band. "And we were listening to a lot more of that sort of stuff... you know: Onslaught, Sacrilege, English Dogs... there wasn't any particular reason, we just gradually went in that direction. I remember Varik used to bring all these riffs to practise and say, 'Just listen to this...!'

"Punk was just a fashion thing most of the time, wasn't it?" he adds, on the thorny topic of 'Leather, Bristles, Studs And Ignorance', the track that so offended the local punk community. "We'd play these festivals in Bradford, and all the punks would get tanked up and start beating hell out of each other, and that wasn't what it was all about! And we got such a lot of flak for that song… mainly from Bradford punks who thought that it was a dig at them… and it was! We still had a lot of people coming to our gigs, but a lot of them were slagging us off too, shouting abuse; there were a lot of people talking shit behind our backs and, as a result, we slagged Bradford off in a few interviews we did with fanzines, because it was turning into such a bad scene. Everywhere else we went, we were thinking, 'Why isn't it like this in Bradford?' We were just fed up with people's attitudes around here…"

With disillusionment and apathy gnawing away at several members, the writing was on the wall for Anti-System almost before the 12" hit the shops, and they split soon after its release during Autumn 1986.

"All the usual reasons," contemplates Phil on their demise. "Everyone went their separate ways; there were musical differences… differences over everything really. I just had enough in the end, couldn't be bothered with all the bickering. And we lost a lot of time when Mick and Mark Keane went to prison as well; they got done for smashing up these butcher shops, and then they broke into an abattoir in the middle of Bradford and let all the cattle out, and they were all running around the streets. So we were doing nothing while we waited around for them to be let out, and then we seemed unable to pick our momentum up again. We were always lazy-minded at the best of times, to be honest, let alone when we couldn't do anything.

"I think the last gig was at [Bradford] Rios, which wasn't great. Although the worse gig we ever did was down in Dover; it was terrible. A lot of people came across from France and Belgium to see us, but it was horrible… the mike on the snare drum kept falling off and bouncing about on the drums… then they started taking the lights down halfway through our set… then there was a big fight with a load of skinheads – it just went from bad to worse. Then we got paid, and Mick and Varik lost the money between them, and were arguing over that, and a load of lads who came with us got arrested 'cos they were bouncing up and down on this war monument of a plane, and one of the wings snapped off it! So they all had to go back to Dover to go to court! It was just a nightmare…

"But I've got really fond memories of the whole time we were together otherwise, though we'll never ever reform. It's like now, when you go and see Discharge – it's just not the same, is it? To do it again now, out of context… well, it's almost like seeing fifty-year-old teddy boys strutting about all over again… it's laughable really. We've even had letters from America, asking us to reform and go over to play some gigs, but I'm just not interested. We were always a good, powerful live band, but it wouldn't work now, and I wouldn't want to cheapen that memory of the band."

SELECT DISCOGRAPHY

7"s:
'Defence Of The Realm' (Pax, 1983)
'Strange Love' (Reconciliation, 1985) – split with Morbid Humour

12"s:
'A Look At Life' (Reconciliation, 1986)

LPs:
'No Laughing Matter' (Reconciliation, 1985)

At A Glance:
Constructive Rebellion's CD version of 'No Laughing Matter' includes the singles and 12", plus all the lyrics and artwork: a storming listen from start to finish.

Nick Toczek, picture by Claire McNamee.

Bradford-born **NICK TOCZEK** (his surname pronounced to rhyme with 'rock check') is a truly renaissance anarchist! Still an accomplished poet and musician, not to mention prolific investigative journalist, these days he is also a successful children's author and spoken word artist, having made over 40,000 public appearances during the last thirty-seven years, visiting en route over 3000 schools around the UK.

From the perspective of this book though, this is also the same Nick Toczek that booked hundreds of alternative shows in pubs and clubs in Leeds, Bradford and Keighley during the Eighties, toured the USA with the Instigators, and released the likes of the 'Britanarchist' demo and 'InTOCZEKated' album through the highly respected (in anarcho circles... no pun intended) Bluurg label.

"What changed everything for me was reading an early '76 interview with Joe Strummer," reveals Nick, who was living in Moseley, Birmingham, during the mid-Seventies and playing with folk/blues band, Stereo Graffiti. "Was it in Sounds or NME? Who cares? What mattered was that it was just so stunningly hard and so utterly uncompromisingly political. It seemed like the first time in years that I'd discovered a rock performer who wanted to wage political war... back in the Sixties Dylan had, even The Stones occasionally did, The Doors and Country Joe in a slightly fake way, The Animals and Janis Joplin via old blues lyrics, The Kinks in an oh-so-genteel English fashion, and – half-heartedly but perhaps more convincingly – The Who and Hendrix. More typical of the whole scene, though, was the utter shit of those lovable mop-tops, The Beatles. Just listen to Paul McCartney sing, 'Don't want no Pakistanis taking other people's jobs... get back... get back... get back to where you first came from,' on 'No Pakistanis' [an early demo version of 'Get Back'] for a measure of their suss. And John going, 'So this is Christmas... another year over, a new one just begun...' No, you drug-addled fuckwit... if it's only Christmas, the year's not over for another week. All hail Mark Chapman!

"What made punk great from the outset wasn't that it was great in itself – much of it wasn't – but it had passion and gave anyone and everyone a chance to get up there. And, in doing so, showed just how complacently crap the whole rock-biz had become.

"During 1977, I saw a string of amazing gigs in Birmingham including The Ramones supported by Talking Heads (at Barbarellas, 24th May), Blondie supporting Television (Odeon, 27th May), The Slits supported by The Prefects (The Bulls Head, 14th September) and The Adverts supported by Steel Pulse (Barbarellas, 20th September)... they were amazing times.

"There was another factor that contributed to my decline into the mad-eyed anarchist that I last saw this morning when I gazed in disbelieving horror at the bald old bastard in my shaving mirror. In 1974, I co-founded Mosley Festival, one of Britain's first community festivals, and for the next few years I ran or co-ran this annual event. The council's sole contribution to the first festival was to take down all our street decorations the day after we put them up. The police tried to declare the entire programme illegal and strove to stop every event... even the concert for pensioners, and the kids' events! I remember that at the early meetings of the first festival committee I was mocked for voicing my support for some of the Liberal Party's policies. By the end of that festival, I was firmly left of mainstream Labour and, very soon after that, totally disillusioned with so-called democratic politics. Within a year, I was resolved to have no-one represent me politically; I'd do it for myself, I'd vote for no-one. And if I wanted something changing, I'd fight for it on my own behalf. It was other people who then labelled me 'anarchist', but I was happy to wear that label and to defend it. Still am. Still do."

Starting his punk career with the Ulterior Motives, who released the 'Y'Gotta Shout' (b/w 'Another Lover') 7" on their own label, Motive Music, in 1979, Nick went on to create an eclectic body of music with many weird and wonderful artists during the Eighties.

"We had a couple of useful breaks," says Nick of the Motives. "The first was having a free rehearsal space that was also a four-track recording studio. It belonged to Yorkshire Arts Association and was run by a guy who was really generous and helpful to us. We could store our gear there too, so recording and rehearsing was easy – much more so than for most bands. The other was that I was also running the local music fanzine, The Wool City Rocker... a monthly which I founded, edited and published, and which John Peel described as one of his favourite zines. Through that mag, I'd a network of local contacts that made gigging so much easier.

"We also had tracks on a couple of samplers, but I actually prefer the stuff I recorded later, working with other bands. I did some cool stuff with Spectre, a local reggae band, and with The Burial, a skinhead ska band from Scarborough – some of that can be found on a 4-track 12" E.P. called 'More To Hate... Than Meets the Eye'. It was supposed to come out on Mortarhate, but they pissed us about, so Red Rhino Records in York put up the money for me to release it myself. I called the label 'Martyrhate' as a joke against Colin... no bitterness though; he was okay, just far too busy at that time to do all the things he promised to do. And he did put another track of mine ['Sheer Funk'], with music by US punks Toxic Reasons, plus Derek [Greening], the guitarist from Peter And The Test Tube Babies, on the Mortarhate sampler, 'We Won't Be Your Fucking Poor'.

"All in all, I did some thirty or forty tracks on sampler albums during the 1980s, both as a vocalist and as a solo poet. One of the best was 'God Save Us From The USA' [Happy Mike Records, 1987], an album for the Nicaragua Solidarity Campaign which included tracks by Zounds, Heresy, Attila the Stockbroker, The Neurotics, Culture Shock, The Instigators, etc. I also had a track on one of the Oi albums, 'The Oi of Sex', on which I was the token anarchist among predominantly far-right-leaning skinhead bands. That was cool though; at least I wasn't preaching to the converted on that track."

Nick eventually hooked up with Bluurg for the aforementioned 'InTOCZEKated' album, which is basically an overview of his Eighties recording career, featuring a wide range of musicians. In more recent years he has even started to host a weekly radio show of the same name.

"I'd regularly booked The Subhumans, and they'd often stayed at my house. I got on well with them, and particularly with their frontman, Dick, who ran Bluurg. We kept in touch and, some time in 1986, I sent him a demo tape by a band I was helping. At that time I'd just finished work on a collection of songs I was going to release as a cassette LP on my own Acrimony (as in 'A Crime Money') cassette label. I included a copy of it with the demo I sent Dick. It was just meant as a present for him 'cos he'd previously released a couple of cassette albums of mine on Bluurg. Later that week, he wrote back to me saying that he didn't like the band's demo, but he did like my tape... and could he release it as an album? I was genuinely gob-smacked; I'd not even thought of a vinyl version of the album. It was just going to be a tape for a few friends and fans. In fact, I'd actually given up gigging with musicians, so by the time it came out, I was into other work. It was odd. I'd spent the past twenty years in various group and solo guises, dreaming of having an album out, and here it was at last, my very own album... and it no longer mattered that much. In a way, that was great. There was no stress, no worry about sales figures. I was just a slightly distanced and marginally interested observer: "Oh, look! An album... and it's got my name on it. Cool!"

"I never listen to it these days, and have no real opinion on it – it's just a piece of my history. Working as a writer and performer isn't a retrospective thing for me. I write every day and gig several times a week, the process of writing and gigging is what I enjoy. A finished gig or a finished piece of writing is just that... finished. And I'm already moving on to the next. It's like this: if I was a painter, the artistry on a painting would end with the final brush-stroke. Getting it into a gallery, pricing it and selling it is pure business and has nothing to do with the creativity. Publishing my work is much the same; by the time a magazine, book or disc comes out, I'm at work on other stuff. Writing and performing is mine; publishing is for anyone else but me.

"As for the radio show, it began years after the album, so I thought it was safe to recycle the crap pun on my name. It's appropriate as well, because I usually record the shows on a Saturday morning, so I'm often hung over. I've done the show every week on Bradford Community Broadcasting for years. It goes out from 6pm to 7pm, Sundays. I just take in a bunch of CDs and play whatever takes my fancy. I never pre-plan it, just line up tracks as I go along, reading poems, talking politics, cracking jokes, playing whatever music I like, interviewing occasional guests, etc. The hour just zooms along. You can listen to it on the web, if you're not in Bradford – just go to www.bcb.yorks.com and find it."

And with his future looking every bit as hectic and diverse as his past, Nick Toczek shows little sign of slowing down any time soon.

"I was, I still am, and I shall (always, I hope) be an anarchist," he closes defiantly. "As I've already said, I represent myself and so have no wish to vote for a representative. Politically, anarchists have much in common with the far left – though the Spanish Civil War demonstrated the limits to that commonality when the lefties rounded on the anarchists and slaughtered them. The key difference, as I see it, between left-wingers and anarchists is that lefties are revolutionary while we're revolutionist. That is, they believe in a post-revolutionary utopia, while we anarchists want continuous revolution – i.e. on-going opposition to whoever's in power. And that's the real value of anarchists. We're here to challenge those in power, those who set themselves above the rest of us. And so we should! Fuck 'em all! Fuck every politician… from Thatcher murdering crewmen on the Belgrano and lying about it, to Blair and Bush murdering tens of thousands of utterly innocent Iraqis… and lying about that. You tell me what's so sacrosanct about democracy when it leaves us led by war criminals, huh?

"As for Nick Toczek's mark on underground punk culture?" he smiles. "Well, I know it's a ridiculous idea, but wouldn't it be cool if a book came out that was all about underground punk culture and in it there was a long and boring interview with him that showed the entire world what a self-regarding and self-seeking little shit he really was. Of course, that'll never happen! So let's just forget he ever existed, huh? But if I was remembered… then what? Well, John Peel always referred to me as 'Nick-whose-name-I-can't-pronounce'. That'll do for me.

"There is another Nick Toczek; I found him on the internet. He used to work as an advertising manager with a local paper somewhere in America. I phoned him up and got his answering machine. It told me that 'Nick Toe-Check' was not at his desk… 'Toe Check'? He makes both of us sound like fucking chiropodists! If that's how it is, then I've a mind not to be remembered at all. Hope that's okay with you? Can I go now? The pub's open…"

SELECT DISCOGRAPHY

7"s:
'Y'Gotta Shout' (Motive Music, 1979) – with Ulterior Motives

12"s:
'More To Hate…' (Martyrhate, 1985) – with The Burial and Spectre

LPs:
'InTOCZEKated' (Bluurg, 1986)

At A Glance:
The 2004 CD, 'Selfish Men', for Not-A-Rioty Records features thirty of Nick's poems.

Kulturkampf's Paul at the Beeston YMCA.

Barnsley's **KULTURKAMPF** may well have only left behind one track – 'Please Help', released on Mortarhate's 1986 compilation, 'We Won't Be Your Fucking Poor' – as their original vinyl legacy, but their two spectacular demos were unsung classics of the time, equal in the poignant song-writing stakes to most of their peers who were signed to labels.

Formed in 1982 in the small mining village of Shafton, just outside Barnsley, Kulturkampf evolved from the remains of the Sub-Zeros, a punk band formed whilst all its members were still at school the previous year.

"As well as myself, there was Mark Wroe on guitar, Paul Kirkwood on bass, Carl Wroe on drums, Neil Hewitt on vocals, and Andy Burden on vocals," explains guitarist Andy Clough of those earliest days. "We must have formed around Christmas time, as that's when I got my guitar and practice amp (thanks, mam 'n' dad!), and I think we split after a couple of gigs at the local youth club; we were probably sick of hearing the same three songs over and over again…

"The first time I can remember listening to punk rock was some music I heard at my uncle's, which turned out to be the Sham 69 album, 'That's Life', and from then on that was it, I was hooked… next it was Stiff Little Fingers, particularly 'At The Edge'. The first punk band I saw play live was The Exploited in Sheffield; I only saw about the first five songs though, as we had to catch the last train home. Another thing that sticks in my mind was watching them on 'Top Of The Pops' through a pub doorway, 'cos we weren't old enough to go inside.

"A major turning point was seeing Crass at Hebden Bridge. I can remember we got there in the afternoon, and they were playing then and also again at night; we watched both sets, and couldn't believe how accessible they were at the time, so approachable, friendly and honest.

"But I suppose I was drawn to punk because I just wanted to be different, wanted to stand out… which wasn't hard coming from such a small village, and I think it was a means to express myself as I'm really shy and quiet by nature."

Sub-Zeros then split into two new bands; Mark and Carl Wroe formed Kulturkampf with Paul Kirkwood and new vocalist Karl Gallear, the unusual moniker being suggested by main songwriter Mark, who came across the word (which basically means the 'struggle for civilisation') whilst studying social history at school.

Meanwhile, Andy Clough and Andy Burden became Societies Vultures, eventually recruiting bassist/vocalist Paul Hutchinson and second guitarist Sean Allen. They recorded an eight-track demo, 'The Dove Has Flown', made the regional finals of a Battle Of The Bands contest, and promptly split in 1983; after playing a squat gig in Sheffield with the Instigators, Andy Burden moved to Sunderland and formed the Famous Imposters.

"The Battle Of The Bands thing at school was interesting," reckons Andy, "as you got to record a couple of tracks in a local studio; we then got through to the regional finals and had to play somewhere in Bradford, which was fun. I think we played two songs of our own, a cover of 'Tube Disaster', and finished with a rowdy rendition of 'Give Peace A Chance'! We had absolutely no chance of winning, but hopefully made an impression on someone?"

Meanwhile, Kulturkampf played a few local gigs – the first one at Barugh Green, a benefit for Barnsley CND supporting the Passion Killers – before Karl left ("After a misdemeanour…," Paul Kirkwood smiles knowingly) to become 'Obesa The Poet', leaving the band as a three-piece for a while… until, after recording their first demo, 'The Struggle', at Barnsley's Street Life Studios with Dennis McGinley during July 1983, and following the demise of Societies Vultures, Andy Clough joined as an additional guitarist to thicken up the sound and give Mark more room for manoeuvre with his vocals.

"We got all our gear for Christmas and birthdays," laughs Paul of Kulturkampf's humble origins. "We rehearsed firstly in Mark's mother's hairdressers, but then moved into an old betting shop owned by Mark's mum and aunt. We got asked to do a lot of gigs with Chumbawamba – some of the Chumbas had even been at our very first gig to show their support, and they were a big influence on us (alongside The Stranglers, Crass, Flux and The System) – and, of course, we arranged a lot ourselves.

"The best ones I think we ever did were the Haddon Hall in Leeds, with Alternative, the Ad Lib Club in Nottingham with Subhumans, and a squat gig we did in Barnsley with Chumbawamba. Those were the shows with the best sound and audiences, anyway.

"The worst show we did would have to have been at the Narrow Boat in Nottingham this one time; it was actually a great audience, but some idiot came along and started up a fight that ended with someone getting stabbed. Luckily the victim survived."

"That squat gig in Barnsley was especially memorable just because it was a squat gig in Barnsley," adds Andy wryly, "Probably the first and the last! Another gig to forget that never was, was supposed to have been an all-day festival thing at the Bierkeller in Leeds… we were all set to go, and were actually getting enough expenses to cover hiring a van for once, but then Carl, our drummer, broke his ankle I think, playing around on – would you believe it? – a kid's BMX bike! It must've been his right leg too, as I recall that we tried to work out some way of still playing, but it never came off, which was a shame."

In November 1983, Kulturkampf recorded their second, and final, demo, 'The Corpse Of Bureaucracy', at Lion Studios, Leeds, with Tony Bonner at the desk. Ten tracks of driving, tuneful, political punk, it included the painfully intense, Rudimentary Peni-esque 'Please Help', which was featured on the aforementioned 'We Won't Be Your Fucking Poor' compilation. Elsewhere, the more subdued strains of 'Let Them Live' and 'Pollution' recalled the glory days of early Mob, whilst 'Third World Holocaust' boasted a disconcertingly melodic chorus hook that perfectly demonstrated the band's keen musical ambition.

Picture taken in Dunfermline, 1984, at Alternative's house (Sned from Blood Robots on left, Andy Burden from Societies Vultures on right).

However, by the time the Mortarhate album was released in early 1986, Kulturkampf had already thrown in the towel, citing the inevitable disillusionment with their progress as the primary reason for their dissolution. They played their last show at the Nottingham Narrow Boat with Famous Imposters and the Scumdribblers.

"That was in 1984," reckons Paul, before admitting, "It was me and another member's fault really; we started missing rehearsals and focused more on our private lives, so Mark went off and joined a new band. In hindsight, I think if we had received more interest from record companies when it mattered, it would possibly have inspired more enthusiasm in us and gave us a reason to carry on. We did actually get some interest from Marcus Featherby, who ran Pax Records, so we gave him our eight-track reel-to-reel master tape… and he was never seen or heard from again!

"I do regret us splitting up when we did though, as we were all getting better as musicians, and the music we were writing towards the end was so much more together and really starting to sound fantastic.

"The passing of the years hasn't changed my ideals," he adds. "I'm still a vegetarian, still a pacifist, and I still perform benefit gigs with my new band, The Thin Kings [a heavy folk/rock outfit who have just self-released their debut album, 'The Middle Ages']."

"I thought we split in early '85 actually," counters Andy. "I don't honestly know why though; nothing dramatic happened, so I think it must have been the usual 'musical differences' thing. Looking back on what we did, I don't regret any of it; we had a great time and the whole experience was basically a good one.

"My ideals haven't changed that much either; I still believe you need to respect other people and that we all deserve to live as we wish without hurting others… although, over the years, you conform more and more, without realising it; getting a job and a house etc., but deep down it's still inside, else you wouldn't have been there in the first place, would you?

"Of course, I'd like the band to be remembered; I still love to see our name on the internet… and, you never know, at some point we may have even made someone stop and think for a moment – and that would be enough for me!"

At A Glance:

At the time of writing, there is no comprehensive Kulturkampf retrospective, although Scarborough-based label, Looney Tunes, is planning to release both demos as one vinyl album late in 2006.

If there was one anarcho-punk band that truly walked the tightrope between melody, power, integrity and intensity, with real aplomb, it would have to be **INSTIGATORS**. The Dewsbury band, whose 'Nobody Listens Anymore' LP for Bluurg remains one of the great unsung classics of the period, were formed in 1980 by drummer Paul 'Hammy' Halmshaw and guitarist Simon Mooney, two school friends from Thornhill High, drawn together by a mutual love of the Sex Pistols. They were soon joined on their quest by vocalist Simon 'Semi' Bridgewater and bassist Nicky Djorjevic.

"We rehearsed in Semi's parents' garage until they could bear us no more," laughs Hammy, "And then I think we moved to Thornhill Youth Club to rehearse, and that was when things began to gel. And because we had an audience for every practise, we started to develop a local following which became quite strong at the time; everyone in Dewsbury had heard of us, in fact. The only other punk band to spring up at the time, Disintegrated, were more from Batley, about five miles away, and they somehow didn't have the same spark we had. They were led by the area's most notorious punk though, Ritchie Calvert, or 'Perv', as he was known to all. He terrified me and Mooney, but he never did anything untoward to us... in fact, he actually seemed to like us a great deal, and be a bit fascinated by these 'posh young punks' (as I'm sure he saw us).

"One day he stopped Mooney in Dewsbury bus station and told him, 'I hear you've got a punk band... well, I was going to use the name 'Instigators' but you can have it instead, if you like?' Mooney wasn't going to say 'No' and neither was I, and anyway it was a superb name, so we took it. Then even Perv was going round writing our name on buses, bus shelters, and town centre shop fronts. It was hardly believable, but soon our name was everywhere you looked – from a bus perspective anyway!"

After their planned public debut at the 1981 school Christmas dance was cancelled due to bad weather (but not before the band had walked all the way there, weighed down with their gear, in the snow!), Instigators played their first show at Morley Youth Club during the summer of '82.

"It must have been pretty awful," admits Hammy, "But no one seemed to mind and we got a few more fans. We were invited to play by some of Mooney's friends from art college, and we did the gig with all these Crass-style backdrops...

"I remember when 'Stations Of The Crass' came out, all the 'really punk punks' had started to wear sinister Nazi-style armbands with a strange circular logo on; it was a new thing and very intriguing, so when I saw their album in the shop for only £3, I had to get it. I was shocked when I got home and read the cover and heard the dreadful music. I wasn't ready for it, but slowly it sank in and I got more and more revelations from the literature and lyrics. Then I started to write to Crass, just letters asking what anarchy meant and how could you have pacifist anarchy and the likes. Unexpectedly, I always got a huge letter back from one of the members explaining their thoughts in great depth. And each time the letter would be accompanied by five or six button badges and a wad of flyers, all containing further explanations and slogans. It all started to make perfect sense to me, and if anyone asked me what it was about, I told them to write to Crass, and those that did got the same back as I did. In the days of distant, disposable pop-stars, this was a huge thing for me and not only that but the writings made a hell of a lot of sense in a world I was struggling to come to terms with. I became a fully fledged 'Crass punk' from thereon in and bought anything and everything that came out on Crass and their associated labels like Spiderleg, Bluurg, Corpus Christi etc.

"I was calling myself an anarchist while not fully understanding the concept... it sounded great though. The rest of the band weren't as into Crass as I was; I think I went off on a little tangent there, but we were all into Flux Of Pink Indians – when 'Neu Smell' came out, it was the first time I'd directly linked the meat I was eating to the slaughter industry, and it really had a massive effect on me. Huge, in fact; I gave up eating meat very shortly afterwards, and so did Mooney and Semi. I've never had any meat since, neither has Mooney, I don't think. Semi lasted a while too, but [bassist] Tab was never a veggie, not even when he joined the band."

Instigators live at Gateshead Station, picture by Scotty.

Before Tab joined though, Instigators parted ways with the volatile Nicky ("He was the Sid Vicious of Dewsbury," chuckles Hammy, "More into prescription drugs and alcohol than learning to play!"), and replaced him with 'Tompo', a friend of Mooney's who only lasted a few months, but long enough to play on the band's first studio demo. A four-song effort, recorded at Lion Studios in Leeds, it helped the band take an important step towards something resembling a national profile.

"We sent it around to loads of people," Hammy recalls, "And, one Saturday morning, I got a call at my parents' house from Colin, the Flux Of Pink Indians singer, asking us to open for them and The System on the 'Guy Fawkes Was Right Night' at Huddersfield Trades Club [November 5th, 1982]. It was like being told you'd won the lottery, 'cos they were one of our favourite bands about then. I was electric with excitement and phoned the rest of the band, who were all gob-smacked. We realised we needed to rehearse big time and this was when everything shifted up a gear. The gig was packed [and organised by a certain Andy 'Tez' Turner, who would later replace Semi on vocals] and all our local fans came to watch us. I remember being so knackered it hurt to play, and we were probably sloppy and amateur, but with a great conviction and heartfelt seriousness we pulled it off and got a brilliant response. Something was certainly happening…"

"We actually went to that gig on the public bus," adds Semi. "I was quite nervous and decided that I was going to open our set with a joke. Hammy thought it would be a good idea, so I began the set with, 'Hello, my name is Margaret Thatcher; Dennis is cooking in the kitchen at the moment, I think he should be ready by now…!'"

Tompo was replaced by Tab [real name Simon Elsey, formerly of Repulsive Honk] on bass (this coincided with a brief period when Semi left and Darren 'Daz' Dean from Sheffield sang for Instigators – Semi then rejoined on the proviso that Tab was recruited as the new bassist), and two further demos were recorded at Lion, the three sessions being compiled onto one cassette and released on Hammy's fledgling record label, Peaceville. A very favourable review in issue two of 'Punk Lives' magazine encouraged a slew of mail orders and ultimately landed the band their first shows outside of Yorkshire.

On May 15th, 1983, Instigators – alongside The Convulsions – supported the Subhumans at

Simon Mooney and Tab of Instigators, picture by Andrew Medcalf.

Bradford's Vault Bar, a gig arranged by Nick Toczek, the punk poet from Leeds. Subhumans singer, Dick Lucas, was so impressed by the band that he recorded and released their set from that very gig as a live cassette through his label, Bluurg, before offering them their own single early the following year. A single the band actually had to record twice…

"Well, quite rightly Dick and [Subhumans guitarist] Bruce wanted us to go to a studio they knew," explains Hammy. "So we went to Warminster one weekend, but the drive really took it out of us and we had to set off back home on the Sunday afternoon as well, which meant we really only had one full day to do it. Also, when we got to Bruce's late on the Friday to stay over, we partied a little with the band and I remember [Subhumans drummer] Trotsky introducing us – well, probably just me really – to the 'blow back', a cool way to consume marijuana. It was slightly messy and way too late, so when we got up the next morning, exhausted, nothing went right and I thought the studio was crap anyway.

"The engineer was at polar opposites to us; we were childish and rubbed him up the wrong way, and it just all sounded dreadful, worse than any of our previous demos. We'd already been to Woodlands Studio in Normanton to record some tracks for Marcus Featherby's Pax compilation, 'Bollox To The Gonads… Here's The Testicles' ['Monkey Man' and 'Old Soldiers'], and they were ace quality, so thankfully, rather than just put out the crap version, Dick and Bruce came up to Yorkshire and we went back into Woodlands [on February 11th, 1984], which was now a big new studio in Castleford. It went a thousand times better than in Warminster and so we finally got the single done.

"We then had disagreements about the artwork internally and came up with a mish-mash of high-end graphics and Crass punk sensibility. Someone also forgot to put 'Pay no more than 90p' on the cover, so initially we were devastated, but that got put right later. It did well enough though, and set us up for our best time ever – the period writing and recording the album. We'd got a bit more professional (a lot more, in Mooney's case) and we took it very seriously, and we had a real song-writing flair at the time; they just seemed to come flying out of us in a way. Superb era! We played gigs everywhere it seemed, with everyone..."

Opening with Semi's high pitched, yet utterly unforgettable, incantation of 'There is no god! There is no god!' on 'The Church Says', 'The Blood Is On Your Hands' is an EP that positively throbs with a vibrant, youthful energy, the whole thing brilliantly simple, and an incredible debut by anyone's standards.

"Religion is something that I find difficult to comprehend," ponders Semi, on the reasoning behind 'The Church Says'. "How, in a developed world, we still believe that something actually exists after death, and that we are all here because of the 'Lord Almighty' is beyond me. As far as I'm concerned, religion is still the biggest cause of hardship in the world, through wars or terrorism, yet we will only really know the truth when we are dead."

The best was still to come from the 'Gators though, in the shape of the aforementioned 'Nobody Listens Anymore'. Recorded at Woodlands again, during early January 1985, and released that summer, the album saw the band working sensibly within their limitations to create a near-perfect melodic punk album, featuring the best Instigators track of all, 'Old Is Sad' – a genuinely ripping tune with lyrics penned by Mooney's then-girlfriend, Victoria Rothwell, who also contributed the spoken word title track.

"Vicky was a very well spoken and educated lady really," reveals Hammy. "I think Mooney wanted something on there to break up the Crass punk feel that I wanted... we were certainly drifting apart as far as our influences by then. It's a very eloquent piece though, something that stands the test of time – more so than the rest of the stuff probably...

"I remember going in to Woodlands knowing that we had to be as tight as hell," he adds, on the sessions for the album. "We had to pull it off as soon as possible 'cos time was limited. And, as drums spill over onto other microphones, I felt that I was under a lot of pressure from Mooney to get it right – he knew I was a piss-head, so didn't trust me a lot of the time to uphold his sense of professionalism. But I think I nailed most of the songs straight away, and felt so relieved to have it out of the way. The sound, because Woodlands was such an ace studio, was great almost straight away too, but, when Dick, Bruce and Mooney had finished with the additional bits and all the mixing, it sounded bloody amazing.

"We knew how good it was immediately, but I don't think most of us could believe that we'd pulled it off in such a style; we went home and listened endlessly to it, had parties to it, played it all live and, for a short while, we really seemed to be on a roll, in control and effortlessly happening. I remember the first week it was out, we were in the Top Five of the Melody Maker Indie charts... it was unreal."

'Dine Upon The Dead' was included on Mortarhate's 'We Don't Want Your Fucking War' album, whilst international recognition was further assisted by the inclusion of 'The Blood Is On Your Hands' and 'Free' on (US label) Pusmort's 1985 'Cleanse The Bacteria' compilation.

Unfortunately all good things come to an end, and the Instigators fell apart rather messily soon after, following a heated argument between Hammy and Semi.

"We had just played with Chumbawamba at Haddon Hall, Leeds," explains Semi. "From what I can remember, we were discussing a tour of Yugoslavia... I can't remember all the details, but I was probably more interested in my girlfriend at the time than the band, and either wanted to take her with us or not go at all... yes, I know! Voices were raised, and I said, 'I'm leaving', and that was that. I still remained friends with the band members, and Tab is still my best mate even today. I stayed close to Mooney for a few years too, but only saw Hammy very occasionally.

"Looking back now, I wish I had stayed and reaped some of the glory from the album which put the Instigators on the map. However, the fact that I'm doing this interview 21 years later speaks volumes, doesn't it?

"It wasn't all a bed of roses though. I remember a gig at a working man's club in Chesterfield. How we got it, I don't know, but our music didn't spark much emotion. I seem to recall we got a few claps at one point, and that was it!

"And we had a couple of gigs with a band called the Seats Of Piss. The singer used to walk around in fishnet stockings, with his willy hanging out. They supported us on a couple of occasions, and he used to rub the microphone all over his genitals and arse crack. Guess who had to use the mike next?"

Tez Turner of Instigators, by Marc Freeman.

When Semi left, the band recruited the aforementioned Tez Turner from The Xpozez to sing for them, but it quickly became apparent that things weren't working out, so Hammy and Tab decided to call it a day too. Mooney and Tez had other ideas though, enlisting bassist Andrew 'Trimble' Turnbull and drummer Steve 'Cuzzy' Curran, to complete what was essentially Instigators MK II, a very different band musically and visually to what had gone before.

"I'd not actually considered that they'd carry on, and I was disgusted for a long while after really," spits Hammy, who went on to front Civilised Society before turning Peaceville into a hugely popular and critically acclaimed international metal label, with feeling. "I saw it as them taking my good reputation down with them, so for me to have any chance of keeping my credibility, I felt that I needed to loudly disassociate myself from them.

"I'll also be honest here and say that I thought everything they did after the first album was pompous, meaningless pseudo-Yank rock drivel. I despised them for taking the name with them… not that I wanted it, but because I wanted it to die with the best line-up after the best release, to go out on a high. As it went on longer and longer, it got even worse in my eyes; Tez really oversold every recording they ever made, and I think they became ponderous rock wank… about as far as you can get from the original intentions we once had. I can talk though, can't I?"

Actually, although Instigators possibly had unveiled their finest material by that point, what followed afterwards was by no means as embarrassing as Hammy might suggest (in 1989, he even released some Tez-fronted re-recordings of early 'Gators songs as the – thoroughly enjoyable –

'New Old Now' album); sophomore full length, 'Phoenix', being an especially fine collection of intelligent melodic hardcore, with both 'American Dream' and 'Dark And Lonely' also being included on the Bluurg compilation, 'Open Mind Surgery'.

The new line-up were not only more slick and melodic than before, they possessed both an incredible work ethic and uniquely energetic stage presence, unrivalled at that point this side of the Atlantic; with Tez and Mooney throwing themselves around the stage with a reckless abandon, they took to concerted touring with an almost evangelical zeal, criss-crossing Europe and America many times.

Undergoing a bewildering string of personnel changes, Instigators flourished long beyond the period covered by this book, unveiling another fine studio album in the shape of 1988's 'Shock Gun' (recorded at Beaumont St. Studios, Huddersfield, by Pete Jones and Chris Ellis) and several live discs before finally splitting in the early Nineties.

"I think I can speak for everyone when I say that we enjoyed just about every minute!" exclaims Tez Turner. "Not only did it build us into what we became as a band, but every one of us used something gained along the way to mould themselves into what they are now... and so much of that was positive energy.

"We were from a time before bands like Green Day and The Offspring, bands that I always use to mark the passing from one era to another. They – and I don't really blame them for it – brought money into the scene, something that wasn't really there before, so was never a motive for any of us. After those two bands went mega, it changed the whole outlook – career moves, management, and all the other vampires there to suck them dry.

"I'm glad that we did what we did, when we did it, and for the reasons why we did it. We still carry that with us today, in everything we do now; an attitude that, after so many years and so much happening, is still the same one we had when we really did see a lot of things that most people could never hope to. I feel grateful for that, and it still gives me today an outlook that seems strange to a lot of people, but it was so pure and honest, it will never leave me."

SELECT DISCOGRAPHY

7"s:
'The Blood Is On Your Hands' EP (Bluurg, 1984)
'Full Circle' (Double A, 1987)
'Invasion' (Super Seven, 1988)

LPs:
'Nobody Listens Anymore' (Bluurg, 1985)
'Phoenix' (Bluurg, 1986)
'Wall Of Sound – Live In Berlin' (Meantime, 1988)
'Shock Gun' (Positive, 1988)
'New Old Now' (Peaceville, 1989)
'Recovery Sessions' (Full Circle, 1990)

At A Glance:
In 2002, Blackfish Records homed in on the band's three strongest releases, compiling the first single and two albums onto a single disc, 'Dine Upon The Dead', complete with a 32-page booklet of exhaustive liner notes from all the band members involved in those recordings. The Peaceville CD version of 'New Old Now' also includes the 'Shock Gun' album, licensed from Positive Records, so is worth searching out, for a decent overview of the latter period of the band's existence.

The Xpozez, live in Huddersfield, May 1983
(left to right: Trimble, Tez and Heppy).

As well as Tez and Trimble, who both turned up in the Instigators, **THE XPOZEZ** also comprised guitarist Nigel 'Nog' Hurst and drummer Anthony 'Heppy' Hepworth. They emerged from the same turbulent Huddersfield punk scene that spawned Criminal Justice and Xocet UK, and prompted the Yorkshire TV documentary 'First Tuesday'; they played their first gig at the Honley Youth Club in late 1980.

"Yeah, it was just down the road from where we lived, and it was packed," elaborates Tez. "Besides the local yokels, a serious amount of hardcore punks turned up, but I can't remember much about it other than we got a serious Aerosmith-style servicing [blowjobs all round, apparently] before we went on, and I got a slap from Trimble's mother who'd snuck in and saw me spitting fake blood all over her son... and the lovely matching T-shirts she'd had specially made for us!

"The Huddersfield scene was very, very violent and parochial," he adds. "It's hard to explain these days, but back then there was a massive touring circuit in the UK, so a lot of people never really had to travel for gigs. Only problem was that, due to a lot of 'punks' also being serious football hooligans, it became a novelty if there wasn't a kick-off at gigs. Cockney Rejects lasted twenty minutes... The Vapors got spray-painted in the face (at first they thought it was that 'silly string' stuff!)... Toyah ran off in tears... even Discharge got a kicking. Although Rainy came back a week later looking for the guys who did it, and he had some serious-looking geezers with him, all tooled-up... don't think he found them though, so we got pissed instead! Adam And The Ants also got a pasting on the 'Kings Of The Wild Frontier' tour... although, in a perverse way, you could say they were asking for it. Eventually someone said enough was enough and bands stopped playing Huddersfield, and due to that you had to travel to see bands, and although we had nothing to do with the violence, it made things 'interesting' in places like Leeds, Bradford and Sheffield..."

After building a strong local following, The Xpozez entered Neil Ferguson's Woodlands Studio – then just an eight-track home-based facility in Wakefield – and recorded the 'Systems Kill' EP, which they released on their own Retaliation Records.

"More due to a general lack of interest than any real DIY ethic," admits Tez. "We had set up a small mail-order company and fanzine, to spread the word and make a little money to finance out-of-town gigs. We pressed the initial 500 copies with a photocopied sleeve, as we'd run out of money to spend on a proper cover, and inside was a slip telling the buyer how they could send in for the real sleeve when the second pressing was ready. We were moving a little faster by then though, so the second pressing never happened, and those 500 people never did get a real sleeve!"

Soon after 'Systems Kill', Nog was replaced by Marcus 'DP' Dosspan, who played on the '1000 Marching Feet' (b/w 'Terminal Case') single for York-based Red Rhino Records, which spent a month in the lower echelons of the Indie charts upon its release during summer 1982.

Early 1983 saw The Xpozez borrowing a new drummer 'Brooky' (real name Andy Brook), from Criminal Justice (Heppy having decided he wanted to concentrate on playing darts semi-professionally), and new guitarist Neil Dickinson, from local comedy punks, All Over The Carpet, creating a relatively stable line-up that made their public debut supporting the Dead Kennedys and MDC in Leeds, and would reign until the band split in '85. Two songs ('Factory Fodder' and 'No Respect') were contributed to Pax's 'Punk's Dead? Nah, Mate...' compilation, before an unauthorised single, '(Be My) New York Doll', was released by Sexual Phonograph, which was promptly totally disowned by the band, who then embarked upon an eventful European tour... well, most of one, at least...

"Stupid as it seems, we took off for a month-long European tour in a Fiat 127," laughs Tez. "We made it to Yugoslavia and back – fuck knows how! – via Switzerland and Italy, where we did a great gig at the Virus squat in Milan... in fact, it was there that I got 'all hippy' and went vegetarian! Sadly, on the second leg, we got turned back at the Hook of Holland, and had to cancel the rest of the dates."

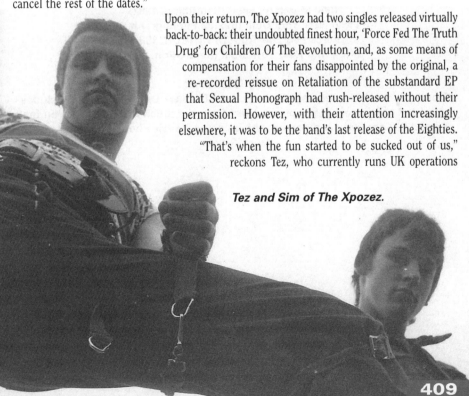

Upon their return, The Xpozez had two singles released virtually back-to-back: their undoubted finest hour, 'Force Fed The Truth Drug' for Children Of The Revolution, and, as some means of compensation for their fans disappointed by the original, a re-recorded reissue on Retaliation of the substandard EP that Sexual Phonograph had rush-released without their permission. However, with their attention increasingly elsewhere, it was to be the band's last release of the Eighties.

"That's when the fun started to be sucked out of us," reckons Tez, who currently runs UK operations

Tez and Sim of The Xpozez.

for the hugely-respected Metal Blade label, "Trawling up and down the country, playing with a bizarre mixture of bands in a weird range of venues… and always a hatful of excuses as to why there wasn't enough money to even cover our petrol costs. We were getting shows with the likes of Subhumans, The System, Zounds, Chumbafuckinwamba, and loads more, in places like the old disused Kwiki Mart, which had no electricity, so you'd set up in the shop window for what little light there was, put your coal in the generator that someone always seemed to have, and get through two or three songs tops, before either the power cut out or the local rozzers [i.e. police] paid a visit…

"I'm gonna probably go against the rose-tinted view of many of your contributors now, and say, with the benefit of hindsight, the bad actually outweighed the good in the anarcho-punk scene. It was great that loads of people wanted an alternative (to an alternative!), and there was an optimistic naivety that made it fun for a while, but later it became cliquey and insular and negative. The 'real world' was approached by people sticking their heads up their arses and hoping it'd all go away; the utopian view of how things should be in anarcho world became ghettoised, and run by a bunch of smelly hippies in badly-dyed German army gear.

"But we didn't really split up as such," he concludes, "It was more a case of other commitments taking over. Me and Trimble joined Instigators… Brooky was already in Criminal Justice, and Neil was in All Over The Carpet. It would have been nice to have done an album, as there were some great songs that never got recorded, but life goes on! Loads has happened since then, and still does. I suppose I'd personally just love to be remembered by the sad grumbling of the people who have to pay for my funeral after they find out any money I ever made had already contributed to my early demise!"

SELECT DISCOGRAPHY

7"s:
'Systems Kill' (Retaliation, 1981)
'1000 Marching Feet' (Red Rhino, 1982)
'(Be My) New York Doll' (Sexual Phonograph, 1983)
'Force Fed The Truth Drug' (COR, 1984)
'(Be My) New York Doll' (Retaliation, 1984)

At A Glance:
Grand Theft Audio's Xpozez retrospective CD, 'Back On The Streets', includes all of the band's recorded output, apart from the much-maligned session for Sexual Phonograph, and comes with a comprehensive booklet of liner notes from Tezzer.

D&V's Jef at the Bingo Hall, Islington, March 1984, picture by Paul May.

Sheffield's D&V weren't to everybody's taste, but once heard, they were never forgotten... how many other anarcho-punk bands comprised just a drummer and a vocalist? And what better way to deliver a pertinent message other than just the words of wisdom you care to impart and a rhythm against which to deliver them? They were also one of the very few bands to do both a single and an album on Crass Records, as opposed to that label's more usual 'one single only' agreement.

"People always used to say, 'What happened to the guitarist and bassist?' But we just wanted to stand out from the crowd really," reckons vocalist Jeff Antcliffe. "There were a lot of bands from Sheffield, lots of avant-garde types... and we weren't into that trying-to-be-cool scene. We were more into the punk thing, bang crash wallop...! And a friend of mine in London invited us down to do a gig, and everyone seemed to like it, and said, 'Cheeky little outfit!' It was good to be different, to have our own sound...

"It was the summer of '78, I think, when I first decided that I wanted to put a punk rock band together... of any nature, didn't matter what it was. So I started writing rebellious poems, but it took a good couple of years, of watching other bands and stuff, before I knew what I wanted to do: a kind of rap almost, with just vocals over a stripped-down drum beat. We were called The Epsilons, to start with, named after an estate near where we lived, and D&V [i.e. drums and vocals] was just a description.

"We met in Sheffield, on the Manor Park Estate... it was me and Andrew Paul Leach, a really cool guy... we weren't at school together, but he was from my neighbourhood, and I convinced him to get a drum kit. He was really up for it, really diligent. And the two of us were D&V basically... a few other people came and went, but all the gigs we did as D&V were me and Andy.

"Every wave [of punk] had its own time," furthers Jeff. "Every time a hurricane hits town, it's brand new, y'know? When it hits you personally, you think it's the first big storm to hit the city, and it ain't; it just feels that way. And there might be another one tomorrow! So it was with music; I was very aware of what was happening at that moment, not concerned with what had been before or what might come after.

"Long before I ever became a punk rocker though, I was hearing West Indian flavours drifting up and down my street, and I'd go and check out sound systems and hang out in blues clubs... and that's always been in me. But the main guy who influenced me to become a vocalist in a band, to get up onstage and scream down a mike, was Tapper Zuki, who was a part of that old DJ scene from Jamaica. I really got into his stuff, his lyrics and how he delivered them, and I'd practise along to his records, and that was way back before I was ever in the band. And, of course, a lot of those Jamaican artists never sold out, 'cos they didn't get chance to, so they remained on the frontline.

"I also took a lot of inspiration from bands like The Clash, and Joe Strummer's writings... you had the music, but it was also like poetry. And later on, Adrian Sherwood was a real gentleman, and he really moved me; I was really big on his sound. And of course, Crass, Flux... even Chumbawamba... I think we had that Yorkshire bond happening with the Chumbas, and we did some crazy gigs together. They were all people who were doing it at the same time as us... oh, and

D&V's Andy at the Islington Bingo Hall, March 1984, picture by Paul May.

THERE IS NO AUTHORITY YOURSELF

Annie Anxiety! She really inspired both me and Andy to lift our game, because her style was in a similar vein to our own. I liked John Cooper Clark and The Fall as well… who were very sarcastic, but with a lot of humanity in their work."

The first D&V gig was in early 1980, at the Grimaldi squat in Pentonville Road, London, with The Eratics, The Epileptics, Rubella Ballet, and many more, a show that went extremely well and helped sear the band deep into the psyche of the emerging anarcho-punk scene.

"Well, there was a lot of symbolism back then, and just putting a circle around your 'A's was only the tip of the iceberg. I was always looking for something more… but as much as I hate labels, as much as I loathe stereotypes, looking back now, if you wanna call it something, call it 'anarcho punk' – 'cos that's what it was! For a good few years of my life, I was an anarchist, because I had to believe in a worthwhile alternative to what was being offered. The left were enticing people in, the fucking right were enticing people in, but it was all fuckin' warfare, you know what I mean? We didn't want anything to do with those extremities, because they weren't healthy… we chose the middle path instead.

"I don't remember all this through any rose-tinted glasses, and neither do I look back angrily at those times… sure, there were a lot of ups and downs, but that wasn't the fault of the movement, that was down to individuals, you know? And for a while, being an anarchist made a lot of sense to a lot of people… but then things change. It's not like everyone suddenly cut their hair and got new clothes overnight, and it is still going on even today…

"All I can say is: anarchy to me was… uh, well that's just it. Anarchy to ME! What's important to me is bullshit to anyone else. Unless you're talking oxygen, or basic food and nutrition and all that, everything is abstract. I could say, as an artist, that it means freedom, a chaos, always being on the edge of it… autonomy is probably a better word to sum up what we were talking about. Going back twenty years, I'd have probably got up on my soap box, y'know? The early D&V lyrics said more than I ever could now anyway… 'Look, you're all bleeding sheep! Wake up and get a life!' They were very direct, and you can't really be that direct when you're trying to explain something from your heart… you come across all cold and clinical, and I'm certainly not like that, I'm as emotional as the next guy. Anarchy is a sense of self, and knowing that you're as free as you want to be. And that scares a lot of people, because it means they have to do something with their life."

And D&V most definitely did want to do something with their lives! A rough demo recorded straight onto sixteen-track tape one rainy Saturday morning in Stoke Newington led to the duo appearing at the Zig Zag squat gig organised by Crass in December 1982, which itself led to the band releasing 'The Nearest Door' single on the Crass label in October 1983. Recorded by John Loder, and produced by Penny Rimbaud, at Southern Studios during March of that year, the single was a quirky, entertaining and intelligent slice of anti-punk, although the spartan sonic landscape created by just drums and vocals didn't exactly lend itself to repeated listens, but nevertheless it made the Indie Top Thirty upon its release and spent a month-and-a-half in said chart.

"Well, there was a demonstration on down in London, and whenever the nurses were on strike or whatever, all these coaches would go down from Sheffield," elaborates Jeff, on how he first hooked up with Crass. "All the trade union dudes and protesters and lefties, would all pile on buses and head down the M1, so every weekend there'd be all these coaches going down to London, and one day, me and Andy, and a couple of other punky chaps, went along – supposedly to go on this demo, but we soon vanished off to a gig at the Moonlight Club, in Hampstead.

"So, we were outside this gig, and it was crazy, punks and skinheads hanging around everywhere, but there were no tickets left, and we were just about to give up and go home, when this dude comes out, chatting to people… and it was Andy Palmer from Crass. When we realised that he had a few tickets on him, me and my mate – being a pair of right likely lads – were straight on him, and he got us in the gig. And it was fucking great; as far as we were concerned, he'd just got us into the coolest club on earth! It was totally packed, and Crass, Poison Girls and The Epileptics played, and we were blown away. We had to leave pretty early though, because we were staying down in Brixton, and we had to catch the tube back, but there were all these fights going on as we left; it was totally crazy.

"A lot of the punk stuff I'd seen before then was at the Top Rank in Sheffield – a lot of bands came through there – but what was happening down in London was another world; it was well scary, and it changed my whole outlook on everything. It was very intense… and that was the first time I met Crass face to face. We had a lot in common; they liked what we were doing, we liked what they were doing…"

Soon after this chance meeting, Jeff relocated to London, moving into a squat in Hackney where he met the likes of The Mob and Zounds, both bands he also cites as a major influence on what D&V was doing. The success of the single led to both a John Peel session and a full album for Crass.

"The term 'D&V' started off as just a description of what we were doing really," reckons Jeff, "Then John Peel started playing the single; he was a lovely chap, who liked what we were doing too, and offered us a session, which was amazing. Most radio stations then were just a fucking joke, but John Peel's show was like an oasis amidst all the shit. And he played our stuff quite a lot, which was a real thrill, hearing your music coming out of the radio in the middle of the night. I used to listen to his shows hidden under my covers when I was a kid, and I'd go out and buy all the records he recommended, so it was amazing to eventually meet the guy, and find that he was a very warm person. So we did the session, and it was an experience, and it went down a treat.

"Anyway, John Peel used to read letters out on his show – he was just great to listen to, I never lost interest – and one day he asked people to write in with suggestions as to what 'D&V' might mean. Of course, most people were like, 'It stands for Drums And Vocals', but this one guy wrote in and pointed out that it was a term used by nurses, that was short for 'diarrhoea and vomiting'… 'Oh, he's got a dose of the D&Vs…!' So, for a while we were known as Diarrhoea & Vomit!"

1984 saw the release of the band's self-titled album through Crass, which was a more adventurous affair in the production stakes, with layers of effects softening the basic abrasiveness of the band's natural sound, and vocal samples coming courtesy of Eve Libertine and Joy De Vivre from Crass. The cover bore the legend 'Inspiration gave them the motivation to move on out of their isolation', which no doubt described D&V's own fortuitous escape from the estates of Sheffield, afforded by the sharing, caring, mutually encouraging network of anarcho-punk rock they were welcomed into with open arms. From rehearsing in a field behind one of their houses, they were now sharing stages nationwide with some of the scene's biggest names.

"Actually, one gig I'll never forget… we were touring with Flux, KUKL and Chumbawamba, a benefit for the striking miners… and we turned up at the Digbeth Civic Hall in Birmingham, a venue where there was always trouble. This particular night, they bashed Martin from Flux, and he had to go to hospital… it was quite gruesome; this isn't a jocular tale! But Andy drummed for Flux that night, even though he only knew one of their songs, 'Tube Disasters'… he played the same beat all the way through the set. And that sums up the whole era really; the gigs were always something else, really crazy. A lot of the other bands no doubt have tons of war stories, but I just used to enjoy the opportunity to get onstage and show off! Dancing around, in another world all my own, getting off on the music…

"There weren't any really bad gigs, because the whole attitude of the period was rough and ready, no pretensions. So, if the PA blew up, or the whole crowd started to try and kill each other, we just got on with it. Sometimes we'd even do a better gig because of it, but we always took it in our stride."

The band's close relationship with Flux no doubt assisted them in landing a deal with their bassist Derek Birkett's fast-rising One Little Indian label, although the 'Snare' 12" they did for him was to be the last D&V release before the duo drifted apart, playing their last show together during the summer of 1986.

"It was the last time I felt like doing what we were doing," claims Jeff. "We'd been out of the country, getting a cheap and cheerful tan in Spain, and we got back and I thought, 'I don't wanna do it like this anymore!' So, that last gig wasn't like what most bands will talk about as their swansong or anything; this wasn't a sad last gig… it was more like a revelation. 'We can't do this anymore, but it's not the end of the line, we can move onto something new and exciting again…'

"It was at the Leadmill in Sheffield… and it really had been a lead mill once upon a time, a big old factory. In fact, I helped build the floor in the bar there! They turned this dangerous old warehouse into a community place, where all these bands would play… we even rehearsed there towards the end. All this was going through my mind as we played that last gig, it felt like we'd come full circle, but it wasn't anything sad… more like, 'Fuck this for a game of cards, I'm off to see the world!' "

And off he went, eventually settling in Australia, where he still resides, pondering occasionally the scene he was once an integral part of.

"It was neither a bed of roses nor a cess-pit full of shite, know what I mean? But I really do think it's important to stay humble and not over-value your own importance in the big scheme of things. I don't really care if anyone remembers what we did then, because deep down I still don't think I've done my best work yet. And never mind how other people remember me… I'm just trying to remember myself! I'm concentrating on checking my own head, keeping my own brain cells together, you know?

"Whenever I feel good about music, I'll try and make music; whenever I feel good about writing prose, I'll write prose. If you wanna do it, do it, but everything's down to interpretation. You could have ten guys in a room, all playing the same tune, but everyone has their own take on things, everyone has their own pain barrier when it comes to putting out art… music can change the world, but it all starts with an idea… and you're lucky if you've got the idea. Then you've got to find a vehicle capable of carrying that idea… then you need a strong engine to maintain the continuity of the idea…

"On the last record we did, 'Snare', there's a line that sums up a lot of what I'd been through and felt at the time. 'It's still out there, and we can still go and get it, if we want it…' And there's another song on there called 'Conscious (Pilot)', a track about death, and I wrote it once when I went home to Sheffield and ended up in this big old city cemetery; I sat up there, huddled in my winter coat with my little note book, writing down ideas as they came into my head… seeing if I could be a poet for the day.

"Something like, 'Please, when I'm dead, don't put me in the ground… you know I could never live with that; please don't burn my bones, these mortal remains, you know I hate it when a fire gets hot; and to be buried at sea isn't my cup of tea, so how's about you leave me in a comfy chair on a hill of my choice?' All the other stuff I did sounded either angry or intense, but this was purely about the place where I grew up, and how it made me feel. I decided it was time to stop moaning about the government and to look deeper into myself."

SELECT DISCOGRAPHY

7"s:
'The Nearest Door' (Crass, 1983)

12"s:
'Snare' (One Little Indian, 1986)

LPs:
'D&V' (Crass, 1984)

At A Glance:
The rather elusive Crass Records compilation CD, 'A-Sides, Part Two, 1982 – 1984', features 'Jekyll And Hyde' and 'Wake Up' from 'The Nearest Door' single.

CHAPTER EIGHT

As detailed in 'Burning Britain', not to mention Sean O'Neill and Guy Trelford's excellent 'It Makes You Want To Spit!' and on the www.belfastpunks.co.uk website, being a punk in Belfast in the early Eighties was radically different to being a punk on mainland Britain. Whereas most anarcho punks here sang about war and police brutality and the heavy-handed military with little or no first-hand experience of such matters, other than what they saw and read in the news, punks in Northern Ireland lived this harsh reality every day. Subsequently, punk rock took on a whole new level of profundity in their lives, colouring the music that originated from there a grim shade of gritty realism.

TOXIC WASTE were one such band, following in the footsteps of The Outcasts, yet furthered inspired by Crass, seizing politically-charged punk rock as the only way to express their anger and disbelief at 'the troubles' intent on ruining their lives.

"I don't think that many people fully understand the impact that the first wave of punk had in a place like Belfast," begins Roy Wallace. "You could not escape being political, as ignoring the cultural signposts might cost you your life, so when punk arrived it was like a huge sledgehammer from left field, which smacked into the hatred of our lives, stuck its finger in the air and screamed, 'Fuck your sectarian war!' This allowed for a significant amount of the provincial youth to capitalise on its potential, and thankfully they did. So, long before the Eighties, enough groundwork had been done by various individuals who spearheaded the punk scene at different times to focus the energies and activities in unique and clever ways which would have a long-lasting effect on all punks from Northern Ireland; the cultural space that was opened up by people like Terri Hooley, SLF, The Outcasts, Rudi and all the other Good Vibrations bands, deeply influenced attitudes in places like Belfast. For most people at that time, punk was their life; it wasn't a fashion accessory down the Kings Road, and it wasn't some form of art. It was a way out of the hatred which permeated every aspect of our existence, and held real significance to many of the punks I came across during that period.

"So when the music press announced that 'punk was now dead', I would argue that it had a profound effect on many people in areas like Belfast. Firstly, it acted as a filtering exercise for those who bought into the fashion and artistic expression that the early punk scene encapsulated in places like London. At this point many of the 'punk poseurs' moved on with their careers and abandoned the potential that punk had offered initially, because many of them felt they had grown up and moved on, and I guess there's nothing wrong with that. However, in Belfast and similar urban environments, many people were finding that punk offered real potential to affect and change their circumstances. The collective anti-politics of punk sidestepped the sectarian circus, and many people were by now working collectively (as before) to organise, communicate and engage with a range of ways to express themselves freely about the situation they were living in. The emphasis was on a shift from 'individual punk star' to 'activist', and the internal dynamics of the previous punk scene faded in favour of a collective approach.

"Crass were an intellectual inspiration who helped many of us understand how to think and act for ourselves, with an understanding that they did not want to constantly be the engine for change. This was both liberating and empowering. The Crass gig in Belfast helped form lasting friendships and relationships, the basis of which helped many new punk bands emerge, and,

Toxic Waste, Bristol 1984, Billy Swain (driver), Stuart Martin, Patsy, and the Bristol promoter.

given the attacks from skinheads outside the event, it helped forge a new sense of solidarity, which acted to re-invigorate the whole scene.

"And, for me at least, many of the influences at this time came through a bookshop called Just Books, who stocked alternative literature, records, and fanzines, and although I would now regard them as more 'internationalist' than 'anarchist' in their outlook, they provided access to thought-provoking information; a small vegetarian café and print press helped spawn a group of anarcho punks who had a profound influence on my life. It was through the bookshop, and other small independent record outlets, that I became familiar with bands like Crass, Dirt, Flux, Zounds, The Mob, and, a bit later on, Conflict. The DIY culture opened up many new ways of communicating, which influenced my thinking and eventually inspired my lyrics."

Formed in and around the Newtownards area of County Down, Toxic Waste initially comprised Dane and Patsy on vocals, Stuart 'Marty' Martin on guitar, Phil Coffey on bass, and Glen 'Grub' Thompson on drums, and played their first gig in Ards, at the West Winds Road House, in late 1982. They released the 'Unite To Resist' demo tape, recorded at Kirkubben Studios, in 1983, a track off which was later included on Mortarhate's 'We Don't Want Your Fucking War' compilation, the very Dirt-like 'Good Morning', that posed the question to the likes of the Royal Ulster Constabulary, 'Will the real men of violence please stand up?'

Roy joined soon afterwards (having previously played with Half Tore and Wardance, the latter of whom contributed 'Stand The Proud' to Mortarhate's 'We Don't Want Your Fucking Law' LP), replacing Dane as second vocalist when the band moved to Belfast; he played his first gig at Du Barry's Bar, where they had also began rehearsing.

"My earliest memories of the other band members? Lentils, TVP [i.e. textured vegetable protein], their pseudo squat in Jerusalem Street, crusty punk, petulia oil, stencils, cassette tapes, enthusiasm and political passion. Those early days were spent addressing the stagnant environment that emerged when punk supposedly 'died', and the hunger strikes began; a lot of time was spent in city centre pubs discussing possibilities, forging new friendships and attending whatever alternative musical or political events were on at the time. Eventually we found a home

through the Belfast Centre for the Unemployed in Donegal Street, tapping into whatever left-wing politics surfaced – CND... the Nicaraguan Solidarity Campaign... the Campaign for Justice etc. We began to use any available assistance to organise and focus our activities on an 'alternative centre' as squatting was impossible, although attempted a few times. This gave birth to the Warzone Collective, Giro's Café, printing facilities and a rehearsal space."

Belfast punks had to work doubly hard to make any headway in their struggle to be heard; fearlessly anti-state in a dangerous environment where state terrorism went hand in hand with sectarian bigotry, and was reinforced with indiscriminate plastic bullets, bands such as Toxic Waste and Stalag 17 helped keep the Warzone collective a relevant, focused means of protest against a backdrop of the bleakest political climate imaginable.

"I later learned that similar circumstances were faced by many punk scenes across the globe [Eastern Europe and South America being prime examples], but for a short period, during the early-to-mid Eighties, it seemed the punks in Belfast ranked No. 1 in the 'worst places to be anarchist and punk' stakes!" recalls Roy, attempting to further illustrate the volatility of the period. "One event that sticks with me was a bizarre incident in the city centre one Saturday afternoon. I had gone into the city centre with a group of friends: Harry, Togsi, Nidge, Roachey, Baker, and a few

Toxic Waste live in London, 1986 (left to right: Stuart Martin, Roy Wallace, Patsy, and Phil Coffey).

others. There was about eight or nine of us walking through this covered arcade between two shops, when two guys walked toward us, looking quite drunk even though it was early afternoon, so we tried to ignore them. However, one of the guys started to hassle Roachey or Togsi about being a punk, and they got into a fight. As there were loads of us, we all tried to break it up before the two guys came off worse.

"But Roachey and Togsi traded some blows with them, and, next thing, one of them hit the ground, but as he did so, a 9mm [hand-gun] fell out of his pocket and onto the ground. We all guessed automatically that these guys might be off-duty cops or military, as they all had these issued for personal protection, but then again it could've been someone on a job in the city centre. So, all the shoppers started screaming and running for cover, as this guy got up and pointed the gun at us. Everyone split in different directions, because we knew he wasn't fucking around and was gonna kill someone. Me and Togsi ran through the BHS [British Home Stores] shop while security and shoppers were screaming and running around like headless chickens, and we made it out the other side to relative safety toward Royal Avenue – the main shopping area in Belfast.

"What we didn't know was that these two guys had decided to chase us both, and were right behind us, which is why everyone was so freaked out – because they could see them pointing the guns at us! Once we realised that we were pretty fucked, and that these guys were determined to kill someone, we made for the middle of the road to attract as much attention as possible and ran like an Olympic athletes through town. I occasionally looked around as chaos followed when we passed, but there was no way we were stopping for anyone, and we eventually made it back to a car park beside St. Anne's Cathedral and the sanctuary of Togsi's car. The police and army had honed in on the spectacle as we progressed through the city centre, so we legged it out of there to a local bar near where we lived. At the time, there were no mobile phones, but we knew people would return there eventually. Everyone made it back with vivid and humorous recollections of the afternoon's events, and we all got very drunk, knowing for real how precious life was that day, and so it was we vowed to always live life for the moment.

"Unfortunately, these kind of events were common place and, over the course of the Eighties, there were loads of similar occurrences which I can recall, happening to other people from different parts of the city. So, I would say that it was a very bold and definitive decision to 'remain punk' after the initial media attention had died down. What was left was the reality of your personal and community circumstances, which you had to conscientiously and continuously oppose on a range of levels. This put the punk scene and the individuals involved in a reasonably precarious situation regardless of background, status or beliefs. By being punk, you were firstly regarded as a freak or a weirdo, same as in the Sixties and Seventies, but, by the time we reached the Eighties, you had punks with 'Crass' stencilled on their backs, with 'Fuck your war' and peace symbols on their jackets, walking down West Belfast at the height of the worst sectarian violence ever, to see the Subhumans play in the Labour Club on a Sunday night, when no other fucker was on the streets except the hoods and the army.

"By the same token, you had pockets of punks sniffin' glue and Lady Esquire, or drinking QC sherry as a precursor to the same gig, from some Loyalist or Republican stronghold, because that made sense in a fucked-up city like Belfast. I wouldn't want to over-dramatise the memories, but I think it is fair to say that the punks who organised small events, attended each other's gigs, slagged each other off, had the odd fight with the skinheads from the New Lodge or Shankill, and then walked each other home through an abandoned city centre to the relative safety of some two-up in the Holy Lands area deserve recognition for the fucking legends they were…

"Often nothing would happen within that environment during that time, yet all around the overbearing sectarian and state killing machine was slowly grinding everyone into apathy. And the punk scene during the mid-Eighties, just like the Sixties or the late Seventies, breathed life into a stagnant hell of adolescent life transition and social turmoil."

A successful, albeit financially ruinous, tour of the UK included a gig with Conflict in London (Toxic Waste had previously supported them at Manhattan's in Belfast), cementing a relationship with Mortarhate that led to them releasing 'The Truth Will Be Heard', a split 12" with Stalag 17, in 1985.

"We recorded our material at a BBC sound engineer's studio in Newtownards; the guy was okay, but the songs were typically overproduced, and we were learning as we went along. Phil and Marty more or less produced the three tracks, while me and Patsy re-arranged lyrics, and Grub went to work in the shipyard during the day, to pay for the studio time.

"It was a great experience, but in hindsight naïve, regarding the overall punk scene, the record-selling side of punk, and dealing with the business which we hoped to avoid. Not everyone we met was as in tune with us as we hoped. The band was 'branding' itself at that time (even if we didn't know it) and this forced us to think more clearly about our short- and long-term aims. Dealing with all the legal, copyright and business aspects threw a spanner in the works, as this was the first 'real' release from the newly-emerging anarcho-punk scene, and the Warzone collective in Belfast, and all sorts of petty bickering ensued.

"This brought both Toxic Waste and Stalag 17 into a position of personal and band scrutiny regarding our beliefs, politics, and lyrics etc., and heralded in external pressures from the punk scene on top of the usual everyday stress. In many ways this pressure was good, but it became dominated by the internal anarcho-punk PC police-force, who basically wanted to determine what

Members of Toxic Waste pictured washing their 'tour bus' on the eve of their first European tour (Marty, Billy Swain and Patsy).

every individual and band should be like. For Toxic Waste, the release on Mortarhate helped stimulate more interest in the band, and provided enough distribution to organise several tours afterwards. We were just happy to have achieved something positive, which helped inspire other bands and people to release their own material, either on cassette or DIY vinyl. It was just another step in our self-education regarding the potential of individual and collective activity.

"The down-side was a dispute with Mortarhate through Jungle, which never really got resolved, and quite a bit of animosity existed within the punk community in Belfast for a number of years over all this. I, however, resolved my differences a long time ago!"

Possibly as a result of the above, Toxic Waste's next record came out through their own label, Belfast, and, in keeping with the ideals of an underground punk brother and sisterhood, 'We Will Be Free' was another split release, only this time a three-way one, with both Stalag 17 and Asylum ("They were a really good band," reckons Roy. "Semi-serious politically, but with a dose of ironic self-debasement thrown in; they played with us and Stalag quite a bit, and we all helped make that early anarcho scene in Belfast").

It demonstrated a marked progression in both the band's song-writing and execution, with 'Tug Of War' ('Two communities set apart, and never the twain shall meet; two kids stare at each other from opposite sides of the street... one more Irish than the Irish, one more British than the British; two perverted, little flag-waving worlds, isolated from every peaceful wish...') being an especially poignant reflection of the tragic reality underscoring the political loggerhead they were suffering under.

Further concerted touring saw the band travelling across the UK and Europe, but they fragmented in 1986, when Patsy moved south, Phil to Bristol, and Roy to London, where he moved into a squat in Andulus Road with Dirty Richard, bassist of Dirt. Marty meanwhile became guitarist with legendary Belfast punk band Pink Turds In Space.

In London, Richard introduced Roy to Gary and Deno from Dirt, who helped him realise the 1987 'Belfast' album (a collection of old Toxic Waste songs, alongside several newly recorded versions that featured Gary on guitar and Deno on vocals), and then, when he returned home in 1990, he reunited with Marty in the brilliantly-named Bleeding Rectum. They released two split albums (one with US 'power violence' combo, Man Is The Bastard, and one with crusty Dutch squatters, Fleas And Lice) but split in late 1991, amidst the storm of controversy surrounding their 'Daniel O' Donnell [i.e. the Irish country music superstar] Must Die' tour.

"I think we named it after we watched that Robbie Coltrane film, 'The Pope Must Die', and because our tour coincided with an all-Ireland tour that Daniel was about to embark upon," smiles Roy ruefully. "Anyhow, talk about bad timing... we had made up posters and publicised the tour as much as possible to create some interest from the local media, when, just a week before the tour, some fucker threatened to kill Daniel O'Donnell while he was travelling around Ireland. So, this then got blamed on Loyalist Paramilitaries, who went into overdrive to demonstrate their disgust at the idea by threatening to shoot whoever had made the threats. Not surprisingly no one owned up to the dirty deed, and the 'Sunday Scumbag' paper did a full article detailing how this 'sick punk band' had made the threats to Ireland's favourite son.

"As we had no way of defending ourselves through any media outlet, the story gathered momentum and spread throughout the assholes who called themselves journalists around Belfast. This in turn put us in a pretty bad situation at the time, as both Marty and I were running a music project based in a Loyalist area of the city. Later, it was made very clear that there was potentially an extremely detrimental situation about to unfold unless we acted, so we were forced to make a public denial that we had nothing to do with the threats, and that basically we were just a 'sick punk band' with 'very bad timing'.

"Daniel cut his tour short due to stress anyway, and we persevered with the punks from around Ireland to make our tour a great laugh, and to celebrate our relief at avoiding impending doom – all due to some crank caller who turned out to be a guy driven mad by his wife playing Daniel

O'Donnell all day. He had phoned in a rage to say that he was going to 'whack' Daniel if he went on tour, so he didn't have to drive his wife to the gigs when the football was on TV or something…

"We [Bleeding Rectum] later paid homage to Daniel on our 'Very Unpleasant Indeed' cassette, which went down a storm with the local community who had supported us through the traumatic events. I personally delivered a copy of the cassette to Daniel's hotel business which he runs in Donegal, but he was unable to see me that day and the barman asked me to leave after I'd downed several Jack Daniels and recounted aloud the whole sorry story to a bus load of tourists in memory of our narrow escape."

Toxic Waste 'enjoyed' one last stint around Europe however, when Roy was forced to reform the band in 1991 to help dig himself out of a desperate financial hole.

"I was finding life increasingly difficult, due to my personal circumstances in Belfast; I had dreadlocks and didn't quite fit in with the local community where I was living, and I was also getting grief because my partner at the time was from Dublin. This later culminated in some veiled threats, and we decided to head off somewhere else to live in peace.

"So, we arrived in Belgium and stayed for eight or nine months, before finding ourselves in trouble again, because I had broken some shitty housing contract, which ended us up in court. I got fined, with court costs, and said, 'Bollocks to that!' but my mate, Gunter, had stood guarantor for me and he would be left with the debt. This totally messed up our lives, as I had no way of paying the money, so I asked Deno and some friends [Marty, Petesy from Stalag 17, and Mickey Death and 'Crispo', both from Bleeding Rectum] if they would help out, so that I could sell off the rest of the 'Belfast' albums I still had available. They kindly agreed to do so, and basically the tour was really a way of resolving yet another legal bullshit dilemma.

"The trip was much more difficult than before; I was stressed out, in need of raising nearly £5,000 in a short period of time, while missing my partner and son. Unlike previous tours, this was not such an enjoyable experience, for obvious reasons, although we still managed to have a good time; I met with loads of good friends, made some new ones, and shot my first ever video, called 'Punk As Fuck', which later inspired me to continue DIY video-making until the present day…"

As well as his video-based endeavours (that include the films 'Big Time', 'Modern Angels' and 'Remembrance Day For The Living', not to mention 'The Day The Country Died' documentary that is a companion piece to this book), Roy is now a full-time teacher, as is Marty, who ended up teaching at his local college after various community-related jobs and even a stint as a sound engineer with the Warzone Collective for several years.

"But I want to make it perfectly clear that I am not in competition with Marty for the 'Best Teacher From Old Punk Band' award! And has punk stuck with us? Yeah, I think so; even though we all took separate paths and had to adjust to various situations that life threw at us, I would say that we are all still as 'punk as fuck' now as we were back then – perhaps just a little more cynical, yet realistic, about negotiating our circumstances."

SELECT DISCOGRAPHY

12"s:
'The Truth Will Be Heard' (Mortarhate, 1985) – split with Stalag 17

LPs:
'We Will Be Free' (Belfast, 1986) – split with Stalag 17 and Asylum
'Belfast' (Belfast, 1987)

At A Glance:
In 1998, Rejected Records released 'We Will Be Free', a twenty-seven track CD compiling all the original vinyl releases of both Toxic Waste and Bleeding Rectum.

Stalag 17, Petesy, Tul and TC supporting Crass at the Anarchy Centre.

66 There's a lot of romanticising about what a way of life punk in the North of Ireland was, but that's certainly how it felt at the time," agrees Petesy Burns, bassist-then-vocalist with the aforementioned **STALAG 17**. "To say punk was a panacea to the small-minded attitudes which twenty years of sectarian violence had engendered is a gross understatement. And given that state of affairs, it was an obvious choice for a wee spide from North Belfast, who knew very little about the outside world.

"Politicising aside, I think it was the fact that the Pistols' 'God Save The Queen' got banned from radio that made me prick up my ears. More so as I grew up in a staunchly Irish Republican area, and here was an English band in Jubilee year, basically saying that the British establishment was full of shit. Okay, so that wasn't exactly an earth-shattering revelation to someone who'd grown up at the nasty end of British justice (oops... I just can't leave the politicising aside, can I?), but it sure was exciting... and they looked great to boot!"

The band formed sometime during 1980, in and around the Pound and the Harp Bar venues, inspired by the thriving Belfast scene then dominated by Rudi, The Outcasts and The Defects. Watching these other bands up onstage, living their dreams (or some of them, at least), it was merely a matter of time before the members of Stalag 17 decided to have a go themselves.

"Yeah, from there it was just a case of finding each other really, and for that I'm afraid the British establishment must take some credit, even though it sticks in my throat to admit it. You see, it was the beginning of the end of good old-fashioned, no-strings-attached dole scrounging, and government training centres sprang up everywhere with the sole purpose of turning out factory fodder. Compared to the shitty training schemes of today it wasn't too bad, I suppose, but still a bag of shite nonetheless.

"Anyway, I happened to find myself in one of these, on a mechanical engineering apprenticeship, and, as it happened, so did two of the other guys, [vocalist] Tul and [drummer] Mickey. Tul had played in a band with another guy, [guitarist] T.C., called Maimed... well, not exactly played; they probably did a gig or two. T.C. was the odd one out in that he didn't work at the training centre: he had a proper job!

Stalag 17, at Coleraine University Battle Of The Bands, picture by John Campbell.

"Mickey was in a band (although I suspect it was more of a concept) called Paranoid, and I'd dabbled with a few Harp Bar boys and Ian [Astbury] from The Cult, who lived in Belfast at the time. That was mostly just jamming around one of my bass riffs, while he read a passage from some book. It was all very avant-garde and short-lived, as he soon buggered off back home – with my bass, I suspect! I'd also been rehearsing, but not playing, with The Stillborns, which had just come to an abrupt end.

"Tul approached me and told me that he and T.C. were putting a band together, and that they needed a bass player. I obliged and we started to practice in Tul's parents' garage. It was as rough as the shucks, and we had very little in the way of gear, but the crack was 90! As Mickey was in the plumbing section of the training centre, we reckoned he'd be the obvious choice for making us a microphone stand, and it was during this process that we found out he was a drummer… we were complete!"

The band's first gig was at the Hillhead Community Centre in West Belfast, although technically their public debut was prior to that when they made an impromptu appearance supporting The Defects at the Pound – Mickey wasn't in the band at that point though, so Defects drummer Kinky kindly filled in.

"It was weird," laughs Petesy, "He [Kinky] knew his shit, and we didn't; I can't remember what it was like, but I'm sure he did us justice. Whatever happened, all of our mates and the other members of The Defects were very encouraging…"

As with so many of the bands featured in this book, a pivotal moment for Stalag 17, and indeed the whole scene they were a part of, was encountering, not to mention opening for, Crass in their local venue.

"When we were offered the Crass gig, T.C. nearly shit himself. I wasn't too fussed, as I had taken the line of the music press: that they were all just a bunch of aging hippies, who were humourless and using punk for their own tired political ends… still, it was a gig and I was up for it.

"The first thing that struck me – apart from how old most of them were – was the fact that a few of them wanted to hang out with the punks the night before the first gig. I don't remember exactly who came to Paddy Rea's, 'our' pub, but Steve Ignorant was one of them. Funnily enough, he struck me as a down-to-earth punk, who was both interesting and interested. Any of the others I got to meet over the course of the weekend were pretty sound too. I even managed to have a good chinwag with Eve, about the nature of intoxication and why people felt the need to get out of it to have fun. I haven't seen a band since who got so involved with their audience, who were so accessible. Dirt and Annie Anxiety were over with them as well, and there was a vibe of togetherness about the whole ensemble that was really infectious.

"The Saturday gig blew my napper, although I was in another dimension anyhow (fungal-induced, shall we say?) When I walked into the venue hall, I thought I'd entered another world. The whole place was adorned with banners; there were screens about the place, projecting wild and disturbing images, and Annie Anxiety was on the stage, looking possessed and making noises that freaked me out of my tits. This however was nothing compared to the spectacle that was Crass. I'd seen more punk bands than you could shake a stick at… I'd seen every pose and sneer and sarcastic scowl in the book, but I had never seen anything like the energy these people belted out to their audience. This wasn't punk for the sake of it… it was punk saying, 'Listen to us, you bastards!' And in no uncertain terms either.

"The highlight for me was watching an RUC officer walk into a hall full of people all shouting, 'Fight war, not wars!' It was all too much for him, and he left with his little piggy tail between his legs. Of course, the fuckers got their own back later, when they called in UDR [Ulster Defence Regiment] reinforcements, blocked off both ends of the street and attempted to provoke a riot. On this occasion, we were all too 'peaced off', and they didn't get a rise from anyone.

"It was only after the Crass entourage left, that we heard how much the band lost from doing the gig. In fact, they knew they would lose it in the first place, but they were committed to playing in Belfast, and willing to put their money where their mouths were. Inspirational stuff to a twenty-year-old who'd watched wave after wave of bands becoming rock stars and chasing the American dream… the seed for what was to happen in the Belfast punk/anarchist scene for the next twenty-odd years was thus planted…"

T.C. and Tul left the band, following a heated disagreement with Mickey at a gig in Port Stewart, so Stalag 17 recruited Gaskey on guitar, and Joe on bass, allowing Petesy to move upfront, behind the mike. They began organising gigs at the Manhattan for other touring anarcho bands such as Subhumans, Dirt and Alternative, and, as the nucleus of people involved in promoting the shows became ever more political in their aspirations, the Warzone Collective, and ultimately the self-ran Giros venue, was born.

"It has to be said that the name 'Warzone' never settled that well with me," admits Petesy, "Even though I bandied it about, and put it on publications and music releases I was involved in. It bought into the besieged mentality of the people of Northern Ireland, as if we're something special because we define ourselves as some sort of war victims. It was sensationalism of the SLF variety, but it stuck and it was probably sexy to those outside of here who didn't know much about what was going on.

"When the people who ran 'Cafe Hideout' in the Just Books building threw in the tea towel, the Warzone Collective jumped in. With as much culinary experience as musical ability, we managed to keep the place running, and it became the first punk drop-in in Belfast – much to the disgust of most of the serious 'booky-types' working at Just Books. We never did get around to giving the cafe a name either, although I seem to remember 'Uncle Dave's Diner' being considered at one point. This was the point where we changed from being a disparate group of punks who got together now and again to arrange gigs, to a group who had the responsibility of making something work on a day-to-day basis. I suppose the old term that keeps cropping up time and again in anarcho-punk circles is the best description: organised chaos! At least it was a base, somewhere from which we could expand on our ambitions of creating a cohesive force for change in Belfast and beyond.

"All along our main goal was to set up our own centre. We had our drop-in at Just Books, we'd a practice space in a disused upstairs room in Dubarry's Bar in Belfast's notorious red light district, and we had a regular venue in the Labour Club. It all worked, but we needed somewhere we could do things on our own terms, whenever we wanted to. I suppose the real momentum for what was to become known as Giro's started in the Unemployed Centre, which opened in the mid-Eighties and proved a perfect opportunity for us. They needed an unemployed group to give them some credibility, and we needed a new practice area as the Dubarry's regulars were getting sick of us. The Rathcoole Self-Help Group, especially Roy from Toxic Waste, were instrumental in getting us a space there, where we could practice, meet, and eventually work out of.

"But Giro's was nothing more than a mirror held up to all of those who were preaching high ideals. It was the culmination of the thousands of hours of pontificating we'd clocked up since the early Eighties. It was the place of our own we'd worked towards for so long… it was also a weight around the neck of the few who ditched their utopian expectations and actually got involved in the nitty-gritty chore of keeping the place open and running. It was no coincidence that, not long after Giro's established itself as something more than a vague hope, heroin hit the Belfast punk scene – that good old punk tradition of the self destructive versus the constructive. To give this some perspective though, Giro's wasn't about the Warzone Collective, or Stalag 17, or any other band for that matter; it was a huge concerted effort which involved many, many diverse elements, most of which had nothing to do with punk, let alone anarcho punk. A comprehensive account of the place will be created one day, so here is not the time or place to go into any further details of it."

As an obvious result of relationships established with bands such as Conflict, Stalag 17 entered Matrix Studios in Kirkubben [which subsequently became Jingle Jangle] and recorded 'Society's Fairytale', which was included on Mortarhate's 'We Don't Want Your Fuckin' War' compilation (prior to then, the band had only ever recorded two-tracks, 'Stalag 17' and 'Smash The Front', on a four-track Portastudio owned by Greg Cowan of The Outcasts). The album shot to No. 4 in the Indie charts, and the ensuing interest in the tracks from Stalag 17 and Toxic Waste led to the split 12" between the two bands on Mortarhate. To promote the record, Stalag 17 embarked on an ill-fated UK tour.

"Well, 'promoting records' wasn't something we were aware of, when we embarked on our tour of Scotland and England; we were just getting favours returned and using whatever contacts we had to get a few gigs for ourselves, Asylum and Anathema [the Belfast version]. It was only really a tour in terms of travelling as well; in terms of gigs, it was mostly playing support slots or having gigs cancelled… but only hearing about this upon our arrival! On one of these occasions, we strongly suspected that there hadn't even been a gig arranged in the first place. None of this mattered though, as we just made the most of it… i.e. got pissed a lot.

"The downside was that we were skint fairly promptly. Even the gigs that did go ahead paid very little, if anything. So, when the cam shaft of our minibus fell off somewhere in Wiltshire, and the flush Fra McGaughey [the band's 'joint No. 1 devotee, alongside Ernie Luney'; he also did a short stint as vocalist for Asylum] bailed us out with his reserves, our last hope for petrol money to get us home were the gigs in Bristol and Telford… both of which – we learned on arrival – had been cancelled. So, it was two nights of nectarine wine, scrumpy [cider], opium poppy tea, and siphoning petrol in Bristol to get us to Telford, where we hung out for a few days more, before we siphoned our way back up to Stranraer.

"We never did tour with Toxic Waste, either, despite the split release, but we played with them

Stalag 17's Mickey at the Anarchy Centre.

a lot, in and around Belfast. I think the only time we actually travelled with them as a band was when we went over for one of the Stop The City demos in London (the one the Subhumans wrote 'Rats' about, in fact) and played with Conflict and the Subhumans [at Dickie Dirt's in Camberwell] together."

Then, in late 1985, Gaskey and Mickey left, just as the band had been offered a place on the very first release from (soon to be) influential Welsh label, Words Of Warning. The 'You Are Not Alone' single was a four-way split, Stalag 17 sharing vinyl space with Oi Polloi, Hex and Symbol Of Freedom, but rather than search for new members, Petesy and Joe handled the recording of their track, 'Harmless Fun', all themselves. Joe played the bass, and the multi-talented Petesy did the rest... although when they undertook a three-week European tour in early '86, Petesy ended up drumming, Joe singing, and Jim and Brian from Asylum were drafted for bass and guitar duties respectively.

Upon their return, Jim became a permanent member, albeit on guitar, allowing Joe and Petesy to resume their former roles and recruit new drummer Molloy. Tracks were contributed to the 'We Will Be Free' split LP with Toxic Waste and Asylum, and two final demos – 'And All The Birdies Sang Fuck This For A Lark' and 'Erection 87' – were recorded on Marty from Toxic Waste's four-track studio, before Stalag 17 disbanded following a disappointing gig on Tayport Beach, near Dundee.

"Some guy... Cody, I think... had asked us to come over for an all-day punk event. En route, we played a gig in Glasgow, that Alan [Axe Of Freedom fanzine] may have possibly helped us out with? Anyway, the Glasgow gig was fine, but I suppose, by this stage, I was ready for something else and Stalag wasn't as much fun as it had been. Then the others disappeared on the day of the Tayport Beach gig, and I had to spend most of the afternoon running in and out of town, and in and out of bars, searching for them, so when we went on, much later than we were supposed to have, and played a set far below par because the boys were pissed, I decided I'd had enough. There was no big blow-out, and no melodramatic showdowns; we just went back to Belfast and the band wasn't mentioned again for a long time."

Petesy went on to form FUAL (alongside Joe for a short while... they eventually released the 'Fuck Up And Live' LP on Ian Armstrong's Meantime Records in 1990), and has played with "a string of bands... too many to mention..." since, although recently he drummed for Shame Academy, alongside ex-members of Rudi and The Outcasts, and is now back with Mickey in an as-yet-unnamed "punk fucking rock group".

"Well, I'm not sure that we were any more outspoken than any of the other anarcho-punk bands really," ponders Petesy on the band's legacy. "After all, surely that was what it was about. I was (and still am!) an opinionated type, and having the opportunity to be this way in front of an audience was just too tantalising. But, as far as I was concerned, I'd ditched my political commitments when I walked away from Irish Republican politics. I regarded my commitments in the anarcho-punk scene as more social than political. A subtle distinction I know, but those social commitments led me to many varied campaigns and actions over the years, the most enduring of which was my continued involvement with Giro's, that sadly closed its doors in 2003 – RIP! These days, I just seethe at the state of the world and wonder where next…?

"I was always a punk, first and foremost. To me, punk was the embodiment of anarchist principles in that it advocated getting off your arse and creating something. I suppose the political anarchist theory missing from this principle was creating something that was constructive, inclusive and open, as opposed to creating self-indulgent chaos, because that was what the papers told you punk was. Getting pissed and 'out of it' was obviously great fun (and still can be), but there had to be something more to punk than that. The anarcho scene created an identity of punk that was defined by ideals rather than outward appearance. Yes, Crass donned their black uniforms before getting onstage – and we all copied them, because copying your rock heroes was what you did – but beyond the image was something of great depth, which wasn't motivated by self-interest. I was glad to leave the ranks of Kings Road-influenced punks and become a fully paid up (DIY dividends, of course!) member of the Epping Forest militia…

"Because anarcho-punk wasn't a trend; it was a community. And through that community, I met people who will be friends for life. I had my ideals challenged and I challenged the ideals of others. It's not so much a case of the ideals staying with me, more the process. It taught me the importance of defending my principles, whilst at the same time being flexible enough to think and act outside the confines of punk.

"And it's a very real possibility that, had I not got involved in punk and in Stalag 17, I would have drifted into a world not of my own choosing. I've watched close friends get sucked back into that world over the years, and when I meet some of them now, they've misery written all over their faces. I'm still pretty far from realising my own dreams, and I still have many demons to face, but so far I'm pretty fucking happy with what I've achieved and who I've achieved it with."

SELECT DISCOGRAPHY

7"s:
'You Are Not Alone' (Words Of Warning, 1986) – split with Oi Polloi, Hex and Symbol Of Freedom

12"s:
'The Truth Will Be Heard' (Mortarhate, 1985) – split with Toxic Waste

LPs:
'We Will Be Free' (Belfast, 1986) – split with Toxic Waste and Asylum

At A Glance:
Petesy one day intends to release a re-mastered retrospective Stalag 17 CD, and he can be contacted directly at: petesyb@yahoo.com

Mining a completely different musical vein to Stalag 17 and Toxic Waste was **HIT PARADE**, the quirky (often irritatingly so) project of Dave Hyndman from the aforementioned Just Books shop, ably assisted by members of Crass, most notably Penny Rimbaud and Eve Libertine. The 7", 12" and LP he released with them were a funky mish-mash of electronics, samples and tape loops that ranged from the great ('Here's What You Find In Any Prison', off the 1982 'Bad News' debut EP) to the frankly horrible (most of the 'Nick Nack Paddy Wack' album!), but they fit well into the eclectic Crass Records catalogue and all pulsed with an almost tangible outrage at the atrocities the British government were perpetrating in Northern Ireland.

"Dave was a bit older than many of us," reckons Toxic Waste's Roy Wallace. "He came through the hippy era and was involved in the Carpenters Club, which later became the Anarchy Centre, and was partly aimed at providing a safe haven for gay men and bewildered punks in Belfast during the late Seventies and early Eighties. He was a bit like your uncle, I suppose, jaded with life and always critical of everything no matter what it was, but passionate and political at the same time, and even though I didn't agree with his Republican views a lot of the time, he was definitely a catalyst for change.

"My impression of Dave was as this one-man-band sat outside of the punk, and anarcho punk, music scene we helped create in Belfast; I would guess he had more in common with Crass and Flux and the political art bands than with any of us really. It was a weird relationship; he came across as critical yet helpful, but never really engaged with any of us politically at that time… then again he was much older, and we were still quite young then, so there was probably a generational challenge!

"And I thought his music was shite!" adds Roy, laughing, "But I liked his approach and his ability to do everything on his own. The lyrics were basically rants, all about Dave's take on life; they never inspired me as such, but he definitely did!"

And that statement from Roy helps explain just why Hit Parade lives on in the memory of so many Ulster punks – apart from the raw, infectious energy of the first single, it certainly wasn't the music that defined Dave Hyndman, but his selfless devotion to helping create an alternative future for the youth of Northern Ireland.

"Yeah, he always struck me as central to a lot of the alternative media activity in Belfast," agrees Roy, "Yet he remained peripheral to any engagement with the Warzone Centre which we set up… always critical of everything we did, but there to help if you asked him. He gave advice and helped facilitate meetings and dialogue, and let us use the resources at both Just Books and Northern Visions [the video production company he later set up]. I think the mixture of youth from all over the city challenged a lot of his generation's politics, which I would attempt to describe as libertarian with Irish Nationalist/Republican tendencies… whereas we were naively opposed to the whole fucking lot of them!

"The same situation existed with Chumbawamba and various other UK bands who would take the safe and easy route of supporting the Republican movement to the detriment of the anarchist scene in Belfast, but Hit Parade, and Dave Hyndman, are not easily categorised into such a neat box, as, although he was very critical of the alternative punk and anarchist movements, he was also active within a whole range of political causes.

"If I'm honest though, I didn't get to know Dave well enough to make any real comment on his politics; I am only offering my opinion formed from observations made during the early Eighties. He was basically a grumpy old bastard who always had something negative to say about the world, but I admired him for his unique ability to criticise you and help you out in the same sentence. He never really made an impact musically, but then I don't think that was his intention or motivation; he preferred to snipe from the sidelines with his sharp, witty observations on life in Belfast… the Lord loved Hit Parade's Uncle Dave – and so did we!"

SELECT DISCOGRAPHY

7"s:
'Bad News' (Crass, 1982)

12"s:
'Plastic Culture' (Crass, 1984)

LPs:
'Nick Nack Paddy Wack' (Crass, 1986)

At A Glance:
Dave's finest moment, 'Here's What You Find In Any Prison', appears on the
1993 Crass compilation CD, 'A-Sides Part 2, 1982-1984'.

A recent picture (2005) of the irrepressible Oi Polloi, live in Sweden.

CHAPTER NINE

Edinburgh's **OI POLLOI** were fairly unique as far as anarcho bands go in that they took the principles and ideologies of anarchism but delivered them via the rousing singalong style of classic Oi! This gave them tremendous crossover appeal between the all-too-often-divided factions of street punk and anarcho punk, and at least allowed them to take their potent lyrical observations to an audience possibly unused to such a positive, intelligent message. They remain one of the most passionate, unique punk bands in the world, nowadays writing and releasing records in their own indigenous Gaelic language, an articulate protest against Anglo-American globalisation.

"In 1976, I was only ten years old, so I just missed getting excited about the Pistols," explains vocalist Deek Allan, on his own introduction to punk rock. "But I got a radio shortly after that and it was listening to John Peel and Mike Read on Radio One at night and hearing stuff like The Jam, Stiff Little Fingers and The Skids that got me into it... 'In The City' by The Jam was the first LP I bought, and 'Into The Valley' by The Skids the first single; fucking magic... the music was just so new and exciting at the time, it really was magic. Then when I heard Peel playing the Cockney Rejects and heard the vocalist just yelling out the lyrics with no attempt at singing, it was such a contrast to most of the totally bland shite in the charts like the fucking Bee Gees or whatever, it just really struck a chord with me. Thank fuck for that too, 'cos the music really changed my life totally: saved me from a life of slaving away in some shitty job for some tosser of a boss anyway. And I know there are thousands more who'd tell you the same thing – for all its faults, we've a hell of a lot to thank punk for."

The band formed in 1981, Deek being joined by school friends, guitarist Spook, drummer Seal and Mark Millar... on keyboards!

"We hadn't been able to find a bassist, and since he happened to have an old keyboard lying around we roped him in and he set the sound to a kind of bass guitar noise," guffaws Deek. "I've still got some classic practice tapes lying around from before our first gig where you can hear these ridiculous synth 'bass lines' in all these Cockney Rejects and 4-Skins songs – fucking classic!

"Our one reason for forming was just that we were totally pissed off with watching these shitty Rolling Stones cover bands or similar, playing at these charity rock concerts our school held every term. Both we and a lot of our mates who went to these things were into punk and Oi!, and we wanted to see that reflected in the school bands that played, but they were almost always just posers from the fifth and sixth year doing fucking covers of Genesis or whatever, and it was doing our heads in. We soon realised that if we wanted to change this, we'd just have to do it ourselves… so we did!"

Indeed, Oi Polloi's first gig was during autumn 1981 in their school assembly hall, which – against all the odds – was a roaring success.

"Everyone thought we wouldn't actually be able to play and would be total shit… in fact, one of the main reasons that we'd got on the bill was because the entertainment committee folk thought we were so bad we'd be really funny! I remember one of the sixth form guys from the committee coming to listen to us practice and just burying his head in his hands as we blasted out the Cockney Reject's terrace anthem, 'East End', with that classic football chant chorus; he thought we were just terrible.

"What the organisers didn't seem to realise though was that a lot of other kids liked our kind of music, and folk also liked the fact that we were lively and energetic; they didn't just want some guitar-wanking bullshit and posing, they wanted some rocking entertainment, and we gave it to them! The place was packed with over 400 folk, so when I first got on the stage under the lights, I was totally shitting it and thinking, 'What the fuck am I doing here?' But there wasn't really any escape, so we just had to go for it. After the first number ('New Song' by the Rejects, I think…), the place erupted with everyone cheering like anything, 'cos they'd never had a band like this at these concerts before, and also 'cos we could actually play – admittedly not very well, but good enough to do the job! So, we battered through our set of Rejects, 4-Skins and Blitz covers and everyone loved it. It was fucking brilliant fun, so afterwards we thought, 'We want to do this again… and again!' Our initial idea of just doing one gig to liven up these charity concerts seemed pretty limited now, so things just took off from there; it's funny looking back on it all now… I never thought it would all get so out of control!"

Oi Polloi lurched on for about a year as little more than a good-time party band, their set nothing but covers, but once they began writing their own material they became very prolific very quickly, at about the same rate they were honing their urgent sense of social justice. Soon they had enough material to justify entering Pier House Studios in Granton, Edinburgh (where they have since recorded all of their releases… "It's used by quite a few local punk bands, but also a lot of folk artists… we even had the pleasure once of recording over an old Proclaimers master!"), to commit their compositions to tape.

"It amazes me sometimes, in some of the places we play abroad, where we might be playing with some young band and they have all their own gear!" says Deek incredulously. "You know, a bunch of seventeen-year-olds with Marshall stacks and so on… we still don't have our own backline after all these years, and their parents have just handed it to them on a plate or something! When we started out, our guitarist only had a shitty wee fifteen-watt practice amp; I had no mike at all so I just shouted, and our drummer had to augment his rudimentary drum-kit, which only consisted of a snare, bass drum and hi-hat, with a couple of buckets of fertiliser in place of tom-toms! Eventually I got a cheap plastic mike for a tenner, and we literally made a couple of mike-stands ourselves in the metal-work class at school, which was pretty DIY looking back on it. We used to practice in our drummer's dad's garage but eventually the inevitable noise complaints forced us to seek other premises and getting a practice place was always a total headache.

"For a while, we had a bassist whose dad had some office out of town on this industrial estate, so we got to practice there at weekends, when there was no one around, and that was great. It all stopped soon enough though, when his dad went mental and decided he hated punks after someone sprayed an anarchy sign over the bonnet of his car one night! Thankfully, we had a few mates whose parents let us practice every once in a while in their houses, so we pretty much had a different practice place every week in various schoolmates' cellars and so on. Then we met this guy, Jason, whose parents were separated and who stayed with his dad who was often away, leaving

Deek of Oi Polloi at the Old Arts Centre, Wood Green, London, Oct 1985, picture by Paul May.

his teenage son on his own... with the inevitable result that every night was party night! And this often coincided with our band practices, which was great; we'd practise for a bit and then get pissed on the contents of his dad's drinks cabinet... or buzz butane lighter fuel to get out of it, which was incredibly fucking stupid, but a lot of fun at the time!

"We played some classically bad gigs, some real crackers, in the early days when we didn't really know what we were doing," laughs Deek ruefully. "One time we played at this community festival in Tollcross in Edinburgh, at this social centre open day, and, as it was during the afternoon, our drummer couldn't make it as he couldn't get out of school. We also had no bassist at the time, so it was just me and the guitarist. He played guitar and sang (into a mike which was held by a mate sticking his arm out from where he was hiding behind a curtain, as we didn't even have a mike stand!) and I attempted to play the drums... which was a very bad idea. I can't play drums at all, and it was so bad that some random guy in the audience just said, 'Look, I'll play the fucking drums – you've got to stop!' That improved things a bit, but then this karate demonstration started in the next room so everyone fucked off to watch that, and we were left playing in this big hall to just one person who must have stayed behind out of pity... pretty ridiculous really.

"A couple of days later, as part of the same festival, we ended up getting booked to play at this under-18s fashion show in this night club, with us as 'special guest live band'. This time, we had three guitarists to make up for the lack of bassist and not very loud amps. We reckoned that three 40-watt amps would be the same as a 120-watt one, but of course it just made this horrendous racket. Added to that was the fact that most of our mates hadn't been let in; we'd only got one in by claiming he was a backing vocalist, and we thought the management would just forget about him, but, just as we went on stage, they thrust a mike into his hand and pushed him on with us. And, as he didn't know any of the words, he just staggered around shouting 'Oi! Oi!' all the way through the set! It really was atrocious, and we ended up getting canned off the stage by angry trendies, who pelted us with soft drinks cans until we had to escape out the back door – classic!"

By the time the band released their debut 'Destroi The System' demo in 1983, comprising nine songs recorded over three sessions at Pier House, Deek was unsurprisingly the only original member left (apart from Spook, who played guitar on just the opening track, 'Punx And Skinz'), with Ozzy now on bass, Guv on drums, and both Rat and Gav on guitars.

"For what it's worth," sighs Deek, "Gav went on to become a biologist who happily took part in vivisection. When I last heard of Spook, he was a smack dealer in Glasgow, and Guv went on to become a neo-Nazi! Rat later became an archaeologist and came back to record with us on later material, and Ozzy, after a couple of years on the road as a traveller, now works in nature conservation; he still drives for us occasionally on tour."

Regardless of where the members who recorded it have ended up, 'Destroi The System' is a fine opening gambit; admittedly it's rough around the edges, and extremely simplistic lyrically compared to what was still to come, but it's gnarly and powerful with the obligatory Rejects influence shining through on all the good, shouty choruses.

"Initially we probably wouldn't have even described ourselves as a punk band," admits Deek, rather surprisingly. "We were just kids listening to stuff like the Rejects, although obviously we did love some punk stuff like SLF and local Scottish groups like The Skids, and The Rezillos from Fife. We mainly liked the fact that folk like the Rejects just looked like us: scruffy herberts and boot boys. We didn't have to have fancy hair or whatever, although the Oi thing, at the start at least, before it became so skinhead orientated, was pretty inclusive of punks and all sorts. Later

Oi Polloi, 1982 (left to right: Rat, Ozzy, Deek, and Guv).

though, as we got more and more dissatisfied with the... er... extremely limited nature of most Oi bands' lyrics, and discovered bands like Discharge, Crass and Icons of Filth, we started to gravitate more and more quickly to the anarcho-punk side of things.

"Seeing Discharge live in '82 really got me and Ozzy totally into them, and seeing Icons Of Filth in Glasgow for the first time had a big influence too; they were fucking amazing, and blew Conflict, who had never particularly impressed us, away. I rushed straight out and got their 'Onward Christian Soldiers' LP, which is a work of genius. That song 'Sod The Children' was actually the trigger for getting me to give up eating meat, and it wasn't that long 'til most of the others followed suit. It really is a tragedy that their singer Stig died so young, when he still had so much to offer.

"Anyway, by 1984, when we were doing miners' benefit gigs during the miners' strike and taking part in the Stop The City protests etc., we most definitely regarded ourselves as part of the anarcho-punk scene, no question about it."

Suitably inspired, Oi Polloi (by now comprising Deek, Rat, Guv and bassist Rab) recorded six songs for the 'Unlimited Genocide' split LP with Loanhead (a small mining village near Edinburgh)'s A.O.A. in 1985, by which time they had honed their sound to a caustic sonic attack that was almost impossible to ignore. The LP didn't actually see the light of day, through Children Of The Revolution, until late summer 1986; it was a modest Indie success upon its release, spending five weeks in the chart and reaching No. 13. By then though, the band had added a second guitarist Mike and had recorded and released not only their debut 7" – 'Resist The Atomic Menace' for Steve Beatty of Plastic Head's Endangered Musik label (aptly enough, it came out just months after the nuclear power accident at Chernobyl in the former USSR, that killed 30 people and resulted in 135,000 Ukrainians being evacuated from their homes) – but also one side of the 'Skins And Punks, Volume Two' split LP with Betrayed, for Roddie Moreno of The Oppressed's Oi Records. So, five years without a vinyl release, and then three records out in the space of eighteen months! Not bad going, but Oi Polloi maintained their considerable momentum with continuous gigging and the release of their first full-length album, 'Unite And Win'.

"That was recorded in two sessions as we never had enough money to do it all at once," reveals Deek. "This time Rat returned on guitar for the first side, and, as Rab had now left, we brought in our old schoolmate Muz on bass. He had been in the band shortly after we had started at school, and he had played drums, bass and guitar with us at various times! He'd later been expelled from school, and his parents had sent him then to a pretty posh, fee-paying school, away from home. We were amazed when he then wrote to us saying that Spike [real name Chris Low], the drummer of London-based punk band, The Apostles, who were famous for all their Class War anti-rich rhetoric, was in his class at this private school, but it turned out to be true. When we met him, the guy was a good laugh though, and certainly no toff, so we got him in on drums and he played on this first side of the album, and toured with us on our first Euro-tour. He now spends most of his time in Japan, where he is going out with some Japanese porn star or something!"

"I was never really an official member of Oi Polloi though," clarifies Chris. "Basically, whenever they were without a drummer, and had a record or gigs coming up, I'd help out. The first record I did with them was the 'Unite And Win' album, on which I was credited as 'Skullhead'... in reality I had my hair down to my arse by then, and was running acid house clubs! I also did their 'Punk Aid' single, and a few other things, plus a month-long European tour, which was a brilliant laugh.

"I suppose the main difference between them and The Apostles was that Oi Polloi were a punk band with a capital 'P', which The Apostles certainly weren't. And also Oi Polloi actually played gigs, which The Apostles generally didn't... well, apart from weird one-off 'musique concrete'-type events, where they'd play amplified printing presses and stuff with feedback and tape cut-ups over the top! So, there was a much more 'social' aspect to Oi Polloi, which I really enjoyed; I met some really nice people on tour..."

"To be honest though," continues Deek, "I think the first side of 'Unite And Win', along with perhaps the 'Omnicide' single, has to rate as one of the worst Oi Polloi recordings... although there do seem to be plenty people who like them well enough. Operating on a DIY shoestring budget, money has always been a problem for us and we've always been recording against the clock, so if anything goes wrong in the studio, it's a total disaster – and that happened in both these cases. I don't think there's anything wrong with the sound or the actual songs really, but for some reason on both occasions we just really couldn't get it together, and both drummers had really bad days, so the tracks came out really sloppy. I've got practice tapes of the stuff where it sounded great, but on the day we fucked up, and we just didn't have money to re-do it, which has always been a source of constant frustration. If we'd had a fraction of the recording budgets of a group like The Exploited, we could've done some real classic stuff, but there you go; beggars can't be choosers, I suppose!

"Another classic low-point, from a lyrical point of view at least, would have to be this ancient song 'Skinhead', although with lines like 'Skinhead on his own, head shaved to the bone, writing skinhead slogans on a public phone', it is thankfully pretty difficult to take too seriously! There've been a few other cringe-worthy moments too, like the infamous 'Whale Song', but then again a lot of people say they liked it, and the rest had a good laugh, so I think everyone's happy really."

By the time they recorded the other side of the album though, Guv was back behind the kit, albeit briefly, with Dave joining on bass, and Arthur playing alongside Rat on second guitar. Arthur added a distinctly metal edge to proceedings that really suited Oi Polloi and stayed with the band for their next two releases, before leaving to join The Exploited. Firstly, yet another split LP in 1987, this time with Aberdeen's Toxik Ephex (entitled 'Mad As…', it appeared on that band's own label, Green Vomit), and then 1988's 'Outrage' 7", both rabid slabs of intelligent, tuneful punk.

"Everyone has their own idea of what exactly 'punk' means, and I suppose, to some people, The Exploited are the epitome of punk," offers Deek, on Edinburgh's most famous punk export. "That's not a view we'd hold now though, and their idea of anarchy as espoused in 'I Believe In Anarchy' is not one we share either! That said though, as a fifteen year old, I did rush out to buy 'Punk's Not Dead', as did the rest of the band, and the first ever song we tried to play at our very first practice was 'SPG' off that same LP. I've seen them live a few times and they are always entertaining, but it's a completely different philosophy from what we're about really… each to their own though.

"I don't know Wattie, but a lot of the other guys from the band I've met have been really sound. His brother Willie is a really nice guy, and Big John even lent us a practice amp from time to time in the early days, which was good of him, but Wattie described us in one 'zine interview as 'a waste of electricity'… pretty good that, actually; made us laugh anyway. They didn't have that much of an effect on us really, except in that, when we first started looking for gigs around Edinburgh in the early Eighties, it was fucking difficult, because as soon as the promoters found out you were a punk band, they didn't want to know, because the aggro at a lot of early Exploited gigs had really made them wary of booking local punk bands; that was a real pain in the arse and it held back a lot of bands here."

Probably the best Oi Polloi album, 'In Defence Of Our Earth' (that saw Muz rejoining on bass, Dan on drums and Chris from Clydebank band State Of Decay on guitar), appeared in 1990 on Welsh label, Words Of Warning; it remains a highlight not only for the band's sterling musical performance, but for some brave, sincere words from Deek. As well as the aforementioned 'Whale Song', you had the likes of 'When Two Men Kiss', that challenged stereotypical homophobic attitudes, 'Free The Henge' that questioned state oppression of the annual Stonehenge free festival, and 'Nazi Scum', a self-explanatory title for a song that has landed the – primarily pacifist – band in a few scary scrapes over the years.

"We've had run-ins with Nazis in several countries, and that has usually resulted in the fash [i.e. fascists] getting a kicking thanks to the locals, but when we played in Tallinn in Estonia it was a very close thing, and we were lucky to get out of it in one piece. We were touring with these Finnish bands at the time, and had been put on the bill with them and a bunch of Estonian bands who we didn't know anything about. Well, we watched some of the bands, including a local punk

Deek live in Edinburgh, 1983.

band who were good and some local rock and roll band, and then went out to our bus to cook up some food. When we came back the Finns told us, 'You're not gonna believe this! They just had some fucking Nazi skinhead band play, with songs like 'Niggers Back To The Jungle'! And, sure enough, when we looked around, we could see that a whole bunch of dodgy-looking bonehead fuckers had come in. It was a pretty fucked-up situation, 'cos we were totally outnumbered in a strange country, but we decided to go on and speak out about how fucked-up fascism and racism are, and so, between every song we gave it all the standard stuff about how they would be the first to go if the fash ever got into power, how the real enemy wasn't 'the Jews controlling the government', as some of these idiots had been claiming, but the rich etc. etc. Well, anyway, after a few numbers, these two boneheads came up to me and said, 'You say you are against Nazis?' And I said, 'Yeah', and explained why, to which they responded, 'Well, we are Nazis!' At which point I lost patience and just said, 'Well, you better fuck off then!'

"They hit me in the face, I hit them back with the mike-stand, and it all kicked off, with us having to try to fight our way out of the venue with absolutely no help from any of the local audience, who seemed to think that this was all part of the entertainment…! In fact, the only folk who lifted a finger to help us were the two ethnic Russian bar owners, these two Josef Stalin look-a-likes in their fifties who produced these lumps of wood from behind the bar and laid into the Nazi fuckers. As none of us are 'hard men', we were really lucky to get out of there. The Finns had windows in their van smashed, and, as we were getting into our bus it was totally surrounded by all these boneheads (who were now joined by half the punks, I might add), kicking fuck out of it as we tried to drive away. I'm just glad we all emerged unscathed while several of those Nazi bastards would have needed hospital treatment afterwards, the fucking dickheads…

"There have been a few other close shaves, like the time we played in Dublin in this upstairs function room and I was just about to get a kicking from these Catholic boneheads for playing our pro-choice song, 'The Right to Choose', when suddenly the pub went up in flames as there had been some argument between a couple of traveller families who had been drinking downstairs. One group left, broke into the other group's van, which was parked up the street, set it on fire and rolled it down the hill straight into the downstairs bar and burnt the place down! Fucking mental…

"We've had full-blown riots at some gigs too – two in particular in Edinburgh which ended in mass violence, both due to police basically attacking folk… the same in Leeds and Potsdam, which ended up with burning police vehicles and hundreds of police from Berlin with water-cannons etc. In Poland recently, outside our gig, we had cops firing plastic bullets at punks armed only with snowballs; it was fucking horrible. And it makes you feel a bit weird when you play at a place like Faslane peace camp, where, last time we were there, playing outside the gate, half the audience were cops armed with machine guns!"

After returning from a tour of the US to find their girlfriends had left them, Chris and Dan decided they'd had enough of lengthy touring, leaving Deek to recruit Gilly, from Airdrie's 4 Past Midnight, on guitar, local drummer Murray (who now plays with the hardcore band In Decades Decline), and Calum, formerly of East Kilbride band Jimmy Saville's Wheelchair, on bass; this line-up gave us 1993's 'Guilty' single and undertook some intensive international touring.

"Then Gilly left due to alcohol problems," explains Deek. "Basically all that free German beer on tour was too much for him; he had a real problem and free booze was the last thing he needed. Around this time I'd met this American guy, Brian [Tipa], from US band Blown Apart Bastards, who was over in Edinburgh on a year's exchange from his university, and when he mentioned that he played guitar and was looking for a band, we just said, 'Well, how do you fancy playing at the 1 In 12 Club in Bradford on Saturday?', as we'd just heard Gilly couldn't do it. One two-hour practice later and he was rocking the kids hard. 'How do you fancy playing in Greece next week then?' we asked, and when the answer was 'Yes!' he was officially in. He then played on our live LP from Berlin, our eponymous EP on [Polish label] Nikt Nic Nie Wie [which translates as 'Nobody Knows Anything']; he also played on and wrote a lot of the stuff for the 'Fuaim Catha' LP [Skuld, 1999] before meeting a French girl on tour, moving to France and marrying her. He's since helped us out on guitar and drums at odd gigs in recent times, and we keep in regular contact.

"After Brian left, we had a short spell with this guy Riley (Murray's brother, who is now strangely enough well on his way to becoming famous with indie band Aberfeldy) on guitar, but he didn't really seem to fit in, and when he uttered the fatal words, 'I think the Oi Polloi guitar sound should have more of an early Cramps feel', it was time to go! We were sad to ask anyone to leave the band but it's obviously worked out for the best for him now."

Riley was replaced by Matt Finch, the author of Harangue fanzine, who now also plays with In Decades Decline; he brought a heavier tinge to the band's sound that manifested itself on the 1999 Ruptured Ambitions single, 'Let The Boots Do The Talking'. Brian rejoined, back from France but this time on drums, and Oi Polloi undertook their most exhaustive touring schedule ever, all across Europe and the States, several years of hard gigging that ultimately took its toll on the band's line-up yet again.

"I remember doing one interview where bassist Calum said, 'My girlfriend lives in America, so I don't get to see her much.' And Matt chimed in with, 'My girlfriend lives in the same room as me, but we're always on tour, so I don't get to see her either!' He eventually decided to leave, so that he could have some kind of ordinary life. His replacement came in the form of long-time Edinburgh underground scene stalwart, Ricky of Rub The Buddha, who had been heavily involved in stuff like the Edinburgh punks picnics and festivals for years; he wrote and played on the 'THC' EP [for German label, Campary], but left shortly afterwards when the two of us fell out over a really stupid incident in the pub. I was drunk and rude to him, and when I tried to apologise he, with some good reason, had been having a go at me… unluckily though, an old mate of mine, the ex-singer of AOA actually, had come out that night, despite having not been to any gigs for years, and when he saw Ricky – who he didn't know and who had short hair at the time, and had just been drinking with some skinheads – shouting angrily at me, he put two and two together and made five and mistakenly thought he was some kind of fascist, and half strangled him before I could make him stop!"

After spending time with a Polish girl, Yaga, on guitar (formerly of Polish band, Disgusting Lies; she later married ex-Oi Polloi drummer, Ade, who played on the 'THC' single, with whom she then played with in Disorder for a while), Ricky rejoined, and Oi Polloi finally settled into a stable line-up around 2001 (not bad going, only twenty years after their inception!) of Ricky and Calum, drummer Cam, with the stoical Deek now a veritable institution behind the mike. This incarnation of the band has already been responsible for the 'Alive And Kicking' CD, recorded at a recent show in Switzerland, a new 7" (2006) on Finnish label Kamaset Levyt, and a split 12" with Israeli band Nikmat Olalim for Campary.

"I think the energy to keep the band going comes from the fact that we all love the music and what we're doing so much," says Deek, of his unwavering dedication to Oi Polloi, "coupled with the fact that none of us have the kind of outside work or obligations that prevent us from doing it. We obviously have to work from time to time (the band actually loses us money rather than making it, which may come as a surprise to some people) but we're not in positions where we can't still get plenty of time to rock, and none of us has kids either, which gives us a lot more free time and energy.

"I mean even I've ended up working now," he laughs incredulously, "as a television producer of all things! But despite my views on TV in general, I work on Gaelic language programmes, which is supporting the indigenous minority culture here in Scotland, so that totally squares with my ideals about supporting diversity and fighting this one-world monoculture that big business wants to foist on us all... and our next project is even a programme about a Gaelic language punk band called Mill a h-Uile Rud, so I'm bringing political punk rock to the masses, and there's nothing wrong with that!"

Indeed, the band's own commitment to save endangered languages that began with the 'Fuaim Catha' LP reached a natural conclusion with the 2003 'Carson?' single, that was entirely in Gaelic, although thankfully also with a translation for the less enlightened souls amongst us.

"Well, there's negative and positive," reckons the vocalist on his lyrical impetus. "Every time I see some fucker like Bush, Sharon or Blair coming out with some of their shite on the TV or whatever, that's an inspiration to stand up and fight back against the kind of evil they're involved in. Every time I hear about some new crime perpetrated by some multinational company etc., that just makes you say, 'Fuck that! We're not taking this shit!' These fuckers are not gonna get away with that without resistance and folk like us raising our voices against it. So, basically, all the shit in the world is an inspiration on the one hand, and, on the positive side, all the kind feed-back and support we get from folk who write to us or meet us at gigs when we're on tour; that really keeps us going too. When you meet folk who tell you that they stopped eating meat as a result of listening to one of your records, or that they formed their own band or got involved in anti-fascist action or hunt-sabbing or squatting, or whatever other kind of direct action, as a result of our stuff, then that really shows you that it's something worthwhile that we're doing.

"We had a couple of letters from folk who told us that they used to be into fascist shit like Skrewdriver until they started listening to us, and to me that alone makes it all worthwhile; if we've changed two people from being potentially active neo-Nazis into anti-fascists that's maybe saved some innocent folk from being attacked and injured or worse by them, and that's reason enough for me to keep going. I read a piece once in some zine too, where the writer talked about how they'd contemplated suicide but how bands like Oi Polloi and the Subhumans had made them realise they weren't alone, and so they'd been able to draw strength from that to carry on etc. Stuff like that is good to know.

"Then again, every fuckin' hypocritical band we see ripping people off, or selling out, is an inspiration to us to keep on doing things the DIY way, to show that there are still some of us here who can't be bought and who are not in it for money, or some kind of fucked-up status. We never broke up and fucked off when things got hard; we've always been here and put our money where our mouth is. People know that and when they tell us that that inspires them, well, that in turn encourages us to keep on going. I should emphasise too that we don't plan on stopping anytime soon either, so you'll have to put up with us for a while yet, I'm afraid, ha!

"People are always knocking punk and saying it can't change anything, but that is bullshit. You look at any political direct action group, like, say, an AFA group, or a hunt sabs group, or a bunch of politically motivated squatters, or whatever, and there are almost always numerous punks or ex-punks involved. Punk music can open people's eyes, make them think and inspire them to action, and that has concrete results in the real world. To think otherwise is to be pretty naive. The dog rescued from a laboratory by activists inspired to direct action and involvement in animal rights by an Icons Of Filth record… the Nazi bonehead kicked to fuck by AFA folk inspired by the Blaggers… the squatted community centre providing cheap nutritious vegan food to the local unemployed and pensioners set up by folk inspired by Crass… the woodland saved from destruction by Earth First activists, first encouraged to get involved in direct action by anarcho punk… these things are all real examples of what political punk has, and can, accomplish. Alright, we haven't bought the system crashing to its knees, but all around the world there are hundreds of thousands of people actively involved in working towards that end, and creating alternatives to it to put into practice in their daily lives, who have been inspired to do so by their involvement in punk. This music changed my life and probably the lives of most of the readers of this book too… don't knock it!"

SELECT DISCOGRAPHY

7"s:
'Resist The Atomic Menace' (Endangered, 1986)
'Outrage' (Words Of Warning, 1988)
'Omnicide' (Words Of Warning, 1991)
'Guilty' (Ruptured Ambitions, 1993)
'Oi Polloi' (Nikt Nic Nie Wie, 1995)
'THC' (Campary, 1998)
'Let The Boots Do The Talking' (Ruptured Ambitions, 1999)
'Carson?' (Nikt Nic Nie Wie, 2003)

LPs:
'Unlimited Genocide' (COR, 1986) – split with A.O.A.
'Skins 'N' Punks, Vol. 2' (Oi, 1987) – split with Betrayed
'Mad As…' (Green Vomit, 1987) – split with Toxik Ephex
'Unite And Win' (Oi, 1987)
'In Defence Of Our Earth' (Words Of Warning, 1990)
'Fuaim Catha!' (Skuld, 1999)

At A Glance:
Step-1's 'Pigs For Slaughter' CD compiles twenty-three of the best Oi Polloi tracks ever, and comes complete with exhaustive liner notes from Deek, making it a perfect introduction to the band. If you can track down the original release on Rejected Records though, it's worth the extra effort, as that included a free DVD-R of guitarist/drummer Brian Tipa's film, 'Global Dissent: Anarchist Music And Action', much of which is about the band and the alternative circles they move in.

ormed in Stirling, Scotland, in early 1982, when all the band members were still at school, **POLITICAL ASYLUM** were an unassuming punk band that released several strong records, some hugely popular demos (their 'Fresh Hate' debut actually went on to sell in excess of 6000 copies!), and did hundreds of gigs across the UK, Europe and America. As brashly melodic as they were politically sincere, the band may not have enjoyed the same profile as some of their more successful counterparts, but they were an integral part of the fiercely independent underground scene that existed at the time.

"It was certainly completely DIY," laughs vocalist Ramsey Kanaan, who teamed up with guitarist Stephen 'Cheesy' Brown when he (Ramsey) was kicked out of the "rather gifted" new wave band, A Change In Blues, for "being too punk!" "We used to practice in each other's bedrooms; we often

Political Asylum, live Dunfermline 1984, picture by Andrew Medcalf.

didn't have a drummer, or a bass player, at various times, so it was often literally just me and Stephen… he'd put his guitar through his stereo for a bit of amplification, and I'd plunk away on the bass unamplified, and sing, or rather shout.

"When we did have a drummer, we'd play in my house… so, our thanks to my long-suffering mother, and neighbours! Of course, we didn't have much gear, but we did have non-punk friends that we could borrow stuff from, when we needed it.

"I honestly can't remember our first gig," he adds. "I think it may have been at a hall, in one of the villages near Stirling. We probably took a minibus full of friends, punks and locals, who all gleefully spat on us… fortunately, gobbing at bands died out soon after that, by and large. Our second or third gig was at our high school; it was shut down by the headmaster after four songs, 'cos he thought the dancing punks – many of whom were not from Stirling High – were 'trying to cause a riot.'

"The gigs we did play were all self-organised, self-promoted; typically they were in non-commercial venues… remember, we were pretty young, and the few bars or clubs that had live music wouldn't have booked a bunch of fifteen-year-olds! I remember booking the community centre on the estate where Stephen lived; my mother used to work voluntarily for Women's Aid, who provided shelter for battered women, and the community centre said we had to provide security, as part of us being able to book it… so me ma and a bunch of women from the shelter were our 'security' that night! Needless to say, there was no trouble!"

Originally named Distraught, at least long enough for Ramsey to paint it on the back of his leather jacket in the time-honoured punk tradition, Political Asylum recruited Chris 'Spike' Low on drums, albeit after "trying out pretty much every kid under eighteen who was vaguely into rock music and/or punk who had a drum kit or a bass", and recorded the aforementioned 'Fresh Hate' demo during late 1982. Under the guidance of engineer Steve Maclean (who enjoyed the limelight himself as part of the late Sixties pop band, Marmalade), Political Asylum tracked fourteen songs in just two days, with Ramsey handling the bass guitar for the live tracking of the music, then Steve re-recording anything that was felt to be sub-standard… which was most of it! A rather impressive debut though, if a little generic and wooden in places, the stand-out track being the anthemic 'Disarm Or Die'; although the introductory bass riff of 'Trust In Me' was instantly recognisable to fans of American hardcore, it being a note-for-note copy of one of Black Flag's finest moments, 'Six Pack'.

"Yeah, we were always happy to rip off tunes from any one, any where, any time," laughs Ramsey. "If one listens not too closely elsewhere, you can hear bits of Public Image, the Damned, Hüsker Dü, Zounds, Black Sabbath… even Dire Straits – eight whole bars of the 'Sultans Of Swing' solo lifted wholesale! I was into, very early on, through the joys of tape-trading, a lot of the stuff that was coming out of America in the early Eighties, and was also getting into some contemporary political folk music. Basically, it's fair to say that we were open to anything that had plenty of harmony and melody.

"All of the music was written by Stephen and myself; when we were growing up, he was into heavy metal and rock, whilst I was into punk and new wave. But we spent a lot of time – even before we were in the band together – hanging out, and playing each other our favourite music. He introduced me to Iron Maiden, Motörhead and Trust… I got him into Black Flag and Amebix.

"However, I suspect the main thing that set us apart from a lot of the bands of the period was that we did everything in relative isolation. We never really had the patronage of other bands, or influential figures to guide us. We never had a track on 'Bullshit Detector'; we really just did it all ourselves. We never bothered releasing a record for several years; our first 7" came out in 1985, by which time we'd in effect already released two albums, in the form of studio demos. And we didn't really care that much about the conventions and traditional stereotypes of the anarcho-punk scene… or any other scene for that matter.

"Also, most of the band weren't even punks. Stephen was never a punker, he was into rock/metal; same with Norman, the longest serving of the early bass players. I remember playing gigs with Stephen and Norman's long hair, Stephen wearing a Status Quo shirt (their 20th anniversary tour shirt, I'm sure!) and Norman wearing his brown leather waistcoat, with the Saxon patch on the back. We all looked pretty normal… we all were pretty normal! We didn't dress the part; we didn't really conform to whatever the conventions were. And while most of the band were vegetarian, some weren't, and we weren't afraid to admit that. Or that we liked different forms of music. And, of course, the music we played wasn't really punk… certainly not the formulaic stuff anyway. But it wasn't really metal either, though we had lots of guitar solos. I'm actually not quite sure why we were embraced by the underground punk scene; in the early Eighties (long before crossover), punks and metallers didn't mix. Motörhead maybe, but that was it! Yet folks really dug our music… especially skinheads, for some reason?"

What was very apparent right from that first recording though was the serious approach Ramsey took towards his lyrics, doing his level best to pen stimulating and cogent words to express his frustration at the injustices so apparent to him in modern society.

"Well, in 1979, when I was thirteen, I got into both punk and anarchism. I got into them separately, but at the same time, and they were very much connected. I bought my first Crass T-shirt that year, even though I'd never heard their music, just because it had 'Anarchy, Peace And Freedom' written on it, and I thought that was what I was into. Henceforth, I always regarded myself as an anarchist… and still do.

"Anarchism, to me, has always been a very common-sense form of theory, history and practice, based on the rather simple idea that folks are best able to organise their own lives – economically, socially, culturally, and politically – without the impediments of authority, hierarchy and the domination of others.

"I was definitely partly attracted to punk because of the politics behind it, the rebelliousness etc. Not just anarcho-punk either; most punk was at least vaguely anti-authoritarian, whether it was the Angelic Upstarts, Ruts, UK Subs, Damned, Black Flag or Husker Du.

"So, I was definitely a punk rocker, but the rest of the band most definitely weren't. Chris Low was the earliest band member that completely identified with the whole anarcho-punk thing; he tracked down and bought lots of the records, did his own anarcho zine etc.

"From an early age, I was into distributing and selling zines myself. At the infamous Zig Zag squat gig in [December] '82, I was peddling my wares out of a polythene bag, whilst this bunch of older dudes, all with beards, were sitting behind a table full of anarcho literature. Transpires they were with Housmans bookshop… I befriended them that night; they put up with me, and in many ways helped 'mentor' me in the ways of anarcho literature. Partly through their help, I started selling all sorts of more explicitly anarchist and political literature – at Political Asylum shows, and anywhere else I could…

"But it's also fair to say that no one else in the band shared my commitment to anarchism… although the rest of them were more or less sympathetic, and we were all into the way we did things… hence, virtually all our gigs were benefits. But it's probably accurate to say that I was the only person in the band that had a real understanding of anarchism, and would have called themselves 'an anarchist' as such. As discussed above, most of the band were never punk rockers… though often through the band, various folks got into various punk bands they weren't into before…"

Recruiting old school friend Norman Thomson on bass, the band relocated to Edinburgh in 1984, replacing Chris Low (who went on to join The Apostles and Oi Polloi) with 'Edinburgh punker' Tam Francis in the process. A new demo, 'Valium For The Masses', showcasing the not-inconsiderable talents of the new line-up was duly recorded, with the fretboard heroics of Brown really stealing the show, the guitarist showboating far more than was widely accepted in a scene that generally poured scorn on such rock clichés as solo spots. It should be noted that two of the songs recorded actually featured lyrics given to Ramsey by another Scottish punk band, Mutual

Political Asylum's Ramsey at an early rehearsal, 1982.

Fear; also, the backing vocals on the metallic chugger, 'A Day In A Life', were provided by Boggy, the singer of Edinburgh band, The Abused, and close friend Dallas, who would later front Darlington band, Dan.

Late '84 saw Political Asylum picked up by Bristol label, Children Of The Revolution, after Tim Bennett, the label boss, was blown away by their set at a show in Belfast, a gig no doubt precipitated in part by the large number of tapes the band were shifting at gigs and through the extensive mail network that maintained the grass-roots scene back then.

"Yes, we played this big show in Belfast (it's actually still the only time I've ever been to Ireland, and then only for a total of 24 hours); I believe it was the show that helped set up the Warzone Collective, at least in terms of money... there was Political Asylum, Subhumans, Disorder, and a bunch of other bands; Tim, who ran COR, was over with Disorder. After our set, this grubby chap came running up to us, and said we were amazing, and that he wanted to put out a record. We couldn't really understand his thick Bristol accent, and we thought he was asking if we had a record. We said, 'Nah, sorry mate, but we do have some demo tapes you can buy...' – which he did! Fortunately, for all concerned, we ended up staying in the same flat as Tim that night, and he made us understand that he actually wanted to release us himself on record, and we said 'Sure!' "

The three-track 'Winter' EP was released by COR in 1985, and sold three thousand copies within a year; a single that captured the band's atmospheric melodies to a tee, not least of all on the dreamy 'Winter Of Our Discontent' 'title track'. By this time one of Tam's Edinburgh friends, Pete Barnett, had joined on second guitar for a brief time, allowing Stephen more room for manoeuvre with some tasteful harmony solos the result.

More personality clashes within the band led to Tam's departure, and Pete walked out in sympathy, meaning that the band were back to a four-piece once they found new drummer Keith Burns. Ralph Hardie, who had overseen the single and previous demo, recorded the 1986 demo, 'Walls Have Ears', live in the band's rehearsal room straight onto his portable four-track machine. For something committed to tape under such limiting conditions, it stands up to repeat listening today remarkably well, the band's spirited performance exuding a real energy.

Norman left soon after its release though, and was replaced by Ewan Hunt, just in time to record the excellent 'Someday' mini-LP "in some studio just outside Edinburgh" with Paddy O'Connel at the helm for German label, We Bite. To promote the release Political Asylum undertook their first European tour, albeit a typically DIY affair that saw Ramsey's long-time sparring partner Stephen Brown departing the band upon its conclusion.

"That was in the days when we used to travel to gigs on National Express buses," recalls Ramsey. "Remember, we were really young and you couldn't rent a van 'til you were twenty-one, even if you had a driving license, so we just carried our guitars, and snare drum and bass drum pedal, with us. We actually did that first European tour in 1987, via train – the same principle, but with Euro-Rail passes. And that was a three week tour!

"A couple of times when we travelled to places (again, often by bus), no-one would, or could, put us up for the night… we slept one night in a bus shelter on West Bromwich High Street… and it was raining, of course! We slept the next night, on the same jaunt, in the Bull Ring Market in Birmingham city centre. That was relative luxury, 'cos we could actually sleep on the tables, so at least we were off the floor.

Later on though, we even bought a van… and blew the engine on the way South, the first time we tried to drive ourselves to a gig. That wasn't too pleasant an experience either… but, we loved to play, and we genuinely didn't mind if we were just playing to five people or 500…

"Anyway, Stephen left at the end of that first tour around Europe; basically he wanted to play more 'rock'… i.e. slower! Whilst we wanted to play more melodic punk… i.e. faster! So, we placed an ad and auditioned some folk, and got Stevie Dewar [formerly with melodic Scottish punk band, Sad Society] in on guitar."

The ensuing 'Window On The World' album saw the band locked formidably tight, and whilst Steven Dewar had some awfully big shoes to fill, he managed more than adequately, bringing some Instigators-like flourishes to his rhythm playing which helped compensate for the lack of shredding lead work. Ramsey's vocal delivery had also come on in leaps and bounds, the restrained, subtle harmonies reminiscent of mid-period works by USHC luminaries Government Issue and Dag Nasty.

But only one side of 'Window…' was studio-recorded (again with Paddy O'Connel in Edinburgh); the other was recorded live in February 1989 at the Woolmington Hall ("somewhere in Dorset"!), during a UK tour with Thatcher On Acid and Danbert Nobacon, and sounds incredibly cohesive and powerful considering that it was recorded with no overdubs onto a portable eight-track tape machine. A track from the same live recording – a cover of Wire's 'The 15th' – was also included on the 'Fuck EMI' compilation album, alongside the likes of (ironically, it would transpire) Chumbawamba.

"That was the only big UK tour we ever did, something like nineteen gigs in twenty-one days; most of the British gigs we played were one-offs, or just three or four in a row, which I guess doesn't really count as 'a tour', as such. That whole trip was pretty memorable though… partly because, by then, we were – in my humble opinion – really fucking good… and partly 'cos the entire tour was a benefit for local anti-poll tax groups. We gave the door money each night to the local group from whichever town we were playing, and we raised a lot of money on that trip…"

When Stevie moved to Holland, right after the band's sole American tour in '89, Political Asylum became a truly European entity, recruiting Leo Van Setten on bass (when Ewan Hunt emigrated to Australia) and Kees de Greef on drums, recording the 'How The West Was Won' 10" for [acclaimed punk graphic artist] John Yates's Allied Recordings label in Holland in 1991. Another great release (this time the regular studio side complemented by an acoustic side, recorded during a live session for a Dutch radio station), it was also the final release for Political Asylum, who ground to a halt when faced with the logistical problems of doing a band with friends who live hundreds of miles away across a considerable tract of very deep water.

"Yeah, the international band thing is hard to do, and it all just kind of trundled to a halt, which was fine... although, if I remember rightly, we did one last European tour in '93, probably a dozen or so gigs. Stevie was actually living in Germany by that time; it was me and him, and we just got these German friends of his, a bassist and drummer, to do it. We rehearsed for a day beforehand, did the tour, and that was that. It was actually pretty good too; I think the last ever Political Asylum show was in Gottingen, in Germany... and it was great!

"I still have all the old ideals," adds Ramsey, who now fronts the protest folk band, Folk This, and runs the alternative publishing house AK Press out in California, where he emigrated in 1994. "I think my politics have matured (understandably) since those teenage years, become more sophisticated, less black and white. But that means I am even more convinced now in my anarchist beliefs and practices. Actually, I don't think that the politics of anarcho-punk in the Eighties had that much to do with anarchism anyway... more like militant liberalism... but that's another story!

"In terms of the punk DIY stuff, I guess I am still involved, somewhat, in that scene. And certainly I still try and practice, as much as one can, living under the dictatorship of Capital, the self-management of my life, work, culture, and music.

"I was in Political Asylum for, I dunno, ten years or so, and obviously it was a great part of my life, and the basis for a lot of where I am today, but I don't really care if people remember us or not, to be honest. I'm proud of what we did, and of the music, and I still really like listening to it. If other folks dug it, or still dig it, that's great, but if they don't, then that's fine too...

"I don't think music alone can change the world, but I think that art, and culture, are a very necessary part of life, and of struggle, and the struggle for a better life for us all. Music can't, and doesn't, change the world then, but it is, or can be, an important part of that process."

SELECT DISCOGRAPHY

7"s:
'Winter' (COR, 1985)

MLPs:
'Someday' (We Bite, 1987)
'How The West Was Won' 10" (Allied Recordings, 1992)

LPs:
'Window On The World' (Looney Tunes, 1990)

At A Glance:
The band's strong musical legacy is thankfully quite well documented on CD, with San Francisco label Broken Rekids having released a colourful retrospective, 'Rock, You Sucker', and Finnish label Passing Bells having compiled most of the band's first three demos and the '85 single for their 24-track 'Winter' disc.

Alternative, picture by Trunt.

Widely regarded by many as 'the Scottish Crass', **ALTERNATIVE** were spawned in the thriving scene centred around Dunfermline (that also gave us The Dissidents, Mutual Fear and The Actives) during late 1979. The very first line-up of the band consisted of vocalist Craig 'Trinity' Nicol, guitarist Rick Bentley, bassist Wilf Shurman and drummer James 'Jaa' Murphy, although by 1980, Rodney 'Relax' Comrie had replaced Rick on guitar, and Eric 'Rice' Beveridge had joined as second vocalist.

"We were heavily influenced by them lyrically," admits Rice, on the constant comparisons to Crass that Alternative have 'endured' over the years. "So were many others around at that time, but we could see the connection and it didn't perturb us unduly. Musically, we did sound quite different to them though; our biggest influence when we started was probably The Clash, I think. We wanted to have our own sound and not get caught up by the whole issue of musical style… we played how we wanted to play and not how others wanted us to, and we had our own way of communicating our views and opinions.

"In the very beginning, we didn't regard ourselves as an anarcho-punk band anyway, but as the band progressed over the years, the ideas behind anarchist values, the struggle for and vision of a better society, became more apparent: the struggle of the oppressed looking for their freedom, the struggle of anyone looking for a new type of society that would put the needs of people before power, and the planet we live on before profit.

"At first we would practice at Rick's house, then we were able to practice at a community centre located in Rosyth… finally we got our own practice place in Dunfermline that we rented from the council. This was later to be known as 'The Pad' and soon became a small autonomy centre, a basic anarcho centre that would facilitate other bands in the area with a place to practice, as well as acting as a meeting place for like-minded individuals. It was used to create fanzines like Lipstick On Your Collar, and many articles and posters. Due to the size of the venue, it was unable to host large events, but smaller events like gigs took place all the time; it was a particularly good place for small local bands to play their first show. As The Pad developed over the coming years, it became a centre where all kinds of people could come from all different age groups and backgrounds, with many different tastes in music, to share their ideas with others in a friendly atmosphere. It became a place where people could escape to share common beliefs and information with each other."

Alternative live, 1981.

The band made their first appearance on vinyl courtesy of Crass, with the track 'Change It' (also known as 'Blind Ones') on 1980's 'Bullshit Detector' album. A simple, rather generic punk ditty, that stood out on the record by virtue of its unassuming yet catchy chorus, it not only helped the band's national profile immensely, more importantly it started a relationship with Crass that would eventually lead to the release of the quietly seminal 'In Nomine Patri' single in early 1983, by which time, Gordon 'Gogs' Smith had replaced Wilf on bass, and Dougie McHale from The Actives had joined as second guitarist.

Recorded at Southern Studios by John Loder, the main thrust of the EP was the potent 'Anti Christ', a powerful statement opening with the unforgettable metaphor, 'I came out of the warm womb into a world of fear and hopelessness, I was given the gift of life, but the package of this gift was opened by someone else...' It spent three months in the Independent charts, peaking impressively at No. 6, and Alternative played many shows, not only with local bands such as Patrol, UK Anarchists and Why?, but also with the bigger acts such as Crass, Flux Of Pink Indians, Poison Girls, The System and The Mob, whenever they ventured north of the border to tour Scotland.

"Most of the bands we played with we enjoyed; those gigs were especially good as we all shared a common interest and similar frames of mind. Playing with some of the better-known bands always made for a good gig, obviously, but Alternative were not just about music or money; we were about communicating with people openly and directly, and every gig we played gave us this opportunity. We used the sounds made by our instruments just like our fanzines, posters, handouts and artwork – as a means of connecting with individuals on a more personal level so they could understand our views and opinions for themselves. So it was never a case of playing with bands that were 'smaller' or 'bigger' (just labels of one's importance that we were not going to associate with); it was about unity, the coming together of like-minded individuals striving for the same cause.

"Of course, not everybody who turned up at the gigs was to be friendly. A memorable gig would be one we played in Livingston, where the crowed formed a semi-circle around the band as we were playing. They were showing no response; there was no clapping, no booing... no anything! When we eventually finished the set, we mentioned to the guy who had organised it that we didn't think we'd gone down too well, to which he replied, 'If they hadn't liked you, they would have kicked the shit out of you and nicked all your gear!'

"The worst gigs were the ones where mindless violence would break out in the crowd. One of the worst gigs was in Bellshill, near Glasgow; we had only just got into our third song and a riot started between local rival gangs. The gig was an all-ages show in a local community centre... there were bottles flying all over the place, one guy was running round hitting people with a hammer... another guy grabbed a heavy-based mike stand and threw it into the audience. He then retrieved the stand and replaced it on the stage, and even said, 'Thanks!' We had to stop the gig and then transport some young guys out of the area in our van as they were in real fear for their lives.

"Another particularly bad gig was in Clydebank at the Hardgate Hall. We were playing with some of the local bands from the Glasgow area, Pract-ex and State Of Decay. I can remember, at the end of our set, we would always play out with the song 'Where Are Your Hiroshimas?' and would invite individuals from the crowd onto the stage, and ask them to hold small banners whilst we played the last song of the set. This was when a small element of the crowd decided to shout abuse at us, and start to throw beer cans and bottles at the band. They were trying to pull the banners from the people who were holding them, and spitting the usual mindless violence these individuals always seem to get off on. Some member of the crowd was hit in the face with a bottle or glass, and the gig ended up with arguments between two of the bands as to who was to blame. Once everything calmed down, we packed up our kit and left Clydebank under a hail of arguments and abuse."

Following the release of the single, Linda 'Linger' Rotherham joined on vocals, briefly making the band a seven-piece, a line-up that was captured on the 'Live At The Bunker' cassette alongside Dirt and Reality Control. By the end of 1983 though, Rice, Trinity and Gogs had all left the band within the space of a few weeks, Rice joining The Actives as vocalist the following year. Neil (AKA C. R. Abbit) and Darren joined on vocals and bass respectively, only to see Dougie replaced on guitar by Billy D-Warf and Jaa superseded on drums (he left to join Reality Control and later became a chef) by David 'Chips' Wood, formerly the drummer with Why?

This was the line-up that recorded the superb 'If They Treat You Like Shit... Act Like Manure' album for Corpus Christi during spring 1984. Recorded again at Southern, only this time with Pete Wright of Crass overseeing production duties (he also contributed some backing vocals, alongside Annie Anxiety, to 'Til Death Do You Part'), the album was an accomplished collection of memorable and provocative protest songs. From the up-tempo – not to mention, sarcastic – opener, 'Another Subversive Peace Song', reminiscent of Conflict at the height of their powers, to the mournful melodies of 'Now I Realise', the album still stands as fine tribute to a criminally-overlooked band that commanded tremendous compositional skills.

By far the most poignant song on the LP, 'Caroline's Carnival' addressed the abduction – and subsequent killing – of five-year-old Caroline Hogg from Portobello, near Edinburgh, on July 18th, 1983. The murder went unsolved until, in 1994, paedophile serial killer Robert Black was convicted and sentenced to ten consecutive life sentences for the heinous crime. Linda's sombre intoning, 'Listen a while, just listen, to the screams of little girls, incestuously loved...', still resonates with hair-raising pathos. Elsewhere on the album, she achieved the terrified, breathless vocals on 'Death Isn't So Sweet' (about the plight of a hunted fox) by sprinting around the studio several times before attempting her take.

After a July tour, and the release of the 'Eat The Rich' demo (comprising live and rehearsal tracks), Billy and Neil left the band, and were replaced by Sean Halliday and Lisa, previously with Edinburgh band, Direct Action. The 'How Dare You!' demo was recorded at Dunfermline studio, Slurpy Gloop, by Pano, who himself played synthesiser on the recording. The band's sound was always evolving, alongside main songwriter Rodney's individual development as a musician, moving ever further away from the harsh distorted style that characterised their earlier recordings and into more experimental areas.

Alternative, 1981.

In fact, it was the resulting musical differences that prompted most of the personnel changes in Alternative, and sure enough, Lisa soon left, with Iain 'Influx' Ball, formerly of A.U.K., then joining on second guitar. After playing on the terrific 1985 demo, 'Just Because The Boot Fits, Doesn't Mean You Have To Wear It', he also left – apparently "not quite seeing eye to eye over the issue of pacifism…" – to join Edinburgh's Slaughterhouse Psychos, before playing with Dundee's Exalt and This Tribe (alongside his brother, John).

Aware that the band had ran its natural course, Rodney and Linda folded Alternative in 1986, after one last seven-track demo, 'Touch The Earth', was recorded on an eight-track portable studio in the practise room of the band's home in Pittencrieff Street, Dunfermline. Chips played alongside Iain in Slaughterhouse Psychos, but sadly died in 2004 following a prolonged bout of ill health.

"He was a very kind man with a huge talent, and he will be sadly missed by all those who knew him, worked with him, and had the pleasure of his company throughout the years," reflects Iain sadly, before adding, on the personal impact his short tenure with the band had. "Being involved with something like Alternative changed us all for the good. We're all still non-conformist to a certain degree within our lives. You can't but be changed when involved with a band like ours, in a movement that meant so much to so many. I like to think there is still a little bit of anarchist left within most of us, although I know for some members that left for personal reasons that the idea of anarchism ever really working began to fade.

"I'd also like to think that the Alternative will be remembered as one of the many UK bands that spoke up against the injustices of the world and helped make some people create an opinion for themselves," he adds proudly. "We used our music as a tool to bring people together, not as a stepping-stone for an ego trip; there were more than enough people doing that at the time to help keep the capitalistic music industry thriving. We stood up for what we believed in, in a vain attempt to provoke a reaction, and we would never rise to those mind-fucked individuals whose sole purpose was to ruin it for everyone else. Certain people had preconceived ideas of Alternative as being blind, unrealistic, grass-eating pacifists, but the truth of the matter is, those individuals were the ones who were most unwilling to look at their own attitudes and circumstances, and to take the appropriate action to find the solution best befitting their situation."

"Our concept of anarchy was a peaceful autonomous way of living, not like many people who thought immediately of a lawless state," clarifies Rice. "We were concerned about politics, religion, war, greed, and the destruction of the planet, and realising that these issues were all interlinked and affecting us all, we believed in a society based on the individual. However, each individual would have different needs, feelings and attitudes to the next, and it would have been unrealistic to think this would have happened overnight… but not unrealistic enough to think we couldn't bring about change within the system we lived in individually.

"Alternative were not dreamers; we believed in a vision, that united struggle that all anarchist bands of our time believed in… a continuous struggle for a better society. We knew that our actions and ideals then could determine what kind of future we would face in years to come, and the idea of sitting back and doing nothing, waiting for the big day to come, was not an option. You had to liberate yourself, change the way you were, and reshape your whole process of thought."

SELECT DISCOGRAPHY

7"s:
'In Nomine Patri' (Crass, 1983)

LPs:
'If They Treat You Like Shit, Act Like Manure' (Corpus Christi, 1984)

At A Glance:
Overground Records included the track 'Where Are Your Hiroshimas?' on their 2006 'Anti-Society' compilation, whilst the single track, 'Anti-Christ', appears on the Crass records compilation CD, 'A-Sides, Part Two: 1982 – 1984'.

I f Alternative were 'the Scottish Crass', Loanhead's **AOA** were surely 'the Scottish Discharge', such was the unbridled ferocity of their sonic attack; indeed, the abrasive fervour with which they applied their craft was even the equal of fellow Scots, the aforementioned Oi Polloi.

Beginning life as Virus (not to mention Self Destruct, Disaster Area and Condemned!), guitarist Scott Paton, bassist Bruce Wagener, drummer Antony Mallin and vocalist Steven Telford finally settled on the name All Out Attack during the summer of 1982, shortening it to just AOA soon thereafter.

"Discharge definitely struck a chord with us musically," agrees Scott, "whilst Crass certainly changed our way of thinking… those were probably our most important influences at the time. The ever-worsening political climate provided more than enough fuel to keep the fire well-stoked and the heat rising, and the situation spiralling out of control from our youthful perspective was a convincing call to the 'A' sign. A real sign of the times, of the early Eighties: unemployment, the threat of nuclear war, misery and pessimism… and, of course, the miners' strike was literally on our doorstep – we were right there, in the thick of it, for better or worse. Anarchist punk seemed like a vehicle for individual thought, a way to express our ideas and feelings through our own distinctive musical meanderings.

"I spawned from a drumming family, which was definitely an advantage for me, pointing me in the right direction, and helping as far as knowing what gear to get etc. We also utilised our connections in the local community for rehearsal space, which changed from a school classroom the one week, to a community hall the next. We were a very noisy lot, as you've probably already gathered! Numerous noise complaints aside though, we managed to secure our first gig at the local town hall in 1982, just us and the disco, which was an interesting experience, but inevitably ended on a sour note with the mindless violence of human nature manifesting itself… a sad sign of things to come. As someone once said, 'It's not the people in power we should worry about; it's the power in people…' "

The band started playing locally on a regular basis, but it was only when they made their 'big city debut' in nearby Edinburgh in 1983, supporting the Threats at The Nite Club, an infamous venue that had previously played host to everyone from Crass to Dead Kennedys, that they really started to get noticed by the Scottish punk fraternity.

"We were meeting both a positive and negative response," admits Scott, "but our message was clear and we had a truly in-your-face 'no compromise' attitude. Our vocalist was becoming quite a notorious figure in the burgeoning local scene with his legendary speeches between songs, and the 'All Out Attack philosophy' started to take shape. Anarchism seemed to be what we were looking for, and we demanded it with passion."

A formative demo, 'Condemned To Destruction', was also recorded in 1983, straight onto four-track tape in a local home studio (sadly no copies remain, not even in the band's own archives), before AOA realised their magnum opus – the blisteringly unfettered material, sonically more Chaos UK than Crass, that would appear on the 'Who Are They Trying To Con?' 12". It was recorded with Pete Haig at his Pier House Studios in Edinburgh, an establishment the band would visit for all ensuing recordings.

"The first tentative steps and the initial experimentation…" Scott recalls the first demo fondly, "An exciting prospect for any budding musician, and a great outlet for teenage angst! I have fond memories of those early studio songs…

"Anyway, 'Who Are They Trying To Con?' was fast becoming a bit of an anthem at gigs," he reckons. "So we had to get a recording done, whatever the cost. As it turned out, we got five tracks down very quickly… time is money in the recording studio… who are they trying to con, indeed! And yes, that probably was our defining moment as AOA; then as now, it still evokes my determination, individualism and freedom of speech.

"The finished article was sent to various record labels, but it was Children Of The Revolution that saw our potential. Originally it was to be a 7" single, but then it was decided that it would do

AOA at the Wood Green Arts Centre, October 1985, picture by Paul May.

better as a 12". However, seeing as the 7" sleeves had already been printed, they were utilised as inserts for the 12" release… never ones to waste anything!"

Tim Bennett from C.O.R helped the band set up a tour of England and Wales, their first shows outside of Scotland, but drummer Mallin left literally days before the dates were due to begin. Undeterred, AOA loaded their transit van ("Thankfully it only broke down once!" laughs Scott) and hit the road regardless, planning to find a replacement drummer en route; thankfully salvation, albeit just for one gig, was at hand, in the guise of Steve Beatty, now the man behind the hugely-successful Plastic Head Distribution, then running Endangered Musik from his own bedroom. He learnt the band's live set in record time, for a show at Bristol's Demolition Diner, and later released their 1988 album, 'Satisfactory Arrangement'.

But first, 'Unlimited Genocide', once again through C.O.R., only this time a split LP with close friends Oi Polloi, followed in August 1986, and spent five weeks in the Independent chart, peaking at No. 13.

"We played gigs with many different bands, but our connection with Oi Polloi stemmed from way back, right to the initial conception of the local punk scene… and we got to know each other very well, some would say! In fact, at one point I was sharing a flat with the Oi Polloi guitarist, the respective vocalists were co-habiting, and the two bass players were brothers! Oh, and as for the drummers, well, we always had a sneaking suspicion of a percussive late night rendezvous…

"It was this tight relationship that eventually culminated in 'Unlimited Genocide', which I had originally wanted to call 'Scotland The Grave', the first release to feature our new full-time drummer, Deek [not to be confused with Deek Allan, the Oi Polloi vocalist]. We had already recorded seven new studio songs for COR, and it was a great idea to bring Oi Polloi onboard and release it as an album."

Much concerted gigging was undertaken in support of the release, including a celebrated appearance at the Scottish punk's picnic held in a disused World War II bunker on Crammond Island, that Scott still cites as one of his favourite ever gigs with the band. AOA finally played some proper shows in England too, even making it as far as London for several gigs, after which vocalist Steven decided to move there permanently. Scott and Bruce had other ideas though, recruiting drummer Loaf and singer Murph from local band, The Degenerates, with whom they recorded 'Satisfactory Arrangement'.

"Yep, it's all in the name!" reckons Scott. "This was the next logical step in AOA's progression;

AOA guitarist Scott Paton, picture by Paul May.

it all sounds like it fell into place, but chaos always had its part to play. Our crowning glory perhaps? It was definitely the most thought-through and experimental recording we did, and, both lyrically and musically, things were becoming more diverse as inevitably we were all tasting different things. There's even an acoustic guitar and keyboard in there somewhere!

"But an unwelcome pattern was beginning to emerge in dealing with record labels… our own naivety, or just plain ignorance? It cuts both ways," he sighs, before adding cryptically, "By their very nature, humans make mistakes and will become endangered… enough said!"

Murph was then replaced on vocals by Degenerates guitarist, Rich, although this incarnation of the band never committed anything to tape.

"A bunch of Degenerates, the lot of 'em!" laughs Scott. "Seriously though, at one point during the proceedings, Loaf and Rich were involved in a horrendous car crash. At that stage, all was looking bad, but thankfully, serious burns aside, they survived more or less intact. In the interim, while they recovered, I handled the vocals and a good friend of mine, Zander, did a grand job as stand-in drummer for a gig or two. After their long, slow recovery process, Loaf and Rich, showing an amazing commitment and dedication to All Out Attack, continued to be positive, even in the ever-present, delicate balance of life and death."

In 1990, AOA had another session booked at Pier House, to immortalise some brand new songs they were especially proud of, but Rich then decided to quit, leaving Scott to re-write the lyrics and handle vocals.

"This was always going to be a natural progression, and not just for me personally either; I think the whole ethos of AOA was that we always tried to look forward and utilise what insight, if any, we had gained through experience, both musically and lyrically. And I still feel that this recording is the most inspiring and thought-provoking material I've written to date, with all the sentiments still ringing true, even after sixteen years.

"Incidentally, the master tape of this final recording, that we called 'All Out Attack', lay in the deepest, darkest recesses of Pier House Studios' basement for over ten years, only to be rediscovered just recently, still wrapped in its original plastic carrier bag shroud. A release is possibly long overdue, one thinks!"

AOA disbanded in 1990, soon after that final recording, although apart from original vocalist Steven who moved to Ireland to start a family, Scott and most of his former band-mates still live in and around Edinburgh and are still involved in music in various guises. The possibility of an AOA reunion may seem remote, but isn't something Scott is prepared to rule out completely.

"Basically we were a tribe of individuals that took a stance against what we saw and felt was the manipulation and total disregard of our liberties. We'd heard all the moaners, and the never-ending chants of the so-called anti-establishment music business and their cohorts. It was, and still is, the easy option to sit back and moan about how life's unfair and how society is to blame, rather than be true to your beliefs and, more crucially, do something positive about it. It takes a bit of effort to change and evolve, and sometimes it becomes all too clear who the real enemy is… always question the cause and effect of humanity's place on this planet and act accordingly.

"We decided to vent our anger through music, and take a more direct approach with our protest, and for the most part it had the desired effect: an all out attack on what we wanted to change. And now, here we are again; the relentless cycle of life and death continues unabated. There will always be something to be angry about… and always a corresponding need for change."

SELECT DISCOGRAPHY

12"s:
'Who Are They Trying To Con?' (C.O.R., 1985)

LPs:
'Unlimited Genocide' (C.O.R., 1986) – split with Oi Polloi
'Satisfactory Arrangement' (Endangered Musik, 1988)

At A Glance:
Until someone sees fit to issue a comprehensive AOA retrospective, the curious reader can contact Scott directly: aoavproductions@msn.com

So, there you have it, a comprehensive overview of the early Eighties anarcho-punk scene in the UK, and what better way to end such a book than with Scott's parting comment? There will always be something to be angry about... and always a corresponding need for change. Yes, anarcho-punk was of its time, a necessary response to very specific stimuli, when an urgent need to loudly voice our dissatisfaction with those that would govern us happily coincided with a watershed moment in underground music, to give us what was surely the most real and challenging incarnation of punk rock ever seen or heard. Most of these bands are long gone, of course, and many of their lyrics were primarily pertinent to their own circumstances and the era in which they confronted them, but the spirit behind those words – that there is a better way, if only we're prepared to stand up and fight for it – remains an indomitable constant as long as there is injustice in the world.

The battle continues...?

Artwork from the back cover of the 'In Nomine Patri' single by Alternative.

The late John Loder, founder of Southern Studios and sound engineer for many of the releases on Crass Records.

APPENDIX 1

COMPLETE DISCOGRAPHIES BY LABEL

Agit-Prop

Agit1	Chumbawamba 'Revolution' 7"
Agit2	Chumbawamba/A State Of Mind 'We Are The World?' 7"
Agit3	Chumbawamba 'Smash Clause 28' 7"
Agit4	Credit To The Nation 'Pay The Price' 12"
Agit5	Chumbawamba 'I Never Gave Up' 12"/CD single
Agit666	Chumbawamba 'Behave' 12"/CD single
Agit7	Credit to the Nation 'Call It What You Want' 12" - unreleased
Agit8	Papa Brittle 'Status Quo/Global Intensified Nationalism' 12"
Prop1	Chumbawamba 'Pictures Of Starving Children' LP
Prop2	Chumbawamba 'Never Mind The Ballots' LP
Prop3	Chumbawamba 'English Rebel Songs' 10"/CD
Prop4	Sportchestra! '101 Songs About Sport' DLP
Prop5	Bassa Bassa 'Bassa Bassa' LP
Prop6	Artists for Animals 'The Sporting Life' LP
Prop7	Chumbawamba 'Slap' LP/CD
Prop8	Thatcher On Acid 'Frank' LP
Prop9	Chumbawamba 'The First Two' CD
Prop10	Chumbawamba 'Jesus H. Christ' LP - unreleased
Prop11	Chumbawamba 'Shhh!' LP/CD/MC
Prop12	Papa Brittle 'Obey, Consume, Marry And Reproduce' MLP/CD

All The Madmen

Mob001	The Mob 'Crying Again' 7" - joint release with Out To Lunch Productions
Rev1	The Review 'England's Glory' 7"
Mad002	The Mob 'Witch Hunt' 7"
Mad003	Andy Stratton 'I Don't Know' 7"
Mad004	The Mob 'Let The Tribe Increase' LP
Mad005	The Astronauts 'It's All Done By Mirrors' LP
Mad006	The Mob 'Mirror Breaks' 7"
Mad007	Flowers In The Dustbin 'Freaks Run Wild In The Disco' 12"
Mad008	Zoskia 'Rape' 7"
Madt008	Zoskia 'Rape' 12"
Mad009	Blyth Power 'Chevy Chase' 12"
Mad10	Clair Obscur 'The Pilgrim's Progress' LP
Mad011	The Astronauts 'Soon' LP
Mad012	Blyth Power 'Junction Signal' 7"
Madt012	Blyth Power 'Junction Signal' 12"
Mad013	The Mob 'Crying Again' 12"
Mad014	Thatcher On Acid 'Moondance' 12"

Mad015	Blyth Power 'ixioni' 7"
Madt015	Blyth Power 'ixioni' 12"
Madt016	We Are Going To Eat You 'I Wish I Knew' 12"
Madlp005	The Astronauts 'The Seedy Side Of...' LP
Madlp006	Blyth Power 'Wicked Women, Wicked Men And Wicket Keepers' LP
Madlp007	Thatcher On Acid 'Curdled' LP
Madc108	Hysteria Ward 'From Breakfast To Madness' tape
Madlp009	Dan 'An Attitude Hits' LP
Foad001	Paranoid Visions 'The Robot Is Running Amok' 7"
Foad002	Paranoid Visions 'Schizophrenia' LP
Foad2u2	Paranoid Visions 'I Will Wallow' 10"

Bluurg

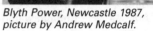

Blyth Power, Newcastle 1987, picture by Andrew Medcalf.

Fish1	Various 'Wessex '82' 7"
Fish2	Subhumans 'Evolution' 7"
Fish3	A-Heads 'Forgotten Hero' 7"
Fish4	Naked 'One Step Forward' 7"
Fish5	Subhumans 'Time Flies... But Aeroplanes Crash' 12"
Fish6	Instigators 'The Blood Is On Your Hands' 7"
Fish7	Faction 'You've Got The Fire' 7"
Fish8	Subhumans 'From The Cradle To The Grave' LP/CD/MC
Fish9	Sears 'If Only' MLP
Fish10	Subhumans 'Rats' 7"
Fish11	Instigators 'Nobody Listens Anymore' LP
Fish12	Subhumans 'Worlds Apart' LP/CD/MC
Fish13	Instigators 'Phoenix' LP
Fish14	Subhumans 'EP-LP' LP/CD/MC
Fish15	Various 'Open Mind Surgery' LP
Fish16	Subhumans '29:29 Split Vision' LP/CD/MC
Fish17	Smart Pils 'No Good No Evil' LP
Fish18	Culture Shock 'Go Wild' LP
Fish19	Nick Toczek 'Intoczekated' LP
Fish20	Culture Shock 'Onwards And Upwards' LP/CD/MC
Fish21	Various 'Stonehenge' 7"
Fish22	Rhythmites 'Integration' LP
Fish23	Culture Shock 'All The Time!' LP
Fish24	Citizen Fish 'Free Souls' LP/CD/MC
Fish25	Subhumans 'Time Flies... But Aeroplanes Crash/Rats' LP/CD/MC
Fish26	Citizen Fish 'Wider Than A Postcard' LP/CD/MC
Fish27	Citizen Fish 'Disposable Dream' 7"
Fish28	Citizen Fish 'Live Fish' LP/CD/MC
Fish29	Citizen Fish/AOS3 'TV Dinner/Conspiracy' split 7"
Fish30	Culture Shock 'Go Wild/All The Time!' CD
Fish31	Citizen Fish 'Flinch' LP/CD/MC
Fish32	Citizen Fish 'Live in London '91' Video
Fish33	Various 'Oriental Transistor' Video
Fish34	Citizen Fish 'Millennia Madness' LP/CD

Fish35	Citizen Fish 'Psychological Background Reports' CD
Fish36	Subhumans 'Unfinished Business' CD
Fish37	Citizen Fish 'This One's For Frank' Video
Fish38	Citizen Fish 'Habit' 7"
Fish38	Citizen Fish 'Active Ingredients' LP/CD/MC
Fish39	Citizen Fish '3rd Psychological Background Report' CD
Fish40	Citizen Fish 'Gaffer Tape' Video
Fish41	Mental/Stupid Humans 'EPs and Demos' CDR
Fish42	Subhumans 'Demolition War, Parts 1-3' CDR
Fish43	Lost Cherrees 'Nothing New' CDR
Fish44	Culture Shock '1st 2 Demos' CDR
Fish45	Various 'The Bluurg EPs: 82-88' CDR
Fish46	Clutton Brothers 'Spring Collection' CDR
Fish47	Citizen Fish 'What Time We On?' CD
Xep1	Subhumans 'Demolition War' 7"
Xep2	Subhumans 'Reason For Existence' 7"
Xep3	Subhumans 'Religious Wars' 7"
XLP1	Subhumans 'The Day The Country Died' LP/CD/MC

Bluurg Tapes

1.	Stupid Humans 'Live Warminster 17-2-80' and 3-track demo
2.	Audio Torture 'Live Bath/Warminster 16/17-2-80'
3.	The Mental 'EP And Demos, June 80'
4.	Organised Chaos 'Live Warminster 9-5-81' and practice
5.	Wild Youth 'Live Trowbridge 21-2-81/Worcester 11-4-81'
6.	Wild Youth 'Live Chippenham 8-5-81'
7.	Subhumans 'Demolition War '81, Parts 1-3'
8.	Subhumans 'Live Worcester 11-4-81'
9.	Subhumans 'Live Warminster 9-5-81'
10.	Subhumans 'Live Bath 20-5-81'
11.	Subhumans/Wild Youth 'Live Melksham 81'
12.	Stupid Humans '2 Demos'

Organised Chaos, live in Swansea St. Phillips Community Centre, November 1985, picture by Dai Joseph.

13. Various 'Wessex 81' (A-Heads/Organised Chaos/Wild Youth)
14. Subhumans 'Live Swindon 11-12-81'
15. Subhumans 'Live Stevenage 81'
16. Subhumans 'Live Skunx, Islington 21-8-82/Bath 10-4-82'
17. A-Heads/Organised Chaos 'Demos 83'
18. Organised Chaos 'Live Skunx, Islington 21-8-82'
19. Subhumans 'London Putney White Lion 1-7-82'
20. The Pagans 'The Cuckoo Has Flown' demo 82
21. Subhumans/Faction 'Live Moonlight Club, West Hampstead 82'
22. Tears of Destruction 'Death Of A Nation, Part 1' demo 81
23. Subhumans 'Live George Robey, Finsbury Park 7-2-83'
24. Flying Fish Band 'Demo 82'
25. Lost Cherrees Nothing New Live and demos 82'
26. Subhumans 'Leeds 11-5-83'
27. Instigators 'Live Bradford 15-5-83'
28. Naked 'Live Holland 4-6-83'
29. Nick Toczek 'Britanarchist' demo 83
30. Sears 'Live and Demo 83'
31. Paranoid Visions 'Blood In The Snow/Destroy The Myths' demos 83
32. Naked 'Live Feltham 29-7-83'
33. Subhumans 'Live Leeds 31-8-83'
34. Ex-Humans 'Demo 83'
35. Various 'Wessex 84' (Smart Pils/Onslaught/Spyin' For Brian)
36. Subhumans 'Live Paris 8-10-83'
37. D&V/Faction 'Paris October 83'
38. Lost Cherrees 'Live Leeds 12-10-83'
39. Mass of Black 'Demo 84'
40. Instigators 'Live Leeds 84'
41. Subhumans 'USAT4: Live San Francisco 24-4-84'
42. Civilised Society? 'Demo'
43. Sears 'Live Wolves/Luton 84'
44. Subhumans 'Live Bathgate 9-8-84'
45. Shrapnel 'Demo/Live London 16-8-84'
46. Mass of Black 'Live Hull/Demo'
47. A-Heads 'Vox Populi Demo 84'
48. Steve L. 'Sliced Bread And The Bomb' demo 84
49. Nick Toczek 'Ulterior Motives' demo 85
50. Phantoms Of The Underground 'Demo 84'
51. End Result 'No Master's Voice' demo 83
52. Paranoid Visions 'From The Womb To The Bucket' demo 84
53. No Policy 'Demo 84'
54. Smart Pils 'Excerpts From The Toxic State' demo 85
55. Rat 'Demo May 85'
56. Freak Electric 'Advance Demo 84'
57. Freak Electric 'Live London 13-7-85'
58. Subhumans 'Live Fulham Greyhound 12-7-85'
59. Subhumans 'USAT5 Live New York'
60. Instigators 'Leeds 24-7-85'
61. Subhumans 'Live Leeds 23-10-85'
62. Subhumans 'Live Fulham Greyhound 31-10-85'

63.	Subhumans/Steve L. 'Live Warminster 10-11-85'
64.	Eyes on You/Pax Vobiscum 'Demo 85'
65.	Blyth Power 'Bricklayer's Arms Demo/Live'
66.	Culture Shock 'Living History' demo 86
67.	Political Asylum 'Walls Have Ears' demo
68.	Funeral Party 'Demo'
69.	Nick Toczek/Ginger John/Seething Wells/Kevin Seisay 'The Intolerance Tape'
70.	Civilised Society? 'All The Demos'
71.	Culture Shock 'Reality Stop No44' demo 86
72.	Smart Pils 'Zen Punk: Demo/Live 86'
74.	Insurrection 'The People Are Starving' demo 87
75.	Rhythmites 'Demo/Live 87/88'
76.	Dick Lucas/Rhythm Activism/Nick Toczek 'The CIA Tape: Live Toronto 87'
77.	Eve of the Scream 'Unbelievable Genocide' demo
78.	Rhythmites 'Can You Feel it?' demo/live 88
79.	Culture Shock 'Hot And Sweaty' live compilation
80.	Internal Autonomy '4th Demo'
81.	Herb Garden 'Live/Demo 89'
82.	Various 'Don't Talk About It-Do It!'
83.	Kendrick Andy 'Wanted For Love' demo
84.	Zygote 'Demo/Live In Germany 90'
85.	Citizen Fish 'Sink Or Swim' demo 90
86.	Citizen Fish 'Live Hereford/Liverpool September 91'
87.	CDS 'Tempo Tantrums/Happy Demos 91'
89.	AOS3 'Owsley' demo 91
90.	Tiny Giants 'Death By Chocolate' demo 92
91.	Useful Idiot/Wordbug 'Demos 91/92'
92.	Blue Meanies 'Banquet' demo 92
93.	Citizen Fish/Blue Meanies 'Live London 17-7-92'
94.	Dirty Headed Bastard 'Both Demos 92'
95.	Ancient Ones 'Antediluvian Legends' demo/live 92
96.	AOS3 'Apparently We Had A Great Time' live/demo 92
97.	Citizen Fish 'First Psychological Background Report 91-93'
98.	Gr'ups 'Almond Tree/Buildings' EPs
99.	Ex Cathedra 'Live Rotterdam 8-3-94'
100.	Rhythmites 'Live Stuttgart April 93 (plus 5 dub tracks)'
101.	Bender 'Live Produce Harlow 7-4-95'
102.	Citizen Fish 'Second Psychological Background Report 94-96'
103.	Ex Cathedra 'Live in Slovenia 2-5-97'
104.	Antibodies 'Kill The Music Live 96/97'
105.	Rhythmites 'Hah!'
106.	Cress 'White Man Destroys Culture' demo 95
107.	Cress 'Live Monuments Manchester 25-6-96'
108.	Cress 'Time: Live at Time Studios 20-7-97 (and Polish demo)'

Crass Records

621984	Crass 'Feeding Of The 5000' LP/CD/MC
521984	Crass 'Reality Asylum' 7"
521984	Crass 'Stations Of The Crass' DLP/CD/MC

521984/1	Honey Bane 'You Can Be You' 7"
421984/1	Crass/Poison Girls 'Bloody Revolutions' 7"
421984/2	Poison Girls 'Chappaquidick Bridge' LP/flexi
421984/3	Zounds 'Can't Cheat Karma' 7"
421984/4	Various 'Bullshit Detector' LP
421984/5	Crass 'Nagasaki Nightmare' 7"
421984/6F	Crass 'Rival Tribal Rebel Revel' flexi – with 'Toxic Graffiti' fanzine
421984/6	Crass 'Rival Tribal Rebel Revel' 7"
421984/7	Poison Girls 'Statement' 7"
421984/8	Poison Girls 'All Systems Go' 7"
421984/9	Poison Girls 'Hex' LP

Deno from Dirt, live at the Mermaid, Birmingham, October 1985, picture by Paul May.

321984/1F	Crass 'Our Wedding' flexi
321984/1	Crass 'Penis Envy' LP/CD/MC
321984/2	Flux Of Pink Indians 'Neu Smell' 7"
321984/3	Annie Anxiety 'Barbed Wire Halo' 7"
321984/4	Snipers 'Three Peace Suite' 7"
321984/5	Captain Sensible 'This Is Your Captain Speaking' 7"
321984/6	Dirt 'Death Is Reality Today' 7"
321984/7	The Mob 'No Doves Fly Here' 7"
221984/1	Conflict 'The House That Man Built' 7"
221984/2	Rudimentary Peni 'Farce' 7"
221984/3	Various 'Bullshit Detector 2' DLP
221984/4	Cravats 'Rub Me Out' 7"
221984/5	Andy T. 'Weary Of The Flesh' 7"
221984/6	Crass 'How Does it Feel?' 7"
221984/7	Dirt 'Never Mind Dirt, Here's The Bollocks' LP
221984/8	Alternative 'In Nomine Patri' 7"
221984/9	Anthrax 'Capitalism Is Cannibalism' 7"
221984/10	Omega Tribe 'Angry Songs' 7"
221984/11	Sleeping Dogs 'Beware Sleeping Dogs' 7"
221984/12	Hit Parade 'Bad News' 7"
121984/1	D&V 'The Nearest Door' 7"
121984/2	Crass 'Yes Sir, I Will' LP/CD/MC
121984/3F	Crass 'Sheep Farming In The Falklands' flexi
121984/3	Crass 'Sheep Farming In The Falklands 7"
121984/4	Crass 'Whodunnit?' 7"
121984/5	MDC 'Multi Death Corporations' 7"
121984/6	Lack of Knowledge 'Grey' 7"
1984	Crass 'You're Already Dead' 7"
1984/1	Kukl 'The Eye' LP/CD
1984/2	Hit Parade 'Plastic Culture' 12"
1984/3	Various 'Bullshit Detector 3' DLP
1984/4	Crass 'Acts Of Love' LP
Catno1	D&V 'D&V' LP
Catno2	Jane Gregory 'After A Dream' 7"
Catno3	Steve Ignorant 'Take Your Elbows Off The Table' 12" - unreleased
Catno4	Kukl 'Holidays In Europe' LP/CD
Catno5	Crass 'Best Before... 1984' DLP/CD/MC

Catno6	Crass 'Ten Notes On A Summer's Day' 12"/CD
Catno7	Hit Parade 'Knick Knack Paddy Whack' LP
Catno8	Various 'A Sides: 1979-1982' CD/MC
Catno9	Various 'A Sides, Part Two: 1982-1984' CD/MC
Catno10	Penny Rimbaud 'Reads From The Book Christ's Reality Asylum' MC
Bollox2u2	Crass 'Christ The Album' DLP/CD/MC
ColdTurkey1	Crass 'Merry Crassmass' 7"

Corpus Christi

Christit's1	UK Decay 'Rising From The Dread' 12"
Christit's2	Very Things 'The Gong Man' 7"
Christit's3	Conflict 'It's Time To See Who's Who' LP
Christit's4	Conflict 'To A Nation Of Animal Lovers' 7"
Christit's5	Omega Tribe 'No Love Lost' LP
Christit's6	Rudimentary Peni 'Death Church' LP
Christit's7	Icons Of Filth 'Used, Abused And Unamused' 7"
Christit's8	Cravats 'The Colossal Tunes Out' LP - with flexi
Christit's9	The Fits 'Tears Of A Nation' 7"
Christit's10	Annie Anxiety 'Soul Possession' LP
Christit's11	Crucifix 'Dehumanisation' LP
Christit's12	Omega Tribe 'It's A Hard Life' 7"/12"
Christit's13	Alternative 'If They Treat You Like Shit... Act Like Manure' LP
Christit's14	Lack Of Knowledge 'The Sirens Are Back' LP
Christit's15	Rudimentary Peni 'The EPs Of RP' LP
Christit's16	Conflict 'The House That Man Built/To A Nation Of Animal Lovers' LP

Annie Anxiety, live in Liverpool 1984, picture by Andrew Medcalf.

Fight Back

Fight1	Vex 'Sanctuary' 12"
Fight2	Legion Of Parasites 'Undesirable Guests' 12"
Fight3	Reality 'Who Killed The Golden Goose?' 7"
Fight4	Exit-stance 'Crimes Against Humanity' 7"
Fight5	Various 'We Don't Want Your Fucking War' LP
Fight6	Lost Cherrees 'All Part Of Growing Up' LP
Fight7	Various 'We Don't Want Your Fucking Law' LP
Fight8	The Arch Criminals 'Hang' 12"
Fight9	The Apostles/The Joy Of Living 'Death To Wacky Pop' 7" - split

Mortarhate

Mort000	Class War 'Better Dead Than Wed' 7"
Mort001	Conflict 'The Serenade Is Dead' 7"
Mortex001	Conflict 'The Serenade Is Dead' 12"
Mort002	Hagar The Womb 'The Word Of The Womb' 12"
Mort003	Lost Cherrees 'A Man's Duty, A Woman's Place' 7"
Mort004	Various 'Who? What? Why? When? Where?' LP/CD
Mort005	Icons Of Filth 'Onward Christian Soldiers' LP

Conflict at Fenders Ballroom, LA, August 1985, picture by Julius from Diatribe.

Mort006	Conflict 'Increase The Pressure' LP/CD/MC
Mort007	Conflict 'Live At The Centro Iberico' 7"
Mort008	Conflict 'This Is Not Enough' 7"
Mort009	The Apostles 'Smash The Spectacle' 7"
Mort010	Icons Of Filth 'Brain Death' 7"
Mort011	Exit-stance 'While Backs Are Turned' 12"
Mort012	Lost Cherrees 'Unwanted Children' 12"
Mort013	Various 'We Won't Be Your Fucking Poor' DLP
Mort014	Stalag 17/Toxic Waste 'The Truth Will Be Heard' 12"
Mort015	Conflict 'The Battle Continues' 7"
Mort016	Flowers In The Dustbin 'Nails In The Heart' 7"
Mort017	Admit You're Shit 'Expect No Mercy' 7"
Mort018	Icons Of Filth 'The Filth And The Fury' 7"
Mort019	Liberty 'Our Voice Is Tomorrow's Hope' 7"
Mort020	Conflict 'The Ungovernable Force' LP/CD/MC
Mort020	Conflict 'Custom Rock/Statement' 7" - promotional
Mort021	The Waste 'Not Just Something To Be Sung' 7"
Mort022	Conflict 'The Final Conflict' 12"
Mort023	The Apostles 'Punk Obituary' LP
Mort024	Potential Threat 'Demand An Alternative' LP
Mort025	Liberty 'People Who Care Are Angry' LP/CD
Mort026	Exit-stance 'While Backs Are Turned' CD
Mort027	Admit You're Shit 'Someplace Special' 12"/CD
Mort029	Various 'We Don't Want Your Fucking War' CD
Mort030	Conflict 'Turning Rebellion Into Money' DLP/CD/MC
Mort031	Conflict 'The House That Man Built' 7"
Mort032	Conflict 'To A Nation Of Animal Lovers' 7"
Mort033	Conflict 'Custom Rock' 7"
Mort040	Conflict 'Standard Issue: 82-87' LP/CD/MC
Mort050	Conflict 'The Final Conflict' LP/CD
Mort060	Conflict 'Against All Odds' LP/CD/MC
Mort070	Various 'A Compilation Of The Deleted Dialogue' LP

Mortcd070	Various 'A Compilation Of The Deleted Dialogue: The Singles' DCD
Mort080	Conflict 'These Colours Don't Run' 7"/CD Single
Mort090	Various 'This Is The ALF' LP/CD
Mortdlp090	Various 'This Is The ALF' DLP
Mort100	Conflict 'Conclusion' LP/CD
Mort110	Conflict 'It's Time To See Who's Who Now' LP/CD
Mort120	Conflict 'In The Venue' LP/CD
Mortcd130	Conflict 'Only Stupid Bastards Help EMI' CD
Mortcd150	Various 'We Won't Take No More' CD
Mort170	Conflict 'Standard Issue 2: 88-94' LP/CD
Mort180	Conflict 'Now You've Put Your Foot In It' 7"/CD Single
Mortcd005	Icons Of Filth 'The Mortarhate Projects' CD
Mort190	Conflict 'Carlo Giuliani' 7"/CD Single
Mort200	Conflict 'There's No Power Without Control' LP/CD
Mort210	Inner Terrestrials 'Guns Of Brixton' CD Single
Mort220	Inner Terrestrials 'X' CD
Mort230	Lost Cherrees 'In The Beginning' CD
Mort240	Conflict 'Rebellion Sucks' CD/DVD
MortTv1	Conflict 'Force Or Service' Video

Mortarhate/Cherry Red

Morta1	Conflict 'It's Time To See Who's Who' CD
Morta2	Conflict 'Increase The Pressure' CD
Morta3	Conflict 'The Ungovernable Force' CD
Morta4	Lost Cherrees 'Free To Speak... But Not To Question' CD
Morta5	Lost Cherrees 'In The Beginning' DCD
Morta6	Various 'Who? What? Why? When? Where?' CD
Morta7	Icons Of Filth 'Onward Christian Soldiers' CD
Morta8	Conflict 'Turning Rebellion Into Money' CD
Morta9	Conflict 'Standard Issue: 82-87' CD
Morta10	Various 'This Is Mortarhate' DCD
Morta11	Conflict 'The Final Conflict' CD
Morta12	Conflict 'Against All Odds' CD
Morta13	Various 'This Is The ALF' CD
Mortdvd1	Conflict 'Live In London' 2DVD
Mortdvd2	Conflict 'Live in England' 2DVD
Mortdvd3	Lost Cherrees 'There Are No Fucking Rules' DVD

Radical Change

RC1	Disrupters 'Young Offender' 7"
RC2	Disrupters 'Shelters For The Rich' 7"
RC3	Icon AD 'Don't Feed Us Shit' 7"
RC4	Icon AD 'Let The Vultures Fly' 7"
RC5	Self Abuse 'Soldier' 7"
RC6	Disrupters 'Bomb Heaven' 7"
12RC7	Revulsion 'Ever Get The Feeling of Utter...' 12"
12RC8	Disrupters 'Alive In The Electric Chair' 12"
RCLP1	Disrupters 'Unrehearsed Wrongs' LP
RCLP2	Destructors 'Armageddon In Action' LP
RCLP3	Disrupters 'Playing With Fire' LP
RCLP4	Various 'Words Worth Shouting' LP

Riot/Clone

Rcr1	Riot/Clone 'There's No Government Like No Government' 7"
Rcr2	Riot/Clone 'Destroy The Myth Of Musical Destruction' 7"
Rcr3	Lost Cherrees 'No Fighting, No War, No Trouble, No More' 7"
Rcr4	Riot/Clone 'Blood On Your Hands?' 7"
Rcr124	Riot/Clone 'Dead... But Not Forgotten' 3x7" - plus 64-page booklet
Rcr5	Riot/Clone 'Still No Government Like No Government' CD
Rcr6	The Glory Strummers 'ESD' CD Single
Rcr7	Who Moved The Ground? 'If Pleasure Was Illegal' CD Single

Spiderleg

Sdl1	Epileptics '1970s' 7"
Sd2	Epileptics 'Last Bus To Debden' 7"
Sdl3	Subhumans 'Demolition War' 7"
Sdl4	The System 'Warfare' 7"
Sdl5	Subhumans 'Reasons For Existence' 7"
Sdl6	Amebix 'Who's The Enemy?' 7"
Sdl7	Subhumans 'Religious Wars' 7"
Sdl8	Flux Of Pink Indians 'Strive To Survive Causing Least Suffering Possible' LP
Sdl9	Subhumans 'The Day The Country Died' LP
Sdl10	Amebix 'Winter' 7"
Sdl11	The System 'Is Murder' 7"
Sdl12	Kronstadt Uprising 'The Unknown Revolution' 7"
Sdl13	Flux Of Pink Indians 'The Fucking Cunts Treat Us Like Pricks' DLP
Sdl14	Amebix 'No Sanctuary' 12"
Sdl15	Antisect 'In Darkness, There Is No Choice' LP
Sdl16	Flux Of Pink Indians 'Taking a Liberty' 7"

Xntrix

Xn2001	Fatal Microbes/Poison Girls 'Piano Lessons' 12" - listed as 'Weeny3'
Xn2002	Pete Fender 'Four Formulas' 7"
Xn2003	Poison Girls 'Total Exposure' LP
Xn2004	Rubella Ballet 'The Ballet Bag' tape
Xn2005	Rubella Ballet 'The Ballet Dance' 7"
Xn2006	Poison Girls 'Where's The Pleasure?' LP
Xn2007	Conflict 'Live At Centro Iberico' 7"
Xn2008	Poison Girls 'Songs Of Praise' LP
Xn2009	Poison Girls 'Real Woman' 7"
Xn2010	Poison Girls 'Real Woman' 12"
Rm101	Poison Girls 'Seven Year Scratch' DLP

Vi Subversa of Poison Girls, picture by Per-Ake Warn.

96 Tapes

96/1   This Bitter Lesson 'Value of Defiance' demo
96/2   Rubella Ballet 'Live at The Starlight'
96/3   D&V 'The New Beginning' demo
96/4   A-Heads 'Live Demos'
96/5   Subhumans/Faction 'Live At The Moonlight Club'
96/6   Faction 'Through The Window'
96/7   A Touch of Hysteria 'Demo'
96/8   Various 'No, No, No, Don't Drop Yer Bombs On Us, They Hurt'
96/9   Faction 'If They Give You Ruled Paper, Write The Other Way'
96/10 Blood And Roses 'Life After Death'
96/11 Omega Tribe 'Live At The Clarendon'
96/12 The Instigators 'It Has To Be Stopped/Live 1984'
96/13 Pandora's Box 'Flickering Candle'
96/14 Flowers In The Dustbin 'All The Best People Are Perverts'
96/15 Blyth Power 'A Little Touch Of Harry In The Night'
96/16 Buld 'Nox Mortis'
96/17 Subhumans/Steve L 'Live In Warminster'

APPENDIX 2

ANARCHO PUNK ONLINE
an incomplete listing of websites...

NAVIGATE TO INFILTRATE

www.1in12.go-legend.net/
www.activedistribution.org
www.akpress.org
www.alternativetentacles.com/
www.amnesty.org
www.anarshite.cjb.net
www.animalaid.org.uk
www.animal-liberation.com
www.animalliberationfront.com
www.anl.org.uk
www.a-o-a.org
www.arkangelweb.org
http://homepage.ntlworld.com/acidstings
www.artofthestate.co.uk
www.atrox.org.uk
www.bdrecs.com
www.belfastpunks.co.uk
www.brokenrekids.com
www.chumba.com
www.citizenfish.com
www.londonclasswar.org
www.conflict-uk.com
www.contemptuk.com
www.thecravats.com
www.earthfirst.org.uk
www.eroding.org.uk/
www.flatearth.free-online.co.uk
www.flowersinthedustbin.co.uk
www.freebeagles.org
www.householdnamerecords.co.uk
www.humaneresearch.org.uk
www.huntsabs.org.uk
www.indymedia.org.uk/en/org.uk/en/

www.keeponfighting.net
www.kronstadt-uprising.co.uk
www.lackofknowledge.com
www.lostcherrees.com
www.mortarhate.com
www.myspace.com/crass_the_biography
www.nochoice.org
www.myspace.com/oipolloialba
www.overgroundrecords.co.uk
www.peta.org
www.pomonauk.co.uk
www.profaneexistence.com
www.punkcore.com
www.punkoiuk.co.uk
www.punkrock.org/
www.punkshitrecords.stigon.com
www.schnews.org.uk/
www.scumville.co.uk
www.shac.net
www.slendermeans.org.uk/
www.speakcampaigns.org.uk
www.steveharnett.com
www.southern.net/southern/label
www.thissystemkills.com
www.toxicwastebelfast.co.uk
www.uncarved.org/music/apunk
www.unit-united.co.uk
www.vegansociety.com
www.vegsoc.org
www.vpsg.org
www.viva.org.uk
www.vivisection.info/ssat
www.zoundsonline.co.uk

*Zig Zag squat gig
graffiti, image courtesy
by Tony Mottram.*

Punk DVDs

FROM CHERRY RED RECORDS

CRDVD 001N	**Dead Kennedys** - DMPO's On Broadway
CRDVD 003N	**Buzzcocks** - Auf Weidersehen
CRDVD 005N	**Johnny Thunders** - Dead Or Alive
CRDVD 006N	**Punk & Disorderly** - The DVD, Various
CRDVD 008	**The Exploited** - Rock N Roll Outlaws / Sexual Favours
CRDVD 10	**Toy Dolls** - We're Mad / Idle Gossip
CRDVD 15	**Peter & The Test Tube Babies** - Cattle & Bum / Live In Manchester
CRDVD 16	**Adicts** - Joker In The Pack
CRDVD 17	**Extreme Noise Terror** - From One Extreme To Another
CRDVD 21	**Slaughter & The Dogs** - Cranked Up Really High
CRDVD 22	**UK/DK & Holidays In The Sun** - Various
CRDVD 26	**One Way System** - No Return / All Systems Go
CRDVD 27	**GBH** - Live At The Ace, Brixton
CRDVD 29	**UK Subs** - Live At The Retford Porterhouse
CRDVD 30	**The Fall** - Perverted By Language / Live At Leeds
CRDVD 41	**GBH** - Kawasaki Live / Brit Boys Attacked By Brats
CRDVD 43	**Chelsea** - Live At The Bier Keller
CRDVD 44	**999** - Feelin' Alright With The Crew
CRDVD 49	**The Exploited** - 83-87 / Live At The Palm Cove
CRDVD 51	**Vibrators** - 1976-2004
CRDVD 54	**The Lurkers** - Bollurks, The European Tour
CRDVD 55	**Young Marble Giants** - Live At The Hurrah
CRDVD 62	**Burning Britain** - The DVD (The History of UK Punk 1980-1984)
CRDVD 65	**Oi! Oi! Oi!** - Highlights from over 2 decades of Oi!
CRDVD 68	**Eater** - Live - Outside View
CRDVD 69	**Punk & Disorderly 2** - Further Charges - Various
CRDVD 72	**The Business** - Surburban Rebels - Live at Rio's
CRDVD 76	**Menace** - GLC
CRDVD 77	**Eddie & The Hot Rods** - Do Anything You Wanna Do
CRDVD 79	**The Drones** - Further Temptations
CRDVD 82	**Holidays In The Sun** - Various
CRDVD 88	**Red Alert** - Take No Prisoners
CRDVD 90	**The Varukers** - Live: Protest and Survive
CRDVD 94	**GBH** - Live in Los Angeles / Live at Victoria Hall
CRDVD 95	**Angelic Upstarts** - Solidarity
CRDVD 97	**Vice Squad** - Last Rockers: The Vice Squad Story
CRDVD 101	**Germs** - Media Blitz, The Germs Story
CRDVD 102	**Subhumans** - All Gone Live
CRDVD 105	**Spizzenergi** - Where's Captain Kirk?
CRDVD 106	**Newtown Neurotics** - The Long Goodbye
CRDVD 115	**Nothin' But Trash** - Various
CRDVD 120	**Wendy O Williams** - Bump 'n' Grind
CRDVD 125	**D.O.A.** - Live at the Assassination Club
CRDVD 126	**The Boys** - Sick On You
CRDVD 130	**Goldblade** - Testify!
CRDVD 131	**The Exploited** - Live in Japan / Live in Argentina
CRDVD 132	**Punk On The Road** - Various
CRDVD 134	**English Dogs** - Psycho Killer
CRDVD 140	**New Bomb Turks** - Reigning on Edinburgh: Live
VISDVD 003N	**Black Flag** - Live

CHERRY RED FILMS

www.cherryred.co.uk

ALSO AVAILABLE FROM CHERRY RED

Anagram Records Punk Collectors Series

CDPUNK 1	BLITZ Voice Of A Generation
CDPUNK 2	CHANNEL 3 I've Got A Gun/After The Lights Go Out
CDPUNK 3	PETER & THE TEST TUBE BABIES Pissed And Proud
CDPUNK 4	PARTISANS Police Story
CDPUNK 10	EATER The Compleat Eater
CDPUNK 11	No Future Singles Collection
CDPUNK 12	CHAOS UK Enough To Make You Sick/The Chipping Sodbury Bonfire Tapes
CDPUNK 13	Secret Records Punk Singles Collection
CDPUNK 14	Raw Records Punk Singles Collection
CDPUNK 15	Riot City records Punk Singles Collection
CDPUNK 16	VIBRATORS Guilty/ Alaska 127
CDPUNK 17	ANGELIC UPSTARTS Reason Why?
CDPUNK 18	THE EXPLOITED Live And Loud
CDPUNK 19	DISORDER Under The Scalpel Blade/One Day Son All This Will Be Yourz
CDPUNK 20	DRONES Further Temptation
CDPUNK 21	SUBURBAN STUDS Slam - The Complete Studs Collection
CDPUNK 22	Punk & Disorderly Further Charges
CDPUNK 23	Punk & Disorderly The Final Solution
CDPUNK 24	A.T.V. The Image Has Cracked - The A.T.V. Collection
CDPUNK 25	BLITZ The Complete Singles Collection
CDPUNK 26	CHAOS UK Total Chaos
CDPUNK 27	CHAOTIC DISCHORD Their Greatest Fuckin' Hits
CDPUNK 28	VICE SQUAD Shot Away
CDPUNK 29	Small Wonder Punk Singles Collection
CDPUNK 30	Fall Out Punk Singles Collection
CDPUNK 31	PATRIK FITZGERALD The Very Best Of Patrik Fitzgerald
CDPUNK 32	Fresh Records Punk Singles Collection
CDPUNK 33	THE ADICTS The Complete Adicts Singles Collection
CDPUNK 34	THE VIBRATORS Fifth Amendment/Recharged
CDPUNK 35	RAPED The Complete Raped Collection
CDPUNK 36	Good Vibrations Punk Singles Collection
CDPUNK 37	Anagram Records Punk Singles Collection
CDPUNK 38	THE NOTSENSIBLES Instant Punk Classics
CDPUNK 39	DISORDER Live In Oslo/Violent World
CDPUNK 40	Rot Records Punk Singles Collection
CDPUNK 41	RIOT SQUAD The Complete Punk Collection
CDPUNK 42	Flicknife Records Punk Collection
CDPUNK 43	THE VIBRATORS The Best Of The Vibrators
CDPUNK 44	ANTI-NOWHERE LEAGUE Complete Singles Collection
CDPUNK 45	Razor Records Punk Collection
CDPUNK 46	DISORDER Complete Disorder
CDPUNK 47	UK/DK Original Soundtrack
CDPUNK 48	ANTI-PASTI The Last Call
CDPUNK 49	RONDELET RECORDS Punk Singles Collection
CDPUNK 50	ONE WAY SYSTEM The Best Of
CDPUNK 51	CHERRY RED RECORDS Punk Singles Collection
CDPUNK 52	ABSTRACT RECORDS Punk Singles Collection
CDPUNK 53	ANTI-PASTI Caution In The Wind
CDPUNK 54	NO FUTURE Punk Singles Collection Volume 2
CDPUNK 55	RIOT CITY Punk Singles Collection Volume 2
CDPUNK 56	VARUKERS Prepare For The Attack/Bloodsucker
CDPUNK 57	THE BUSINESS Complete Punk Singles Collection
CDPUNK 58	VIBRATORS Meltdown/Vicious Circle
CDPUNK 59	ANGELIC UPSTARTS The Independent Punk Singles Collection
CDPUNK 60	SECRET RECORDS Punk Singles Collection Volume 2
CDPUNK 61	BEAT THE SYSTEM Punk Singles Collection
CDPUNK 62	OUTCASTS Punk Singles Collection
CDPUNK 63	VARIOUS Punk Rock Rarities Voume 1
CDPUNK 64	PETER AND THE TEST TUBE BABIES Complete Singles Collection
CDPUNK 65	CHAOS UK Floggin' The Corpse
CDPUNK 66	UK SUBS/URBAN DOGS/CHARLIE HARPER Punk Singles Collection
CDPUNK 67	999 The Biggest Prize In Sport
CDPUNK 68	VARIOUS Live At The Vortex
CDPUNK 69	THE LURKERS Powerjive/King Of The Mountain
CDPUNK 70	SMALL WONDER Punk Singles Collection Volume 2
CDPUNK 71	CHAOS UK Short Sharp Shock
CDPUNK 72	CHAOTIC DISCHORD Fuck Religion, Fuck Politics, Fuck The Lot Of You/ Don't Throw It All Away
CDPUNK 73	Beggars Banquet Punk Singles Collection
CDPUNK 74	THE VARUKERS The Punk Singles 1981-1985
CDPUNK 75	Pax Records Punk Singles Collection
CDPUNK 76	VIBRATORS The Independent Punk Singles Collection
CDPUNK 77	RUDI Big Time - The Best Of Rudi
CDPUNK 78	999 The Albion Punk Years

ALSO AVAILABLE FROM CHERRY RED

**Available from all good record stores, distributed by Pinnacle, or via mail order from Cherry Red
with Visa, Mastercard or Switch.
Call 0044 (0) 20 8740 4110 for details,
email info@cherryred.co.uk or write to:
Cherry Red, 3a Long Island House, Warple Way, London W3 0RG**

**CD prices including post and packaging
£9.95 UK, £10.45 Europe, £10.95 Rest of World.**

www.cherryred.co.uk

Burning Britain – A History Of UK Punk 1980-1984

Ian Glasper's mammoth tome has won praise from all quarters.

"I can't recommend this book enough…Glasper's done his research well and got the opinions of the bands involved."
Punknews.co.uk

"Packed with tour stories, gossip and little-known facts. Anyone who's ever spiked their hair needs to read this."
Terroriser magazine

"Not content to rehash old **** about Discharge, Exploited, etc, Glasper also covers excellent bands like the Wall, Erazerhead, Dead Mans Shadow and the Insane…a good source of information."
Rock Sound magazine

"If you want to read it, buy your own – this is way too valuable to lend to any ****!"
Anarchoi website

At £14.99, this is a must-buy for punks, post-punks and the merely curious. For ordering information, please see the Cherry Red website.

www.cherryred.co.uk

ALSO AVAILABLE FROM CHERRY RED

**Indie Hits
1980-1989**

The Complete UK
Independent Chart
(Singles And
Albums)

**Compiled By
Barry Lazell**

Paper covers,
314 pages,
£14.99 in UK

**Cor Baby, That's
Really Me!**

(The New
Millennium
Hardback Edition)

John Otway

Hardback,
192 pages and 16
pages of
photographs
£11.99 in UK

**All The
Young Dudes,
Mott the Hoople
and Ian Hunter
The Biography**

Campbell Devine

Paper covers,
448 pages and 16
pages of
photographs
£14.99 in UK

**Embryo - A Pink
Floyd Chronology
1966-1971**

**Nick Hodges and
Ian Priston**

Paper covers,
302 pages and
photographs
throughout
£14.99 in UK

**Johnny Thunders
In Cold Blood**

Nina Antonia

Paper covers,
270 pages and
photographs
throughout
£14.99 in UK

**Songs In The
Key Of Z**

**The Curious
Universe of
Outsider music
Irwin Chusid**

Paper covers,
311 pages, fully
illustrated
£11.99 in UK

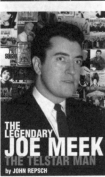

**The Legendary
Joe Meek
The Telstar Man**

John Repsch

Paper covers,
350 pages plus
photographs,
£14.99 in UK

**Random Precision
Recording the
Music of Syd
Barrett 1965-1974**

David Parker

Paper covers,
320 pages and
photographs
throughout
£14.99 in UK

www.cherryred.co.uk

ALSO AVAILABLE FROM CHERRY RED

Those Were The Days

Stefan Granados

An Unofficial History of the Beatles' Apple Organization 1967-2002

Paper covers, 300 pages including photographs £14.99 in UK

The Rolling Stones: Complete Recording Sessions 1962-2002

Martin Elliott

Paper covers, 576 pages plus 16 pages of photographs £14.99 in UK

Goodnight Jim Bob – On The Road With Carter The Unstoppable Sex Machine

Jim Bob

Paper covers, 228 pages plus 16 pages of photographs £12.99 in UK

Our Music Is Red - With Purple Flashes: The Story Of The Creation

Sean Egan

Paper covers, 378 pages plus 8 pages of photographs £14.99 in UK

Bittersweet: The Clifford T Ward Story

David Cartwright

Paper covers, 352 pages plus 8 pages of photographs £14.99 in UK

The Secret Life of a Teenage Punk Rocker: The Andy Blade Chronicles

Andy Blade

Paper covers, 224 pages and photographs throughout. £12.99 in UK

Burning Britain

Ian Glasper

Paper covers, 410 pages and photographs throughout £14.99 in UK

Truth... Rod Stewart, Ron Wood And The Jeff Beck Group

Dave Thompson

Paper covers, 208 pages plus four pages of photographs. £14.99 in UK

www.cherryred.co.uk

available on dvd from Cherry Red Records

CRDVD 144
The Day The Country Died

The rise of anarcho punk in the wake of Crass finally saw punk rock become the movement it always threatened to be in the late Seventies. Suddenly punk wasn't about the clothes that you wore, the music that you played, it was about what was in your head, what was in your heart. Bands like Conflict, Flux Of Pink Indians, Subhumans, The Mob, Zounds, and quite literally hundreds more, took the sentiments of Crass in myriad musical directions, but always maintained as their primary motivation a desire to offer a genuine alternative to the mainstream.

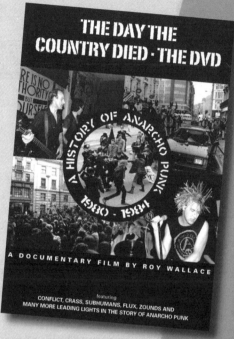

Such purity of purpose was not sustainable forever, of course, and by the mid-Eighties, anarcho punk had almost became a parody of itself, the scene having adopted - for the most part - a standardised look, sound and stance that almost rendered it as redundant as that which it had set out to overthrow. But, for a few short years back then, anarcho punk was the most vital, exciting and downright subversive music to ever spring forth from a loudspeaker, its power and passion a far cry from what is so often passed off as revolutionary music today. Yet so little has been done to seriously document that ground-breaking period of the UK underground, even massive-sellers like Crass seemingly swept under the carpet, out of sight, out of mind, the 'poor relations' of the infinitely safer bands laughably lauded by the media as 'true punk'.

Until now, that is, and the publication of Ian Glasper's book, 'The Day The Country Died', which peels away the myths one by one, through all-new interviews and exhaustive research. This DVD, by renowned maverick filmmaker Roy Wallace (himself one-time vocalist with Belfast band, Toxic Waste) is the visual companion to that work, concisely relating the real story of anarcho punk via a wealth of exclusive new interviews and ultra-rare archive footage. Between this disc and that book, anarcho punk finally gets a fair hearing, and not before time!

Available in all good record stores, distributed by Pinnacle. Alternatively, they can be ordered directly from Cherry Red Records mail order department on 0208 740 4110 or via the website *www.cherryred.co.uk*

CAN YOU HELP? Have you any suggestions for releases that would work as part of our DVD series or as a Cherry Red release? If so, please e-mail *ideas@cherryred.co.uk* or write to Cherry Red Records, Unit 3a, Long Island House, 1-4 Warple Way, London W3 0RG

CHERRY RED
FILMS

CHERRY RED BOOKS

We are always looking for interesting books to publish.
They can be either new manuscripts or re-issues of deleted books.
If you have any good ideas then please
get in touch with us.

CHERRY RED BOOKS
A division of Cherry Red Records Ltd.
Unit 3a,
Long Island House,
Warple Way,
London W3 0RG.

E-mail: iain@cherryred.co.uk
Web: www.cherryred.co.uk